A POLITICAL HISTORY
OF SCOTLAND

A POLITICAL HISTORY
OF SCOTLAND
1832–1924

Parties, Elections and Issues

I. G. C. HUTCHISON

Department of History
University of Stirling

JOHN DONALD PUBLISHERS LTD
EDINBURGH

ISBN 0 85976 117 7

Exclusive distribution in the United States of
America and Canada by Humanities Press
Inc., Atlantic Highlands, NJ 07716, USA.

The publisher acknowledges the financial
assistance of the Scottish Arts Council in the
publication of this volume.

Phototypeset by Quorn Selective Repro,
Loughborough.
Printed in Great Britain by Bell & Bain Ltd.,
Glasgow.

Preface

It is advisable to state that this book does not purport to be a comprehensive history of all aspects of Scottish politics between 1832 and 1924. Its ambit is indicated by the subtitle. That is to say, it examines developments within the main political parties in Scotland, looking in particular at their electoral fortunes. It also studies the manner in which political issues impinged on the parties, and how the latter responded to these policy demands. There are several areas on which little is said in this work. One, for instance, is that of working-class political movements in the nineteenth century. These are passed over cursorily not because they are deemed unimportant, but for the reasons just outlined. Moreover, the historiography of the Scottish working class is in a fairly advanced state, whereas some of the factors investigated here are perhaps less well developed. Again, there are certain topics which do not receive a thorough discussion, even although they might be held to fall, in part at least, within the scope of this book. Two such items are the crofters' electoral revolt in 1885 and the unrest on Clydeside during the First World War. In defence of their brief treatment here, it may be pointed out that both of these episodes have recently been fully and convincingly explored by other historians, so that it would merely be heaping Pelion on Ossa to go over the ground again.

An aim of this work is to seek to broaden the geographical spread of evidence. There have been several useful studies of some of the topics discussed here, but sometimes their overall applicability has been limited. Too often, it seems, either generalisations have been based on restricted samples, which might prove to be unrepresentative, or a movement in one part of the country has been the focus of intense scrutiny, on the grounds of uniqueness, without attention being paid to similar trends at work elsewhere. Another, perhaps related, problem lies in the natural tendency of political historians to concentrate on using the resources of the main record repositories in Edinburgh (the National Library of Scotland and the Scottish Record Office) and London (the British Library and the Public Record Office). While these collections are utterly indispensable for any interpretation of the period, they do have some limitations. Firstly, they do tend — quite properly — to portray two types of politics more than others, viz. the political operations of the great landed estates and the 'high politics' of front-benchers. There is not, however, a great deal to be found on middle-class urban politics or on constituency party activities. Secondly, these collections are not always fully representative of the various parts of Scotland, and display a tendency to be preponderantly drawn from the Lothian and Border regions. As the nineteenth century advanced, the economic and social experiences of other regions increasingly diverged from those of the south-eastern Lowlands. To attempt to overcome these difficulties, attention has been paid to a variety of source material held in private hands or in local record centres.

A second objective has been to suggest in what ways and for what reasons political trends in Scotland varied from or conformed to the broad British pattern. By adopting this approach, the study of Scottish politics may offer, amongst other things, an opportunity to test interpretations of British political history as they apply to one part of the United Kingdom. It is hoped that because Scotland in many respects resembles the rest of Britain, yet in other ways possesses distinctive traits, it may provide an illuminating perspective, and at the same time serve as a corrective to both Scoto-centric and Anglo-centric interpretations.

I. G. C. Hutchison

Acknowledgements

Most generous financial assistance towards the costs of undertaking the research for this project was provided by the British Academy and the Carnegie Trust for the Universities of Scotland. Dr P. Anderson, the Secretary of the National Register of Archives (Scotland), displayed admirable patience and efficiency in securing access for me to numerous collections of papers in private hands. I have to thank all the owners of manuscripts for permitting me to consult them, especially those who admitted me into their homes. The staff of many record repositories and libraries, both national and local, were universally helpful. A number of people gave me hospitality which permitted my research to be carried out more cheaply and more comfortably: Dr and Mrs I. Gibbs, Mr and Mrs P. Hartnell, Mr and Mrs J. M. K. Hutchison, Mr and Mrs T. Whiteman. My publisher, John Tuckwell, allowed me to draw heavily on his apparently inexhaustible reserves of tolerance. Professor R. H. Campbell, by a judicious mixture of exhortation and friendly prodding, encouraged me in the enterprise of writing this book. Dr D. W. Bebbington read a draft with a critical eye, and Mr J. M. Simpson, Dr C. J. Wrigley and Professor J. C. Williams gave me help and advice in varying forms. None of them, of course, are at all responsible for errors of fact or oddities of opinion which remain. Evelyn Whyte processed my draft, a pot pourri of execrable typing and illegible handwriting, with remarkable speed, accuracy and good humour. She assures me it is entirely coincidental that she has decided to take up a new position immediately after completing the typescript which will lead to her working abroad. Finally, I must thank my wife and family for acquiescing cheerfully (on the whole) in my frequent decisions that the past should take precedence over the present. I must also thank them for insisting from time to time that my priorities be reversed.

I am deeply grateful to those named for permission to quote from the following manuscript collections: Adam of Blairadam MSS. (Mr K. Adam); Asquith MSS. (Mr M. Bonham-Carter and the Bodleian Library); Balfour (Whittingehame) MSS. (Lord Balfour); Ballindalloch MSS. (Mr and Mrs O. Russell); Brodie of Brodie MSS. (Mr M. N. A. Brodie of Brodie); Austen and Joseph Chamberlain MSS. (University of Birmingham Library); Clerk of Penicuik MSS. (Sir John Clerk); Craigmyle MSS. (Lord Craigmyle); Crawford and Balcarres MSS. (Lord Crawford); Dalhousie MSS. (Lord Dalhousie); Stormonth-Darling MSS. (Mr M. Stormonth-Darling); Derby MSS. (Lord Derby); Devonshire MSS (The Trustees of the Chatsworth Settlement); Disraeli MSS. (The National Trust); Elgin MSS. (Lord Elgin); Lloyd George MSS. (The Beaverbrook Foundation and the House of Lords Record Office); Glasier MSS. (The Librarian, University of Liverpool Library); Glynne-Gladstone MSS. (Sir William Gladstone); Glen & Henderson MSS. (Messrs. Glen and Henderson, and the West Lothian Conservative Association); Hatfield House MSS. (Lord Salisbury); Hunter of

Hunterston MSS. (Mr N. A. K. Hunter of Hunterston); Johnson MSS. (Independent Labour Publications — the successor to the Independent Labour Party); King MSS. (Sir James King); Bonar Law MSS. (The Beaverbrook Foundation and the House of Lords Record Office); Lothian MSS. (Lord Lothian); MacKenzie of Gairloch MSS. (Mr J. MacKenzie); MacLeod of MacLeod MSS. (Mr J. MacLeod of MacLeod); Mansfield MSS. (Lord Mansfield); Moncrieff MSS. (Lord Moncrieff); Morel MSS. (British Library of Political and Economic Science); Newcastle MSS. (University of Nottingham Library); Novar MSS. (Mr A. B. L. Munro Ferguson); Oswald of Dunnikier MSS. (Mrs D. Bruton); Ponsonby MSS. (Lord Ponsonby and the Bodleian Library); Portland MSS. (University of Nottingham Library and the Trustees of His Grace the Duke of Portland); Pringle MSS. (the House of Lords Record Office); MacCallum Scott MSS. (the late Mr J. MacCallum Scott); Selborne MSS. (Lord Selborne and the Bodleian Library); Telfer-Smollett MSS. (Mr P. Telfer-Smollett); Strathcarron MSS. (Lord Strathcarron and the Bodleian Library); Wemyss MSS. (Lord Wemyss).

I am also most grateful to the following political organisations for allowing me to quote from their records:—

The Co-operative Party, Scottish Section; the Labour Party; the Scottish Liberal Party; the Scottish Conservative and Unionist Party; Kincardineshire Conservative Association; Kirkcaldy Burghs Unionist Association.

The owners of copyright in the undernoted books are thanked for granting me permission to make quotations:—

Lord Tweedsmuir, for J. Buchan, *Andrew Jameson, Lord Ardwall*; Messrs Hutchinson Publishing Group, for T. N. Graham, *Willie Graham. The Life of the Rt. Hon. W. Graham* (London, n.d.); Messrs Secker and Warburg, for J. Paton, *Left Turn!* (London, 1936).

Contents

Tables

Abbreviations

BSP	British Socialist Party
EHR	*English Historical Review*
ESLA	East and North of Scotland Liberal Association
ESLUA	East of Scotland Liberal Unionist Association
FC	Free Church
GCOA	Glasgow Conservative Operatives' Association
HJ	*Historical Journal*
ILP	Independent Labour Party
LRC	Labour Representation Committee
NAC	National Administrative Council (ILP)
NEC	National Executive Committee (Labour Party)
NFU	National Farmers Union
NLF	National Liberal Federation
NLFS	National Liberal Federation of Scotland
NUCAS	National Union of Conservative Associations of Scotland
P.P.	Parliamentary Paper
SAC	Scottish Advisory Council (Labour Party)
SDF	Social Democratic Federation
SHR	*Scottish Historical Review*
SHRA	Scottish Home Rule Association
SLA	Scottish Liberal Association
SLF	Scottish Liberal Federation
SLRL	Scottish Land Restoration League
SNCA	Scottish National Constitutional Association
SPBA	Scottish Permissive Bill Association
STL	Scottish Temperance League
STUC	Scottish Trades Union Congress
SUA	Scottish Unionist Association
SWRC	Scottish Workers' Representation Committee
T & LC	Trades and Labour Council
UFC	United Free Church
UP(C)	United Presbyterian (Church)
WSLA	West and South of Scotland Liberal Association
WSLUA	West of Scotland Liberal Unionist Association

The Conservatives in the Age of Reform: 1832–1841

I

The passing of the Reform Act of 1832 presented the Conservative party with a formidable challenge to re-establish itself as the majority party in Britain. In Scotland, however, the task was especially daunting, for two broad reasons. Firstly, the electorate had been more profoundly changed in Scotland, and secondly, the Tories were far more unpopular than in England. The unreformed electorate had been exceptionally restricted in extent, even compared to England. While there were perhaps 366,000 voters before 1832 in England and Wales (or 1 in 8 adult males), there were only 4,500 in Scotland, a ratio of 1 voter to 125 adult males. Although the introduction of the new system (based, as in Enland, primarily on the £10 urban householder franchise) left the percentage of voters among adult males in Scotland (1 in 8) still below the English level (1 in 5), in comparison to the previous position the proportionate increase was far greater in Scotland. In England there were 652,777 voters after the bill, an increase of around 80%; in Scotland, with a new electorate of 64,447, the increase was 1,400%.[1] The consequences of this change were twofold: firstly, the Whigs, as the leaders of the Reform campaign, had won the support of a more numerous and socially more extended part of the Scottish electorate precisely because of the narrowness of the old system. Secondly, the value placed on the hard-won right to vote created a long-enduring sense of gratitude towards the Whigs. 'The complete change in the constituency of Scotland', Peel was told by Sir George Clerk after the 1832 elections, 'and the importance attached by the newly enfranchised Reformers to the privilege now conferred on them rendered the chance of any Conservative, especially one who had taken part in opposing the Reform Bill, extremely doubtful'.[2]

Clerk's analysis also reveals the other factor inhibiting a Tory revival, namely the widespread hatred of the party both for ruthlessly manipulating unreformed Scottish politics over a period of some fifty years and for using their power to sustain a Toryism more reactionary (or so the Scottish opponents claimed) than its English equivalent. This had been particularly the case in the 1820s when Liberal Toryism was seen to develop in England, but not in Scotland. This record of resistance to progress culminated in the almost monolithic opposition to the Reform Bill evinced by Scottish Toryism, whose pamphleteers claimed with greater accuracy than political sensitivity that the unreformed system had not prevented either prosperity or civil liberties from flourishing in Scotland, while the new system would only encourage, on the one hand, greater influence by mighty landlords and the creation of fictitious votes, and on the other, rule by cliques of village shopkeepers, accompanied by mob intimidation. The growth in the power of the great aristocrats and the lower middle class would extinguish the role of the gentry in county seats and debauch the purity of contests everywhere.[3] To wind up this catalogue of predicted disasters by denouncing the bill as 'calculated to revolutionise Scotland, to overturn her political establishments and to abolish her vested interests' simply revealed the gulf between Scottish Tories and the overwhelming body of quite moderate opinion in the country.[4]

As a result, the Tories were subjected to virulent and passionate hostility. Occasionally this took the form of physical threats. When the Duke of Buccleuch, the epitome of Tory reaction, appeared in Edinburgh in July 1832, missiles were flung at his carriage, breaking his windows, and a journeyman baker went further: 'It appears that this fellow had the impertinence to hold out a rope in the presence of the Duke, calling out, 'I'll give anybody 5s (25p) to hang the Juck' '.[5] The candidate for Fife in 1832 was expressly warned against entering several towns in the county, as feeling was said to be running very high after his opposition to the Reform Bill.[6] More often the dislike was confined to political opposition but was not less unremitting. Repeatedly, Conservative agents remarked that only a candidate without a record of resistance to reform would have any prospects of success in a Scottish seat. Thus, in Lanarkshire in 1837, the prospective candidate Buchanan was ruled out: 'But such are the prejudices against him in consequence of his conduct at and preceding the Reform Bill that it is in vain to hope for success with him'.[7] A new candidate was found and the seat gained from the Liberals. This drawback was alluded to as operating in a wide range of constituencies, including Glasgow, Ayrshire, Perthshire and the Haddington Burghs.[8] These assertions were not entirely the products of a near-paranoia which was induced in Tory managers by the comprehensive defeat in the 1832 election. When Sir George Clerk solicited the support of a prosperous paper mill-owner in the succeeding general election, he received a clear exposition: 'Those who advocated [the Reform Bill] are entitled to the approbation and gratitude of all classes of society. Had you, Sir George, been amongst its supporters you should have commanded not my vote only but that of many others who with pride and pleasure would have hailed you as their Honourable Representative. You declared however in Parliament that I ought not to possess the Elective Franchise, and yet request me to exercise it on your behalf, to the prejudice of those who aided me in obtaining it. Figure yourself in my position — How would you have acted?'.[9]

This basic anti-Toryism sometimes became the sole device used by Whigs to win support, and it worked because it reflected a widely held sense of distrust. In the 1835 election, the main thrust of the Whig appeal to the voters in the Kirriemuir part of Angus was that: 'if the electors returned such Representatives as Col. O[gilvy — Tory] they must surely now wish to overturn the Reform Act and the many great national blessings it has given rise to'.[10] The short-lived Tory administration of 1834–5 evoked widespread expressions of dismay, and public meetings in numerous towns protested against the King's decisions first to put the Tories in office and then to accede to a request by Wellington for a premature dissolution of Parliament. The Tories were accused, as *The Scotsman* put it, of organising 'a conspiracy against the people, their interests and rights' by trying to secure a Tory House of Commons — a conspiracy, moreover, led by Sir George Clerk and Sir George Murray, 'the old system personified', with its record of oppression and injustice throughout the fifty years it had controlled and exploited Scotland.[11] Reformers everywhere closed ranks, as at Kinross: 'Whigs and Radicals have instantly agreed to waive their minor differences and unite in one grand phalanx to save the country from Wellington dominance'.[12] Hence the Whigs could contemplate the outcome of the 1835 election as better than anticipated six months previously, when no Tory bogey could be raised.[13] One of Peel's Scottish advisers stressed after recounting the many firm displays of anti-Tory opinion during that election: 'In short, in Scotland, the Reform Bill has produced a more permanent change than anywhere else, amounting to a complete revolution in the Government'.[14]

In the face of this massive corpus of opposition, it was not to be expected that the broadly based and skilfully engineered Conservative recovery, which led to a decisive majority in England in 1841, would be repeated in Scotland.[15] Yet although the Tories in Scotland did do less well, it should be noted that considerable gains were made in the shires in 1835 and 1837, in almost the same proportionate rate of increase as in the English counties. 1841 was not so successful in the Scottish counties, and in burgh seats throughout, Scotland lagged badly.

Table 1.1.   Conservative Seats, 1832–41

		(N)	1832(%)	1835(%)	1837(%)	1841(%)
All	England	(464)	117(25)	200(43)	238(52)	277(60)
	Scotland	(53)	10(19)	15(28)	20(38)	22(41)
Counties	England	(144)	42(30)	73(51)	99(69)	124(86)
	Scotland	(30)	9(30)	14(47)	19(63)	20(67)
Boroughs	England	(320)	75(24)	127(40)	139(43)	153(48)
	Scotland	(23)	1 (4)	1 (4)	1 (4)	2 (8)

The most clearly identified cause of the Tory resurgence in the counties was the manufacture of votes. As a seminal article by Ferguson demonstrated, this old practice survived the Reform Bill. Faulty draughtsmanship in 1832 left untouched the legal entitlement of the owner of the superiority in a property to break down his rights into £10 units of value and to assign these to nominees, who were then entitled to vote. It should be borne in mind that in Scottish law, where the feudal inheritance remained strong, ownership of the superiority was quite separate from the physical ownership of land or property, and was frequently retained by large landowners when selling off land.[16] Brash has shown that this device was used by the Tories in the South-East of Scotland (i.e. Roxburgh, Peebles, Selkirk, East and Mid Lothian) to build up voting strength, and there is abundant evidence to show that the practice was tried in other county seats — including Angus, West Lothian, Stirling, Inverness, Kincardine and Renfrew.[17] But fictitious votes were not deployed everywhere, nor was their existence necessarily related to Conservative victories. Some of the seats where manufacturing of votes was used either remained robustly Liberal — as for instance, Angus, even although the Earl of Airlie was actively engaged in this exercise — or, conversely, were in no danger of slipping from the Tory grip. Kincardineshire was the subject of one of the earliest schemes to make votes, yet no Liberal stood after 1832 until 1865.[18] Vote creation was not universal, and in several seats where it was not seriously proceeded with the Tories were still able to capture them — e.g. Dumfriesshire, Perthshire and Ayrshire.[19]

Even where vote-making operations were conducted more aggressively, this could be counterproductive. In Roxburghshire, Lord Lothian pointed out that while some 250 extra Conservative votes were needed to render the seat safe, the Whigs had more property in the county and could not therefore be overtaken in this way. In 1841, after the Whigs had won the seat back, a pact between the two camps was suggested to prevent vote creation being extended endlessly.[20] The main period of vote making seems to have occurred in a spell between 1835 and 1839–40, and by 1840 F. R. Bonham, Peel's party manager, was bemoaning the failure of Scottish Tories to make gains in that year's county registration.[21] Part of the reason for stopping the process in 1840 may have been the belief that the objective of securing county seats had been achieved, but the 1841 elections did not demonstrate the onward progress of rural Toryism. An equally important factor was probably the negative impression that the perpetuation of faggot voting, one of the notorious abuses of the pre-1832 system, would create among potential recruits, particularly in urban areas. As a moderate Tory argued, 'anything like an extensive creation of votes would be unjustifiable and would decidedly do harm'.[22] The motives for adopting vote manufacture were not entirely based on an atavistic desire to return to the old pattern of politics. One advocate of the practice contended that the Scottish Reform Act was less satisfactory than the English one in that it gave the vote to £10 householders in county seats, so admitting 'small shopkeepers, weavers, shoemakers and other Tradesmen' to the electorate. In England, the Act had been designed, by drawing constituency boundaries with care, to exclude these urban elements from being over-represented in county seats. The 'Ten-pounders' were widely seen as the main barriers to a Tory recovery, inasmuch as they were 'steady only in opposing the agricultural interest on every occasion'. Hence the grounds for creating votes were to redress this imbalance and they were therefore, in the eyes of Tories, legitimate.[23]

The effectiveness of fictitious voting is not easy to determine. Even where it was carried out with gusto, it was not crucial to Tory success. West Lothian was claimed by Tories in 1836 to have been 'swamped' by paper votes.[24] Yet an analysis of voting in the 1832 and 1837 elections shows that whereas the Conservative majority had been increased from a bare 14 to 138, only 58 of the new majority — less than one half — was due to the net gain of Conservatives added to the register, and not all of these were necessarily faggots. The rest of the majority came from the normal processes of political change: some Liberals switched parties, abstainers in 1832 came out in 1837 for the Tory.[25] Similarly, numerous Tory paper votes were enrolled in Renfrewshire prior to the party seizing the seat in 1837, yet of the 1832 voters who turned out in 1837, the Tories had a majority of 62.[26] This is quite remarkable, as no Tory stood in 1832.

One of the most striking features of the Conservative recovery in the 1830s was their capture of the larger county seats. Of the five constituencies with over 2,000 voters in 1832, only one — Aberdeenshire — was Tory in 1832, but by 1841 only one — Fife — was not, whereas Perthshire, Ayrshire and Lanarkshire had been won. The scale of vote creation needed, and the risk of Whig reprisals, made such activity unlikely to be significant, and in two of these three large seats the evidence points to no substantial faggot element. (There is no clear evidence either way for Lanarkshire.) In Ayrshire a Tory scheme to form paper voters in 1839 met with a lukewarm response from local supporters, and the Liberal county paper, while claiming some manufacturing had gone on, stressed intimidation as the key to the Conservative victory in the 1839 by-election.[27] In Perthshire, in 1837, Lord John Russell told the Queen, 'the superior organisation of the Tory party have enabled them to gain the appearance of change of opinion which has not in fact taken place'. Cockburn explained the Whig defeat in the 1834 by-election by the formation of a 'confederacy of Lairds to domineer over their dependents. It is the victory of the owners of the soil achieved by the forced services of their helots and serfs'.[28] Neither invoked the traditional Whig cry at a Tory win of vote making, a point implicitly reiterated by the Liberal agent in Blairgowrie, when he argued that the Conservative registration drive was ending because 'our opponents, who depended almost entirely on their tenantry, are nearly exhausted'. One of the few references by Liberals to Tory vote making occurs in 1838, after the seat had been decisively won by the latter.[29] In 1840, the Tory M.P. issued instructions that qualified voters should be added to the rolls wherever possible, but that fictitious creations were emphatically not to be used.[30]

Thus whereas vote making made an important contribution to the Tory revival, it was effective only when taken with other factors. In no more than a handful of cases, with an adventitious conjunction of very small electorates and the majority of superior titles held by Tory lairds — as perhaps in Selkirk and in Peebles — was it decisive on its own. Other elements also have to be taken into account to explain fully the Tory performance in the 1830s: the use of influence; organisation; and the broad movement of opinion from Whiggery to Conservatism.

Political influence and social deference — the two sides of the control exercised by a landlord over those economically and socially dependent on him to secure their votes for the candidate of his choice — have been seen as the major determinants of voting behaviour in English counties in the era between the first and second Reform Acts. Out of respect for the acknowledged leaders of their agricultural community, tenant farmers and others connected with an estate would vote subserviently in accordance with the declared wishes of the landowner.[31] Evidence of this type of influence is not hard to find in Scotland. Lord Airlie was assured in 1840 that his tenantry would comply with his wishes at an election 'without the *least* reluctance'; in Inverness-shire, the Dochfour factor intended to keep the estate voters neutral until the laird expressed his political preference; in Fife, Lord Moray's agent promised to deliver the tenants' votes to the Tory now that Moray had converted to Conservatism.[32] The prevalence of influence may be gauged from the flourish with which some landlords announced they would leave their tenants free to vote at will: 'I have never interfered with my Tenants on the occasion of any former election with regard to the disposal of their votes and it is not my intention to do so now'.[33] A great deal of care was taken by lairds to prevent the opposition from canvassing estates without prior permission (which was not invariably given), presumably lest contrary opinions might conflict with deferential respect.[34]

While it can thus be accepted that deference played its share in explaining voting patterns, and would probably help Conservatives, as most landowners were of that party, it was not always exercised effortlessly or without countervailing pressures. Deference was more likely to apply if a well-known local man stood: defeat in Angus in 1832 was predicted for the Tories because, while the gentry could probably have induced their farmers to vote for one of the Airlie family, they could not guarantee support for the outsider eventually chosen. Not all Tory landlords were prepared to utilise their powers of influence, as in Argyll, where the Duke 'has taken no part whatever in the late contests in that county', being not in good health, of a retiring disposition and preoccupied with running his extensive estates. In Ayrshire, the Tory candidate complained that in neither the 1832 nor the 1835 contests were the lairds willing to use their influence over the tenantry.[35] A significant difference between Scottish and English villages and small towns tended to reduce the extent of deference in the former. Not only was there, as has been noted, a sizeable number of villages qualified to vote in counties on the £10 suffrage, but also the English type of estate village was relatively rare in Scotland. Instead the Scottish village served a wider area, and so the shopkeepers and tradesmen were not so beholden to one or two estates for their business. Peel was reminded of this by a Scottish Tory M.P.: 'In Scotland, you are perhaps aware that the inhabitants of the Towns and Villages are generally less dependent upon the neighbouring proprietors than in England'. Two years later the same M.P. gave an instance of this: 'In two villages of Berwickshire, Earlston and Neidpath, situated apart from any large towns, on the lands of three beneficient, resident Conservative proprietors, out of 34 electors, 30 went to a distance to vote for the *Liberal* candidate, Sir Francis Blake, a stranger to the County, in a contest got up a few days before the election'.[36]

It is not always easy to reconcile the concept of deferential voting with the frequent allegations that coercion and threats were used by landlords against their dependants. Most of this evidence of course comes from defeated Liberals, who spoke in dark but generalised terms of jobs, tenure and contracts being at risk, although very few instances were actually adduced.[37] Some indications of these tactics emerge in the Perthshire contest of 1840, when Lord Airlie put great pressure on tenants and shopkeepers, but the only concrete claim found by the present writer that a tenancy had been lost by voting against the landlord's wishes came (ironically) from a Tory in Inverness-shire.[38]

Several factors worked against the untrammelled use of deference and influence. Anti-Tories, especially the non-electors, sought to deploy alternative techniques of influence and coercion. Sometimes it took the form of exclusive dealing against Conservative shopkeepers, an excuse used by an ingenious Stirlingshire baker to justify retaining the custom of Tory lairds despite charging higher prices for bread.[39] Frequently uglier devices came into play, as in Stirlingshire in 1837: 'Your tenant Forrest has had a dog shot and been threatened to be smoked out of the mill'.[40] In Fife, landlord influence was countered by committees of Liberal electors and non-electors which were formed in small towns like Ceres, Limekilns and Charlestown with the aims of both publishing lists of Tory voters (presumably to encourage exclusive dealing) and of keeping the Whig support intact by convening meetings of delegates from nearby villages to pledge to vote solidly against the Tory.[41] Allegations of intimidation were made frequently by Tories, and the greatest outbreak of violence came in 1837 at the Roxburghshire contest when Tory voters in Hawick were stripped and thrown into the river. The upshot of such attacks was that the Tories could not get all their voters to the poll. In 1835, only the tenants of the most ardent Ayrshire Tories, like Lord Eglinton, voted; 'fear of Hawick' was stated to be a serious obstacle to Tory prospects in Roxburghshire after 1837; while in Fife in 1837 one third did not vote, because, the Tory claimed, of past intimidation. Indeed in the 1835 Fife contest, the party's canvassing agents reported that many farmers declined to vote for fear of being beaten up by radicals.[42] It may well be that tenants not of the same political persuasion as their landlords found the fear of intimidation argument a useful pretext for at least abstaining, a suggestion hinted at by a Liberal manager who noted that the Inverness-shire tenantry were finding excuses not to vote Tory.[43]

Deference and influence, moreover, were most likely to apply if there were no great contentious issues of principle, as a Tory laird observed: 'I have had a good deal of experience in county canvassing and I have been led to the conclusion that the Tenants of Scotland are on the whole very indifferent to points of mere civil politics. They feel no great interest in either party and therefore they will not quarrel with their landlord on such subjects — but vote along with them, and this you will see is the case on both sides all over the Country'. He went on, however, to stress that there was at least one very fundamental question developing in the later 1830s whose gravity would induce normally compliant tenant-farmers to resist lairdly influence: 'But in this Church Question I am firmly persuaded that the influence of the Landlords will be *absolutely* nothing over those who are Non-Intrusionists. On points of religion and Presbyterian principles the Tenantry of Scotland will be as inflexible as their forefathers'.[44] Confirmation of this came when in 1841 the Buteshire electors, normally the most docile in the land, were stirred to protest, as Rae explained: 'Lord Bute's tenants will not vote against me, but considering the question is of a religious nature, they refuse in many circumstances to come to the poll at all'.[45] But even before the upheaval in the Church of Scotland, religious feelings were the source of protest against landlords. Roman Catholics would defy their lairds to oppose Toryism, as the ultra-Protestant candidate, The Chisholm, found in Inverness-shire in 1835: 'A few minutes before the final close of the poll, when his success was beyond all doubt, some of his tenants, members of his clan and bearing his name, who were Roman Catholics, came up and recorded their votes against him. As the act itself could not possibly have affected the result of the contest, the performance of it under such circumstances was calculated to make it partake of the character of a personal insult'. Similarly, a list of voters in the Lochaber area in the same contest shows voting by estate blocks, with the exception of Roman Catholics, who were all Liberal.[46] Dissenters, too, were non-subservient. In Wigtownshire, Lord Galloway's influence was less extensive than appeared, because a good number of his tenants were 'dissenters, and extremely liberal, and will vote according to their own inclinations and in spite of their Tory landlords'.[47]

Organisation played a substantial part in the Tory advance, but within clear limitations.[48] No nationwide body existed. A Scottish Conservative Association was formed in May 1835 with the aim of forming branches in all constituencies to attend to registration work. With club premises in Edinburgh and a full-time secretary to handle administrative and political affairs, it was patently modelled on the Carlton Club. Despite being sponsored by the foremost Scottish Tories —Buccleuch, Mansfield, Lord Ramsay, Alexander Pringle, Sir George Clerk, C. L. Cumming Bruce and Sir Francis Drummond — it came to little, and by August 1836 an Edinburgh Tory complained that it lacked adequate cash to function effectively, while its interference in constituency matters was resented.[49] The collapse of the Scottish Association revealed two related forces inhibiting the growth of Conservatism. Firstly, it was too much the creature of Tory notables from the pre-Reform era, with minimal middle-class involvement. This left it open to *The Scotsman's* charge that its object was 'to provide resources and organise agencies for the employment of bribery, influence and intimidation throughout Scotland'.[50] Secondly, as Mansfield lamented, 'many of our friends, who were otherwise good men and true, might hesitate from timidity or excess of caution on [sic] joining a Society whose political objects are so plainly designated in its name'.[51]

As a result, little central assistance was available, certainly not from London: 'not a guinea has been given by the Carlton Club for any Scotch election and none is expected', grumbled an Inverness-shire Tory in 1835.[52] In the mid-1830s some efforts were made by Sir Francis Drummond to co-ordinate the party's work in Scotland, acting on the request of the Duke of Buccleuch, whom Peel had made general overseer for Scotland.[53] Drummond's main duties were to try to assist constituencies to find candidates and to help raise the finance to meet the costs of electioneering.[54] After 1837, Drummond's role rather faded out and greater interest in Scottish matters by London became apparent, as Sir James Graham and F.R. Bonham assumed many of Drummond's responsibilities. This was probably an effort to reach the middle-class West of Scotland Conservatives on whom Peel had made such an impact at the start of 1837, as discussed below. While there are no letters of any importance from this social group in either the Buccleuch or Drummond papers, Bonham, Graham and Peel himself were by 1838 in regular contact with Robert Lamond, the Tory agent in Glasgow and district.[55]

But very little attention was paid by these national figures to strengthening the structure of organisation: this was left very much to each constituency to find its own way forward. Two results ensued from this local devolution. Firstly, the transmission of organisational skills depended on informal, personal communications and was thus sporadic and patchy in its distribution. The West Lothian registration agent received a very detailed and knowledgeable set of instructions from John Hope explaining how to work the registration procedure; but invaluable though the information was, it seems not to have been made generally available to party agents throughout Scotland.[56] Similarly, the idea of vote making was raised in Ayrshire only after a local Tory laird had had a conversation with the Town Clerk of Ayr, who remarked that 'this is now in operation in the County of Mid-Lothian'.[57] Secondly, local jealousy and parochialism were strongly felt and were unchecked by any wider concept of promoting the Conservative interest. Several committees refused to make money available to help contests elsewhere, even in winnable seats. Glasgow Tories, on being asked to contribute to a planned fight at Perth Burgh, replied: 'we have but small funds, and [we] don't think the members will consent to send them so far away'; and Ayrshire Tories were likewise reluctant to subsidise their fellow partisans fighting the Kilmarnock Burghs.[58]

In some county seats, the organisation of the party was vested in the hands of a few large landowners, the most notable instances being in the Borders, where Buccleuch and a handful of others ran Tory affairs in Roxburghshire, Selkirk and Dumfriesshire, and in the North-East, where Lords Aberdeen and Arbuthnott were all-powerful in Aberdeenshire and Kincardineshire respectively. But not all counties were like this. In Perthshire, the M.P. recorded in 1843, 'the expense and trouble of preserving the Conservative interest in Perthshire have chiefly fallen on a very limited number of private gentlemen, ... the aid given by the Aristocracy was comparatively small'.[59] Ayrshire too was run by a committee of twenty to thirty lairds.[60] In Perthshire, the lairds controlled the choice of candidates, for it was a committee which invited Lord Stormont to stand.[61] In these county seats, which would also include Fife, Stirling, Angus, and Lanark — that is, the larger county seats which were being won in 1837 and 1841 — the party finances were on a broader basis than the purses of a few grandees. Stirling had an elaborate rating system for contributions based on 1% of the annual value of property which revealed 75 contributors, many with very small estates; Perthshire had a fund to defray registration charges to which at least 26 lairds contributed; and Ayrshire had 31 subscribers meeting registration bills of nearly £400.[62]

The raising of cash to develop registration work was very important. *The Scotsman* perceived only sinister grounds behind this development: 'in the Conservative vocabulary this is synonymous with the fabrication of fictitious votes'.[63] But that paper tended to be obsessed with vote making by Tories, and anyway there were other gains to be derived by a well-organised registration system. The West Lothian agent was alerted to the advantage of lodging Conservative claims ahead of the Whigs, so that the latter could be opposed in court without the Tories being retaliated against, while the delay caused by the consideration of the Conservative applications would cause the Whigs much loss of time, frustration and expense.[64] An even more striking bonus was shown in Roxburghshire, where the gains from expunging Liberals over the four years between 1837 and 1840 were greater than those chalked up from creating fictitious votes. Of a net gain in Tory additions of 65 over these years, 76 came from removing Liberals, who made 11 more faggot voters than the Tories. In Inverness-shire, too, the Liberals ruefully noted that the Tory gains in registration came from the same techniques, and the same process was to be found in Fife.[65]

These county committees were not preoccupied with registration to the exclusion of all else. At elections, much work was put in. Most counties were divided into districts, with local committees conducting canvassing of voters and identifying qualified but unregistered voters.[66] Outvoters had arrangements made to convey them to polling places: in the case of Perthshire, London outvoters received their travelling expenses, plus £5 as an indemnity for loss of time.[67] Outwith elections, other work was undertaken. Several committees strove to disseminate party principles through newspapers. This was done sometimes by floating new ones, as was considered for both the South-East and for Ayrshire, and was achieved in 1835 by the Glasgow Tories when they established *The Glasgow Constitutional.*[68] Elsewhere, efforts were made to keep alive existing ones by expanding the subscription lists. This was urged on Fife Tories, who were warned of the urgency of keeping their paper, the *Fifeshire Journal,* in business: 'the case in this county is essentially similar to that of almost every county in Scotland, in most of which the newspaper advocating conservative principles is likely to cease unless it is supported by those professing similar opinions'.[69] Another form of propaganda was considered in Kincardineshire, where the two leading Tories planned a counterblast to a pro-government manifesto circulating in the area, and agreed that a pamphlet should be produced to expose 'the false pretentions' of Liberal M.P.s.[70]

Several of the bigger counties had, as has been noted, extended their active supporters beyond a narrow handful of great landowners, but in some there was a deliberate bid to establish a very broad scale of participation. In the West Kilbride district, an Association (not a Committee, which had different overtones) had been founded, open to all who were both Conservative and respectable, 'however humble their station'. There were, in 1839, 120 members, making donations at the low level of from 1/-(5p) to 20/-(£1), with a committee to administer the work of registration and canvassing. Significantly, of the 18 on the committee, not more than 7 or 8 could be deemed gentry.[71] Stirlingshire had a similar body in the Polmont Constitutional Association; but it was in the burghs that formal organisation was particularly required.[72] Some of the smaller urban seats could be managed by a few local potentates — as in the Ayr Burghs, where Lords Eglinton, Bute, Argyll and Buccleuch co-operated to uphold the Tory cause. But the practice of grouping towns that were often widely dispersed geographically made this difficult to sustain, and could ruffle the feathers of the increasingly self-confident bourgeoisie in the towns. So even the Haddington Burghs, generally submissive to the will of nearby landowners, had their Conservative Association by 1838, although the magnates had vetoed a similar body for the county three years earlier.[73]

Glasgow possessed the most advanced popular organisation in the Conservative Operatives' Association, formed in the excitement of Peel's visit to the city in 1836–7, of which more later. With an attendance of 270 at its first A.G.M., it was clearly a sizeable body, and it claimed a steady growth in membership subsequently. Indeed by 1841 it was felt necessary to divide the city into districts to help keep the members in contact with each other, as apparently the existing unified structure could not deal with the large numbers involved. The Operatives' Association's work consisted in part of 'purifying' the registers and enrolling party voters, and in part of canvassing on behalf of candidates. In addition it tried to inculcate Conservative opinions among the populace by holding quarterly lectures on political issues, and its annual dinner was also the occasion for an exposition of Conservative ideas.[74] Edinburgh too had its Operatives' Association, with premises in the High Street and receiving small annual subscriptions from leading city Conservatives.[75] Although little direct evidence exists regarding the activities of the middle-class 'official' Conservative party organisations in Glasgow and Edinburgh, they must have been quite substantial and efficient institutions, for in both cities the party was making great advances in municipal politics, implying a high degree of co-ordination and direction. For six years (i.e. two terms) after 1837 Conservatives held the Lord Provostship of Glasgow, and in 1840 Edinburgh also installed a Tory Lord Provost.[76]

In general, the commitment of the Tories to organisation work was impressive and suggests that devices such as vote creation should be seen in the wider perspective of a general desire to resist radicalism by all possible means. The resolution of the Angus Tories after the 1835 election was all the more impressive because it was another 51 years before the Liberals lost the seat: 'It has generally been thought advisable among our friends that the Party in the county should be kept together and the inrollments [sic] attended to'.[77] Perhaps the best judges of the merits of Tory organisational qualities were the Liberals. Publicly, it was usually alleged that Tory victories were caused by vote making, and this was obviously designed to foment fears that the Tories had not abandoned their notorious pre-1832 practices. In private, and in odd moments of public candour, while vote creation was referred to, much emphasis was placed on the better spirit and machinery of the Conservatives. In Roxburghshire, the Whig M.P. praised the Tories to his brother: 'They certainly work much better together than we do, and are more willing to put their shoulders to the wheel'. In the same year, Sir John Dalrymple told Earl Grey that Mid Lothian and Stirlingshire were not lost because of Tory faggot voters, but because of more energetic and prompt Conservative electioneering machinery. Lord John Russell's comment to Maxwell on the loss of Renfrewshire in 1837 had a broader applicability: 'I understand the Tories were far better prepared than the Liberal Party'. Similarly, the Liberal press commented that the increased Tory vote in Ayrshire in 1837 was due in part to influence, but also to 'exertions unparalleled in the history of electioneering in this County — that as a party they are better organised than their opponents'.[78]

II

Another factor contributing to the progress of Conservatism was, simply, the changing views of many moderate Whigs.[79] Gaining such recruits was a staple claim made by enthusiastic candidates, sometimes based on flimsy evidence, and it may be discounted as a natural confidence-boosting device.[80] That there was, however, a genuine movement by actual voters seems clear. In West Kilbride, one-fifth of those who had voted Whig in 1832 supported the Tory in 1837; while in Inverurie — part of the Elgin Burghs — a Whig vote of 60 in 1832 fell to 39 in 1835, and the Tories correspondingly rose from 5 to 20.[81] West Lothian showed a clear pattern of Tory converts between 1832 and 1837. In sum, if there had been no switches in voting in 1837 by those eligible to poll in both contests, the Tory majority would have been 43 (211–168) among this category, whereas in fact it was nearly doubled to 81 (205–124). Fourteen Whigs in 1832 (9% of the 1832 Whig poll on the register in 1837) turned Tory in 1837, but only one Tory (0.5%) crossed to the Whigs in 1837. Eighteen abstainers in 1832 were Tory voters in 1837, double the eight who went Whig. While the abstainers in 1837 among those who polled in 1832 — an early indication of movement away from one's original party — were numerically even, with 37 Tories and 39 Whigs, proportionally they represented 1 in 6 of the surviving 1832 Tory voters, but 1 in 4 Whigs.[82]

Individuals who declared their grounds for switching party support afford possible insights into these broader movements of opinion. Several abandoned Whiggery because they felt it was becoming too radical in challenging the existing order. Lord Ailsa was one such, informing Earl Grey that he found the Liberal Ayrshire candidate in the 1835 general election 'a positive Radical', and in the by-election later in the year he backed the Tory since 'the County of Ayr is becoming quite Radical, and unless it is stemmed in some way, Landowners will be mere cyphers among their Tenantry'.[83] Peers and landowners who went along the same road included The Chisholm, Lord Moray, William Berry of Tayfield, all in 1834, and Lord Elcho in 1837, while in 1840 the Duke of Richmond, hitherto ostentatiously neutral, declared himself a Tory.[84] Less socially elevated men behaved likewise. A Fife businessman, who was also factor to Moray's property in that county, announced in 1834: 'I became a Reformer in the hope of witnessing the *improvement* of certain portions of the constitution of my country. Instead of which I have seen the most reckless and wanton attempts to effect the destruction of *every part of it,* accompanied by the most undisguised endeavours to drag the country into Revolution'.[85] Hugh Miller recalled in 1847 that 'when many of my respected friends in the north country, alarmed, some ten or twelve years ago, by the Whig measures of the day, were casting their influence into the Conservative scale, I remained a Whig still'.[86] The other main motive for becoming a Conservative was the belief that the Whig policy threatened the Church of Scotland. An important coup for the Tories was the defection of Sir Andrew Agnew, the Whig M.P. for Wigtownshire and an ardent sabbatarian. He found it impossible to support Melbourne's Church and State reform proposals and in the

1837 election endorsed the Tory against the ministerialist candidate for his old seat.[87]

These twin themes of the threat of radical changes leading to republicanism and the cry of the Church in danger became the props of a carefully orchestrated bid by Peel and his senior political advisers to woo the Scottish urban middle class to Conservatism, just as in England. It is symptomatic of the attenuated social base of Scottish Toryism in the mid-1830s that the initiative had to come from England. The landed Tories in Scotland were frequently parochial and snobbish in their approach to building the party. Montrose displayed the envy of old wealth for the *nouveau riche* when he rejected an appeal from nearby Glasgow to help defray the cost of the 1841 contest in the city: 'I really think that Glasgow is rich enough to pay their own Elections and although the Provost was very reluctant to stand he can well afford not to go a-begging'.[88] Ignorance of, or indifference to, the bourgeoisie was prevalent. Having between them chosen a middle-class candidate for the Ayr Burghs, neither Eglinton nor the Duke of Argyll could recall his name. Also in Ayrshire, a local laird confessed himself unable to offer any advice about choosing a suitable political agent, since he had little occasion for personal acquaintance with the lawyers and men of business in the town of Ayr.[89] A Stirlingshire baronet showed minimal interest in social nuances when considering how to raise an election subscription list: 'If more money should be wanted, the list might be circulated among the middle class, none of whom has as yet added their names'.[90] To be fair, some landed Tories did have an inkling of what was possible. Lord Rosslyn had high hopes of tapping this seam: 'My reliance is upon the returning good sense of the middle ranks of people who have some property to save and upon the interested feelings of tradesmen who must be convinced that times of trouble must put an end to all profitable trade'. Within two months he was earnestly coaxing a wealthy Liberal banker and manufacturer into seeing that his future prosperity lay with a Conservative victory.[91] Sometimes good intentions could misfire. Lord Stormont, seeking to win Perthshire, set out to ingratiate himself with the 'middling and lower classes in this quarter [Perth town] by patronising football and so forth'. Fifteen thousand gathered on the burgh's North Inch grounds to watch a fifty-a-side match between teams chosen by Stormont and the Provost. Uproar ensued when Stormont protested at the crowd's behaviour, and violence broke out when he bit a man who was arguing with him.[92]

By the end of 1835 it had become plain to Peel and his entourage that more direct action on their part was required in Scotland. The election of 1835 had not gone so well there as in England, at any rate in the urban constituencies, as Table 1.1 shows. Part of the blame for the poor performance was ascribed to the feeling that Peel's appointments to the main Scottish legal and administrative posts were made on the recommendation of three pillars of the old jobbing system — Lord Melville, Sir William Rae and John Hope. In one seat, East Lothian, it was claimed that the animus this had created very nearly destroyed the Conservatives' election effort.[93] These old Tories were concentrated in Edinburgh, but the natural constituency analogous to those middle-class moderates won over by Peel in England was in the industrial West of Scotland. Peel was assured in 1836 that there were indeed marked stirrings of sympathy in the Glasgow region towards progressive Conservatism.[94] Indeed, a candidate had been put up for the city in the 1835 election by a determined local group. Moreover, a new paper, the *Glasgow Constitutional,* had been launched by city businessmen in 1835 to articulate moderate Conservative principles, in distinction to the existing organ of older Toryism, the *Glasgow Courier.*

This tentative realignment, it was contended, was far more advanced in the West than in the East: 'In the West of Scotland the distinction between the old Tory Party and the Conservative Reformers is much less strongly marked and maintained than in Edinburgh, and I am assured that many most respectable persons, who were friendly to the Reform Bill, will be found in Glasgow ready to meet you and bury all past differences in the earnest desire of making common ground against a republic ... But in *Edinburgh* the case is different. There the High Tory feeling is unmingled and unmitigated: no alliance has taken place between the old Party and the more moderate of their former opponents'.[95] An ideal opportunity to hasten this process presented itself in the Glasgow University Rectorial Election of November 1836. The previous incumbent, Lord Stanley, had won in 1834 with an alliance of moderate Whig and Tory support, but although he had left the Whigs in May 1834, he did not openly join the Conservatives until 1836, so his victory could not be considered an index of Conservative feelings. Peel stood in 1836 and was elected handsomely, his victory being hailed as a portent of a major shift in political attitudes in the West, as the three rectors immediately previous to Stanley had all been staunch Reformers: Jeffrey, Cockburn and Brougham. The crusty Tory sheriff of Lanarkshire stressed how significant it was 'that Glasgow College, filled with the descendants of the inveterate Whigs of Bothwell Brig and the Ayrshire Covenanters, or the sons of the reforming Merchants of Glasgow who were so deeply imbued with democratic principles in 1832, should so soon have reverted to Conservative principles'.[96]

The promotion of the new Conservatism did not end with the Rectorial victory, but was skilfully built upon with the address given by Peel at a banquet of Conservatives held in Glasgow in January 1837, on the occasion of his installation as Rector. The old high Tories of Edinburgh were consciously and ostentatiously snubbed. An invitation to speak in Edinburgh as well as in Glasgow was turned down by Peel, since that would undo any benefits derived from a visit to Glasgow. The admission to the Peel banquet of a large number of Tories of pre-1832 vintage would drive moderates away, and even receiving a deputation of Edinburgh Conservatives was a dubious proposition as, unlike the Glasgow body, the group contained no converts from Whiggery.[97] Then Peel's speech was carefully constructed. Graham read it in advance: 'I collected he was resolved to risk the displeasure of the High Tories and to hold out the Hand of Friendship to all Reformers who with him were now willing to resist the democratic impulse'.[98]

The effect of the oration was successful on a large scale. The banquet itself had been attended by 3,500 diners, sitting in a specially constructed hall of huge dimensions and served by 137 waiters. Peel had been invited to the banquet by a group of local operatives incensed at the Town Council's refusal to grant him the freedom of the city. Two thousand working men were said to have signed the address to Peel, and this led directly to the formation of the Glasgow Conservative Operatives' Association, dedicated to spreading Peelite Conservatism among the urban proletariat. Its first committee had 23 members, and their occupations indicate a reasonable working-class presence: 2 wrights; 7 printers; 4 warehouse and shop men; 4 cloth lappers; 1 sawyer and 1 fringe maker.[99] More relevantly, Peel had equally caught the mood of the middle classes, as all testified, and the political benefits rapidly showed themselves. At the 1837 election, the Glasgow Tories felt strong enough to run two men, and powerful challenges were mounted in the burgh seats of Kilmarnock, Greenock, Perth and Ayr. Only one burgh seat, Kilmarnock, was won, but the party agent in the West blamed the results on the unexpectedness of the dissolution and promised that seats like Glasgow would be safe after the next registration courts.[100] After 1837, the momentum was sustained: Sir James Graham, Peel's lieutenant, won the Glasgow University Rectorial contest in 1838, confirming the trend set in 1836. Moreover Graham was accorded the honour denied to Peel, as the Town Council voted to make him a freeman of the city. As previously noted, Graham and Bonham took a very close interest in running Scottish affairs. After the 1839 registrations they were predicting good results in most urban lowland seats, and were still buoyant after the 1840 registrations.[101] The normally safe Liberal seat of Greenock was felt by a local Whig to be at risk: 'unless we move, some influential mercantile Tory will be invited to stand and probably would sit'.[102] But these ambitious and confident expectations were comprehensively shattered in the 1841 election. This is in signal contrast to England where, as Table 1.1 shows, marked advances by the Tories were made in the boroughs. No sizeable gains were made in the urban West: Kilmarnock and Renfrewshire were lost, and Falkirk was the only gain, while Glasgow and Greenock remained comfortably in the Whig camp. The failure to carry Peel's strategy to a successful conclusion was in glaring contrast to the pattern south of the border, as Graham observed to his collaborator in Scottish organisational matters: 'In Scotland we have been least successful'.[103]

III

This setback at the final hurdle in 1841 was deeply disappointing after the careful exertions made over the previous years. The irony was that the Tories' electoral rebuff occurred because their assiduous support for the cause probably closest to the hearts of the moderate urban middle class in the 1830s led to an irreconcilable tension between the differing strands of the party's policy and of its social bases. The source of the problem was the revived assertiveness within the Church of Scotland in the 1830s of an Evangelical wing, determined to remove the blemishes which had, as they saw it, been allowed to disfigure the state church over the preceding half-century. The dominant party, the Moderates, were depicted by the Evangelicals as lax in their theological standards, indifferent to improved worship and unwilling to proselytise. Instead they preferred a quiet life, acquiescing in the control of church appointments by the political rulers of the country who deployed this patronage with ruthless skill to maintain their dominance and stifle opposition. As a result, the Moderate clergy were lacklustre preachers, subservient to the landowning class — the lay patrons — and generally ill-equipped to respond to the social changes attendant on industrialisation and urbanisation. Accordingly many of the urban middle class, finding the Church of Scotland unsatisfactory, became increasingly attracted to those churches which had seceded from it. The Secession churches rarely showed any substantial theological differences from the state church, firmly retaining the full panoply of Presbyterianism. Their disputes with the national church were generally over the extent of lay patronage, as control of the appointment of the minister was vested in one man (usually the local laird), which meant that the selected candidate would be virtually certain to propound opinions consistent with the patron's. As many of the landed class were Episcopalian, much dissatisfaction with the ministers' insufficiently warm espousal of John Knox's views grew among the evangelically minded members of the congregation. Moreover, as the middle class grew more assertive, they did not find it easy to accept the right of one man to make the nomination, especially as traditional deference was less extensive in an urban setting. The growing wealth of this new class made it financially possible for the congregation to support a church, and so to appoint ministers whose preaching commanded popular esteem, without relying on the state for cash aid. These independent, or Voluntary, churches became prevalent in the expanding urban centres, where the Established Church was unable or unwilling to operate. By the 1820s the Voluntary churches were developing steadily, while the Church of Scotland seemed stagnant, languishing in rural backwaters and impervious to the evangelical yearnings of congregations. Led by the Rev. Thomas Chalmers, a movement sprang up in the state church anxious to counter these trends. Chalmers, deeply impressed by his experiences in a working-class Glasgow parish in the post-Napoleonic era of social unrest, became convinced that without the resources and support of the state, Christianity could not hope to retrieve the lapsed urban masses, but that only a vigorous evangelicalism would recapture the cities for God. Thus Chalmers, and the young evangelical clergy and laity who rapidly grouped around him, wished to draw the lesson of the Voluntary upsurge, viz. that evangelicalism was appealing to the urban population, but sought to graft that onto the existing state church, largely by eradicating the defects of moderatism and restoring the Church of Scotland to its pristine condition, shorn of erastian control.[104]

The 1830s therefore saw a complicated three-way struggle to establish the pattern of religion in Scotland: between the Voluntary and the Establishment principles, and within the latter between the Evangelical and the Moderate position. To a large extent the outcome of the first conflict depended on whether the Evangelicals won the second; for if they did so, the Church of Scotland would become very appealing to many otherwise attracted to Voluntaryism. The political dimensions of this battle were wide-ranging, not least because fundamental questions regarding the national institution of the state church were involved. The national church Evangelicals were of particular interest to both Whig and

Conservative, as they were heavily drawn from the dynamic aspirant newer bourgeoisie.[105] A few landowners were strongly identified with the Evangelical churchmen — Sinclair of Ulbster, Agnew of Lochnaw, Fox Maule, Breadalbane, Campbell of Monzie, Colquhoun of Killermont, Thomson of Banchory — although some of these, e.g. Colquhoun, were actually Evangelical Anglicans. It was, however, mostly manufacturers, merchants and professionals who formed Chalmers' lay army: in Glasgow, William Collins, printer, Henry Dunlop, cotton spinner, Hugh Tennent, brewer, William Campbell, warehouse man; in Greenock, John Dunlop, banker; in Edinburgh, F. B. Douglas, advocate, Charles Cowan, paper manufacturer. Voluntaries tended to be radical in politics in part perhaps because of their democratic ecclesiastical structure, in part probably because they had suffered until the 1820s from religious discrimination embodied in legislation, and also because the Scottish state church was identified with the unreformed political regime. Evangelical churchmen were inclined to moderation in politics, as one of them — a Whig — portrayed the general outlook of the type: '[they] approved the Reform Bill and may wish for the practical reform of abuses generally, but [their] great object is good government without attaching any great importance to the circumstances of which party it may be from whom it is obtained'.[106] This was a precise picture of the very sort of men Peel was hoping to lure to his party, and the additional point that Evangelical churchmen were differentiated from Voluntaries largely by their absolute commitment to the establishment principle naturally suggested a close affinity to moderate Conservatism, with its proclaimed role of stopping rash and destructive assaults on existing institutions. Indeed Chalmers himself was always a Conservative, and had opposed the Reform Bill.

From the passing of the Reform Bill until 1834–5, the church Evangelicals generally gave their backing to the Whigs. It was natural for a pressure group aiming to make sweeping changes in the nature and structure of a state institution to seek to establish close relations with a party which looked likely to be in office for a long time. Also, the Whigs were embarking on a wave of reform measures, and so might reasonably be expected to respond positively to requests to alter and democratise the Scottish Church. Thirdly, the Moderates, still vigorously fighting the Evangelicals in the Church, were intimately identified with the Tory party. It was reported that many Evangelicals otherwise sympathetic to Conservatism were still suspicious because they believed that on Scottish church matters Peel was overly influenced by John Hope, the leading lay Moderate and pre-Reform *éminence grise* of the Tories.[107] From 1834–5, however, these attitudes towards the Whigs were reappraised, and the Conservatives came closer to the Evangelicals. In part, the natural convergence of views on state churches was recognised, and Episcopalian landowners were urged on these grounds to subscribe to the Presbyterian state church's church-building programme.[108] More important was disillusionment with the Whig administration after its reluctance to grant at once and in full the demands of the Evangelicals. Chalmers complained after one confrontation: 'Nothing could exceed the strength of the general assurances that we received from the Government in favour of our Church. But I am much staggered by their subsequent proceedings since I left London'.[109] The grievance was not merely that the Whigs were hostile to the Evangelical wing's requests, but that they seemed utterly submissive to the Voluntaries. Whig resistance to the Church Extension Scheme adopted by the Evangelicals was ascribed by Chalmers to the excessive influence of Dissenters.[110] The appointment of a commission to investigate the condition of the national church was denounced as being packed with anti-Church of Scotland individuals by the Whigs at the behest of Voluntaries.[111] The Universities Bill of 1836 was seen as too pro-Voluntary, and an Education Bill of the same year was attacked as the first step to Voluntaryism by threatening the state church's control of the parochial schools.[112] Hence, Peel was told in late 1836, the Church of Scotland was deeply suspicious of Melbourne's ministry: 'They [Church of Scotland] consider that they [Whigs] are on all occasions ready to sacrifice the interests of the Established Church in order to conciliate the Dissenters'.[113]

Wedded to this surge of unease at the Whigs' handling of the Scottish Church issue was the apprehension aroused by the government's apparent willingness to contemplate a drastic solution to the Irish Church problem, which some saw as tantamount to disestablishment. Thus Stanley's victory in the November 1834 Glasgow University Rectorial election was credited to the skilful co-ordination by Professor Sir D.K. Sandford of an alliance of both wings of the state church, hitherto hostile to each other.[114] Emboldened by this, the church cry was openly worked in the ensuing parliamentary elections in January 1835. In Fife, the Tory was advised to drive the Whig candidate into the Radical camp by supporting the Church Extension Scheme since 'the great thing is to catch the moderates'. An erstwhile supporter wrote to the Whig candidate in Fife, complaining: 'Matters have greatly changed since I last tendered my support', specifically instancing the threat to the national church posed by the government's policy.[115] In Mid Lothian, a Whig confessed, Church questions, 'as to which a great proportion of our Electors here are literally frantic, occasion the greatest difficulties — and the Elections will depend more on Ecclesiastical than Political considerations'. In Glasgow, the journal of the Evangelical church party advised that the Tory should be supported by 'those friends of the Church of Scotland who conceive that in the maintenance of Christian principles of legislation and the extension of our church and schools are involved at once the Christianity, the constitution and the peace of their country'. Fox Maule was warned that 'the game is up here in Perthshire' unless he could assure Churchmen that despite voting against further grants to it, he was a true friend of the Church, and not a tool of Dissenters.[116] The process was continued in two by-elections held in 1835, because the Whigs had decisively repudiated the Evangelicals' calls for financial assistance to the Church. In Inverness-shire, 'The general opinion is (among Mr. Grant's old staunch supporters too) [i.e. Liberals] that the Church question will complete his downfall in this County', as it permitted many Whigs to defect in response to 'the Church in danger' cry. The Chisholm campaigned as a Tory exclusively on the religious issue and won.[117] In Ayrshire, where the Liberal vote fell by one-third — 700 votes — from 1832 and the Tory rose from 324 in 1832 to 829, 'the now sickening 'twaddle' of 'the Church in danger' was urged not without success on the minds of the over-sensitive in religious matters'.[118]

Public interest in the Church crisis became all-absorbing hereafter, and there was a mounting drive by the Chalmers camp to see a party sympathetic to its aspirations returned to power. The fervour was intense, not to say lunatic. Sir John Bowring, defeated in Kilmarnock in 1837 by an ultra-Evangelical Tory, recalled: 'In one of the Clyde Burghs [i.e. Kilmarnock burghs] a letter was shown to me in which were the words 'we will have a religious man to represent us, even if we go to hell to find him' '.[119] Peel's Glasgow banquet speech in 1837 won acclaim and struck a warm response more for its stress on the rights of the state church than its exposition of moderate reform. The address of the 2,000 working men, while acknowledging the due role of well-considered reform, reserved its full literary powers for the coda: 'Sir, we love the Church of Scotland, for all it has suffered and all it has done to provide the poor with religious instruction and to afford their children a Bible education in its Parish Schools'. The Conservative Operatives' Association's objects were to uphold the British Constitution as established in 1690, with a significant ordering of priorities. First, 'a prominent object of the Association shall be to defend the Ecclesiastical and Educational Establishments of Scotland as an integral part of that Constitution', and then it added, the Association would seek to promote purity of administration.[120] There was, then, little vestige of Tory Radicalism behind working-class Conservatism in Scotland. As J.T. Ward demonstrated, the factory reform movement did not attract any sizeable degree of support from Scottish Tories. Most Conservative M.P.s voted against factory legislation, and only a few Tories outside Parliament — Thomson of Banchory and John Hope, the Evangelical philanthropist — displayed any commitment.[121] There was an active movement in Glasgow agitating for this reform, but it was led by working-class radicals and had no strong contacts with city Tories.[122] The absence of the New Poor Law in Scotland meant that a vital linkage between Tory Radicals and working classes in the North of England was not available in Scotland.

In the aftermath of Peel's speech, the progressive wing of the Glasgow Conservatives called on all Tories to be actively organised to defend, in sequence, the Established Church, then the House of Lords, since abolition of the latter would be a prelude to disestablishment, and thirdly to oppose plans to appropriate the revenues of the Church of Ireland. The pro-Chalmers paper in Glasgow was even franker, warning beforehand that if Peel's banquet simply consisted of an array of Conservative notables, it would have little impact, whereas if the principles of the national church were advocated, success was assured. After the event it professed itself well pleased at Peel's forthright acceptance of the Evangelical churchmen's demands.[123] The General Election of 1837 continued the identification of Conservatism with the Church of Scotland. In Glasgow, where fourteen Established Kirk Sessions were said by a Whig to be canvassing with their congregations on behalf of the Tory, the link was explicit. No Church of Scotland clergyman voted Liberal in Mid Lothian, and only one in Roxburghshire, while the Ross and Cromarty Presbytery received a resolution accusing Liberal voters among the state church clergy of being covert Roman Catholics.[124] More generally, Non-Intrusionist leaders were assured by local Tory managers that the rise in the Conservative vote in this period was largely due to the support of their Church party.[25]

However, this relationship, in which both the ecclesiastical and the political wings fed off each other's success, became steadily more ambivalent after 1837. While the Conservatives were jubilant at the accession to the party of so vigorous and dynamic a force as the Evangelicals, gradually the party leadership grew less happy at the potentially disruptive impact of the Evangelicals. Firstly, the apparent insatiability of Chalmer's importunate demands roused fears as to who was controlling whom. 'I can no longer trust his prudence or believe his promises', confided Graham in 1839, after Chalmers had put greater pressure on the Tories to endorse the single-minded pursuit of his goals.[126] This concern had sharpened in 1838, when the focus of the Evangelicals' campaign shifted direction. In general until then the main thrust of their strategy was firstly to preserve the state church's sphere of activity in education and the poor law, and secondly to extend the scope of the Church of Scotland's work by the Church Extension Scheme, which was designed to build established churches in those areas of demographic growth hitherto the stronghold of the Voluntaries. Church Extension, paralleling the work of the Church of England in the great cities, was warmly applauded by Conservatives as politically desirable.[127] From 1838, however, the Evangelicals opened up a new line to spike the Voluntaries, which soon became the predominant theme. This was the assault on the institution of lay patronage in the Church, a principle which had been upheld by the courts in a series of decisions, thereby invalidating the Veto Act, passed by the General Assembly in 1834 to give congregations some veto over a patron's choice. The Evangelicals upheld the concept of the Veto Act, namely that a patron should not be allowed to force his choice of minister onto a parish against the wishes of the congregation. Thus they espoused the cause of non-intrusion, a term which gave them their usual name until 1843. Moreover, the Non-Intrusionists asserted the principle of spiritual independence, claiming that the Church could not accept dictation by the state courts in matters affecting its spiritual integrity, notably the terms on which ministers should be appointed. Thus the Church put itself above the law courts in certain areas.[128]

The Non-Intrusionists were now striking at a fundamental principle of Toryism, the rights of property, and the party leaders drew back in alarm from endorsing this. Graham protested that Chalmers' claim for unlimited public cash to further the goals of the Church of Scotland with no restrictions on its use and also for an end to lay patronage were causes 'for which no Man and no Party can contend with propriety or consistency at the same time'.[129] Wellington was perturbed at 'the alarming strides' made by Voluntary-like doctrines in the Scottish Established Church, and worried lest it be a prelude to similar trends in the Anglican Church: 'When one's neighbour's house is on fire, one's own is in danger. We shall have it in England, if not extinguished in Scotland'.[130] The Non-Intrusionist campaign had a further serious aspect: it widened the rift within the state church, and the Moderates who were loyal Tories of long standing grew aggressive in resisting the pretensions of the Chalmers party. In 1839 John Hope rallied the old Tory Moderates with a scathing pamphlet exposing the stance taken by the Non-Intrusionists. It was reading Hope that led Wellington to express his concern, and Graham was worried from another standpoint by it, fearing that the patronage issue 'is likely to produce the most fatal divisions in the Conservative ranks of Scotland'. Thus, the giving of £300 to the Non-Intrusionists' funds by the father of a potential Tory candidate for Perthshire was deplored as likely to split the county Conservatives and so was 'a step so obnoxious to many of your friends'.[131]

Not only was the total adoption of the Non-Intrusionist's menu of demands antipathetic to many of the ideas of Conservatism, as well as dividing the party in Scotland, it by no means guaranteed the full support of the Non-Intrusionists. Many leading members were staunch Liberals, and there was a powerful desire to keep the group as a whole distant from either Whigs or Tories in order to play both off, as well as retain unity. 'We were, and are, most anxious to keep the question free from politics', said one of Chalmers' closest clerical henchmen.[132] The Tory leaders were thus trapped in a horrendous dilemma. Chalmers, as they were very well aware, was extremely popular, yet he could not be supported after his generally deceitful and intransigent conduct.[133] As the Non-Intrusionists pushed their anti-patronage views to their logical extreme, it became ever more difficult for Peel to back them, and accordingly vital electoral support was dissipated. This process worked itself out relentlessly between 1839 and 1841.

By 1839, with the court cases regarding lay patronage well developed, the Tories were moving to define their position on the principles at stake. Graham warned that the concept of democratic control being advocated by Tories such as J.C. Colquhoun was 'more affined' to Radical than to Conservative doctrines, and if the Non-Intrusionists persisted in their course, the party would be split: 'they will surrender the Key of our strength in Scotland'.[134] An indicator of the dangerous cross-currents to which the Tories were exposed by collaborating with rampant Non-Intrusionism was revealed by the Perthshire by-election in February and March 1840. This seat had been highly volatile since 1832: the Whigs won it then, lost it in 1834, then won it back in 1835, only to surrender it again in 1837. To complicate matters, two of the three court cases testing the issue of lay patronage versus non-intrusion concerned parishes in the county — Lethendy and Auchterarder. Much bitterness was created by these cases. The third, Strathbogie, case was at a crucial stage in February 1840. On the 14th the Court of Session issued an interdict against the Non-Intrusionists, and on the 28th Chalmers defied the Court with a powerful vindication of spiritual independence at an emotional public protest meeting.[135] Polling in the Perthshire contest was on March 9th. Although the Tories did manage to keep the seat in the by-election, the conditions under which they succeeded disturbed many party adherents. Home Drummond, the Tory candidate, began by announcing in his election address that he saw it as a 'sacred duty' of the government to enact legislation 'to effect the principle of Non-Intrusion'. Yet he was deemed 'evasive' in his answers to questions on the issue, with dire results. 'I understand', wrote a Tory, 'all the '*Non-intrusion*'

Voters, Whig and Tory, have resolved to vote for Stewart [the Liberal]'. 'Mr Stewart's party', another reported on the same day, 'are making all they can of that distressing Church question'.[136] A leading Non-Intrusionist paper accused Drummond's address of 'vagueness' on the lay patronage question and on the eve of polling announced its 'conviction that *Mr. Home Drummond is unworthy of the confidence of the Perthshire Non-Intrusionists*'.[137] This lack of confidence in the Tory was skilfully exploited by the Liberals, whose candidate also endorsed Non-Intrusionism, but in a fuller version than Drummond's. Dunlop, a Liberal and the legal adviser to the Non-Intrusionists, went to Perth to stem any Tory support among 'our people', which he did by persuading a meeting of clergymen to pronounce against Drummond.[138] The Tory's continued reluctance to commit himself to the full demands of the Non-Intrusionists so weakened his prospects that ultimately he capitulated to them on nomination day. His new stance paid electoral dividends: ' . . . the church question has done us no harm. There were several I was afraid of, but we have succeeded in removing the impression which was, at the first blush of the matter, made upon them'.[139] The Non-Intrusionists were exultant, thoughtful Tories less exuberant. Drummond, cried the Non-Intrusionist paper, 'at last came to the full and utmost length which the ministers desired'. Two conclusions were drawn by the paper: firstly, 'all Parliamentary candidates, even in the most Tory counties, must come up to Mr. Drummond's non-intrusion mark'. Secondly, the Non-Intrusionists' demands were entitled to special consideration since they had abandoned their political partisanship for the greater ecclesiastical cause: 'There are devoted friends of the Church who feel so warmly that they are prepared to make the greatest sacrifices of feeling and of general politics and to expose themselves to no small misrepresentation and odium on behalf of this momentous question — a class of men surely whose feelings are not lightly to be regarded'.[140]

Elated by their gain in Perthshire, the Non-Intrusionists ignored plain evidence of Conservative unease. While Lord Aberdeen called on Chalmers to disown Dunlop's intervention in the by-election, Chalmers was more anxious to warn the Tories that one lesson of the contest was that they might be outbid by the Whigs. So he asked whether the Conservatives could 'not only be upside with the Whigs, but if they could so far outrun them as to make the measure their own'. Aberdeen's efforts to provide a legislative compromise on the Veto question foundered in May 1840 when Chalmers, evidently believing that the tide of opinion was running in his favour, pronounced the bill unsatisfactory because it still subordinated the Church to civil authorities in spiritual matters.[141] Aberdeen was enraged and denounced Chalmers' committee for being 'dishonest and unscrupulous' in dealings with him. Chalmers retorted that the whole episode constituted 'a severe blow on the moral weight of Conservatism in Scotland', in that it revealed that the Tories conceived the role of the Church to be an engine of the state, not an agent of spiritual progress, and he therefore anathematised them: 'I am bound to declare that, for aught like right church principles, I have discovered the Conservatives to be just as bad as [the Whigs]'.[142] The Moderate churchmen, guided by Hope, began to regain influence with the Tory leadership throughout 1840. Graham explained to a Non-Intrusionist supporter that Chalmers had forfeited respect by his conduct in inducing the General Assembly to 'bid defiance' at the state and for rejecting all reasonable compromises.[143]

An explicit opportunity for official Conservative displeasure to be shown came late in 1840, when Chalmers applied for the post of professor at Glasgow University. By academic criteria Chalmers was widely acknowledged to be outstanding, but Graham, who as Rector sat on the appointing committee, cast his vote against Chalmers as a reprisal for the collapse of the Aberdeen bill. 'No other ground was open to me without a departure from the line laid down by you on the subject of Lord Aberdeen's bill', he told Peel, who agreed.[144] This decision was taken in the face of reports that such an action would cripple the party in Scotland and perhaps drive Non-Intrusionists to opposition. 'Sir William Rae informs me that Dr. Chalmers and his followers threaten 'war to the knife' at a general election against the Conservative party if I venture to declare against them by my vote at Glasgow', Graham reported, adding that it was nevertheless necessary to demonstrate to Chalmers that his agitation was not 'all-conquering', but rather antagonised friends.[145] Chalmers was indeed loosening his ties with the Tories at that very time, as when he reprimanded a sympathiser for putting party before Church: 'At present I should tremble for the return of the Conservatives to power. I dread the one party and distrust the other'. These were not mere feelings of personal disappointment but a response to Peel's apparent endorsement of the Moderate pro-patronage section of the Scottish Church.[146]

On the eve of the 1841 general election, however, dissatisfaction with the Melbourne administration's handling of the Church grievances had somewhat mollified the Non-Intrusionists, and Conservative hopes were higher than in the previous year. This recovery operation was then shattered by an incautious interview given by Peel to a group of Chalmers' supporters in June 1841. Peel, a despondent correspondent stressed, should have been wary of any deputation led by Dunlop, the veteran of the Perthshire by-election. Peel was reported by Dunlop as having called for the submission of the Church to the civil courts and to have rejected Argyll's compromise bill as conceding too much to popular control of clerical appointments. Although it was claimed that Peel's opinions had been distorted, it was difficult to rectify the impression of decided hostility.[147]

The dismay among the Scottish Conservatives was immediate and widespread. Sir George Clerk told Peel, 'As many of our candidates are disposed to pledge themselves to support some bill resembling the Duke of Argyll's bill this statement of the Non-Intrusionists has placed them in some difficulty, particularly in the West of Scotland'. The Glasgow agent confirmed Clerk's reading: 'It is with a heavy heart that I see the labours of years thrown away'. He passed on correspondence from supporters, adding that on a visit to Ayrshire he was 'besieged' by aggrieved Conservatives.[148]

The reality of these fears materialised as the campaign developed. Several seats were not won because the Non-Intrusion issue pushed many out of the Tory camp, usually into the Whig one. In Renfrewshire, Glasgow Non-Intrusionists began by aiming to defeat the Whig, Patrick Stewart, either by supporting the sitting Tory, Mure, or by running one of their own interest, Henry Dunlop. Candlish — Chalmers' heir-apparent — and A. M. Dunlop warned Henry Dunlop of the damage which would ensue from letting Mure in, as he had been a firm opponent of their cause, and Peel's remarks at the notorious interview clinched it: 'Sir Robert Peel's avowal of extreme views against us would almost make it indispensable to require of all his supporters that they should suspend their support of him' until he modified his position.[149] Henry Dunlop then withdrew his candidature, but in the interim Mure lost the support of Moderate churchmen by approving of Argyll's bill, and the Whig won handsomely. Mure told Peel his statement had destroyed his prospects, as the Non-Intrusion men 'are chiefly *staunch Conservatives* in state politics', but were implacably opposed to him.[150] In Kilmarnock the strenuously Non-Intrusionist Tory M.P., Colquhoun, was faced with a demand from the Chalmers faction that he oppose the return of Peel to office if Peel persisted in rejecting their views on the Church. This seat too was regained by the Liberals.[151]

Seats that were initially expected to be won were lost heavily, largely on this issue. Glasgow was a case in point. The defeated candidate, Campbell, reported: 'I am sorry to say that this untoward Church question has damaged us not a little'. The *Glasgow Constitutional* agreed, rebuking those who declined to vote for Campbell because of a difference of opinion on the Church, and it added a reference to 'similar errors elsewhere committed on the part of Non-Intrusionists'.[152] In another winnable prospect, Greenock, the candidate complained that Peel's interview 'is playing the devil here', imperilling his otherwise good chances of success 'should this all exciting Church question not throw me over'.[153] In Banffshire, where the Tories had high hopes, twenty Conservative voters in Mortlach parish went against the party because of the Church question, and had that score of voters been loyal, the voting would have been nearly equal. Strathbogie, the subject of the bitterest confrontation in the lay patronage struggle, was in Banffshire.[154]

Elsewhere, although the Conservatives were not defeated, they faced much stiffer opposition than anticipated even in very safe seats, and the need to defend their own strongholds impaired the vigour of their assault on Whig seats. Bute, safest and loyallest of Tory constituencies, was the object of an all-out Non-Intrusionist challenge from Henry Dunlop against Peel's Lord Advocate, Rae. Sir William wrote in some trepidation to Peel: 'in this, what has hitherto been regarded as one of the most secure seats in Scotland is in the greatest peril of being lost'.[155] In Haddington Burghs a certain Tory gain was suddenly felt at risk because of the circulation of a copy of the Peel interview: 'If Robert Steuart [Liberal] succeeds at Haddington, I understand it will proceed from this document'.[156] In Roxburghshire, where the Whigs had withdrawn their candidate early in the campaign, violent Non-Intrusionist protests at Peel's interview revived their hopes, and they re-entered the contest, winning the seat.[157] A further category of constituencies comprised those where in the end no Tory opposition to the Liberals was mounted. St. Andrews was a walkover for Ellice, because, the Tory press explained, 'the non-intrusion controversy has here waxed so warm'. The Tory candidate, Maitland Makgill, was an enthusiastic upholder of the Chalmers position who in 1835 had declined to support the Conservative candidate in Fife because of the gulf between their opinions on the Church issue. He had made himself unacceptable to the bulk of St. Andrew Tories: 'it would seem that his recent course of agitation and repeated declarations of hostility to a Conservative government have alienated the only friends he had'.[158] A further vitiating aspect of the divide within the party was that if a candidate did move to accommodate the Non-Intrusionists, he ran the risk of offending Moderate churchmen. As we have seen, this affected the Renfrewshire result, but Lord Aberdeen voiced his disgust with Rae for trimming on the issue in Bute. In Glasgow, Campbell, himself a solid Moderate, paid the price of trying to placate Non-Intrusionists, for John Hope then declined to make a public appeal to Church Moderates, so displeased was he with Campbell's wobbling.[159]

The Scottish results were therefore a major deviation from the national trend, and many Tories ascribed this to the church difficulty.[160] The Conservatives were in fact saved from greater setbacks in Scotland only by Whig weaknesses and, occasionally, countervailing forces. Of the latter, Roxburghshire provides a vivid instance. Buccleuch's election manager analysed the poll and concluded: 'it may be pretty confidently stated that the Conservatives lost at least as many votes on the Church question as they gained by the not voting of the Liberals in consequence of the Corn question'.[161] But only a few other seats were influenced by protection. Elsewhere the absence of Whig candidates alone protected the Tories: 'Had the Whigs contested Lanarkshire on non-intrusion principles it was theirs', remarked the Glasgow agent.[162] A number of seats formerly held by Whigs were not fought by them in 1841, and this reflected tensions and conflicts within their party as much as a sweeping tide of Conservatism carrying counties such as Ayr, Dunbarton and Perth. The reasons for this Whig-Liberal weakness must next be examined.

Of the Conservatives returned to Westminster, very few were at all associated with Non-Intrusionism. Only Campbell of Monzie (Argyll) could be so described. In general, the old gang seemed to have regained the upper hand in Scottish Conservatism, typified by the continuing influence of John Hope on men like Lord Aberdeen. Hope had in the immediate pre-election phase insisted that very few Tories were Non-Intrusionists, and he urged Aberdeen to induce Peel to oppose Argyll's bill, as such a stance would not cause any loss of support. When J. C. Colquhoun protested at the direction being taken by party leaders on the Argyll proposals, Hope dismissed the only Scottish Conservative then sitting for an industrial burgh seat: 'he is a most awkward friend, and has in various ways injured the Conservatives greatly in Scotland since he joined them'.[163]

NOTES

1. J. Cannon, *Parliamentary Reform, 1640–1832* (London, 1973), pp. 258–9, discusses these figures.

2. Sir George Clerk to Sir R. Peel, 23 Dec. 1832, Peel MSS., Add. MS. 40403, ff. 150–1.

3. [F. Scott], *View of the Representation of Scotland in 1831: A Letter to the Scottish Landed Proprietors* (London, 1831), pp. 5–17; (A Conservative), *Letter to the Lord Advocate on the Scotish (sic) Reform Bill* (Edinburgh, 1832), pp. 5–28.

4. *Letter to the Lord Advocate,* p. 5.

5. 'Attack upon the Duke of Buccleuch', contained in a collection of *Edinburgh Electioneering Broadsides* (n.p., 1832), held in the British Library (Cat. No. 826.1.28).

6. T. Anderson to Col. Lindsay; J. Thomson to same, 1 Jul., 24 Nov. 1832, Crawford & Balcarres MSS., 40/5/10, 561.

7. J. C. Douglas to Sir F. W. Drummond, 17 Mar. 1837, Drummond MSS., GD 230/577/2.

8. Same to same, 23 Nov. 1834, Ibid., GD 230/580/52 (Glasgow); W. Blair to A. Scott, 28 Nov. 1834, ibid., GD 230/580/1 (Ayrshire); J. Miller to F. Maule, 23 Jan. 1836, Dalhousie MSS., GD 45/14/630/44 (Perthshire); Sir F. W. Drummond to Buccleuch, 19 May 1841, Buccleuch MSS., GD 224/581/8 (Haddington).

9. J. Brown to Sir G. Clerk, 23 Dec. 1834, Clerk MSS., GD 18/3350.

10. Report of remarks by Hallyburton, the Liberal candidate, made by D. Wilkie, to Capt. Kinloch, 28 Nov. 1834, Airlie MSS., GD 16/64.

11. *Scotsman,* 10 Jan. 1835, cf. Ibid., 22, 29 Nov. 1834 for meetings, also the copy of resolutions passed at a Lochwinnoch meeting, 13 Jan. 1835, Ardgowan MSS., T-ARD 1/6/373.

12. *Scotsman,* 22 Nov. 1834.

13. E.g., Minto to Grey, 28 Jan. 1835, Grey MSS.

14. A. Pringle to Sir R. Peel, 19 Jan. 1835, Peel MSS., Add. MS. 40410, ff. 269–72.

15. R. Stewart, *The Foundations of the Conservative Party* (London, 1978), pp. 93–6 for this.

16. W. Ferguson, 'The Reform Act (Scotland) of 1832: intention and effect', *SHR,* 45 (1966), pp. 105–14.

17. J. Brash, *Scottish Electoral Politics, 1832–54* (Edinburgh, 1974), especially pp. xl-xlvii.

18. Airlie MSS, GD 16/40/65; Lord Arbuthnott to Sir J. Forbes, 28 Jan. 1833, Fettercairn MSS., Acc. 4796/Fl/58.

19. J. J. H. Johnstone to Buccleuch, 18 Feb. 1838, Buccleuch MSS., GD 224/582/ 'Dumfriesshire 1838'; H. H. Drummond to Sir W. Stirling, 23 Apr. 1840, Stirling MSS., T-SK 29/3/123; W.P. Neill to A. Hamilton, 27 Jan. 1839, Hamilton MSS., P/CN 49.17/20.

20. Lothian to Buccleuch, 26 Dec. 1839, Buccleuch to D. Horne, 26 Jul. 1841; H. F. H. Scott to Buccleuch, 20 Jul. 1841, Buccleuch MSS., GD 224/582/'Roxburgh & Selkirk Politics, 1834–9', 224/581/11 (twice).

21. F. R. Bonham to Sir G. Sinclair, 9 Jul. 1840, Sinclair MSS., XVII, Pt. 4, ff. 372–3, RH 4/49/6.

22. J. J. Hope Johnstone to Buccleuch, 18 Feb. 1838, Buccleuch MSS., GD 224/582/'Dumfriesshire, 1838'.

23. 'A Plan for Extending and Securing Political Interest', n.d. (c.1834–5?), Airlie MSS., GD 16/40/65.

24. P. Robertson to Sir F. W. Drummond, 31 Aug. 1836, Drummond MSS., GD 230/572/11.

25. Based on 'List of Linlithgowshire Electors' compiled after the 1838 registration, Glen and Henderson MSS.

26. W. Barr to D. Crawford, 7 Jan. (1837), Ardgowan MSS., T-ARD 1/6/369; *Glasgow Constitutional,* 22 Feb. 1837.

27. W. P. Neill to A. Hamilton, 27 Jan. 1839, Hamilton MSS., P/CN 49.17/20; *Ayr Advertiser,* 2 May 1839.

28. Lord John Russell to Queen Victoria, 15 Aug. 1837, Russell MSS., PRO 30/22/2, ff. 12–15; *Letters chiefly concerned with the Affairs of Scotland from Henry Cockburn to Thomas Francis Kennedy, M.P.* (Edinburgh, 1874), p. 507 (10 May 1834).

29. J. Miller to F. Maule, 25 Apr. 1835, Dalhousie MSS., GD 45/14/630/13; F. Maule to A. Rutherfurd, 16 Oct. 1838, Rutherfurd MSS., MS. 9697, ff. 171–6.

30. H. H. Drummond to Sir W. Stirling, 23 Apr. 1840, Stirling MSS., T-SK 29/3/123; cf. D. Horne to Buccleuch, 9 Jun. 1836, Buccleuch MSS., GD 224/526/1/36 for obstacles to making votes in Perthshire.

31. D. C. Moore, *The Politics of Deference* (London, 1976), esp. pp. 5–15, 103–13, 312–3, 432–6, 446–7. Cf. N. Gash, *Politics in the Age of Peel* (London, 1953), pp. 42–3, 177–83.

32. J. MacNicol to Airlie, 28 Feb. 1840, Airlie MSS., GD 16/40/78/26; A. MacPherson to J. Grant, 19 Dec. 1834, Bught MSS., GD 23/689/1; J. MacDonald to Col. Lindsay, 15 Dec. 1834, Crawford & Balcarres MSS., 40/5/345.

33. W. Dundas to H. H. Drummond, 3 Mar. 1840 (scroll); and copy of circular to the Ochtertyre tenantry in W. Dundas to Sir G. Murray, 30 Nov. 1832 (scroll), Dundas of Ochtertyre MSS, GD 35/276 (both); cf. J. H. Callender to H. MacColl, 11 Oct. 1835, Murray of Polmaise MSS., GD 189/1/153.

34. H. Wedderburn to G. Simpson, 26 Dec. 1834 (copy), Dundee MSS., 35.

35. B(readalbane) to Melbourne, 27 Oct. 1839, Dalhousie MSS., GD 45/14/640/13; W. Blair to A. Scott, 28 Nov. 1834, Drummond MSS., GD 230/580/1.

36. A. Pringle to Sir R. Peel, 6 Feb. 1833, 19 Jan. 1835, Peel MSS., Add. MSS. 40403, ff. 174–6, 40410, ff. 269–72.

37. E.g. A. Currie to F. Maule, 1 Feb., 14 Mar. 1835, Dalhousie MSS., GD 45/14/626/1, ff. 3–6, 23–7; *Ayr Advertiser,* 2 May 1839; *Letters from Cockburn to ... Kennedy,* p. 505 (10 May 1834); *George Hope of Fenton Barns. A Sketch of his Life compiled by his daughter* (Edinburgh, 1881), pp. 61–2.

38. Cf. the correspondence in Airlie MSS., GD 16/40/78; W. Fraser to J. MacLeod, 14 Mar. 1833, MacLeod MSS., 7/781.

39. S. D. Stirling to W. Forbes, 26 Apr. 1835, Forbes MSS., GD 171/43; for an Ayrshire parallel, W. Hunter to (A. Hamilton?), 10 Jul. 1835, Hamilton MSS., P/CN 49.17/20.

40. J. Lucas to W. Forbes, 23 Jul. 1837, Forbes MSS., GD 171/44.

41. 'Resolutions of Non-Electors of Ceres', 15 Dec. 1834; 'Resolutions of Meeting of Captain Wemyss' Friends', 14 Jan. 1835; J. MacDonald to Capt. Lindsay, 27 Dec. 1834; Crawford & Balcarres MSS., 40/5/682, 689, 347.

42. W. Hunter to (A. Hamilton?), 2 Jul. 1835, Hamilton MSS., P/CN 49.17/20; Sir J. Graham to F. R. Bonham, 3 Oct. 1839, Peel MSS., Add. MS. 40616, ff. 97–8; Sir J. Oswald to Sir R. Peel, 20 Dec. 1837 (copy), Oswald MSS., VI/A.2; J. Balfour to Col. Lindsay, 15 Dec. 1834, W. Drummond to same, n.d. (Jan. 1835), Crawford & Balcarres MSS., 40/5/36,211. Gash, *Politics in the Age of Peel,* pp. 140–52 for violence at elections, including the Hawick incident.

43. See A. Currie to F. Maule, 5 May 1835, Dalhousie MSS., GD 45/14/626/2/8.

44. A. Thomson to Lord Aberdeen, 14 Aug. 1841, Aberdeen MSS., Add. MS. 43237, ff. 270–7.

45. Sir W. Rae to Sir R. Peel, 5 Jul. 1841, Peel MSS., Add. MS. 40485, ff. 46–7.

46. J. S. M. Anderson, *Memoir of The Chisholm, late Member of Parliament for Inverness-shire* (London, 1843), p. 227. Cf. 'List of Voters of Fort William, 20 and 21 July 1835', in Cameron MSS.

47. A. Murray to J. Dalrymple, 13 Jun. 1835, Stair MSS., GD 135/109/16/13.

48. Stewart, *Foundations of Conservative Party,* pp. 130–45 for the role of organisation, mainly in England.

49. Based on 'Scottish Conservative Club' Bundle in Buccleuch MSS., GD 224/582; MS notes on the Scottish Conservative Association (by Lord Ramsay), Dalhousie MSS., GD 45/1/251; J. C. Douglas to F. W. Drummond, 7 Dec. 1834, Drummond MSS., GD 230/580/53.

50. *Scotsman,* 13 Jun. 1835.

51. MS notes regarding the Scottish Conservative Association, Dalhousie MSS., GD 45/1/251.

52. J. Nairn to A. MacTavish, 13 Feb. 1835 (copy), MacLeod MSS., 7/664.

53. D. Horne to Buccleuch, 22 May 1837, Buccleuch MSS., GD 224/582/'Roxburgh and Selkirk Politics 1834–9'; Buccleuch to Sir R. Peel, 6 Jan. 1835, Peel MSS., Add. MS. 40409, ff. 172–4.

54. P. B. Ainslie to Col. Linday, n.d. (1834–5), Crawford & Balcarres MSS., 40/5/2. Much of the material in Drummond MSS., GD 230/572,577,579,580 deals with these questions.

55. E.g., R. Lamond to Sir J. Graham, 21 Jun. (1841); R. Lamond to Sir R. Peel, 9 Jul. 1841, 14 May 1837; Graham to F. R. Bonham, 27 Dec. 1838, Peel MSS., Add. MSS. 40318, ff. 263–5, 40485, ff. 121–2, 40423, ff. 203–4; 40616, ff. 38–42. For Bonham as party manager: Gash, *Politics in the Age of Peel,* pp. 413–8.

56. J. Hope to R. B. Glen, 29 Jun. 1839, Glen & Henderson MSS.

57. D. Campbell to A. Hamilton, 5 Sep. 1838, Hamilton MSS., P/CN 49.17/20.

58. J. C. Douglas to F. W. Drummond, 24 Dec. 1834, Drummond MSS., GD 230/580/51; Lord Eglinton to A. Hamilton, n.d. (1837), Hamilton MSS., P/CN 49.17/20.

59. H.H. Drummond to Sir J. Graham, 7 Jul. 1843 (draft), Abercairney MSS., GD 24/1/535/2, ff. 209–11. Cf. 'Meeting of Gentlemen connected with the Conservative interest in Perthshire', 6 Jul. 1841, Ibid., GD 24/1/1068.

60. 'Minutes of meeting of Gentlemen of Conservative Principles ... ', 27 Dec. 1834, 22 Apr. 1837, Hamilton MSS., P/CN 49.17/20.

61. Stormont to Mansfield, 14 Dec. 1834, Mansfield MSS., 18/5.

62. 'List of Persons ... ' (c.1840), Forbes MSS., GD 171/46; Conservative Registration Fund papers for Perthshire (1837–38?), Airlie MSS., GD 16/40/74/2; H. H. Drummond to (A. Stirling), 24 May 1839, Stirling MSS., T-SK 29/75; 'Minute of Meeting of Gentlemen of Conservative Principles', 22 Apr. 1837, Hamilton MSS., P/CN 49.17/20.

63. *Scotsman,* 13 Jun. 1835.

64. J. Hope to R. B. Glen, 29 Jun. 1839, Glen & Henderson MSS.

65. G. Cameron to J. MacPherson Grant, 9, 20 Aug. 1836, Ballindalloch MSS., 685; 'Report on Registration, 1840', in Buccleuch MSS., GD 224/581/11.

66. E.g., T. Carnaby to J. MacNicol, 10 Jul. 1839, Airlie MSS., GD 16/40/77/5 for Angus; Airlie to F. W. Drummond, 5 Dec. 1834, Drummond MSS., GD 230/580/27.

67. T. Watson to Lord Mansfield, 18 Jul. 1837, Watson to J. Miller, 20 Jul. 1837 (both copies), Mansfield MSS., 125.

68. D. Horne to Buccleuch, 27 Mar. 1835, Buccleuch MSS., GD 224/582/'Roxburgh & Selkirk Politics 1834–9'; 'Minutes of Meeting ... ', 27 Dec. 1834, Hamilton MSS., P/CN 49.17/20.

69. Circular letter by Col. Lindsay, and replies thereto, 28 Oct. 1835, Oswald MSS., VI/A.2.

70. Lord Arbuthnott to Sir J. Forbes, 12 Nov. 1833 (incomplete), 16 Nov. 1833, cf. 28 Jan. 1833; Fettercairn MSS., Acc. 4796/Fl/58.

71. R. Hunter to A. Hamilton, 25 Jun. 1839, Hamilton MSS., P/CN 49.17/20; 'West Kilbride Conservative Association' (1839?), Hunter MSS., 562.

72. W. Findlay to W. Forbes, 9 Sep. 1835, Forbes MSS., GD 171/43.

73. Haddington to Buccleuch, 25 Apr. 1838, Buccleuch MSS., GD 24/581/8; Haddington to G. W. Hope, 20 Jun. 1835, Hope MSS., GD 364/1025A. J. Brash, 'The Conservatives in the Haddington District of Burghs, 1832–52', *Trans. East Lothian Antiquarian and Field Naturalist Society*, 11 (1968), pp. 37–70, is illuminating.

74. G.C.O.A. Min. Bk., 17 Mar., 14, 20, 28 Jun. 1837; — Oct. 1838, 17 Apr. 1839; 17 Feb. 1841; *Short Review of the Political Events of the Past Year, as contained in the second Annual Report of the Glasgow Conservative Operatives' Association* (1839), esp. pp. 15–16. J. T. Ward, 'Some Aspects of Working Class Conservatism in the Nineteenth Century', J. Butt & J. T. Ward, *Scottish Themes* (Edinburgh, 1978), pp. 147–51.

75. D. Horne to Buccleuch, 16 Dec. 1839, Buccleuch MSS., GD 224/581/9.

76. Graham to Bonham, 27 Dec. 1838, Peel MSS., Add. MS. 40616 ff. 38–42; cf. D. Horne to Buccleuch, 13 Dec. 1839, Buccleuch MSS., GD 224/581/9.

77. T. Carnaby to J. MacNicol, 24 Jan. 1835, Airlie MSS., GD 16/40/68/9.

78. Admiral G. Elliot to Lord Minto, 17 Jan. 1834, Minto MSS., MS. 11750, ff. 116–7; Sir J. Dalrymple to Lord Grey, 25 Dec. 1834, 3 Jan., 7 Feb. 1835, Grey MSS; Lord J. Russell to J. Maxwell, 6 Feb. 1837, Maxwell of Pollok MSS., T-PM 116/361; *Ayr Advertiser*, 10 Aug. 1837.

79. Stewart, *Foundations of Conservative Party*, pp. 152–3 for this.

80. E.g., Lord Ramsay to F. W. Drummond, 27 Dec. 1836, Drummond MSS., GD 230/572/4.

81. R. Hunter to A. Hamilton, 25 Jun. 1839, Hamilton MSS., P/CN 49.17/20; A. MacLean to W. Brodie, 20 Jan. 1835, Brodie MSS.

82. 'List of Linlithgowshire Electors' (1838), Glen & Henderson MSS.

83. Ailsa to Grey, 13 Dec. (1834), 5 Jan. (1835), 24 Jun. 1835, Grey MSS; Grey to Sir J. Dalrymple, 29 Jun. 1835, Stair MSS., GD 135/110/10/44.

84. G. to J. MacPherson Grant, 27 Dec. 1834, 13 Mar. 1840, Ballindalloch MSS., 160, 182; W. Berry to Col. Lindsay, 28 Nov. 1834, Crawford & Balcarres MSS., 40/5/52.

85. P. B. Ainslie to Col. Lindsay, 28 Nov. 1834, Crawford & Balcarres MSS., 40/5/3.

86. P. Bayne, *Life and Letters of Hugh Miller* (London, 1871), II, p. 278.

87. T. McCrie, *Memoir of Sir Andrew Agnew of Lochnaw, Bt.* (London, 1850), pp. 318–24.

88. Duke of Montrose to Sir A. Campbell, 26 Jul. (1841), Campbell MSS., TD 219/11/82.

89. Eglinton to Buccleuch, 3 Dec. 1840, and reply, 8 Jun. 1841, Buccleuch MSS., GD 224/581/9; A. Smith to J. Smith, Lord J. Campbell to same, 20, 12 Feb. 1840, Smith of Jordanhill MSS., TD 1/645/1, 1/638; Col. M. Cathcart to A. Hamilton, 20 Mar. 1838, Hamilton MSS. P/CN 49.17/20.

90. Sir A. Edmonstone to W. Forbes, 20 Feb. 1838, Forbes MSS., GD 171/45.

91. Lord Rosslyn to Sir J. Oswald, 30 Oct., 10 Dec. 1834, Oswald MSS., VI/A.2.

92. G. Gardiner to R. Graham, 4 Jan. 1836, Lynedoch MSS., MS. 16143, ff. 143–4.

93. Buccleuch to Peel, 12 Jan. 1835, Peel MSS., Add. MS. 40410, ff. 26–9; W. Burn to Buccleuch, 12 Aug. 1835, Buccleuch MSS., GD 224/582/'Scottish Conservative Club'.

94. Haddington to Peel, n.d. (c.Nov. 1836), Peel MSS., Add. MS. 40422, ff. 234–5.

95. Graham to Peel, 11 Dec. 1836, Peel MSS., Add. MS. 40318, ff. 49–52; A. Dunlop to Sir G. Sinclair, 3 Dec. (1836), Sinclair MSS., Letterbook Vol. XVI, RH 4/49/6, cf. Graham to Stanley, 12 Dec. 1836: 'In Glasgow the Tories and Conservative Whigs make common cause, in Edinburgh the High Tories stand aloof, are rampant, unpopular', Graham MSS., 32.

96. A. Alison to Peel, 19 Nov. 1836; W. Boyle to Peel, 17 Nov. 1836, Peel MSS., Add. 40422, ff. 190–1, 185–6.

97. J. Hope to Peel, 27 Nov. 1836, Peel MSS., Add. MS. 40422, ff. 249–51; D.K. Sandford to Stanley, 23 Nov. 1836, Derby MSS., 132/1; A. MacOnochie to Peel, 2 Dec. 1836, Peel MSS., Add. MS. 40422, ff. 271–3.

98. Graham to Stanley, 15 Jan. 1837, Graham MSS., 33; J. Cleland, *Description of the Banquet in Honour of the Rt. Hon. Sir Robert Peel, Bt., M.P.* (Glasgow, 1837), pp. 57–71.

99. G.C.O.A. Min. Bk., 23 Dec. 1836; Ward, 'Nineteenth Century Working Class Conservatism', pp. 147–51.

100. R. Lamond to Peel, 1 Jul. 1837, n.d. (Jun. 1837), Peel MSS., Add. MS. 40423, ff. 297–8, 244–5.

101. Graham to Bonham, 5 Sep. 1839, 21 Oct. 1840, Peel MSS., Add. MS. 40616, ff. 69–72, 171–2.

102. P. M. Stewart to F. Maule, 31 Dec. 1839, 9 Jan. 1840, Dalhousie MSS., GD 45/14/646.

103. Graham to Bonham, 29 Jul. 1841, Peel MSS., Add. MS. 40616, ff. 214–5.

104. S. J. Brown, *Thomas Chalmers and the Godly Commonwealth in Scotland* (London, 1982), esp. pp. 211–25, is a lucid and balanced survey.

105. A. A. MacLaren, *Religion and Social Class* (London, 1974), Ch. 3, also pp. 208–10, for Aberdeen; P. Hillis, 'Presbyterianism and Social Class in Mid-Nineteenth Century Glasgow: a Study of Nine Churches', *J. Eccles. Hist.,* 33 (1981), pp. 47–64.

106. A. Dunlop to Sir G. Sinclair, 3 Dec. (1836), Sinclair MSS., Letter Book, Vol. XVI, RH 4/49/6.

107. J. C. Colquhoun to Aberdeen, 23 Dec. 1839, Aberdeen MSS., Add. MS. 43237, ff. 114–5.

108. D. Maitland Makgill to H. Wedderburn, 31 Oct. 1836, Dundee MSS., 33.

109. T. Chalmers to Lord Moncrieff, 28 Jul. 1835, Moncrieff MSS., 6/24; cf. W. Hanna, *Memoirs of the Life and Writings of Thomas Chalmers, D.D., L.L.D.* (London, 1851), III, p. 461.

110. Hanna, *Chalmers,* IV, pp. 18ff.

111. Brown, *Chalmers,* pp. 250–5.

112. Rev. R. Buchanan to H. H. Drummond, 15 Jun. 1836, Abercairney MSS., GD 24/1/529/9; cf. Lord Haddington to Drummond, 24 Jun. 1836, Ibid., GD 24/1/529/10; Dr. Welsh to Lord Moncrieff, 19 Oct. 1836, Moncrieff MSS., 6/24.

113. Sir G. Clerk to Peel, 25 Nov. 1837, Peel MSS., Add. MS., 40422, ff. 221–2; *Glasgow Constitutional,* 1 Feb. 1837.

114. D. K. Sandford to Stanley, 8, 16 Oct., 15, 22, 28 Nov. 1834, Derby MSS., 132/1.

115. W. Drummond to Col. Lindsay, 11 Dec. 1834; T. G. Skene to Capt. Wemyss, n.d. (copy); Skene to Lindsay, n.d., Crawford & Balcarres MSS., 40/5/207, 367, 483.

116. J. Gibson Craig to Sir. J. Dalrymple, 13 May 1834, Stair MSS., GD 135/111/10/10; *Scottish Guardian,* 16 Jan. 1835; A. Currie to F. Maule, 7 Apr. 1835, Dalhousie MSS., GD 45/14/626/1, ff. 42–4.

117. W. Stewart to D. Grant, 18 Apr. 1835, Bught MSS., GD 23/6/684/6.

118. *Ayr Advertiser,* 2 July 1835.

119. *Autobiographical Recollections of Sir John Bowring, with a Brief Memoir by L. B. Bowring* (London, 1877), pp. 79–80.

120. G.C.O.A. Min. Bk., 23 Dec. 1836.

121. J. T. Ward, 'The Factory Reform Movement in Scotland', *SHR* 41 (1962), pp. 100–23.

122. F. Montgomery, Glasgow Radicalism, 1830–48 (Glasgow University Ph.D. Thesis, 1974), pp. 234–64 is illuminating.

123. *Glasgow Constitutional,* 1 Feb. 1837; *Scottish Guardian,* 6, 20 Jan. 1837.

124. J. Cunningham to F. Maule, 27 May 1837, Dalhousie MSS., GD 45/14/625, ff. 75–6; *Journal of Henry Cockburn, Being a Continuation of the Memorials of his Time, 1831–54* (Edinburgh, 1874), I, pp. 147–8 (27 Aug. 1837).

125. N. Walker, *Robert Buchanan D.D. An Ecclesiastical Biography* (London 1877) p. 192; Brown, *Chalmers,* pp. 264–7 for Tory-Non-Intrusionist links.

126. Graham to J. C. Colquhoun, 25 Dec. 1839 (copy), Graham MSS., 139A.

127. D. Maitland Makgill to H. Wedderburn, 31 Oct. 1836, Dundee MSS., 33.

128. Brown, *Chalmers,* pp. 276–302.

129. Graham to Stanley, 21 Oct. 1838, Graham MSS., 36; Graham to Chalmers, 30 Dec. 1839: C. S. Parker, *Life and Letters of Sir James Graham, 2nd Baronet of Netherby* (London, 1907), I, pp. 378–80.

130. C. Arbuthnot to Graham, 10 Dec. 1839, Graham MSS., 37B. Cf. Graham to W. E. Gladstone, 8 Dec. 1839: 'It is but one step from the Veto to Voluntaryism': Parker, *Sir James Graham,* I, pp. 375–6.

131. Graham to Bonham, 13 Dec. 1839, Peel MSS., Add. MS. 40616, ff. 130–2; H.H. Drummond to A. Stirling, 27 Feb. 1841; M. Napier to W. Stirling, 22 Jan. 1841, Stirling MSS., T-SK 29/75, 29/4/26.

132. Rev. R. Buchanan to Aberdeen, 5 Mar. 1840, Aberdeen MSS., Add. MS. 43237, ff. 122–3.

133. Graham to Bonham, 6 Oct. 1840, Peel MSS., Add. MS. 40616, ff. 169–70.

134. Graham to J. C. Colquhoun, 25 Dec. 1839 (copy); Graham to Stanley, 21 Oct. 1838, Graham MSS., 139A, 36.

135. Brown, *Chalmers,* pp. 308–10.

136. Election Address of H. H. Drummond, 22 Feb. 1840, Abercairney MSS., GD 24/1/1068; D. Matheson, J. Fleming, C. Clark to J. MacNicol, 5 Mar., 29 Feb. (twice) 1840, Airlie MSS., GD 16/40/78/23,12,13.

137. *Scottish Guardian,* 13, 3 March 1840.

138. A. M. Dunlop to F. Maule, 25, 23, 28 Feb. 1840, J. Ivory to Maule, (25 Feb. 1840), Dalhousie MSS., GD 45/14/658/1, GD 45/14/14/651.

139. J. MacNicol to J. Miller, 5 Mar. 1840 (copy), Airlie MSS., GD 16/40/78/5.

140. *Scottish Guardian,* 13, 10 Mar. 1840.

141. Aberdeen to T. Chalmers, 10 Mar. 1840; Chalmers to Aberdeen, 10 Mar., 12 May 1840; *The Earl of Aberdeen's Correspondence with the Rev. Dr. Chalmers and the Secretaries of the Non-Intrusion Committee from 14 January to 27 May 1840* (Edinburgh, 1840), pp. 34–41, 54–5; M. Chamberlain, *Lord Aberdeen* (London, 1983), pp. 290–2 for a recent account.

142. T. Chalmers, *What Ought the Church and the People of Scotland to do Now? Being a Pamphlet on the Principles of the Church Question* (Glasgow, 1840), pp. 53–7; Brown, *Chalmers,* pp. 316–20.

143. Graham to J. C. Colquhoun, 6 Sep. 1840 (copy), Graham MSS., 40.

144. Graham to Peel, 20 Sep. 1840, Peel MSS., Add. MS. 40318, ff. 222–5; Peel to Graham, 30 Sep. 1840, Graham MSS., 40.

145. Graham to Peel, 20 Sep. 1840, Peel MSS., Add. MS. 40318, ff. 222–5; cf. A. Alison to Graham, 17 Sep. 1840, J. C. Colquhoun to Graham, 9 Sep. (1840), Graham MSS., 40, 139A.

146. T. Chalmers to Sir G. Sinclair, 29 Sep., 20 Nov. 1840, Sinclair MSS., Letterbooks, XVI, RH 4/49/6; Hanna, *Chalmers,* IV, p. 191.

147. Graham to Bonham, 24, 25 Jun. 1841; A. Dunlop to A. Smollet, 19 Jun. 1841 (copy, extract); R. Rae to Cochrane, 21 Jun. 1841, Aberdeen to Peel, 25 Jun. 1841; Graham to Peel, 25 Jun. 1841; Peel MSS., Add. MSS. 40318, ff. 261–2; 40616, ff. 202–3; 40318, ff. 266–7; 40429, ff. 349–52; 392–3; 40318, ff. 277–8; 277–8; Brown, *Chalmers,* p. 323.

148. Sir G. Clerk to Peel, 22 Jun. 1841; R. Lamond to Graham, 21 Jun. 1841; A. Wingate to R. Lamond, 22 Jun. 1841; Lamond to Graham, 22 Jun. 1841), Peel MSS., Add. MSS. 40429, ff. 364–5; 40318, ff. 263–5, 273–4, 269–70.

149. R. S. Candlish to H. Dunlop, 21, 25 Jun. 1841, A.M. Dunlop to H. Dunlop, 24 Jun., 4 Jul. 1841, New College MSS., Box 25; cf. Rev. R. Burns, *Free Thoughts addressed to the Electors of the County of Renfrew, with special reference to the Church Question* (Paisley, 1841), pp. 14–15.

150. W. Mure to Peel, 22 Jun. 1841, Peel MSS., Add. MS. 40429, ff. 368–9.

151. J. C. Colquhoun to Graham, 22 Jun. 1841; Graham to Bonham, 25 Jun. 1841, Ibid., Add. MSS., 40318, ff. 275–6, 40616, ff. 202–3.

152. J. Campbell to Peel, 7 Jul. 1841, Ibid., Add. MS. 40485, ff. 79–80; *Glasgow Constitutional,* 7 Jul. 1841.

153. M. MacKenzie to F. R. Bonham, 21 Jun. (1841), Peel MSS., Add. MS. 40617, ff. 99–100.

154. Seafield to Peel, 16 Jul. 1841, Ibid., Add. MS. 40485, ff. 204–5; Aberdeen to J. Hope, 4 Jul. 1841, Lord Stanmore, *Correspondence of Lord Aberdeen 1838–43* (priv., n.d.), pp. 453–4.

155. Sir W. Rae to Peel, 5 Jul., 25 Jun. 1841, Peel MSS., Add. MSS. 40485, ff. 46–7, 40339, ff. 373–4.

156. Sir W. Rae to Peel, 25 Jun. 1841, Ibid., Add. MS. 40339, ff. 373–4.

157. See below, p. 51.

158. *Glasgow Constitutional,* 19 Jun. 1841.

159. Aberdeen to J. Hope, 11 Jul. 1841, Stanmore, *Correspondence of Lord Aberdeen,* pp. 458–9; J. Campbell to Peel, 7 Jul. 1841, Peel MSS., Add. MS. 40485, ff. 79–80; J. Hope to Aberdeen, 5 Jul. 1841, Stanmore, *Correspondence of Lord Aberdeen,* pp. 454–7.

160. C. Arbuthnot to Bonham, 23 Jul. 1841, Peel MSS., Add. MS. 40617, ff. 101–2.

161. 'Report by the Edinburgh Agent on the Result of the Last Election of the County of Roxburgh, July 1841' Buccleuch MSS., GD 224/581/11.

162. R. Lamond to Peel, 9 Jul. 1841, Peel MSS., Add. MS. 40485, ff. 121–2.

163. J. Hope to Aberdeen, 19 Jun. 1841, Stanmore, *Correspondence of Lord Aberdeen,* pp. 451–2.

2
Whigs, Radicals and the Liberal Party: 1832–41

I

The very comprehensiveness of their victory in the first general election held under the reform dispensation — they won all but 10 of the 53 Scottish seats —posed, paradoxically, several potential problems for the Whigs. As those responsible for handling the affairs of Scotland, the Whigs would be blamed for a failure to carry through a broad tranche of reforms modernising the institutions of the country. Disaffection might also occur if the Reform Act did not appear adequate to ensure the end of political chicanery. The demands of Radicals both for more substantial reforms and for a speedier rate of progress towards change could easily link with these discontents and create conflict within the party. This tension would be most evident in burgh seats, where the Radical element was more prevalent, and the competition to sit for burghs would be intensified if Conservatives began to recapture the counties, so squeezing Whigs rather than Radicals. However, any bids to effect a compromise with the Radicals — whether in policy or in choice of M.P.s — might stimulate an exodus or, at least, abstentions among moderate reformers, a natural component of the Whigs' support. From 1832 until 1835 the general pattern was for the Radicals to drift away from collaboration towards confrontation with the Whigs, while moderates grew more alarmed at the steepening Radical programme. From 1836–7, however, the Radical threat was not sustained, as the church question emerged. The challenge then for the Whigs was to avoid alienating both Dissenters and Non-Intrusionists, while still retaining the attachment of traditional Whigs, who were averse to all manifestations of religious zeal, the more so when it inserted itself into party politics.

The Radical drive to widen and accelerate the reform scheme was in full tilt by the 1835 general election, having clearly shown itself to be a serious problem at the Edinburgh by-election of June 1834. Two solid Whigs, Jeffrey and Abercromby, had won comfortably in 1832, and a Radical had been obliged to withdraw his candidature before polling day, due to insufficient support. Now, however, there was much uncertainty about Jeffrey's replacement among the Whigs: 'I grieve to say that Edinburgh is far from safe', Cockburn fretted, and the city's Whig leader warned that time was needed to find a suitable Whig. If the election was held precipitately, either a Tory or a Radical could win.[1] The Radicals, who had joined with the Whigs eventually in 1832, now positively declined to do so. The Whigs put up the Attorney General, a Scot, and won in what Cockburn claimed would be 'the greatest victory of Whiggism, if it shall prevail, over both Tories and Radicals'.[2] To some degree, the discord in Edinburgh was not typical of the

33

general Scottish picture, for the church problems existed in an exceptionally acute form in the city: 'It is not a matter of politics — the absorbing question is church matters and it is almost impossible to say what effect these disturbing elements will have on the calculation'.[3] The grievance specific to Edinburgh was the Annuity Tax, a local assessment imposed to subsidise the city's state churches and raised on all the citizens, except Church of Scotland clergy and advocates. A movement of civil disobedience to repeal the tax had been launched, and the resistance encountered among Whigs to a reform which to Dissenters seemed to be an almost automatic concomitant of the Reform Bill heightened the conflict. Nevertheless, it is significant that while the Annuity Tax was an issue in the by-election, the Radicals chose James Aytoun to fight the seat. Aytoun was the Radical opponent of the Whigs in the 1832 election, contending that Jeffrey was not suitably advanced in his political principles.[4] The choice of a Radical in political as well as religious matters indicates that the Annuity Tax was seen in the perspective more of extending political reform than merely as a sectarian grievance.

The location of religious reform within a broader political context was confirmed by the demands of the Radicals in this period. The failure to achieve rapid and substantial reforms partially contributed to stimulating demands for more profound change. As Lord Advocate, Jeffrey was felt to be obdurate and conservative. Finding his illiberal views on the Church of Scotland to be out of line with those of most M.P.'s, he tried to make amends in a clumsy manner, and only compounded M.P.'s criticisms. 'He really is too bad', said a staunch Whig, 'and is either laughed at or abused by them.' His refusal to consider amendments to the Reform Act to provide for the elimination of fictitious vote making alienated many.[5] His successor, J. A. Murray, was able to carry only a few bills through to statute during his five years' tenure of the Lord Advocateship. Proposals for reform of the Court of Session, the Universities, the magistracy, Sheriff Court procedure and debt imprisonment were all brought forward, but most foundered in the welter of pressure of parliamentary business. Fox Maule, who as junior minister at the Home Office was much involved in Scottish business, complained to Rutherfurd, Murray's Solicitor General, that Murray's over-sensitivity to criticism and his preoccupation with detail were responsible for these delays: 'Some plans must be adopted to get our business into a state of less intricacy and *more prominency* in the house and ere another session comes we must seriously consider this point'. Maule was too bound up with his own departmental work to do much, while Cockburn's suggestion that a Secretary of State be created, so leaving the Advocate to concentrate on legal matters, was not taken up.[6]

Two types of Radical demand arose from this governmental inertia. One was the emergence of Radicals interested in a single issue, such as Robert Wallace, M.P. for Greenock, who immersed himself in the revision of Sheriff Court procedures and became the bane of ministers as he pursued the topic relentlessly in the House. A second form of analysis concluded that major abuses remained untreated because the Reform Act had not proved the expected cure-all and that its fundamental defects would frustrate further change. Thus the persistence of fictitious votes and intimidation by landlords were seen as the main props of the

Tory recovery which should be stamped out. The Whigs simply retaliated by adopting the same techniques to cancel out Tory gains, while making noises of protest at having to stoop to such measures. Radicals, however, seeing that the government seemed incapable of drafting legislation worded tightly enough to close these loopholes, called for other remedies. They contended that only by introducing the ballot and widening the franchise to include a very broad band of the working class could these devices inimical to the spirit of the Reform Act be rendered irrevocably void. Thus an address from Glasgow working men to Lord Durham in October 1834 complained that the sole fruit of Reform so far realised was the emancipation of slaves and argued that only a wider suffrage, the ballot and shorter parliaments would produce desirable policies such as the abolition of placemen (which many Scottish Whigs were), repeal of the Corn Laws and abolition of the taxes on knowledge (Newspaper Tax). Likewise, a public meeting in Edinburgh to advocate the ballot and wider franchise was stimulated by Conservative intimidatory tactics in the 1835 and 1837 elections.[7]

The growth of this climate of opinion troubled the Whig section. Many were already uneasy at several aspects of the government's policy. A dinner in Edinburgh for O'Connell, intended to foster closer liaison with the Irish M.P.'s, was deemed likely to split Scottish Liberals, and measures to reform the Church of Ireland were unpopular because they were regarded as a partial disestablishment. '[Church reform] has made more impression than I imagined, and with a better class of People', a Whig M.P. brooded.[8] The Whigs were equally unhappy at the Radical demands in Scotland. For some, it was quite unreasonable to press the ministry for legislation which could not conceivably be got through Parliament.[9] The style of Radicals was deplored by an ex-M.P. as 'that brutal debasing and mob-courting Radicalism which at present too much disgraces the political *manners* (I will not say *character*) of our country'.[10] The Radicals were going well beyond anything which the Whigs could accept: for the latter, the Reform Act marked a great step forward, and should therefore be preserved rather than overturned because it had not at once been fully successful.[11] The image of the Radicals held by Whigs was expressed in extreme language by Cockburn, who urged a young Whig hopeful to seek an English seat 'so that you may be independent of the follies of any constituency in the country [Scotland] whose follies it must often be your duty to resist ... The best proof of your state will be if you vomit, and largely, whenever you hear the Members for Greenock and Airdrie [i.e. Falkirk Burghs] speak ... Urinate upon him [the Greenock M.P.] whenever he chatters about his resident sheriffs and other d-d nonsense'.[12] One factor in this tension was a social gulf, for the Whigs, mainly landowners and advocates, had little contact with Radical manufacturers and shopkeepers. Cockburn observed that Sir T. Dick Lauder alone of the Edinburgh Whigs had any rapport with the populace: 'He is the greatest favourite with the mob that the Whigs have ... He is one of the persons whose Whiggism is so Liberal that it enables him to keep the Radicals in some order. The chief part of his influence, indeed, is owing to his being very much one of themselves'.[13] There is an unmistakable sneer in Maule's toying with standing for Glasgow: 'much good might be done by having a person in for Glasgow interested in the general concerns of Scotland, not one of their *mercantile* selves'.[14]

The most open and deep conflicts came at the general elections of 1835 and 1837. Lauder had pointed out at the time of the 1834 Edinburgh by-election the existence of 'several difficult and complicated questions which divide the freeholders by *shades* of difference of opinion requiring great care and attention to be able to be blended'.[15] This became a general problem at the 1835 elections, although the struggle took different forms. In some places the Radicals ousted the Whigs and took over the nomination of candidates, as in Kilmarnock where the diplomatist and social reformer Sir John Bowring replaced the lukewarm Captain John Dunlop. Elsewhere, a Radical challenge was made to an incumbent Whig, generally unsuccessfully, as in the Stirling and Ayr Burghs, and in Renfrewshire. The Whigs seemed powerless to resist the onward push of the Radicals. One index of the enfeebled state of the Whigs was that in their strongholds, the county seats, there was a widespread dearth of candidates. 'The cry everywhere is for *Candidates*', reported a Whig agent. As an instance of this, no candidate could be found for Mid Lothian until three weeks before polling, yet he won the seat.[16] The trend of the 1835 elections in Scotland troubled Earl Grey: 'perhaps there is too great an infusion of Radicalism in the new members quite to suit my fancy'.[17] This apprehension grew increasingly acute as most of the Tory gains were at the expense of the Whigs in county seats. The Whigs were not generally disposed to side with the Tories in 1835, although, as noted earlier, seepage to Conservatism had begun in certain instances. In Renfrewshire, a leading Whig laird denounced Radicals unreservedly as 'the Clique of Blackguards who try to domineer over our wretched county', and announced he would rather see the Tory win 'than have to pull in a boat of which that '*Liar*' Mr. Muir was Palinurus or that Quaker Ruffian stroked oar'. Nevertheless, he confessed, 'All minor questions, I think, now merge with the great one of Tories or no Tories — Peel or no Peel — I shall use my feeble endeavours to try to get rid of them and him'.[18]

By 1837, the Radicals looked to be even more in the ascendant. In Renfrewshire, where a Radical had come third in 1835, Sir John Maxwell fought as the sole Liberal on a quasi-Chartist platform. By now the Whigs were unwilling to sacrifice their conscience for party unity. Maxwell's advocacy of a sweeping measure of suffrage extension overstepped the mark: 'Never was there such a production as Sir John's address ... It was too radical by far and lost him some Whigs without winning others more than he had at any rate'.[19] In Lanarkshire the Whig candidate recalled that if he withdrew, 'the leading men who had asked me to stand would give the Tory candidate their votes rather than have a possible Radical'.[20] In Glasgow, the Whigs felt that the greatest threat now came from Radicals: 'We did not fear the Tories, but we had some dread of the Radical opposition'.[21] The abstention or defection of Whigs was used to explain the defeats sustained in several seats in 1837, and the Whig leaders were reduced to a sense of helplessness when contemplating the wreckage after the election. 'The Radicals have been smote Hip and Thigh — will they never learn?' exclaimed Rutherfurd in biblical mood, citing the loss of Kilmarnock as an instance of Radical excesses driving voters away. Maule reiterated this point later in the year: 'The evil spirit of radicalism is making efforts to shake off the control of reason to which it has been subjected for the last three years, and there is no saying what may be the consequences of their infatuation'.[22]

II

However, soon after these defeatist remarks were uttered, the Radical surge seemed to be checked, and even put into reverse. Two by-elections in 1839 revealed the new context. A vacancy arose at Glasgow on the death of the Whig, Lord William Bentinck. As we have seen, the threat of a Radical challenge there in 1837 had disturbed the Whigs, and the unity of the Liberal party in the city had accordingly been described by the Whig agent as somewhat tattered.[23] Although some of these fears still existed among the Whigs, there was no opposition to James Oswald, who had sat as M.P. for the city from 1832 to 1836 and who was not regarded as very Radical. In Edinburgh, even more surprisingly, T. B. Macaulay was elected without a contest, despite being the most eloquent intellectual exponent of the Whig doctrines, and therefore hardly acceptable to the Radicals. Several features arise from these two by-elections. Firstly, the return of Macaulay imparted a major fillip to the flagging spirits of Whiggery: 'The greatest triumph the Whig cause has obtained in Scotland since your own return in Perthshire [in 1835]', Maule was told, and from Edinburgh a cautious lawyer reported: 'We are here in a slight *revival* of Whiggery'.[24] The rejoicing was in part because the dwindling band of talented Scottish Whigs in Parliament had been replenished, a problem which had worried some for nearly five years: 'It would be of some advantage to the Liberal cause in Scotland generally to get William Gibson Craig properly trained and brought up to Parliamentary business, as our younger Liberals of respectability are really getting very scarce'.[25] Moreover, Macaulay's masterly advocacy of their principles reinvigorated the Whigs after a period of creeping disillusionment with the government shilly-shallying to Radicals. Macaulay, a correspondent stressed, had enunciated his political principles with spirit, energy and frankness and without truckling to Radicalism.[26] The second aspect of these by-elections was the evident desire of the Radicals to avoid provoking a serious schism in the party, a conciliatoriness not previously apparent. Duncan MacLaren, the leading Edinburgh Radical, and a thorn in the flesh of the Whigs for half a century, turned down an offer from his Glasgow admirers to provide £500 p.a. as a salary if he became M.P. for the city. In Edinburgh itself, although several possible Radicals were initially suggested as candidates, 'all fortunately are apparently set upon avoiding a split, so that we shall come all right in the end', recorded an amazed Whig.[27]

Several reasons for this collapse of Radical pressure may be suggested. The main factor was the development of a divergence between those who saw political reform as the main goal, and those who were becoming more concerned to act politically in order to protect their religious position. The latter were almost entirely to be found among the Dissenters, most of whom were Voluntary Presbyterians. The Dissenters had a great deal of political weight, which derived both from their numbers and distribution and also from the tight-knit cohesiveness which they had built up. Voluntaries were primarily, as seen in Chapter I, an urban middle-class group, wielding considerable influence in many burgh seats. For instance in Perth in 1841, Dissenters claimed to form rather over one quarter of the voters, with 200 out of 760.[28] They were also significant in a spread of county constituencies where economic growth had created small towns and villages, such as Kirkintilloch, whose numerous Dissenters were held to be crucial for Whig hopes of victory in Dunbartonshire in 1841. They also constituted 'a most numerous influence' in Mid Lothian and carried weight in Perthshire.[29] As is frequently the case with minorities, Voluntaries had evolved a certain sense of solidarity of outlook and action which was institutionalised with the formation of the Scottish Central Board of Dissenters in 1834. The Board was largely created by Duncan MacLaren and immediately became the recognised vehicle for voicing the political demands of Dissent in Scotland. The main initial call by the Board was for the 'immediate, total and eternal' separation of Church and State, but this issue was at first easily subsumed under the general umbrella of demands for other reforms — such as the ballot, wider suffrage, repeal of the Corn Laws — upon which Radicals could easily unite in the early post-Reform Act years.[30] Thus at the Stirling Burghs, Lord Dalmeny was opposed in 1835 by Radicals both because he was alleged to be favourable to the further endowment of the Church of Scotland, so affronting Dissenters, while his Whiggish outlook on political change upset that section of Radicalism.[31]

The split between political and religious reformers was mostly caused by the fightback by the Evangelical party in the Church of Scotland, expressly designed to regain those Presbyterians who had left the state church for the Voluntaries, as has been discussed earlier. As the Evangelicals became more confident and vigorous in the mid-1830s, their challenge led Dissenters to view the defence of their ecclesiastical position as the dominant issue in politics. The further endowment of the state church, which Chalmers' Church Extension Scheme required, was the first subject of protest, and one of the earliest expressions of discontent revealed the deep unease felt: '[Dissenters] consider it one [question] in which their feelings and their principles are involved ... [and they oppose] even a partial though small grant to the Church, as they will conceive that this was letting in the *principle* that the State was bound or inclined to support their opponents and to neglect themselves'.[32] By 1837 the question of state grants to the Church of Scotland had become the all-consuming topic for Dissenters: in November the Solicitor General met a deputation from the Central Board and reported: 'They said the feeling was determined and very general ... '[33] The Board pressed its case by calling a public meeting in December, at the same time despatching to Parliament 362 petitions containing 148,000 signatures opposed to the demands 'so pertinaciously made' for endowments. Deputations were sent to meet government leaders, prominent Scottish politicians and the political spokesmen for English Dissent. The climax of the campaign came in March 1838 with a mass rally in Edinburgh, attended by leading English Dissenters. At the end of 1838 the Central Board felt contented — '[we] cannot avoid congratulating Dissenters on the success which has hitherto attended their labours' — and pointed out that they had succeeded in exposing the fallacies in the Church Extension propaganda and in showing that the attitude of the state church was aggressive and sectarian.[34]

By 1839 the Dissenters felt more secure, noting that the government had made it plain that they would not yield to renewed Church requests for additional endowments. As a result, the Central Board wound down its activities, and its subscriptions fell to £38 in 1839, from £192 in the previous year.[35] But although the frontal assault had been repelled, other issues were thrown up between 1839 and 1841 which prevented the Voluntaries from re-integrating with the other streams of Radicalism because they were seen as affronts to religious liberty. Guided by MacLaren, who felt 'that nearly all the public interests he held dear were the objects of Established Church intolerance', the Dissenters maintained their pressure with, as Macaulay described it, heat and passion.[36] These grievances, as enumerated endlessly and ubiquitously, included the continuing exclusion of Dissenters from holding university chairs — a practice begun in 1690. Moreover Dissenters descried a tendency in the government's policy between 1839 and 1841 to favour the state church, so that they feared that the Test Acts, repealed in 1829, were being restored by stealth. The creation of a Bible Board for Scotland, with only the Established Church represented on it; a clause in the Prison Act debarring Dissenters from serving as gaol chaplains; the restriction of the School Inspectorate to members of the National Church; worries that further state aid might be provided for the teaching of religion in State Church schools — these were all pointed to as evidence of a pattern of discrimination against those outside the Church of Scotland.[37]

Absorbed with these matters, the Voluntaries withdrew from the broad Radical alliance to become a single-interest group. By 1841 a meeting of Edinburgh Dissenters was convened to consider getting 'their opinion properly represented in Parliament'. This, it was agreed, would best be attained by getting a Dissenter elected as M.P. for the city, as he 'should possess that intimate knowledge of their principles and their attachment to their cause which will secure their entire confidence, and entitle them to expect that he will constantly exert himself to prevent the recurrence of similar aggressions [to the recent encroachments on their civil liberties]'.[38] In Dundee, too, the segmentation of Radicalism was well in train by 1841. In 1837, there had been general discontent at the sitting member's lack of commitment to radical policies, and so the Dundee Political Union had sought in vain to persuade a more congenial candidate, such as Col. T. P. Thompson, the suffrage and Corn Law reformer, to stand. In 1841 the contest was between George Duncan, a local merchant and town councillor, and J. B. Smith, the leader of the Anti-Corn Law League. On most political issues, such as free trade, the two men were virtually indistinguishable, and the only detectable gulf came over church matters. Duncan was the nominee of the Non-Intrusionist wing of the state church while Smith, a Unitarian, was the Dissenters' man. Easson, the leader of the Political Union, who in 1837 had been trying to find a politically advanced candidate, now indicated that advocacy of free trade alone was not criterion enough for choosing a candidate: support for 'civil and religious liberty' (a code phrase for Voluntaryism) was a further prerequisite. Edward Baxter, the city's largest manufacturer and a Voluntary, who had been prominent on the committee of the Whig Parnell in 1837, and so opposed to Easson, was instrumental in 1841, working closely with Easson, in luring Smith to fight the seat. The journals of both groups agreed that the Church issue was, as the Voluntary journal put it, 'at once all and all and a *sine qua non* in judging the public qualifications of a public officer'. The Non-Intrusionist organ echoed this: 'The views of any candidate upon the Church question will however determine our support and the support of a large section of the voters'. The alignment of partisanship along sectarian lines was further shown by the fate which befell the candidature of George Kinloch. He was the son of the city's first post-Reform Radical M.P., and he too advocated a vigorous programme of radical political reforms including suffrage extension, the ballot, shorter parliaments, and abolition of the Corn Laws. Kinloch, however, said almost nothing about church matters, and despite his impeccable credentials was compelled to stand down, leaving the two church contenders in straight conflict. At the poll, Duncan was successful.[39]

An additional part of the process of divorce between Radicals stemmed from the Chartist movement. Voluntaries, mostly drawn from the ranks of the middle class, would have little truck with a movement designed to transfer political power totally to the working classes. Moreover, identification with Chartists might weaken the Dissenters' influence on the Whigs, who, as the party in office at the outset of the agitation, were anxious to minimise its appeal and to dampen any impact it might make.[40] So when MacLaren tried to argue at a meeting of the Edinburgh Liberals that Macaulay should not be selected as candidate without some alternatives being offered, he was promptly supported by some 'semi-Chartists', whereupon MacLaren tried to withdraw his motion in embarrassment. At a private meeting a week before, Radicals — probably including MacLaren — had expressed their distaste for the Chartists and their unruly conduct at meetings.[41] In Glasgow, the rift left George Mills politically vulnerable. Early in 1838 Mills, as an earnest Radical, had warned the Whig M.P. Bentinck of the dangers to the Liberal party of alienating Dissenters (and Radicals generally) if more concessions were made to the Non-Intrusionists.[42] In 1841, Mills stood as a Chartist for the city, and was the target of a pamphlet listing the Chartists, Churchmen and Tories who had given their votes to him and the sole Conservative candidate. Clearly the significant noun was the first one, and Mills' poll of 353 (while the other three all got around 2,500) shows the limited backing he could command once identified with Chartism, even although he argued for religious liberty in a bid to woo Voluntaries.[43]

The political weight of the Voluntaries doubly benefited the Whigs: firstly it deprived the Radicals of their most disciplined and sizeable section, and secondly the Dissenters found themselves inexorably driven to vote for the Whigs almost willy-nilly, thereby reducing their bargaining power with the Whigs. Certainly the

Whigs did not always go out of their way to entice the Voluntaries with lavish promises or sympathetic responses. When MacLaren submitted to Macaulay the list of complaints alleging religious discrimination described earlier, the reply was harshly insensitive to the social nuances implicit in the Voluntary position. 'Consider then to what the provocations enumerated by Mr. Alexander amount. Some trifling matters of punctilio — some little slight about the printing of a bible, or about the appointment of school inspectors. Are these things seriously to be maintained as aggressions on religious liberty?'[44] Despite this indifference of the Whigs — indeed at times the Voluntaries went further and objected to pandering by the government to 'please a section of a sect' (i.e. Non-Intrusionists) — in the 1841 contests the Whigs normally obtained the votes of Dissenters.[45] The alternatives were to abstain or to vote Conservative. The latter was admittedly held out in one of the earliest protests by Dissenters as a consequence of Whig support for extending the endowments of the Established Church: 'nothing would be more likely to alienate them from the present ministry and to throw them into the hands of their rivals [i.e. Tories, not Non-Intrusionists]'.[46] This was not really a probability in view of the fundamental discrepancies between the views of Tories and Voluntaries on the Church-State relationship.[47] By 1837 the stance of the Dissenters had therefore altered to one of threatening abstention, as a deputation conveyed it to the Solicitor General: 'They said the feeling ... would lead not indeed to the Dissenters supporting the Tories but to a very lukewarm and partial support, if not abandonment, of the Whigs'.[48] The implication, that the withdrawal of Voluntary votes would result in the loss of many seats to the Tories, became less credible as developments in the late 1830s, as shown earlier, indicated that the Tories seemed willing co-operators in the onward drive of the Non-Intrusionists.

The resulting reappraisal of tactics pushed the Dissenters into giving support to the Whigs as a rule, only threatening to abstain in specific seats. The Whigs and Dissenters were brought closer in practice late in 1840 by manoeuvres in Glasgow and Edinburgh municipal politics. In both cities, Tories and Non-Intrusionists formed alliances to install their choice of Lord Provost against a Whig-Dissenter nominee. In Edinburgh this crisis was especially acute as Adam Black, who was both a Whig and a Dissenter, lost to James Forrest, an influential Non-Intrusionist. The Dissenters not unreasonably saw this as an attack not just on Black, but on all Dissenters *qua* Dissenters, and drew closer to the Whigs. Black was given a large public dinner by his followers, which was attended by Lord Dunfermline, who as James Abercromby had been the first Whig M.P. for Edinburgh, and Sir James Gibson Craig, the moving spirit behind Edinburgh Whiggery. Black spoke at the dinner, taking the occasion to emphasise the natural and close alliance which existed between Dissenters and Whigs because the latter had always promoted civil and religious liberty.[49] In letters to Maule, Gibson Craig placed the blame firmly on the Non-Intrusionists, totally exonerating Black and even MacLaren from any sectarian or dishonest motives. Macaulay also denounced the manipulations of the Non-Intrusionists and pledged his sympathy for Black.[50] As a result of this rapprochement, the Dissenters in the 1841 Edinburgh election decided to remain loyal to the local Liberal organisation, rejecting any move to form a separate party. When a vacancy arose in one of the two Edinburgh seats, the Dissenters urged their claims to nominate the second Liberal candidate to run with the Whig Macaulay. Significantly, given a choice between Sir Culling Eardley Smith, whose only interest was undiluted Voluntaryism, and Joseph Hume, who advocated a broad range of political as well as religious reforms, the first preference of the Dissenters was for the former. But, faced with the argument that Smith would antagonise all except pure Voluntaries, while Hume was acceptable even to Church Liberals, they somewhat reluctantly picked Hume. Perhaps understandably, Hume however opted to fight Leeds, and at short notice Gibson Craig's son, William, was put up as the second candidate. No other candidates stood as Liberals, and MacLaren was prepared to work for Macaulay and Craig, although, as we have seen, the sitting M.P. made few concessions to Voluntary susceptibilities.[51]

But whereas Whiggery was apparently tolerable, Dissenters were less ready to accept Non-Intrusionists, as the Dundee episode demonstrated. In the 1840 Perthshire by-election, the Dissenters were reported to have determined to abstain, considering the Liberal too warm towards Non-Intrusionism.[52] The loss of Perthshire led influential Voluntaries to argue for persisting with the policy of general neutrality at elections except where a candidate was explicitly and genuinely in favour of the separation of Church and State. Accordingly, they were now urged to vote for the veteran radical Aytoun solely because of his Voluntary, and not his political, principles.[53] In the aftermath of the Edinburgh Lord Provostship dispute, 'the Dissenters had a meeting last night and unanimously determined that they would recommend to every one of their members throughout Scotland to vote for *no* person who was a Non-Intrusionist ... '[54] One man in particular was identified as a bogeyman: Fox Maule. Maule was a firm adherent of the Non-Intrusionist tendency, and as the minister jointly responsible for handling Scottish matters, he was regarded as the prime culprit behind what the Dissenters saw as a systematic and cumulative series of assaults on their religious rights in the later 1830s. At the meeting of Dissenters in November 1840 to lay down general policy, Maule learned, they resolved that 'they would not vote for you because you were not only a Non-Intrusionist but had treated Dissenters, as a proscribed party, on every occasion, excluding them from Commissions, etc.' When Maule was mooted as a possible candidate for Edinburgh, the Dissenters made known their total resistance to this project, and he decided not to proceed.[55]

On the whole, then, centripetal forces drove the Voluntaries to support the Whigs in 1841. The Whigs had indeed for most of the time felt fairly confident of keeping the Dissenters in line. As early as 1837 Rutherfurd had argued that the protests by the Central Board would not lead to defections — but he was close to the Non-Intrusionists. On the eve of the 1841 election, Gibson Craig prophesied: 'In Leith, the dissenters are likely to *heckle* the Advocate and tell him, at last, that they will vote for him, not on his own account, but for the sake of the Government'. In Edinburgh MacLaren informed Macaulay that the government still had his support, though not, to be sure, his uncritical adulation.[56] In Perth burgh, the Voluntaries, after initially expressing reluctance, came down in favour of voting for Maule. In part they feared to do otherwise would let the Tory win, and in part Maule's satisfactory liberal record on non-ecclesiastical issues swayed them.[57]

III

Non-Intrusionism presented problems of a different order for the Whigs. Emotionally and intellectually most found the Evangelical wing of the Church of Scotland unsettling. In a display of hitherto undetected expertise in theology, psychiatry and criminology, Melbourne expressed the attitude of many Whigs in analysing Chalmers: 'Chalmers, I feel certain, knows no divinity . . . I particularly dislike Chalmers. I think him a Madman and all Madmen are also Rogues'.[58] Macaulay of course was able to communicate Whig reservations about the Non-Intrusionists' position on state support for established churches in a more elevated conceptualisation. The claims for the independence of the Church of Scotland from any state control he castigated as 'high pretensions put forth by a portion of the church', adding for good measure: 'I think the question a question of expediency, to be decided on a comparison of good and evil effect . . . [In Scotland] I find a Kirk established. I am not prepared to pull it down. I will leave it what is has, but I will arm it with no new powers. I will impose no new burdens on the people for its support'.[59] This epitome of erastianism highlighted starkly the gulf between the Whigs and the militant Evangelicals.

On the other hand, there were links. Several leading Non-Intrusionists were politically, socially and professionally very close to the Whigs. There were a few Whig landlords like Breadalbane who were identified with the High Church party. Also, a group of promising and able lawyers were involved with the Chalmers element. This was particularly important because the Bar was the recruiting ground for the key political posts in Scotland, the Lord Advocate and the Solicitor General. As has been shown, the Whigs were facing grave difficulties finding talented members of the younger generation to replace such doyens of legal Whiggery as Jeffrey and Murray. Two of the most impressive younger luminaries at Parliament House were James Moncrieff, whose uncle, the Rev. Sir Henry Wellwood Moncrieff, was a central figure in the Evangelical party, and Alexander Murray Dunlop, who acted as legal adviser to the Non-Intrusionists. A third rising barrister associated with the Chalmers camp was Speirs, later to be very distinguished Sheriff of Mid Lothian.

Moreover, as already stressed, the Non-Intrusionists straddled party lines. There was a strong group of Liberals among the Evangelicals, led by the three lawyers just mentioned, who strove, albeit at times ambiguously, to maintain influence with and support for the Whigs.[60] Indeed neither of the factions in the state church offered much attraction to the Whigs. Although the Moderates in certain respects approximated quite closely to the Whigs on church-state relations, they were, as noticed above, unappealing for cogent historical grounds. In addition, the Moderates infuriated the Whigs by their obduracy in refusing to make any concessions on lay patronage, which seemed as repellent as the high-handedness of the Evangelicals. Most Whigs doubtless agreed with Macaulay in regarding the principle of lay patronage as no longer tenable in its pure state, instead accepting the institution of congregational veto, but simultaneously denying the grander claims to spiritual independence championed by Non-Intrusionists.[61]

The difficulties of coping with this intricate political network were further exacerbated by differing views of the church controversy adopted by Whig politicians. Among Scottish ministers, Maule's espousal of Non-Intrusionism has been noted, and Rutherfurd also leaned to that side, as evidenced by his appearing for them in the major legal cases involving the competing claims of lay patronage and popular veto. Melbourne, of course, was not well-disposed toward the High Church party.[62] His attitude was the despair of Evangelical church Liberals like Dunlop and Maule, the latter blaming the Premier's Scottish adviser, Robert Stewart, for tendering 'injudicious' counsel.[63] Lord John Russell was no warmer: his stance on Scottish questions was probably derived from his father-in-law, Lord Minto, no admirer of Non-Intrusionism.[64] Hence there was a veritable minefield to be traversed: Non-Intrusionists might be driven totally into the Tory fold, so toppling many Liberal seats. A Renfrewshire laird who stood for the county in 1841 summed up the problem. In January 1840 he noted: 'The Church question is going like a tropical turnip'; and by April 1841 the consequences were apparent: 'To you I may say confidentially that I have felt it to be my duty to write lately to both Lord Melbourne and to Lord John R that unless Govt do something toward settling the Kirk's wrongs we are gone as a party in the West of Scotland. No man indifferent to the Question need attempt either County or Town there, and I believe this is the general state of affairs throughout the majority of our Counties and many of our most important Towns'.[65] Yet they could not permit the Non-Intrusionists to seem too influential, or else, firstly the Dissenters would become disaffected (as when Maule contemplated running in Edinburgh) and, secondly, Melbourne and Russell, in the light of their views, would decline to make concessions, so effectively alienating the Non-Intrusionists.

What saved the Whigs from this acute dilemma was their lack of principle on the issue, and Peel's over-abundance of principle. The former may be seen at work in cameo in the conduct of the MacPherson Grants, one of the main Whig families in the Eastern Highlands. Their Ballindalloch estates lay in three county seats (Banff, Inverness, and Moray and Nairn), and there was also some interest in two burgh groups (Elgin and Inverness). In general, Non-Intrusionists were regarded with distaste by the laird, both because of the principle and because of their conduct. In Banffshire, George MacPherson Grant displayed his adherence to Whig principles during the 1841 election. He responded to an appeal from the Earl of Seafield for his vote on behalf of the earl's son, Lord Reidhaven, who was the Conservative candidate, by saying that while his 'private and personal feelings' ranged him with the chief of the clan Grant, since Reidhaven was opposed to a

Government whose measures Ballindalloch had long approved of, 'public duty and conscience' forbade him to do other than decline to vote Conservative. However, he did not support the Liberal at the hustings because of the latter's approval of Argyll's bill, which to Grant was excessively favourable to Non-Intrusionists.[66] Yet the MacPherson Grants were quite willing to countenance receiving the electoral support of Non-Intrusionist clergy and laity against the Tory candidate in Inverness-shire who was unpopular on account of his church opinions. The only reservation expressed by MacPherson Grant was whether these Evangelical voters would actually carry through their declarations by going to the poll.[67]

The events of 1840–1 suggested that however pragmatic the line adopted by the Whigs toward the Non-Intrusionists, there were no grounds on which harmony could be reached. At the start of 1840 Maule was apprised of the feelings of the latter by Dunlop, known to be pro-Whig: ' . . . you must remember that as yet the Liberal party have not . . . given us greater grounds of confidence than the Conservatives. Some of our greatest adversaries are Whig peers. Except Lord Melbourne (sic), yourself and the Advocate [Rutherfurd] we have hardly any [Ministers] friendly to us. In regard to the press, the Whig papers have been decidedly more hostile than the Conservative journals'. Hence there was 'a less open and confident reliance' on the Liberals than might be expected, and Maule was warned that if the Government did not act promptly to seize the initiative from the Conservatives, many Non-Intrusionists would cross party lines to vote for upholders of their principles.[68] The Perthshire by-election reinforced attitudes on both sides; the High Church Liberals bewailed the administration's 'coldness' to their cause, while the Tories' response encouraged 'the prevailing belief that the Conservatives are as a party more favourable than the Government', with the result that the Liberals were 'throwing' the seat away.[69] The loss of the seat did not persuade the Liberal party leaders to be more accommodating to the Non-Intrusionists: on the contrary two broad conclusions were drawn, both counselling no rapprochement. Firstly, the full advocacy of these principles would cause many Liberals to stay aloof. The Whig manager in Perthshire complained that their candidate's outright support for Non-Intrusionism backfired: 'All is coldness, nay worse, for plainly there is a feeling in the minds of many of our friends that their sense and judgment and candour might be brought into question by their taking any active part in this business', an interpretation endorsed by *The Scotsman* in its post-mortem on the result.[70] Secondly, the Non-Intrusionists were patently trying to play off both parties in order to enhance their electoral indispensability. Dunlop protested to Rutherfurd that despite his valient efforts to mobilise Whig Non-Intrusionists against the Tory, he was doomed to fail because of the equivocations of the ministry: 'If your friends had had a spark of manly courage and openness what a victory we might have won'.[71] The Tory Non-Intrusionist laird, Alexander Thomson of Banchory, made this point in 1841 when he warned Lord Aberdeen: 'I am quite aware that in most places among the electors the High Church party are far inferior to the Conservatives or the Whigs, but when in a contest between two parties a third is introduced, it is clear that this third party, though far less strong than the others, may yet be able to decide betwixt them, and turn the election in favour of the candidate who will adopt their peculiar views'.[72]

The biography of the Rev. Dr. Robert Buchanan, who served as Chalmers' main clerical emissary to politicians in London, shows how justified the Whigs were in fearing that the Non-Intrusionists were engaged in an auction with the two parties. In March 1838 Buchanan led a deputation to seek an easing of the conditions imposed by the government on church-building by the state church. After a rather unprofitable interview with Melbourne, Buchanan promptly entered into discussions with Peel, Wellington and Graham as to how the Church's case might best be presented to Parliament. Disillusioned with the government's handling of the Scottish Church question, 'at this period of this history, Mr. Buchanan was strongly inclined to Toryism'. However, he just refrained from publicly avowing his partisanship, and his closest collaborator on these missions to London, A. M. Dunlop, became most concerned lest Buchanan should be seen to be too closely allied to the Tories. While presumably this was partly because Dunlop was a Whig, it may also have arisen from a desire to keep options open in dealing with both parties.[73]

The fullest manoeuvres emerged in February-March 1840 when Buchanan and Dunlop engaged in simultaneous negotiations with all political leaders over the patronage crisis. The two Non-Intrusionists found that some Tories feared the Whigs would outbid them in the extent of their concessions, so, displaying a deviousness worthy of Chalmers himself, Buchanan was clear as to the course to be pursued: 'I am thoroughly convinced that our wisdom and duty is this — to bring the Conservatives up to the highest point we can, and ascertaining what that is, to use our whole influence to bring the Government to the proposing of a measure as near to it as possible, without, of course, hinting what the Conservatives will do'. When this plan was followed in an interview with the Lord Advocate, Rutherfurd angrily charged them with double dealings. The Government dragged its feet over giving a firm answer because it was finding difficulty in arriving at a compromise which would be acceptable alike to Parliament and the Non-Intrusionists. Buchanan and Dunlop meanwhile, evidently concluding — correctly — that no satisfactory solution would be hit upon by the Whigs, opened discussions with Lord Aberdeen in the hope of inducing him to promote legislation.[74]

The cooling of relations with the Whigs which came with the Non-Intrusionists' liaison with the Tories at the start of Aberdeen's bill was moderated in early summer. The ministry had opposed the bill, Melbourne making a particularly strong speech against it, and, as discussed above, the Non-Intrusionists then vehemently repudiated Aberdeen's scheme as inadequate. 'We have got quit of any reliance on the Tories who have deceived so many of our adherents and there is no risk of any half or quarter measure that would divide', the arch-intriguer Dunlop reported to Maule. But as Dunlop indicated, the terms for co-operation with the Whigs were still high, in that total acquiescence in their demands was expected.[75]

The Liberals were quite quickly confirmed in their distrust of the new-found Non-Intrusionist desire to draw closer. The episode in the autumn of 1840 when the latter allied with the Tories to install a Non-Intrusionist as Lord Provost of Edinburgh was taken by men like Gibson Craig as positive proof that the High Church faction were conspiring against the other sections comprising the Liberal party. Again there were fairly blunt efforts by Dunlop and his allies to coerce the rest of the Liberals. He argued that the Dissenters had little political weight, but that their activities would offend his own grouping, who might transfer to the Tories. He gave an ominous indicator of this prospect from the West: 'In Glasgow we have also carried [the Lord Provostship], but as we have no Whig non-intrusionists there, the triumph is also of necessity a Conservative triumph'. However, as we have seen, the Non-Intrusionists had overreached themselves, for as Macaulay explained, the incident simply fuelled suspicions that the Chalmers faction were seeking coalition with the Tories.[76]

A further rift was opened up by the formation in 1840 of a 'Church Defence and Anti-Patronage Electorial Association', which became a source of irritation to Liberals. To help maintain the state church principle against both its internal and external foes (i.e. erastians and Voluntaries), the Association claimed that it was essential to exercise the municipal franchise with great care, since town councils had considerable powers over the established churches within their jurisdiction. Nowhere was this electoral role more vital than in Edinburgh, where enemies of the Association's goals had become too powerful. 'It is a matter of comparative indifference what political opinions a candidate may profess, so he be sound in regard to the Church and religion', contended the Association, concluding that voters should therefore be willing to sacrifice normal party preferences to this end. It must have seemed not improbable to the beleaguered Liberals that this tactic might well be extended from municipal to parliamentary contests.[77]

Thus by the beginning of 1841 the Non-Intrusionists seemed to have become estranged from the Liberals and increasingly meshed in with the Tories again. Even so, the Liberal-inclined group within the High Church party still strove not to break their ties with the Liberals entirely, since, it may be presumed, the bargaining power of the Non-Intrusionists as a voting bloc would be gravely diminished if they were thought to be irrevocably committed to one side. In February 1841 Dunlop predicted to Maule that severe setbacks would afflict the Liberals in the event of a speedy dissolution because of 'the unsettling of the confidence of our people in the Govt.' Melbourne's intransigence only reinforced Dunlop's pessimism: 'I fear more and more therefore the result of a dissolution in Scotland'.[78] By April, Dunlop put heavier pressure on the Liberals. No longer had they merely lost the Non-Intrusionist vote — it had now gone across from abstention to support for the Tories: 'I rather believe that after all the Conservatives will be the party to take advantage of our position'. Through May and early June Dunlop reiterated the theme. In the counties of Stirling and Dunbarton, as well of course as Perth, the Tory candidates had declared their approval of Non-Intrusionist principles, while in Glasgow the two Tories bade fair to win on the same plank. Dunlop, needless to say, assured Maule that despite his earnest wish to act as an honest broker, he lacked any means: 'As far as I can, I shall of course seek to throw the balance to the Whigs, but they have by their own efforts paralysed my sinews'. The Liberals were now charged by Dunlop with acting 'at the dictation of the Voluntaries', so disillusioned Non-Intrusionists not unnaturally looked elsewhere. If a Tory sympathetic to the High Church party were to stand in Edinburgh, he remarked darkly, 'you can guess' how his friends would cast their votes.[79]

As most Liberals remained impervious, by mid-June the Non-Intrusionists had virtually entered into a coalition with the Tories, and the Liberals were spared serious electoral defeat only by the high scruples of the Conservative leadership and their own opportunism. Dunlop returned from the famous interview with Peel 'furious' at the leader's refusal to budge.[80] In protest against the Tory position, Dunlop, Moncrieff and other High Church Liberals moved rapidly to try to switch support to Liberal candidates. As Macaulay saw it, neither Non-Intrusionist nor Whig had any illusions about the new arrangement. After a conference with the church party leaders, he reflected: 'though we do not exactly agree they own that they shall get more from me than from a Tory and are now cordially on my side'.[81] A good illustration of the intricate tacking operations carried out by Non-Intrusionist Liberals is revealed by the Renfrewshire contest. A. M. Dunlop was instrumental in persuading the out-and-out Non-Intrusionist Henry Dunlop to withdraw his candidacy, so letting the broadly sympathetic Liberal have a winnable fight, and instead direct his energies to Bute. What Dunlop may have been aiming at was to show the Liberals how grave the opposition of his church party could be, and also he may have hoped to build up support in the Commons from all sides for the Non-Intrusionist cause, in order to give the latter a wider field to play.

The chastened return of many Non-Intrusionists to the Liberal fold, thus finding themselves on the losing side, had an important side-effect. The Dissenters, who had been ostentatiously loyal to the Liberals throughout 1840 and 1841, now saw themselves deprived of their expected heavy claims on the party by the re-entry of their bitterest rivals. Accordingly, within a month of the election, a new campaign was launched to ensure the return to Westminster from Edinburgh (at least) of a Dissenter quite independent of the official Liberals in order to have their interests and viewpoint represented. The mover of this resolution, Rev. J. McGilchrist, beseeched Dissenters to sink any internal differences and to unite to stop the Non-Intrusionist wing of the Established Church exerting political influence far out of step with its numerical size, and far more than the numerically larger Dissenters enjoyed. The committee appointed at the meeting was instructed to ensure that all those with voting qualifications were placed on the register.[82] Thus the 1841 election did not herald the dawn of an era of Liberal unity, and the threat of rupture seemed if anything greater afterwards.

IV

One major reason why the Liberals were unable to press home their advantage in the 1841 election, and which substantially explained their electoral slide after

1832, was that their organisation was in almost every respect inferior to that of the Conservatives. Whether these weaknesses contributed to the internal Liberal conflicts or vice versa is not easily resolved. But there were few who denied that the Tories ordered their affairs better, more especially in county constituencies. In the 1835 election, Earl Grey was reliably informed, county seats such as Mid Lothian and Stirling were lost 'through idleness' and want of prompt action on the Liberals' part.[83]

The causes of this poor performance were diverse. One was the almost total absence of any central co-ordination of effort either from London or Edinburgh. The obvious orchestrator was the Lord Advocate, but after the passing of the first Reform Act none took any great part in stimulating party organisation, with the exception of a modest advisory circular sent out by Murray after the 1835 election which recommended close scrutiny of the registers and greater efforts to return Liberals to Parliament. Only one seat — Lanarkshire — took the trouble to respond, and for only one seat — Orkney and Shetland — did a candidate provide the Advocate with an analysis of the causes of his defeat.[84] Again, the Scottish legal officers played remarkably little part in another obvious area, that of finding candidates. In 1833 Murray said he knew of no one who could stand for Berwickshire, but he did tentatively suggest one name — which turned out to be that of the Conservative candidate.[85] Yet the absence of a good (sometimes just any) candidate was a recurrent complaint. Even in 1832, it was a problem in Mid Lothian; in 1835 Murray complained, 'There is a great want of candidates'; and this posed difficulties in the solidly Liberal Fife seat in 1837. In 1841 Gibson Craig located Dunbartonshire and Lanarkshire as outstanding prospects for re-capture provided a strong candidate was found. None was, and the Tories had walkovers in two seats they themselves were apprehensive about.[86]

Cash from central sources was very limited, and its availability was not publicised. One Stirlingshire laird — the Liberal candidate for the seat in 1841 — told another: 'Bannerman, our Aberdeen M.P., told me Rutherfurd the Solr. Genl. had sent him something handsome he believed out of some general fund he acts for'.[87] So shadowy was this kitty that while on occasions something was doled out of it — Kincardineshire and Aberdeenshire were both beneficiaries in 1837 — much confusion existed as to where applications for aid should be submitted. Two leading Whig aristocrats, who might be presumed to be well informed, Lords Minto and Lovat, were convinced that London was the likeliest provenance for subsidies.[88]

A group of Edinburgh-based Whigs did try to furnish some broad organisational conspectus, and as they included all the main managers and politicians — Sir John Dalrymple, Sir James Gibson Craig, Fox Maule — together with several legal worthies, dividends seemed probable. However, as a rule they seem to have achieved nothing, doing little more than grumble to each other about the problems of managing the party's electoral affairs, and certainly demonstrating minimal leadership. Thus an attempt by these party leaders to form a Scottish Liberal Association to deal with registration matters in 1835–6 produced no constructive results.[89] The national leaders of the Whig party (i.e.

Melbourne, Grey and Russell) do not seem to have felt the need to use one of the professional managers from London, such as Coppock, to tighten up the Scottish party. This is of course in marked contrast to the Tories, for whom Graham and Bonham immersed themselves in Scottish organisational details. Liberals bewailed this neglect, pointing to the profusion of cash being scattered by the Tories, which was believed to emanate from the Carlton Club, while no money came from the Reform Club to Scotland. At the outset of the 1841 election, it was reported that there were many complaints by Liberals about the lack of a top-class organiser or party manager in Scotland to whom local agents could turn for advice and help. In the absence of a general Scottish organiser, it was feared that there might be electoral rebuffs.[90]

Much was therefore left to local initiative, but here the Conservatives did better. In several counties, e.g. Perthshire and Roxburghshire, there was a conscious desire not to run the constituency through the agency of county writers, who were notoriously expensive and highly inefficient. If these lawyers were used, it would mark a reversion to the pre-1832 practices, for they would 'again rally round [them] all the Harpies of [their] profession whom we have shaken off with so much difficulty'.[91] By dispensing with such services, two trends became apparent. One alternative to using paid agents was to build up local committees of activists. Contributions made by Liberal voters in Roxburghshire to help defray the cost of the 1832 election were welcomed not just for the cash value but also for promoting involvement in organisation: 'small sums indeed, but will help them to keep up an interest in the thing as well as to keep them together'.[92] The advantages were obvious — enthusiasm, a willingness to be adventurous, unlike the caution of professional lawyers, and, above all, cheapness. The best instances of this model of organisation was probably in Ayrshire, where bodies like the Cunninghame and the Beith Reform Associations throve, drawing delegates from every parish, holding regular meetings, appointing subcommittees to cover all polling stations at elections and assuming local responsibility for frequent registration drives.[93] Other examples included East Lothian, where similar parochial committees were vital to the capture of the seat in 1835, and Perthshire, where local committees handled electoral business.[94]

The defects of this voluntary activism, which became more evident as the 1830s advanced, were twofold. Firstly, much of the impetus depended on eager leaders, but all too often these were very few, and if they lost their sense of commitment, no obvious replacement was available to provide direction. In Perthshire, the Marquess of Breadalbane was alleged to have allowed Whig organisation to slide badly between 1832 and 1834, so letting the Tories win the seat at a by-election. Prompted by Maule, Breadalbane then quickly acted to galvanise the party machinery, and the seat was reclaimed in the 1835 general election. After 1837, when Maule lost, decline set in, and by 1840 Breadalbane had apparently lost all enthusiasm for maintaining an efficient level of organisation, and the Liberal defeat in that year's by-election was ascribed in part to neglect of the register and a general sloppiness in machinery.[95] In Inverness-shire, lost to the Tories in 1835, a feeble registration effort was made in 1836, but soon came to a stop when the

Liberal candidate, Grant of Glenmoriston, would not settle the expenses.[96] Again, in Renfrewshire, one factor which helped the Tories to take the seat in 1837 was the utter absence of organisational and registration work on the part of the late Liberal M.P., Sir Michael Shaw-Stewart.[97] Kirkcudbrightshire had also been so badly run down by the incumbent Liberal, Alex Murray, that in 1840 a local Whig warned that the Conservatives had reasonable prospects of winning.[98]

The second weakness inherent in relying on local committees was their tendency to disintegrate, usually from discouragement or disunity. Being seen to be on the losing side was felt to have grave consequences, so frequently no opposition would be offered after a seat had been decisively won by the Tories. Breadalbane used this argument to justify his non-participation in the 1840 Perthshire contest.[99] Once it was felt undesirable to fight a seat, local committees would soon dwindle away, as their sole *raison d'être* had been removed. Disunity also became a significant factor, especially as the church question was thrust to the fore, and reconciling conflicting interest groups — never an easy task — became almost impossible. As early as 1834 the tensions in the party were manifest, as the Roxburghshire M.P., Admiral the Hon. Gilbert Elliot, ruefully pointed to the greater unity and spirit of resolution to be found among Tories than Liberals.[100]

As the local committee structure fell apart, the burden of keeping organisation in existence devolved upon a few notables. After their majority fell from 940 in 1832 to 200 in 1835, Lanarkshire Liberals intimated their intention to form a popular association to place the constituency on a well-organised footing, and with a firm financial base to fight elections. By the 1837 contest these local associations appear to have been defunct, and a reversion to the older pattern occurred. C. A. Murray recorded that he was approached in that year to run by a group of local gentry on a fairly informal basis. Murray at first declined because his uncle, the Duke of Hamilton, was disinclined to foot the bill, but when the Duke was prevailed upon to change his mind, Murray consented to stand.[101] The drawbacks of over-dependence on a handful of leaders like Hamilton were seen in 1841, when several of these individuals decided to retire from active engagement in Liberal politics. Hamilton himself, who had paid 'several hundred' pounds each year since the 1837 election, stated that he would support only his nephew, Murray, and no other candidate. Murray, having made three bids to enter Parliament, had lost the appetite for electioneering, the Duke was adamant, and, so the seat was abandoned to the Tories without a contest.[102] Breadalbane and Lovat in Perthshire and Inverness-shire respectively declared themselves no longer active, and both seats put up no Liberal. In Roxburghshire, the Duke of Roxburghe's decision to pull out of the Liberal effort (because he wished to employ paid agents to administer constituency politics) was a major consideration in deciding the Liberal candidate to withdraw. However, the candidate, John Elliot, was persuaded to re-enter after intervention by a group of Non-Intrusionist Edinburgh Liberals, an almost unique piece of activity by a non-local body. With the Edinburgh group's help, and not a little assistance from a disastrous campaign by an egregious Tory, Elliot won, and this feat served only to underline the defects of party organisation in most seats.[103]

In addition to a degree of disaffection arising from the policies pursued by the Liberal government, one of the causes of the reduced level of commitment was that the financial burden was borne by a very few individuals in most seats. When the Duke of Roxburghe withdrew, the Minto family calculated that the cost of fighting Roxburghshire (a sum running into thousands) would have to be met preponderantly by them, as the lairds could be relied on to produce only £2–300, while the small subscriptions of 1832 had obviously vanished.[104] In Inverness-shire, where a contest was reckoned to involve expenditure of £1500, along with £600 annual 'running costs', Lovat demurred at this being met by a handful of proprietors.[105] In a number of seats, the cost of fighting elections had been met in the first euphoria of the Reform Act by public subscription among the electors, and agents had offered their services free, as in Perthshire. But as enthusiasm waned and the frequency of elections — there were four general elections in nine years — imposed heavy cost burdens, this practice seems to have dried up. Whereas the Tories devised a form of levy on property to keep in good financial health, the Liberals did not follow suit.[106] Relying on a clutch of rich proprietors could stave off crisis for the Liberals, but even this was frequently only a temporary respite. Perthshire set up a registration finance committee in 1835, which in practice meant that four peers put up £450 p.a., but misunderstandings and disputes over how the money should be spent vitiated the committee's work and sapped support. As a result the Liberals of Perthshire, a populous county of great wealth, were reduced in 1837 to begging for financial assistance from Edinburgh.[107]

In burgh seats, much greater variety of circumstances was to be found affecting organisation. In only a very small number of burghs did patronage, still less corruption, play a role of any moment. The Inverness burghs were widely regarded as falling into this category, as MacPherson Grant revealed in explaining to his brother why James Morrison would carry comfortably in 1840 a seat which had been Tory until 1837, and then won by the Liberals with a majority of only 19. 'He is just the man who has it in his power to make a return for the services of that description of voters, in forwarding their sons in Clerkships, etc. as I understand his business employs several hundred young men' and, moreover, he had influence with the East India Company. 'I believe', added Ballindalloch some days later, 'that the Liberal Party in the Burghs are well pleased at the prospect of getting their fingers into a purse as heavy as that of Mr. Morrison.' Morrison duly won the by-election by 351 votes to 307 and was not opposed at the subsequent general election.[108] But Inverness does seem to have been exceptional, for an Englishman who fought burghs in Scotland (Kilmarnock and Kirkcaldy) and in England (Blackburn and Bolton) remarked: 'In Scotland, since the Reform Act, the constituencies are infinitely less corrupt than in England, expectations of reward for electoral services being by no means usual ... Such was the purity of elections in those days in the newly enfranchised Scottish burghs that my election [in 1835] did not cost me a farthing'.[109] It is striking that the Tories never seriously raised the cry of corruption to explain their abject failure to win burgh seats.

In a small number of burghs, patrons could exercise influence. The Earl of Stair was probably in control of the Wigtown collection in the far South-West; and at Kirkcaldy Ferguson of Raith was secure as M.P., thanks to his influence as the local laird. But in many even of the smaller seats, no influence can be discerned. Partly this was because the groupings of towns into one burgh seat, as noted, made influence difficult; secondly, the fierce independence displayed by the voters made them especially vigilant against any hints of manipulation. Such manipulation was more likely to come after 1832 not from a patron but from the Government, seeking to place ministers in safe seats, which were mostly burghs. But resistance to having a placeman intruded upon them was strongly felt by constituents. T. F. Kennedy warned his successor as a Lord of Treasury, Robert Graham, that he could not also expect to take over his seat, the Ayr Burghs: 'Although as a stranger out of office you might do, but as a *stranger in office* I am certain you would be beat. *We are very radical* and the idea of using these Burghs as a Treasury seat would never go down'.[110] The major grounds for fearing that the Attorney General would not be successful in Edinburgh in 1834 were that he was a ministerialist; Glasgow accepted Lord William Bentinck, but not over-enthusiastically, and when Maule angled to come to Glasgow in 1841, he was firmly turned aside. Whereas at the end of the nineteenth century Scotland was to become a safe refuge for prominent English Liberals, very few sat for Scottish seats in the 1830s and even fewer of these sat comfortably. Parnell, the Paymaster General, was supported by Dundee Radicals in 1837 only because a Tory stood. With Whigs being squeezed steadily out of county seats by the Tory gains, the desire of officeholders to be installed in burghs, still impregnably Liberal, was much sharper. It is ironic that they should run up against such implacable opposition from the voters, as the reason given by the latter, namely to preserve their seats from becoming controlled by the Government, was precisely one of the major articles of grievance levelled by Whig reformers against the pre-1832 Tory corruption of Scottish political life. The Whigs were now hoist with their own petard.

NOTES

1. *Letters chiefly concerned with the Affairs of Scotland from Henry Cockburn to Thomas Francis Kennedy, M.P.* (London 1874), p. 508 — Cockburn to Kennedy, 10 May 1834; cf. J. Gibson Craig to Brougham, 2 May 1834, Brougham MSS., 17616; P. Miller to Earl Grey, 15 May 1834, Grey MSS; J. Cunningham to Sir J. Dalrymple, 7 Mar. (1834), Stair MSS., GD 135/112/7/14.

2. *Letters ... from Cockburn to Kennedy,* p. 510, Cockburn to Kennedy, 23 May 1834.

3. W. Murray to Sir J. Dalrymple (17 May 1834), Stair MSS., GD 135/109/12/24.

4. See Collection of Electioneering Broadsides for the 1832 Edinburgh City Election in the British Library, Cat. No. 826.1.28. E.g. *'Hurrah for Aytoun'* and Aytoun's *'Address to the Independent Electors of Edinburgh and Its Vicinity'*.

5. G. Elliot to Minto, 2 Jun., 9 Jul. 1833, 17 Jan. 1834, Minto MSS., MS. 11750, ff. 47-8, 64-6, 116-7.

6. F. Maule to A. Rutherfurd, 31 May 1837, Rutherfurd MSS., MS. 9697, ff. 20–3, cf. Lord Melville to F. Maule, 24 Jul. 1839, Dalhousie MSS., GD 45/14/629/7; *Journal of Henry Cockburn, Being a Continuation of the Memorials of his Time, 1831–54* (Edinburgh, 1874), Vol. 1, pp. 125–7 (12 Aug. 1836).

7. *The Durham Festival, Glasgow, Wednesday October 29th 1834* (n.p., n.d.), p. 3, Cockburn, *Journal,* Vol. I, p. 152 (8 Dec. 1837).

8. J. Cunningham to F. Maule, 22 Aug. (1835), Dalhousie MSS., GD 45/14/625/21; J. H. Callender to W. Murray, 20 Jul. 1837, Murray of Polmaise MSS., GD 189/1/163; G. Elliot to Minto, 17 Feb. (1837), Minto MSS., MS. 11751, ff. 25–6.

9. J. Gibson Craig to A. Millar, 20 May 1839, Edinburgh Public Library MSS., YJN 1531.839.

10. J. H. Callender to W. Murray, 11 Oct. 1835, Murray of Polmaise MSS., GD 189/1/152.

11. F. Tytler to J. MacPherson Grant, 16 Feb. 1840, Ballindalloch MSS., 182.

12. H. Cockburn to E. Horsman, 8 Feb. 1837, Stair MSS., GD 135/114/13/5–6.

13. Cockburn, *Journal,* Vol. I, p. 102 (25 Aug. 1835).

14. F. Maule to A. Rutherfurd, 3 Oct. 1837, Rutherfurd MSS., MS. 9697, ff. 63–6.

15. T. D. Lauder to J. MacPherson Grant, 16 May 1834, Ballindalloch MSS., 141.

16. J. Cunningham to Sir J. Dalrymple, 26, 11 Dec. 1834; J. A. Murray to Dalrymple, (1), 15 Dec. 1834, Stair MSS., GD 135/112/7/28–9, 23–4; GD 135/109/6/5, 135/110/17/48–9.

17. Grey to Dalrymple, 15 Feb. 1835, Ibid., GD 135/10/10/41.

18. A. Spiers to R. Bontine, 15 Jun., 7 Jan. 1835, Cunninghame Graham MSS., GD 22/1/583.

19. A. Currie to F. Maule, 28 Jan. 1837, Dalhousie MSS., GD 45/14/626/5/54, cf. J. Cunningham to Maule, 29 Jan. 1837, Ibid., GD 45/14/625/48/9.

20. Sir H. Maxwell, *The Hon. Sir Charles Murray, K.C.B. A Memoir* (Edinburgh, 1898), p. 153.

21. G. Crawfurd to Lord W. Bentinck, 20 Jul. 1837, Portland MSS., Pw Jg 82.

22. A. Currie to F. Maule, 16 May 1837, A. Rutherfurd to Maule, 29 Jul. 1837, Dalhousie MSS., GD 45/14/626/5/75–7, 45/14/642/1; Maule to Rutherfurd, 23 Nov. 1837, Rutherfurd MSS., MS. 9697, ff. 73–4.

23. G. Crawfurd to Lord W. Bentinck, 20 Jul. 1837, Portland MSS., Pw Jg 82.

24. A. Currie to F. Maule, 1 Jun. 1839, Dalhousie MSS., GD 45/14/626/6/75–6, J. Ivory to A. Rutherfurd, 25 Jan. 1840, Rutherfurd MSS., MS. 9694, ff. 271–4.

25. J. Cunningham to Sir J. Dalrymple, 11 Dec. 1834, Stair MSS., GD 135/112/7/23–4.

26. A. Currie to F. Maule, 1 Jun. 1839, Dalhousie MSS., GD 45/14/626/6/75–6, cf. T. Macaulay to Mrs. C. Trevelyan, 29 May 1839: T. Pinney, *Letters of Thomas Babington Macaulay* (London, 1976), Vol. III, p. 290.

27. J. Ivory to Rutherfurd, 26 May, n.d. (May), (24 May) 1839, Rutherfurd MSS., MS. 9694, ff. 79–87, 210–4, 76–8; cf. J. Gibson Craig to Maule, 17 May 1839, Dalhousie MSS., GD 45/14/628.

28. *Perthshire Courier,* 10 Jun. 1841.

29. J. G. Craig to Maule, 19 Feb. 1841, Dalhousie MSS., GD 45/14/628; Craig to Sir J. Dalrymple, 20 Feb. 1833, Stair MSS., GD 135/114/12/4–7; W. Drummond to R. Stewart, 28 Feb. 1840, Stewart MSS.

30. J. B. Mackie, *The Life and Work of Duncan MacLaren* (Edinburgh, 1889), Vol. I, Ch. 8 and p. 170; cf. *George Hope of Benton Barns. A sketch of his life compiled by his daughter* (Edinburgh, 1881), pp. 24–5.

31. J. Cunningham to Dalrymple, 2 Jan. (1835), Stair MSS., GD 135/112/7/33.

32. 'Statement regarding Protestant Dissenters of Scotland' (c. 1836), Portland MSS., Pw Jg 404.

33. Rutherfurd to Maule, 20 Nov. 1837, Dalhousie MSS., GD 45/14/642/1.

34. *Scottish Central Board for Extending the Principle of Voluntary Churches and Vindicating the Rights of Dissenters,* 4th, 5th Ann. Reps. (1837-8, 1839).

35. Ibid., 5th Ann. Rep. (1839).

36. Mackie, *MacLaren,* I, pp. 211-3.

37. D. MacLaren, *Substance of a Speech delivered at a Public Meeting of Dissenters held in Edinburgh on the 14th July 1841 ...* (Edinburgh, 1841), esp. pp. 9-14, 4-6; Mackie, *MacLaren,* I, Ch. 10; *Scottish Central Board of Dissenters,* 5th Ann. Rep. (1839).

38. MacLaren, *Speech ...* , p. 3.

39. This is based on: *Dundee Advertiser,* 23 Jun.-4 Aug. 1837, 11 Jun.-9 Jul. 1841; *Dundee Warder,* 22 Jun.-6 Jul. 1841: J. B. Smith MSS., 923.2 S336/13-42.

40. For the Whig ministers' views and of the Chartist challenge, see the Rutherfurd-Maule correspondence: Dalhousie MSS., GD 45/14/642/1 and 2; Rutherfurd MSS., MSS. 9697-8.

41. J. G. Craig to Maule, 23 May 1839, Dalhousie MSS., GD 45/14/628; cf. Macaulay to Mrs. C. Trevelyan, 29 May 1839, Pinney, *Letters of Macaulay,* Vol. III, p. 290; cf. A. Nicolson, *Memoirs of Adam Black* (2nd ed., Edinburgh, 1885), pp. 117-20.

42. Mills to Lord W. Bentinck, 10 Jan. 1838, Portland MSS., Pw Jg 258.

43. *List of Tories, Chartists and Churchmen who united at the Late Glasgow Election and Voted for James Campbell and George Mills* (n.p., n.d. — 1841). This identifies 296 voters, leaving Mills, presumably, with 57 plumpers. A. Wilson, *Scottish Chartism* (Manchester, 1970), pp. 33-46, 53, 121, 153-65 traces the complex relations between middle-class reformers and Chartists. Also, F. Montgomery, 'Glasgow and the Movement for Corn Law Repeal', *History,* 64 (1979), pp. 363-79, which stresses the extent of co-operation.

44. Macaulay to MacLaren, 5 Dec. 1840 in Mackie, *MacLaren,* Vol. I, pp. 215-7.

45. MacLaren, *Speech ...* , p. 10.

46. Statement re Protestant Dissenters in Scotland (1836), Portland MSS., Pw Jg 404.

47. G. I. T. Machin, *Politics and the Churches in Great Britain, 1832 to 1868* (London, 1977), pp. 128-9.

48. A. Rutherfurd to F. Maule, 20 Nov. 1837, Dalhousie MSS., GD 45/14/642/1.

49. Nicholson, *Black,* pp. 106-8.

50. Craig to F. Maule, 8 Oct., 5 Aug., 24 Nov. 1840, Dalhousie MSS., GD 45/14/628; Macaulay to: J. F. MacFarlane, 22 Nov., D. MacLaren, 5 Dec. 1840, Pinney, *Macaulay Letters,* III, pp. 347-8, 350-2.

51. *Scotsman,* 22 May, 2 Jun. 1841; Mackie, *MacLaren,* I, pp. 222-4.

52. W. Drummond, Lord Abercromby to R. Stewart, 22 Feb., 9 Mar. 1840, Stewart MSS.

53. J. McFarlane, *Dissenting Neutrality, or the Perthshire Election* (Edinburgh, 1840).

54. J. G. Craig to F. Maule, 14 Nov. 1840, Dalhousie MSS., GD 45/14/628, but see Cockburn, *Journals,* I, pp. 270-3 (20 Dec. 1840) for a version suggesting the Voluntaries were also against the Whigs, not just the Non-Intrusionists.

55. J. G. Craig to F. Maule, 14 Nov. 1840, 14 Feb., 17 May 1841, Dalhousie MSS., GD 45/14/628.

56. Rutherfurd, Craig to Maule, 20 Nov. 1837, 8 Jun. 1841, Ibid., GD 45/14/642/1, 45/14/628; Mackie, *MacLaren,* I, pp. 222-4.

57. *Perthshire Courier,* 10 Jun., 8 Jul. 1841.

58. Melbourne to F. Maule, 28 Oct. 1840, Dalhousie MSS., GD 45/14/640.

59. Macaulay to A. Black, 20 Nov. 1840, Pinney, *Macaulay Letters,* III, p. 346.

60. E.g. A. Rutherfurd to F. Maule, 22 May 1838, Dalhousie MSS., GD 45/14/642/1; J. E. Elliot to Minto, 19 Jun. 1841, Minto MSS., MS. 11754, ff. 170–1 for a pledge by Moncrieff and Dunlop to do all in their power for the Liberal cause at the elections.

61. Macaulay to A. Black, 20 Nov. 1840, Pinney, *Macaulay Letters,* III, p. 346; cf. Cockburn, *Journals,* I, pp. 296–8 (23 Jul. 1841).

62. Melbourne to Lord Dunfermline, 20 Apr. 1841, L. C. Sanders, *Lord Melbourne's Papers* (London, 1889), pp. 416–7.

63. Maule to Rutherfurd, n.d., Rutherfurd MSS., MS. 9697, ff. 294–7; Dunlop to Maule, 11 Feb. 1841, Dalhousie MSS., GD 45/14/658/1.

64. S. Walpole, *Life of Lord John Russell* (London, 1889), II, p. 329.

65. P. M. Stewart to F. Maule, 9 Jan. 1840, 20 Apr. 1841, Dalhousie MSS., GD 45/14/646.

66. J. to G. MacPherson Grant, 18 Mar. 1840; G. to J. MacPherson Grant, 17 Mar. 1840, 5 Jul. 1841; G. MacPherson Grant to Seafield, 24 Jun. 1841 (copy), Ballindalloch MSS., 688, 182, 185, 656. *The Scotsman* (21 Jul. 1841) cites a North-East Liberal for a claim that the fall of 35 in the Liberal majority was in part due to dislike of the Liberals' zealous espousal of Non-Intrusionism.

67. J. to G. MacPherson Grant, 1 Feb. 1840; G. to J. MacPherson Grant, 17 Mar. 1840; T. Falconer to G. MacPherson Grant, 18 Mar. 1840; Ballindalloch MSS., 688, 182, 688.

68. Dunlop to Maule, 3 Jan. 1840, Dalhousie MSS., GD 45/14/658/1.

69. Same to same, 23, 24, 25, 28 Feb. 1840; J. Ivory to Maule, 22, 25, 26 Feb. 1840, Dalhousie MSS., GD 45/14/658/1; 45/14/651.

70. A. Currie to F. Maule, 26 Feb. 1840, Ibid., GD 45/14/626/7/7; *Scotsman,* 11 Mar. 1840.

71. Dunlop to Rutherfurd, 25 Feb., also 24, 27 Feb. 1840, Rutherfurd MSS., MS. 9689, ff. 236–7, 232–5, 238–41; cf. G. Speirs to F. Maule, 22 Feb. 1840, Dalhousie MSS., GD 45/14/641/2; J. Ivory to Rutherfurd, 20 Feb., 6 Mar. 1840, Rutherfurd MSS., MSS. 9694, ff. 222–30, 9695, ff. 10–13.

72. Thomson to Aberdeen, 14 Aug. 1841, Rev. G. Smeaton, *Memoir of Alexander Thomson of Banchory* (Edinburgh, 1869), pp. 231–2.

73. N. L. Walker, *Robert Buchanan, D.D. An Ecclesiastical Biography* (London, 1877), pp. 77–80, 102 and Ch. 6 *passim.*

74. Buchanann to Dunlop, 26 Feb. 1840, in Ibid., p. 187, and Ch. 9 generally for this episode.

75. Dunlop to Maule, 20 Jun. 1840, Dalhousie MSS., GD 45/14/658/1.

76. Craig to F. Maule, 5 Aug. 1840, Dalhousie MSS., GD 45/14/628; Dunlop to Maule, 5 Nov. 1840, Ibid., GD 45/14/658/1; cf. Dunlop to A. Rutherfurd, 5 Sep. 1840, and n.d., Rutherfurd MSS., MS. 9689, ff. 266–9, 278–9.

77. *To the Electors of the City of Edinburgh, Address by the Church Defence and Anti-Patronage Electoral Association* (n.p., n.d. — c. 1840), unpag.

78. Dunlop to Maule, 6, 11 Feb. 1841, Dalhousie MSS., GD 45/14/658/1.

79. Dunlop to Maule, 3 Apr., 15, 24, 19, 24, 27 May 1841, Ibid., GD 45/14/658/1, 2.

80. J. Elliot to Minto, 19 Jun. 1841, Minto MSS., MS. 11754, ff. 170–1.

81. T. B. Macaulay to F. Macaulay, 28 Jun. 1841, Pinney, *Macaulay Letters,* III, pp. 348–50.

82. *Scotsman,* 17 Jul. 1841.

83. Sir J. Dalrymple to Grey, 25 Dec. 1834, 3 Jan., 7 Feb. 1835, Grey MSS.

84. J. Hamilton, T. Muir, G. Traill to J. A. Murray, 14, 16, 10 Feb. 1835; T. Muir to Messrs. Wilson and MacIntyre, n.d. (copy); Rev. J. Barclay to G. Traill, 6 Feb. 1835; J. A. Murray MSS., MS. 19735, ff. 175, 176–7, 165–8, 178–9, 169–71.

85. Murray to Minto, 19 Nov. 1833, Minto MSS., MS. 11808. ff. 97–8.

86. Murray to Sir J. Dalrymple, — Jun. 1832, 1 Dec. 1834, Stair MSS., GD 135/110/17/9–11, 135/109/6/5; J. Cunningham to F. Maule, 29 Jun. (1837), Dalhousie MSS., GD 45/14/625/81–2; Craig to Maule, 9, 12, 21 Jun. 1841, Ibid., GD 45/14/628.

87. Sir M. Bruce to W. Murray, 24 Nov. 1838, Murray of Polmaise MSS., GD 189/1/169.

88. L. Crombie, A. Bannerman to A. Rutherfurd, 5, 13 Aug. 1837, Rutherfurd MSS., MS. 9686, ff. 188–9, 198–201; J. Elliot to Minto, 15 Jun. 1841, Minto MSS., MS. 11754, ff. 155–60; J. to G. MacPherson Grant, 1 Feb. 1840, Ballindalloch MSS., 688.

89. *Reform Registration of Scotland, Address to the Counties of Scotland* (Edinburgh, 1836). There is a copy of this, and a discussion of the inutility of such projects between J. Campbell, J. Dobie and J. Dunlop in March 1836, in Beith Parish MSS., P/CN 49.1/673, 667–9.

90. J. Cunningham, A. Currie to F. Maule, 6 Jan. 1837, 27 May 1841, Dalhousie MSS., GD 45/14/625/33–6; 626/7/30–1.

91. Minto to J. Elliot, 5 Feb. 1841, Minto MSS., MS. 11754, ff. 123–6; G. Goodman to Lynedoch, 16 Jan. 1835, Lynedoch MSS., MS. 16143, ff. 58–9.

92. Admiral G. Elliot to Minto, 29 Dec. 1832, Minto MSS., MS. 11749, ff. 72–4.

93. J. Dobie to J. Campbell, 14 Mar. (1836) (copy); *Regulations of the Reform Association of the District of Cunninghame in the County of Ayr* (12 Sep. 1835); poster, dated 7 Sep. 1835, summoning a meeting to form a branch in Beith, Beith Parish MSS., P/CN 49.1/668, 628, 622.

94. *Hope of Fenton Barns*, p. 32; J. Miller to F. Maule, 3 Mar. 1835, Dalhousie MSS., GD 45/14/630/4; G. Goodman to R. Graham, 11, 16 Jan. 1835, Lynedoch MSS., MS. 16143, ff. 43–4, 58–9.

95. G. Gardiner to R. Graham, 17 Jun., 8 May 1834, Lynedoch MSS., MSS. 16142, ff. 67–8, 16141, ff. 206–7; A. Currie to F. Maule, 14 Jun. 1835, Dalhousie MSS., GD 45/14/626/2/57–60; R. Graham to W. Anderson, 28 Jun. 1839 (draft), Lynedoch MSS., MS. 16144, f. 82; Currie to Maule, 24 Feb. 1840, Dalhousie MSS., GD 45/14/626/7/3–4.

96. G. Cameron to Lovat, 20 Aug. 1836, to G. MacPherson Grant, 9 Aug. 1836; G. to J. MacPherson Grant, 21 Jul. 1839, Ballindalloch MSS., 685, 151.

97. J. Cunningham, A. Currie to F. Maule, 6, 29 Jan. 1837, Dalhousie MSS., GD 45/14/625/33–6, and 45/14/626/5/55–6.

98. T. Maitland to A. Rutherfurd, 20 Jul. 1840, Rutherfurd MSS., MS. 9700, ff. 44–7.

99. Breadalbane to R. Stewart, 22 Feb. 1840, Lynedoch MSS., MS. 16144, ff. 97–8.

100. G. Elliot to Minto, 17 Jan. 1834, Minto MSS., MS. 11750, ff. 116–7.

101. J. Hamilton, T. Muir to J. A. Murray, 14, 16 Feb. 1835; J. A. Murray MSS., MS. 19735, ff. 175, 176–7; H. E. Maxwell, *The Hon. Sir Charles Murray, K.C.B. A Memoir* (Edinburgh, 1898), pp. 152–6.

102. A. Currie to F. Maule, 27 May 1841, Dalhousie MSS., GD 45/14/626/7/30–1.

103. J. Elliot to Minto, 15, 18, 26, 27, 29 Jun. 1841, Minto MSS., MS. 11754, ff. 155–60, 166–9, 174–9, 180–3, 188–9.

104. Elliot to Minto, 15 Jun. 1841, Ibid., MS. 11754, ff. 155–60.

105. J. to G. MacPherson Grant, 1 Feb. 1840, Ballindalloch MSS., 688.

106. J. Dobie to J. Campbell, 14 Mar. (1836) (copy), Beith Parish MSS., P/CN 49.1/668.

107. A. Currie to F. Maule, 14 Jun. 1835, Dalhousie MSS., GD 45/14/626/2/57–60; Maule to A. Rutherfurd, 19 Jun. 1837, Rutherfurd MSS., MS. 9697, ff. 33–4.

108. G. to J. MacPherson Grant, 27 Jan., 1 Feb., 1840, Ballindalloch MSS., 182, 688.

109. *Autobiographical Recollections of Sir John Bowring, with a Brief Memoir by L. B. Bowring* (London, 1877), pp. 81, 85.

110. T. F. Kennedy to R. Graham, 25 Jan. 1834, Lynedoch MSS., MS. 16140, ff. 9–10.

3

Early Victorian Politics

In English politics, the 1850s have been interpreted as a period of stability and, eventually, of an absence of acute political acrimony. The former is demonstrated by the containment of the radical challenges to the basic elements of the Constitution: the House of Lords and the state church were not subverted, as had appeared likely in the 1830s, and the resolution of the Corn Law crisis reinforced this.[1] By the 1850s, few issues seemed prominent enough to divide the parties, so that the 1857 General Election became, in *The Times'* table of results, merely a contest between Palmerstonians and anti-Palmerstonians, not Liberals versus Conservatives. While some of these trends did apply to Scotland too, there were considerable divergences. Lord Aberdeen, as Prime Minister, was exasperated and worried by political turbulence in Scotland. 'The violence of party rancour in Scotland has been frequently apparent', he stated in August 1853, adding five days later that he 'lament[ed] the violence of political differences in Scotland'.[2] The party conflict which was so upsetting to Aberdeen was not that of Conservative against Whig, for the Conservatives, as is discussed below, were abnormally weak in Scotland after 1846, even by their standards. The disputes raged within the broad umbrella of the Liberal party, and the issue which reflected most clearly the nature of the turmoil was also accurately identified by Aberdeen: 'This education question is likely to become a real torment, as indeed everything Scottish is ... I see very clearly [Education] is destined to give us much trouble'.[3] The education difficulty in Scotland was of wider significance, for if the proposed reforms were put through, there were many on both sides of the issue who believed it would lead to the disestablishment of the Church of Scotland. If the state church in Scotland were placed in jeopardy, the survival of its English counterpart might become equally uncertain.

I

In England, the major dislocation to the pattern of political alignment was caused by the split in the Conservative party over the introduction of legislation to repeal the Corn Laws. But Scottish politics experienced an earlier and deeper fracture to the two-party system. The emergence of a new ecclesiastical body in 1843, the Free Church, led to the creation of a separate voting bloc, composed of adherents of that Church. In 1847 in the Haddington Burghs, a possible candidate was told, 'Since the Free Church party has gained a firm footing and a high standing, and as much will depend upon this party being satisfied as to the views of candidates [on various questions] ... a less correct idea can be formed as to the probable success of any candidate whatever'.[4] The basis of the existence of the Free Church vote was, firstly, a desire to promote the interests of the Free Church, and secondly, to wreak some vengeance on those politicians and parties deemed responsible either for permitting the Disruption to occur or for being hostile to their Church's interests. A major source of complaint was that many landowners were alleged to have refused the new church sites on which to build its churches, even although the secessionists might constitute the majority of the community. Ross and Cromarty was gained by the Liberals in 1847, despite a considerable amount of feeling against the repeal of the Corn Laws among the larger farmers on the eastern side of the county. The main reason for this victory was stated to be that the Conservative incumbent, MacKenzie of Applecross, had the reputation of having denied sites to the Free Church, while his Liberal opponent, James Matheson, although not a Free Churchman, had been most co-operative in providing ground on his Lewis estates.[5] But support was not given unconditionally to Liberals. *The Witness,* the main organ of the Free Church, was explicit in its assessment of the political affiliation of the Church. Whereas up until the Disruption, those who were to become Free Churchmen had often been Conservative-inclined, Peel's handling of the crisis altered things and so, 'our great ecclesiastical question, and more especially the Disruption, have altered this position and placed us on a safer and freer ground'. But as the Whigs had no more supported them in the crisis of 1843 either, there was no reason to vote for them. The newspaper's conclusion, articulated a fortnight earlier, was that 'the days of the great party questions have, we repeat, gone by, and what the country wants is neither Whigs nor Tories ... '[6] This non-partisan stance could lead to great confusion. In Roxburghshire in 1847, the leading Free Churchman in politics told one of the few members of the Whig government sympathetic to the Church that the votes of his fellow churchmen would go to the Tory, partly because he was a brother-in-law of the Earl of Breadalbane, who had been an ardent champion of their cause, and partly because the Whig candidate was the uncle of Lord Melgund, who was challenging the Free Church's claim to control the Liberal nomination in Greenock.[7] However, Melgund's uncle had formed the distinct impression that the Free Church vote would go to him, in order to break the power of the Duke of Buccleuch, particularly in the matter of granting church sites. Without the accession of Free Church votes, the Liberals had no hope of winning the seat, as the Tories had a large majority on the registrations, he explained.[8] In the event, no Tory stood, the Whigs walked the course, and so Free Church pretensions remained untested.

Distaste for the existing parties was not the sole factor behind the presence of a Free Church vote, however. It very soon became apparent that one of the more optimistic scenarios predicted by the secessionists was not going to occur. The expectation was that the departure of one third of the Church of Scotland's membership — and that, at least in their own estimation, being the brightest and the best third — would lead to the rapid disintegration of the state church, with further waves of defecting elders, teachers and clergy, reducing the national church to a pathetic and unsustainable rump, so that the Free Church would become in fact *the* national church. As this failure to destroy the Church of

Scotland became evident, the impulse to use other means — notably electoral weight — to weaken further the established church became ever more pressing. The defect in this political tactic soon became apparent: in very few constituencies was the Free Church on its own able to exercise a decisive influence on the outcome of a contest. This was witnessed in the three by-elections (Kilmarnock, Greenock and Kirkcudbrightshire) which occurred in the two years or so after the Disruption. At Kilmarnock, in May 1844, the Free Church elements brought forward a candidate, who withdrew before polling, while in Greenock in 1845 a Free Church man did run but lost to another Liberal. The lessons of these contests are significant. In Kilmarnock, the Free Church candidate, Robertson, found it impossible to broaden his support sufficiently to challenge the other Liberal, although he strove to woo the Voluntaries by claiming in his election address to uphold religious liberty 'on behalf of both of the new Seceders, who by refusal of sites may be prohibited the free worship of God, and of older Seceders [i.e. Voluntaries] kept out by religious test from academic situations'. However, the emergence of a Tory candidate led many Free Churchmen to respond to calls to rally to the other Liberal and stopped Voluntaries from backing Robertson.[9] In Greenock, A. M. Dunlop, the leading Free Church lawyer, opposed the Provost, Baine, but could not beat him, in part because Voluntaries were unwilling to co-operate, and also because Baine put Free Trade as the more important issue, while Dunlop wished to stress ecclesiastical questions.[10]

Thus the Free Church had difficulty in exerting any leverage on politics. The drawbacks were numerous. Firstly, the existence of a major party issue, Free Trade, tended to push religious grievances to the side, and to promote loyalty to Whigs or Liberals as the main proponents of the abolition of the Corn Laws. Secondly, as a result of the bitter conflict of the pre-Disruption decade, relations between the two non-established Presbyterian churches were very poor. The Free Church was committed to the ideal of an established church (to be achieved by purifying the existing corrupt and erastian one); the Voluntaries believed all establishments to be wrong. So while the Dissenters had little reason to be the allies of the Whigs, upholders of the present corrupt state churches, they had, in a sense, even less motive to work with those in the Free Church, as a reformed and dynamic establishment could be held to present a more serious threat to the disestablishment doctrines of the Voluntaries.[11] Thirdly, so long as the Conservatives seemed to be a serious threat, the Free Churchmen were open to wounding allegations of letting in those who had forced them out of the national church.

All of these retarding forces were removed in the course of 1846, and the formation of an alliance between the two non-established Presbyterian churches in 1846–7 was to alter the political complexion of Scotland for a decade. What could be done, and how it might be attained, were suggested by the third by-election in the 1844–5 period. On the death of the M.P. for Kirkcudbrightshire in July 1845, the Liberals chose Thomas Maxwell of Terregles. The news that he was not only a Roman Catholic, but that he also approved of the government giving a grant to the Roman Catholic seminary at Maynooth in Ireland, drove the Free Church and Voluntaries in the county into paroxysms of anger. They induced the Tories to run a candidate on the cry of No-Popery and forced Maxwell to withdraw. His replacement, Thomas Maitland of Dundrennan, was a Whig, and not opposed to the Maynooth grant, but presumably as a Presbyterian was more acceptable, winning the seat after what he termed 'as good a stand-up fight against bigotry and oppression as I ever witnessed'.[12] Over the next ten years there were to be relatively few such victories as the anti-Maynooth movement became dominant.

Moreover the confusion and disarray in the Tory camp over Protection rendered inapplicable the argument that challenging a Whig candidate with another Liberal was simply opening the seat to a Conservative victory on a minority poll. The passsage of the Corn Law Repeal legislation also removed the leading issue which united both Whig and Radical. *The Witness,* whose views on the erosion of party lines have been referred to, went on to call for a new type of representative. The paper looked for 'members untrammelled by the influences of the aggrandizing class from whom the demanded concessions have to be wrung . . . and at one with the preponderating Protestantism of the community in the religious views and feelings'.[13] Of course, the difficulty of the divergence of views over the correct role of the state in supporting religion still remained beteen Free Churchman and Voluntary, but this was circumvented by the expedient of co-operating on issues in which they shared a common view, and studiously avoiding debate on the unresolved conflict about state endowment.

The initial step towards closer relations came through the Evangelical Alliance, a stoutly anti-Catholic body formed in 1845. Initially the Free Church was uneasy at participating in this movement, because members of the state church were also involved, but Chalmers endorsed it, and Candlish, the emergent successor to Chalmers, was active in its work. The Voluntaries were equally zealous supporters of the Alliance, and this area of collaboration had direct political benefits. The candidate around whom both non-established Presbyterian churches could rally at the Edinburgh by-election of 1846 — the first at which the strength of the new voting alignments became clear — was Sir Culling Eardley Smith, the leader of the Alliance. In 1841, Smith had been rejected as a candidate for the city by the Voluntaries on the grounds that he would not attract broad suppport. The successful nominee of the Free-Voluntary party in the 1847 general election at Edinburgh, Charles Cowan, had been a prominent worker on behalf of the Evangelical Alliance in Edinburgh. In Greenock, the defeated Free Church candidate in the 1845 election stood again in 1847, believing his chances were much enhanced by what he saw as a drawing together of his own church with Voluntaries 'after the lapse of another two years when their feelings of brotherly love had been greatly advanced, and when they had received additional countenance and made greater progress — he meant by the evangelical alliance . . . '[14]

While the Evangelical Alliance was of cardinal (if such an adjective be appropriate) importance in forging common bonds, it lacked a precise issue on which some political movement could be generated. This need was provided by resistance to the Maynooth grant as the Kirkcudbright episode had foreshadowed. It was not relevant that the Voluntaries opposed the financing of the Catholic seminary in Ireland on the grounds of the high principle that all state endowment of religion was wrong, whereas the Free Church simply abhorred subsidising 'erroneous' teaching; the common ground was that both Tory and Whig politicians were acting wrongly. Several consequences flowed from the Maynooth question. Firstly, the old enmities were dropped. At a mass meeting in Edinburgh to oppose the grant, A. M. Dunlop noted that relations between the Voluntaries and his own church were now of 'cordial union'. Candlish, one of the arch-opponents of the Voluntaries before 1843, spoke warmly of the need for unity between both churches in order to prove it was possible to overturn bad legislation, and he argued that the issue at stake was not the rightness of the Voluntary or the Establishment principle.[15] Secondly, Maynooth permitted both sides to justify modifying their hitherto rigid and doctrinaire positions on church-state relations. At Greenock, the Free Church's candidate skilfully refined his Church's views in the wake of Maynooth: 'he had long held it to be the duty of nations as such, to support and maintain the true religion, but if it be the case that Government cannot endow truth without at the same time endowing error, then he would say, by all means endow none'. Moreover, he added at another meeting, for the Free Church to accept state support would lead 'to the breaking up of that friendly relation which had been formed among evangelical bodies'.[16]

The Voluntaries too reappraised their stance. In 1844, the British Anti-State Church Association, a Voluntary pressure group, expressed strong criticisms of the Free Church for persistence in upholding the state connection.[17] By 1846 the tone had changed, and the recognition of past political weakness was used to vindicate moderating the firm line in favour of co-ordinating efforts with the Free Church. This was reflected in an address issued in that year by the Scottish Board of Dissenters: 'the candidates who have hitherto solicited your suffrages have virtually treated Dissent as a weak and extravagant folly', it began, adding: 'The weakness of Dissent lies in the paucity of suitable candidates'. However, Maynooth had altered this: 'At a crisis like the present all friends of religious liberty should study to the utmost harmonious co-operation ... surely there may be an amicable co-agency in a parliamentary conflict. Where the same measures are approved of, there may be a mutual forbearance as to abstract opinion, and parties may unite in supporting this or that man, as the qualification of the individual and the circumstances of the locality render desirable.To be more specific, unless Dissenters can vote for Free Churchmen and Free Churchmen for Dissenters, union is impossible and defeat certain'.[18] Hence the Dissenters and the Free Church had gingerly negotiated themselves into a political coalition, based on the argument adumbrated by Candlish at the great anti-Maynooth meeting, and reiterated by him in an article in *Lowe's Magazine* for January 1847, namely that what was necessary was to elect men who would enact Christian legislation, not pander to error.

The first indication of this political force was seen at the Edinburgh by-election in July 1846, when Macaulay sought re-election upon being appointed Paymaster-General. The leader of the Evangelical Alliance, Culling Eardley Smith, was chosen to run against Macaulay, partly, it would seem, because he possessed the inestimable advantage of belonging to neither sect and so being acceptable to both. Smith failed, but the real significance lay in the leaking to the press during the contest of a private memorandum of a meeting held in March and attended by prominent figures in the Free and Voluntary churches. This constituted the plainest declaration of the new political disposition. Their aim was stated to be to secure the return as M.P. for Edinburgh of an individual of 'sound Protestant and Evangelical character'. The churches themselves should not act directly, nor should a public committee be set up. Instead a private committee was to be formed, 'to be composed of gentlemen of different religious denominations who possess entire confidence in each other', to alert the voters to the needs of the situation. Again, long-term ideological differences were glossed over by stressing immediate agreed abuses. 'In regard to the religious principles sought to be promoted by the committee it was thought enough to describe them under the general designation of 'Sound Evangelical Protestantism'. The efforts of the committee will of course be directed against the errors and machinations of Popery, and against the growing influence and power of that system, both general and political, and specially against its endowment and encouragement by the state. And as regards State endowment of other religious systems — it may be sufficient to state that — while a difference of opinion exists in the committee as to whether it is, or is not, the duty of the State to countenance and promote the objects of the Christian Church in a manner consistent with its spiritual independence, all the members are agreed in regarding existing religious institutions as unsound, and in thinking, *first* that the utmost exertions should be used to resist the further extension of these establishments, whether at home or in the colonies, and *secondly,* that in the event of a proper occasion arising, the entire removal of such establishments may be sought, as a legitimate and desirable end.'[19] The use of the subjunctive in the last verb is revealing.

The Edinburgh Committee was the prelude to a broader movement, which was not secret, but open. An address *To the Electors of Scotland* was issued in the summer of 1846, and was alleged to have been written by Candlish himself. The Committee was composed (as well as Voluntaries) of Free Church worthies, both Liberal and Conservative, such as Campbell of Monzie, Thomson of Banchory, Sir James Forrest, an ex-Provost of Edinburgh, and Francis Brown Douglas, a future candidate in the city. It too emphasised the urgency of returning Evangelical Protestants to Parliament in the cause of opposing Popery and waived the question of the principle of establishment as less important than resisting extensions of the existing establishments. The appearance of this document created alarm among the Whig party managers in Scotland, who feared the importation of religious questions into politics as being as divisive as in the 1830s. They deplored especially the 'disgusting' tone adopted by the pamphlet against the Government, which seemed to be regarded as having either no religion at all, or 'at best as open advocates of Puseyism and leaning to the Church of Rome'. Unless prompt action were taken, it was feared that many 'well-meaning' people would join the movement in large numbers. The basis of this fear was the coda to the leaflet: 'It is more certain, that the giving of public countenance and support to

Popery will be an immediate subject of contention. And whatever a false and spurious Liberalism may think, no religious man can look on such a proposal without the utmost alarm'.[20]

The general election held in July 1847 soon put the fears of the Whig managers to the test, and amply confirmed their deepest misgivings. In those seats (mainly urban) where a substantial portion of the electorate belonged to the Free or Voluntary churches, the Whiggish candidates found themselves swept aside, or at best barely clinging on to their seats. In all of these seats, the reason for their defeat was a firm Free Church-Voluntary alliance, and the cement bonding them together was almost invariably Maynooth. The most spectacular advance was made in Edinburgh where Macaulay was defeated by the Free Church paper manufacturer, Charles Cowan. Macaulay, who had memorably dismissed the anti-Maynooth movement as 'the bray of Exeter Hall', was confronted with an organised opposition, constructed primarily of Free Churchmen and Voluntaries and styling itself the Independent Liberal Committee.[21] The target was Macaulay, and not his fellow-Whig, Gibson Craig, and Cowan's voters were instructed to use their second vote for anyone other than Macaulay, because of his conspicuous hostility to the anti-Maynooth movement, since the basis of the Cowan coalition consisted of 'the common plank of resistance to endowments'. Five years later, an Edinburgh Voluntary paper recalled these events: 'The earnest Voluntary, equally with the zealous Free Churchman was scandalised at [Macaulay's] unprincipled latitudinarianism. The establishment of the 'Independent Liberal Committee' was the result of that common feeling of moral reprobation, and of the craving for union to repel a common danger'.[22]

In Glasgow, the two sitting Whig M.P.s were defeated by the first Voluntary to become Lord Provost of the city, Alexander Hastie, in tandem with another Dissenter, in a contest in which much turned on the failure of the sitting men to resist Maynooth. It was this factor which was cited by the Glasgow Tory Free Church paper for supporting the two Voluntaries.[23] In Aberdeen, a Free Church candidate, Dingwall Fordyce, defeated a state church Liberal with the backing of the Voluntaries, whose Religious Freedom Society (i.e. for the promotion of disestablishment) met and endorsed Fordyce because his views on state endowment were 'so nearly approximate' to theirs. Or, as the Whig organ paraphrased it, the Voluntaries 'continued to bore a hole in Captain Fordyce's endowment principle, and then shrink their own Voluntaryism into such dimensions as would fit it'.[24] Fordyce had adopted the same line as Dunlop at Greenock, rejecting further extensions of religious endowments to existing churches. In the Stirling Burghs, opinion was so hostile that the sitting M.P., Lord Dalmeny, who 'has rendered himself very unacceptable by the course he has taken on ecclesiastical questions', withdrew from the contest.[25] The replacement Whig was beaten by the preferred candidate of the Voluntaries. The only seat where the coalition failed to make headway was Greenock, for reasons discussed later. Elsewhere, the success of the Free-Voluntary alliance lay not in gaining seats from Whigs, but in averting contests in seats which one or the other already held. This was the case in Dundee, Paisley and Perth, where three Free Church sympathisers consolidated their position, although in the past they had been in acute conflict with Dissenters. Now the need for unity was paramount.

In almost all the victories gained by the new alliance, other issues also entered, and indeed in places the anti-Whigs had constructed a coalition out of diverse interests, not primarily ecclesiastical. Thus in Edinburgh, Macaulay's arcane dispute with the drink industry over the mode of collecting the malt tax was deployed by Cowan to advantage. In Glasgow, there had been personal antagonisms in the ruling Whig junto which contributed to the running of Hastie and MacGregor. Moreover, MacGregor's prime case for being elected was his expertise in Free Trade matters. Similarly in Stirling, the new M.P. put great emphasis to the electors on 'your desire to have a Commercial Representative', and as the President of the (British) Anti-Corn Law League ('the man whom his fellow-citizens deemed worthy to lead the van in the conflict with a proud and selfish aristocracy'), his claims were obvious.[26] Two points may be made about these other issues. Firstly, they were normally subordinate to Maynooth. When the seat-hunting Lord Melgund sought nomination first at Haddington and then at Greenock, Maynooth was the question on which assurances were sought as to his views.[27] Secondly, it seems that the uncertainty as to the extent of support to be derived from a purely ecclesiastical campaign counselled opening as broad an anti-Whig front as possible. By 1852, when the degree of backing which a narrower sectarian contest would secure was apparent, most of these trappings were discarded.

Grants to Maynooth were still being made when the general election of 1852 came round, and the Free-Voluntary alliance exploited this to the full. All the seats gained in 1852 were retained, and Greenock was seized. Increasing confidence was shown in the expansion into new seats — notably Perth, where the succession of Fox Maule to the peerage removed one of the Free Church's strongest supporters in Parliament. His replacement was to be the brother of Lord Kinnaird, a strong supporter of the state church, and so a Voluntary was run against him, though without success. The 1852 elections were particularly notable for the intensity with which the religious issue was pursued. As Cockburn noted of the Edinburgh contest, the 'striking characteristics' on all sides were the 'prevalence and intensity of our bigotry', and with every city candidate 'the religious element was far more powerful than the political'.[28] The most impressive instance of this heightened feeling occurred at Stirling. The M.P. elected in 1847, J. B. Smith, was a Unitarian, and his victory had not been met in Free and Voluntary circles with unconfined joy. *The Witness* was horrified to contemplate that 'the burghs of the two Erskines may possibly have the unenviable distinction of sending a Socinian to Parliament', and Smith himself was aware of these feelings, which induced several clergymen on whose support he was counting to desert him at the poll. Smith stood down at the 1852 dissolution, citing as a major factor the continuing hostility to his religious opinions.[29] He found a seat at Stockport, where, presumably, religious feeling ran less high. In his stead was chosen an orthodox Voluntary, James Anderson, who managed to stave off a severe challenge from a Whig nominee. Elsewhere, Maynooth continued to dominate the voters' predilections. In Greenock, the incumbent M.P., Lord Melgund, reported that his Free Church opponent in 1847 had received a very numerously signed requisition: 'Maynooth is the great point of opposition. What the nature of the opposition will be upon points other than that of Popery is not very plain ... I had little idea that the public mind was so deeply imbued with hostility to the Maynooth Grant but when we consider the untiring efforts that have been used to produce this effect it is not altogether a matter of surprise'. Withdrawing from there to fight Glasgow, he was hounded by the same issue: 'There has been throughout the greatest miscalculation ... of the strength of the anti-Maynooth feeling'.[30] In Edinburgh, 'no candidate could win who did not unreservedly avow his intention of rescinding the Maynooth Grant', remarked a Whig.[31]

The general election results of 1852 were thus of considerable significance. The Whig counter-offensive had been, in general, unsuccessful, and in some places quite humiliatingly repulsed. Melgund's retreat from Greenock to Glasgow was the most glaring instance. If the fight was hopeless on the lower reaches of the Clyde, it was as bad upriver, where his committee were accused of poor preparation: 'It seems pretty clear that you never had a chance from the first, and that therefore the whole thing was a goose chase'.[32] Where Whigs did retain seats, it was often alleged they did so only by the grace of Tory voters, as in Perth where nearly 70 of Kinnaird's majority (of 100) over his anti-state church opponent was held to have come from those who had been Conservatives in 1841.[33] While the Whigs had by 1852 been largely driven from most urban seats (with the likelihood that those few remaining bastions would not survive another assault from the Free-U.P. alliance), little direct attack had been made on the Whig county seats, indicating the absence of that solid phalanx of militant, self-confident middle-class men so typical of the larger towns. But even in the fastnesses of rural Angus, rumblings were making themselves felt, to the evident panic of the Whig candidate: 'He is anxious to know what he is to say about Maynooth, as the Free Kirk is making that a great point'.[34]

There were, however, two seats where the alliance failed to work smoothly. In 1847 at Greenock, A. M. Dunlop ran with full Free Church backing for the seat he had fought in 1845. He was opposed by the Whig, Lord Melgund, who, in a bitter and complex contest, won the seat. One of the determinants of the outcome in 1847 was the behaviour of the Voluntaries, and although Dunlop tried to persuade them that he came quite close to their views in practice, he had to confess that he had not won their wholehearted support at the polling booth.[35] The reason for the refusal of the Voluntaries to vote for Dunlop was that although he gave answers to their questions which revealed that he would not favour the Free Church accepting state endowments, that was — according to Melgund — regarded 'merely as jesuitical, because Dunlop is thought to be much the representative of the bigotry and ambition of the Free Church as O'Connell of the Catholics'.[36] Moreover, Dunlop was remembered as a militant anti-Voluntary in the 1830s, and a grudge was long harboured against him for his court appearance in 1835 on behalf of a Voluntary minister in Campbeltown who was pressing a claim against his church over the ownership of church property. One of the foremost Greenock Voluntaries, Bailie Duff, announced that he could not support Dunlop because of the Campbeltown case, and Dunlop himself acknowledged that this had damaged his vote.[37] By 1852 the position had altered. Many of the moderates who had preferred Melgund in the previous election were now less keen to do so. Shipowners in particular were said to be moving towards protectionism, and a Conservative ran, probably attracting votes given before to Melgund. Dunlop mobilised a very wide range of support by concentrating exclusively on his opposition to Maynooth, thus glossing over the rift so apparent in 1847. Melgund, unwilling to abandon both Free Trade and support for Maynooth, withdrew, leaving Dunlop to defeat the Tory.[38]

The second seat was Edinburgh. In 1852 it was argued by the Voluntaries that, as the surviving Whig, Gibson Craig, was retiring, he should not be replaced by another Whig, but that the Independent Liberal Committee, which had secured the return of Cowan, should aim to capture the second city seat. This time, moreover, the man chosen should represent the U.P. Church since Cowan was a Free Churchman, and since Cowan's victory was in large part due to the crucial support of Dissent. As a speaker at the Independent Liberal meeting succinctly expressed it, 'The Free Churchman had the nomination of one candidate, and the Dissenters [i.e. Voluntaries] ought now to have the nomination of the other'.[39] This claim was pressed in order to thwart a maturing arrangement between Cowan's committee and the Whig committee to run Cowan in conjunction with a nominee of the latter — ironically, E. P. Bouverie, who had withstood an early Free Church challenge at Kilmarnock in 1844. The Voluntaries persisted in their claim and chose as their candidate, MacLaren. He was the obvious man as the lay Voluntary leader since the 1830s, and he had been elected Lord Provost in 1851. Furthermore, he had masterminded much of the tactical operation that had given Cowan victory in 1847. There was only one disadvantage: as probably the greatest exponent of cant in mid-Victorian Scottish public life (a title won in the face of intense competition from virtually every prominent cleric), MacLaren had made too many enemies to be acceptable as an M.P. The voice of Edinburgh Free Churchism protested against the MacLaren-Cowan ticket as an 'ill-omened attempt' to 'thrust upon Free Churchmen their old, and as they used to think at one time, and as many of them still think, a not very scrupulous opponent'. MacLaren, *The Witness* reminded its readers, had been the most vigorous antagonist of the Non-Intrusionist wing of the State Church in the 1830s, and the paper warned its fellow-Churchmen against being 'overreached and baffled by men wilier, though certainly not wiser, than themselves'.[40]

The Witness, however, underestimated the shrewdness (but not the saintliness) of the Free Church politicians. A rupture within the Independent Liberal Committee followed upon MacLaren's nomination, with a number of Free Churchmen leaving and then picking a second Free Church candidate, Alexander Campbell of Monzie. The choice of Campbell was instructive: as a Conservative M.P. who resigned his seat in protest at his government's handling of the Disruption crisis, he was chosen to stop defections by Cowan's voters who found

MacLaren too radical.[41] Faced with this coup, MacLaren's camp proclaimed the end of the Free Church-Voluntary alliance. The break was exacerbated by the abusive tone adopted, especially on the Voluntary side. Their journal exulted that the departure of the Free Church element from the Independent Liberal Committee meant 'the excision of a troublesome corn ... part(ing) company with a warty excrescence'.[42] At this point the Whigs, with the other Liberals in disarray, launched Macaulay as their candidate. MacLaren, amazingly enough, made overtures to the latter to form some sort of voting arrangement, but he was quite unpalatable to the Whigs, who had been the objects of his bitterest attacks and manoeuvrings, the culmination of which had been to contrive the deposition of the very man he now proposed to run with. 'He has such a multitude of irreconcilable enemies', the editor of the Whiggish *Scotsman* observed, ' — owing to his personal bitterness and malignity — that for the Whigs to support him would be to disgust far more of their own supporters that they would gain of his.'[43] MacLaren's camp, despite the Whig rebuff, strove in the immediate pre-polling period to attach his candidature to Macaulay's, inviting Voluntaries to reverse utterly all they had done in 1847 and now cast their votes for Macaulay and MacLaren.[44] Macaulay was elected, as was Cowan, and MacLaren was beaten into third place. The pattern of cross-voting revealed how this result came about. Of Cowan's 1754 voters, over a quarter — 491 — also voted for Campbell, the second Free Church candidate. Of the rest, 501 also voted for Macaulay, twice as many as the 230 who voted for MacLaren. Very few (133) plumped for Cowan as compared to Macaulay and MacLaren plumpers (327 and 439 respectively). Half of MacLaren's votes (798 out of 1561) went to Macaulay, without which the latter would not have succeeded. At the same time the use of second votes by Cowan's supporters worked to defeat MacLaren.[45]

The general upshot was that in Edinburgh the Voluntary-Free Church collaboration seemed to be in tatters, but this was mainly due to personal, rather than ideological, factors at this stage. A Free Church supporter at the Independent Liberal Committee's discussion of the choice of second candidate expressed the position when he stated that he did not object to another Voluntary standing, but that he found MacLaren personally unacceptable.[46] MacLaren's biographer asserted that a last-minute surge of Conservative voters came to cast their second votes for Cowan, so displacing MacLaren, who was then second, and Cowan confirms this in his autobiography: 'I am not ashamed to say that I owed the support which I received, in a great measure, in the latter part of the day, not so much on the ground of my being deemed worthy of the honour as that I was deemed a degree less objectionable in my political creed than Mr. MacLaren'.[47] The rage of the MacLaren group at this tactical vote amused the Whigs, who had suffered from MacLaren's deployment of it in 1847.

What the Edinburgh and Greenock elections of 1847 and 1852 suggest is that the relationship between the two non-established Presbyterian churches was not a total convergence, and that memories of the previous decade's antagonisms could not easily be erased if either side insisted on putting forward candidates who were centrally identified with that conflict. A portent of the eventual disintegration of

F

the alliance was that in the cases of Dunlop and Maclaren, the underlying differences on church establishment were brought to prominence to justify the refusal to co-operate, whereas normally that gulf was not referred to. Thus in Greenock in 1847 the Voluntaries took exception to Dunlop's refusal to accept the abandonment of teaching religion in schools receiving state finance. 'It is in reference to Education that they propose to fetter [?] themselves not to vote for anyone who won't oppose all grants under Minutes of Council requiring religious teaching', Dunlop explained.[48] In Edinburgh, Cowan's views of Establishments were assailed by Voluntaries in 1852, though they had not altered from five years previously, when he had won their ardent backing. 'With Mr. Cowan's opinions on Establishments we in no respect sympathise', their paper explained. 'They are those, however, of the majority of Free Church who cling to an abstraction, while rejecting Establishments in bodily form, and they reject Voluntaryism, while clinging to it as their only real stay.'[49] But in neither instance did the lack of total harmony lead to permanent breach: in 1852 Dunlop won, and MacLaren was, as we shall see, one of the firmest advocates within his Church of the policy of supporting the education bills which were largely inspired by Free Church doctrines.

II

The political threat to Scottish Whiggery was matched by a growing menace to the Church of Scotland. For one thing, the close electoral collaboration between the Free and United Presbyterian churches had led to the concept of union being seriously bruited among influential figures on both sides. In 1854 an exuberant Lord Panmure (formerly Fox Maule) informed a doubtless aghast Edward Ellice: 'I have another matter in hand which is not unimportant and of which I see some fair prospects of success', viz., the union of these two churches. He stressed there was no probability of the Free rejoining the state church, using a most unScottish image: 'The thing is impossible. You might as well essay to put a cricket ball into a hen's egg'. The main reason he gave for this is interesting: the difficulty of compromising principles, implying that it was now easier for the Free Church to reconcile its principles with the Voluntaries.[50] This point had been stressed by the Liberation Society in 1850, when it urged the Free Church to acknowledge that it was in practice a Voluntary church and should therefore embrace the disestablishment doctrine to the full.[51] The challenge of the union to the state church was explicitly developed by Panmure: it would probably comprise a majority of the Scottish people, but in any event: 'If this union be accomplished the new body will far outnumber the Established Church and for good or evil in all matters which refer to Ecclesiastical or Educational policy will be far more powerful with the great body of the people'.[52] Panmure was writing at a time when the two non-state churches were at maximum harmony — as Sir James Gibson Craig put it, 'anxious to waive differences and endeavour to act together'.[53] But within two years all these political and ecclesiastical aspirations were destroyed.

The reasons for propelling Education to the political forefront as the chosen vehicle for the final push on both Whiggery and the erastian established church were numerous but cogent. In 1836 George Lewis had published a polemical pamphlet arguing that Scotland was a half-educated nation, and by the early 1850s the deficiencies in the educational system, so far from having been remedied, had arguably been compounded by the effects of the Disruption. By statute each parish had to have a school provided by the heritors (landowners) and controlled by the Church of Scotland. Admirable and acceptable as this scheme had been in earlier centuries, by 1850 it was hopelessly inadequate and inequitable. The gist of the difficulties was expressed at a meeting held in Edinburgh in 1850 to press for a substantial re-casting of Scottish education.[54] Firstly. the immense demographic changes induced by industrialisation were not catered for: each parish was required only to have one school, not to provide schooling for all children in the parish. Private (both charitable and commercial) ventures had attempted to repair the gaps, but these were by definition uneven in their spread, so that in the more densely populated urban areas it was contended that not more than 40% of children received any schooling. Moreover, the quality of education provided at the non-parochial schools was extremely uneven and largely unsupervised. Financial provision was haphazard and low: the heritors were reluctant to pay for improved facilities in the parochial system, and the private schools were always short of cash. There was thus a clear case for sweeping away the patchwork system with its conflicts, duplications and omissions, and replacing it with a national scheme of administration which would impose and maintain uniformly high standards. A further cause for disquiet was the control of the parochial schools by the state church. This meant, in practice, firstly that teachers had to be members of the Churches of Scotland since they had to affirm their acceptance of the Church's doctrines; secondly that religious instruction was an integral part of the school curriculum; and thirdly that the form of instruction given conformed to the established church's tenets. These three facets of the parochial school system made them unacceptable to many, who wished to see the national system free of sectarian control and devoid of any religious teaching component.

These goals — a national, unsectarian, secular education — were promulgated by the National Education Association of Scotland, which was formed in 1850. The interests involved in the Association were remarkably broad. They included Whigs, true to the tradition of administrative efficiency and social reform which had prevalence in the 1830s, and was now represented by John Hill Burton, the prominent historian and writer on economic and legal matters; Lord Melgund, of the Whiggish Minto family and brother-in-law to Lord John Russell; and Alexander Russel, editor of *The Scotsman*. Leading figures from the teaching profession were also active in the movement — university professors like Sir David Brewster, Sir William Hamilton, J. S. Blackie, G. Traill, W. Gregory, W. Thomson; the President of the Educational Institute of Scotland (the teachers' organisation), the rectors of several academies, and so on. A third body consisted of prominent individuals with a record of social concern, such as William Chambers of Edinburgh, George Combe the phrenologist, John Tennant of St.

Rollox, and several sheriffs, notably Innes and Crawfurd. All of these could be termed, broadly, 'secularists' in the sense that their main aim was to solve Scotland's educational difficulty by removing the religious element from schooling. The final group, and the most troublesome (it follows automatically), were the representatives of the non-established churches. Voluntaries were very much committed to these precepts. They were categorically against state funding for religious purposes, be it in church or school, and so they supported the non-sectarian secular principle fully. Prominent clergymen such as Harper, Renton and Eadie were firm in their support of the objectives of the Association, and most of the leading laymen were likewise committed — Adam Black, Duncan MacLaren, Sir James Anderson, Alexander Hastie, M.P.

The more surprising participant in the reform agitation was the Free Church. At the Disruption, consistent with its pretensions to be a national church, Free Church schools were to be set up to provide proper education for the sect's congregations. This ideological imperative was reinforced by the practical and moral obligation to provide employment for the 360 or so teachers who had come out of the Church of Scotland schools in sympathy with the principles of the new church. As a result, by 1851 there were 712 Free Church schools in Scotland. But this remarkable success in providing so many schools and teachers in a short space of time concealed worrying features which led many in the church to argue that simply replicating the state church was unsatisfactory.[55]

For one thing, the provision of schools by the church covered only about two thirds of the congregations, and the concentration of schools was in the Highland areas, whereas in the Lowlands there was considerable under-supply. This of course reflected the geographical distribution of the secession in 1843 by teachers, rather than any allocation based on proven need. The five crofting counties had 189 Free congregations and 225 schools, while five Lowland counties — Ayr, Renfrew, Lanark, Dunbarton and Stirling — had 179 congregations and only 111 schools. The state church had a better balance: in the five Highland counties, 216 schools and 140 churches were provided; in the same Lowland counties, the figures were 299 schools for 198 congregations.[56] Apart from demonstrating that it had not emulated the Church of Scotland in its educational provision, the Free Church faced the further disturbing implication that many of its adherents might not only be deprived of their own church schools, but might well be sending their children to state church schools where they would be exposed to indoctrination. Moreover the financial burden of maintaining the Free Church Educational scheme was onerous in the extreme. The salaries of Free schoolteachers were cut by one third as an economy, which placed them well below the level of parochial masters, thus aggravating the distinction. But even this, and the acceptance of government grants, was not enough to stave off impending ruin, as Hugh Miller predicted in 1850: 'there awaited on her Educational Scheme — ominously devoid of that direct Divine mandate which all her other schemes possessed — inevitable disastrous bankruptcy ... the Government grants have wholly failed to preserve the Educational Scheme from the state of extreme pecuniary embarrassment which we too surely anticipated'.[57]

Having failed to destroy the state church's educational role by direct competition, the Free Church turned to embracing the case for replacing the existing system by a national scheme, an argument espoused by Begg and Miller. A national scheme would relieve the Free Church of a heavy financial commitment and also safeguard the employment of its teachers, while simultaneously knocking away a prop from the still shaky established church. While it retained its control over a substantial portion of education provision in the country, the Church of Scotland could still attach some vestige of credibility to its claim to be a national church. Its other main non-religious function, the administration of the relief of poverty, had been swept away in 1845, and with the schools stripped from it, the state church would be seen as just another sect, of similiar size to both the Free and U.P. Churches. Indeed, many contended that, deprived of its schools, it would lose many adherents who worshipped before its altars either because of their jobs as teachers or in order to secure favourable educational treatment for their children. Thus advocacy of the national approach to educational provision could lead, from both the Free and Voluntary viewpoint, to the extinction of the existing established church. Voluntaries were by 1850 calling on the Free Church to recognise that in practice it had become Voluntary, and the dropping of the bid to emulate the state church's educational scheme doubtless heightened this feeling and may have contributed to the impressive solidarity generally displayed in the 1852 election.[58]

This, so to speak, backdoor disestablishment created great alarm among supporters of the national church. Buccleuch warned the Prime Minister: 'It is not Education but Political Power which under that guise many of them seek to obtain'. In a coded message, the Church of Scotland schoolteachers petitioned against the elimination of parochial schools which 'could not fail to give an impetus to the democratic element in this country of which past history affords no parallel'.[59] Sir James Graham, himself intimately involved in the Disruption crisis, was emphatic as to the interconnectedness of these trends: 'The dissolution of the exclusive connections between the Parochial Schools and the Established Church of Scotland is the inevitable consequence of this Schism ... [it] was clearly foreseen by me and regarded as one of the Evils inherent in that disruption. The Roots of Dissent have struck so deep and have spread so wide, that the secular portion of the Establishment can no longer be maintained in its integrity ... I am quite sure that if an attempt be persevered in to uphold the Parochial Schools on their present footing, a struggle will ensue in which the Church will be worsted and its existence endangered'.[60]

While the Free Church felt compelled to forsake its original educational project, thereby allying itself with the other forces which sought the introduction of a national system, there was still room for differing views as to the detail of the new model. The major point of contention was whether the provision of religious instruction should be part of the curriculum or not. The secularists believed it should not, as did the Voluntaries, as also did a powerful body in the Free Church, led by Miller, Begg and Guthrie. Candlish took a contrary view, claiming that the state could not abandon its duty to promote the inculcation of Christian principles

in the nation's children, a position fully consistent with the general tenets of the
Free Church. In the debates within the Church it was, as usual, Candlish's opinion
which prevailed.[61]

The result of this new tack in Free Church manoeuvring was seen in the fate of
the efforts in 1850 and 1851 by Lord Melgund to carry an education bill which
would both withdraw the parochial school system from control by the Church of
Scotland and also impose a policy of purely secular instruction in the new national
schools. The two bills, although endorsed by the National Education Association,
were not successful. Melgund and his associates were quite clear that a major
responsibility for their non-passage lay with a skilfully orchestrated Free Church
lobby.[62] In April 1850 Melgund felt that his bill's prospects were good, but warned
that 'a hot blast from Candlish taken up by Fox Maule will produce a sirocco in
Downing Street, which will paralyse the energies of those who are inclined to
forward the good cause'.[63] In 1851, the Free Church's role was even more explicit,
as it strove to stop secular education being introduced. A deputation headed by
Candlish was very active in persuading Lansdowne, the Home Secretary, not to
pledge government support for the bill. As Melgund complained: 'He [Candlish]
and others in white neck-cloths have prowled about London for some weeks . . . It
is not the practice of the holy men of Scotland to observe very conscientiously the
line of demarcation which they say is so easily distinguished between secular and
religious matters'.[64] A petition was also got up by the Free Church leaders with the
apparently laudable demand of calling for a bill which would remove state church
presbyterial control over schools, but with the rider that the teachers should still
be required to give religious instruction. This was denounced by Melgund's
associates as designed to ensure that only Free Church teachers would be
employed in the new system (in addition to existing Church of Scotland masters),
and yet also avert secular education since no Voluntary or secularist could accept
the idea of the state financially assisting in the support of religion.[65] The strength
of the Free Church's proposal was that it went further than Melgund's in
destroying the role of the state church. Thus it won the support of men like Begg,
who felt very bitterly about Established Church control, so re-uniting the Free
Church, while its thoroughness attracted some Voluntaries who did not pay too
close attention to the demands for the maintenance of religious teaching.[66] As a
result the National Education Association found itself hopelessly split on which
reform scheme to support, and by December 1851 Melgund lamented: 'The
'Association', as they call themselves, are at sixes and sevens and I believe will
never act together in real harmony'. The failure of supporters of Melgund's bill to
mobilise support enabled the Free Church petition to influence the Government
and halt its legislative progress.[67]

The confidence of the Free Church and the discomfiture of the secularists were
increased by the appointment of James Moncrieff as Lord Advocate in April 1851.
The Free Church now had one of its eminent laymen at the very heart of the
Scottish political process, after a period when it had lacked direct political
influence on the governmental machine. Maule, who as noted earlier had been
deeply involved in Scottish affairs in the 1830s, was, much to the chagrin of his

Free Church admirers, shifted to deal with military matters when Russell formed his administration in 1846. Moncrieff's predecessor, Rutherfurd, although not hostile, had done little to promote Free Church interests after 1846. Moncrieff, with his distinguished connections at the core of the Free Church, was to many merely the puppet of Candlish, as Minto warned his son-in-law, the Prime Minister: 'The good and amiable Lord Advocate . . . is such an amateur of Church and Churchmen that I almost despair of obtaining a tolerable bill . . . the Advocate being too deeply imbued in his own feelings to see his way readily in any other direction'.[68]

Moncrieff, however, did not bring forward any education bill until late in 1853, two and a half years after being appointed. There are several possible reasons for the delay. Firstly, it was very difficult to get Scottish legislation accorded any priority in the timetable for putting bills through Parliament. But it was equally important that any new bill be couched in terms which would satisfy both Free and Voluntary churches, where Melgund's strongly secularist proposals had failed. Here delay was helpful — as well as necessary — for while the two churches were growing steadily closer, the abuse of Church of Scotland control of the parochial schools grew more glaring, and the secularist elements in the virtually defunct National Education Association increasingly lost influence. The 1852 general election results, moreover, sustained the advances made in representation by the non-established churches and so would validate any reform scheme.

Moncrieff wisely concentrated his first bill's central aim on destroying the power of the national church, by appointing locally elected boards to administer the school system in the localities. He evidently calculated that this was an overriding objective for most critics of the existing regime, to the extent that they would accept the retention of religious instruction in the school curriculum, a major objective of the Free Church, as already noted. This was a soundly based assumption. Even Melgund, in 1849 an inveterate opponent of the latter ('to give to local bodies a power of prescribing confessions of faith and shorter catechisms and other remnants of barbarism and Priestly domination is more than I can stomach'[69]), had by 1852 been chastened into accepting it as a *pis aller:* 'I do not know that a good measure including such a provision [i.e. religious instruction] would not be an improvement on the present state of things'.[70] More importantly, it seemed likely that the leading U.P.s would accept this flagrant breach of their principles, or so Moncrieff was assured by that Church's clerical expert on education, Dr. John Taylor. Taylor did admit that if local boards were given powers to enforce religious instruction in schools, 'not a few' Dissenters would be unhappy. But, he continued, it should prove straightforward to shape the legislation so as to circumvent this. Provided 'a really good system of education' was outlined, it would be 'cordially welcomed' by Voluntaries, even if it meant leaving religious instruction on its present footing. This apparent abandoning of Voluntary principles was explained by Taylor as tolerable since the need for immediate action was so immense.[71]

Thus it was alleged by critics of the bill that it was the product of a pact of kinds between Candlish and Harper, as leaders of the two non-established churches, with which Moncrieff was confronted and which, as a loyal Free Churchman, he simply incorporated into legislative form.[72] Moncrieff naturally hotly denied these calumnies. He assured Lord Aberdeen that no communications between the two churches and himself had taken place regarding the contents of the bill, nor had they submitted proposals which 'shadow out some intended scheme on the part of Government'. While he did agree that the views of the two churches 'are much nearer than I ever hoped to see the case', he claimed for his bill that it 'gives no undue weight to any particular section'.[73] In early 1854, the bill's success seemed unquestionable. The Free and Voluntary churches held a series of mass meetings to uphold the bill's principles — in the case of Glasgow, arranging the meeting before the bill's details were made public. It is significant that these meetings were held by the sects and not by the National Education Association, indicating the total eclipse of the secularist wing and the triumph of the ecclesiastical one in the education reform agitation. The Church of Scotland found itself in a hopeless minority: in Edinburgh, reported the Whig Gibson Craig, only the state church opposed the reforms, while all other groups were enthusiastically favourable. The squeals of the established church received little sympathetic hearing, for as the Prime Minister tartly noted, Parliament would not support the perpetuation of a school system based on exclusive principles.[74]

Both supporters and opponents of Moncrieff's first bill recognised that the crucial determinant of its success or defeat lay with the Voluntaries. As Maule put it: 'If he can get the Voluntaries to accept it cordially he will have a good chance of carrying it'.[75] The weak point in the bill, which its critics sought to exploit, was that it could be depicted as simply a device to subsidise the Free Church by transferring the cost of its educational scheme from its own supporters on to all ratepayers, while at the same time restricting the supply of teachers in the national system to either Established or Free Church members, who alone would give Bible teaching in the classroom.[76] And indeed, as details of the contents of the bill seeped out, the Voluntary warlords found a great deal of discontent among their followers. By the middle of March 1854, U.P. opposition to the bill was growing vociferous, particularly in Glasgow, 'which', as the biographer of the rising star in that Church observed, 'has always been the Headquarters of the United Presbyterian Church',[77] but also in Edinburgh. This protest manifested itself through three agencies of opinion. Firstly, the press advocating the Voluntary position — *The Glasgow Chronicle, The Edinburgh News,* and *The Scottish Press* (also of Edinburgh) — were all strident and immediate in denouncing the bill. Secondly, public meetings were held — most notably one convened in Edinburgh by the British Anti-State Church Association — to condemn roundly the proposals in the bill, and deputations were sent to London to lobby M.P.s and government ministers. Lastly, the church courts also pronounced on the legislation: the U.P. Presbyteries of Paisley and Greenock, Cupar, Perth, Kirkcaldy and Annandale all submitted declarations of protest to the Lord Advocate, and in May 1854 the Synod (the U.P. equivalent of the General Assembly) resolved that the bill, with its 'obnoxious provisions, . . . is not only unworthy of the support, but demands the strenuous opposition of the Synod and of the Members of the United Presbyterian Church'.[78]

The main focus of what *The Glasgow Chronicle* described as the 'disappointment and dissatisfaction' entertained by Voluntaries was the conjuncture of clauses 27 and 35.[79] The former stipulated that certain times of the school day would be set aside for religious teaching, which would be given by the schoolmaster. The rider that parents could withdraw their children from such classes was Moncrieff's device to placate Voluntary scruples, but this was counterbalanced by the final portion of that clause, which stated that 'no additional or separate Charge shall be made in respect of the Attendance of Children at such separate Hours'.[80] In other words, the cost of religious teaching would come out of general school costs which would be met by taxing ratepayers, irrespective of denomination. This outraged the great Voluntary doctrines of no state support for religion, and it was additionally unjust to expect them to pay for this blatant affront to their consciences. Thus the Anti-State Church Association meeting in Edinburgh called the intention to retain Bible teaching 'unsound in principle, hostile to liberty and opposed to the word of God', and these points were reiterated at all times, both in presbyterial protests and the press.[81] MacLaren's brother-in-law, the Rev. Henry Renton, found clause 27 so objectionable that he became the organiser of the U.P. opposition to the bill.[82] Moreover, clause 27 had the additional consequence that as no Voluntary teacher could possibly accept it, it would 'practically operate as a test, limiting the selection of masters almost exclusively to persons in communion with the Church of Scotland or the Free Church'.[83]

These various aspects of the bill stimulated the Voluntaries to have recourse to what a Free Church minister referred to as 'very violent language', but the target of their campaign broadened from a passionate defence of Voluntary principles to an attack on those perceived as posing the threat.[84] On the one hand, the guilty men were the leaders of the U.P. church, who were castigated for betraying their principles: 'the zeal of some rev. gentlemen, who still call themselves Voluntaries, to aid their Free Church brethren in their work is certainly something very astonishing', cried *The Glasgow Chronicle.* The paper then turned its fire on MacLaren, who supported the bill, and William Duncan, who had resigned as chairman of the Anti-State Church Association because of its hostile stance on the bill: 'Other indications also appear that the Voluntaries are in imminent danger of being sold by those whom they have been accustomed to acknowledge as their leaders'.[85] The most vituperative phrases, however, were earmarked for the other enemy of the Voluntary principle, the Free Church, which was seen as having framed the bill for its sole benefit. 'A more disgraceful crochet never disgraced sectarianism', opined *The Edinburgh News;* and *The Glasgow Chronicle* echoed this: 'He must be rather defective in mental vision who does not see that the whole movement is in the direction of Free Church interests and Free Church principles'.[86] The bitterness had several dimensions. Firstly, the Free Church was accused of having eliminated its financial embarrassment over the provision of education by transferring the burden of maintaining its schools on to the ratepayer: 'It is a scheme ... for taxing the entire people of Scotland to the benefit of the Free Church', in the words of *The Edinburgh News*.[87] More importantly, the bill was not evenhanded; besides promoting Free Church goals, it was positively anti-Voluntary; and if passed, 'a blow will be given to their [Voluntary] distinctive principles heavier by far than they have experienced for a generation back, and from the effects of which it may be more than one generation before they recover'.[88] This rage is perhaps partly explained by the shock it afforded the confident expectation among U.P.s that the Free Church was steadily moving towards Voluntaryism, largely through the reality imposed by financial self-sufficiency. This analysis had been prevalent, as we have seen, by 1850, and as late as May 1853 *The Glasgow Chronicle* hailed the generosity of Free Church lay subscribers as evidence of the spread of the Voluntary ideal.[89] Now the utter insensitivity of the Free Church to U.P. tenets would, if persisted in, weaken the working alliance established in 1846–7. A sign of U.P. disenchantment was the charge levelled by *The Edinburgh News* that in accepting the right of government-appointed (rather than church-appointed) inspectors to regulate the teachers of religious instruction, the Free Church stood convicted of erastianism. As this was the very sin which had led to the departure of the Free Church from the established church, the gibe was wounding in the extreme.[90]

The discontent of the Voluntaries at the 1854 Education Bill was the vital ingredient which brought about its defeat.[91] English nonconformist M.P.s voted against it, in league with supporters of the state church, both English and Scottish versions.[92] The English established church M.P.s were fully seized of the implications of the possibly fatal erosion of the Church of Scotland which could well follow upon the passage of the bill, and the fear that this might rejuvenate English Dissent's assault on the Anglican Church was worrying.[93]

Moncrieff came back to Parliament in 1855 with a new Education Bill.[94] He had been faced with the choice of either placating the Church of Scotland by leaving the parochial schools under their purview, and only abolishing the religious test for schoolmasters, as a sop to the other churches, or of wooing the Voluntaries by responding to their objection to paying rates to uphold religious instruction.[95] He chose the latter course, no doubt persuaded by the advice of moderate Voluntaries like Adam Black who had affirmed in 1854 that amending clause 27 of that year's bill would 'convert the greater part of the bitterest opponents of the bill to its hearty supporters'.[96] In the 1855 bill, accordingly, clause 27 omitted the offending final section proposing that Bible teaching should be given at no extra cost. The reaction among Voluntaries was not at first hostile: *The Scottish Press* intimated that most of its objections had now been met. However, on closer perusal, defects began to emerge, and within ten days of according its initial *imprimatur,* the *Press* withdrew its support, and as amendments were moved in the Commons to the Bill which resulted in compromises judged necessary to ensure its passage, but weakening the overall Voluntaryism of it, the vehemence of protests by that group mounted.[97]

Again, the newspapers were in the van, while the church courts seemed less averse, and the U.P. Synod voted by nearly two to one in favour of the bill.[98]

However, there was still considerable unease among Voluntaries, despite these official pronouncements, and a large meeting held in Glasgow on 31 May 1855 summoned U.P. opponents of the bill to continue their resistance.[99] The grounds of objection were in general similar to those levelled at the 1854 measure. It was contended that the apparent improvements were mere camouflage, since the bill 'contains a principle that wounds the consciences of Dissenters', namely, government control of religion and religious teaching paid out of the rates. Moreover the insertion of an amendment carried in the Commons meant that the teacher had to have a certificate of his competence to give religious instruction — which would clearly exclude all Voluntary teachers. Until persons other than the schoolmaster, whose salary came from generally raised rates, were given the duty of providing religious instruction, Voluntary principles were being broken.[100] Those Voluntaries who had supported the new bill on the grounds that its imperfections could be cured as it proceeded through Parliament were rebuked for 'act[ing] as a jackal to the Free Church on these matters', for the outcome of the committee stage of the bill was that the Free Church had managed to tighten the regulations on Bible teaching.[101]

The conviction that the 1855 bill was just as much the product of the Free Church lobby as its predecessor led the Voluntaries to remount their vigorous disparagement of that Church. Outrage was added to by the decision to accept an amendment permitting Episcopalian and Catholic schools to remain outside the projected national system, yet still receive government grants. This was interpreted as a ruse to buy off opposition to the bill from these quarters on the part of the Free Church, which was now exposed in the eyes of the Voluntaries as having double standards: 'No doubt meetings against the Maynooth Grant will continue to be held by those whose participation in Government grants form [sic] the excuse for so mischievous and immoral procedure as indiscriminate grants'.[102] The litany of denunciation was as extravagant and as unremittingly critical of the Free Church as in 1854: 'a monster job on behalf of the Free Church', said *The Edinburgh News;* and *The Scottish Press* agreed: ' ... we denounce the whole arrangement as paltry, disgraceful and unprincipled, and we wash our hands of [it]'. The most comprehensive anathema came from a clergyman who deemed it 'a Bill exclusive, latitudinarian, erastian, secularist and indefinite'.[103] The case presented by the bill's opponents gradually persuaded M.P.s of a Voluntary inclination to resist. The currents of change can be traced in the reactions of Sir James Anderson, M.P. for the Stirling Burghs, and a U.P. stalwart. In April, he was a willing supporter of the bill: 'To-night the Lord Advocate's Bill comes up for a second reading and I hope may safely get through this time'. The only hostility, he stressed, came at this point from the state churchmen. By July, doubts had not so much crept up on Anderson as run amok: 'I began lately to be rather unfond of the measure, and to doubt if, as a sound Voluntary, I could with consistency give it my support ... I am strongly of the opinion that if the Bill passed it would create strife and debate among our Ministers and people and not answer the good intended by it. If I had voted for it I could no longer have had the face to oppose Maynooth and suchlike grants'.[104] He therefore voted against it, as did Hastie and

Baxter, both U.P.s, and G. Thomson, described as a Free Churchman with strong Voluntary leanings. With the fulsome co-operation of upholders of the Established Church and of English Dissenters, the latter led by Edward Miall, the bill fell, to the exultation of the Voluntary press.

III

A year later, the significance of the education controversy in altering the relationship beteen the two non-established churches became quite apparent. *The Edinburgh News* recalled that in the later 1830s Candlish and his friends, then in the Church of Scotland, had been very active in seeking to maintain that church's supremacy in education, and they had hoped to kill off Dissenting schools. That time had been, the paper noted, 'the highest days of their crusade against freedom of opinion as embodied in Dissent! Dr. Candlish and his party are eminent examples of that liberty taught us in our state-paid schools'.[105] The results of the disagreement between the Free and United Presbyterian Churches over education were manifold. Firstly, the advance towards a union of the two churches was stalled. In 1854, Guthrie, one of the least political or narrowly sectarian of the Free Church leaders, had expounded frankly the implications: 'We were getting on most favourably, preparing the way for a union (in the long run, and I would have hoped at no very distant period) between us and the U.P.s. This Education question had in Providence rather come as an obstacle, men would say ... Adam Black and I spoke very plainly to Dr. Harper and Mr. Duncan of the violence of their Voluntary friends about Education. I told them distinctly that, unless in some way or another they presented Voluntaryism in a less offensive light than as an obstruction in the way of saving our perishing masses they would stink in the nostrils of patriots and enlightened Christians for a century to come, and put an end to all hope of union'.[106] By 1857, the high hopes of three or four years previously were severely curtailed. A printed declaration in 1857 urging a 'contemplated union' between the Churches admitted that the differences over 'the power and the province of the State' in educational matters were large, but it argued that since there were divisions among other churches too, 'it is not necessary that any fixed principle on the subject be laid down in the event of a Union being happily effected'.[107] This was somewhat unrealistic in the light of the rift just opened up on this precise topic. A U.P. leader was more practical when he told Panmure: 'the matter evidently is not to be precipitated. It will be enough if the Free Church, or the party in it favourable to union, simply secure an open ground for the future'.[108] Little further was attempted to bring about a union until 1863, by which time much else had changed.

Politically, too, disengagement followed the demise of Moncrieff's major educational reform legislation. The alliance still seemed to be holding as late as March 1855 — just four months before the decisive parliamentary vote — when a by-election occurred in the Montrose Burghs. Initially, the only Liberal in the field was Sir John Ogilvy, but as a friend of the Church of Scotland and a supporter of the Maynooth Grant, his candidature provoked W. E. Baxter, the prominent Dundee Voluntary, to stand, also as a Liberal. Baxter partly stressed his business background (he was one of the largest manufacturers in Dundee) as more apposite to the representation of the seat than Ogilvy's status as a landowner, and he linked this to his attack on the ineffective conduct of the Crimean War, which he blamed on aristocratic incompetence. But he also stressed that 'I disagree *in toto caelo* with the religious views of Sir John Ogilvy', notably on Maynooth, and succeeded in winning the seat.[109] By 1856, when the next by-election came, the context had altered dramatically. Macaulay's retiral through ill-health occasioned a contest at Edinburgh. Piloted by Gibson Craig, the Whigs shrewdly forestalled opposition by picking as their candidate Adam Black, 'as he was a citizen, and no lawyer or placehunter, and as he was well-known to the 'religious' — that sort of thing', explained the editor of *The Scotsman*.[110] Faced with a Voluntary Whig, MacLaren, no longer interested in continuing the link with Whiggery which he had unsuccessfully striven to forge in 1852, made a bold counter-move. He and his associates nominated as candidate Francis Brown Douglas. Douglas was a Free Churchman, and, more surprisingly, an advocate, a breed normally detested by MacLaren as much as Church of Scotland clergy. He also had a strong tinge of Conservatism, standing in 1857 at St. Andrews as a Tory.[111] Black cantered home to win comfortably, partly because 'the enemy [did] not [work] as well as usual as the different parts of the Coalition wanted confidence in each other' and partly, as one of Douglas's press allies put it, because his anti-disestablishment views kept the Voluntary vote down. He was also too closely identified with the Free Church to make his return along with Cowan acceptable.[112] A U.P. minister found himself in the minority and on the defensive when justifying his voting as a Voluntary for Douglas: 'My own views and leanings, however, point to a closer political and ecclesiastical alliance with the Free Church, though it is unpopular with multitudes of Dissenters'.[113] Within a year Cairns, as noted above, had abandoned even these modest hopes for a coming together of the two churches.

A further sign of the deterioration of the alliance came with the Glasgow by-election in March 1857. Here the old Whig clique, so ignominiously bundled out of control in 1847 by the Free-U.P. church alliance, and even more humiliatingly repudiated in 1852, retrieved some of their power by securing the return of their old leader, Walter Buchanan, without any opposition at all from the victorious party in the previous two contests. The general election of 1857, coming a month later, underlined this trend, as nearly all the seats held by the Free-U.P. alliance were lost. In Edinburgh, the sitting M.P.s were unopposed, not because of unanimous support for them throughout the city, but because the Independent Liberal Committee could not find a suitable candidate. The Committee's fire was directed at Cowan, the man for whose return to Parliament it had been formed, but who was now accused of having struck a bargain with the Whigs. Now the Committee was described as almost totally barren of Free Churchmen, and it was made plain that this time Douglas would not get the votes of advanced Radical Dissenters.[114] Opponents of the Cowan-Black candidacies were reduced to jeering impotence at the hustings: 'probably nothing more grotesque in the annals of electioneering ever took place', remarked *The Scottish Press*.[115] In Dundee, the retiral of the Free Churchman George Duncan opened the way for the defeat of George Armitstead by Sir John Ogilvy, who had been beaten two years earlier at Montrose by Armitstead's brother-in-law and co-religionist, Baxter. While Ogilvy continued to defend the national church principle and represented Whiggery, Armitstead had stood as a Radical on the ballot and, more importantly, perhaps, as a stout opponent of Maynooth and a general critic of Puseyism.[116] In Aberdeen, the sitting M.P., Thomson, a man on the Voluntary wing of the Free Church, stood down, and none of his prominent supporters could be induced to run in his stead, mainly because, as the Dissenters' newspaper reported, 'not only do the ties of political party seem fairly dissolved, but even the stronger bonds of ecclesiastical connexion and sympathy'. As for the two Liberals who eventually contested the seat, the same paper complained: 'to Voluntary Dissenters the professions of both are, so far as elicited, somewhat uncertain and decidedly unsatisfactory'. Both — Sykes and Leith — were favourable to the state church and supported the principle of religious endowments, yet no united front could be formed against them.[117]

In Glasgow, the M.P. surviving from the 1847 anti-Whig alliance, Alexander Hastie, lost to Robert Dalglish, who, while he had the support of franchise reform radicals, was staunchly against the sectarian parties, and was moreover the son of a prominent member of the Whig junto in its heyday. Hastie's defeat was generally ascribed by both friendly and hostile journals to his forthright Voluntary stand on the Education Bills, which was deemed to have lost him the backing of many former friends (i.e. the Free Church).[118] Thus in Glasgow by 1857 two old-style Whigs were reinstalled as M.P.s, a remarkable reversal of their near-total annihilation over the previous decade. In Paisley, divisions also occurred. The sitting M.P., the Free Churchman Archibald Hastie, resolved to retire, and in lieu of him H. E. Crum Ewing offered himself. Ewing, who had been one of the leaders of the West of Scotland ultra-Voluntary assault on Moncrieff's bills, stressed during his campaign his record of opposition to the Education Bills and also his attachment to pure Voluntaryism. As Hastie had warmly welcomed the bills, Ewing's stance angered the Free Church members of the former's committee, and they induced him to withdraw his retiral. At the hustings both men emphasised their views on education: as one of Ewing's team phrased it: 'The Lord Advocate's bill has been made the test-point of this election'.[119] Ewing lost, but when Hastie died later in the year, Ewing won easily against an ex-Chartist, presumably because there were fears that running a Free Church nominee against Ewing might have let the extreme Radical in on a split vote. The only seats to escape this reaction against the non-established churches' alliance were Stirling Burghs and Greenock, where the incumbent M.P.s were returned. When, however, Sir James Anderson retired from the former in 1859, his old committee could put up no one to oppose the return of James Caird, whose impeccable Whig credentials precluded any sympathy for those religious tendencies outwith the established churches. In other seats, not held by the alliance, but where in the past a challenge to the sitting M.P. had been mounted, there was no fight. This was the case in Perth Burgh and Kilmarnock, and in the counties.

The split in 1857 was heightened because in that year Maynooth was no longer the unifying issue which it had been for the non-established Presbyterians in the previous two elections. Although it was raised in some constituencies, it never predominated as before, and it was no longer a certain vote-catcher. With relief, *The Scotsman* detected that 'one nuisance has been considerably abated at this election, though still rather pestilent — Maynooth is not emitting so much smoke as on former occasions ... The Maynooth clamour is no longer even a bigotry, but has become a mere cloak of hypocrisy and a weapon of malignity'. [120] The paper's latter point was well illustrated by an incident which demonstrated how wide was the chasm between Free and Voluntary. When the Lord Advocate, standing for Leith, intimated in his election address that he would not oppose the Maynooth grant, this provoked the prominent U.P. clergyman, Principal Harper, to issue a public letter to the burgh electors calling on them not to vote for that apostate Free Churchman. Those Voluntaries who defended Moncrieff and chided Harper for clerical dictation were in turn denounced by the Voluntary journal for surrendering their principles. [121]

Thus in 1857 the Whigs regained most of the political ground which had slipped away from them in the preceding decade. Equally significantly, the danger to the national church also subsided, largely through the own goals of its opponents, as *The Scotsman* noted. [122] The Church of Scotland retained its control of the parochial schools, but perhaps more important, it won an extended breathing space in which it could recover from the damage inflicted in 1843 and began to consolidate its position. By the early 1870s, when the attack on the state church was re-opened, the Church of Scotland was in a vigorous, confident condition, quite unlike its health in the early 1850s. An additional consequence of the process was that the church did not find itself looking naturally to the Conservatives for protection. The Whigs, with their pre-eminence restored, offered surer defence against Radical Dissent, and Liberal Churchmen were to be found firmly entrenched at the heart of power in Scottish Liberalism in the next generation.

The major casualty of these events was of course Scottish education, which was left to limp along unreconstructed until 1872, some twenty years after the deficiencies had been widely identified and measured. Some trifling reforms were carried out, to be sure: in 1861 the religious test imposed on parochial schoolmasters was removed. Nevertheless the Argyll Commission in the late 1860s could identify only one Free Church member teaching in a Lowland parochial school. But as a rule, two generations of children were left educationally seriously underprovided, and the social fabric was presumably thereby gravely damaged. For leading ecclesiastics like Principal Harper this was a lesser cost to weigh against the risk of violating cherished precepts: 'But it was immeasurably better to have waited even this long for a measure containing so many excellencies, than to have consented at an earlier period [i.e. the 1850s] to an Act of compromises that would ever have been entailing new controversy and new legislation'. [123]

IV

The depletion which the split over the Repeal of the Corn Laws produced in the strength of the Conservative party in England is well known, and the same issue had perhaps an even more severe impact on Scottish Conservatism. To compound the crisis for the party in the late 1840s, Scottish Tories had already been confronted with a serious difficulty over the Disruption from the Church of Scotland in 1843. The result of these twin problems was to contribute materially to leaving the Conservatives in Scotland an impotent rump for a far longer period than south of the border. The humiliating failure of John Inglis, the Lord Advocate in Derby's 1852 and 1858 administrations, to find a Scottish seat was ascribed to these two factors.[124]

Although the 1841 election had dented the more extravagant hopes of the Tories about integrating the Non-Intrusionists into their party, hopes still flickered that some rapprochement might be achieved by acts of statesmanship on the part of Peel, Graham and company. These were comprehensively confounded. The Government refused to make any concessions to stop the Non-Intrustionists seceding from the Church in 1843.[125] The impact on the Tory party was profound. The only M.P. in the party identified with the Chalmers tendency, Campbell of Monzie, resigned his Argyllshire seat, and subsequently preferred to term himself a Liberal-Conservative. It was under these colours that he stood for Edinburgh in 1852, allied with Charles Cowan, another Free Churchman, and opposing an orthodox Tory. The particularly disturbing aspect of the Free Church crisis for the party managers was that, as we have seen, in the Lowlands the class most closely associated with the new sect was precisely that socio-economic stratum which Peel's progressive Conservatism was designed to reach — the prosperous middle classes. Thus men like Henry Dunlop, cotton spinner of Glasgow, and James Forrest, the ex-Lord Provost of Edinburgh, were hereafter to be identified with Liberalism, whereas before they had been inclined to Toryism. The Glasgow Conservative Operatives' Association — which, despite its name, contained several middle-class members — was another casualty of the Disruption. In 1842 it had carried by 70 votes to 15 a resolution fully endorsing the policy being pursued by the Non-Intrusionist party, and warning that a schism would occur in the Church if these ideas did not prevail. The seconder of the motion was William Collins Junior, whose father had been one of Chalmers' most ardent workers in Glasgow. By the 1860s the young Collins had become a leading Radical in Glasgow politics, and subsequently helped found the Glasgow Liberal Association. When the Conservative Operatives wound up their organisation, only two months before the Disruption actually took place, they defiantly suggested that their rooms be offered to the Young Men's Evangelical Church of Scotland Society (a Non-Intrusionist body), provided the premises were designated the 'Free Presbyterian Reading Rooms'.[126]

The Tories expressed little sense of awareness of, far less contrition for, what happened in 1843, thereby greatly exacerbating relations. Within three weeks of the secession, a leading Perthshire Tory laird reassured his M.P. as to the temporary nature of the upheaval: 'I think we have now got the Church in a good state and I have no doubt but in a year or two everything will fall into its former regular and quiet state . . . '[127] This attitude, taken with the great vexation caused to the Free Church by the refusal of landlords — most of whom were Tories — to release sites for church-building led to the total collapse of a segment of potential Conservative support. In major cities like Glasgow, where serious expectations had been entertained of a gain in 1841, the Conservative agents had ceased to attend to registration by the mid-1840s.[128] The ill-will aroused by the Disruption was mentioned by more than one candidate as a prime factor making the outcome of the next general election likely to be unfavourable to the Tories.[129]

The Free Church difficulty perplexed the Tories for a considerable period. If they were to adhere resolutely, as in 1843, to the principle of supporting the Established Church, they ran the risk of alienating what they felt was only a temporarily estranged group. Yet overtures to the Free Church Conservatives were likely to create panic in the neurotically insecure Church of Scotland. Nearly ten years after the formation of the Free Church, this dilemma was starkly illuminated by the problems foreseen in a seemingly simple proposal to have a toast to the Church of Scotland at a Conservative dinner in Edinburgh: 'We were told we must not bring forward the Church of Scotland in those decided terms which I would wish to . . . It is a sad consideration that in a company united by a political bond to maintain established institutions of the country it should not be considered safe to toast the Church of Scotland, but so it is . . . '[130]

The abandonment of Protection by Peel compounded the Tory crisis in Scotland. Most of the great territorial magnates who were publicly active on the Conservative side came out on the side of Peel. The party thus lost both a section of its leadership (probably more significantly so than in England, because there were fewer Scottish Tory M.P.s and so the peers were thrust into greater political prominence) and also a sizeable amount of electoral influence. Leading peers who stayed loyal to Peel included Buccleuch (with influence in the counties of Dumfries, Selkirk, Roxburgh, Peebles and the Dumfries Burghs), Aberdeen (Aberdeenshire), Argyll (Argyll, Dunbartonshire and Ayr Burghs); Dalhousie (East Lothian, Perthshire, Angus, Montrose and Haddington Burghs), Wemyss (East Lothian and Haddington Burghs), and Queensberry (Dumfriesshire). As the retiring Selkirkshire M.P. reported early in 1846: 'so far as I can gather, the chief proprietors are not inclined to resist but rather to support the present ministry'.[131]

It was frequently contended that while the large wealthy landlords were cushioned against any hardships created by the ending of Protection, resistance was stronger among both the gentry, whose sources of income were less diversified, and the tenantry, whose livelihood was threatened. Thus it was alleged that in Perthshire, Roxburghshire, and Selkirkshire there was much unease at the direction of Peel's policy toward Free Trade.[132] In practice these discontents rarely came to very much. Partly, the power of the grandees was too great for the lesser lairds to force their views on a candidate, as in Roxburghshire where Buccleuch's territorial interest prevented the Protectionist gentry from acting in the 1852 election.[133] Also, gentry opinion was not wholly united on the merits of returning to tariffs: in Ayrshire, where the lairds held a good deal of political power, the replacement of a Peelite by a Protectionist in the 1852 election resulted in a bid by some Conservative landowners to put up a Free Trader.[134] Although this scheme did not materialise, at a by-election in 1854 the new Tory emphasised his acceptance of the Repeal of the Corn Laws, and despite his defeated opponent, Oswald, having been the Peelite M.P. for the county until 1852, the real dispute between the two candidates was over the threat of Popery.[135] Similarly, in Perthshire, where gentry unrest has been alluded to, the Peelite M.P., Home Drummond, retained his seat in 1847 with no murmur of dissent, and in 1852, upon his retiral, he was replaced by another opponent of Protection, William Stirling, the laird of Keir.

A serious impediment to the gentry forming an effective force to defend agriculture from the imposition of free trade was the attitude of the tenantry. The farmers were portrayed as the real opponents of the repeal measures, as a circular issued in 1850 by the Scottish Protective Association argued. It called on resistance to free trade to be based on market towns and grain centres, and urged that 'where landlords and others are not yet prepared to join in the movement against free trade', farmers should act independently to force a restoration of Protection and so save the agricultural community.[136] This could be read as an admission that proprietors were lukewarm in the cause, but its assumption that farmers were eager for Protection may have been optimistic.[137] After all, one of the most strenuous advocates of the repeal of the Corn Laws had been George Hope, a famous progressive tenant in East Lothian.[138] It must be borne in mind that arable farming was much less prevalent in Scotland than in England. In the mid-1850s — when accurate statistics are first available — grain was grown on 168,000 acres in Scotland (rather under 1% of the total agricultural acreage), as against some three million acres (around 8%) in England. In only two Scottish counties was the proportion of acreage given over to grain as high as the English average — East Lothian and Fife. Only in the other two Lothians, Berwickshire, Roxburghshire, Moray, Nairn and Easter Ross was the arable element remotely significant.[139] Even in these counties there was little solidarity among the different types of farmers. In Roxburghshire livestock farmers 'don't seem to care *one farthing*' about repeal, the Duke of Buccleuch was told, because stock prices were high.[140] Likewise in West Lothian, the farmers went out of their way to record their acquiescence in the abolition of the Corn Laws. After being defeated by a Protectionist in South Nottinghamshire, and apparently unable to find a seat in England, Lord Lincoln contested a by-election in the Falkirk Burghs seat (one of whose component parts was Linlithgow town) as a member of Peel's Cabinet in the very middle of the passage of the Repeal legislation. Lincoln was invited to join the West Lothian Agricultural Society, a tenant-farmers' organisation, 'the largest proportion of whose members entertain the same sentiments as your lordship upon the great question'.[141] At the general election the following year, when Lincoln faced a severe challenge from a Liberal, 'a number of the tenantry', including the most influential, in West Lothian proposed sending him a requisition inviting him to stand for the county seat, and in 1852 a potential Peelite candidate for the shire was authoritatively assured that his free trade views would do him no harm among the farmers.[142]

In both Fife and East Lothian, where tenant-farmers' economic interests were most heavily at risk from free trade, there was indeed serious electoral activity by them in the general election of 1847. But in neither seat was Protection the issue in contention; rather it was the Game Laws, which were deemed to be affecting the tenants adversely and, by implication, far more critically than Repeal. In Fife, John Fergus was induced to run by a committee almost exclusively comprising farmers and issued an address concentrating heavily on the iniquities of the Game Laws. As the local journal commented, 'In this election it must be borne in mind that the Game Law is beyond all doubt the bone of contention which has led to the present contest'.[143] Tory landlords were pressed to drop their political differences of opinion and rally round Balfour, who would support the Whig administration and so resist 'the movement party' represented by Fergus.[144]

In East Lothian, the tenant-farmers also moved to bring forward a candidate after a meeting in June 1846 carried a resolution calling for the return of an M.P. who would amend the Game legislation to their satisfaction. By the time of the dissolution in 1847, the farmers had found a suitable champion in R. G. Welford, an English barrister, and *The Scotsman* predicted that so strongly held were feelings about the loss of crops due to the game that the question would overshadow all else.[145] But fear of splitting the anti-Tory vote led to Welford's retiral in favour of a local proprietor who had however to give an undertaking to espouse the farmers' game grievance before the Anti-Game Laws Committee would endorse him.[146] It is instructive that the Conservative candidate, Frank Charteris, was a Peelite, but that the opposition to him from the farmers was not based on Protection, but his hostility to amending the Game Laws. Similarly, in Stirlingshire, on the eve of polling, farmers held protest meetings against the Game Laws.[147]

If Protection did not stimulate much support among rural voters, it was hopelessly unpopular in most urban seats. The Anti-Corn Law League had been resoundingly popular in the Scottish burghs, even amongst those of a Conservative inclination. Thus, as we have seen, Lincoln found Falkirk a safe haven of Free Trade Toryism in 1846. William Baird, who vacated the seat for Lincoln, fought the 1841 election on an anti-Protectionist manifesto, as did his brother James who won in 1851. Only in Greenock in 1852 was there any detectable groundswell of support for Protectionism. Here shipowners felt threatened by the repeal of the Navigation Laws, and a Conservative was induced to stand. But this sentiment did not spread very far. In Glasgow, for instance, attempts to launch a Tory Protectionist movement in 1848–49 failed, Disraeli was told, because the old party leaders were not interested. The Conservative who did stand for the city in 1852 acknowledged the impossibility of re-imposing the Corn Laws, a line which was cordially endorsed by the moderate Tory organ, which had announced on the eve of the dissolution that 'the representatives of Glasgow must be staunch Protestants and Free Traders'.[148]

The result was that the basis for a Conservative regrouping such as occurred in the 1850s in England was not really available in Scotland.[149] In 1847, while the Tories appeared to do reasonably well north of the border in winning 20 seats as against 22 in 1841 (whereas in England they fell from 277 to 252), this performance concealed weaknesses. Firstly, the party contested far fewer seats: while in 1841 the Liberals were allowed a walkover in only four of the ten county seats they held, they were not challenged in any of the eleven they won in 1847. In the burghs, where the Tories had fought twelve (winning two) in 1841, they put up a mere three candidates in 1847, only one of whom was elected. Indeed, Haddington Burghs, Conservative in 1841, passed without a contest to the Liberals in 1847.[150] Moreover, many of the Conservatives were returned unopposed in 1847 because the Liberals chose not to fight a Free Trade Tory and, in order not to alienate Liberal support, several Peelites stressed their independence from any intensely partisan Conservative position. This was notably the case with Home Drummond in Perthshire and Charteris in East Lothian. As Cockburn remarked: 'The Tories are extinguished — at least old Toryism is. The term is generally taken in a bad sense by themselves, and they won't even call themselves Conservatives. I have scarcely been able to detect any candidate's address, which if professing Conservatism does not explain that this means '*Liberal* Conservatism' which signifies something very like Whiggism, even if it does not mean Radicalism'.[151]

The predicament of the Tories became clearer in 1852, when no seats changed hands, but a stronger Conservative challenge proved a complete failure. Two Liberal counties were contested in an effort to win Protectionist support. In Banffshire a bid to woo the tenantry by the Tory gentry was unsuccessful.[152] In Ross-shire a similar bid to attract the grain-growers of the eastern seaboard was in one sense more rewarding. To keep his seat, the Liberal, James Matheson, was pressed by his local supporters to acknowledge 'that nothing will go down among the farming community but a distinct declaration of your willingness to support Protection'.[153] Matheson obliged by allowing it to be reported that he would support measures, if not to reimpose Protection, at least to relieve agricultural hardship, and he deplored Russell's 'having taken into his Councils the leaders of the Anti-Corn Law League whose agitation I disapprove of'.[154] Matheson then won comfortably. In the burghs, the Tories contested nine seats in a bid to retrieve the abysmal performance in 1847 of standing in only three. In almost every seat, except Falkirk, which they kept, and Ayr, where they came within nine votes of winning, their results were disappointing. In the others, their vote was normally well down on 1841: in the four constituencies where Conservatives stood in 1841 and 1852, the total vote fell from 3477 to 2423, while the Liberals rose from 3892 to 4479. This urban setback in 1852 blighted the party: only four burghs were fought in 1857, and none of the unsuccessful ones contested in 1852 was re-fought, while the solitary Tory seat, Falkirk, passed to the Liberals. This rundown in Conservative activity persisted in many burgh seats for a long period. Aberdeen was not fought after 1841 until 1872, Ayr — so narrowly lost in 1852 — not again until 1865; Glasgow was left alone after 1852 until 1868, Edinburgh from 1852 to

1874, Greenock from 1852 to 1878, Perth from 1841 to 1874, and Kilmarnock (Conservative between 1837 and 1841) from 1852 until 1880.

The causes of this decay were not far to seek. As has been noted, except in a very small number of places, such as Greenock, Protection had no urban appeal, and the alternative cry used in England, that of anti-Catholicism — based on resistance to Maynooth and 'Papal Aggression' — produced few dividends in Scotland.[155] Firstly, the fears of 'Papal Aggression' related to the restoration of the Catholic hierarchy in England, and this had a less immediate relevance in Scotland, which was not directly affected. More importantly, resistance to Maynooth, as has been seen, was the foundation of the Free-U.P. political alliance of 1847 and 1852. Thus in Scotland the challenge to the Whigs for truckling to Catholic demands was more convincingly presented by earnest evangelicals in the Liberal camp, whereas the Tories, after the shedding of Free Church support in 1843, were identified either with the erastian Church of Scotland or with the semi-Catholic (in Presbyterian eyes) Episcopalian Church.

The retardation of the Tory recovery in the 1850s was also a result of the strength of the Peelite wing. As noticed above, Protectionism did not have the same economic or social props as in England, and this was reflected in the balance of the leanings of the Tory M.P.s returned in 1847. In England there were about 170 Protectionists and roughly 90 Peelites, but in Scotland Peelites outnumbered Protectionists by 12 to 8.[156] A curious co-existence obtained between the two Tory camps in Scotland. In 1846 and 1847 the Peelites were utterly scathing in their appraisal of the Protectionists' policies: 'We should strive to avoid the risk of having to undergo a period of Protectionist imbecility, which, tho' it might be brief, would produce many evils', Buccleuch warned Dalhousie.[157] Nevertheless, Buccleuch was adamant that no permanent rupture should occur if at all possible, since re-union was not inconceivable. He advised against opposing the Protectionist in Roxburghshire, 'especially [when] at this moment there are so many elements of discord, which may alienate friends and divide an otherwise strong party. For what with Free Kirk and Free Trade, both of them exciting topics, we should have men committing themselves in every foolish way, saying and doing things they would regret for the rest of their lives'.[158] Buccleuch insisted that 'I have as concerns myself indicated most unequivocally my desire for reconciliation', stressing that in Roxburghshire he went so far as to offer the Protectionist Francis Scott support which he had earlier withdrawn, but also pointing out that even when he had initially distanced himself from Scott, he had plainly indicated that he would countenance no Peelite opposition to the candidate.[159] Dalhousie replied to Buccleuch, agreeing that while he could not rejoin the Protectionists at the cost of sacrificing his principles, he would not regard them as his enemies.[160] In Dunbartonshire, the sitting M.P., Alexander Smollett, was a Peelite, but was ready to stand down if his re-election 'would be distasteful to a considerable number of my former supporters, who might prefer to run a Protectionist'.[161] On the other side, Eglinton was insistent that the Ayrshire Protectionists would not challenge Oswald, although he refused to endorse their position on tariffs, since a split in the Tory vote would only produce a Whig victory.[162]

But this was a static, not a dynamic compromise, and gradually in the early 1850s the Peelites either drifted over to the Liberal side or withdrew completely from active politics, often letting their seats in either event slip out of the Tory grip.[163] The advent of the Aberdeen ministry in 1853 was a significant moment, since Peelites sat in government beside Liberals. Thus the Dumfriesshire M.P., Lord Drumlanrig, accepted office under Aberdeen as Comptroller of the Household, and accordingly offered himself for re-election. Many local Tory Protectionists were unhappy at Drumlanrig's presence in a Free Trade administration, the more so as he had been thought to be in favour of their policy. A group of dissident lairds therefore contemplated mounting a candidate of their own political outlook against the apostate. Their project drew forth a magisterial rebuke from Buccleuch. Firstly, their cause was dead: 'Protection was ingloriously smothered and ignominiously buried by its former nurses, upon them is the blame if this [?] is defunct. It was killed, but it should lie'.[164] Secondly, and critically, he expressed his full confidence in his old colleague, Aberdeen: 'upon *public grounds* and consideration for the welfare of the country I have decided to support the present government, looking to the measures that will be brought forward rather than to the men who proposed them'.[165] Thus by 1853 the premier Conservative peer in the post-Reform era had effectively moved to a non-partisan position. Elsewhere, too, the same process of disengagement from Conservatism was in train. Aberdeenshire, still largely controlled by the Earl of Aberdeen, returned his son in place of his brother in 1854, the more important change being that the party label was altered from Conservative to Liberal. In 1857 in Argyllshire, the Tory Campbell of Succoth was deposed as M.P. in favour of A. S. Finlay, a Liberal, thanks to the machinations of a group of lesser gentry, acting with the connivance of the Duke of Argyll and the Marquess of Breadalbane, because of Campbell's refusal to support Palmerston.[166] In Ayrshire, many Tories, such as the Duke of Portland and Alexander Oswald, Peelite M.P. for the county between 1843 and 1852, were observed to cross in 1857 to the Liberals. This was partly because the Conservative, Sir James Fergusson, declined to endorse Palmerston's foreign policy, and partly because he had not supported the Church of Scotland in its struggles to defeat Moncrieff's Education Bills.[167] Even though Fergusson contrived to recapture the county in a by-election in 1859, it was only by a very slender majority, and was achieved with no great gentry support, as he complained to one landowner who had exerted himself: 'It was in great measure owing to you, among a few others, that we fought at all'.[168] This was a grave falling off from the heyday of the Tory party in Ayrshire in the later 1830s, when the serried ranks of the lairds controlled the seat, to an embattled group with a frail hold on the constituency. Fergusson's problem in 1857 was replicated in Lanarkshire that year, where the Disraelite Baillie Cochrane lost his seat, largely because the Tory party was no longer united behind him.[169]

Thus by 1857 the Conservative share of the representation of Scotland had shrunk to 15, the lowest level since 1835, and it was shorn of many of its leaders. Symbolically, *The Glasgow Constitutional,* launched in the heady days when the new middle class were flocking to Peel's new Conservatism, closed down in 1855.

One result was to leave the Liberals with a hold on seats which was more tenuous than was always apparent, as the only reason for their remaining Liberal was the absence of any concerted Conservative opposition. The sitting M.P. for Roxburghshire admitted this on the eve of the 1857 election, when he was unopposed in what had long been one of the most keenly contested counties: 'Nothing can be more unsatisfactory than the State of the County. No gentlemen left on our side, and the Register containing so many new names that nobody can say how things would go in the case of a contest'.[170]

V

One of the first flickers of modern Scottish nationalism began in the 1850s, with two features characterising the movement. Firstly, there was a desire to restore some of the historical rights and trappings of Scottish national identity — notably heraldic and emblematic aspects. Secondly, there was a demand to give Scotland better representation in Parliament and a wider franchise system as the prelude to getting social reform legislation for Scotland carried. This strange alliance, in Hanham's phrase, of romantic and radical nationalism, is less surprising than it initially appears.[171] Virtually all of the leaders of these campaigns were men who had recently been marginalised from the political mainstream and had lost influence within their respective interest groups. Hence they sought to re-order the basis of Scottish politics with the aim of re-integrating themselves at the centre.

W. E. Aytoun, one of the foremost romantics, had had high aspirations. He had been an assiduous exponent of Protectionism and High Toryism in the columns of *Blackwood's Magazine* over many years, and had also tried to prod the Conservatives in Orkney and Shetland (where he held legal office) to organise themselves efficiently. The advent of the Derby-Disraeli ministry in 1852 was expected by Aytoun to restore Protection and sweep away any Peelite remnants in the party. He was soon sharply disabused of his vision. 'You may judge of my surprise and, I may say, indignation', he expostulated upon learning that the Tory Solicitor-General ('an arrant jobber') intended 'to replace [i.e. restore] the whole Peelite staff of Parliament House in office, just as if nothing had occurred since 1846'.[172] As a result of this, Aytoun was not awarded the post of Advocate-Depute which he believed his abilities and his political opinions merited. Within a few more days, his dismay was total, for it was quite apparent that 'the set in office here' were hostile to, not in favour of, Protection.[173] Hence it may be suggested that one factor in Aytoun's launching of the National Association for the Vindication of Scottish Rights in 1853 may have been his loss of faith in the existing political system. The attitude of a fellow High Tory contributor to *Blackwood's*, Sir Archibald Alison, was in good part similar. Alison, the Sheriff of Lanarkshire, recorded in his memoirs that he had declined the offer of Scottish Solicitor General made on Derby's behalf, and was given a baronetcy by the Tories in recognition of his support for them.[174] But Aytoun reported on Alison's distaste for the Scottish law officers eventually appointed, and the speedy departure from Protectionism by the party leaders greatly upset Alison, who remained a staunch critic of Free Trade. By the end of the 1850s he was in despair at the growing Liberal spirit of the age, and lamented that the Conservatives had yielded totally to it.[175] Dislike of Disraeli, who portrayed him as Mr. Wordy in *Coningsby* (because of his 15-volume history of the French Revolution), probably contributed to Alison's loss of faith in the traditional party system.

Aytoun and Alison were attached more to the symbolic wing of Scottish nationalism and gradually withdrew from the National Association's activities in 1854 as the political radicalism of Begg and MacLaren became the primary concern of nationalist feeling. The Rev. Dr. James Begg, who in the 1840s had been one of Chalmers' chief lieutenants, found himself in the 1850s increasingly in permanent opposition within the Free Church as Candlish tightened his control. Moreover Begg began to be regarded by many in the Free Church as a nuisance, rather than an asset, hindering the Church's deliberations. His biographer candidly stated: 'In one respect the General Assembly of 1852 may be said to form an epoch in Dr. Begg's history as an ecclesiastic. Hitherto he had often been engaged in controversy on matters arising within the Free Church ... But with scarcely an exception the combatants had not regarded one another as opposing partisans, but each had been ready to give his opponent the fullest credit for honesty of desire to promote the interests which all admitted to be the interests of all ... But the hisses with which he was greeted before opening his mouth and [an] absurd interruption ... indicate there were some members who were disposed to offer him a factious opposition'.[176]

Begg was consistently outvoted on a whole series of internal Free Church issues in the 1850s, as Candlish established his general ascendancy as Chalmers' undisputed successor, flanked by Drs. Buchanan and Cunningham as the Church's top administrators.[177] Begg's frustration at his isolation found expression in a pamphlet produced in 1855 entitled *The Crisis in the Free Church,* in which he intimated his concern at the many grave errors committed since the death of Chalmers, particularly instancing various important decisions taken recently by the Church which demonstrated that 'Probably there is no corporation in Britain so despotically governed at this moment as the Free Church of Scotland. A limited number of men notoriously manage all our affairs in any way they please ... The Free Church is as completely managed by an oligarchy as ever the British Government was'.[178] It may be relevant that while he had spoken with approval of the need for greater Scottish self-government as early as 1850, his involvement in first the Scottish Rights and then the Scottish Freehold movements came only in the mid-1850s, when his disenchantment with the Free Church had arisen. His case for political reform has, indeed, clear parallels with that outlined in his philippic against his own Church, inasmuch as he ascribed harmful effects to over-centralised and undemocratic forms of government. There was also a similarity in his assumption that the ordinary mass of the Scottish people shared his views, so that franchise reform would facilitate housing and other social reforms. This belief lay behind his argument that the Education Bills of the early 1850s did not require the provision of religious instruction to be written into them (as the vast bulk of the Free Church contended) because popularly elected school boards meant that a pious populace would ensure that the Bible remained in the classroom. This cause, of course, was firmly rejected by mainstream Free Church opinion, just at the time Begg turned to Scottish nationalism.

Duncan MacLaren after 1852 was also something of an outcast from his natural community, and his isolation if anything increased steadily over the rest of the decade. After his repudiation by the Free Church at the Edinburgh poll in 1852, he had amassed considerable sympathy among the Voluntaries, but this groundswell of loyalty he dissipated, firstly by supporting the 1854 and 1855 Education Bills of Moncrieff, which to most of his fellow Churchmen were Free Church engines, and then by putting forward a Free Church candidate in the 1856 by-election for the city against the veteran Voluntary, Adam Black. The upshot of his actions was that MacLaren alienated large sections of Voluntary support without the compensating gain of securing the wholehearted backing of the Free Church. The denunciations of his conduct were specially robust in the columns of the Voluntary press, as we have seen. Again, there is the near-simultaneity of MacLaren's deepening commitment to Scottish nationalist agitation and the eroding of his power base in the U.P. Church. For MacLaren an attack on the existing arrangements for governing Scotland would weaken the control exercised by the legal elite, the object of his perpetual animus (with the exception of F. Brown Douglas in 1856).[179]

Further evidence of the peripheral nature of the nationalist movement came from the response of broad sections of the political community to its demands. Glasgow, the centre of the most advanced, dynamic economic and social region of the country, makes a useful case-study. Hardly any prominent citizens were involved in the National Association — the most important exception being William Campbell of Tullichewan. The main figures in the Glasgow wing were political lightweights, such as William Burns and some middle-ranking councillors.[180] The attitude of those Glaswegians who wielded influence in shaping and articulating opinion was not simply one of indifference: frequently a preference was displayed for trends which actually worked toward greater assimilation with England, rather than a re-assertion of Scottish distinctiveness. The vital importance of maintaining historic Scottish values was not seen as a goal to be placed above others. Thus, many of the business and professional men in the West of Scotland were more exercised during the early 1850s with a movement to reform the Scottish legal system — one of the fundamental pillars of a separate Scottish identity — by integrating it more thoroughly with English law. This movement, styling itself the Glasgow Law Amendment Society, highlighted several areas where Scottish law contrasted unfavourably with English, and urged that speedy action was imperative. 'The fitness of the Scotch laws to the Scotch people has scarcely ever been less than at present', a pamphleteer complained, and the Glasgow Law Amendment Society asserted that this parlous situation arose because of economic and social change, which meant that Scottish laws, 'however just and expedient in a poor community and a rude state of society are, to say the least, of questionable propriety in the present social condition of the people of this country'.[181] What made this indictment the more powerful was that the Law Amendment Society was so representative of the Glasgow business world. Its inaugural meeting was attended by prominent men of all political views. Three former Lord Provosts (Sir James Campbell, Henry Dunlop and Sir James Anderson) and three future M.P.s (Anderson, Walter Buchanan and H. E. Crum Ewing) were present along with the Dean of the Faculty of Procurators (i.e. Glasgow lawyers), and the heads of three of the most important banks.[182] The key business institutions of the city, the Chamber of Commerce and the Merchants' House, collaborated with the Law Amendment Society (as did the Faculty of Procurators) in framing its objectives.[183] Most of these men, notably Walter Buchanan, had been prominent in the Anti-Corn Law League, and clearly saw this campaign as a further step towards rationalising the socio-economic framework within which business could function at optimum efficiency. But their great Scottish leader of the Corn Law Repeal days, MacLaren, was now divorced from these erstwhile followers. The Law Amendment body attracted the support of the main Glasgow newspapers, several of whom, like *The Glasgow Herald* and *The North British Daily Mail*, ran series of articles on the various facets of this question.[184] In 1853, the Society claimed its case for Sheriff Court reform had been supported by thirty-six newspapers in all parts of Scotland.[185] The student of the Scottish press could find twenty papers supporting the Scottish Rights movement at its peak.[186]

The specific charges against the Scottish legal system fell under two general headings. Firstly there were complaints about the inadequacies of the administration of justice in Scotland, which had recently become more glaring because the English courts had improved their conduct of business. The insistence in Scotland on the use of written evidence and pleading, even at the Small Debt Court level, seriously impeded the processing of cases, as did the country's greatly extended appeal procedure which allowed all cases to be taken right up to the Court of Session, whereas in England the right of appeal was strictly controlled. Also, the presence in Scotland of non-resident Sheriffs placed over and above the Sheriffs-Substitute was an added and confusing judicial level not present in England.[187] The second ground of complaint was the discrepancy between English and Scottish mercantile law, a problem which had become more worrying as commerce between the two countries grew. Decrees issued in one country could not be enforced in the other; a non-domicile could not sue in the other country's courts; and different rules and procedures made legal dealings very complex. Nowhere were these problems more sharply seen than in a co-partnery functioning in both countries, since the form of business entity was regulated by quite different laws. The inadequacy of the bankruptcy laws in Scotland as compared to those in England was another topic which aroused much concern among business and professional circles in Glasgow.[188] Faced with these problems, the Glasgow businessmen had no doubt where their energies should go: 'The time has therefore come when the laws of the two divisions of the Island should be gradually assimilated and the exertions of [the Law Amendment Society] cannot be more usefully applied than in forwarding this truly national object'.[189] The approach adopted was clearly stated. While a 'spirit of free enquiry' would determine which country's law should prevail, 'where the Law of England is not objectionable in principle, it will probably be found expedient to give it the preference, particularly in Mercantile matters'.[190] This is a world removed from the concerns of the Scottish Rights Association.

In this atmosphere of critical appraisal of Scottish institutions prevalent in places like Glasgow, calls to preserve national traditions and values were not likely to appeal. Indeed, the Glasgow lawyers wished to diminish Edinburgh's position as the legal centre of Scotland: 'Is it to be supposed that this large and influential community will always submit to the supreme Courts having their seats in Edinburgh?', rhetorically asked the head of the Glasgow lawyers in 1856.[191] Another aspect of this tendency was shown in 1856 when the Faculty of Procurators considered the appellate jurisdiction of the House of Lords in Scottish cases, an issue which perturbed those who felt that Scottish law was not fully understood by English law lords. William Burns contended that this level of appeal should be abolished as an anomaly, so keeping Scottish cases entirely within the Scottish legal system, but he found no supporters at all. Sixteen supported a call for the Lords to keep their powers, with the proviso that a Scottish legal expert be in attendence to advise on matters of Scottish law. Twenty-two, however, endorsed the successful motion that the *status quo* be left, as it was working perfectly well.[192]

Moreover, the other main argument used by the early nationalists, viz. that Scottish business at Westminster was neglected and poorly managed, appealed little to Glasgow opinion. The implementation of Sheriff Court reforms in 1852 and 1853 did a good deal to placate the Law Amendment Society and also confirmed that Parliament was neither deaf to, nor incapable of responding to, Scottish demands. The passage of a major Scottish bankruptcy measure in 1856 went far to satisfy the other leading demand raised by law assimilators in the West of Scotland. The major legislative failure of the period was in education, and here the problem, as we have seen, was ascribable not to indifference in Whitehall, but to difficulties entirely confined within the boundaries of Scotland.

NOTES

1. N. Gash, *Reaction and Reconstruction in English Politics 1832-52* (London, 1965).

2. Aberdeen to J. Moncrieff, 25, 30 Aug. 1853, Aberdeen MSS., Add. MS. 43201, ff. 227-8, 254-5.

3. Aberdeen to Lord Justice Clerk (J. Hope), 3 Feb. 1854, same to Buccleuch, 1 Feb. 1854, Ibid., Add MSS. 43206, ff. 290-1, 43201, ff. 131-2.

4. J. Haldane to Lord Melgund, 10 May 1847, Minto MSS., MS. 12340, ff. 46-7.

5. J. Matheson to D. Monro, 31 Jul. 1846, Monro MSS., GD 71/333/8; *Inverness Courier*, 20 Jul. 1847.

6. *Witness,* 11 Aug., 28 Jul. 1847.

7. A. M. Dunlop to F. Maule, 1 Jul. 1847, Dalhousie MSS., GD 45/14/658/3.

8. J. Elliot to Minto, 21, 27 Jan. 1846, Minto MSS., MS. 11754, ff. 224-7, 232-7.

9. *Kilmarnock Journal*, 16, 23, 30 May 1844; G. Spiers to F. Maule, n.d., A. M. Dunlop to same, 10 Feb. 1844, Dalhousie MSS., GD 45/14/641/21; 45/14/658/2; J. Robertson, *The Macaulay Election or the Design of the Ministry* (Edinburgh, 1846), pp. 3-4.

10. Dunlop to Maule, 11, 15 Aor. 1845, Ibid., GD 45/14/658/3; G. MacPherson Grant to —, n.d. (April 1845), Ballindalloch MSS., 143; *Greenock Advertiser*, 15, 18 Apr. 1845.

11. Cf. P. Bayne, *The Life and Letters of Hugh Miller* (London, 1871), II, pp. 282-6, for this point made by Miller, the chief Free Church propagandist.

12. T. Maitland to A. Rutherfurd, 26, 8, 12 Aug. 1845, J. Mackie to Maitland, 6 Aug. 1845, Rutherfurd MSS., MS. 9700, ff. 121-2, 113-6, 119-20, 117-8; *Scotsman*, 6, 13 Aug. 1845.

13. *Witness*, 28 Jul. 1847.

14. *Greenock Advertiser*, 23 Jul. 1847.

15. Dunlop to Maule, 11 Apr. 1845, Dalhousie MSS., GD 45/14/658/3; *Scotsman*, 12 Apr. 1845.

16. *Greenock Advertiser*, 18, 15 Apr. 1845.

17. *Scotsman*, 13 Apr. 1844.

18. 'Address by the Scottish Board of Dissenters', *Scottish Congregational Magazine* (1846), unpaginated.

19. *Caledonian Mercury*, 13 Jul. 1846.

20. *To the Electors of Scotland* (Edinburgh, 1846), J. C. Brodie to Maule, 11 Aug. 1846, Dalhousie MSS., GD 45/14/665.

21. J. B. Mackie, *The Life and Work of Duncan MacLaren* (Edinburgh, 1888), II, pp. 29-30; C. Cowan, *Reminiscences* (priv., 1878), pp. 212-5; G. O. Trevelyan, *Life and Letters of Lord Macaulay* (London, 1876), II, pp. 156-9; *Scotsman*, 12 May 1852; *Scottish Press*, 22 Sep. 1847.

22. Mackie, *MacLaren*, II, p. 30; *Edinburgh News*, 15 May 1852.

23. *Scottish Guardian*, 2, 25 Jul. 1847.

24. *Aberdeen Herald*, 31 Jul., 7 Aug. 1847.

25. A. Johnstone to J. B. Smith, 29 Aug. 1846, J. B. Smith MSS., MS. 923.2 S335/10.

26. J. B. Smith, *Address to the Electors of Stirling Burghs*, 4 Sep. 1846, and an undated pamphlet, written by Smith's supporters, J. B. Smith MSS., MS. 923.2 S335/1, 7.

27. J. Irvine to Capt. Stewart, 16 Feb. 1847, Minto MSS., MS. 12340, ff. 6-7.

28. *Journal of Henry Cockburn, Being a Continuation of the Memorials of His Time, 1831-54* (Edinburgh, 1874), II, pp. 284 (20 Jul. 1852).

29. *Witness*, 28 Jul. 1847; J. B. Smith to D. MacLaren, 11 Aug., 6 Sep. 1847; Smith to E. Beveridge, n.d. (copy), J. B. Smith MSS., MS. 923.2 S335/37, 38, 68.

30. Melgund to Minto, 12, — Apr. 1852, Minto MSS., MS. 11758, ff. 261-2, 263-4.

31. J. Gordon to A. Rutherfurd, 9 May 1852, Rutherfurd MSS., MS. 9693, ff. 267-9.

32. Lord Mounteagle to Melgund, 12 Jul. 1852, Minto MSS., uncat.

33. *Northern Liberal*, 22 May 1852.

34. Sir J. Carnegie to Maule, n.d., Dalhousie MSS., GD 45/12/278.

35. Dunlop to Maule, 7 Jun., 4 Aug. 1847, Ibid., GD 45/14/658/3.

36. Melgund to Minto, 10 Jun. 1847, Minto MSS., MS. 11758, ff. 62-3.

37. *Greenock Advertiser*, 30 Jul., 3 Aug. 1847; Melgund to Minto, 19 Jun. 1847, Minto MSS., MS. 11758, ff. 66-8; *Greenock Telegraph*, 3 Dec. 1885.

38. R. Steele to Melgund, 29 Feb., 27 Mar., 3 Jun. 1852, T. O. Hunter to Melgund, 1, 31 May 1852, Minto MSS., MS. 12340, ff. 257-8, 275-6, 310-11, 304-5, 308-9.

39. *Scottish Press,* 14 Apr., *Edinburgh News,* 3, 17 Apr., *Scotsman,* 12 May 1852.

40. *Witness,* 10 Jul. 1852, cf. Mackie, *MacLaren,* I, pp. 294–6.

41. *Scotsman,* 12 May, 2, 9 Jun. 1852.

42. *Scottish Press,* 30 Jun. 1852.

43. A. Russel to E. Ellice, 9 Jun., 14, 22, 29 May 1852, Ellice MSS., MS. 15049, ff. 17–18, 8–9, 10–13, 14–16, J. G. Craig to Ellice, 24, 26 May 1852, Ibid., MS. 15009, ff. 103–4, 105–8.

44. *Scottish Press,* 3, 7, 10 Jul. 1852.

45. *The Approaching General Election* (Edinburgh, 1866, i.e. 1865), pp. 26–33.

46. *Scotsman,* 12 May 1852.

47. Cowan, *Reminiscences,* p. 256; Mackie, *MacLaren,* II, pp. 34–5; *Scotsman,* 16 Jun. 1852.

48. Dunlop to Maule, 7 Jun. 1847, Dalhousie MSS., GD 45/14/658/3; *Greenock Advertiser,* 23 Jul. 1847.

49. *Scottish Press,* 9 Jun. 1852.

50. Panmure to E. Ellice, 3 Feb. 1854, Ellice MSS., MS., 15048, ff. 65–8.

51. British Anti-State Church Association, *Scotland and The Kirk* (London, 1850), pp. 7–11, 27–30.

52. Panmure to E. Ellice, 3 Feb. 1854, Ellice MSS., MS. 15048, ff. 65–8.

53. W. G. Craig to Ellice, 28 Feb. 1854, Ellice MSS., MS. 15009, ff. 121–4.

54. *National Education Association of Scotland* (n.p., n.d.).

55. D. J. Withrington, 'The Free Church Educational Scheme, 1843–50', *Records of the Scott. Church Hist. Soc.* 15 (1963–5), pp. 103–15.

56. *1851 Census, Great Britain, Report and Tables on Religious Worship and Education in Scotland,* P.P. 1854 (1764), LIX, Table 0.

57. H. Miller, *Thoughts on the Educational System or 'The Battle of Scotland'* (London, 1850), p. 52.

58. E.g. British Anti-State Church Association, *Scotland and Its Kirk, passim.*

59. Buccleuch to Aberdeen, 25 Jan. 1854, Aberdeen MSS., Add. MS. 43201, ff. 124–9; 'Memorial to the Nobility, Gentry and Heritors of Scotland by the Parochial Schoolmasters of Scotland', 15 Sep. 1853, Lord Advocates' MSS., AS 56/47/1.

60. Graham to Sir G. Clerk, 16 May 1854, Clerk MSS., GD 18/3926.

61. T. Smith, *Memoirs of James Begg, D.D.* (Edinburgh, 1888), I, pp. 150 ff; W. Wilson, *Memorials of Robert Smith Candlish, D.D.* (Edinburgh, 1880), pp. 436–7; D. K. & C. J. Guthrie, *Autobiography and Memoir of Thomas Guthrie, D.D.* (pop. edn., London, 1877), pp. 592–3.

62. Melgund to Lord John Russell, 23 Jan. 1850, Russell MSS., PRO 30/22/8C, ff. 268–9, for an early intimation of this difficulty.

63. Melgund to J. H. Burton, 22 Apr. 1850, Hill Burton MSS., MS. 9410, ff. 35–40.

64. Same to same, 3 Mar. 1851, Ibid., MS. 9410, ff. 84–9.

65. J. H. Burton to Melgund (enclosing the Free Church petition), 3 Mar. 1851, Minto MSS., MS. 12348, unfoliated.

66. W. Duncan, J. H. Burton to Melgund, 19 Mar. 1851 (both), Ibid., MS. 12348, unfol.

67. Melgund to Minto, 3 Dec. 1851, Ibid., MS. 12348; Minto to Burton, 14, 25 Apr., 17, 29 May 1851, Hill Burton MSS., MS. 9410, ff. 90–1, 92–5, 98–100, 101–4.

68. Minto to Lord J. Russell, 14 Dec. 1851, Russell MSS., PRO 30/22/9J (1), ff. 157–60.

69. Melgund to Burton, 3 Dec. 1849, Hill Burton MSS., MS. 9410, ff. 1–4.

70. Melgund to Minto, 28 Jan. 1852, Minto MSS., MS. 11758, ff. 253–6.

71. Rev. J. Taylor to Lord Advocate (Moncrieff), 30 Mar. 1853, Lord Advocates' MSS.,

AD 56/47/1.

72. A. Russel to Melgund, 18 Nov., Melgund to Minto, 16 Nov. 1853, Minto MSS., MSS. 12358, ff. 92–3, 11759, ff. 10–11.

73. Moncrieff to Aberdeen, 1, 27 Dec. 1853, Aberdeen MSS., Add. MS. 43201, ff. 310–5, 317–9.

74. W. G. Craig to Ellice, 28 Feb. 1854, Ellice MSS., MS. 15009, ff. 121–4; Aberdeen to Buccleuch, 1 Feb. 1854, Aberdeen MSS., Add. MS. 43201, ff. 131–2.

75. Maule to Rutherfurd (27 Feb. 1854), Rutherfurd MSS., MS. 9699, ff. 167–8, cf. Rutherfurd to Maule, 26 Feb. 1854, Dalhousie MSS., GD 45/14/642/2. For the other side, Melgund to Burton, 2 Feb. 1853 (should be 1854), Hill Burton MSS., MS. 9410, ff. 121–2.

76. Buccleuch to Sir G. Clerk, 9 Apr. 1854, Aberdeen MSS., Add. MS. 43252, ff. 316–21; Melgund to Minto, 6 Mar. 1853 (should be 1854), Minto MSS., MS. 11759, ff. 42–5.

77. A. R. MacEwan, *Life and Letters of John Cairns, D.D., LL.D.* (London, 1895), p. 387.

78. Copy in Lord Advocates' MSS., AD 56/47/1, as are the presbyterial motions.

79. *Glasgow Chronicle,* 1 Mar. 1854.

80. *A Bill to make further provision for the education of the people in Scotland, and to amend the laws relating thereto,* P.P. 1854 (37) II, 317.

81. A copy of the proceedings at a meeting held on 24 Mar. 1854 by the British Anti-State Church Association is in Lord Advocates' MSS., AD 56/47/1.

82. Rev. H. Renton to Melgund, 1, 10, 24 Mar., 7 Apr., 6 Jun. 1854, Minto MSS., MS. 12349, unfol.

83. A copy of the proceedings at a meeting held on 24 Mar. 1854 by the British Anti-State Church Association is in Lord Advocates' MSS., AD 56/47/1.

84. Rev. A. Blair to Lord Advocate, 22 Apr. 1854, Lord Advocates' MSS., AD 56/47/1.

85. *Glasgow Chronicle,* 15 Feb., 29 Mar. 1854.

86. *Edinburgh News,* 4 Mar. 1854; *Glasgow Chronicle,* 15 Mar. 1854.

87. *Edinburgh News,* 29 Apr., cf. 28 Jan., 25 Mar. 1854.

88. *Glasgow Chronicle,* 29 Mar., cf. 12 Apr. 1854.

89. *Ibid.,* 25 May 1853.

90. *Edinburgh News,* 4 Mar. 1854.

91. Sir J. Anderson to Lady Anderson, 2, 3 May 1854, Anderson MSS., MS. 11/29, 30.

92. Cf. E. Ellice to A. Rutherfurd, 16 May 1854, Rutherfurd MSS., MS. 9690, ff. 232–3.

93. *An Educational Retrospect. Being an Address delivered by the Rt. Hon. Lord Moncrieff, Lord Justice Clerk of Scotland, on the Occasion of the Opening of the Kent Road Public School* (Glasgow, 1886), pp. 11–13.

94. *A Bill to provide for the education of the people in Scotland.* P.P. 1854–55 (69), II, 269.

95. Memorandum by Lord Advocate, 22 Feb. 1855, Lord Advocates' MSS., AD 56/47/2.

96. Black to Palmerston, 10 Apr. 1854, Ibid., AD 56/47/1.

97. *Scottish Press,* 27 Mar. 1855 for a favourable approach, 6, 10, 13 Apr., 15 May, 3 Jul. 1855 for adverse views.

98. Rev. J. Taylor to Lord Advocate, — May 1855, Lord Advocates' MSS., AD 56/47/2.

99. *State Education at Variance with Civil and Religious Freedom. Report of the Speeches delivered at a public meeting held in Glasgow on Thursday, 31 May 1855 to oppose the Lord Advocate's Education Bill for Scotland* (Glasgow, 1855); H. A. Bruce to

Lord Advocate, 4 Jun. 1855, Lord Advocates' MSS., AD 56/47/2.

100. *State Education ...*, pp. 36–7; J. Edmonds, *Voluntaryism in the House of its Friends, being a Review of Answers by the United Presbyterian Synod to Reasons of Dissent from the Resolutions of May 11, 1855 on the Subject of National Education* (Glasgow, 1855), pp. 4–14; *Glasgow Chronicle,* 11 Apr., *Scottish Press,* 6 Apr., *Edinburgh News,* 28 Apr. (all 1855).

101. *Edinburgh News,* 16 June, 7 Jul. 1855.

102. *State Education ...*, pp. 28–9, *Scottish Press,* 3 Jul., *Glasgow Chronicle,* 27 Jun., 4, 11 Jul. 1855.

103. *Edinburgh News,* 7 Jul., *Scottish Press,* 3 Jul. 1855, *State Education ...*, p. 38.

104. Sir J. to Lady Anderson, 27 Apr., 13 Jul. 1855, Anderson MSS., MS. 11/46, 51.

105. *Edinburgh News,* 26 Apr. 1856.

106. Dr. T. Guthrie to Provost Guthrie, 17 Apr. 1854; Guthrie, *Autobiography & Memoirs,* p. 605.

107. J. Cairns to Panmure, 25 May 1857 (enclosing the leaflet on union), Dalhousie MSS., GD 45/13/401.

108. Ibid.

109. *Northern Warder,* 1, 3, 8 Mar. 1855.

110. A. Russel to E. Ellice, 13 Feb. 1856, Ellice MSS., MS. 15049, ff. 39–40.

111. J. Stalker, *Francis Brown Douglas* (Edinburgh, 1886).

112. A. Russel to E. Ellice, 13 Feb. 1856, Ellice MSS., MS. 15049, ff. 39–40; *Scottish Press,* 12 Feb. 1856.

113. J. Cairns to Mrs. Balmer, 13 Feb. 1856, MacEwen, *John Cairns,* p. 420.

114. *Edinburgh News,* 7 Mar. 1857; *Scotsman,* 14, 18, 21, 28 Mar. 1857.

115. *Scottish Press,* 24 Mar. 1857.

116. *Report of the Proceedings at the Non-Electors' Festival on the Occasion of presenting a Time-Piece to George Armitstead, Esquire* (Dundee, 1857), esp. pp. 12–20.

117. *Aberdeen Free Press,* 27, 20 Mar. 1857.

118. Lumsden Diary, 17, 31 Mar. 1857; *Scottish Guardian* (Free Church), 3 Apr; *Glasgow Chronicle* (Voluntary), 1 Apr; *Glasgow Commonwealth,* 4 Apr. — all 1857.

119. *Paisley Herald,* 21, 28 Mar., 4 Apr. 1857.

120. *Scotsman,* 28 Mar. 1857.

121. A. Thomson, *Life of Principal Harper, D.D.* (Edinburgh, 1881), pp. 192–7; *Scotsman,* 28 Mar. 1857; *Scottish Press,* 31 Mar. 1857.

122. *Scotsman,* 4 Apr. 1857.

123. Thomson, *Principal Harper,* p. 192.

124. J. C. Watt, *John Inglis, Lord Justice General of Scotland* (Edinburgh, 1893), pp. 138–54.

125. Brown, *Chalmers,* pp. 329–32; G. I. T. Machin, *Politics and the Churches in Great Britain 1832 to 1868* (London, 1977), pp. 136–43.

126. Glasgow Conservative Operatives' Association, Min. Book, 10 Mar. 1842, 30 May 1843 (Reading Room Comm.); cf. J. Ward, 'Working Class Conservatism', pp. 157–61.

127. R. Smythe to H. H. Drummond, 8 Jun. 1843, Abercairney MSS., GD 24/1/535/2, ff. 141–2.

128. E.g. *Scottish Guardian,* 24 Jul. 1846, states that of 1065 claims to be put on the register, 864 came from Liberal agents, 201 from individuals. *Glasgow Saturday Post,* 24 Aug. 1847, divides that year's claims (4595) as 3810 Liberal, 785 neutral.

129. F. Scott to Buccleuch, 8 Apr. 1847, Buccleuch MSS., GD 224/581/11; cf. A. Pringle to Sir G. Clerk, 3 Feb. 1846, Clerk MSS., GD 18/3808.

130. A. Pringle to J. Brown, n.d. (1852), Mansfield MSS., 74/2.

131. A. Pringle to Sir G. Clerk, 3 Feb. 1846, Clerk MSS., GD 18/3808.

132. H. H. Drummond to W. Stirling, 31 Jul. 1846, Stirling MSS., T-SK 29/78; Polwarth, F. Scott to Buccleuch, 12 Jan. 1846, Buccleuch MSS., GD 224/581/11; A. Pringle to Sir G. Clerk, 3 Feb. 1846, Clerk MSS., GD 18/3808.

133. Lt. Col. MacDonald to Buccleuch, 10 Apr. 1852, Buccleuch MSS., GD 224/582/ 'Roxburgh & Selkirk Politics, 1851–2'.

134. Col. M. Cathcart to T. Cuninghame, and reply, 21, 23 Feb. 1852, Cuninghame of Caprington MSS., GD 149/403/4, 5.

135. *Ayr Advertiser,* 14, 21 Dec. 1854.

136. Printed circular, 24 May 1850, Ardgowan MSS., T-ARD 1/6/700.

137. R. Stewart, *The Foundation of the Conservative Party* (London, 1978), pp. 206–10 makes this point for England.

138. *George Hope of Fenton Barns,* esp. pp. 85–9, 95–102, 111–23.

139. J. H. Dawson, *Abridged Statistical History of Scotland* (Edinburgh, 1862), pp. 285–303. Cf. E. S. Whetham, 'Prices and Production in Scottish Farming, 1850–70', *Scott. Jnl. of Political Economy,* 9 (1962), pp. 233–43.

140. W. Ogilvie to Buccleuch, 26 May 1846, Buccleuch MSS., GD 224/581/11.

141. P. Thomson to Lincoln, 6 May 1846, Newcastle MSS., Ne C 12411.

142. W. Murray to C. Hope, 29 May 1847 (copy), Linlithgow MSS., 9/8; J. Hope to G. Hope, 3 Mar. 1852, Hope MSS., GD 364/173.

143. *Fife Herald,* 22, 15 Jul. 1847; cf. Fergus' Address, 20 Jul. 1847, a copy of which is in the Berry MSS., 51/4.

144. Sir R. Anstruther to W. Berry, 2 Aug. 1847, Berry MSS., 51/4.

145. *Caledonian Mercury,* 22 Jun. 1846, 10 Jun. 1847; *Scotsman,* 26 May 1847.

146. *Scotsman,* 19 Jun., 10 Jul. 1847; *Caledonian Mercury,* 21 Jun. 1847; *Hope of Fenton Barns,* pp. 152–61.

147. A. Buchanan to W. Forbes, 16 Jul. 1847, Forbes MSS., GD 171/47.

148. There is a copy of W. Baird's Address in Robertson-Aikman MSS., 1/1/11; for J. Baird, see *Glasgow Herald,* 14 Feb. 1851. G. Sutherland-B. Disraeli correspondence, 8 Nov . 1848–17 Feb. 1849, Disraeli MSS., MS. Disraeli, Box 144, B/XX1/S/715–724; *Glasgow Constitutional,* 7 Jul., 3 Apr. 1852.

149. Stewart, *Foundation of Conservative Party,* pp. 256–87 for England.

150. Brash, 'Conservatives in Haddington Burghs', pp. 60–1.

151. Cockburn, *Journals,* II, pp. 190–1 (22 Aug. 1847).

152. Sir R. Abercromby to H. MacD. Grant, 29 Oct. 1851; Circular letter by Grant, 17 Jul. 1852, Abercromby MSS., GD 185/31/168, 149.

153. D. Monro to J. Matheson, 15 Mar. 1852, also 10 Mar., 1, 10 Apr. 1852, Monro MSS., GD 71/333/15, 14, 22, 26.

154. J. Matheson to D. Monro, 9 Apr. 1852, Ibid., GD 71/333/25.

155. R. W. Stewart, *The Politics of Protection* (London, 1971), pp. 191–205 for this point.

156. *Scotsman,* 28 Aug. 1847, identifies the twelve Scottish Peelites as: Baillie; Charteris; Drummond; Drumlanrig; Gordon; Lincoln; A. E. Lockhart; McNeill; Mure; Oswald; Smollet; Wortley. The eight Protectionists would then be Arbuthnott; Bruce; G. Dundas; Forbes; Sir J. Hope; W. Lockhart; MacKenzie; Scott.

157. Buccleuch to Dalhousie, 31 Dec. 1846, Dalhousie MSS., GD 45/14/578/33–5.

158. Buccleuch to W. Maxwell, 15 Jul. 1847, Buccleuch MSS., GD 224/504/1.

159. Buccleuch to G. W. Hope, 15 Apr. 1847, Hope MSS., GD 364/1047.

160. Dalhousie to Buccleuch, 13 Jan. 1847, Dalhousie MSS., GD 45/14/578/37–9.

161. A. Smollett to Marquis of Lorne, 25 Jul. 1846 (copy) and draft (27 Jul. 1846), Telfer-Smollett MSS.

162. Eglinton to P. Boyle, 8 Jan., 9 May 1847, Earl of Glsgow MSS.

163. J. B. Conacher, *The Peelites and the Party System, 1846–52* (Newton Abbot, 1972) discusses this.

164. Buccleuch to W. Maxwell, 5 Jan. 1853, Buccleuch MSS., GS 224/504/1.

165. Buccleuch to Sir J. H. Maxwell, 2 Jan. 1853, Ibid., GD 224/581/7.

166. W. G. Craig to E. Ellice, 12 Mar. 1857, Ellice MSS., MS. 15009, ff. 131–4.

167. W. Mure to P. Boyle, 13 Mar. (1857), R. Hunter to Boyle, c. 28 Mar. 1857, Earl of Glasgow MSS., where there are several other letters in the same vein.

168. Sir J. Fergusson to J. Hamilton, 21 Nov. 1859, Hamilton MSS., P/CN 49.17/59.

169. A. B. Cochrane to W. Stirling, 6, 9 Nov. 1858, Stirling MSS., T-SK 29/8/33, 32.

170. J. Elliot to Minto, 7 Mar. 1857, Minto MSS., MS. 11754, ff. 427–9.

171. H. J. Hanham, 'Mid-Century Scottish Nationalism: Romantic and Radical', in R. Robson, *Ideas and Institutions of Victorian Britain* (London, 1968), pp. 143–79.

172. W. E. Aytoun to W. Blackwood, 28 Feb. 1852, Blackwood MSS., MS. 4097, ff. 78–83.

173. Same to same, 2 Mar. 1852, Ibid., MS. 4097, ff. 84–5.

174. A. Alison, *Some Account of my Life and Writings* (Edinburgh, 1883), II, pp. 46–8.

175. Ibid., II, p. 237.

176. T. Smith, *James Begg*, pp. 183–5.

177. *Ibid.*, Ch. 31.

178. J. Begg, *The Crisis in the Free Church* (Edinburgh, 1855), pp. 4, 5.

179. E.g. D. MacLaren to W. E. Gladstone, 1 Oct. 1853, 14 Aug. 1866, W. E. Gladstone MSS., Add. MSS. 44376, ff. 77–80; 44411, ff. 151–4, for attacks on the Edinburgh legal establishment.

180. Hanham rather overstates Burns' importance when he refers to him as a leading Liberal in the West of Scotland. Burns took no active part in the various political committees of the period. Moreover, as legal representative of the iron and coal owners, many of whom, e.g. the Bairds, were Tory, he would be unlikely to be prominent on the Liberal side. Cf. Hanham, 'Mid-Century Scottish Nationalism', pp. 161–2.

181. A Scotch Lawyer, *The Amendment of the Law* (Edinburgh, 1853), p. 5; *Report of the Committee of the Law Amendment Society of Glasgow* (Glasgow, 1851), pp. 5–7.

182. *Glasgow Herald,* 11 Aug., 22 Sep. 1851.

183. *Ibid.,* 29 Oct. 1852; *A Letter to James A. Anderson, Esq., Banker, from James Reddie, Advocate* (Glasgow, 1851), p. 3; *North British Daily Mail,* 19 Jan. 1853.

184. *North British Daily Mail,* 17 Oct. 1851–23 Jan. 1852; *Glasgow Herald,* 25 Oct., 12 Nov. 1852; *The Demand of the Country for Sheriff Court Reform Attested by the Resolution of Public Bodies and the Voice of the Press* (Glasgow, 1853).

185. *The Demand of the Country* ... lists these, together with town councils who also approved of the demands.

186. R. M. W. Cowan, *The Newspaper in Scotland, 1815–60* (Glasgow, 1947), p. 326.

187. *Address delivered by Andrew Bannatyne to the Glasgow Legal and Speculative Society* (Glasgow, 1856), pp. 15–19; *Demand of the Country* ..., *passim;* A Scotch Lawyer, *The Amendment of the Law, passim; Glasgow Herald,* 25 Oct. 1852.

188. E.g. *North British Daily Mail,* 19 Jan., 29 Oct. 1853; *Report of Committee of Glasgow Law Amendment Society,* pp. 7–8.

189. *Report of Committee of Glasgow Law Amendment Society,* pp. 8–10.

190. *Ibid.,* pp. 10–11; cf. *North British Daily Mail,* 24 Feb. 1855, for an editorial welcoming legislation to bring mercantile law closer in the two countries.

191. *Address ... by Andrew Bannatyne,* p. 19.

192. *Glasgow Herald,* 18 Apr. 1856. Hanham, 'Mid-Century Scottish Nationalism', pp. 161–2 suggests that the Glasgow Faculty was on the defensive against English pressure for assimilation, but this does not seem to be fully borne out by the evidence.

4

The Conservatives in the Age of Disraeli: 1865–1881

I

The Conservative advance in Scotland in the 1874 General Election was not so total as in England, but the party did still turn in, on the surface, a very creditable performance. From the miserable seven seats won in 1868, the total went up to twenty, almost exactly one third of the Scottish total. Equally revealing, three of the 1874 gains were in burgh constituencies, the first recorded in this category since Falkirk was lost in 1857. The most striking Tory urban victory came in the capture of one Glasgow seat, and this was hailed as proof that the new phenomenon of urban Conservatism obtained in Scotland as in England, an argument reinforced by the additional evidence of contesting twelve burgh seats, and polling well in most. In 1868 only five burghs had been fought, and the average vote per candidate increased by around 33% in 1874. But these results must be put in perspective. Firstly these three gains in burghs (out of a total of 26) were not only minimal compared with England, where 137 out of 285 borough seats were won, but they included largely artificial victories. Glasgow returned a Tory because of a plethora of Liberals. Four Liberals, plus a candidate appealing to Roman Catholics, stood, so splitting the anti-Tory vote badly, and with a secret ballot in operation for the first time, no scheme had been devised for ensuring that Liberals would capture all three seats. The two Conservatives received 26,667 votes, the four Liberals 43,989, and the Roman Catholic 4,444. The result was:

Cameron	(Lib)	18,455
Anderson	(Lib)	17,902
Whitelaw	(Con)	14,134
Hunter	(Con)	12,533
Crum	(Lib)	7,453
Kerr	(R.C.)	4,444
Bolton	(Lib)	169

In the opinion of Gorst, Disraeli's chief adviser, Ayr Burghs was an 'unexpected bonus', while the third seat, the Wigtown Burghs, was lost on petition.[1] Secondly, winning 15 county seats, doubling the seven held in 1868, is less impressive if it is remembered that in 1859, one of the worst elections for the party, there were 15 shire Tory M.P.s, out of a smaller total of 30 (against 32 after 1868). In 1865, the Tories held only ten county seats, so the decline had begun before the new franchise, which in any case did not alter the rural electorate.

The erosion of support in their rural power base was deeply worrying for the traditional landed Tories, and tended to divert their energies from helping to build up city Toryism. This was in clear contrast to England, where the political harmony between landlord and tenant-farmer was a feature of these years.[2] The major reason for the loss of so many county seats — together with close shaves in four or five others — over the 1865 and 1868 elections was the disaffection of the tenant-farmers, who had two major grievances which induced them to revolt. The first was the operation of the Game Laws, particularly in respect of hares and rabbits, which were treated as the property of the landlord, not the farmer. Developments in the early 1860s suggested (at least to the tenant-farmers) that farmers were being more adversely treated than in the past, as proprietors began to perceive the economic benefits to be derived from the growing interest in field sports. 'Of late years more especially', claimed a pamphlet written in 1866, 'hunting has been so very much in fashion among the rich classes as to have made the preservation of low country game a source of considerable income to needy and greedy landlords'.[3] Farmers were unable to curtail, or to secure compensation for, the depredation wrought on their crops by hares and rabbits, which was described by Wigtownshire farmers as 'absolutely destructive'.[4] Moreover, the landlord profited either by selling the carcases to butchers or by letting shooting rights, thereby, it was argued, extracting a double rent from the tenant-farmer. Further, as game became more valuable, landlords cracked down more severely on poaching. Through a loophole in the 1862 Scottish Police Act, gamekeepers could be sworn in as special constables at the instance of the lairds, who were normally the local magistracy. These gamekeeper-constables, of whom 43 were appointed in Perthshire alone in ten years, dealt solely with poaching offences, and the right to search without warrant conferred upon the special police by the 1862 Act caused a sharp deterioration in landlord-tenant relations in the countryside.[5] As virtually all poaching cases were heard before the local bench, the proprietors' power was reinforced. The position in Scotland was in contradiction to that in England, where the tenantry's right to deal with rabbits and hares was well-established.[6] The feelings of the farmers were summed up in a petition to the Lord Advocate which denounced the Game legislation as 'injurious to morals, and hurtful to the best interests of Rural Society; an Obstacle to the progress of Agriculture and the development of the productive resources of the Country'.[7]

The other farmers' issue was Hypothec — 'which no Englishman can pronounce and few Scotsmen defend', as a Tory landlord M.P. informed Disraeli.[8] Hypothec was a legal right giving the landlord absolute security for rent over a tenant's crop and livestock, and furnished far more effective protection than the English right of distress.[9] The economic result of hypothec, according to aggrieved farmers, was that landlords could impose very steep rentals in the confident knowledge that they would always be able to extort payment, while the high rents prevented farmers from fully applying their capital to agricultural improvements. Moreover, the abolition of the Corn Laws had removed the main defence of hypothec, viz. that tenants' incomes were protected, yet agricultural wages had doubled in the twenty years since the Repeal of the Corn Laws, so that the tenants' tight profit margins were being doubly squeezed.[10]

Hypothec had a further dimension to it. The above aspects only really affected tenants, and so had an impact on merely a part of the county electorate. The same was true of the Game Laws grievance, although all farmers, not just arable ones, were affected, as the greatest stockbreeder in the north-East, William McCombie, testified when reporting that his winter feed was repeatedly ravaged by ground game. Sheepfarmers claimed their grazing land was adversely affected by heather-burning and by incursions of deer from the expanding deer forests.[11] Poachers may also have been upset by the operation of the Game Laws, but they probably had little political power — although one bank manager did darkly confess to having suffered through the Game Laws.[12] Two facts about hypothec broadened opposition to it to include those interests servicing the needs of the agricultural community, and so mobilised a wide front for political change. Firstly, a case in 1864 (Allen v Burns) determined that the landlord had the right to invoke hypothec over the tenant's produce even if it had been sold to a third party. The second matter was that hypothec established the landlord's status as a preferential creditor ranking above most general creditors, a fact which created great unease among the suppliers of goods and services to farmers. Hence auctioneers, corn and manure merchants, seedsmen, bank managers, blacksmiths and other village tradesmen were all to be found actively supporting the agitation to abolish hypothec. Thus at a large protest meeting held in Easter Ross in 1873, the banker at Tain, Mr. Ross, led the denunciations of the evil of hypothec.[13] Analysis of the evidence presented before the Select Committee on Hypothec reveals this gulf: 41 witnesses were broadly favourable to the existing system, and 57 advocated substantial diminution. Landlords divided 6 for the status quo, 2 against; their factors, 27 for, 3 against; tenant farmers came out 7 for, 31 against; while merchants, auctioneers, bankers and maltsters were 1 for, 21 against.[14]

While these economic arguments probably had a degree of validity, of themselves they do not explain the political revolt of the tenantry. In the first instance, there were presentable arguments for retaining both laws. The Game Laws, in view of the weak law of trespass in Scotland, in fact served to protect farmers from damage done by poachers. Hypothec encouraged landlords to take the risk of letting to small farmers, so stimulating the prospects of upward social mobility among farm servants. Moreover, both laws had been in force for many years, and the evidence for an intensification of their operation in the 1860s is not fully convincing. Significantly, there had been (as discussed in Chapter 3) moves by the tenantry in the 1847 general election to secure a promise from the candidates to seek the relaxation of the Game Laws in the East Lothian and Fife seats. However, at least in East Lothian, the power of the lairds was a partial factor in forcing a withdrawal by the farmers of their nominee from the contest.[15] The change in the 1860s may have stemmed not so much from an objective deterioration in the farmers' experience of these two laws, as from a new feeling among them. The farmers wished to reject deference and to assert their due political weight, and the Game and Hypothec questions became the most evident and repellent reminders of their social subordination. This theme is repeatedly stressed. The ablest tenant-farmer of the age, Hope of Fenton Barns, ran against Lord Elcho in East Lothian in 1865, alleging in his election address that Elcho regarded Hope's action as 'a piece of presumption ... the rebellion of a servile race'.[16] An equally eminent farmer — the pioneer of the Aberdeen-Angus breed — argued in the same year that raising these issues constituted part of the age of emancipation. There had been the emancipation of trade, of slaves, and now came 'the emancipation of the tenant farmer from that craven spirit of subserviency which has too long characterised the majority of us'.[17] Rural middle-class consciousness had thus been formed among these prosperous, innovative and intelligent farmers, as the editor of *The Scotsman* testified. Of their revolt, he noted: ' ... there is a little touch of class in it. They thought, as a class, they did not hold their proper position, and they are men of capital and education generally'.[18] This emergent sense of common identity was institutionalised in two bodies both founded in 1864. One was the Chamber of Agriculture which aimed to discuss topics of interest to farmers and to lobby for their interests.[19] The other was the Scottish Farmers Club, with premises at South St. Andrew Street, Edinburgh.

The rejection of political deference was an automatic conclusion of these developments, fuelled by the analysis of the perpetuation of these injustices, which was ascribed to the return to Parliament by farmers of landlords indifferent to the interest of the tenantry when the latter's conflicted with the former's. This resolve to end social subordination was widespread, as when in 1872 the Angus farmers insisted on running J. W. Barclay, a merchant and farmer, against a cadet branch of the Dalhousie family, in order to establish the rejection of the political control of Brechin Castle.[20] Similarly, the Liberal in Perthshire in 1868 was praised as a model candidate for visiting not the mansions of the lairds, but the farmhouses of the tenantry.[21] These attitudes were sharpened by the conclusions of the Select Committee on Hypothec in 1865 that there were only minor defects in the law. A Kincardineshire farmer told the Tory candidate in the county that the evidence was socially biased: 'Na, na they took guid care to seek nane o' my class (laughter and applause)'.[22] A flurry of pamphlets and meetings all stressed the point that the franchise should be deployed to end these injustices.[23] The changed mood and resolution were summed up by a Cromarty farmer in 1873: 'The day is gone by when the so-called farmers' friends, when soliciting our votes, would pat us on the back and call us a set of jolly good fellows, highly intelligent and all that sort of thing, and then when subjects affecting our interests came on before Parliament would vote dead against us, and explain their conduct away by saying that we were a set of clod-hoppers who hardly knew the difference between a cow and a pig, and rudely add that we should mind our clods, and not meddle with politics ... We have got power now if we care to use it'.[24]

This process shifted the political balance in county seats. In 1868 the Dumfriesshire tenants of the Duke of Buccleuch voted against his party, to his factor's consternation: 'I scarcely expected this and it shows what a change has taken place in the county', so that the Liberal victory was interpreted as 'a sort of mutiny of [Buccleuch's] supposed influence'.[25] The candidate for the next general election intimated that he would run only if his own tenants would not oppose him: a far cry from the previous confident assumption of unwavering support.[26] In Perthshire, a similar situation existed: 'One thing is clear', remarked the ex-M.P., 'that the political power of the County is — for this Election at least —wholly in the hands of the farmers'.[27] In the election which deposed the writer of that letter as M.P., a landowner with estates in both countries drew a distinction between England and Scotland: 'I have taken means to let our Perthshire Tenantry know our interest in your success, but I have little faith in the effects of a landlord's wishes in a political question among Scotch tenants'.[28] By 1880 things had reached such a state that a prospective Liberal candidate for Kirkcudbrightshire had to be rejected, with a revealing order of priorities: 'The objections to Knocknalling are insuperable . . . He *is* unsound on Rabbits and he *is* (or at least *was*) unsound on the Trinity'.[29]

Simply because they held so many rural seats, rather than through any ideological repudiation, the Conservatives were the primary casualties of the new political current among tenant-farmers. In 1865, Kincardineshire was the bellwether: a seat held by the Conservatives since 1832, and unopposed in every election after 1832, was lost. The new Tory candidate, Sir Thomas Gladstone, had a reputation as a fervent game preserver: he was alleged to sell shot rabbits to his tenantry at one penny below shop prices.[30] The Liberal, J. D. Nicol, fought the contest almost solely on farmers' grievances, of which, as a Tory clergyman informed Gladstone, 'the Game Laws in their present form were now their chief hardship'.[31] Gladstone's choice of the Game Law Procurator Fiscal as his election agent was less than diplomatic, and even his own tenants declined to vote for him. The farmers in the constituency organised local meetings to discuss the leading questions of the day, they heckled Gladstone vigorously and, as a Conservative agent observed, were dedicated electioneers: 'We must never lose sight of the fact that, above and beyond all, Mr. Nicol has the immense advantage of the most active and energetic assistance of a number of very influential young farmers who is [sic] making his case their own, are working night and day for him'.[32] Nicol won by the convincing margin of 490 to 288.

Elsewhere, the process was also in train in 1865. Stirling County, Tory and uncontested for twenty-five years, was lost. The sitting M.P., Peter Blackburn, was dislodged because, said the local Conservative newspaper, the Game Law 'has really been the bugbear in this election', the more so as Blackburn had assisted actively in passing the Night Poaching Act.[33] In East Lothian, Hope of Fenton Barns claimed that most of the larger tenants voted for him, or abstained in a contest fought 'between landlord and tenant, with game-preserving and the law of Hypothec as the bones of contention'.[34] Elcho managed to repulse Hope's assault, but not without difficulty. In West Lothian, a candidate acceptable to the farmers was selected by the Tories, 'after long and anxious debate', in preference to both a landowner and a prominent industrialist on the grounds that he had the greatest prospect of success.[35] The candidate, Peter MacLagan, won the seat, and when in Parliament pronounced himself a Liberal and became a staunch critic of the Game Laws, thus rendering himself impregnable for thirty years against Conservative hopes of regaining the seat: 'We stupidly *sold* ourselves to a turncoat . . . and since 1868 have paid the penalty'.[36]

The momentum was maintained by a by-election in Tory Aberdeenshire in

1866, a seat which until 1861 had been tightly controlled by Haddo House. A Liberal landowner, William Dingwall-Fordyce, who urged the farmers to unite and organise against the unjust Game and Hypothec laws, won comfortably, to rejoicing at the end of landlord influence in rural seats.[37] Two seats were created by the 1868 redistribution in Aberdeenshire, and at the ensuing election, Fordyce retained the Eastern seat, while McCombie, a leader in the farmers' movement, won the Western constituency, having campaigned on these grievances to telling effect.[38] The 1868 general election saw further bastions of Conservatism collapse in the face of tenant-farmer unrest. In Dumfries the farmers defeated the Tory, as has been noted. In both Ayrshire seats, Liberals won with the aid of the agricultural vote in a campaign which prominently featured Game and Hypothec reform.[39] The most stunning instance of the extent of the farmers' protest came in Perthshire, still seen as one of the most important county seats, with agricultural interests predominant. Here Sir William Stirling-Maxwell, a man of culture and distinction, a good landlord and a long-serving M.P., was cast aside in favour of a latecomer fighting a short campaign begun ten weeks after the Tories launched theirs. The Liberal chief whip had confessed himself as 'being at his wits' end' trying to pick a candidate for this 'very difficult' or, at best, 'not hopeless' seat.[40] The Liberals decided that the only policy to fight on was the Game Law question, and their candidate, C. S. Parker, plugged that issue relentlessly and to great effect, so that, as a Tory agent stated, at Callander 'Shepherds' dogs and game laws were his trump cards'. From all parts of the county it was reported by local Conservatives that, as in Methven, 'the Game question is the one great point with the tenant farmers', and several farmers wrote to Stirling-Maxwell to explain their objections at length.[41] Although Stirling-Maxwell stressed that in 1867 he had supported a bill to modify the Game Laws, he could not offer so much as Parker, inasmuch as he would not interfere by legislation with existing leases which reserved game rights to the landlord. To this his questioner, William Scrimgeour, a Crieff farmer, riposted that when passing the Factory Acts the Tories had been willing enough to interfere with the contractual relations between employer and labourer.[42] Stirling-Maxwell was decisively beaten by 279 votes in a seat last fought by the Liberals in 1840. Elsewhere, Conservatives held on by slender margins: in Peebles and Selkirk, by three votes, while in East Lothian their majority was cut in half, from 126 to 65.

II

Despite the severity of the setback, the 1865 and 1868 results only gradually weaned the Scottish Tories from indifference to the political trend. At the outset of the 1868 campaign a Perthshire laird argued that there were no serious problems among the farmers — 'except want of rain'.[43] Likewise, the Stirlingshire Conservatives blamed their loss of the seat in 1865 on their candidate's railway interests having upset several voters.[44] A good number in many seats shared Lord

Ailsa's view of the defeat in South Ayrshire in 1868: 'Our failure was brought about by the revolutionary spirit of the ministers of the Free and U.P. churches who domineered over the members of their congregations'.[45] While it is true that the disestablishment of the Church of Ireland was electorally popular, these setbacks cannot be attributed solely to that issue. Support for the non-established churches was probably weakest in the rural areas of the North-East, while Wigtownshire, long a centre of Presbyterian dissent, actually swung to the Tories in 1868. What these statements by the Tories reveal is the gulf in understanding between landowners and their tenants which had opened up in this period. Disraeli had shrewdly detected it in 1865: 'The state of Scotland alone is most serious. All influence appears to have slipped away from its proprietors . . . '; and he feared that if matters were not promptly redressed, the Conservatives' aspirations of holding office would be fatally damaged.[46] Sir James Fergusson, Disraeli's consultant on Scotland, took up the theme in 1868: 'I am strongly of opinion that if the Scottish country gentlemen have sufficient energy to profit by the lessons of the late elections their defeat may easily be reversed'.[47]

By the 1874 election, Fergusson's predictions seemed correct as eight net gains were logged up in shire seats. Part of these gains arose from dissatisfaction among farmers at the inaction of the Gladstone government over their grievances. The Lord Advocate had warned Gladstone that C. S. Parker was right to claim that 'the Scotch farmers may manifest their disappointment unpleasantly at the next election if nothing is done for them before that event'.[48] The Lord Advocate himself had received from politically sympathetic farmers expressions of dismay at the Liberals' failure to act.[49] This neglect was partly because, as at times in the past, Scottish legislation occupied a low priority in the Government's timetable, so that the Lord Advocate's programme was not brought to the Commons until three months before the dissolution of the Parliament.[50] Moreover, reform of the Game Laws in particular was no more palatable to Whig than to Tory landlords, and the challenge of tenant-farmers to the political influence of proprietors had equally distasteful implications for Whig magnates. So, as we have seen, the victory of J. W. Barclay in Angus in 1872 was directed against the Liberal Lord Dalhousie's power. In 1874, the Inverness-shire farmers insisted that they would support the laird of Ballindalloch as Liberal candidate only if he adopted their demands. When he declined, they opted to field a radical London barrister, Augustus Smith, against him. This scheme was firmly squashed by the Liberal managers in Scotland, W.P. Adam and A. Craig Sellar, both of landed background.[51] Sellar indicated the Whig estimate of the farmers: 'The Liberal committee means I fancy the four or five farmers who frightened Grant away. I do not think the Govt. should have anything to do with Smith'.[52]

In 1874, therefore, Tories were able to exploit the deafness to farming demands shown by the Liberals in office. Stirling-Maxwell based his election campaign strategy in Perthshire heavily on this point, and won by that means, as did the Tories in South Ayrshire and Inverness-shire.[53] In addition, it was felt on both sides that the Gladstone administration was guilty of sins of commission as well as of omission. The imposition of gun and dog taxes irritated farmers, as, more obscurely, did the tax on cards. Furthermore, the introduction of an education rate to finance the new national school system laid down by the 1872 Act upset the tenantry by adding to their financial problems, especially as in many rural areas the deficiencies of the old parochial schools were less apparent than in towns.[54] So in the Blairgowrie area, a Tory paper reported, excitedly abandoning the rules of grammar: 'The school rate is acting like an irritant poison upon Liberal palates, and every ratepayer is imprecating the rash man and the unwise Government who has [sic] made such an attack upon their [sic] trouser pocket'.[55] A Liberal journal in Roxburghshire, a seat lost by its party, agreed: 'farmers feel aggrieved at being taxed for education under the recent act, nor can they forget that the questions of game and hypothec are no further advanced toward a settlement than they were in 1868'.[56]

But the Tories had gone beyond simply playing upon the iniquities of the Liberals: they also stressed that they had now accepted the demands of the tenantry on these two issues. 'Who would have thought', pondered the farmers' paper, 'that in this year of grace, loud as the complaints have been against the Law of Hypothec there should not be a single aspirant to Parliamentary honours, whether Radical, Whig or Tory, who was not ready to vote for the total abolition of Hypothec ... It is so far gratifying that every candidate in the counties north of the Tweed declaring that as the tenants don't wish a continuation of that law, the landlords don't require, and therefore it need no longer stand in the way'.[57] The formulation employed by Conservatives was instructive, as in North Ayrshire where the Tory, after starting his personal opinion that the law of hypothec was fair to tenants, added: 'but as it is entirely a question for them [the tenants], I am quite willing to meet their views on the subject'.[58]

This new realism marked a significant shift in political relations between landlord and tenant, which was epitomised in the change in attitude between the 1873 by-election in Berwickshire and the general election eight months later. In the former, the Liberals kept the seat, doubtless partly because of the insensitivity to farmers' status anxieties expressed by the chairman of the Conservative meeting at Duns who, upon the candidate indicating a willingness to answer questions, quickly interposed: 'I think he has answered everything [in his speech], there is no use putting off time with questions, for some of you will be asking questions that you don't understand anything about'. To compound this, at a later meeting in Aytoun, the local laird, Captain Mitchell-Innes, defined the Tory candidate's credentials in terms which tenant-farmers found grating, given their views on landowners noted earlier. The Captain said: 'They knew very well that Lord Dunglass was not experienced in political matters ... They knew ... that he was not only a noble but a gentleman bred and born, that he had all the principles, tastes and views which befit his high station in life. He thought that when they considered these claims they could hardly hesitate to say that he ought to be sent to Parliament to represent that county in which he had so much interest'.[59] His successor as Conservative candidate in the general election of 1874, the Hon. R. B. Hamilton, struck a note perhaps more calculated to appeal to the self-importance of the farmers when, in contrast to Dunglass's declaration that he was inclined to give the existing system of hypothec a longer trial, Hamilton announced that he would support the abolition of that law 'in deference to what I have ascertained to be the general wish of the tenant-farmers'.[60] Deference was thus inverted, and the Tory seized the seat, increasing his poll by 20%.

Thus, county Tories had to spend the late 1860s and early 1870s mending fences (literally and metaphorically) with their tenants. A local agent explained to Stirling-Maxwell what was involved in this process in Perthshire, where the Liberal was working skilfully: 'He seems to go to the smallest village and speaks to everyone as if he had been born and bred in Perthshire. People will expect you to do some work of that kind'.[61] The Conservative paper in that county stressed that this reassertion of rural community bonds was the key to the party's victory there in 1874: 'The lairds and tenants have for the most part gone hand in hand ... They have common interests which require they should stand together, not apart ... They have done much to help the welding together of the two sections of the community ... The Perthshire election of 1874 will have failed to achieve the good which it ought to achieve if it does not have upon the minds of the lairds of Perthshire a deep and strong conviction that the best interests of the county require, not only at the moment of a contest, but at all times, that they and their tenants should make common cause'.[62]

In addition to establishing close ties with the farmers, the shire Tories improved organisation in their seats in various ways. Firstly, there was a shift from the loose informal structure which was prevalent until the reverses of 1865 and 1868.[63] In 1864, with a by-election looming in Fife, a local landowner and ardent hunter recalled: 'I found a fox and ran a bit, but had to stop, as I had to go to a Conservative meeting in Cupar. Before going in to the meeting I met John Cairns and Peter Dingwall, my tenants, who said, 'You will be asked to stand for the county to oppose Sir Robert Anstruther.' ' After agreeing to stand, the laird discovered that the party had done no registration work for years and had few agents of calibre. As a preliminary sample canvass was depressing, he withdrew: 'I hated the whole business, and I was awfully tired and I had a buzzing in my ears, from which I have never recovered'.[64] If a committee did exist, it comprised, as in West Lothian in 1865, about ten self-selected proprietors who met infrequently to choose a candidate, and did little else.[65] These defects were promptly remedied, as local committees were set up, on a broad representative footing. In Stirlingshire, after the seat was lost in successive elections, the old party leaders met to institutionalise and expand the party: 'We then formed ourselves into a Stirlingshire Conservative Association to include any Conservatives who may wish to join ... '[66] It was particularly the object of these bodies to bring in tenant-farmers, as in Perthshire after the 1868 defeat: 'Let there be an influential General Committee consisting of the Proprietors and a very limited sprinkling of Farmers etc., and local committees of Gentlemen and Farmers'.[67] To aid this, subscription fees were either not charged, as in Stirlingshire, or kept very low, as in the West Kilbride association, where the bulk of the thirty-two subscribers paid 2/- (10p) or under annually, and seem to have been drawn from the ranks of the tenantry.[68] The Wigtownshire Association, formed in 1873, had a tariff of subscriptions which specifically identified tenant-farmers as a category of subscribers and this body helped to retain the seat won in 1868.[69] The Earl of Galloway recognised the necessity of formal organisation to stimulate participation when he described the Kirkcudbrightshire Conservative Association: 'It is my own thing and I am proud of it. It is the only way of keeping a party united'.[70]

The second aspect of organisational improvement was that efficiency was imposed where previously ignorance and incompetence had held sway. In Stirlingshire in 1865 the registers had been hopelessly neglected by the Conservatives during their long ascendancy. Moreover, there was no agent, and so, as before, estate factors were requested to canvass — probably an unwise procedure in light of the growing independent-mindedness of the tenant-farmers.[71] In the aftermath of the defeat in 1868 in Dumfriesshire, the call was for 'a first-class agent trained in England to organise the canvass', and other counties adopted the same professionalism.[72] Perthshire best exemplified this new businesslike approach. Instead of the previous type of *ad hoc* body summoned for the duration of an election and then stood down, a central committee was created to keep organisation functioning continuously between the 1868 and 1874 elections, which it did mainly by establishing twelve district committees with local agents and squads of enthusiastic local workers.[73] For example, in 1872 in the Crieff area, copies of pamphlets outlining Conservative principles were distributed to all who had voted Tory in 1868, to all doubtful and to all new voters. Perhaps even more important, the Crieff local agent succeeded in at last establishing that the chairman of the central committee was Sir Thomas Moncrieffe, and not, as he had until then believed, John Smythe. Things could only move upwards thereafter.[74] These new associations were especially successful in registration work: in Liberal-held Roxburghshire, by 1869 the incumbent party was extremely disturbed at the advances being made in this department by the Tories.[75] Indeed, the seat fell to the Conservatives in 1874. The main organ of the tenant-farmers ascribed the Tory gains in 1874 in large measure to superior organisation.[76]

This evidence of organisational efficiency in shire seats is somewhat at odds with the picture painted by Crapster, who, basing his argument on a survey conducted in 1876 on Disraeli's behalf into local Conservative parties in Scotland, highlighted the unrepresentative dominance of lairds and the utter lack of expertise as endemic characteristics.[77] However, most of the survey is devoted to the North-East and the Highlands, with a much smaller portion looking at Angus, Fife, Stirling and East Lothian. There is nothing on Perthshire, the Borders or the Western Lowlands. The report therefore concentrates overwhelmingly on those parts where the Conservative recovery in 1874 was not manifest: of the fifteen Tory county seats in 1874, only one was in the North-East and Highland regions, but these districts gave the Liberals ten of their seventeen shire constituencies. One of the major compilers of the report was Horace Skeete, who was instrumental in resurrecting Conservative organisation in Perthshire after 1868. His strictures on the inadequate performance of local proprietors seem to be true of Northern Scotland (for instance, Cameron of Lochiel repeatedly lamented the apathy of his fellow-lairds in the Inverness-shire seat he held), but not generally applicable in the Lowlands.[78]

III

Preoccupied with retaining and then holding their own county fastnesses, the gentry took little interest in sponsoring the growth of urban Toryism in Scotland, and they had little appreciation of its nature and aspirations.[79] The organisational link set up in England between town and country in 1867, the National Union, had no real counterpart in Scotland until 1882.[80] There was formed — also in 1867 — the Scottish National Constitutional Association (SNCA), but it remained passive and dilatory in its role. In the 1868 election it declared its work had been unobtrusive, but critics might have termed it non-existent. It repeatedly stressed that, apart from diffusing information, it would not seek to direct local parties, but only offer assistance on request. It did not produce model rules for local party associations until 1878, and it seems to have made no effort to follow up its general circulars suggesting means of improving organisation in order to check whether they were being implemented. There was something rather lukewarm in the President's defence of the SNCA on the eve of its dissolution: 'It did a great deal of good'.[81] The Association failed to play the same role as the English National Union, partly because it apparently lacked any representative framework to encourage local bodies to participate in its deliberations, as membership was on an individual basis.[82] The Association may also have been limited in its efficacy by essentially consisting of the landed classes and Edinburgh advocates. In 1872 it had 321 members, 51 of whom were titled and 113 gentry; 101 of the total had Edinburgh addresses, with only 8 Glasgow ones. By 1882 there were 19 more peers and only 3 more Glaswegians in the membership, and on the 24-man management committee in that year there were 14 landowners, 8 advocates, 1 publisher and 1 Glasgow businessman. Indeed, only 5 of the 24 had any obvious links with the West of Scotland, the basis for any urban Tory breakthrough. Small wonder that a leading Glasgow-based business Tory, while sending a subscription in 1868, in response to a request to drum up others, wrote: 'This matter has been taken up among friends here who have received your communication, and while wishing to be with you they have had doubts as to the policy of the Association'.[83] If the SNCA found it difficult to get on a firm footing with the new school of middle-class Conservatives, its attitude to working-class Tories was that of having unearthed a zoological curiosity. Noting the emergence of Working Men's Conservative Associations in Dundee and Glasgow, the SNCA hastened to reassure members: 'Conservatism has nothing to fear from, but on the contrary, much to gain by the criticisms of its professions and practice by thinking men in the few hours they have of relief from labour — hours which it has been the privilege of Conservative legislation to secure'.[84] Typically, the SNCA produced model rules for counties a year ahead of those for burghs. Its loose grasp of the sociological aspects of urban life is suggested by the contrast in its recommendations as to the social composition of local committees in county and burgh seats. In the former, it stipulated they should consist of one half landlords, the other tenants and villagers, while in towns it was evasive as to the social structure to be mirrored in organisation: 'Friends of all classes acquainted with the neighbourhood' was all it could offer.[85]

The absence of close contact between the social wings of Scottish Conservatism is further illustrated by the efforts to found a party newspaper. It was a general refrain that the dearth of Conservative journals was in considerable measure the cause of the party's difficulties in Scotland.[86] 'Our great need at present is undoubtedly a newspaper, and I should be very glad to see one started', Brodie of Brodie wrote in 1874, explaining why he felt unable to stand as a candidate in Moray and Nairn with any chance of victory.[87] Before 1873 the only reliably loyal paper was *The Edinburgh Courant,* but it was unsatisfactory in several respects. A candid critique of the *Courant* by a Tory journalist in London predicted that 'ruin is inevitable', since 'the prevailing characteristics of these Articles are Confusion of idea, Looseness of expression and wordiness ... The tone seems as objectionable as the style'. Also — 'perhaps more fatal' — the type was too small for train passengers to read.[88] The *Courant* did not have a wide circulation and had in particular little readership in the West, where the *Glasgow Herald* and the *North British Daily Mail,* both Liberal, were the staple reading diet of the very middle classes the Tories hoped to win over. The response of the lairds to this crisis was simply to concentrate on saving the *Courant,* which had been in a parlous financial condition since the death of its principal benefactor in 1864. A group headed by Sir James Fergusson, Graham Montgomery of Kinross and A. C. Swinton of Kimmerghame launched a rescue bid. By late 1868 they had raised £8,000 out of the necessary £10,000, and it was confidently predicted that on the attainment of Lord Bute's majority the remainder would be forthcoming.[89]

The recurring problems of the *Courant* led the SNCA, long disturbed at the absence of good propaganda sheets, to initiate the formation of the Scottish Newspaper Company in early 1872, with the objective of taking over the *Courant* and also promoting provincial weeklies. The managers and owners of the company were mainly landowners and Edinburgh lawyers and, inspired by their enterprise, a daily Tory paper was begun in Aberdeen on capital of £16,000, and a weekly was also started in Inverness.[90]

These efforts, it will be seen, were focused largely on the East of Scotland. In the West, in 1873, a daily Tory paper, *The Glasgow News,* was first published. The main finance for the *News,* which was floated with a healthy capital of £50,000, came from James Baird, a wealthy ironmaster, and his nephew, Alexander Whitelaw, who put up £35,000 between them, along with leading city businessmen Tories like James Campbell, a warehouse owner, and William Kidston, an iron broker. A few gentry with intimate Glasgow links, such as A. Campbell of Blythswood and Sir G. Campbell of Garscube, also participated, but it proved difficult to raise much from other landed Tories. Buccleuch, for all his wealth, put up only £2,500; the Earl of Moray gave £1,000 to the *Courant,* nothing to the *News.* In Perthshire, Stirling-Maxwell admittedly gave £6,000 to the *News,* but James Baird's urgent request that Stirling-Maxwell should also approach 'the rich noblesse and landed gentlemen of Perthshire' did not produce results.[91] On the other hand, the proprietors of the *News*, it appears, chose not to be associated with the bid to salvage the *Courant*, keeping aloof because they felt the *News* would be better able as an independent organ to take readers from the Glasgow Liberal press.[92]

The *News* was reasonably successful, selling 10–13,000 copies a day, but by 1879 it was in acute need of financial aid, partly because Baird had died some years previously. The editor, rather than directly approach any landowners, went to Disraeli's secretary to ask for his aid in raising the cash, and pointed out that a number of leading landowners — Fergusson, Sir Charles Dalrymple and Lord Glasgow — had already declined to help, because they disliked the paper's tone. A specific complaint by the editor was that Tory proprietors were reluctant to advertise in the paper, whereas if Conservative agents could ensure that town and country advertisements were inserted solely in the *News*, and not in Radical organs, it would induce farmers to read the paper, 'with the natural result that Conservative opinion would spread and the landed interest would be conserved'.[93] The rescuer of the paper, however, proved to be a wealthy Glasgow shipbuilder, William Pearce, who pumped a vast amount of money into the *News*. The *Courant* in the meantime continued to ail, while the *News* found it increasingly hard to bite into the *Herald's* readership, and so finally in 1886 the two Conservative papers merged, mainly through pressures of economic reality rather than because of any east-west harmony, to become *The Scottish News*. This did little to stop the protests about the lack of decent Tory journals, but with both *The Scotsman* and the *Herald* turning Unionist, there was no scope in either city for *The Scottish News*, and it folded in 1888.

Another episode demonstrating the gulf between the traditional Tories and the newer groups moving towards Conservatism was the decision by Disraeli's 1874 government to legislate for the abolition of lay patronage in the Church of Scotland. This of course had been the central issue over which the Disruption had taken place, and it had become widely believed in both Tory and state church circles after 1869 that its abolition would facilitate the return to the national church of a large number of Free Church adherents. The Free Church constitutionalists had by their fervent opposition to the negotiations for union with the U.P. Church asserted very clearly their commitment to the establishment principle, and might well decide to quit a Free Church now openly Voluntary. The extent of this pro-establishment feeling was hard to quantify, but it was noted that in the Glasgow Free Presbytery, where the union case was carried by 63 votes to 40, the majority for merger was much larger among the clergy (36 to 20) than among the laity (27 to 20).[94] The surprisingly large body of Free Church opinion (again, the Tories noted, bigger among laity than ministers) which was engaged alongside the Church of Scotland in the agitation to retain Religious Instruction in schools heightened expectations, as the Lord Advocate, E. S. Gordon, told Disraeli: 'The discussion of this question [patronage] and of the Education question has done much to obliterate animosities'.[95] Within the state church, a sizeable section felt that the removal of patronage was not so much desirable as necessary. Norman MacLeod concluded that there was a need to combat fears that a merged Free and U.P. Church would revive the demand for disestablishment, since the existing national church would be numerically inferior. The best solution, for MacLeod, was to seek a large intake into the established church of anti-Voluntary Free Churchmen.[96] As the Liberals were hardly likely to accommodate these demands of the Church of Scotland, leading Scottish Tories, like Fergusson, Sir J. C. Dalrymple Hay, A. C. Swinton and, above all, E. S. Gordon, all stressed to Disraeli that this gave the Tory party a great opportunity to widen and consolidate its hold on the middle class. 'I believe,' said Gordon, 'however that if carried out it will effect great benefit both to ecclesiastical and political interests'.[97]

While the Disraeli administration procrastinated over redressing tenant-farmer grievances for its entire life, it immediately acted to abolish patronage, eliciting at the Church of Scotland General Assembly in 1874 a warm reception. The Lord High Commissioner assured the Prime Minister that the bill 'will add to the strong hold exercised and affection felt by the Scottish Church for the Conservative Party', and a year later he confirmed that expectations of a numerous Free Church influx were widely held.[98] In practice, hardly any F.C. clergy and a very few laymen came back to the national church, and the leaders of the anti-Union movement, such as James Begg and William Kidston, did not budge. This abject miscalculation in large part arose because all the Tories urging the abolition of patronage, as identified in the preceding paragraph, were of landed background, none had any direct Free Church links, and few were even in the Church of Scotland. Those nearer to the feelings of the anti-union Frees were less sanguine. Whitelaw, the only Tory M.P. for a major urban seat (Glasgow), had very close ties with the Free Church constitutionalists because of the education campaigns, and he was ultra-cautious: 'I am sorry to have to confess to an uneasy feeling on the issue of the moment [i.e. patronage abolition] which is being conducted. I wish it may turn out well for the Church and country'.[99] Michael Connal may be taken as the archetype of the anti-union Free Church man who should have been attracted by this bill. Connal was a wealthy Glasgow merchant, a Tory in politics and an ardent Free Church constitutionalist, yet he wrote in his diary: 'I cannot be a party to Disestablishment, as on the other hand, I cannot join the Establishment . . . But for the existence and prosperity of the Free Church she would never have got rid of patronage, and the State has never acknowledged the wrong she did to the party who left in 1843'.[100] Thus there was a complete failure to grasp the sense of injustice so powerfully felt by the Free Church, both because it was not consulted in any way over the bill and because it received no recognition of the sacrifices it had made over thirty years for the principle now enacted. The Tory mishandling of this complex problem was emphasised by the impact of the Patronage Abolition Act on the pro-union Free Church elements. They were now driven by the Act towards openly accepting the need for disestablishment, and the Free General Assembly pronounced in favour of disestablishment on the evening of the day on which the state church General Assembly endorsed the bill. The Free Church formed the Scottish Disestablishment Association to agitate for redress of the grievance felt to be produced by legislative benefits conferred on a minority church.[101] The Conservatives thus instigated the major crisis of later nineteenth-century Scottish politics which challenged the survival of the very church they were seeking to make secure.

Nor did the Tories' bill win the united support of the established church, as had been intended. Many in the Broad Church camp — that is, those of liberal theological opinions — were distinctly alarmed lest the accession of hordes of Low Church Frees would tilt the balance within the state church sharply against the progressives. In 1873 James Baird had set up a trust fund of £500,000 to install evangelical clergymen in Church of Scotland pulpits and so to counter Broad Church tendencies. The Baird Trust was administered by Baird himself and Whitelaw, with prominent progressives like John Caird, William Tulloch and R. H. Story as the targets of the scheme. In view of the political colouring of Baird and Whitelaw, the conclusions drawn about the motives for ending lay patronage were straightforward. Thus R. H. Story, a leading exponent of the new theology, was exceptionally and vociferously unhappy about these political and ecclesiastical trends.[102] The Broad Churchmen were, by and large, in positions of influence over the solid prosperous middle classes. Caird had been minister of the elite Park Church in Glasgow before becoming Principal of Glasgow University in 1873, a post in which he was followed by Story, while Tulloch was a renowned Principal of St. Andrews University. Hence the respectable middle classes, the potential voters the Tories hoped to reach, were probably swayed by the anti-conservatism (theologically) of these ministers. *The Glasgow Herald,* a staunch defender of the rights of the Church of Scotland, and widely read by the better-off in the West of Scotland, was bitterly hostile to the Patronage Abolition Act. It argued that because the bill pandered to High Tory Lawyers and ultramontane theologians, it would assuredly not promote Presbyterian reunion but rather incite Liberals of many hues to advocate disestablishment. The bill was roundly condemned as 'retrograde legislation', and the paper praised the opposition's stance: 'Most of the reason and the argument have been on their side, but reason, facts or statistics have not in the least degree influenced the Ministry'.[103] Thus while urban Conservatism remained in the eyes of the respectable citizens tainted with Orangeism (for reasons discussed below) and as long as upper-class Tory leaders in Scotland seemed to out of touch with the real sentiments of the solid bourgeoisie, there were good reasons for this class to stay on the Liberal side.

IV

Conservative leaders and managers in Scotland looked with foreboding at their party prospects in urban seats under the widened franchise introduced by the Second Reform Act. As they held no burghs in the last Parliament before the new franchise came into play, this seemed extremely negative thinking. Sir Graham Montgomery, M.P. for Peeblesshire, told Disraeli in 1867: 'As for the Boroughs

[sic], their case is well-nigh hopeless, one or two might however be contested'.[104] Yet at least one glimmer of hope could be discerned in the 1868 results: Fergusson pointed out to Disraeli the 'remarkable fact' that 10,000 voted in Glasgow for 'a very indifferent Conservative candidate'.[105] The formation of working men's Conservative Associations was a characteristic of the early years of the new franchise: Dundee, Edinburgh, Glasgow and Greenock all possessed such bodies.[106] The Conservative vote rose markedly in 1874 in burghs, most notably in Montrose (over 80%) and Ayr (up some 60%). Although, as noted earlier, the victory in Glasgow was a fluke, it should not mask the clear advance in voting numbers — from 10,000 in 1868 to 14,000 in 1874 — and the membership of the city Conservative Association in 1874 numbered 2,800.

The basis for this increase in support was not an appeal to the social reform tradition of radical Toryism. Smith and Blake have convincingly demonstrated that this was not a major strand in the thinking of the party leadership.[107] However, in some urban areas local leaders were more sympathetic. The emergence in Manchester of W. J. Maclure and W. R. Callender, upholding trade union rights, temperance legislation and the principle of cooperative societies, is a case in point.[108] This was at times indeed stressed, notably in an address given in 1867 to the Edinburgh Workingmen Tories by Charles Scott. He claimed that working men were deeply patriotic, not revolutionary, instancing their involvement in the Volunteer movement, so Conservatives did not fear anarchy as a result of the new enfranchisement. On the contrary, Tories looked to the vote being used to produce social reform in housing and sanitary conditions, in which they, who 'have never identified themselves with the laws of political economy' — the cause of much of the distress — would support working men. Education should be compulsory, with free higher education for the brightest. Legal and judicial reform should be enacted to eliminate the oppression which fostered criminality. The great class gulf now so evident in Scotland, said Scott, could best be closed if the working class sought to regain the cultural traditions of the past, and in this they would be supported by the aristocracy and the Tory party.[109] But Scott was atypical, and was not embraced by the party leadership as representing a central strand in Scottish Toryism. E. S. Gordon described Scott to Disraeli's secretary in terms of awe, as one who did understand the working class, implying the uniqueness of this ability.[110] Scott was never given a winnable seat, instead being sent in 1874 to fight Perth city, one of the safest Liberal strongholds.

But Edinburgh may be misleading, for, as Lord Dalkeith told Disraeli: 'there is a stronger Conservative feeling among the lower classes in the West than in the East'.[111] Here, too, however, commitment to social reform was limited. Of the five Tory candidates for Glasgow in the three general elections of 1868, 1874 and 1880, only one candidate explicitly referred to such issues in his election address. He was Whitelaw, the only successful candidate, but he did not win on these grounds, and once in Parliament, he spoke on only five occasions. In four of these he made brief contributions on local, church and educational matters, but never on any of the numerous major social reform bills of the 1874–76 era. His sole major speech was to second the motion on the Queen's Speech in 1875. Here Whitelaw first surveyed foreign, imperial, colonial and Irish affairs before turning to domestic reforms, and although he did dwell at some length on housing standards, he clearly regarded such issues as of secondary importance: 'The need for such legislation is clamant, and it is well that Parliament should, in the absence of exciting policies, devote itself to these problems'.[112]

On labour questions, *The Glasgow News* spoke for the leading West of Scotland business Tories who owned it. It argued that wages and conditions of work could not be artificially controlled by legislation, denounced strikes as self-defeating, and reviled trade unions as 'despotic and restless . . . a drag upon commerce and an element of danger to social and domestic order'.[113] Thus there was little sympathy for the approach typified by the aristocratic Lord Elcho, M.P. for East Lothian, who was a friend of Alexander MacDonald, the Scottish miners' leader, and who was a warm supporter of the campaign by West of Scotland trade unionists to repeal the Master and Servant Act. In recognition of his services, Elcho was the guest of honour at a dinner given by Glasgow area trade union leaders to celebrate the success of the agitation, and the working-class paper *The Glasgow Sentinel* pointedly contrasted Elcho's conduct with that of local employers who universally shunned the issue.[114] Elcho was invited to speak under the auspices of Glasgow Conservatism on only one occasion, possibly because the industrial interests most inclined to Toryism in the area were coal, iron and steel, and shipping, in all of which industrial relations were unsatisfactory. Coal and iron, which produced three of the first five Conservative candidates for Glasgow — along with some half-dozen vice-presidents of the city Conservative Association—had an especially poor record on labour. James Baird, the most lavish financial supporter of the party in the West of Scotland, was the part-owner of a firm widely regarded as one of the most notoriously ruthless exploiters of its workforce. Shipowners were ferociously opposed to legislative attempts to ensure the safety of British seamen. John Burns, the head of the shipping lobby's resistance, was often spoken of as a future Tory M.P.[115]

Recent historians of the Tory party in this era have tended to see a good portion of the party's appeal as reposing on its claim to be the 'national' party, which it achieved by inheriting Palmerston's mantle of patriotism.[116] The reaction in Scotland to Disraeli's speech of 1872, which established the Tories as the party of Empire, was slight. On only one occasion in the 1870s was Imperialism discussed at a meeting of the Glasgow Conservative Association, and it scarcely featured in election manifestos for the 1874 or 1880 contests in the city. In an address given in 1876 Whitelaw indicated the interest in Imperialism among urban Conservatives. In explaining why working men should vote for his party, he made a solitary reference to the topic, placing it well below such matters as 'the preservation of national insitutions, their social privilege [sic], their Protestantism and their Sabbath'.[117] Again, jingo feeling during the Bulgarian Crisis was muted. In 1876 the Glasgow Tories decided not to hold meetings on the issue, and in 1877, at the peak of the controversy, the city party was even more subdued: 'in no other year since its formation has there been so little to excite attention or discussion in politics'.[118]

The central and binding factor for Scottish urban Conservatism was, rather, religion. At times it seemed that nothing else counted, as in 1872 when five of the seven lectures given to Glasgow Conservatives were on the theme of defending established Protestant churches.[119] In its inaugural editorial, *The Glasgow News* took up that theme: 'There is one point upon which public feeling here is deeper than in the East. Now, as in the past, Glasgow is the head and heart of Protestantism in Scotland, and also keeps firmly and unwaveringly in the 'old patterns', despite all the lecturings of the new lights'.[120] The significant part of the *News*' comment is the latter half, for there were plenty of Church Liberals who, as the next decade was to show, were equally dedicated to the establishment principle. The paper well illustrates the stress on fundamentalist Protestantism which characterised West of Scotland Toryism. This factor permitted Free Church constitutionalists like Kidston to co-operate with those they had left in 1843 against the common enemies of Voluntaryism and creed revision. At a mass meeting in Glasgow of Free Churchmen opposed to union, fears of Broad Churchism within the U.P. Church were conveyed in a resolution moved by a minister: 'In the present struggle there are involved important questions which affect soundness of doctrine, purity of worship, the Sabbath, and scriptural education in national schools . . . '[121]

As indicated in the last phrase, the unity between anti-union Free Church elements and Church of Scotland Conservatives was forged over the issue of religious instruction in state schools, which played a decisive role in the emergence of urban Conservatism, especially in the West of Scotland. The 1872 Scottish Education Act posed an acute challenge to the tradition of clerical control of schooling by providing for popularly elected school boards with full management powers. The Established Church would not only lose direct oversight of staffing and curriculum, but it also seemed certain that the non-established churches would win the board elections in many towns where the Church of Scotland was weak. An alliance of the Church of Scotland and the constitutional Free Church party stood for continuing the existing practice, or 'use and wont', whereby Bible readings and catechism constituted an integral part of the educational process. The clearest exposition of the political dimension of this question came from a clergyman who pointed out that, deprived of classroom religious teaching, the people would be less resistant to the message of Roman Catholicism, and this would make possible the severance of the link between the Crown and Protestantism, upon which the entire palladium of civil liberties was held to repose.[122]

Fears that, on the analogy of English Nonconformity, the Voluntaries would seek to end religious instruction, roused the anti-union Free Church, since this threat summed up the whole trend towards error which they saw being opened up by the union proposals. As the leading lay anti-unionist and ardent Tory, William Kidston, put it: 'The obstacle in the way of getting proper security for religious instruction in the bill, according to use and wont, arises *not* from irreligious secularism, which has no power in this country, but from religious voluntaryism run mad. These are the practical secularists in Scotland'.[123] Hence both anti-

Voluntary groups joined to form the Scottish Educational Association in 1871, led by E. S. Gordon, the future Tory Lord Advocate and instigator of the Patronage Abolition Act. The Association aroused a huge wave of public support at mass meetings held throughout the West of Scotland for its sole aim of securing the inclusion of religious instruction in the provisions of the Scottish Education Bill during its parliamentary process.[124] When the Association failed to amend the bill to its satisfaction, it encouraged the running of use and wont candidates drawn from both Free and State Churchmen at the first School Board elections in 1873, and proved strikingly successful. Thus in Glasgow, five of their six nominees won places on the fifteen-man board, against only three Voluntaries. Elsewhere, the pattern was repeated. In Edinburgh, ten of the fifteen seats were won by the use and wont party, who also swept into power in most towns including Aberdeen, Dundee, Perth, Kirkcaldy, Hawick, Dunfermline and Kilmarnock.

The relevance of 'the Bible in the School' controversy had wider ramifications than the merely educational, for it promoted the advance of the Conservative party in towns and cities by a number of methods. Firstly, it produced new local leaders and broadened the appeal of others. In Glasgow itself, Whitelaw, previously not a public figure, became first chairman of the city's board, and this was his passport to standing for Parliament in 1874. William Kidston and James A. Campbell, hitherto mainly confining themselves to, respectively, Free and Established Church matters, now emerged as influential forces in the Tory party upon election to the Glasgow board. Both Whitelaw and Campbell published only one political statement, in each case reprinting speeches delivered on education and the necessity of use and wont Bible teaching therein.[125] Secondly, the results showed plainly how religious issues could promote the party's growth. The SNCA reported in 1872 that support for the Tories had risen in the previous year because of the Bible in the Schools campaign, which 'has aroused a spirit which has already achieved important results by uniting in defence of constitutional principles all sections of the community. This spirit is notably evinced in the Scottish Education Association'.[126] The Glasgow Conservatives recorded for 1871 that 'the most important effort of your Association has been in conjunction with other agencies in defence of THE BIBLE IN THE SCHOOL'. This involved organising meetings, getting signatures to petitions and so on.[127] In the 1874 general election most West of Scotland Tory candidates followed the example of the two Glasgow men by putting their support of the use and wont principle as the first item in their election address, with defence of church establishments usually put second. For instance, the local press of both party persuasions agreed that the Liberals lost the Ayr Burghs because of the allegation that their candidate was hostile to the use and wont doctrine, while the Conservative trumpeted his adherence to it.[128]

The School Board elections were also a decisive pointer to the existence of a sizeable vote which would need to be carefully organised. From 1873 there was a mounting interest in places like Glasgow to get the maximum number of School Board voters who were eligible put on the parliamentary register. Also, at subsequent School Board contests, efforts were made to discipline the use and wont voters to support only candidates on that slate. There was a semi-secret body operating in the east end of Glasgow styling itself, appropriately, the Knoxites, which undertook this task with considerable effect, so that its champion, Harry Alfred Long, normally topped the poll.[129] It is possible that this electoral machinery was made available to the Conservatives at parliamentary contests, for the Knoxites were largely composed of Orangemen and sympathisers, with whom the Conservatives in many parts had exceptionally close ties.

The role of the Orange Order in Conservatism in the West of Scotland was most explicitly manifest in Glasgow at the 1880 General Election, when the Order was able to thrust its chosen candidate, Sir James Bain, upon the party in the face of patent reluctance on the part of most respectable leaders of the local association. In 1879 Bain presided at the Orange Lodges' annual soirée, resplendent in an orange sash, and was there referred to as the Orangeman's candidate.[130] The Orange Provincial Grand Master, George MacLeod, was also vice-chairman of Bain's election committee, and many leading Orangemen were also prominent on the committee. On polling day, a press notice urged Orangemen to vote for the other Conservative candidate as well as Bain himself.[131] This was the culmination of a decade-long process whereby the Orange movement had become well integrated with the Tory party. The Order had disappeared in Scotland after its proscription in 1836, and although some early stirrings were detectable in the mid-1860s, the real upswing in support came in the early 1870s. By 1878 it was calculated that out of 90,000 members in England, Wales and Scotland, some 15,000 were to be found in Glasgow alone, and it may be surmised that there were as many more in surrounding areas.[132] Along with growth in numbers, politicisation occurred: at the simplest level, Lodge No. 690 styled itself 'Beaconsfield Purple Guards'. Press reports on almost every Orange meeting in the 1870s contained explicit references to their affinities with the Tories. Provincial Grand Master MacLeod himself exulted at the 12th of July meeting in 1874: 'they had returned a Conservative member for Glasgow ... they had got a good sound solid Conservative Government (Cheers) in place of a mixty-maxty government of Churchmen, Ritualists, Quakers, Jews, Infidels, Papists ... every sound Orangeman was a Conservative and if there were any Radicals in their ranks they were as rare as black swans'.[133]

Again, education was a major ingredient in this link. The Glasgow Conservatives praised MacLeod for his 'vigorous and manly stand' in 1871 in defence of the use and wont principle.[134] As has been noted, the School Board elections of 1873 resulted in the Orangeman's choice, Long, coming top of the poll, securing 4,000 more individual votes than any other candidate. The main feature of Orange support was that it was essentially working-class, and it is no coincidence that Sir James Bain's 1880 election committee was significantly different to that of Pearce, his orthodox Tory fellow-candidate. Firstly, Bain had far more newcomers than Pearce, who relied on those who had already been on the 1874 committee. This could imply that Bain was attracting a different type of Conservative supporter. Secondly, Bain had a far larger working-class element on his committee, and had support more evenly spread across the working-class strata.

Table 4.1.   Social Analysis of Glasgow Conservative Candidates' Election Committees,
1874 and 1800

	1874		1880: Bain		1880: Pearce	
	N	%	N	%	N	%
Upper Business and Professional	455	38.5	167	17.8	564	38.0
Lesser Business and Professional and Clerical	425	36.0	346	36.9	589	39.7
Manual Workers: Skilled	170	14.4	219	23.5	192	12.8
Semi-Skilled	60	5.0	99	10.6	64	4.3
Unskilled	73	6.1	105	11.2	77	5.2
	1183	100	936	100	1486	100

Table 4.2   Continuity and Recruitment in Glasgow Conservative Election Committees,
1880

	Bain				Pearce			
	Old		New		Old		New	
	N	%	N	%	N	%	N	%
Upper Business & Professional	48	28.8	119	71.2	168	29.3	396	70.7
Lower Business & Professional and Clerical	53	15.5	293	84.5	122	20.1	467	79.9
Manual Workers: Skilled	24	10.9	195	89.1	41	21.3	151	78.7
Semi-Skilled	7	7.1	92	92.9	9	14.1	55	85.9
Unskilled	10	9.6	95	90.4	8	10.3	69	89.7
	142	15.1	794	84.9	348	23.4	1138	76.6

'Old' means served on the 1874 Committee.
See Appendix for classification details.

This link between the Conservative party and the Orange Lodges became more apparent and more institutionalised in the early 1880s. Prominent Tories like Col. A. C. Campbell of Blythswood and J. N. Cuthbertson alternated between attending party and lodge meetings in these years. When Salisbury came to Glasgow in 1884, he was presented with an address from the Grand Orange Lodge of Scotland immediately after one from the Glasgow Conservative Association, and before any other Tory body.[135] From the start of the 1880s, the Glasgow Orange Lodges had a representative on the city Conservative Association's executive, an arrangement which ended only in 1922.

The upsurge in Orangeism was due to several factors. In part it may be due to the close links with Ulster, whence many West of Scotland Irish immigrants originated: between 1876 and 1883, 83% of all Irish immigrants to Scotland came from Ulster, as against only 33% of those Irish going to England.[136] Moreover, in the late 1850s Harland's Belfast shipbuilding yard imported many Clydeside workers to train native Ulster labour in the new skills of iron ship construction. The Belfast shipbuilding areas were among the most vehemently Orange sections of that city, and either through Scots returning, or Belfast men going across to the Clyde yards, there may well have been some, so to speak, cultural transmission. Certainly Greenock, Glasgow, Govan and Dumbarton had strong pockets of Orangeism among these workers, as a Glasgow paper noted: 'There appears to be a considerable number of 'the brethren' among the numerous workmen engaged in the shipyards'.[137] The apparent resurgence of Roman Catholicism in the later 1860s and through the 1870s probably stimulated Orangeism. There was initially the declaration of papal infallibility which so disturbed Gladstone, and then in 1878 the Scottish hierarchy was reintroduced, fully twenty-five years behind England. These developments led to the formation of several organisations dedicated to combating this challenge, all of which had overlapping personnel and close links with the Orange Order. In 1873 — the best year for the Tory party in Scotland for a very long time — the West of Scotland Protestant Alliance was formed and proceeded to hold meetings over the years to protest against all indications of growing Catholic activity, be it Vaticanism, Ultramontanism or the restoration of the Scottish episcopate. Of the ten vice-presidents, seven were active Conservatives, including one M.P., and only two were Liberals. The secretary was a noted Orangeman, as were a good number of the directors.[138]

A less polished body conveying the same message, but carrying perhaps greater weight in the lower echelons of society, was the Working Men's Evangelistic Association, which was created in 1870 'by pious operatives to stem the tide of Popery in Glasgow and to offer effective opposition to the infidel propaganda coming to Glasgow at selected intervals from London'.[139] It was this body which first provided the launching pad for the pivotal figure in this intricate network of religio-political relationships — H. A. Long, who was its director, and who operated in the intensely working-class east end of Glasgow. Long was a demagogue of some stature, and was immensely popular with the local working class, as was shown in the 1874 election when he was called by acclamation to address east-end audiences on behalf of the Conservative candidates.[140] Long was a regular speaker at Orange meetings, and his Evangelistic Association included among his directors J. N. Cuthbertson — already identified as a Tory with Orange leanings — who went on to be chairman of the Glasgow School Board and stood as a Conservative candidate for Kilmarnock in 1880. Another director was Thomas Wetherall, a top officebearer in the Orange Lodges who was also influential in Tory politics. Long himself became a vice-president of the Glasgow Conservative Association in 1887 after serving on the general committee for over a decade. This incorporation into official Toryism of men like Long represented a clear decision by the party after the 1880 elections that the best method to seek to cope with the mounting working-class popular Protestant political movement was to embrace it and co-operate with it as fully as possible.

But the cost of permitting these quasi-Orange elements to assume a prevailing influence in the Conservative party was considerable. It made it almost certain that their presence would repel the accession of middle-class suburbanites, those areas of recruitment so adroitly tapped by the Tory party in England in the same period. These more sophisticated groups, often attending, as noted above, churches where liberal theological currents were well represented, would find utterly repugnant the unquestioning fundamentalism of men like Long, who believed every word in the Bible to be literally true. The middle classes, as respecters of law and order and proper public conduct (one of the reasons why they found the proposal to grant Irish Home Rule in 1886 so obnoxious) would have been deeply unhappy at the violence which frequently accompanied Orange demonstrations. The most notable example of this was the rioting in Partick, a strong shipbuilding area, in 1875, which it took the police three days to quell. The language of public debate used by the popular Protestants was both ludicrous and extreme, and so unlikely to appeal to more sober-minded bourgeois citizens. One ardent Tory at an Orange meeting solemnly intimated that Gladstone was a covert Jesuit, while the Rev. Robert Thomson, Tory candidate for Kilmarnock Burghs in 1868, claimed at an Orange meeting that 'he believed that he was the only Protestant that ever preached a sermon in St. Peter's at Rome. He preached on the occasion of his visit, when a number of Protestants present were about to follow the example of the Romanists in kissing the Pope's toe'.[141] Even moderate Conservatives, still more presumably Whigs, were disturbed by these elements. When Bain projected himself into the Glasgow candidacy, the Tory already selected, J. A. Campbell (whose brother was the Liberal M.P. Campbell-Bannerman), quickly turned his attention to another seat. No doubt Campbell shared the views articulated by a prominent civil servant, later a Scottish Tory M.P., to a leading Conservative West of Scotland industrialist, who had himself declined to stand for Stirlingshire in 1880: 'Bain is a disgrace both to our city and our party'.[142] Hence the movement of moderate Liberals into Conservatism was delayed in Scotland, and as long as the Liberals avoided ultra-Radical control and in particular seemed able to contain demands for disestablishment, moderate Liberals would remain aloof. This calculation probably operated until 1886, and then gradually changed, so helping to explain why the growth of Unionist support was so dramatic in the last fifteen years of the century.

Appendix : Notes to Tables 4.1 and 4.2.

1. The candidates' Committees were printed in the *Glasgow News* on most days throughout the election campaigns. Occupations, when not indicated in the press, were checked from the electoral registers or the *Post Office Street and Trades Directory for Glasgow*.

2. The principles and methods used in determining the social groupings are based on W. Armstrong, 'The Uses of Census Information regarding Occupations', in E. A. Wrigley, *Nineteenth Century Society* (London, 1972), pp. 198–225. Armstrong's categories have, however, been modified in one important respect: clerical workers and minor functionaries have been put in Group II. This leaves Group III confined to the skilled working class, a rearrangement which seems to reflect more accurately the realities of social division in the city, as described by contemporaries.

NOTES

1. J. E. Gorst to Disraeli, 7 Feb. 1874, Disraeli MSS., MS. Disraeli, Box 59, B/XIII/255.

2. H. J. Hanham, *Elections and Party Management* (London, 1979), pp. 3–19; J. P. D. Dunbabin, *Rural Discontent in Nineteenth Century Britain* London, 1974), pp. 173–4.

3. *The Present Position, Prospects and Duties of the Scotch Farmer viewed in Relation to the Landlord's Right of Hypothec, the Operation of the Game Laws on Grass and Corn Lands and the New Reform Bill* (Edinburgh, 1866), p. 5.

4. Enclosure in A. McCracken to Lord Advocate, 11 Mar. 1870; *The Game Laws. Report of a Discussion at the Chamber of Agriculture, Edinburgh* (held on 17 May 1865). Lord Advocates' MSS., AD 56/10.

5. 'List of Perthshire Gamekeepers', n.d. (c.1875); J. Bartlemere to Lord Advocate, 11 Jun. 1874; *The Game Laws . . .* , p. 19, Ibid., AD 56/10.

6. See a draft Memorandum on the Game Laws, 5 Mar. 1870, Ibid., AD 56/10; cf. *North British Agriculturist,* 29 Mar. 1865.

7. Enclosure in A. McCracken to Lord Advocate, 11 Mar. 1870, Lord Advocates' MSS., AD 56/10.

8. Sir J. C. D. Hay to Disraeli, 11 Mar. 1876, Disraeli MSS., MS. Disraeli, Box 131, B/XXI/H/317.

9. There is a full account in the Report of the Select Committee on Hypothec, P.P. 1865 (3546) XVII, 441.

10. Scottish Chamber of Agriculture, *Discussion on the Report of Her Majesty's Commissioners on the Law Relating to the Landlord's Right of Hypothec in Scotland . . . in so far as regards Agricultural Subjects and the Minutes of the Evidence on which it is based* (Edinburgh 14 Nov. 1865), *passim; The Present Position, Prospects and Duties of the Scotch Farmer . . .* , pp. 3–6, 7–9; *North British Agriculturist,* 11 Jan.–1 Feb. 1865.

11. *North British Agriculturist,* 24 May 1865; G. Hope, 'Hindrances to Agriculture', Sir A. Grant, *Recess Studies* (London 1870), pp. 400–9.

12. A. Lindsay to Sir T. Gladstone, 8 Mar. 1865, Glynne-Gladstone MSS., 9/1.

13. *Inverness-shire Advertiser,* 2 Sep. 1873, cf. *The Present Position, Prospect, Duties etc . . .* , pp. 9–10.

14. *North British Agriculturist,* 12 Apr. 1865.

15. *George Hope of Fenton Barns. A Sketch of his Life compiled by his Daughter* (Edinburgh 1881), pp. 157–74.

16. Hope's Election Address (21 Jul. 1865), Wemyss MSS., RH 4/40/1/55.

17. W. McCombie, in *North British Agriculturist,* 28 Jun. 1865.

18. Select Committee on Parliamentary and Municipal Elections, P. P. 1868–9 (352) VIII, q. 5913.

19. Hanham, *Elections and Party Management,* pp. 32–3. The Farmers' Alliance was the nearest equivalent, but only functioned after 1879.

20. *Dundee Courier,* 30 Nov., 5 Dec. 1872.

21. *Ibid.,* 9 Dec. 1872.

22. *North British Agriculturist,* 5 Apr. 1865.

23. Scottish Chamber of Agriculture, *Discussion on the Report . . . on . . . Hypothec . . .* , p. 37; *The Present Position, Prospects and Duties of the Scotch Farmer . . .* , p. 10.

24. *Inverness Advertiser,* 2 Sep. 1873.

25. J. G. Clark, Lord H. Scott to Buccleuch, 3 Nov. 1868, (8 Dec. 1868), Buccleuch MSS., GD 224/505/1.

26. Clark to Buccleuch, 29 Mar. 1872, Ibid., GD 224/505/2.

27. W. Stirling-Maxwell to W. Smythe, 12 August 1872 (copy), Stirling MSS., T-SK 29/22/477.

28. Lord Childs to Stirling-Maxwell, 27 Oct. 1868, Ibid., T-SK 29/80-2.

29. J. J. Reid to W. P. Adam, 10 Jul. 1879, Adam MSS., 4/425.

30. *Fifteen Reasons for Voting against Sir Thomas Gladstone, By a Mearns Farmer* (n.d., but 1865), Glynne-Gladstone MSS., 9/1.

31. Letter of thanks to constituents by J. D. Nicol (18 Jul. 1865); Rev. R. M. Spence to Sir T. Gladstone, 13 Mar. 1865; Ibid., 9/1.

32. A. G. Monro to Gladstone, 10 Mar. 1865, Ibid., 9/1.

33. *Stirling Journal and Advertiser,* 21 Jul. 1865.

34. *Hope of Fenton Barns,* pp. 263–77; Hope's Election Address (21 Jul. 1865), Wemyss MSS., RH 4/40/1/55; *North British Agriculturist,* 19 Jul. 1865.

35. Minutes of Meeting of Conservative Voters in the County of Linlithgow, 12 Apr. 1865, Glen & Henderson MSS.

36. Sir W. Baillie to H. Hope, 29 Jan. 1874, cf. J. D. to H. Hope, 6 Oct. 1868, Hope MSS., GD 364/288,671.

37. *Aberdeen Free Press,* 11, 18 May 1866.

38. *North British Agriculturist,* 25 Nov. 1868.

39. Mrs. E. H. Perceval, *The Life of Sir David Wedderburn, Bt.* (London, 1884), pp. 96–100, 178–9; *Ayr Observer,* 27 Oct. 1868.

40. G. Glyn to W. E. Gladstone, 17, 22, 23 Sep., 3 Oct. (3/5 Nov.) 1868, W. E. Gladstone MSS., Add MS. 44347, ff. 170–8, 187–9, 228–9.

41. J. C. Waterfield to A. Young, 10 Nov. 1868; J. Smythe to W. Stirling-Maxwell, 19 Oct. 1868, Stirling MSS., T-SK 29/80-2.

42. *Perthshire Journal and Constitutional,* 22 Oct. 1868.

43. J. Graham Stirling to Sir W. Stirling-Maxwell, 15 Jul. 1868, Stirling MSS., T-SK 29/80-2.

44. W. Stirling to P. Blackburn, 25 Nov. 1865 (copy), Ibid., T-SK 29/15/11A; Chrystal & MacFarlane to W. Forbes, 28 June 1868, Forbes MSS., GD 171/44.

45. Lord Ailsa to Col. Alexander, 28 Sep. 1868 (draft), Ailsa MSS., GD 25/9/30; for Dumfriesshire: J. G. Clark to Buccleuch, 17 Nov. 1868, Buccleuch MSS., GD 224/505/1; Perthshire: *Perthshire Journal,* 26 Nov. 1868.

46. Disraeli to Derby, 28 Jul. 1865, Derby MSS., 146/1.

47. Fergusson to Disraeli, 27 Nov. 1868, Disraeli MSS., MS. Disraeli, Box 127, B/XXI/F/105.

48. G. Young to Gladstone, 13 Oct. 1873, W. E. Gladstone MSS., Add. MS. 44440, ff. 189ff.

49. A. Taylor, H. Rankin to Lord Advocate, 3, 27 May 1870, Lord Advocates' MSS., AD 56/10.

50. G. Young to Gladstone, 5 Nov. 1873, W. E. Gladstone MSS., Add. MS. 44441, ff. 18ff.

51. Telegrams to W. P. Adam from G. MacPherson Grant, A. Smith, Sir G. Balfour, and J. Colvin, 30, 31, 30, 28 Jan. 1874, Adam MSS., 4/564.

52. A. C. Sellar to W. P. Adam, n.d., ibid., 4/578.

53. *Perthshire Journal,* 28 Jan. 1874; *Ayr Observer,* 31 Jan. 1874; *Inverness Advertiser,* 27 Jan. 1874.

54. *Kelso Chronicle,* 20 Feb. 1874; P. Haggart to — Haggart, 2 Feb. 1874, Stirling MSS., T-SK 29/83/32; D. Cameron to B. Disraeli, 9 Feb. 1874, Disraeli MSS., MS. Disraeli, Box 122, B/XXI/C/21; *Berwickshire News,* 24 Jun. 1873. Hanham, *Elections and Party Management,* pp. 36–8 notes this factor in England.

55. *Perthshire Journal,* 30 Jan. 1874.

56. *Kelso Chronicle,* 20 Feb. 1874; *Perthshire Journal,* 16 Feb. 1874.

57. *North British Agriculturist,* 28 Jan. 1874.

58. R. Montgomerie's address, *Ayr Observer,* 31 Jan. 1874; cf. D. Cameron's address, *Inverness Advertiser,* 27 Jan. 1874; Stirling-Maxwell's *Perthshire Journal,* 28 Jan. 1874.

59. *Berwickshire News,* 24 Jun. 1873.

60. Election addresses of R. B. Hamilton, 27 Jan. 1874, and of Lord Dunglass, 16 Jun. 1873, in Hope MSS., GD 364/288.

61. D. Williamson to W. Stirling-Maxwell, 7 Dec. 1873, Stirling MSS., T-SK 29/23/563.

62. *Perthshire Journal,* 16 Feb. 1874.

63. Hanham, *Elections and Party Management,* pp. 17–21 for English parallels.

64. J. Anstruther Thomson, *Eighty Years Recollections* (London, 1904), I, pp. 295–304.

65. Minute of Meeting of Conservative Voters in the County of Linlithgow, 12 Apr. 1865, Glen & Henderson MSS.

66. H. Erskine to W. Forbes, 25 Sep. 1873, Forbes MSS., GD 171/44.

67. J. Smythe to W. Stirling-Maxwell, 12 Dec. 1868, J. Miller to Stirling-Maxwell, 24 Sep. 1868, Stirling MSS., T-SK 29/80-2.

68. Manuscript notes (by R. W. Cochran-Patrick) on the annual meeting of the West Kilbride Conservative Association held on 29 Mar. 1870. These notes are on the reverse of the Report of the West Kilbride Conservative Association for 1839, Hunter MSS., 562.

69. There is a copy of the rules of the Association in Maxwell of Monreith MSS., Acc. 7043/HEM 1.

70. Galloway to Lord Inverurie, 8 Apr. 1879, Kintore MSS., 190.

71. P. Blackburn to W. Stirling, 29 Jun. 1865, Stirling MSS., T-SK 29/15/10; Duke of Montrose to W. Forbes, 21 Jul., 7 Aug. 1865, Forbes MSS., GD 171/44.

72. J. G. Clark to Buccleuch, 28 Nov. 1868, Buccleuch MSS., GD 224/505/1.

73. H. Skeete to W. Stirling-Maxwell, 7 Nov. 1873, 6, 14, Feb. 1874; R. C. Chapman to Stirling-Maxwell, 13 Feb. 1874, Stirling MSS., T-SK 29/83/85,91–2; 29/84/20.

74. D. Williamson to W. Stirling-Maxwell, 26 Feb., 28 Aug. 1872, Ibid., T-SK 29/22/571-2.

75. Circular letter by G. Elliot, 5 Oct. 1869, Minto MSS., MS. 12354, ff. 75 ff.

76. *North British Agriculturist,* 18 Feb. 1874.

77. B. L. Crapster, 'Scotland and the Conservative Party in 1876', *Journal of Modern History,* 29 (1957), pp. 355–60.

78. H. Skeete to Sir J. Fergusson, 12 Jun. 1876, also Dr. Mackie's Report, Disraeli MSS., MS. Disraeli, Box 59, B/XIII/261-3; D. Cameron to C. Innes, 6 Aug. (1874), 21 Aug. 1875, Innes & Mackay MSS., GD 296/156.

79. E. J. Feuchtwanger, *Disraeli, Democracy and the Tory Party* (London, 1968) for England.

80. Feuchtwanger, *Disraeli, Democracy and the Tory Party,* pp. 105–220.

81. SNCA *15th Annual Report* (1882), pp. 8–9.

82. Feuchtwanger, *Disraeli, Democracy,* pp. 124–31, 167 for the English body.

83. A. Whitelaw to F. Pitman, 12 Feb. 1868, Whitelaw MSS., UGD 101/1/1.

84. SNCA *4th Annual Report* (1871), p. 4.

85. There are copies of these documents in Glen & Henderson MSS.

86. Hanham, *Elections and Party Management,* pp. 109–13 notes this problem for England.

87. H. Brodie to J. Sime, n.d. (Feb. 1874) (draft?), Brodie MSS., 48/3.

88. R. Leslie-Melville to W. Stirling-Maxwell, 20, 22 Jan. 1872, Stirling MSS., T-SK 29/22/304–5.

89. Printed Memorandum, 1 Dec. 1866 on the *Edinburgh Courant,* Innes & Mackay MSS., GD 296/158/17; Sir J. Fergusson to Duke of Portland, 1 Sep. 1868, Portland MSS., Pw K 1675.

90. Prospectus of Scottish Newspaper Company, 1 Feb. 1872, Innes & Mackay MSS., GD 296/158/7; SNCA *5th Annual Report* (1872), pp. 5–6; Memoranda as to proposed daily newspaper to be established in Aberdeen and in Inverness (n.d., c. 1874–5); D. Cameron, J. Winchester to C. Innes, 19 Feb. (1876), 13 Oct. 1874, Innes & Mackay MSS., GD 296/158/8,13; 296/157,156.

91. Baird to Stirling-Maxwell, 23 Nov. 1871, Stirling MSS., T-SK 29/22/14; F. Wicks to M. Corry, 11 Jun. 1879, Disraeli MSS., MS Disraeli, Box 88 B/XX/A/47, which gives the capital at £100,000. Moray, J. Baird to W. Stirling-Maxwell, 2 Nov. 1871, 17 Jan. 1872, Stirling MSS., T-SK 29/21/240, 29/22/15.

92. C. Dalrymple to R. W. Cochran-Patrick, 20 May 1872, Hunter MSS., 28/143.

93. F. C. Wicks to M. Corry, 11 Jun. 1879, Disraeli MSS., MS. Disraeli, Box 88, B/XX/A/47; Private Memorandum from the Proprietors of the *Glasgow News* to Conservative Agents Throughout Scotland, 12 Apr. 1880, Ibid., MS. Disraeli, Box 88, B/XX/A/50.

94. *Union on the Basis of the Standards, explained and vindicated by Rev. Dr. Buchanan and Rev. Dr. Adam* (Edinburgh, 1870), Appendix.

95. Gordon to Disraeli, 18 Jan. 1872, Disraeli MSS., MS. Disraeli, Box 129 B/XXI/G/202.

96. Rev. N. MacLeod to Rev. A. H. Charteris, 6 Apr. (1869/70), 1 Apr. (1870), New College MSS., X 14a 1/5.

97. Gordon to Disraeli, 30 May 1870, Disraeli MSS., MS. Disraeli, Box 129 B/XXI/G/201; Sir J. Fergusson to C. Dalrymple, 29 Jan. 1874, Newhailes MSS., Acc. 7228/214, ff. 174–6; Sir J. C. D. Hay to Disraeli, 11 Jun. 1868, 24 Aug. 1871, Memorandum by A. C. Swinton on Scottish Politics, n.d. (Oct. 1867), Disraeli MSS., MS. Disraeli, Box 131 B/XXI/H/305,309; Box 42 B/X/A/12.

98. Rosslyn to Disraeli, 27 May 1874, 21 May 1875, Ibid., Box 141 B/XXI/R/174–6.

99. A. Whitelaw to Rev. Dr. R. W. R. Pirrie, 20 Jan. 1874, Whitelaw Letterbooks, UGD 101/1/3.

100. J. C. Gibson, *The Diary of Sir Michael Connal, 1835–93* (Glasgow, 1895), p. 161 (22 May 1876); cf. pp. 151, 152 (5 Jun., 12 Aug. 1874).

101. See the manifesto of the Scottish Disestablishment Association (24 Oct. 1874) in Adam MSS., 4/416.

102. C. L. Warr, *Principal Caird* (Edinburgh, 1926), p. 246; *Principal Story: A Memoir by his Daughters* (Glasgow, 1909), pp. 129–31.

103. *Glasgow Herald,* 29 Jul. 1874, cf. 6, 19 May, 3, 10 Jun., 8, 9 Jul, 1874, 22 May 1875. Many of these editorials were probably written by Story.

104. Montgomery to Disraeli, 21 Jan. 1867, Disraeli MSS., MS. Disraeli, Box 137 B/XXI/M/485.

105. Fergusson to Disraeli, 27 Nov. 1868, Ibid., MS. Disraeli, Box 127 B/XXI/F/105.

106. Feuchtwanger, *Disraeli, Democracy,* pp. 191–5; Hanham, *Elections and Party Management,* pp. 284–9 for instances of this in Lancashire.

107. P. Smith, *Disraelian Conservatism and Social Reform* (London, 1967); R. Blake, *Disraeli* (London, 1966), pp. 553–6, 762–3.

108. Hanham, *Elections and Party Management,* pp. 314–8.

109. C. Scott, *What Should the Working Man Do With his Vote? A lecture delivered by request to the Working Classes of Edinburgh by Charles Scott in the Queen's Hall, on Tuesday 25 Jan. 1867* (Edinburgh, 1867), pp. 30–41, 47–8.

110. Gordon to Corry, 26 Oct. 1867, Disraeli MSS., MS. Disraeli, Box 42 B/X/A/21.

111. Memorandum by Lord Dalkeith to Disraeli (c. 15 Dec. 1879), Ibid., MS. Disraeli, Box 124, B/XXI/D/1a.

112. Hansard, *Parliamentary Debates,* 3rd Series, ccxxii, cols. 46–53.

113. *Glasgow News,* 30 Jul. 1874, 16 May 1877, 17 Sep. 1879; cf. F. Wicks to W. Blackwood, 15 Oct. 1877, Blackwood MSS., MS. 4367, ff. 195–6 for an attack on the printing unions for holding a strike in the paper's premises.

114. *Glasgow Sentinel,* 2, 30 May 1868.

115. *Glasgow Herald,* 1 Jan. 1876, 1 Dec. 1883; *Glasgow News,* 25 Dec. 1884.

116. R. Blake, *The Conservative Party from Peel to Churchill* (London, 1970), pp. 124–9.

117. *Glasgow News,* 15 Feb. 1876.

118. Glasgow Conservative Association, *8th, 9th Annual Reports* (1876, 1877), unpag.

119. Glasgow Working Men's Conservative Association, *4th Annual Report* (1872), unpag.

120. *Glasgow News,* 15 Sep. 1873.

121. *Full Report of the Great Free Church Meeting of those upholding Free Church Principles, and Unfavourable to Union on the Proposed Basis, in the City Hall, Glasgow on Wednesday 11 Jan. 1871,* (Glasgow 1871), pp. 45–53, also speeches by J. Begg, pp. 53–69 and W. Kidston, pp. 9–13.

122. *Scottish Education Bill. The Bible in the School. Report of a public meeting in the City Hall, Glasgow on 13 Apr. 1871* (Glasgow, 1871), pp. 38–45.

123. *Ibid.,* pp. 22–30. Cf. W. Kidston, *The Captious and Ensnaring Question* (Glasgow, 1871), where he argues that on national education, 'their (U.P.s') voluntaryism is driving them over to practical Secularism'.

124. *Glasgow Herald,* 14 Apr., 21 Dec. 1871.

125. A. Whitelaw, *National Education* (Glasgow, 1871); J. A. Campbell, *The Education Question. An address to the Glasgow Working Men's Conservative Association on 30 October 1871, introductory to a Course of Popular Lectures* (Glasgow, 1871).

126. SNCA, *5th Annual Report* (1875), p. 3.

127. Glasgow Working Men's Conservative Association, *4th Annual Report* (1872), unpag.

128. *Ardrossan & Saltcoats Herald,* 14 Feb. 1874; *Ayr Observer,* 7 Feb. 1874.

129. *Reasons for Organising a Protestant Confraternity to be called 'The Knoxites'* (n.p., n.d. — c.1881); H. A. Long, *Glasgow School Board Elections. 2nd Edition of 'Wrinkles', showing how the Glasgow Knoxites can capture the poll head at all future elections while the cumulative vote is legal* (Glasgow, n.d. — c.1900).

130. *North British Daily Mail,* 8 Nov. 1879. Cf. Hanham, *Elections and Party Management,* pp. 304–8 for Orangeism in Lancashire in 1868; P. Waller, *Democracy and Sectarianism* (Liverpool, 1981), pp. 30–2, for Liverpool parallels.

131. *Glasgow News,* 2 Apr. 1880.

132. *Ibid.,* 13 Jul. 1878.

133. *Glasgow Herald,* 13 Jul. 1874.

134. Glasgow Working Men's Conservative Association, *3rd Annual Report* (1871).

135. *Glasgow News,* 1–4 Oct. 1884.

136. E. G. Ravenstein, 'The Laws of Migration', *Journal of the Royal Statistical Society,* 48 (1885), pp. 167–235.

137. *North British Daily Mail,* 12 Jul. 1869, 9 Aug. 1875.

138. West of Scotland Protestant Alliance, *1st Annual Report* (1873–5).

139. Glasgow Working Men's Evangelistic Association, *10th Annual Report* (1879), p. 5.

140. *Glasgow News,* 31 Jan., 2 Feb. 1874.

141. *Ibid.,* 17 Nov. 1884.

142. H. Craik to J. King, 15 Mar. 1880, King MSS.

5

The Mid-Victorian Liberal Party: 1865–1881

I

The implications of the passing of the Second Reform Act seemed to present formidable challenges to the Scottish Liberal party. In the first place, there was the rapid and massive increase in the urban electorate: in Glasgow, for instance, up from 18,000 to 47,000. Secondly, the new voters came preponderantly from the working classes, as a breakdown of the social composition of the new and old Glasgow electorate reveals.

Table 5.1. *Socio-Economic Groupings of the Glasgow Electorate, 1867–8 and 1868–9*

| | 1867–8 | | 1868–9 | |
	N	%	N	%
Upper Business and Professional	317	17.3	436	9.1
Lesser Business and Professional and Clerical	860	47.0	1,209	25.2
Manual Workers: Skilled	413	22.9	1,659	35.0
Semi-Skilled	167	8.5	831	17.1
Unskilled	79	4.3	650	13.6
	1,836	100	4,785	100

See Appendix for the statistical and classification basis.

This meant that canvassing could no longer be physically carried out, and also that whereas the old £10 householder frequently had some personal contact with party workers, this was no longer the case.[1] To complicate matters, the agitation for the passing of the 1868 bill showed that there existed a disciplined body possessing substantial claims to represent the opinion of the new working-class majority. This was the Scottish National Reform League, which was particularly strong in the West of Scotland. Within four months of its inception in September 1866, it had reached a level of support proportionate to that which its English counterpart had taken two years to reach. The monster rally held by the League in October 1866 was the largest public demonstration seen in Glasgow since 1832, far outnumbering any Chartist demonstration. Above all, the League was superbly well organised: even hostile press observers commented on the peaceableness of the crowds at its mass meetings, and the efficient marshalling techniques used.[2] The League's Secretary, George Jackson, although only in his mid-twenties, having demonstrated these admirable administrative talents, now turned the League's attention to consolidating the gains made in obtaining the franchise.

From as early as autumn 1867 they resolved to secure some representation of their interest in the new Parliament.[3]

Yet this demand by the League, ostensibly threatening to the Liberal party's prospects, proved to have little real weight behind it. No sitting Liberal lost his seat to a candidate sponsored by the League. In Glasgow, where an additional third seat was created, this was earmarked by the League as reserved for its nominee. The two sitting M.P.s assented to this claim, as they were in return guaranteed delivery of working-class votes by dint of a joint scheme agreed upon by all three Liberals to allocate the votes evenly between all of them. This agreement — 'an understood compromise', as John Stuart Mill was informed —precluded any support being given to extra Liberal candidates. None stood against this trio, and all three easily saw off a Tory challenge.[4] In Kilmarnock, there was clearer evidence of the feebleness of the League's pretensions. Alexander MacDonald, the Scottish miners' leader, initially stood here, but withdrew when it became plain that he had no prospects. However, the Reform League's Secretary, Jackson, visited the component burghs in order to smooth the way for Edwin Chadwick to stand against the sitting M.P., E. P. Bouverie. Bouverie, the son of the Earl of Radnor, was a right-wing Whig in political outlook and, allegedly, not very diligent in the discharge of constituency business. Nevertheless, Chadwick, facing a weak opponent, endorsed and championed by John Stuart Mill as well as the Reform League, still failed to win. Indeed the great advocate of urban social reforms could only narrowly win second place from a rabid Protestant clergyman who stood as an unofficial Tory.[5] A third venture came at Edinburgh, where the leader of the English Reform League, Beales, was tentatively suggested, but withdrew due to patent lack of support.[6]

Thus the Reform League did not in the event prove a serious disruptive factor to the established Liberal powers. Very rapidly after the 1868 election, the decline of the League was reinforced. Jackson failed in the 1869 Glasgow municipal elections to win a solidly working-class ward against a Tory Church of Scotland cotton master. In the 1873 school board contests, further setbacks occurred. Many of the members of the Scottish Reform League formed the Scottish National Education League, modelled on the very successful English body, and put up candidates in the larger cities. In Glasgow, only one of their candidates won, and in Aberdeen also, only one representative, a university professor, won. In these elections, by contrast, the vast bulk of the working-class vote seemed to be going to crypto-Conservatives running on the 'use and wont' ticket.

In sum, the new electorate in 1868 largely shared the same political proclivities as the existing middle-class voters. W. E. Baxter, the Radical middle-class M.P. for Montrose, and A. F. Kinnaird, the Whig aristocratic M.P. Afor Perth burgh, both used very similar language to describe the climate at the polls. As Baxter reported to Gladstone: 'Nothing could be more admirable than the conduct of the workingmen here. Their zeal, demeanour and intelligence are beyond all praise'.[7] The major preoccupation in Scotland for the Liberal Chief Whip was in finding suitable men to fight county seats, while W. P. Adam, already emerging as the expert on Scottish electioneering, was more concerned at a possible threat by

Conservatives to stand in Liberal county strongholds than with any potential disorders in urban constituencies.[8] Indeed the more profound onslaught on the power structure of Liberalism in Scotland came not in 1868 but in 1874, and from middle-class radicals, who were quite different from, and indeed frequently hostile to, working-class radicals. The most graphic example of this new force came in Glasgow in 1874. Here two of the sitting M.P.s, both somewhat Whiggish, retired, and, as Adam's adjutant in Scotland reported, the city Whigs naturally put up two of their own to replace them: 'Two good men got for Glasgow — Bolton and Crum'.[9] However, on the eve of polling, the Whig committee was obliged to withdraw Bolton, but Crum still failed to be elected, thus depriving Whiggery of two M.P.s.[10] One of the three city seats fell, through Liberal disarray, to the Tories, one was retained by George Anderson, the Reform League's choice in 1868, and the third seat was won — and the poll topped — by a Liberal, Dr. Charles Cameron, standing as the voice of dissenting evangelical radicalism, regenerated after a lapse of nearly twenty years as a potent force.

Glasgow was merely one segment of a general pattern which also embraced Dundee, where Sir John Ogilvy, a Whig who had sat since defeating a Dissenting radical in 1857, lost to a new representative of middle-class radicalism, Edward Jenkins. In Kilmarnock, too, where working-class radicalism had failed to budge E. P. Bouverie in 1868, a radical of the middle-class variety, J. Fortescue Harrison, triumphed in 1874. In Greenock in 1878 James Stewart, another of the same hue as these three, saw off a Tory and a moderate Liberal to win a by-election, while in Aberdeen in 1880 Dr. Webster seized the city for the same interest group. Somewhat similar developments occurred at Leith, Falkirk and Inverness burghs.

The timing of these conflicts is interestingly belated, in that the breakthrough did not occur in 1868, immediately upon the new franchise coming into play. Many Tories of course believed that the new electorate would be mere catspaws of the Dissenting clergy.[11] The U.P. Church itself stated in 1865 that any political advances were conditional upon a wider suffrage.[12] The only successful advance made by middle-class radicals before 1874 came in Edinburgh, and that had been set in train in 1865, under the old franchise dispensation. The element which had long made Dissent more political and politics more ecclesiastical in the city was the Annuity Tax, and the 1865 election constituted the final episode in the struggle to abolish it. The tax had indeed been commuted in 1860, at the instance of Lord Advocate Moncrieff, one of the Edinburgh M.P.s, supported by the other city M.P., Adam Black. The failure to repeal the tax *in toto* merely intensified the campaign to abolish it entirely. Duncan MacLaren ran with John Miller, a Free Churchman also eager to extinguish all relics of the Annuity Tax, and while Moncrieff was able to stave off the attack mounted by his fellow Churchman Miller, MacLaren unseated his fellow-Voluntary Black. In 1868 the process was accelerated. Moncrieff had not fully supported MacLaren's efforts to eliminate the Annuity Tax, and so MacLaren again ran in tandem with Miller, whereupon Moncrieff chose to retreat from his exposed position and opted for the safer Glasgow and Aberdeen Universities seat.[13] But the special circumstances of

Edinburgh did not obtain elsewhere, and so the Free Church-Voluntary radical alliance could not be created elsewhere as early as 1865 or 1868.

The groundwork for this reconstitution of the alliance of Free and U.P. elements into a new political upsurge was in part laid by the negotiations for union between the two churches. The merger talks had begun in 1863, reflecting the changes in personnel, both lay and clerical, in the two churches as the older generation implicated in the sometimes bitter controversies of the past quarter-century passed from prominence. They also were a response to the realisation that the state church was beginning to mount something of a recovery, particularly in the bigger towns, as a new generation of liberal, dynamic clergymen came to the fore. These men were inspired by Norman MacLeod in Glasgow and Robert Lee in Edinburgh, and included the rising leaders of the national church, like Tulloch, Caird, Story and Marshall Lang. The Free and U.P. discussions produced close and protracted encounters at a long series of joint meetings which involved not only ministers but also lay members. Almost immediately they had embarked upon the Union talks, one of the benefits of a merger was pointed out by an elder: 'Supposing, for instance, that when they came to choose a member of Parliament they could get a man of talent who was also a *consistent* Christian [i.e. not Church of Scotland], we could more easily get him elected'.[14] Although the Union talks collapsed in 1873 in a welter of threatened legal actions on the part of a minority within the Free Church, the so-called constitutional Free Church party, a new unity had been found by both the U.P. and the bulk of the Free Church who had reached accord. As the ecclesiastical road forward was effectively blocked, however, many turned to politics as a means of securing advance toward their goals. It is perhaps significant that the Union talks came to an end in 1873, so that much of the energy and preoccupation of both sides was committed to church matters during the 1868 election, but these forces were released in good time for the 1874 election. But the anticlimactic collapse of the high hopes and efforts invested in the negotiations could have led to apathy and withdrawal from public life. The new-found *élan* of the radical evangelicals had deeper roots. James Fitzjames Stephen, the eminent jurist, was humiliatingly beaten in the Dundee by-election of 1873, which was partly created in order to find him a seat. Stephen managed to get under 10% of the poll, despite being the Government's preferred candidate, and referred aptly to the views of his radical opponent, Edward Jenkins, as 'unctuous philanthropic enthusiasm'. His biographer relates that Stephen's exposure to this style of politics was one of the factors which drove him over from Liberalism to becoming one of the foremost exponents of late Victorian Conservative thinking.[15]

'Unctuous philanthropic enthusiasm' was connected directly with a reappraisal in the later 1860s of the best means of tackling the problem of irreligion in urban Scotland. This new interest in the topic stemmed in part from the implications of a wider electorate after 1868 with little religious feeling, and from the exposure by the Argyll Commission of 1867 of the absence of educational provision in the great cities.[16] But there were additional factors to these. Firstly, it was stressed that the mere building of churches or providing of domestic missions would not in themselves end godlessness, unless social reforms were also undertaken. In April 1871, the significantly titled Association for the Promotion of the Religious and Social Improvement of the City was founded in Glasgow, and in explaining the urgency of coping with the utter lack of religion amongst one-fifth of the city's population, the Association listed three hindrances. They were, firstly, want of education, followed by intemperance and bad housing, and then, lowest in importance, lack of church accommodation.[17] Many of the evangelicals behind Cameron's candidature in Glasgow in 1874 possessed this socially aware missionary emphasis. A highly successful charitable scheme to provide substantial lunchtime meals for working men who might otherwise succumb to the temptations of the public house was pioneered by Thomas Corbett, whose son, Alexander, became a Radical M.P. for one of the city seats in 1885.

Corbett senior was also involved in endeavours with the central figure in West of Scotland evangelical philanthropy, William Quarrier, who launched his most enduring project, a scheme to rescue destitute and orphaned children, in 1871. Quarrier's work was seen by him and others as reclamatory work of a social and religious nature: 'The dirty and over-crowded streets and lanes of the city', he reported in 1874, 'have as before, been the scenes of our labours and from them we have gathered many a rough but precious jewel which will, we have no doubt, shine brightly in the Crown of our blessed Saviour'.[18] Quarrier and some of the directors of his Orphanage Trust were instrumental in running Cameron. Cameron had opened the pages of his newspaper, *The North British Daily Mail,* to a whole series of exposures of social problems in the Glasgow area, many of which were clearly written in collaboration with Quarrier himself.[19] Eventually Cameron became the Chairman of Quarrier's Orphans Homes Committee. Others involved in Quarrier's various charitable ventures included men with considerable political influence in seats apart from Glasgow itself. One such was Thomas Coats, the largest employer in Paisley, and another example was J. C. White, later Lord Overtoun, who played an active part in securing the return of Harrison for Kilmarnock, through his important industrial interests in Rutherglen, one of the component burghs.[20]

The evangelical context within which these men worked was markedly elevated by Moody and Sankey's first revival tour through Scotland. This important event began in November 1873 and lasted until the summer of 1874, thus coinciding exactly with the general election period: indeed they were in Glasgow during the peak of electioneering frenzy. Their work in Scotland, which was mainly in the Lowland cities, was by common consent of wider and deeper impact than in England.[21] Their meetings were everywhere packed to capacity and many were enthused by their preaching, especially in the Free and U.P. congregations. The biographer of the leading Free Churchman of the period, Robert Rainy, a man not easily swayed by emotion, pointed out the effects of the Americans, stressing in the course of his remarks the impetus to charitable works which their preaching prompted: '[Moody] in Scotland refreshed the religious essentials of the Gospel — the love of God, the freeness of forgiveness, the power for holiness and, it should be noted, the Christian call to righteousness and even philanthropy'.[22]

Strikingly, the life of Cairns, the U.P. leader of the day, similarly testifies to the energising effects wrought by Moody and Sankey, and also notes the call for a public display of religious belief contained in their message.[23] The reaction in Scottish cities was remarkable, and in Glasgow can justly be described as electrifying, with 3,000 converts being claimed. One episode is worthy of fuller consideration. At a meeting in Ewing Place Church, 101 young men openly testified to their conversion, and this was followed by intense prayer sessions over a nine-month period, during which many more were converted. Out of this spectacular incident came the Glasgow United Evangelistic Association, formed in 1874: 'The Mission was the means of begetting throughout the Christian community a new sense of responsibility and deeper compassion in relation to the spiritual and temporal needs of the City's poor and its social outcasts'. Free breakfasts for derelict sleepers-out and day refuges for destitute children were organised, as well as prayer missions and bible fellowship classes.[24] Again, three of the key figures in Quarrier's circle of supporters — Alex Allan, J. H. N. Graham and J. C. White — were stalwarts of this by-product of Moody and Sankey. In Greenock, Gourock and Paisley, the response to Moody and Sankey was fervent, and in these places similar political movements emerged. Although the revivalists' campaign attracted support from the Church of Scotland, it stirred the greater excitement in the Free and U.P. Churches. In general, it seems that apathetic members, not the irreligious masses, were reached by Moody and Sankey, and this re-entry of erstwhile communicants may well have boosted Dissenting confidence.[25]

With a sharpened perception of the social barriers to religious advance, it was a short step to desiring an increase in truly Christian influence in the legislature, in order to pass laws of a properly moral quality. The Contagious Diseases Act was a major focus of evangelical discontent on this score, for it was construed as condoning prostitution.[26] Quarrier praised Cameron's opposition to the measure and called on Christian voters to elect parliamentary representatives 'who value Moral Legislation as a first consideration'.[27] In addition, the impatience of the new moral force at the obstructive attitude shown by local authorities may have contributed to the mood of protest and direct political action. Quarrier complained bitterly of Glasgow Corporation's refusal to make sites available for his refuges unless he competed on the open market with speculative builders.[28] As a result new men entered local politics in several places in an effort to change the policies of the municipality. In Dundee after 1868, among those coming on to the Council with this objective was F. Y. Henderson, leader of Jenkins' 1873 and 1874 election committees, while in Glasgow, William Collins, a leading member of Cameron's committee, entered the Council to fight against existing policies.

While these emotional spasms gave the evangelical radicals the urge to exercise dominance in Liberal politics, such powerful emotions were not easily translated into electoral power. The crucial determinant for this latter success came through the electoral organisational drive contributed by perhaps the most vibrant component of this general religious social reform movement — Temperance. The older temperance tradition of moral suasion, embodied in the Scottish Temperance

League, had settled into complacent stagnation after the passage in 1853 of the Forbes MacKenzie Act, which restricted the hours of public drinking. In 1858, the more dynamic Scottish Permissive Bill Association was established, as a wing of the militant United Kingdom Alliance (which, despite its name, did not operate in Scotland). The SPBA called for positive action rather than total abstinence in order to suppress drink, which it saw as an offence against society, and its remedy carried an overt incitement to political action: 'Prohibitive Legislation alone can be effectual against the public sources of Intemperance'.[29] But no major political progress was made by the SPBA before 1874, as it lamented on the eve of the 1868 General Election: 'In the coming contest temperance reformers . . . cannot make our views a turning point upon which the election will hinge. We are only a small minority and therefore cannot anticipate that the larger section of the electorate will defer to us'.[30] But in 1874 the situation was altered: in Dundee, Jenkins' candidature was described as triumphant largely because he attracted the adhesion of the local SPBA, and in Leith the unqualified backing given by temperance bodies to Dr. MacGregor was crucial to his unseating the incumbent M.P. In Glasgow, Cameron's victory was, as will be seen, ascribed to the same factor, and at Greenock in 1878 the endorsement of the temperance party was seen as decisive in winning the seat for the radical, who was a Vice-President of the Permissive Bill Association.[31]

There were several reasons for this breakthrough by the temperance section. Firstly, Moody and Sankey, abstainers both, provided a major impetus: 'Although their mission is not distinctly to promote the Temperance cause', remarked the Temperance League's paper, 'it has operated powerfully in this direction . . . The increase in the temperance reformation manifested in connection with the great religious revival with Glasgow and other parts of Scotland experienced in the early months of 1874 has not only continued but increased in intensity and extent'.[32] John Cairns, the leader of the U.P. church, became a Permissive Biller in 1874, at the same time as he was profoundly affected by Moody and Sankey.[33] This growth was reflected in subscriptions to the SPBA. From £752 in 1865–6, they rose to £1,224 in 1870–1, and by 1875–6 were at £2,037, a level which held for a decade.[34] In addition, a new temperance body, the Scottish Grand Lodge of the Independent Order of Good Templars, was formed in 1870. By 1876 there were 62,334 members claimed in 804 branches, a striking testimony to the upsurge of temperance support in the early 1870s.[35] Equally importantly, the gulf opened up between the Scottish Temperance League and the Permissive Bill Association by the rift in the 1850s over tactics was fully closed upon the accession of William Collins to the Presidency of the League in 1872. Collins was on good terms with many Permissive Bill leaders, and the latter welcomed Collins' appointment as President in effusive terms.[36] Between these two bodies and also the Templars, there was much overlap of personnel and considerable pooling of effort in the 1870s.[37] Five men were Directors of both main bodies in the 1870s.

The SPBA was, however, the driving force in the temperance campaign, and from around 1870 it shifted its emphasis, which had hitherto been devoted to propagandist and educational ventures, to political involvement. 'The great truth should ever be kept in view', its annual report for 1871–2 stated, 'that all temperance efforts should culminate at the ballot box. Moral suasion is a great principle, but it does not meet all the wants of this particular question.'[38] This goal, the SPBA felt, was to be attained by organising sympathetic voters, and accordingly it worked on this task throughout 1872 and 1873. The SPBA claimed some six months before the 1874 elections that it had completed a thorough scheme of organisation designed to allow it to '[come] to a thorough understanding with members of Parliament and of thoroughly removing from their minds any uncertainty regarding our electoral strength'.[39] The SPBA's model rules for these political activities stressed the necessity of canvassing all electors, of then registering all friendly eligible voters and above all of trying to ensure the selection of candidates favourable to Prohibition.[40] The emphasis was placed on early and decisive moves to secure the choice of the proper type of man: 'Hitherto in no small way we have begun at the end,' said the SPBA journal two months before the 1874 elections. 'We first voted for men hostile to the Permissive Bill and then petitioned them to pass the bill. We propose to alter all that. The temperance question being of all questions the most momentous, we urge that it shall have the first place'.[41]

Looking back over a quarter of a century later, the Secretary of the SPBA in the 1870s argued that 'An electoral committee to every Temperance Society is indispensable. The active work required will be in consonance with the interest which most people take in political affairs ... Committees formed for such a patriotic purpose have found pleasure in the arduous work pertaining to electoral effort ... What has been done by committees in the early days of the agitation [i.e. the 1870s] can be done as easily at least to-day. Canvassing was carried on then in a way which elicited the admiration of Social as well as Temperance Reformers'.[42] Given the rise of a mass electorate and the innovation of the secret ballot, the temperance movement held a strong vantage point with its commitment to political activism, the highly charged enthusiasm of adherents to the cause, and highly developed techniques of organisation designed to identify and deliver a body of votes. These qualities were amply demonstrated in Glasgow in 1874: 'Dr. Cameron, having pledged himself to the influential deputation that waited upon him, the moral and social reformers of Glasgow wrought nobly for him — leaders and led vying with each other for his return. The result was his elevation to the senior membership for Glasgow'. Cameron's committee claimed to have distributed 53,000 circulars by voluntary labour, and one of his temperance supporters testified how he and two or three friends worked one evening to communicate with about one hundred sympathisers who gathered the next day to sort and deliver 4,000 letters to voters in one locality.[43] Cameron held seven public meetings during the election. Of the four men who sat on the platform at five or more of them, three were temperance leaders (the other was Quarrier); of the ten individuals who were on the platform at three or four meetings, six were temperance men.

This tilt in the political balance of Scottish Liberalism was of course paralleled by a similar pattern in major English cities, typified by Chamberlain in Birmingham, with whose policies and organisational methods the Scottish Radicals identified themselves. But there were salient differences between the two. In Chamberlain's Birmingham, the civic gospel of municipal service and urban renewal initiated the emergence of advanced Liberalism. The civic gospel tended to be low in evangelical content, with minimal church overtones (lectures, not sermons, were delivered), and was pragmatic in tone.[44] This clearly had little in common with the sweeping emotional revivalism associated with Scottish Radicalism's origins. Then, the education issue, which acutely politicised English Nonconformity after the passage of the 1870 Act, had no equivalent in Scotland. One of the two major non-established churches, the Free Church, as has been shown for the 1850s, had absolutely no objection to the principle of state-financed religious instruction in schools. The other one, the U.P. Church, was split between those willing to accept the use of rates to support religious teaching, provided a conscience clause allowed Voluntaries to withdraw their children from the class, and those utterly opposed to the state subsidising religion. The U.P. organ regretfully wrote in 1872: 'there is no disguising the fact that our Church is not united on this question'.[45] Thus Henry Calderwood, emerging as the heir to John Cairns as leader of the Church, stood for the Edinburgh School Board on a platform of being willing to retain the use and wont system.[46] The Scottish National Education League was a coalition of working-class reformers, some university dons like Professor J. P. Nichol of Glasgow and some Whigs, but, quite at variance with its English analogue, it contained almost no Dissenters. Thus, when R. Dale, the English Nonconformist minister most centrally involved in the Education struggle in England, came north in 1872 to rally opposition to the Scottish bill, he failed abjectly to rouse any kindred spirits to action. Indeed men like John Cairns advised him not to come to Scotland at all.[47] In the School Board elections, the Dissenters' candidates ran quite separately from those sponsored by the Scottish National Education League.

A further divergence between the English and the Scottish patterns was in attitudes to organised labour. In the former, Chamberlain made 'free labour' (i.e. trade union rights) one of his cardinal demands in the 1870s and A. J. Mundella forged close links with Sheffield working men by his support of their trade union demands. In most of Scotland, though not in Dundee and Leith, the new Radicals displayed no avid desire to establish close ties with working-class reformers. Cameron's attitude to trade unions was not that of the new model employers so prominent in England, as he showed when observing that the Dublin office of his printing firm 'is open to Trades Union men, but they don't choose to come into it (Laughter and cheers) ... All I contend for is justice and I say if union men have a right to fight against offices, offices have a right to fight against union men (cheers)'.[48] One of the leading figures in Cameron's circle, J. C. White — later Lord Overtoun — was to be the subject of a bitter dispute over allegations made by the ILP in the 1890s that workers in his chemical factory were appallingly treated. In Edinburgh, MacLaren's running mate in 1868 was dropped from the joint ticket with alacrity in 1874 when he adopted a programme of trade union rights. MacLaren, who staunchly declined to endorse the demand for a repeal of the anti-union Criminal Law Amendment Act, was content to be returned with an old-fashioned Whig. The radical journal in the city pointed out that MacLaren had captured the solid middle-class vote, 'the backbone of Edinburgh Society', and the result had given 'eloquent testimony' to the futility of trade union agitation in the city.[49] In Greenock in 1878, while the temperance movement pushed a candidate forward, the working-class Liberals protested volubly at the manipulation by local middle-class radicals 'who were ever ready to ignore the workingmen', and they asserted their desire to find a candidate 'who could not only look over ship and sugar houses, but over the country generally'.[50]

The civic gospel concept stimulated the execution of sweeping urban reform measures in England, most clearly exemplified by Chamberlain's work as Mayor of Birmingham. There was much less evidence of these trends in Scotland. In Glasgow, for instance, the initial irruption into municipal affairs by radical Dissenters was mainly in reaction to the cost of the City Improvement Trust's work, which was designed to raise housing standards by facilitating slum clearance. The Lord Provost responsible for the scheme, John Blackie, lost his seat in 1866 to an ardent teetotaller, who campaigned against the expense incurred by the Improvement scheme, and the regime of the first of the new radicals to become Lord Provost, William Collins (1877–80), was characterised by strict economy and absence of initiative, a stark contrast to Chamberlain's expansive enterprising approach.[51] Likewise, when a group of radical Dissenters acquired seats on the Glasgow School Board in 1882, it was not a victory for the issue of opposition to religious teaching in schools, for the main cry of the radicals was a promise to cut back the extravagant expenditure levels permitted by the existing use and wont majority on the Board.[52] Thus, the Scottish radicals were usually cast as 'economists', the party whom Chamberlain had overturned in Birmingham.

II

The combination in 1874 of an electoral setback, along with a new and potentially disruptive element within the Liberal party, resulted in a complex set of manoeuvres between the competing wings of the party. These operations were largely conducted around matters of organisation.[53] The 1874 results had exposed quite plainly the failure of Liberal party machinery to adjust to the difficulties presented by the innovation of the ballot, which rendered redundant the old style of electioneering. Most constituencies had no permanent structure of organisation: most M.P.s or candidates had a legal agent who attended to registration matters and summoned together supporters upon a dissolution. Where some more coherent organisation did exist, it had frequently atrophied, as in the case of the Roxburghshire Liberal Registration Committee, which by 1867 was sustained by only four subscribers.[54] This inertia may well have been due to the virtual collapse of the Tory party presence in many seats from the mid-1850s, as we saw. Under W. P. Adam's direction, however, attempts were made to improve the standard of

Liberal organisational work in the constituencies. Soon after the 1874 general election reverse, enquiries were made by Adam to ascertain the degree of administrative competence obtaining in Scottish seats. At times, little could be accomplished, especially when the response from a sitting M.P. was testy. Edward Ellice replied that the St. Andrews Liberals 'have managed their own affairs quite satisfactorily without asking for or receiving interest from without ... I should advise my friends to adhere to the same independent position they have hitherto maintained and to decline the suggested interference of an English agency in their local political affairs'.[55] Gradually, however, constituencies were induced to set up formal associations. In Roxburghshire, this had occurred after the 1865 election, and it was a question of reviving it, but elsewhere the new system often came about on the retiral of an M.P. or a change of candidate, as happened in Fife in 1878 and in East Lothian in 1879.[56]

This somewhat crablike advance acquired urgency as organisation began to be perceived as a powerful means of furthering policy changes as well as being desirable merely to enhance efficiency. Urban middle-class radical M.P.s had in certain places been aware even before 1874 of the broader gains to be derived from a formal organisation. This was best developed in Edinburgh, where the Whiggish Aggregate Liberal Committee dated from the 1830s and the radical Independent Liberal Committee from the 1840s. By the later 1860s MacLaren identified the latter body as the main contributory factor to his electoral success. In 1865 the committee had mobilised its voting power against Adam Black, and in 1868 it had united MacLaren with Miller to stop second votes being cast for Moncreiff, who promptly retired from the contest.[57] The Dundee radicals who put Jenkins into Parliament in 1874 also had an Independent Liberal Committee to discipline and deliver their vote. Out of this influence wielded by the committees there flowed an important corollary: than an M.P. should acquiesce in the expressed opinion on policy of these organisations which had secured his return to Westminster. As MacLaren, the most eminent and individual of the radicals of this period, phrased it: 'I will always consider myself in their hands and will cordially act with them in all circumstances, whatever they may be ... I hold that my individuality is now merged with the committee'.[58] This was said in a private letter to his son, not a public speech, and so may not be just a classic instance of radical persiflage.

Although at first the opinion of these committees was mainly pronounced on matters such as joint candidature, two important extra arguments stemmed therefrom. Firstly, it was an obvious way of legitimising the claim of a contender to be designated as the official Liberal candidate if he were endorsed by a body styling itself as the Liberal Association of the constituency, especially when the other candidates had no more than self-appointed *ad hoc* structures. So when a vacancy cropped up in late 1877 in Greenock, the town's Liberal Association was resuscitated by a group of local radicals after it had been in abeyance for nearly nine years.[59] Likewise, rumours in 1878 of the resignation of one of the city M.P.s led to the hurried formation of the Glasgow Liberal Association by Collins and other leaders of Cameron's election committee.[60] Both these moves were clearly described, and openly acknowledged, as bids to pre-empt the choice of candidate, rather than to heighten the efficiency of party machinery in either seat.

In addition to annexing the power of selecting a candidate, the new Liberal associations asserted the right both to formulate policy decisions and to make these decisions binding on the local party. Thus whereas the reconstituted Roxburghshire Liberal Registration Society — where an old Whiggish element prevailed, as its title suggests — defined its role in a strictly administrative capacity, the Glasgow Liberal Association vested the determination of the policy stance of the Association on public affairs in a mass meeting of branch delegates, and charged the executive with the task of implementing these policy decisions.[61] This right to pronounce on policy was vigorously taken up in Glasgow: in the third annual report of the Liberal Association, delegates were recorded as having passed resolutions at each quarterly meeting of the '600' on a range of issues such as the Game Laws, the Deceased Wife's Sister Marriage Bill, the Irish Franchise Bill and a proposal to erect a statue to Louis Napoleon (which last they opposed).[62]

The example of the Birmingham Liberal Association was of course ever-present as a model and inspiration for the radicals, but added impetus was given by the emergence of disestablishment as a leading issue in Scottish politics in the 1870s.[63] It had not been a prominent factor before the summer of 1874, and in the 1868 election the topic was barely mentioned. In the 1874 election campaign in Glasgow, even Cameron's own paper commented: 'The question ... is not occupying very largely the public mind'.[64] The final collapse of the Free-U.P. Church Union talks in 1873 was an important factor, but, as already pointed out, the introduction of legislation to abolish lay patronage in the state church in 1874 gave a badly needed stimulus to the disestablishment campaign. Thus the Liberation Society was able to report after an autumn campaign in 1874 that 'generally the meetings indicated a decided progress of the movement in Scotland'.[65] Particular stress was laid by veteran disestablishers on the participation in this new agitation of members of the Free Church, who for the first time since the Disruption were willing to declare themselves Voluntaries in principle, as well as in practice. Although the Free Church kept itself organisationally distinct from the Liberation Society by forming the Scottish Disestablishment Association as its own vehicle, close collaboration was promptly established.[66] The rise of the disestablishment cry on so broad a front was a novel development, but initially Church of Scotland Liberals were not over-anxious, regarding the campaign as confined to the clergy, while 'the public remains apathetic', which explained, according to the editor of *The Scotsman,* 'the rather cool reception of the agitation'.[67]

However, Hartington's tour of Scotland as leader of the party late in 1877 forced a reappraisal by Church Liberals. Hartington had told Rosebery, 'I shall expect you to give me a safe sentence or two on Scottish Church matters'.[68] Hartington, whatever Rosebery's briefing, declared his approval of the demand being made for disestablishment. This meant that the advanced Liberal wing could justifiably claim to have the endorsement of the leadership, and now had to bend their energies to demonstrating that the bulk of Scottish public opinion also demanded disestablishment.[69] The momentum seemed irresistible, as the bulk of Liberal grassroots activists in the 1870s were drawn from the ranks of the two churches clamouring for an end to the Church of Scotland's privileged status.

Very quickly after Hartington's declaration, Fife radicals acted, both in the county seat and the St Andrews burghs. In the first, a local party organiser told the Liberal Chief Whip, 'From all I can hear the Nonconformists will not support our present member'.[70] The M.P. was Sir Robert Anstruther, who had long been one of the doughtiest apologists of the Church of Scotland, and who had been an earnest advocate of the abolition of patronage. In his place, it was alleged, some Kirkcaldy Free Churchmen — 'a group of fanatical Dissenters' — had designs to put up a Voluntary.[71] At St Andrews, the retiral of the long-serving anti-disestablisher Ellice allowed what Church Liberals described as 'the extreme wing' to press the candidature of a staunch opponent of the state church principle, Stephen Williamson.[72] Yet the challenge did not materialise in a substantial form. At the general election of 1880, a survey of the contents of Liberal candidates' election manifestos concluded: 'It will be seen that the almost universal desire of Liberal candidates was to express no definite opinion on the subject'. Only eight out of the sixty candidates came out unequivocally in favour of disestablishment.[73]

This containment of the disestablishment lobby and the concomitant retention of Church Liberals within a united party was achieved in two ways. Firstly, organisational means were adopted to counter the workings of advanced Liberals, and two actions were taken to this end. One was at constituency level by the participation of moderate Liberals in the new party machinery constructed by radicals. This involvement was undertaken with the aim of seeking to prevent control from being monopolised by one faction. This at any rate was the reason Principal Tulloch, the arch Church Liberal, gave for his somewhat surprising decision to enrol in the St Andrews Liberal Association.[74] This tactic was decidedly stiffened when hostility existed between working-class Liberals and Dissenting radicals. At the 1878 Greenock by-election the local Working Men's Liberal Association backed Donald Currie, who was lukewarm on disestablishment, in preference to the choice of the temperance and disestablishment lobbies, who, as has been seen, were hostile to labour's demands.[75]

This arrangement also functioned in Glasgow, but in a more extended form. When the Dissenting radicals decided, in circumstances already noted, to found the Glasgow Liberal Association, both the Whig committee and the Liberal Working Men's Electoral Union (a sort of transmogrified Scottish Reform League) declined to join it, as the new body was regarded as over-dominated by sectional radical interests. Because of these sizeable abstentions, the Glasgow Liberal Association was at the outset treated as the product of a narrow clique, and in order to repudiate allegations by critics that it was a mere catspaw of the militant radicals, it agreed to drop from its constitution a programme of demands which included disestablishment, temperance and so forth. The removal of the policy content succeeded in encouraging a broader intake of membership, and the election in 1879 to the Presidency of the Association of Charles Tennant, a representative of one of the great old Whig families in the city, was hailed with delight. When a vacancy in the representation of Glasgow was created by the death of Whitelaw, the anti-radicals moved with speed and skill. Tennant was nominated as the Liberal candidate by the Working Men's Electoral Union, which remained aloof from the Liberal Association, before the latter could convene a meeting of delegates to consider the choice of a candidate. When the Association did meet, confronted by the *fait accompli* of its President being already in the field, it voted by 127 to 119 to endorse Tennant rather than its originally preferred nominee, R. T. Middleton, who was a radical in the disestablishment-temperance mould. Thus an alliance of Whigs and working-class Liberals had outflanked advanced Liberals.[76] In Edinburgh, the advanced radical forward movement was stymied by a circuitous but effective train of events in 1879. In the face of strong working-class support for a third Liberal candidate, there arose the rich irony of Duncan MacLaren's son, John, writing desperately to the Scottish Whig managers to urge concerted action to avert a Liberal split in the city. Whereas in 1877 Duncan had thundered his defiance — 'The members of the Liberal Independent Committee will never unite with the old Whig committee, called the Aggregate ... ' — two years later John MacLaren canvassed, as one option, an agreement by the two sitting M.P.s to offer themselves for a further Parliament, even although one of them was a solid Whig, normally anathema to any MacLaren.[77] This in fact happened, and the third candidate, feeling it would be difficult to dislodge M.P.s in occupancy, retreated. But the price of this was of course that the Whigs retained the seat the radicals had targeted as winnable.

A second level of machinery at which the thrust of Dissenting radicals could be held down was through the creation of a central organisation for Scotland. In England in 1877 the National Liberal Federation (NLF) had been formed to promote and project on a national scale the political programme advocated by Chamberlain and his allies. W. P. Adam was trenchantly clear about the threat such a body posed in his native land: 'Chamberlain is the last man of the party whose advent to Scotland should be celebrated ... We don't want him and his Birmingham schemes here, and can manage our own business without his instructions'.[78] In fact two bodies had been set up in 1876–7, but in composition and function they were quite unlike the English organisation. They were the East and North of Scotland Liberal Association and the West and South of Scotland Liberal Association: ESLA and WSLA respectively. The personnel of both were overwhelmingly Whiggish. The ESLA had Adam as chairman, with the Perthshire laird Maxtone Graham and Rosebery the other leaders, while the WSLA had a prominent urban Whig, James Grahame of Auldhouse, as secretary and moving spirit, accompanied on the executive by fellow-Whigs like Breadalbane, Sir T. E. Colebrooke, J. G. C. Hamilton of Dalzell — three wealthy landowners — and also Bolton and Crum, the defeated Whigs in the 1874 Glasgow election.[79] There was to be found, however, in both associations a smattering of advanced radicals. These included two of Cameron's committee, J. C. White of Overtoun and James Roberton, the M.P.'s agent, as well as John MacLaren and the future radical M.P. for Aberdeen, Dr Webster. These were adroitly balanced by the presence of working-class Liberals, of whom the most eminent was George Jackson, of the Glasgow Liberal Working Men's Electoral Union. In addition, many of the great Whig magnates held themselves aloof from these bodies, finding them too democratic for their taste. Such men included Minto, Bowmont, Sutherland and Reay, and their absence may possibly have made the two bodies more acceptable in the eyes of many non-Whigs.

The two Associations took a less exalted view of their powers and responsibilities than the NLF. Thus the ESLA defined its scope as advisory and supportive: 'While the Council will not in any way whatever interfere with the independent action of the various Liberal Associations for which it is formed, it will be prepared at General or other Parliamentary Elections or upon such other occasions as may seem to call for action, to afford all information and advice to the several local Associations or Constituencies ... '[80] Adam expounded his conception of the policy-forming role of the ESLA at its first annual general meeting when he insisted emphatically that it should concentrate on developing party machinery to a peak of efficiency, while also counselling against seeking to impose policy programmes upon the party leadership.[81] The activities of both these regional associations in practice seem to have extended well beyond these vague outlines. For one thing, they were instrumental in ensuring that within the first two years of their existence almost every seat had a constituency association set up. It is probable that many of these local bodies were guided away from being dominated by cliques of radicals. As the ESLA described the fruits of its labours, these were 'committees of a character more or less completely representative'.[82] Secondly, at the General Election of 1880, both regional associations claimed a main part in finding candidates for the numerous local parties who had no-one to bring forward. This sphere of activity proved to be merely a figleaf for further manipulation by Adam to regulate the quality and political character of candidates. The growth in democratic sensitivities produced by the creation of constituency party associations made it no longer possible for him to control the process, as in 1874, through the medium of telegrams to his Edinburgh acolyte, Craig Sellar. In 1880 Adam instead worked through the ESLA secretary, J. J. Reid. Reid visited many constituencies in the six months prior to the dissolution, and he also interviewed and approached a fair number of aspiring candidates. But all of his work was done under the direction of and in full consultation with Adam. Sixteen seats were assessed and allocated candidates, and this was probably in addition to an unknown number of seats in the Glasgow area, which would be dealt with by Reid's counterpart in the WSLA, James Grahame.[83]

It should be noted that Whiggish candidates were not always installed in vacant constituencies by Adam and Reid. Thus Principal Tulloch led the complaints about manipulation against Church Liberal interests at the hands of Adam, Rosebery and *The Scotsman.* Nor was Tulloch's case entirely groundless, for Reid discouraged him and others from challenging the candidature of the zealous disestablisher Williamson in St Andrews, Tulloch's own constituency.[84] Also sometimes desperation, not Machiavellian cunning, dictated the choice of candidate. Sir Leonard Lyell, an Angus landowner, was bruited for Inverness

County by Reid: 'We have *no local man whatever,* and the next best thing is a laird and a Scotchman ... I hope he wears a kilt; if he is up Glenisla way he very likely does'.[85] But in a number of places it was possible to finesse matters in a preferred direction. In the Ayr Burghs, where 'The P.B.s [Permissive Billers] gave trouble', Reid addressed the local committee and quietened the radicals down. As a result the nomination was gained by R. F. F. Campbell of Craigie, a mainstream Whig.[86] In South Ayrshire the pressure to produce a local man was resisted by Reid, on the grounds that 'if we gave in to that we should be in a nice mess, I am afraid'. Instead, the son of the Earl of Stair, the most prominent Whig in the south-west, stood after Stair had consulted with Reid.[87] Adam and Reid were substantially assisted in their endeavours by the existence of a secret fund which in January 1881 totalled £2,000.[88] The use to which this could be applied was shown most plainly in Roxburghshire. Here secret fund money was made available to bolster the claims of A. R. D. Elliot, a younger son of Lord Minto, to be appointed as candidate. This maintained Whig representation in a seat where radicals from the burghs within the county had for a decade been restive at the domination of magnatial figures like Lords Minto, Roxburghe and Napier.[89]

There was a third method by which the regional associations could curb the pretensions of radical bodies. As both the ESLA and the WSLA were patently sanctioned by the official party leadership, the status of more than one organisation in a constituency claiming sole legitimacy could be determined by how the central association viewed the rival claims. Thus, as already noted, the Glasgow Liberal Association found it well-nigh impossible to acquire the mantle of the recognised representative organisation of city Liberalism. In good measure this was because the Liberal Workmen's Electoral Union had affiliated to the WSLA, and so was recognised by the latter as a, if not the, valid voice in Glasgow Liberalism. When the ESLA and the WSLA were merging in 1881 to form the Scottish Liberal Association, one of the most protracted squabbles broke out over the attempt by the Glasgow Liberal Association to assume the status of the sole Glasgow body entitled to participate. The Workmen's Union protested vociferously at their exclusion, and in the end their demands were accommodated, with the Union getting the right to have one delegate sit on the national association's executive, alongside the Glasgow Liberal Association's two delegates.[90]

Although quite different techniques were used by the Whigs to stave off the threat to unity presented by the disestablishment lobby down to 1880, they were equally successful. The method applied consisted, largely, of ensuring that the party leaders did or said nothing more after Hartington's first dictum to encourage the pressure for disestablishment. At the same time, great care was taken not to alienate Dissenters by pandering to the neurotic appeals from Church Liberals for copperbottomed assurances that the state church's position would remain unaltered. The demands of the latter proved extremely irritating, because they were treated as both irrational and unappeasable. A Church Defence Association was formed in August 1879 by prominent Church Liberals such as Lord Stair, Sir George MacPherson Grant, A. B. McGrigor, a Glasgow Whig, A. Asher, M.P., and J. Guthrie Smith, another West of Scotland Whig. As the secretary of the WSLA — himself highly sympathetic to their stance — reported to Adam, they were 'resolved no longer to be under the imputation of coquetting with the Disestablishment party'. The Church Defence Association produced a manifesto which reiterated this attitude, expressed their alarm at the use of party organisational reform as a guise to promote disestablishment candidates, and disclosed their reluctance at having to vote for such unappetising Liberals.[91] Adam found this all too much, remonstrating with a leading Church Liberal: 'I cannot understand what madness of suspicion seems to possess the Liberal Churchmen of Scotland'.[92]

Adam's outburst stemmed in part from frustration at continued sniping from the Church wing of the party after he had managed to get Gladstone to adopt a stance broadly compatible with the anti-disestablishment viewpoint. He had urged Gladstone to confirm that 'you have no intention whatever of bringing Scottish Disestablishment to the front but on the contrary would keep it in the background as far as possible at present'.[93] Gladstone replied to Adam that he felt Hartington in 1877 had gone very far indeed on the question, and should accordingly have the gratitude of the anti-state church camp. While he fully upheld Hartington's position. Gladstone could 'see no occasion to, and have no intention to press forward the Church question in any manner', especially as he foresaw that sorting out the legacy of Beaconsfield's financial and foreign policies would preoccupy an incoming Liberal administration.[94] In this context Gladstone's pledge given at the same time to Principal Rainy, the head of the Free Church, that the issue would not be raised by the Liberal party until the Scottish people had pronounced upon it 'in a manner which is intelligible and distinct' seems to have envisaged a timescale more protracted than that contemplated by the Rainy faction.[95] Another incident shedding light upon the influence over Gladstone enjoyed by Scottish Whigs came at the end of 1879. Charles Tennant sent him a copy of a memorandum compiled by a 'good Liberal' in the Tulloch mould which sketched the worries felt by Church Liberals at the pro-disestablishment construction which might be placed upon a recent speech by Gladstone on the church-state relationship. Tennant felt depressed at the prospect of seats being lost by Church Liberal abstentions or defections on this matter, but added, 'I do not see however what you can do to help us'. Gladstone promptly sent a clarification of his speech, which to Tennant's delight mollified the doubter: 'I think his mind is easier in consequence and his condition altogether happier'.[96]

Thus by a set of strategems and by exploiting fundamental weaknesses in the posture of the advanced Liberals, the balance between the various factions in Scottish Liberalism remained largely undisturbed at the general election of 1880. Church Liberal and Voluntary radical were still in the same fold, united behind the inspirational oratory of Gladstone during his Mid Lothian campaign in a common desire to oust the Tories. The relegation of disestablishment from the forefront of political priorities was confirmed in 1881. At an early meeting of the Council of the Scottish Liberal Association, the Chairman, Maxtone Graham, alluded to the candidature in the East Lothian by-election of R. B. Finlay, a tenacious defender of the Church of Scotland: 'On one particular point, the relations between Church and State, that gentleman held opinions different from many other Liberals — indeed very different from his own, but, as they knew, it was not a burning or pressing issue in the country at this time. What they were really looking forward to were questions of the tenure of land, the relations between landlord and tenant and so on, and questions of the procedure of the House of Commons to enable the representatives of the country to do their duty more effectively. These were the real pressing questions of the day'.[97]

Appendix: Notes to Table 5.1.

1. The principles and methods used in determining social groupings is described in the Appendix to Chapter 4.

2. A simple random sample of 10% of the electoral register was used — i.e., every tenth name was taken from the electoral rolls for each year. The voters' registers for the Scottish burghs were widely acknowledged to be reliable, and very few appeals were made to the registration counts on the grounds of error. This was not, of course, the case in England. The registers also recorded the occupation of every voter, but in cases of doubt — particularly in ascertaining whether the elector was an employer or an employee —recourse was had to the *Post Office Street and Trades Directory* for Glasgow.

3. The total electorate in 1867–8 was 18,363, and in 1868–9 it was 47,854. Copies of the electoral registers are kept in the Mitchell Library, Glasgow.

NOTES

1. D. MacLaren to J. MacLaren, 24 Jul. 1868, Oliver MSS., Acc. 7726/14, ff. 111–2.

2. Lumsden Diaries, 17 Oct. 1866; Scottish National Reform League, *Great Reform Demonstration at Glasgow on Tuesday 16th October 1866* (Glasgow, 1866).

3. G. Howell to G. Jackson, 14 Sep. 1867 (copy), Howell MSS; *Glasgow Herald,* 17, 18 Sep. 1867. W. H. Fraser, 'Trade Unions, Reform and the Election of 1868 in Scotland', *SHR,* 50 (1971), pp. 138–57 discusses this.

4. J. P. Nichol to J. S. Mill, 12 Jul., 1868, Chadwick MSS. 1401/99; E. Smith to W. Melvin, 24 Jun. 1868 (copy), David Murray Letterbooks.

5. J. P. Nichol to E. Chadwick, 6 Aug. 1868; J. Henderson to Chadwick, 17 Aug. 1868; Chadwick MSS. 1485; 979; 1401/99,100,112.

6. Beales to A. Russel, 11 Jul. 1868, Russel MSS., MS. 1845, ff. 48–52.

7. W. E. Baxter, A. F. Kinnaird to W. E. Gladstone, 23 Nov. 1868 (both), W. E. Gladstone MSS., Add. MSS. 44416, ff. 220–1; 44230, ff. 51–4.

8. W. P. Adam to Sir G. Montgomery, 8 Aug. 1868, Adam MSS., 4/430; G. Glyn to Gladstone, 17 Sep. 1868, W. E. Gladstone MSS., Add MS. 44347, ff. 170–3.

9. A. C. Sellar to Adam, n.d. (Jan./Feb. 1874), Adam MSS., 4/578.

10. Lumsden Diary, 3 Feb. 1874.

11. E.g., Ailsa to Col. Alexander, 29 Sep. 1868 (draft), Ailsa MSS., GD 25/9/30. The Select Committee on Parliamentary and Municipal Elections heard conflicting evidence on the role of the clergy in the 1868 election. Liberals like A. Russel and J. H. MacGowan

L

stressed that the influence of the Scottish minister in political matters over his flock was very slight, P. P. 1868–9 (352) VIII, 99, qq. 5871–83; 5987; 6051. Tory allegations are at qq. 7352–4; 7836–8; 7871–6.

12. *U. P. Magazine,* 9 (1865), pp. 331–2.

13. J. B. Mackie, *Life and Work of Duncan MacLaren* (Edinburgh, 1888), I, pp. 192–202; II, pp. 38–48; *Scotsman,* 5 Jun. 1865; A. Nicolson, *Memoirs of Adam Black,* (2nd edn., Edinburgh, 1885), pp. 227–33. In 1868, MacLaren also secured working-class support for his advocacy of franchise reform: R. Q. Gray, *The Labour Aristocracy in Victorian Edinburgh* (London, 1976), pp. 156–7.

14. *Union Soiree* (n.p., n.d.), p. 4. This was held on 15 Apr. 1868.

15. L. Stephen, *Life of Sir James Fitzjames Stephen* (London, 1895), p. 345. The by-election is incorrectly dated 1874.

16. In Glasgow, the churches organised Sanitary Visiting Committees to stem cholera and fever scares: *Glasgow Herald,* 4, 13, 25 Sep., 2 Oct., 27, 28 Nov. 1866, 2 Jan., 20 Apr. 1867; 27 Dec. 1869, 15 Mar. 1870. On educational provision, the Argyll report revealed only one-third of children in cities like Glasgow were receiving schooling (P. P. 1867 (3845) XXV).

17. Association for Promoting the Religious and Social Improvement of the City, *Report on the Religious Condition of Glasgow,* (n.p., n.d., c.1871–2), pp. 10–12.

18. [W. Quarrier], *A Narrative of Facts relative to the Work done for Christ in connection with the Orphan and Destitute Children's Emigration Homes in Glasgow* (1874), p. 36.

19. *The North British Daily Mail* published 97 such articles between July 1869 and June 1874, with a further 40 appearing between March 1876 and the end of 1879.

20. For the Kilmarnock contest generally, cf. E. P. Bouverie to E. Ellice, 8 Feb. 1874, Ellice MSS., MS. 15005, ff. 144–7.

21. A. L. Drummond and J. Bulloch, *The Church in Later Victorian Scotland* (Edinburgh, 1978), pp. 9–16 discusses the visit, but rather concentrates on theological aspects.

22. P. C. Simpson, *The Life of Principal Rainy* (London, 1909), I. pp. 408–9.

23. A. R. MacEwan, *Life and Letters of John Cairns, D.D., LL.D.* (Edinburgh, 1895), pp. 587–91.

24. *A Book of Remembrance: The Jubilee Souvenir of the Glasgow United Evangelistic Association's Evangelical and Ameliorative Schemes, 1874–1924* (Glasgow, 1924), pp. 13–19; cf. the Association's *Annual Report,* 1875.

25. *A Book of Remembrance,* p. 10.

26. P. MacHugh, *Prostitution and Victorian Social Reform* (London, 1980) and J. R. Walkowitz, *Prostitution and Victorian Society* (London, 1980) both discuss these aspects.

27. See an advertisement inserted by Quarrier, *Glasgow Herald,* 4 Feb. 1874, and Cameron's election address, *Ibid.,* 29 Jan. 1874.

28. [Quarrier], *Narrative of Facts* (1875), pp. 34–6.

29. Scottish Permissive Bill Association, *Address to the Electors and Ratepayers of Scotland* (Glasgow, 1861), p. 9.

30. Scottish Temperance League, *Journal,* 8 Aug. 1868; SPBA *Annual Report,* 1868–9.

31. *Dundee Weekly News,* 7 Feb. 1874; *Dundee Courier,* 6 Feb. 1874; *Scotsman,* 7 Feb. 1874; *Greenock Telegraph,* 11, 21, 22 Jan. 1878.

32. STL *Annual Reports,* 1875, p. 66, 1876, p. 51; SPBA *16th Annual Report* (1873–4), n.p.

33. MacEwen, *Cairns,* pp. 586–91.

34. SPBA *8th–27th Annual Reports* (1865-6 — 1884-5).

35. T. Honeyman, *Good Templary in Scotland: Its Work and Workers, 1869–94* (Glasgow, 1894), pp. 27-30.

36. SPBA *16th Annual Report* (1873-4), unpag.

37. E.g. a joint meeting of eight different organisations was held to discuss the vacancy in the Glasgow constituency in 1879. SPBA *21st Annual Report* (1878-9).

38. SPBA *14th Annual Report* (1871-2), p. 3; cf. J. L. Selkirk — an active Prohibitionist at this time — in G. L. Hayter, *The Prohibition Movement* (Newcastle, 1897), pp. 266-7.

39. *Social Reformer,* 7 (Aug. 1872), pp. 60-1; 8 (Apr. 1873), p. 1. This journal was the organ of the Permissive Bill movement.

40. These were printed in the *15th Annual Report* (1872-3) of the SPBA.

41. *Social Reformer,* 8 (Dec. 1873), p. 136.

42. Hayter, *Prohibition Movement,* pp. 264-5.

43. SPBA *16th Annual Report* (1873-4), pp. 10-11; *North British Daily Mail,* 6 Feb. 1874.

44. E.g. E. P. Hennock, *Fit and Proper Persons* (London, 1973), pp. 61-176; A. Briggs, *History of Birmingham* (London, 1952), II, pp. 67-70.

45. *United Presbyterian Magazine,* 16 (1872), p. 141. Cf. *Ibid.,* 15 (1871), pp. 62-4, 150-5.

46. *The Life of Henry Calderwood, LL.D., F.R.S.E.* by his son and the Rev. D. Woodside (London, 1910), pp. 226-30.

47. *Glasgow Herald,* 18 Apr. 1872; A. W. Dale, *Life of R. W. Dale of Birmingham* (pop. edn., London, 1902), pp. 289-93.

48. *North British Daily Mail,* 2 Feb. 1874.

49. *North Briton,* 7 Feb. 1874 Gray, *Labour Aristocracy,* pp. 162-3 seems to think the rupture was not very serious.

50. *Greenock Telegraph,* 12 Dec. 1877, also 15 Dec.

51. *Glasgow Herald,* 21 Sep. 1880, for a critical appraisal of Collins' Provostship. The *Herald* was a firm Liberal opponent of advanced Radicalism.

52. *Glasgow Herald,* 20, 25 Mar. 1882.

53. H. J. Hanham, *Elections and Party Management* (London, 1959), pp. 158-65, gives a useful survey.

54. J. Ord to Lord Minto, 23 Oct. 1867, Minto MSS., MS. 12354, ff. 71-2, and cf. f. 73.

55. A. C. Sellar to Ellice, 1 Aug. 1874, and reply, 11 Aug. (copy), Ellice MSS., MS. 15104, ff. 65-6, 60-1.

56. W. Smith to W. P. Adam, 12 Jun. 1878; J. Y. Guild to J. J. Reid, 2 Aug. 1879; D. Roughhead to Adam, 7 Aug. 1879; Adam MSS., 4/968, 4/425 (twice).

57. Mackie, *MacLaren,* II, pp. 45-53.

58. D. to J. MacLaren, 25 Jun. 1868, Oliver MSS., Acc. 7726/14, ff. 80-1; cf. same to same, 20 Sep. 1872, Ibid., Acc. 7726/15, ff. 79-80.

59. *Greenock Telegraph,* 7 Dec. 1877, 21 Jan. 1878.

60. Glasgow Liberal Association, *1st Annual Report* (1878-9), pp. 2-3.

61. Roxburghshire: there is a printed scheme by W. Elliot of Benrig, dated 5 Oct. 1869, in Minto MSS., MS. 12354, f. 75. Glasgow Liberal Association, *Constitution and Rules* (n.p., n.d., c.1878).

62. Glasgow Liberal Association, *3rd Annual Report* (1880), Appendix.

63. J. G. Kellas, 'The Liberal Party and the Scottish Church Disestablishment Crisis', *EHR,* 79 (1964), pp. 31-46, is the standard account.

64. *North British Daily Mail,* 10 Feb. 1874.

65. Liberation Society Minute Books, Minute 396, 17 Dec. 1874, A/LIB/5.

66. Liberation Society, *The Established Church and the People of Scotland* (London, 1879); Scottish Disestablishment Association, *Statement by the Executive Committee* (Edinburgh, 1874).

67. A. Russel to Rosebery, 17 Feb. 1875, Rosebery MSS., MS. 10074, ff. 146–7.

68. Hartington to Rosebery, 2 Nov. 1877, Ibid., MS. 10074, ff. 230–1.

69. J. Grahame to W. P. Adam, n.d. (Oct. 1877); Adam MSS., 4/421. There is more in the same vein in Ibid., 4/420.

70. W. Smith to W. P. Adam, 12 Jun. 1878, Adam MSS., 4/968.

71. Smith to Adam. 20 Jun. 1878; J. Morton to Adam, 13 Jun. 1878, Ibid., 4/968; J. Tulloch to E. Ellice, 28 Jul. (1879), Ellice MSS., MS. 15057, ff. 108–13.

72. Tulloch to Ellice, 28 Jul., 29 Sep., 29 Oct. (1879), Ellice MSS., MS. 15057, ff. 108–13, 114–7, 118–9.

73. *The Scottish Liberal Members and their Pledges on the Church Question in 1880* (Edinburgh, 1880).

74. Tulloch to Ellice, 28 Jul. (1879) Ellice MSS., MS. 15057, ff. 108–13.

75. *Greenock Telegraph*, 12 Dec. 1877, 1, 11 Jan. 1878.

76. Glasgow Liberal Association, *1st Annual Report* (1879), p. 3.

77. J. MacLaren to J. J. Reid, 27 Jul. 1879, Reid MSS., MS. 19623, ff. 72–3; Reid to MacLaren, 17 Jul. 1879 (copy), Adam MSS., 4/425. D. to J. MacLaren, 16 Mar. 1877, Oliver MSS., Acc. 7726/15, ff. 168–71 for Duncan's disavowal of Whiggery.

78. Adam to J. J. Reid, 3 Sep. 1879, Reid MSS., MS. 19623, ff. 87–8.

79. J. G. Kellas, 'The Liberal Party in Scotland, 1876–95', *SHR*, 44 (1965), pp. 2–3, tends to exaggerate the Radical influence in the Western Association.

80. ESLA Minute Books, printed rules (June 1877).

81. Ibid., *Report of 1st Annual General Meeting* (1879), pp. 3–10.

82. Ibid., *Report of 1st Annual General Meeting* (1879), pp. 3–10.

83. Reid MSS., MS. 19623 *passim* and Adam MSS., 4/425 *passim* for this correspondence.

84. Tulloch to E. Ellice, 28 Jul. (1879), Ellice MSS., MS. 15057, ff. 108–13; J. J. Reid to W. P. Adam, 5, 17 Jul. 1879, Adam MSS., 4/425.

85. Reid to Adam, 17 Jul. 1879, Adam MSS., 4/425.

86. Reid to Adam, 10, 5 Jul. 1879, Ibid. 4/425.

87. Reid to Adam, 5 Jul. 1879, Ibid. 4/425; Stair to Reid, 8 Jan., 9 Mar. 1880, Reid MSS., MS. 19623, ff. 121–7, 132–3.

88. Reid to Adam, 17 Jan. 1881, Adam MSS., 4/430.

89. Adam to Reid (10 Oct. 1878), Reid MSS., MS. 19623, ff. 31–2; G. Hilton to Minto, 26 Apr., 14 Dec. 1870, Minto MSS., MS. 12354, ff. 157–8, 181–2; J. Anderson, J. H. Waterston to A. R. D. Elliot, Elliot to Waterston, 9 Jan. 1878 (really 1879), 26 Nov., 3 Dec. 1878, Elliot MSS., MS. 19485, ff. 70–1, 123–4, 125–6. In fact, Elliot did require to use Adam's subsidy — Elliot to Minto, 26 May 1880, Minto MSS., MS. 12245, ff. 66–7.

90. J. Patten to Rosebery, 7 Jun. 1881 — 21 Jan. 1882, Rosebery MSS., MS. 10042, ff. 29–94 *passim*. Kellas, 'Liberal Party', p. 4, gives a rather different version of the Glasgow difficulty.

91. J. Grahame to W. P. Adam, 1 Aug. 1879; Adam MSS., 4/416. This letter includes a copy of the Church Defence Association's manifesto.

92. Adam to A. B. McGrigor, 10 Dec. 1879 (copy), Reid MSS., MS. 19623, ff. 111–2.

93. Adam to W. E. Gladstone, 10 Apr. 1879, Gladstone MSS., Add. MS. 44095, ff. 79–80.

94. Gladstone to Adam, 12 Apr. 1879, cf. 23 Sep. 1879, Adam MSS., 4/431.

95. Gladstone to Principal Rainy, 24 May 1879 (copy), Ibid., 4/431.

96. Tennant to Gladstone, 15, 19 Dec. 1879, W. E. Gladstone MSS., Add. MS. 41461, ff. 245–6, 265–6.

97. SLA Minute Book, 12 Oct. 1881.

6

The Liberal Party under Strain: 1881–1900

I

The split induced in Scottish Liberalism by Gladstone's plan to give Home Rule to Ireland was very sharp, with substantial defections both among leading Whigs (Minto, Stair, Fife) and Radicals (MacLaren, Cameron Corbett, Boyd Kinnear). This breakaway has frequently been seen as the culmination of a growing sense of unease among moderate Liberals at the leftward drift of the party, and it is not hard to find examples of this sentiment. The Earl of Fife told his local M.P. in 1885: 'I have been utterly disgusted with the miserable rubbish with which Birmingham has deluged the whole country during the contest. Doctrines of ransom and confiscation will shatter our party unless resisted by honest men. I have been quite sickened lately and have felt very strongly about it'.[1] At a less exalted social level, the Professor of Medicine at Glasgow University recorded that his Liberalism was undermined by Gladstone's handling of South Africa and the death of Gordon, but was finally shattered by Home Rule.[2] But these remarks may be, as with Gairdner, retrospective justification or, as with Fife, an outburst of immediate feelings, for the Earl was still happy to meet much of the Banffshire Liberals' election bill.[3] Perhaps the degree of alienation from Liberalism before 1886 among Liberal Unionists can be assessed better by a study of the impact of various crises which might test their commitment to the Liberal party.

The Irish policy of Gladstone's administration between 1880 and 1885 was seen by some as too radical, most notably by the Duke of Argyll, who left the Government in protest at Gladstone's 1881 Land Bill. Yet despite Argyll's importance, very few in Scotland seem to have followed him. Two members were stated to have quit the Scottish Liberal Association; only a couple of speakers opposed the Bill at a packed meeting of Edinburgh Liberals held specially to discuss the matter; Inverness was similarly reported content.[4] Most tellingly, the Glasgow Liberal Association, which had at its head a future Whig Unionist, Dr A. B. McGrigor, overwhelmingly endorsed the Government's bill.[5] One of Argyll's fears about Irish land legislation was that its principles (fixity of tenure, free sale, fair rent) might in future be applied to Scotland, where the Highland crofters were mounting a powerful campaign to secure similar rights. The political climax of the crofters' struggle was the triumphant return in the 1885 election of candidates standing on the crofters' platform in four of the five Highland counties, defeating in the process orthodox Liberals, often of a landed background.[6] Moreover the public support given to the crofters' cause by Chamberlain during the election campaign was an aggravating factor to moderate Liberals. Yet there was a widespread belief that the crofters had a reasonable case, and were not lawless anarchists. The Whig party agent in Inverness recounted to Rosebery the views aired in a conversation he had had at his club with a Liberal laird, the Sheriff Clerk, a Tory journalist and two lawyers. All were agreed that 'the small tenants in the West Highlands have been ill-used' and that 'the landlords must be curbed'.[7] When the elections approached, there was a clear acceptance by moderates of the priority of electing a Liberal, albeit a Crofter, rather than let a Tory win. In Argyll Whigs were initially ready to support William MacKinnon, who seemed to be a Liberal, in preference to MacFarlane, the crofters' candidate. Nevertheless, when it became plain that MacKinnon was in reality a Conservative, the moderate Liberals withdrew their support for him and let MacFarlane carry the day.[8] Not all those who opposed the crofters' movement became Unionist in 1886. Munro Ferguson, the owner of vast estates in Ross-shire, who had exulted when smashing the crofter candidate in a by-election in the county in 1884 — only to be humbled in the ensuing general election — remained a loyal Gladstonian.[9] Another defeated Whig, MacKenzie of Gairloch, did become a Liberal Unionist, but then joined forces with Chamberlain to urge the necessity of running Unionist land reformers for Highland seats.[10]

Similar fears of letting in the Tories inhibited critics of Gladstone's management of imperial problems. Even although many Scottish Liberals were reliably reported to be incensed by the Egyptian bungles of 1884, Rosebery was assured by the secretary of the Scottish Liberal Club that the prospect of Salisbury taking office was a sufficient deterrent to stifle revolt.[11] Fears of the irresistible onrush of radicalism were also generally contained without much difficulty. On the one hand, the panic seemed on closer inspection to be groundless. The editor of *The Scotsman,* whose alarm had been mounting in the early part of 1885 at the prospect of a Dilke-Chamberlain takeover, confessed himself reassured by the actual characteristics of most Liberal candidates in the general election, and this view was echoed by the Whig candidate for Edinburgh West who discerned no radical spirit among the electorate: ' ... with the exception of Glasgow and the Highlands there does not seem much demand for entirely new programmes'.[12] Where radicalism did prevail, however, the position taken by moderates was to acquiesce and not to abandon the party. In East Fife the Whiggish gentry found themselves confronted with the ultra-radical J. B. Kinnear as candidate, after their preferred nominee withdrew. Their first reaction was to predict the break-up of the party, but after a week the Whig leader, R. Cathcart of Pitcairlie, noted a change of thinking. Now they would remain in the party, hoping to expose the fallacies of radicalism over time and looking forward to regaining control at the following election. Cathcart at that point planned to abstain, but by polling day he cast his vote for Kinnear. 'It was a bitter pill to swallow', he observed, but 'I had to think of the party ... the more I think of it, the more I am convinced that, as a Liberal, and as the supposed leader of the Liberals in East Fife, I could not remain neutral and give the Tories a chance of winning'.[13]

There does not seem to have been much ground for the allegation sometimes made by radicals that the less advanced Liberals were drifting out of the party because of the increased demands for working-class representation. In Glasgow in

1885, George Jackson, the hero of the Scottish National Reform League in the 1860s, was selected as candidate for Glasgow Central. Far from being alarmed at this, Whigs in the city were delighted, for Jackson had beaten Gilbert Beith, one of the most outspoken disestablishers, for the nomination.[14] In Edinburgh, the Trades Council summoned a meeting of trades delegates to consider the propriety of putting up a *bona fide* working man for one of the four city seats.[15] But the party managers, moderate Liberals, were doubly placated. Firstly, the tone in which the unions couched their bid was conciliatory. They 'wish to know', Rosebery learned, 'whether a proposal to start a working man candidate for the South-East [sic] Division of Edinburgh would meet with acceptance from the party. They won't do anything to the injury of the party interest, or in opposition to any other good man who may be started'. Secondly, after meeting the delegation, the Whigs were further delighted to note that working men were less interested in disestablishment than local government reform and land reform.[16]

The struggle to acquire control of party organisation in the early 1880s had the appearance of an irreconcilable conflict, with the radicals on the offensive. A case in point was the resignation of A. B. McGrigor as President of the Glasgow Liberal Association in 1882. Having installed McGrigor as president in a bid to woo Whigs to participate in the Association, the radicals, who controlled it, then passed a resolution calling for the disestablishment of the Church of Scotland. McGrigor found this intolerable, and many Whigs interpreted the whole episode as a calculated humiliation, devised to show how little support Whiggery had.[17] More importantly, the formation by radicals just before the 1885 election of the National Liberal Federation of Scotland (NLFS) — quite consciously echoing the title of Chamberlain's English vehicle — was taken to herald the prelude to the eclipse of the Scottish Liberal Association (SLA), because it was too moderate.[18]

In fact it appears that the SLA leaders were rather relieved, not despondent, at the formation of the NLFS. Throughout the early 1880s the SLA directorate had two broad aims. Firstly, the Association should accommodate all party organisations of whatever political complexion. This was carefully maintained, with the most delicate problem being that of the rival Glasgow organisations, discussed earlier, which was resolved by agreeing to let both be affiliated. The second area of difficulty was the growing demand, associated with the crescendo of the disestablishment agitation, that policy issues and party policy be discussed at the SLA meetings. Begun in 1882, this campaign reached its full height at the A.G.M. of the SLA held in January 1884. Despite demands put by Calderwood, backed by Brown Douglas, Pullar and Taylor Innes, Elgin, the new chairman of the SLA, took the line that the national body did not interfere with local parties, so that it was not a caucus in the way that the NLF in England was, and accordingly it should not prescribe or even discuss policy, which could be highly disruptive.[19] Despite this, Calderwood and his associates kept up the demand throughout 1884, but when they failed to get agreement at the next A.G.M. to open up the SLA to political debate, they formed the NLFS to fulfil that role.[20]

Although this seemed a grave rupture, from another angle it did have the merit of avoiding a power struggle within the SLA itself. The NLFS existed almost solely as a resolutionary body, while the bulk of the organisational work remained firmly in the hands of the SLA, thereby avoiding the dangerous (in Whig eyes) English precedent. There the NLF's power derived from being the locus of both organisation and policy determination, the former endowing the latter with greater significance. In Scotland, by contrast, the NLFS's opinions were not representative of every Liberal association, and the SLA had a stronger right to assert itself as all-embracing. To a degree, the NLFS seems to have taken this view, for by the beginning of 1886 its creators had decided to accept a compromise. The NLFS would disappear, and in return policy questions would be ventilated at SLA meetings, but any resolutions passed would not be binding on the SLA. Elgin remained unhappy about even holding policy debates in the SLA, but in the light of a widespread desire on all sides for compromise, he acceded. Unity and amity had, it seemed, been restored. Elgin was praised by Munro Ferguson in March 1886:'I think you have done marvellously well in keeping things together.'[21]

By far the most profound factor making for disunity in Scottish Liberalism before the Home Rule crisis was disestablishment, and the general succession of events has been well discussed in several recent studies.[22] Although, as noted earlier, the election of 1880 caused little perturbation among the ranks of Church Liberals, the effects of that contest were nevertheless to alter the situation. A group of single-minded disestablishers were returned from Scotland, the most assiduous of whom was Dick Peddie, the M.P. for Kilmarnock, who introduced disestablishment bills in Parliament. Also, there was the simultaneous accession to the ranks of the English Liberal M.P.s of a number of advanced radicals who saw the settlement of the Scottish Church issue as the prelude to breaking the state-church relationship in England. Moreover the Free Church became even more set upon obtaining revenge on the Church of Scotland, and Rainy, who was fully dedicated to the cause of disestablishment, was now firmly installed as the unchallenged head of the former. The Free Church had been inhibited in the 1870s from all-out advocacy of disestablishment by the presence of its Constitutional wing, but the eruption of the crofters' revolt altered the Free Church's strategy. The Highlands had been the stronghold of the Constitutional Free Church, and most of the crofting communities were solidly Free Church. Now the land question, which had politicised the crofters, was adroitly linked to the church issue. A special meeting of the Scottish Council of the Liberation Society was held in Edinburgh on January 15 1884, presided over by Dr. Cameron, a firm disestablisher and the M.P. most sympathetic to the crofters' cause. The meeting urged franchise reform in order to accelerate the 'reform' of the Church of Scotland in the Highlands, where 'churchmen-landlords' were charged with harrying the crofters.[23] This theme was extensively developed by the Free Church Highlander, Gilbert Beith, who argued that although the Church of Scotland was public property, its funds in the Highlands were distributed for the exclusive benefit of landlords, while the crofters, as Free Church adherents, were denied any share. Should disestablishment and disendowment occur, the £3.8 million tied up in maintaining Established churches in the Highlands could be released to provide free education, build harbours to develop fishing and, above all, enable a land bill on the Irish model to be enacted for the benefit of the whole Highland population.[24]

The disestablishers stepped up their tactics in the 1880–85 era. M.P.s were diligently lobbied;[25] deputations went to harangue Gladstone;[26] petitions and memoranda rained down on the Prime Minister.[27] Increasingly the anti-state church men strove to put the issue as the overriding political topic before the Liberal party. Gladstone was warned not to rely on the unwavering loyalty of Dissenter votes, and a meeting of the Scottish Disestablishment Association resolved 'to press it as a testing question on the electorate of the country'.[28] As the general election became more imminent, the pressure on Church Liberals was increased, as Principal Cairns declared war on them in May 1885 ('They may be in the Liberal party, but they are not of it'),[29] and local parties were increasingly assertive in selecting disestablishers as candidates. In Edinburgh South, where Calderwood was very influential, a disestablisher who on all other radical issues —temperance, the Unauthorised Programme — was pretty Whiggish was selected by 89 votes to 2 in preference to an ex-Lord Provost who was a Church Liberal.[30] In Inverness another Church Liberal was opposed by Duncan MacLaren's son, the latter supported by the local Liberal Association, 'which was formed by the Disestablishment party'.[31]

The response of those who were not ardent disestablishers was mixed. A group of phlegmatics was disposed to dismiss the whole agitation as got up by a hysterical minority. No one was more phlegmatic than Campbell-Bannerman, even although he sat for a seat with a long record of hostility to the state church. 'If I analysed my constituency', he told a Tory, 'I should say it was composed of: .80 Voluntary in principle; .10 Militant Churchmen; .10 Passive Ditto. But of the .80 I should say the immense majority are against urging the question — 'The Auld Kirk's daeing nae harm.' Thus an accurate analysis would be — .10 Rampant Churchmen .10 'It'll come by and by, but ye needna hurry it' .10 'down with her' .70 'Ca canny'. I am one of the .70'.[32] A variant of this approach was typified by a group of young upper-class moderate Liberals with Parliamentary aspirations. These men — T. R. Buchanan, A. R. D. Elliot (Minto's son), R. P. Bruce (Elgin's brother) — took the line in a triangular correspondence that the agitation on both sides was produced by clergymen, while the laity were not particularly interested in disestablishment as an overriding priority.[33] Some confirmation of this view came from West Perthshire where a bid by clergymen to oppose Donald Currie as the candidate because of his state church opinions was heavily defeated by lay Liberals in the constituency association.[34]

But these men, though not radicals, were not Church Liberals: indeed Elliot was in favour of disestablishment as a principle, but did not agree with the proposed mode of attaining it.[35] Church Liberals were less stoical about the orchestrated disestablishment campaign in the 1885 election campaign. A major incident arose from the leaking of a letter from Chamberlain to Taylor Innes, indicating that the return of a majority of Scottish M.P.s who supported disestablishment would be taken as proof of the Scottish electorate's demand for its enactment.[36] The SLA in October carried a resolution calling for disestablishment, further agitating the

Church Liberals. The political conduct of the latter now became problematic. As early as 1882 they were understood to have reached some sort of electoral arrangement with the Tories, and in 1884, with the disestablishment campaign at full tilt, a bout of public meetings was held to uphold the case for the state church. 'There is no doubt a desire on the part of an influential section of the Establishment Liberals not to let things slide any further', Rosebery was warned.[37]

Although contacts were undoubtedly made with the Tories, this was done — in the eyes of Church Liberals — solely to defend the Church, and rarely indicated an intention to vote Conservative, even in those circumstances. At a mass rally held in Glasgow in late October 1885, when feelings were at their highest, A. B. McGrigor (who as noted above had resigned from the presidency of the Glasgow Liberal Association over the issue) spoke clearly of the extent to which the protest would be carried: 'While I — and I speak, I believe, for thousands of true-hearted Liberals throughout the country — am not prepared to support by my vote the party against whom I have honourably and consistently contended throughout my life, I am not prepared by that vote to swell the number of those who will vote for [disestablishment]'.[38] Indeed, it was as a rule the Tories who agreed to stand down and instead pledge support for a Church Liberal against a radical, as for instance at Edinburgh East, where Goschen faced a Chamberlainite, B. F. C. Costelloe. Very rarely was the right to face a disestablisher given to a Tory if a Church Liberal was in the field. In one of the few seats where two Liberals faced a Conservative — Kilmarnock — the Established Liberals' man, North Dalrymple, reiterated his resolve to fight the architect of disestablishment legislation, Dick Peddie, even if it meant allowing a Tory to win. Evidently Dalrymple felt his supporters could not be counted on to vote Conservative for the Church's sake if he were to retire.[39] The results in Kilmarnock bear him out. In 1886 the Conservative vote increased by only 135, while the staunch disestablisher standing as a Gladstonian got 1,151 extra votes. As Dalrymple polled 1,862 in 1885, even on the unlikely assumption that all the 1885 radical voters remained Gladstonian, two-thirds of Church Liberals still voted for Home Rule, and only some 8% went Unionist. Thus Church Liberals were by no means all incipient Liberal Unionists.

Polling in the 1885 contest more generally suggested that Liberals put party before church, and the Tory expectations were not at all met. Only 8 Conservatives were returned out of 70 Scottish M.P.s, whereas in 1880, one of the worst elections for the party, there were 6 out of a smaller total of 58. Gladstone's opponent in Mid Lothian noted that he was certain that the Tories had not received the Church Liberal vote and that they should not have expected to do so.[40] The Conservative loser in Banffshire agreed: 'One thing is evident: that the Church people swallowed Gladstone's soothing syrup; and I doubt whether even if the question were put directly, disestablishment or not, they would not prefer their own party'.[41] Gladstone's 'soothing syrup' was a speech he made in early November which set the fears of the Church Liberals at rest, and confirmed that they still exercised powerful leverage within the party. Gladstone had been subjected to entreaties from many of his closest Scottish political advisers, all stressing the importance of dissociating the party leadership from the clamant demands for disestablishment.

Rosebery was particularly insistent on this in his discussions with Gladstone, but this merely reflected the volume of correspondence flowing in to him from alarmed Church Liberals. The candidate in North-East Lanarkshire reported the mood of Church Liberals there just prior to Gladstone's speech: 'They go the length of saying Liberal principles will ultimately triumph, even if they are checked at the next election. But the Church once gone cannot be set up. The important thing appears to me to be this. If these men can be assured in any way that the decision on Disestablishment will be deliberate, that the country will have the time and opportunity to express an opinion, they will acquiesce loyally in the verdict. . . . But the attitude of the Churchmen will I expect mainly be determined by Mr Gladstone's utterances on the question'.[42] Rosebery passed some of these letters on to his leader, while other candidates wrote directly to Gladstone predicting the loss of anything up to fifteen seats because of the Church difficulty, and even the Chief Whip pitched in.[43] The message was simple, as Rosebery told Gladstone: Church Liberals needed reassurance that this election was not a plebiscite on disestablishment. Only one man could deliver this message, and that was Gladstone.[44]

Gladstone's mind had been moving that way, as he disliked the rival candidatures cropping up in Scotland, and also found the plan of disestablishment being peddled 'outrageous'. Therefore he determined to 'deprecate making Disestablishment a test question', just as he had done in England, and made a speech to that effect.[45] The response was instantaneous and gratifying (to Church Liberals). In North-East Lanarkshire, it was reported that the disestablishment lobby were stilled and the leading Church Liberals were now pacified and ready to vote Liberal.[46] The Tories were downcast at the warm reception accorded the speech, and Gladstone himself a week later reported from Edinburgh: 'All pleased and sanguine. Disestablishment scare nearly over'.[47]

There were several reasons behind Gladstone's decision to come down on the side of the Church party, apart of course from his own personal inclinations. Firstly, the importance of the Liberal Churchmen's vote was recognised even by disestablishers and led some, particularly candidates, to be reluctant to sustain the demand to the end. Rosebery recorded with amusement how Cameron Corbett, one of the Glasgow extreme radicals, drove out in a panic to Dalmeny when faced with the threat of Church abstentions.[48] The voting power of the two camps may be deduced from the six seats where two Liberals stood along with a Tory. In these cases the Church Liberal vote would not be greatly swelled by Tory support, as probably happened elsewhere when the latter stood down. Of the six, two were won by Church Liberals (Moray & Nairn and Perth City), and while three were won by disestablishers (Mid Lanark, Montrose and Edinburgh Central), the Church Liberal vote in these seats was impressive. In Mid Lanark they polled 67% of the disestablisher's vote, and in both Montrose and Edinburgh Central they were as high as 80%. The sixth seat, Kilmarnock, was won by the Conservative, the Church Liberal getting 53% of the radical's poll. In sum, Church Liberals were a not inconsiderable voting bloc. Brutal *realpolitik* dictated that it was less risky to offend the radicals than the moderates, for the former were not nearly so likely to abstain (still less vote Conservative) if they did not like party policy. Moreover, the disestablishers lacked the monolithic determination of the Church Liberals to have their line accepted. There were some ultras, like Taylor Innes, who would countenance no fudging of the demand for full and immediate disestablishment. But Innes's intransigence at the SLA conference in October 1885 alarmed pragmatic figures like Alexander Cross, who was willing to accept a milder formulation.[49] Among the latter was Calderwood, who in 1884 was seeking a *via media*: 'It may be possible for us to guide the movement in such a way as to be conciliatory on all hands, and carry the approval of the more moderate men of our party, with the acquiescence of the more advanced'.[50] Consistent with this standpoint, Calderwood loyally agreed to the decision pronounced by Gladstone on the grounds of unity and took it upon himself and his friends to deal with the Taylor Innes faction 'and keep them quiet'.[51]

Another aspect affecting Gladstone's stance was that very few of his Scottish political confidants were supporters of disestablishment. Rosebery, his main consultant, had little time for the issue; Sir Charles Tennant was a strong Church Liberal; and Edward Marjoribanks, later to be his Chief Whip, was utterly hostile to all fads, as his protest in 1887 against a Home Rule for Scotland motion being presented at a party conference revealed: 'Some means should be devised to stop all sorts and conditions of men from moving strange and gruesome resolutions'.[52] The Chairman of the SLA for most of the 1880s was another friend of the state church, Lord Elgin, and his skill in restoring unity to the Scottish party after 1886 gave him considerable weight. Above all there was Lord Aberdeen, grandson of the Premier under whom Gladstone first held Cabinet office, and himself converted to Liberalism by Gladstone's Mid Lothian campaign of 1879. Gladstone was a frequent visitor to the Aberdeens' Scottish estate and to their London residence, Dollis Hill.[53] Aberdeen had served in the sensitive office of Lord Lieutenant of Ireland under Gladstone, and equally important, he was Lord High Commissioner to the General Assembly of the Church of Scotland in 1885, and so would have very clear views to pass on to Gladstone.[54] Indeed, much of the failure of radicalism to capture the Scottish Liberal party in the 1880s and 1890s may be ascribed to the influence of this group, and more especially to the extraordinary nexus of blood and marriage ties based on Lord Aberdeen. His wife was the sister of Marjoribanks; his daughter married John Sinclair, Bannerman's Scottish Whip, 1900–5, and then Secretary of State for Scotland; his third son, Archie, was engaged to Violet, Asquith's daughter, but died before the marriage took place. The Aberdeen group provided a solid centre weight in Scottish Liberalism, balancing not just the radicals but also the Liberal Imperialist section of the 1890s. It may be significant that the Liberal Imperialist most prepared to place party unity before all else was Asquith, the only one to be connected to the Aberdeen network.

The outcome was that between the 1885 election results and the introduction of the Irish Home Rule measure Church Liberals appear to have felt quite secure, and indeed on occasions were ready to go on the offensive. In Edinburgh South, a by-election was caused in January 1886 by the death of the Church Liberal M.P.

In this seat whose Liberal Association had voted overwhelmingly to choose a disestablisher as candidate in 1885, furious manoeuvres by MacLaren and company failed to prevent the nomination going to an out and out upholder of the state church principle, H. C. E. Childers.[55] At the beginning of 1886 Church Liberals acted to form a specifically Liberal Church Defence grouping. One plan, proposed by R. V. Campbell, an Edinburgh advocate and future Liberal Unionist, was to set up a 'National Liberal Union' with the objective of curbing the excesses of the disestablishers at the local level, which was where, in his opinion, they had caused the most damage.[56] A separate proposal was to create a Liberal Church Defence Association, and meetings to launch it were held in both Edinburgh and Glasgow in January 1886. This body intended to compile a list of candidates with acceptable opinions on the state church and to install a corresponding secretary in each seat, ready to organise a local committee should the need arise.[57] Although neither of these ventures seems to have come to fruition, the instructive point shared by both is their confidence that only *Liberal* Churchmen need be involved. Campbell stressed that the existing Church Defence Association, although supposedly non-partisan, had been abused by the Tories as a party vehicle, so discrediting it.[58] Some percipient Conservatives had come quite independently to the same conclusion, and Balfour of Burleigh had warned Salisbury of just this danger.[59] The Liberal Church Defence Association felt pretty certain that its existence would be adequate to deter the enemies of the Church of Scotland from making additional gains within the Liberal Party. 'The mere existence of such a Committee could be sufficient to prevent the Member going over to the Disestablishment party. In others it would be necessary to organise a fight, but the probability is it would not be so in many. The effect of this organisation I believe would be to keep Candidates from bringing forward this question and this would certainly be most desirable'.[60] A further sign of confidence was the onslaught made in the Commons early in 1886 by R. B. Finlay on disestablishment.[61] This spirited speech rallied the Church Liberals and suggested that, rather than imminent departure, a counter-attack by them was in the offing at the very moment when Irish Home Rule occluded the other policies of the day.

II

The impact of the introduction of the Irish Home Rule Bill in 1886 upon the Scottish Liberal party has been well documented, and its most tangible effect was seen in the return of 27 Unionist M.P.s to Parliament, easily the worst result for the Liberals since the passage of the First Reform Act. Moreover, of these 27, the larger number (17) were Liberal Unionists rather than Conservatives. Much of the strong support for Liberal Unionism has been shown to stem from factors which applied with especial force in Scotland. The religious bond between Irish and Scottish Presbyterianism was a leading factor, and was certainly one upon which the Ulster Unionists laid great stress. Another ingredient was the close economic relations, both industrial and agricultural, between Ulster and the western

Lowlands, and a third was the extensive presence of Ulster Protestants in Scotland, characterised by men as diverse in their contributions to Scottish society as William Thomson (Lord Kelvin) and Sir Thomas Lipton.[62] But the strength of Liberal Unionism was not the only predicament which faced the Gladstonian Liberals after 1886, for the situation was complicated by the presence of a sizeable and aggressive Radical Unionist wing. This was something of a rarity in England outside the well-known Chamberlain stronghold of the West Midlands.

The extent of the loss among the landed and urban Whig figures in the party has already been alluded to. However, as Cooke and Vincent have shown, it was vital for Gladstone's strategy that not all Whigs should depart, and in Scotland this aim was in good measure achieved.[63] Among non-radicals who accepted the Home Rule package were such landowners as Rosebery, Elgin, Dalhousie, Aberdeen, Reay, Breadalbane, Munro Ferguson, Gibson-Carmichael, the Master of Elibank, Sir Charles Tennant, J. C. G. Hamilton of Dalzell and Maxtone Graham of Cultoquhey. In addition a group of key centre and right-of-centre politicians generally inimical to radicalism remained. These included Campbell-Bannerman, Haldane, C. S. Parker (the most outrageously Whiggish of all Scottish M.P.s), Bryce, R. W. Duff, R. T. Reid, Dr Farquharson and P. MacLagan. If the split was not clear-cut on the Whig side, it was not so among the Radicals either. A good proportion came out against Gladstone. Among these were: in the Highlands, Fraser-Mackintosh, an ultra-radical crofters' M.P; in Dundee, the sons of W. E. Baxter, long the radical Pooh Bah of that city; in East Fife, J. B. Kinnear, whose election in 1885 was looked upon by Whigs as tantamount to the implementation of the Communist Manifesto. Among Glasgow radicals to leave were A. C. Corbett, the son of Quarrier's associate and a long-standing temperance advocate, along with local caucus stalwarts such as Alexander Cross and Walter MacFarlane, whose radical credentials included assuming the presidency of the city Liberal Association when McGrigor resigned over disestablishment in 1882. James Caldwell, who worked closely with Chamberlain after 1886 to develop radical Unionism in Scotland, was another Glaswegian. Edinburgh had its quota of radical Unionists too, including Thomas Raleigh who incurred the wrath of *The Scotsman* for running against a moderate Liberal in 1885 at Edinburgh South; Calderwood, so prominent in disestablishment circles; and, the biggest catch of all, Duncan MacLaren, who occupied the position of doyen of Scottish advanced Liberalism. Moreover, unlike his English counterpart (and quondam brother-in-law) Bright, who had been elbowed aside by Chamberlain and was essentially a figurehead, MacLaren remained active and very much at the centre of Scottish radicalism.

Two elements seem to explain the large weight of radical Unionists. For several it was the belief that disestablishment would never be realised while Gladstone retained the leadership of the party. McLaren for instance regarded the rebuffs endured by his wing in Edinburgh in the 1885 elections as due 'largely to the influence' of Gladstone's excision of the church question from the Scottish programme, and Calderwood's bitterness at Gladstone's conduct on this issue led him to regard Gladstone no longer as the head of Scottish Liberalism.[64] For others it was the proposal to buy out Irish landlords which proved the unacceptable element of the Home Rule scheme. As James Caldwell stated in 1892: 'The defeat of the Home Rule bill in radical constituencies especially was largely — if indeed in many cases not wholly — owing to its being necessarily accompanied by a Land Purchase Bill'.[65] Caldwell's argument seems justified. At a debate in the Paisley Liberal Club, most of the opponents of the bills cited their dislike of the Land Purchase measure as their basis of objection, and a survey of Glasgow radicals conveyed the same impression, which in turn was confirmed in the assessment of opinion in Edinburgh prepared by the Secretary of the SLA for Rosebery.[66] The land scheme was unpopular on several counts, but given the widespread interest among radicals in the Scottish land question and the crofters' campaign, the reaction was always likely to be stronger than in England. So while some complained at landowners being compensated but businessmen not receiving the same treatment, and others objected to British finance buying out Irish landlords, the differentiation in treatment as between Ireland and Scotland may well have jarred with many.[67]

There are also difficulties in treating the Home Rule split as a watershed in that there is evidence to suggest that the outcome of the 1886 election was determined in many seats not solely by the opinions of the electorate on the merits of Gladstone's scheme. There is for instance no consistent economic or social pattern to the seats won by the Liberal Unionists in 1886, even in the industrial West of Scotland, where several gains were made. Thus while Greenock, a shipbuilding centre with a large Orange element, went Unionist, this was not so in the Kilmarnock burghs, which included Port Glasgow, a town adjacent to Greenock, and identical in its economic and social basis, and also two other Clyde shipbuilding towns, Rutherglen and Dumbarton. Of all the Glasgow seats, there were two most likely on paper to fall from Gladstonianism. The first was College, a seat with a large middle-class component and also housing many university professors, large numbers of whom, led by Lord Kelvin, were hyperactive Liberal Unionists. The second was Bridgeton, where a Protestant working class was likely to be swayed by the religious arguments. In reality, these were held fairly comfortably by the Liberals.

As significant as anything else in shaping the outcome of the election was the decision made by the incumbent Liberal M.P., for whichever side he came down on, there was marked reluctance on the part of opponents within the constituency to act against him. Thus in West Perthshire, the sitting M.P., Donald Currie, informed the Liberal Association in May that he would oppose Home Rule. The meeting expressed no views on Currie's stand, but voted its 'unabated confidence' in him as their M.P. At the end of June, the Association gave full consideration to the Irish proposals, and voted by 21 to 10 in support of Gladstone. However, a motion to look for another candidate, apparently the logical conclusion, split the meeting in half with 17 voting to drop Currie, and 16 to retain him. The final decision was deferred until a meeting a week later, when by 28 to 16 it was carried that no opposition should be offered to Currie. So, an Association which had decisively backed Home Rule rested content with an M.P. who had voted against the bill.[68] Although a Home Rule Liberal ran in the 1886 election, he received almost no help from the constituency Liberal Association. On the other side, the foremost Liberal Unionist in Stirling stated, 'I am of the decided opinion' that Campbell-Bannerman 'is entitled to receive my continued support', and it was the certainty that Liberal Unionists would fight if he were to go to another seat that persuaded Bannerman not to leave: 'If I were removed a lot of manufacturers and others, who are at present neutral or at least not active against me, would throw away the scabbard and plunge into the fight against us'.[69] A kindred process may have been at work in the Edinburgh West by-election of 1888, which was brought about by the reversion to Gladstonianism of the sitting Liberal Unionist, T. R. Buchanan. Buchanan kept the seat, improving on the previous Liberal's poll by 900 votes, while the Unionist vote dropped by only 200. In other words, many Liberal abstainers came out to vote once Buchanan returned to their side, but while he was in the other camp, they stayed at home. This line of analysis is also suggested by the performance of Liberal Unionist candidates in the 1886 election. In those seats where the Liberal Unionist was the sitting M.P., 13 were won and 6 lost, but where the sitting Gladstonian was standing again, only 2 were taken by the Liberal Unionist, 23 remaining Home Rule Liberal.

One of the factors explaining the willingness of Liberal voters (whether Unionist or Home Rule) to accept without great protest an M.P. of the opposing views was a sense of personal affection.[70] Another force appears to have been that the minds of many voters had not been firmly made up by the polling date, and so they either abstained or gave the incumbent the benefit of the doubt. A wide range of reports indicated that after initial blanket hostility to the Home Rule Bill, grassroots Liberal opinion was gradually swinging round to acquiescence. In April, the Secretary of the Liberal Club (a Home Ruler) reported from Edinburgh: 'I have never on any former subject in my time listened to opinion so adverse and so unanimous', claiming that neither he nor any SLA official had met a Liberal who backed Gladstone.[71] At the same time, Stirling and Dunfermline Liberals were stated to be firmly critical too.[72] But several correspondents were confident that these adverse responses could be modified. The party agent in Banffshire wrote to this effect to his M.P., while a loyal Glasgow M.P. stressed to Gladstone in early May that the sceptics there 'only require a little lucidity and earnestness expended on them to bring them right'.[73] The presence from the middle of May of Members back in their constituencies helped to drag opinion round to regarding Gladstone's project in a more favourable light. In Dunfermline, Bannerman successfully wooed leading doubters at a private luncheon, and in Stirling he won an important convert when the President of the Liberal Association, who in April had intimated his decision to oppose Gladstone, responded positively to a speech by Bannerman some three weeks later: 'Although I was 'sitting on the fence' for a time over this momentous Irish question, I got down on the side I found you were on'.[74] In Mid Lothian, Gladstone was told how a prominent opponent had lately been won over by 'a full discussion in his own parish'.[75] Gladstone's speeches in June encouraged this movement: 'he has said just the things to please and satisfy Scotland', remarked the now pleased and satisfied Liberal Club Secretary. A Liberal Unionist candidate noted a falling-off of support in June because 'they now think the popular wind is blowing the other way'.[76] But while this conversion campaign may have turned the tide in some places, several Gladstonians felt that it had not quite peaked by the polling date: 'The shortness of the contest of course accounts for the large number of abstentions ... ', reflected Asquith. 'With another week we could have added largely to our majority'.[77] It may be that in this unsettled and volatile context, many electors decided either to stay away or to support the sitting M.P. as a gesture of sympathy. Thus a fervent Liberal Unionist pledged his support to Campbell-Bannerman, acknowledging how difficult a decision it must have been to declare in favour of Home Rule.[78]

An added complication of the Home Rule crisis was that a number of M.P.s and candidates in Scotland later changed their minds and crossed the floor. C. C. Lacaita was the only Gladstonian M.P. to lose faith in Home Rule, and he accordingly resigned from his Dundee seat in 1888. On the other side, those who reverted to Gladstonianism included T. R. Buchanan, G. O. Trevelyan, W. Jacks and James Caldwell. It should be noted that two of these — Trevelyan and Buchanan — were Whiggish, while the other two were radicals, showing no distinct trend even here. For many on both sides of the issue, moreover, the conflict over Irish Home Rule was not treated as a permanent rupture, and because of this widespread sentiment it was easier for voters to continue to support a candidate who happened to differ from them over this item only, while in all other respects remaining an upright, solid Liberal. Very many Liberal Unionists were reluctant to break formally with the official party agencies, either at constituency or national level. This sense was strongly held not just among radical Unionists, but also among a surprising number of Whigs. Arthur Elliot, who had been much involved in building up Liberal Unionist organisation, could still write in October 1886 to another Whig Liberal Unionist, who had been if anything still more active in organising the revolt against Gladstone: 'At present the split in the party is widening here [Roxburghshire] and elsewhere, and I am very sorry'.[79] Similarly, the head of the Stirling Burghs Liberal Unionists felt it would be 'fratricidal' if Home Rule Liberal fought Liberal Unionist in the 1886 election, and as late as November 1886 he was resisting pressure from headquarters to form a Liberal Unionist party in the seat because he felt it would perpetuate a regrettable gulf.[80] Two Whig Unionists, the Fife laird, R. Cathcart, and the Earl of Stair, urged Elgin, a Home Ruler, to remain as head of the SLA in April 1886 in an effort to keep the party united at a time of great stress.[81] Cathcart remained chairman of the East Fife Liberal Associations, although it was firmly Gladstonian, until mid-1887.[82] East Fife was fairly typical of the coexistence which obtained for quite some time among local parties: in Gladstone's own seat this persisted until at least 1889, and fully a year after his return as a Liberal Unionist M.P. Donald Currie delivered an address to the West Perthshire Liberal Association with no apparent animosity on either side.[83] The Scottish Liberal Club, very much a Whig institution, remained mixed for a remarkably long time. In 1891 the Liberal Unionist Dean of Faculty agreed with the Secretary when at a club dinner the latter confessed his confidence that the party would be re-united once the Irish difficulty was set aside.[84] In 1895, it is clear that Liberal Unionists were still a powerful force in the club. In that year too, James Grahame, one of the major Whig figures in West of Scotland Liberal Unionism, responded to the decision of Devonshire and Chamberlain to join Salisbury's administration with the startling affirmation that he was a Liberal Unionist *'virgo intacta'*, who would in no eventuality go with the Tories.[85]

Given these strong manifestations of a desire on all sides not to create a long-term divorce, the reasons why the split became permanent are hard to explain. Here the explanation for the Liberal break-up in 1886 offered by Cooke and Vincent might be seen to have a bearing. The crucial decisions as to the extent and timing of the schism were taken in the realms of 'High Politics' by party leaders. The rank and file, presented with a *fait accompli,* had no means of asserting an alternative resolution of the crisis. For Scottish Liberalism the decisive point after which the likelihood of patching-up became slimmer was the carrying at the SLA conference in October 1886 of a resolution which made it impossible for Liberal Unionists to take any further part in the Association. This was a similar stance to that taken at the English NLF's momentous conference which resulted in the expulsion of the Radical Unionists. There were certain differences in context between the two bodies, however. Firstly, there was not in Scotland anything akin to the regional tensions which derived in England from the tight grip held by Birmingham radicals on the reins of power in the NLF. Accordingly there was no semblance of that prime motive behind the Yorkshire Liberals' determination to oust completely Chamberlain and his entourage. On the other hand, the English NLF was almost entirely radical in its composition, while the SLA remained a careful balance of the various sections under the broad umbrella of Liberalism. It was a natural conclusion on the part of many to see the SLA resolution as a move to dislodge Whigs: 'extreme men were determined to drive out the moderates if they could', was how one Whig Home Ruler read the proceedings.[86]

If, as Ivory's interpretation suggests, the SLA after the Home Rule split had indeed been seized by radicals, Elgin and Marjoribanks, the leading Whigs in the Association, reacted with surprising equanimity. Marjoribanks saw the situation as one which might be turned to advantage by moderates to curb the radicals, rather than let them dominate. 'A crisis sooner of later was inevitable and if instead of the Association going to pieces it can be utilised as the foundation of a new organisation to swallow up the Federation, a great success will be scored', he told Elgin shortly after the SLA conference.[87] Both the SLA and the NLFS had been heavily depleted by the withdrawal of Unionists, and the merger which was mooted at the time had attractions for the two bodies. Marjoribanks summarised these benefits pithily: '[It] will be of benefit to both:- the one [NLFS] will gain prestige, the other [SLA] life, in which it has been sadly deficient'.[88] The NLFS believed that it had a superior hand to play, for while the SLA was suffering from a cessation of subscriptions in the second half of 1886, the NLFS claimed to be 'sweeping in the Liberal Associations now at the rate of two to five a week'.[89] But an extra assumption beyond those outlined by Marjoribanks seems to have lain the merger: that it would perhaps be possible to confine the radicals by incorporating them into the SLA, as preferable to leaving them to function unchecked in the NLFS. In this way, radical demands for new policy directions could be deflected, and the party's national leadership would be given a free hand, so continuing the principle for which Elgin himself had contended through the early 1880s. Hence Marjoribanks' reference to 'swallowing up' the NLFS, which was crucial to the strategy of containing the damage caused by radicals at the October meeting of the SLA. Two points were made by the moderates. Firstly, for some eighteen months following the merger there would be so much detailed organisational work to be undertaken in restoring the health of Liberal machinery that all other considerations would be pushed to the side.[90] Secondly, as Elgin explained to Rosebery, it was far better to maintain close and direct contact with activists by means of involvement in the SLA than leave them to their own devices. Because he was sceptical of the claims of activists to represent the views of the wider Liberal electorate, Elgin argued that the very existence of the SLA was essential to allow moderating influences to be deployed. Rather than quit in protest if an adverse resolution were passed, the important thing was to seek to exercise influence on the executive, where, Elgin remarked, 'I have always found them extremely willing to listen to anything I had occasion to say'.[91]

These objectives were pursued in the negotiations held at the end of 1886 between the two Liberal bodies. The NLFS demanded that while Elgin retained the chairmanship of the new organisation, the vice-chairman should be their leader, Gilbert Beith, as a 'visible recognition' of the achievements and importance of the Federation.[92] On the question of the powers of the new SLA, Elgin was adamant that while the proposed constitution provided for full discussion of any topic, no resolutions arising therefrom had any binding force whatsoever on any individual or affiliated association. Elgin and Beith reiterated their well-rehearsed respective positions, the former arguing it would be 'insubordination' to proffer guidance to the party leader, the latter claiming that even if the executive moved ahead of the conventional wisdom, because of the representative structure of the SLA they would still carry great weight.[93] Elgin's position prevailed, however, thus safeguarding the line adopted by himself and Marjoribanks. However, this did not in itself mean that in the long run they would succeed in limiting the role of the radicals.

III

After the immediate dislocation caused by the Home Rule crisis, there were several pressing problems confronting the Liberal party in Scotland. The one most easily dealt with was the point made by many during the 1886 election campaign, namely that the issues involved had not been fully expounded to the party faithful. This was remedied partly by convening a series of regional conferences to outline the policy and partly by having Irish Nationalist M.P.s make speaking tours. The latter were regarded as of 'high value' by the SLA, and in 1888 alone half-a-dozen such trips were arranged to the West of Scotland.[94] The second task was to repair the depredations wrought on organisation by the Home Rule split, which, as Elgin reminded Gladstone late in 1887, were acute: 'our difficulties in Scotland especially in the matter of organisation are neither few nor trivial'.[95] A major worry for the party was finance. In the year after the schism the SLA set itself a target of raising £2,000, but reached only halfway, and much of that lower sum came not from regular subscribers but from one-off donations, suggesting that the sum the Association could rely on normally was much smaller. In 1887 the Secretary was reported to be contemplating resignation, as the shortage of cash bedevilled all his efforts to improve the efficiency of central and of constituency machinery.[96] Lack of money was a serious headache at constituency level, too, as Gladstone learned from his party chairman in Mid Lothian: 'I wished as before that your friends should defray these [election expenses]. But on looking over the list of those who had subscribed most liberally before, I was ashamed to find that nearly all had turned aside from us — for a time only I hope'.[97] In West Perthshire, subscription income plummeted from £271 in 1885-6 to £117 in 1887-8, while in Ross-shire the local Secretary refused to do registration work in 1889 because there were insufficient funds to meet the previous year's fees.[98]

The financial problems accentuated a difficulty created by the loss to Liberal Unionism of a key group of constituency officials, most of whom were lawyers. 'Most of the former agents have ceased to take an active part, or are engaged on the other side', a party manager reported, and local instances from as far apart as Stornoway and Dunfermline confirmed this.[99] Where it was possible to find replacements, they were generally inexperienced: as one long-standing Liberal agent remarked of the new man in Crieff, he was keen but inclined to be over-optimistic in his assessments.[100] But the SLA had no resources to instruct these tyroes in the technicalities of party work. One casualty was registration, which was neglected for several years in many seats. In 1891 'a considerable number' of constituencies had a smaller electorate than in the 1886 contest, and as the Tories had been assiduous in attending to their supporters, it was highly likely that the Liberals had lost quite a drastic number of voters through organisational deficiencies.[101]

As a result, Liberal grassroots organisation was highly defective. Three years after the Home Rule election Campbell-Bannerman was informed that there was still no party machinery in West Perthshire apart from a few unco-ordinated branches.[102] So uncertain were headquarters about the existence of constituency associations that a special enquiry was mounted by the SLA to ascertain the true state of affairs in seats.[103] Campbell-Bannerman went to see Provost Walls of Dunfermline on party business, but then 'the horrid thought occurred to me that I was not sure that Walls was now Chairman of my Committee — nor do I know who is'.[104]

These considerable barriers were gradually but effectively overcome, with the SLA directing the recovery. A key advance came at the end of 1887 when four men (Marjoribanks, Beith, Robert Pullar and John Wilson) undertook to guarantee any deficits incurred by the SLA. Thus the financial constraint which had so depressed the Association's secretary earlier that year was removed, and organisational work could be expanded without stinting.[105] By 1889 the whole picture was much better, as subscriptions had doubled the previous year's figure.[106] The SLA now embarked on a series of initiatives. In 1890 a briefing document on organisational matters was distributed to constituencies. A sub-committee was set up to promote registration work, and again 1890 was a decisive point, with substantial Liberal additions made to the rolls for the first time since 1885, while outvoters were identified and organised after a period of neglect.[107] The SLA had by 1889 been so successful in resuscitating local parties that 301 were affiliated (against 180 in 1887), with a total membership well in excess of 60,000.[108] In 1889, the first Scottish branch of the Women's Liberal Federation was formed in Glasgow, and by 1890 a Scottish section was established, with special attention being paid to involving working-class women.[109] By the start of 1892 the Secretary of the SLA (a successor to the dismayed individual of 1887) was almost complacent: '[1891] has been a year more of consolidating in a quiet and unostentatious way the various organisations — so far as we could get at them'.[110]

The other problems were in the realm of policy. Here the exercise required of the party was to adopt positions which would keep united the Whig and radical wings of Gladstonian Liberalism without appearing so moderate as to enhance the prospects of the vigorous radical Unionists winning over advanced Liberals by deploying the argument that Home Rule was being used as a device to prevent the introduction of domestic reform. One difficulty was the Highlands, where the crofters' demands, although overshadowed by Ireland in the 1886 election, were by no means settled, so that there was no assurance that these M.P.s would re-enter the Liberal fold. The Liberal party indeed was virtually defunct in the north thanks to the dual defections of the crofters in 1885 and of the landlords in 1886. In Argyll, Inverness and Ross-shire activity had ceased after 1885, and Caithness was active only because 48 of the 60 Committee members were Land Leaguers.[111] The orthodox Liberals were still unpopular: Caithness Liberals pointedly observed that there was 'not much attachment' to the party because of so little having been done for the crofters' cause. Moreover, Caithness added, there was felt to be more on offer from radical Unionism, an opinion endorsed by Ross-shire and Inverness-shire Liberals.[112] Chamberlain, Caldwell and intimates were indeed making a real challenge to win the Highlands, having been given *carte blanche* by Whig Liberal Unionists to advocate a progressive land policy, and Chamberlain claimed to have received many promises of support from crofters.[113]

In the light of these organisational difficulties and the prospect of letting radical Unionists win seats if Liberals persisted in challenging Land League M.P.s, the SLA simply abandoned the Highlands to the Crofters' party. Whereas in 1887 there had been calls by SLA activists 'urging the importance of Liberal Organisation in the Highland constituencies', in 1890 the Scottish organiser of the SLA was despatched to the annual conference of the Land League to determine what course Liberals should pursue in the Highlands.[114] His report emphasised 'the desirability of allowing all the Highland Counties to make their own arrangements for candidates', which in practice meant leaving the Crofters' party unchallenged.[115] This proved a successful decision, as no further gains were made by radical Unionists in Highland seats in 1892. In addition, by leaving Land League crofters in sole possession, the salient questions at post-1886 contests were naturally land-related, while a fully-fledged Liberal might well have lost votes over disestablishment. Despite the high hopes held out in 1885 by Free Church disestablishers of a change of attitude by their Highland co-religionists, the latter remained totally opposed to the separation of church and state, and when an election was fought on that issue in the Highlands, Unionists could do well, as Campbell-Bannerman explained in 1890: 'Ayr was a bad loss. The Tory whips did not expect to win, and what is the thing they confidentially say gained them the seat? Routledge going so hot for disestablishment! It was in Oban and the other Highland burghs [i.e. Campbeltown and Inveraray] that we were beaten and the Auld Kirk did it. So say the Tories and our agents and friends agree'.[116]

Disestablishment was a delicate topic everywhere, not just in the Highlands, and here again the radical Unionists created much of the uncertainty. As has been noted, a whole clutch of eminent disestablishers had broken with Gladstone over Irish Home Rule, but also over the church issue. Accordingly, one of the fears expressed by Gladstonian disestablishers after 1886 was that any pusillanimity on the part of the Liberals could quite feasibly permit radical Unionists to bid for that vote.[117] Gladstone was warned by his Chief Whip that this was a real threat: 'I have no doubt that the attitude taken up [by you] in 1885 had the effect which he states of depressing the ardour of some of our best supporters'.[118] Then they had no other party to vote for, now they had. It was therefore felt desirable to deliver an open commitment to Scottish disestablishment (which Gladstone did in a speech at St Austell on 12 June 1889) in order to staunch any haemorrhaging of support. This proved a successful ploy: the consequence of this was that the Radical Unionists were shorn of another attractive policy. Leading disestablishers changed tack, and now men like Calderwood preferred to stress the case for a merger of all three Presbyterian churches, so that none would harbour any grievance of inequitable treatment.[119]

A third policy area into which the Liberals found themselves moving after 1886 was Scottish Home Rule, which indeed became a party plank in 1888.[120] Espousal of this cause had several advantages. Firstly, it was regarded as placing Irish Home Rule in a more acceptable framework for effecting constitutional change, so that it was possible to argue that while Ireland, because of the exceptional conditions prevailing there, would receive priority, Scotland would follow.[121] Secondly, it was extremely and spontaneously popular, generating real enthusiasm. ' ... My experience is that *everywhere* I go the body of the meeting favour Scotch H.R.', Campbell-Bannerman noted, ' ... the great bulk of our best supporters are in favour'.[122] Bryce was warned that one of the main reasons being given by Aberdeen socialists for opposing him in 1892 was his failure to support this proposal warmly enough.[123] Thidly, by emphasising that one of the essential elements of any measure granting self-government would be the consideration of local option, the temperance lobby was offered a way out of the impasse it faced in trying to have such a bill passed by the Imperial Parliament.[124] Further, the demand for a greater degree of self-government for Scotland was one which the Liberals could proclaim with consistency (unlike Irish Home Rule, where the wounding charge was that the party had totally changed its stance), since the establishment of the Scottish Office and the appointment of ministers to deal specifically with Scottish affairs had been initiated by the second Gladstone administration. Lastly, of course, by taking up the issue so wholeheartedly, the Liberals trumped the inclination of Radical Unionists like Fraser-Mackintosh to promote it.

But while the adoption of these policies acted to curb Radical Unionism, a threat was posed to the unity of the Gladstonian Liberal party, for the latter's alliance of Whigs and radicals risked being capsized by these advanced Liberal nostrums. Indeed Whig unease had been heightened by the speedy rebuttal of Elgin's and Marjoribanks' calculation that the new SLA would avoid contentious policy issues. Radical activists began raising such questions, particularly by the device of tacking policy resolutions on to the end of a series of regional and district conferences convened in 1887 to stimulate the renewal of organisation in constituencies. For instance, a Scottish Home Rule motion was carried at such a meeting held at Castle Douglas in September 1887, to Marjoribanks' dismay.[125] When the Whigs insisted that the SLA had no powers to bind local parties on policy issues, this was neatly circumvented by sending delegates from Scotland to the English NLF to urge the inclusion of Scottish radical demands in the latter's policy pronouncements. This was first adopted over disestablishment in 1887, and repeated in 1888 for Scottish Home Rule.[126] These trends left Marjoribanks in deep gloom by the spring of 1888, when he prophesied that within another year most of the moderates would have been driven out of the SLA, and he blamed the radical leader Gilbert Beith for manoeuvring to this end.[127]

In reality, the radicals were not so advantageously placed to sweep through the party as they initially seemed. Firstly, the SLA could not be regarded as truly representative in its deliberative functions. Most of those attending the Council, the policy debating body, were drawn from one area only. For example, the 1890 Council was attended by 84 delegates, with 29 coming from Glasgow and another 37 from the four surrounding areas of Renfrew, Lanark, Ayr and Dunbarton, so that the rest of Scotland contributed a mere 18 delegates.[128] The west-central region had of course been the stronghold of the NLF of Scotland, but the preponderance of this region at Council meetings left it unclear what the remainder of the country's Liberals felt. The tactic of seeking English NLF commitment to radical Scottish issues was not particularly profitable. As Barker shows, the English Liberals were lukewarm, preferring the demands of Welsh Liberals, because the latter did not insist on organisational independence, but willingly submitted to accepting guidance and leadership from England.[129] But other factors were also at play to limit the advances made by the radicals.

Scottish Home Rule's progress was impeded firstly by the misplaced tactics adopted by its advocates, which were assertive and insensitive. Late in 1889, the SHRA, encouraged by the resolution passed by the Scottish Liberals, sought a conference with the SLA, 'with the view of arranging a *modus vivendi*'. Although the Liberals agreed to discuss the matter, throughout 1890 and 1891 they declined to countenance any moves to advance beyond the limited Home Rule for Scotland set forth by them in 1889. It is likely that the SLA was reluctant to be too closely identified with the whole programme of one pressure group, lest this would encourage other sectional interests to make the same demand. The SLA refused to send any delegates to the SHRA conference in 1892 because the Home Rulers aimed to make their cause a test case in every Scottish constituency. In an interesting emulation of Gladstone's technique for dealing with such demands, the SLA stated that while it had indeed declared in favour of Scottish self-government as a general principle, it could not of course be associated with attempts to bind candidates to a specific scheme.[130]

A further check on the self-government movement stemmed from the hostility shown by several of the key personnel in Scottish Liberalism. Marjoribanks was particularly averse to the idea. It is indicative of his position that just after the SLA-NLFS merger was carried through at the end of 1886, with so many problems still facing the party, he could say to Elgin, 'The only real rock ahead that I can see is this Scottish Home Rule business'.[131] Rosebery and Campbell-Bannerman were also opposed, as was James Bryce, whose reputation with Gladstone was high in this period, because of his enhanced stature as one of the most cogent exponents of the case for Irish Home Rule. Two difficulties were stressed by these men. Firstly, as Rosebery argued, 'It is difficult to go far in the direction of Scottish H R without doing an infinity of harm in England, where we shall hear the cry of the 'Heptarchy' again'.[132] Secondly, Bryce contended that the case for Irish Home Rule would be seriously damaged if the weaker issue of Scottish devolution were linked to it.[133] This latter argument naturally was of concern to Gladstone, and it was relatively easy for Marjoribanks to ensure that the leader did not proceed far with Scottish Home Rule. In the administration of 1892, Gladstone readily acceded to Marjoribanks' recommendation that the institution of a Scottish Grand Committee was sufficient to meet the needs of Scottish legislation.[134] Scottish Home Rule was thus effectively shunted aside.

Similarly, disestablishment's blanket endorsement by the SLA and the GOM did not ensure its automatic triumph, and several factors prevented it being carried into legislation by the 1892 Government. Firstly, it was seen as electorally unpopular. Arnold Morley, Gladstone's Chief Whip, blamed the party's relatively poorer showing in the 1892 election in Scotland on the church question.[135] This argument had a particular impact on Gladstone, whose majority in Mid Lothian fell from 3,931 in 1885 (there was no contest in 1886) to a fragile 690 in 1892. His constituency agent, P. W. Campbell, concluded that this sharp and unforeseen decline in Gladstone's support was mainly due to the 'determined and continued' efforts of the state churchmen. Campbell put four-fifths of the fall in the Liberal vote down to disestablishment, and only one fifth to Irish Home Rule.[136] Gladstone was patently affected by this Mid Lothian verdict, which stopped any headlong rush to legislation, for it was apparent to him that the Scottish people had after all not spoken unequivocally.

However, it seems possible that Gladstone was being presented with, or was adopting, a slanted view of the role of disestablishment in the 1892 election in Scotland. Campbell had in 1890 warned that five seats in particular would be lost if the church question were prominent in a general election.[137] Yet of these five, two (Ayr Burghs and Argyll) were won, despite having gone Unionist in 1886. The other three (Bute, Kirkcudbright and Wigtown) were Unionist in 1892, but they had not been Liberal even in 1885, and in the landslide of 1906, Wigtown still remained uncaptured. Indeed the Church Defence movement seems to have presented a challenge which was both feeble in its impact and narrow in its scope. As noted elsewhere, Chamberlain was scathing about the lack of impact made on Liberal voters by the Church Defence campaign.[138] The reasons for this poor performance seem to have been twofold. Many Church Liberals would not vote against a Gladstonian who adopted a reasonably conciliatory stance toward the Church of Scotland. A Tory party manager complained that in Kincardineshire the local Church Defence Society was ready to support J. W. Crombie as the new Liberal candidate provided he satisfied them on church politics.[139] This episode, which occurred in 1890, when the pro-disestablishment agitation was at its peak, revealed how resistant the Church Defence people were to being incorporated into the Conservative party. In 1891, the Church Interests Committee met the east of Scotland Tories to reveal plans for putting forward Church Liberal candidates in some half-dozen seats, but declined to support Conservatives in other places, such as West Lothian, where the Liberal M.P., Peter MacLagan, was deemed sound on the topic.[140] In the event, no such intervention took place, and it may be deduced that either most Liberal candidates were not seen as hostile to the Church of Scotland, or the Church Defence lobby was too weak to act on its threats.

Certainly there was a distinct absence of a feeling that the Church stood in mortal peril in 1892. Another prominent anti-disestablishment group, the Laymen's League — which drew some of its support from outwith the state church — reported that although it had distributed 700,000 leaflets during the contest, it had to confess that it had discovered a widespread opinion among electors that the Church of Scotland was not actually in any serious danger from its enemies.[141] It was, however, in the interests of both camps to present the pro-establishment pressure as active and serious during the 1892 campaign. For the Churchmen the object was to dissuade the party leaders from action by warning of the electoral damage which would ensure. For the disestablishers, the decisive rejection at the polls of the intensive propaganda war waged by the Church Defence elements vindicated the call for immediate and total legislation, while the vigour of the Church of Scotland's agitation should alert Liberationists to the need for renewed vigilance.[142] In practice it seems that by 1892 the disestablishment issue was regarded by Liberal party strategists as having passed its zenith. It had served its purpose in outflanking Radical Unionism, and while there could be no major retreat in rhetorical commitment, there would equally be no concrete advance. This approach was reinforced by the belief that the cause had no wider appeal. A plea by the leading English Nonconformist clergyman, J. Guinness Rogers, that the prospective Liberal candidate in Argyllshire should not be backed by the party because he was 'not definite' on disestablishment drew a brutal assessment from Schnadhorst, the party's electoral and organisational expert. 'I very much doubt', he told Gladstone, 'if we have anything more to gain in Scotland from this question, but I am quite sure that apart from a very small section of Liberationists no one in England cares two pence about it as a question of practical politics'.[143]

It was a further weakness of the disestablishment campaign that its unity was created only rather belatedly, and was always paper thin. Until 1886 there were three quite separate bodies urging the case in Scotland. Efforts were made in that year to amalgamate in the interests of both economy of costs and clarity of purpose, as well as in order to exploit the anticipated receptiveness of the Gladstonian Liberals to the question. But the merger foundered on the refusal of the Scottish Disestablishment Association (which was closely identified with the Free Church) to sacrifice its separate identity. Although an umbrella body, the Scottish Disestablishment Council, was formed, the three component parts continued to exist and operate independently.[144] These profound differences, which revolved over the best plan for disestablishing the state church and over the degree to which political means could be used to secure the desired end, remained to blunt the assault of the disestablishers. Indeed, the former difficulty undermined the claims of the Liberationists to have the support of the overwhelming number of Scottish M.P.s. Although 47 out of 70 had indicated their approval of ending the state church, this was a misleading picture of the real amount of support on offer. A good number were quite willing to affirm the broad principle of disestablishment, but were unable to associate themselves with the details of proposed legislation. The major obstacle was the demand made by more extreme disestablishers that the Church of Scotland should be disendowed as well as disestablished. R. B. Haldane was taxed by Principal Rainy with failing to champion disestablishment in the Commons, despite having approved the policy in his 1886 election campaign. The M.P. retorted that while he accepted that there was a firm desire to eliminate the 'political grievance' of the state church, he would only agree to vote for such a measure if it erred generously on the side of a disestablished church. Haldane went on to denounce the disendowment scheme contained in the bill on offer as far too harsh, and, being therefore unacceptable to 'a moiety' of the Scottish people, it would not provide a permanent solution.[145] This argument was also Gladstone's ground for refusing to go forward when in office with a suspensory bill for Church Endowments along the lines suggested by a backbencher. The Prime Minister found that the scheme amounted to nine tenths of a total disendowment, and would accordingly be unacceptable.[146]

IV

The sharp electoral setbacks suffered by the Liberals in the 1895 and 1900 elections were regarded as very serious in Scotland, since even in 1886 the party had been comfortably ahead by 43 seats to 27, but in the 1895 contest their lead narrowed from 39 to 31, and 1900 actually marked the first Conservative majority since 1832. 'We have been hopelessly smashed in Scotland,' wailed a party official in 1895.[147] The divergent interpretations of the causes of these cumulative setbacks and the differing solutions proffered merely deepened the crisis in the party. It may not be too fanciful to wonder how far the specific Scottish circumstances contributed to the emergence of Liberal Imperialism in the later 1890s.[148] The leader, Rosebery, was the pre-eminent Scottish Liberal, still very much in touch with affairs in Scotland, even although he had moved out of strictly Scottish politics, for he retained the presidency of the SLA. Two of the most effective Liberal Imperialists. Haldane and Asquith, sat for Scottish seats, and a third leader, Grey, had a good knowledge of Border Liberal trends. Other Scottish 'Limps' were Munro Ferguson, formerly Rosebery's private secretary, and Scottish whip in the late 1890s as well as treasurer of the SLA, Sir Charles Tennant, Asquith's father-in-law, Sir Thomas Glen-Coats, Andrew Ure and Sir Thomas Gibson-Carmichael. The last became vice-president of the SLA in the 1890s and was its effective director, as well as being M.P. for Mid Lothian in succession to Gladstone, a position of symbolic value.[149]

Following diagnosis of the causes of the 1895 and 1900 defeats, the central tenets of Liberal Imperialism were clearly established in Scotland. Firstly, the faddists — disestablishers, teetotallers, etc. — who predominated in the Scottish party had driven many voters away.[150] Then Irish Home Rule was a vote-loser too, especially as it, along with faddist issues, had so dominated the Liberal government between 1892 and 1895 that Scottish matters were not dealt with. Thus moderate middle-class and working-class electors had been driven off.[151] In 1900, Gibson-Carmichael ascribed the further election losses to a different factor: 'war-fever'.[152] The attractions of Liberal Imperialism were therefore obvious: the pull of jingoism, apparently so strongly felt in the Clyde area in 1900, when the Liberals were whitewashed in all seven Glasgow seats (an exact reversal of the 1885 result), could be countered only if the party adopted a less negative stance on Imperialism. Discarding faddist policies would win back those unhappy at the party's sectional image, but the main dividends would accrue from jettisoning Irish Home Rule. This belief had several bases. Firstly, several Liberal Unionists were displaying a willingness to reconsider their position, as the case of Grahame showed. The most important businessman in Fife, the Liberal Unionist Michael Nairn, 'spoke to me', wrote Munro Ferguson, 'most seriously last Friday about Ireland. He is in favour of National Councils in the three capitals but could not stand Mr Gladstone's Bills. I tackled him well and found him all right on everything else'.[153] But not only would middle-class defectors drift back, it was felt the removal of the Irish barrier to domestic social reform would retrieve the lapsed masses of working men. The Liberal Imperialist preference for federal Home Rule all round had of course a particular attraction for Scotland, and helped win many Scots to their side.[154]

The centre of the party, represented by Campbell-Bannerman after he inherited the leadership in 1898, wished to steer a middle course between the faddism of the early 1890s and Liberal Imperialism. Their analysis of the political trends in Scotland not unnaturally deviated from the other two camps. On the one side, they contended that faddism was in eclipse. The disestablishment issue, for them, had subsided after 1895, mainly because of the Free-U.P Churches' merger negotiations, and partly, as the disestablishers themselves confessed, because the Boer War had preoccupied people's attention.[155] However, the centre could not accede to regarding the Boer War as a major factor in the 1900 results, since such an interpretation would reinforce Rosebery's Liberal Imperialist explanation of the way forward. So, as Bannerman saw it in his own seat, which included two of the largest military centres in Scotland: 'There were of course a few influenced by the war, but not many'.[156] His general survey of the results was as follows: 'The wretched result in Scotland is partly due to bread and butter influences, especially in the Clyde district, where warlike expenditure is popular, partly to the turnover of the Catholic vote, which was the main cause in my diminished majority, partly to Khaki, and partly to our own factions which have taken some of the heart out of us'.[157] The loss of the Irish Catholic vote was the point most stressed by the centre, and this was ascribed to Catholic anger at the Liberals' resistance to Unionist proposals both to found a Catholic University in Ireland and to protect the position of the teaching of Catholic doctrine in British schools.[158]

But the last ingredient, the lack of Liberal unity, seemed the most distressing and the least soluble problem. The chosen battlegrounds were the SLA iself and the selection of candidates in 1900. The Liberal Imperialists blamed the sectional intransigents for the electoral debacles. Munro Ferguson assured Rosebery that only 'middle class faddists or enthusiasts' were against Rosebery's return as leader of the party.[159] Unfortunately these men, typified by A. L. Brown of Galashiels, dominated the SLA, and Ferguson's scorn for that body knew no bounds: 'ruffians ... that tribe of Dervishes' were his descriptions to Bannerman.[160] However, what rendered the plight of the SLA more critical than that of its English equivalent was that the SLA was heavily permeated by Liberal Imperialism, whereas the failure of the Roseberyites to secure a major foothold in the NLF is often seen as a fatal flaw, explaining their eventual demise. In Scotland the President, the two Vice-Presidents and two prominent subscribers (Pullar and Glen-Coats) gave Liberal Imperialism a firm base inside the SLA. Friction with the A. L. Brown-led faddists was inevitable. The latter attempted in 1897 to get Harcourt, the arch-enemy of Rosebery, to speak under SLA auspices and then recognise him as leader of the party.[161] Rosebery announced he had only just restrained himself from cancelling his subscription, but shortly afterwards another stormy meeting persuaded Munro Ferguson, at the prompting of Bryce, Tennant and Lord Reay, to cancel his considerable donation to the Association. Ferguson's aim was to strike fear into the faddists. He hoped that it would be seen that if he withdrew completely from the SLA most of the repairs to the party organisation which he had helped achieve would be thrown away. This threat he believed would rally moderate opinion against the A. L. Brownites.[162] But power seesawed, to the general detriment of morale. By 1899 Ferguson was happier —'our fight on the Executive is fought out ... we are a very sizeable entity' — and

Brown was quieter. However, by late 1900 Ferguson was back to denouncing the disorder in the SLA.[163]

In his other capacity as Scottish Whip, Ferguson's main responsibility was to find candidates, and his efforts there caused further controversy. Campbell-Bannerman learned that it was felt in Scotland that Ferguson and Gibson-Carmichael were manipulating the selection process to further the interest of the Rosebery faction: 'What is alleged is that all their official candidates are of the militant Imperialist type and if another sort of man is adopted no help is given but much cold water'.[164] As an instance of this Bannerman cited the Clackmannan and Kinross by-election of 1899. Ferguson reported that although 'the Teetotallers are of course on the warpath', J. A. Dewar, the whisky magnate and Liberal Imperialist, had made more impact, whereas Bannerman regarded him as 'an all but impossible candidate'. Finally, Eugene Wason, a temperance advocate and ex-M.P. for South Ayrshire, was chosen, to Ferguson's ill-feigned distaste: '[Wason] is doing better than might have been expected as the Teetotaller candidate'. When Haldane publicly deplored the preferring of Wason to Dewar, Bannerman saw this as proof of an organised conspiracy to undermine all who were not Liberal Imperialists.[165] When Ferguson told Bannerman in 1899 that, in the field of prospective candidates, for the first time since 1886, 'there are green shoots to be seen', it is quite clear that he had in mind Limps like C. M. Douglas or Glen-Coats (whom he persuaded to run for West Renfrewshire).[166] J. A. Murray MacDonald, who had been close to Hardie in Parliament in the early 1890s and became a social radical in the next decade, was dismissed by Ferguson as a 'lame duck' who 'can fill up any blank in the Highland seats'.[167]

These two forces intertwined to leave the Liberal party disorganised, internally wracked and consequently deeply dispirited in the 1900 election. The SLA was accused of playing little active part in the election campaign because it was preoccupied with internal wranglings. These disputes were so acute that the party's most experienced organiser, Lord Tweedmouth (formerly Edward Marjoribanks), declined to become chairman of the executive.[168] It was felt, by Tweedmouth among others, that Ferguson and Gibson-Carmichael were too remote from the rest of the executive and that generally the SLA was out of control.[169] Also, the ruthless billeting of Liberal Imperialist candidates on reluctant constituencies created unrest, as Ferguson tacitly acknowledged: 'Douglas is just about what we need, whatever view North West Lanarkshire may make of him'.[170] The widespread belief that Ferguson employed the SLA's financial recources exclusively to help Liberal Imperialist candidates exacerbated relations. Ferguson discovered that Campbell-Bannerman shared many of these hostile opinions, and especially felt that Ferguson was not keeping him fully informed of candidate selection developments. He promptly resigned as Scottish Whip, and while this would normally be hailed as a welcome event, as he quit only three weeks before polling started, the party was left in even greater disorder.[171] This catalogue of mishaps and frictions not surprisingly depressed the level of commitment shown by party workers, and this was a crucial flaw, as the election was being fought on an old register, a circumstance which invariably called for considerable effort on the part of Liberals to track down the new addresses of voters. However, 'Voluntary aid was hard to get, tho' needed more than usual because of the removals'.[172]

While official Liberalism could console itself by believing that imperialist sentiments were not the main cause of the 1900 result, the problems confronting the party were still immense. Though Munro Ferguson had lost his grip on the levers of power, Liberal Imperialism remained an influential current within the party in Scotland, and their exclusion from the orthodox party institutions would only encourage Rosebery's followers to organise a separate, rival body and so widen the rift. As Haldane expressed this approach: 'I hear on all sides that there are, North of the Tweed, all the indications of a growing body of Liberalism which the official organisations fail to represent. It is the old story of the difference between religion and dogma'.[173]

V

The Liberal party in the 1890s appeared to be facing remorseless decline in its electoral popularity, and that downturn seemed to be thrown into very sharp relief in Scotland by the election results of 1895 and 1900. Firstly, it appeared introverted in its reluctance to embrace new policies, instead reiterating the assorted collection of sectional demands pulled together in the Newcastle Programme. Secondly, its preoccupation with these issues and its indifference to emerging economic and social questions — typified by the general hostility to the demand for an eight-hour day in the coalfields — resulted in the growing alienation of working-class voters, who in the 1890s were being offered an attractive alternative in the socialist ideas of the ILP.[174] Buckley's study of Aberdeen reveals how the organised labour movement there moved from Lib-Labism in the mid-1880s to a more socialist position by the early 1890s, in reaction to Liberal hostility to the economic, social and political demands of the Trades Council.[175] This trend received its initial impetus in Scotland in 1888 when Keir Hardie contested the Mid Lanark by-election as a Labour candidate, an event which led directly to the formation of the Scottish Labour Party.[176] This early start, and the obstinately faddist image of the Liberals in Scotland in the 1890s, gave an impression of circumstances being highly propitious for the movement towards independent working-class representation.

It is not difficult to find Liberal comments in the 1890s which confirm the threat of Labour. In 1892 Bryce faced a challenge in Aberdeen South from the socialist H. H. Champion, and several Liberal correspondents warned Bryce that his alleged indifference to labour questions and his party's neglect of local social injustices would together constitute the grounds for a sharp drop in his vote.[177] In the 1895 General Election, the Chief Whip reported: 'Accounts from Scotland are good except in the West where, especially in Glasgow, there is much trouble with the Labour people'.[178] In 1899 there were grave fears about the party holding West Fife, for long one of the safest Liberal seats in Scotland. Augustine Birrell wished to transfer to Manchester North East because he 'finds his Fife miners reluctant and a bit sore'. His agent, however, was alarmed at Birrell leaving: 'what he fears is a Socialist or some such man being started among the miners'. He added that if Birrell's replacement lacked local standing, 'the mass would either go for the Socialist or pass over to the Tory'.[179]

The Liberals, in addition, made few bids to court the working-class vote in Scotland by any display of commitment to the demands made by Labour. In response to the demand for the direct representation of Labour, Rosebery's reply to a Dundee working man seemed less than a full-blooded endorsement of the concept: 'I have only to say that every person who thinks the least about politics must wish to see the labour [sic] classes freely and fully represented in Parliament, and by persons who possess their confidence on solid grounds. The difficulty of ascertaining who are the real and trusted mouthpieces of the working classes constitutes one of the main perplexities of politics'.[180] On the eight-hour day, the litmus test of sensitivity to working-class demands, the SLA was virtually silent, and the policy resolutions debated at the Association's General Council meetings in the 1890s were more concerned with defining the party's stance on Home Rule for Scotland, disestablishment, and so on. In the period of the 1892–95 Liberal governments, the two issues which preoccupied Scottish Liberals and which the SLA executive pressed Rosebery to concentrate on in the 1895 election campaign as the most important political questions facing Scotland were 'Registration and Disestablishment'.[181] It can be concluded therefore that Scottish Liberalism made no warmer or clearer reply to the Labour challenge than English Liberalism, and it might accordingly be expected to face as serious a threat.

Hardie's conduct of the Mid Lanark contest opened up several directions in which the cause of Labour representation could be pursued. One method, of course, was by the spread of socialist beliefs among the working classes; another was to win the allegiance of organised labour; a third was to woo the Irish nationalists; a fourth was to strike some electoral bargain with the Liberals. Socialist ideals clearly had a potential audience in Scotland, given the official Liberal party's reluctance to criticise the injustices of the capitalist system, some of the most glaring examples of which were to be found in the industrial Lowlands. William Morris, on his visits to Glasgow in this period, never ceased to comment on the appalling social conditions in the city, which he pronounced certain to create a mass socialist movement.[182] The ILP, with several Scots, notably Hardie, MacDonald, and Glasier, involved in its foundation, evidently had high expectations of growth in Scotland, yet by 1900 these had not, on the whole, been realised.[183] In 1893 the Scottish Labour Party (which became part of the ILP) was reported to Hardie as being weak, many of its branches displaying 'a very poor specimen of organisation'.[184] While a fortnight's tour by Tom Mann in 1895 produced indications of growth and enthusiasm, from 1897 onwards there were unmistakable signs of decay and disintegration.[185] In the outlying areas, as far apart as Inverness and Dalbeattie, 'a few earnest socialists' struggled to keep their vision alive, but numerical and financial weaknesses were overwhelming.[186] Yet even in the industrial Clyde valley, there was no marked difference. In 1897 the

Glasgow Women's section could not afford to meet the affiliation fee, so low was membership. This was echoed by Glasgow Central and Clydebank branches, both complaining that only two or three of the nominal membership did any actual work.[187] The experience in the exclusively working-class area of Possilpark sums it up: 'I am instructed to acquaint you with the fact that after a Precarious struggle of about two years duration. We Have Been Compelled to Bring the Existence of the Branch to A Close. I may say that of the beginning there Had Been a Continual Dwindling of Members who Knew nothing about Socialism who would neither attend Lectures nor Read Literature to Learn till Latterly the work of Carrying on the Branch was left Intirely in the Hands of one or Two'.[188]

Securing the support of organised labour was for much of the 1890s little more successful. There were two connected problems. One was that the unions could not necessarily deliver their mass vote. This emerged clearly at the second Mid Lanark by-election, in 1894. Although Hardie had not received many miners' votes in 1888, with Smillie, the Lanarkshire men's leader, as candidate, he felt confident. 'There is a strong likelihood of winning if a good show is made', Hardie told John Burns. His optimism was based on a resolution taken at a meeting of 5,000 miners in the area to run a Labour candidate at the contest.[189] The secretary of the steelmen's union — of whom there were many in the constituency — also believed Smillie would win, and pledged: 'We will support any man that the Labour Party will bring forward'.[190] However, Smillie came third, admittedly doubling Hardie's 1888 vote of 617 to 1,221. But in percentage terms this was only 13.7% of the turnout, and as the electorate had increased by 2,000 since Hardie stood, with many of the new voters probably working men, it was apparent that the pull of organised labour over its members was uneven. Many trade unions and trades councils were reluctant to work with the ILP. At Dundee the seamen's union persuaded the Trades Council not to run Tom Mann in 1892, and the Greenock Council also refused to put up a candidate.[191] Even the miners, frequently regarded as the socialist vanguard in Scotland, were not yet won over. Weakly unionised and still riven by sectarianism, especially in Lanarkshire, the Scottish miners were less responsive to socialism than many of their English and Welsh counterparts.[192] The Tories ascribed their failure to win Mid Lothian in 1892 and 1895 to the miners' union 'interfering' on behalf of the Liberals.[193]

Hardie had made much of the initial headway in Mid Lanark in 1888 by forging a political relationship with the Irish Nationalists. Although on polling day most of the Irish voted Liberal, the strategy remained an attractive approach, both to build up Labour support and to detach a sizeable working-class component of the Liberal vote in many Scottish seats. Moreover, the cooling of relations between the Irish and the Liberals after the Parnell divorce seemed to provide an opportunity for Labour. Yet the Irish stayed with the Liberals. Cunninghame Graham was despondent in 1890: 'The Parnell split has, I fear, killed the Labour movement in Scotland. All the fools are united in Gladstone'.[194] The head of the Irish Home Rulers in Scotland, John Ferguson, remained an active figure on the executive of the SLA, which body invited Irish Nationalist speakers to tour Scotland during the 1892 election.[195] The Liberal government, the Irish decided, deserved all support between 1892 and 1895 as they strove to get Home Rule on the statute book. Michael Davitt, who had been a key element in Hardie's 1888 Mid Lanark bid, now reproached Hardie for putting up Smillie in that seat in 1894, as this would only let the Tory in.[196] In this forbidding context, the socialists turned from wooing the Nationalists to abusing them roundly. Cunninghame Graham called on Glasgow socialists to protect him in his bid for the Camlachie seat in 1892 from 'the attacks of reactionary priestcraft'.[197] Only in Edinburgh Central, inspired by James Connolly, was an attempt at an electoral alliance seriously made, but by 1894 this effort was abandoned, and no Labour man stood.[198] Even when relations between Liberals and Irish Nationalists became frayed in the 1890s, the ILP rarely extracted any benefit. In Edinburgh East, the Irish party was said to be a sizeable part of a body of dissident Liberals opposed to the re-election of the sitting M.P., Robert Wallace. The objectors vowed that in no circumstances would they support Wallace, yet he was nominated as candidate and won the seat, with no Labour party opposition.[199] When the Irish did cut themselves adrift from the Liberals in 1900, the recipients of their votes were not Labour, who put up no candidates. In Blackfriars and Hutchesontown, won by Labour in 1906, Irish Nationalists voted for the Tory, Bonar Law, in 1900.

The fourth option available to Labour was that counselled by Davitt to Hardie in 1894: 'What I would strongly urge you to do at this juncture is to try to come to some understanding with the Liberal Party in Lanarkshire about the claims of Labour to one of the seats in that county at the General Election'.[200] In the aftermath of Hardie's Mid Lanark intervention, an electoral arrangement was reached in 1890, but this soon foundered when the Liberals discovered that the ILP had very little voting strength.[201] In three Scottish constituencies this approach was seriously proceeded with subsequently, but to no gain for Labour. In Tradeston, where a Labour intervention denied the Liberals the seat in 1892, discussions were held in 1894 to settle upon one candidate, but these broke down when Labour selected their candidate in advance of a final agreement. The Liberals then chose a man of their own, and both sides fought in 1895.[202] Camlachie represented the best advance by Labour. Here in 1900 A. E. Fletcher was endorsed by the Liberals, the ILP and the Trades Council, and so stood with the backing of both parties.[203] At a by-election in Aberdeen North in 1896, the Liberals were initially equally accommodating. Fletcher received a private approach from the chairman of the Liberals asking if he would accept nomination, as 'he thinks I should receive the united support of all the progressive sections in the division'. Fletcher, who defined his position as an 'advanced radical', and did not accept the ILP programme in its entirety, intimated that he would not stand against a Labour candidate. When Tom Mann entered the election, Fletcher stood down. The Liberals chose D. V. Pirie, described by Fletcher as a 'military plutocrat', who fought against Mann.[204]

These attempts to reach an electoral understanding provide significant pointers to the relative strengths of the two parties. Firstly, there was no general pact, and the Liberals felt under no duress. A conference held in 1894 in Glasgow, where Labour candidatures were most prevalent, to assess the prospects for an arrangement failed because the Liberals trenchantly rejected any compromise on their part. The Liberals argued that on payment of M.P.s and the removal of barriers to working-class representation there was no difference between the two. However, they added: 'the difference is one of principle. The programme of the Independent Labour Party is purely socialistic, their leaders declare unqualified opposition to the Liberal Party and do all they can to break it up. The Committee therefore do not see that there is any basis upon which united action can be taken'. Instead they advised petitioning Parliament to introduce the Second Ballot system.[205] By highlighting the socialist content and the threat to Liberal electoral success, the Glasgow Liberals showed shrewd skill in probing the weakest parts of the ILP. This assurance was derived from two factors: the electoral impact of Labour in Scotland was less than in England, and the Liberal party in Scotland, however depleted compared to its Unionist rivals, was apparently still in a healthier condition than in many areas of England, where the Liberals had abandoned several constituencies, so letting Labour become the anti-Unionist party; nowhere in Scotland was this to be found.

The number of Labour candidates in each country in the elections of 1892, 1895 and 1900 is revealing. In both England and Scotland, six candidates stood in the first contest, but thereafter the pattern diverges: in 1895, eight stood in Scotland, thirty in England and Wales; in 1900, no candidate stook in Scotland, as against sixteen in England. No Scottish seat was held by Labour before 1906, whereas in England and Wales the tally was two in 1892, one in 1895, and two in 1900. An important consideration was taking away votes from Liberals, so denying them crucial seats: thus a pact would be of more interest to Liberals. On the assumption that all Labour votes would have been cast otherwise for the Liberal, several English constituencies were lost to the Liberals because of Labour intervention in the general elections between 1892 and 1900. In Scotland, only Tradeston and Camlachie in 1892 fell into this category. In Camlachie, Labour got 906 votes and the Liberals fell 371 behind the Unionist. It may be no accident that this was the only Scottish seat to operate a quasi-pact in 1900. Moreover, in terms of votes gained, England was ahead of Scotland. Taking three-cornered contests as the only instances where the true Labour vote can be gauged, in 1892 the average Labour vote in Scotland was 689 (7.8%), in England 1,386 (17.5%); in 1895 it was 561 (7.0%) and 956 (9.0%) respectively.

It must be borne in mind that the English support is probably understated because of the second factor far more prevalent in England, namely that in certain seats there Labour had supplanted the Liberals as the main anti-Unionist force. In Scotland only three seats in 1895 and 1900 were not fought by Liberals. These were Bute, Glasgow Central, Wigtownshire and East Renfrewshire (the last two left alone in both elections). None of them was natural Labour territory, and indeed not one of these was fought by Labour before 1914. In England, in 1892 Labour stood without a rival Liberal candidate in ten seats, in 1895 only in two and in 1900 in ten. In several English seats the Liberals, after fighting Labour in one election, gave them a free run thereafter (e.g. Bradford West in 1900), but in others the decline of the Liberals was even more precipitous. In Hanley, Blackburn, and

Bow and Bromley, where the Tories had faced only Liberals in 1892 and 1895, Labour alone challenged Unionists in 1900. In some double-member seats, like Derby, by 1900 one Liberal and one Labour stood, presumably reflecting the perceived risk of splitting the anti-Unionist vote if both parties or either of them insisted on fighting the two seats. In Dundee, the only two-man constituency in Scotland, Labour fought two Liberals in 1892 and 1895, but abandoned the effort in 1900.

Even where Labour did seek to fight, there was a marked lack of optimism. Cunninghame Graham decided to withdraw from Camlachie in 1892, because his supporters refused to help him, many of them emphasising the great difficulty of defeating the Liberal.[206] Nor did the Liberals on close scrutiny of the election results have very much to fear from the challenge of Labour in the 1890s. Bad as was the setback delivered by the 1895 election, when a dozen seats were lost, not one was attributable to Labour's intervention, and in 1900 when a further half-dozen seats turned to Unionism, not a single Labour candidate had stood. Even in terms of votes lost, as distinct from seats at risk, the Liberals were not badly damaged by Labour. Of the nine seats for which comparative data are available,[207] the Liberal vote actually increased in three, and in one it fell by only 23. Of the other five, while the Liberal vote did fall when Labour stood, this was not the major cause of the drop in four cases. Dundee was the sole exception, where Labour in 1895 rose by nearly 1,000 and the two Liberals fell by around 600 and

Table 6.1.   The Labour Vote in Scotland before 1901

	General Elections				Other Contests		
	1892		1895				
	Votes	%	Votes	%	Date	Vote	%
Aberdeen, N.			608	12.8	(1896)	2479	46.0
Aberdeen, S.	991	15.8					
Dundee	354	n.a.	1313	n.a.			
Edinburgh, Cent.	434	7.3					
Glasgow:							
Blackfriars			448	7.1	*(1885)	1156	14.4
Bridgeton			609	9.4	*(1885)	978	12.1
Camlachie	906	11.9	696	10.9			
College			225	2.1			
St Rollox			405	4.0			
Tradeston	783	10.7	368	5.7			
Lanarkshire:							
Govan			430	4.9			
Mid					(1888)	617	8.4
"					(1894)	1221	13.7
Stirlingshire	663	6.3					

* Candidates of the Scottish Land Restoration League

900 respectively. Elsewhere abstentions or conversions to Unionism constituted the bulk of the decline and may therefore have appeared the most pressing problem for the Liberals to grapple with. Nor need the Liberals have had any lingering worries about the trend of support for Labour. Not only did Labour's vote fall in the only two Glasgow seats it fought in successive elections, but an illuminating standard of measurement was afforded by the performance of the Land Restoration League candidates in 1885. These men, who were semi-socialist, stood in two seats which were contested by Labour in the 1890s. In Bridgeton, 978 (12.1%) voted for the SLRL in 1885, but by 1895 this had fallen to 609 (9.4%). In Blackfriars and Hutchesontown — where the same man, J. Shaw Maxwell, stood on both occasions — the SLRL vote of 1,156 (14.4%) dropped to 448 (7.1%) to Labour in 1895. Indeed so lamentable was the party's result in Bridgeton in 1895 that no candidate was entered in the Bridgeton by-election of 1897. Yet Labour had recorded its second highest poll of the 1895 election in the seat, and it would have been hard to find a more appealing seat for them. The constituency was a blackspot, even by Glasgow's demanding criteria, for both unemployment and social conditions, and the Liberals chose Sir Charles Cameron, the veteran faddist who had lost College in 1895.

NOTES

1. Fife to R. W. Duff, 30 Nov. 1885, Fetteresso MSS., GD 105/635/5.

2. G. A. Gibson, *The Life of Sir Willliam Tennant Gairdner* (Glasgow, 1912), p. 240.

3. Fife to R. W. Duff, 31 Dec. 1885, Fetteresso MSS., GD 105/635/6.

4. J. Patten to Rosebery, 9, 10 May 1882, W. Burns to Rosebery, 10 May 1882, Rosebery MSS., MS. 10042, ff. 102–3, 104, 107–10.

5. *Report of the Annual General Meeting of the Glasgow Liberal Association Held in the Trades Hall on Monday 27 February 1882* (Glasgow, 1882).

6. J. Hunter, 'The Politics of Highland Land Reform, 1873–95', *SHR* 53 (1974), pp. 45–55.

7. W. Burns to Rosebery, 10 May 1882, Rosebery MSS., MS. 10042, ff. 107–10.

8. J. Patten to Rosebery, 12, 22 Sep., 29 Nov. 1885, Ibid., MS. 10042, ff. 192–3, 194–5, 204.

9. Cf. Munro Ferguson to C. Munro, 21 Aug. 1884, Monro MSS., GD 71/333/39; also Munro Ferguson to Rosebery, 26 Dec. 1885, Rosebery MSS., MS. 10017, ff. 15–16.

10. J. Chamberlain to K. MacKenzie, 9 Sep. 1889, J. P. Grant to MacKenzie, 16 Sep. 1889, MacKenzie to Lord Wolmer, 1 Sep. 1889, MacKenzie MSS.

11. H. Ivory to Rosebery, 20 Mar., 17 Jun. 1884, Rosebery MSS., MS. 10037, ff. 96–8, 109–10.

12. C. Cooper to A. R. D. Elliot, 18 Jan. 1885, Elliot MSS., Acc. 4246/14; Cooper to Rosebery, 24 Aug. 1885, Rosebery MSS., MS. 10011, ff. 107–8; T. R. Buchanan to R. P. Bruce, 14 Sep. 1885, Elgin MSS., 41/84.

13. R. Cathcart to R. P. Bruce, 25 Aug., 2 Sep., 1, 2 Dec. 1885, Elgin MSS., 41/24,10,84 (twice).

14. *Glasgow Herald,* 13, 14 Mar. 1885 praises Jackson lavishly.

15. There is a copy of the Trades Council's circular letter of 30 Mar. 1885 in the National Library of Scotland, catalogue number Pt.Sm. 1(5).

16. J. Patten to Rosebery, 17 Mar. 1885, Rosebery MSS., MS. 10042, ff. 186–7.

17. Glasgow Liberal Association, *4th Annual Report* (1882); *Glasgow Herald,* 13 Jun. 1882.

18. This episode is discussed in J. G. Kellas, 'The Liberal Party in Scotland, 1876–95', *SHR* 44 (1965), pp. 5–9; D. C. Savage, 'Scottish Politics, 1885–86', *Ibid.* 40 (1961), pp. 123–9.

19. SLA Minute Book, 23 Jan. 1884.

20. H. Calderwood to Elgin, 3, 5 Feb. 1885, Elgin MSS., 41/7; SLA Minute Book, 16 Jan., 17 Feb., 15 Jul. 1885.

21. J. Patten to Rosebery, 14 Dec. 1885, 9 Jan. 1886, Rosebery MSS., MS. 10042, ff. 205–6, 208–9; R. C. Munro Ferguson to Elgin, 23 Mar. 1886, Elgin MSS., 41/8.

22. J. G. Kellas, 'The Liberal Party and the Scottish Church Disestablishment Crisis', *EHR* 79 (1964), pp. 33–46; J. F. McCaffrey, 'The Origins of Liberal Unionism in the West of Scotland', *SHR* 50 (1971), pp. 48–52; Savage, 'Scottish Politics', pp. 121–3.

23. Scottish Council of the Liberation Society, *Annual Report 1883* (sic), pp. 17–19.

24. G. Beith, *The Crofter Question and Church Endowments in the Highlands, viewed politically and socially* (Glasgow, 1884), pp. 9–16.

25. E.g. Rev. G. Whyte to Sir G. MacPherson Grant, 1 Mar. 1882, Ballindalloch MSS., 635.

26. W. E. Gladstone MSS., Add. MS. 44629, ff. 103 ff. for a verbatim minute of a meeting held on 29 Aug. 1884.

27. A. R. McEwen, *Life and Letters of John Cairns, D.D., LL.D.* (London, 1895), pp. 733–6.

28. W. E. Gladstone MSS., Add. MS. 44629, ff. 103 ff., esp. pp. 8–23 of the Verbatim Report; Scottish Disestablishment Association, *Address by the Rev. Principal Cairns, D. D., United Presbyterian College, Edinburgh at the Conference Held at Edinburgh on 21 May 1885* (n.p., n.d.).

29. Scottish Disestablishment Association, *Address by Cairns,* p. 7.

30. T. Raleigh, *Annals of the Church of Scotland* (London, 1929), pp. xix–xx.

31. Sheriff A. Mackintosh to Rosebery, 27 Oct. 1885, W. E. Gladstone MSS., Add. MS. 44288, ff. 258–63.

32. Campbell-Bannerman to H. Craik, 18 Nov. 1885, Craik MSS., MS. 7175, ff. 31–2.

33. E.g. A. R. D. Elliot to R. P. Bruce, 17 Sep. 1885, Elgin MSS., 41/84; T. R. Buchanan to A. R. D. Elliot, 7 Nov. 1885, Elliot MSS., Acc. 4246/14.

34. West Perthshire Liberal Association Minute Book, 2 Jul., 16 Oct. 1885, DG/YG/Li.

35. Elliot to Rev. T. Burns, 5 Nov. 1885 (copy), Elliot MSS., Acc. 4246/14; cf. A. R. D. Elliot, *The State and the Church* (2nd edn., London, 1899).

36. Sheriff A. Mackintosh to Rosebery, 27 Oct. 1885, W. E. Gladstone MSS., Add. MS. 44288, ff. 258–63.

37. J. Patten to Rosebery, 3 Jun. 1884, Rosebery MSS., MS. 10042, ff. 161–2; cf. J. K. Donaldson to Rosebery, 9 Jun. 1882, Ibid. This letter was formerly in Box 58, but I have been unable to locate in the new classification.

38. *The Church of Scotland. Report of a Meeting of Scottish Laymen of Different Religious Denominations opposed to the Disestablishment and Disendowment of the Church of Scotland held in St Andrew's Hall, Glasgow, 20 October 1885* (Glasgow, 1885), p. 24.

39. N. Dalrymple to Rosebery, 25 Nov. 1885, Rosebery MSS., MS. 10084, ff. 195–6.

40. C. Dalrymple Diary, 28 Nov. 1885, Newhailes MSS., Acc. 7228/273.

41. M. T. Stormonth-Darling to P. Stormonth-Darling (29 Nov. 1885), Stormonth-

Darling MSS., 64.

42. D. Crawford to Rosebery, 1 Nov. 1885, Rosebery MSS., MS. 10084, ff. 103–8.

43. Sheriff Mackintosh to Rosebery, 27 Oct. 1885; T. R. Buchanan to W. E. Gladstone, 5 Nov. 1885; C. Tennant to Gladstone, 23 Oct. 1885; Rosebery to Gladstone, 6 Nov. 1885; J. Grahame to Lord R. Grosvenor, 4 Nov. 1885; W. E. Gladstone MSS., Add. MSS. 44288, ff. 258–63; 44493, ff. 42–4; 44492, ff. 228–9; 44288, ff. 265–6; 44316, ff. 89–93.

44. Rosebery to Gladstone, 6 Nov. 1885, Ibid., Add. MS. 44288, ff. 265–6.

45. Gladstone to Lord R. Grosvenor, n.d., 6, 8 Nov. 1885, Ibid., Add. MS. 44316, ff. 96, 97–8, 100–1.

46. J. G. C. Hamilton to Gladstone, 12 Nov. 1885, Ibid., Add. MS. 44493, ff. 68–9; cf. J. Patten to Rosebery, 11 Nov. 1885, Rosebery MSS., MS. 10042, ff. 200–1 for Sheriff Mackintosh's positive reaction.

47. Gladstone to Lord R. Grosvenor, 18 Nov. 1885, W. E. Gladstone MSS., Add. MS. 44316, f. 110; C. Cooper to Rosebery, 13 Nov. 1885, Rosebery MSS., MS. 10011, f. 130.

48. Rosebery to Gladstone, 6 Nov. 1885, W. E. Gladstone MSS., Add. MS. 44288, ff. 265–6.

49. G. W. T. Omond to Rosebery, 24 Oct. 1885, Rosebery MSS., MS. 10084, ff. 50–3; Rosebery to Gladstone, 6 Nov. 1885, W. E. Gladstone MSS., Add. MS. 44288, ff. 265–6.

50. Calderwood to Elgin, 16 Jul. 1884, Elgin MSS., 41/7.

51. J. Patten to Rosebery, 14 Nov. 1885, C. Cooper to Rosebery, 11 Nov. 1885, Rosebery MSS., MSS. 10042, ff. 202–3, 10011, ff. 128–9.

52. Marjoribanks to Elgin, 9 Sep. 1887, Elgin MSS., 41/84.

53. J. Morley, *The Life of William Ewart Gladstone* (London, 1903), III, p. 517.

54. *'We Twa': Reminiscences of Lord and Lady Aberdeen* (London, 1925), esp. pp. 216–7.

55. J. B. Mackie, *Life and Work of Duncan MacLaren* (Edinburgh, 1888), II, P. 249.

56. R. V. C(ampbell), *Scottish Liberals and Disestablishment: A Proposal for a National Liberal Union* (n.p., 1886).

57. L. Mackersy to D. Murray, — Jan. 1886, in Murray Collection, Glasgow University Library, Mu 44-e-20; *Constitution of the Liberal Anti-Disestablishment Association for Scotland* (n.p., n.d.).

58. Campbell, *Scottish Liberals and Disestablishment,* pp. 2–3.

59. Balfour of Burleigh to Salisbury, 5 Dec. 1885, Hatfield House MSS., 3M/E.

60. L. Mackersy to D. Murray, — Jan. 1886, Murray Collection, Glasgow University Library, Mu 44-e.20; *Liberal Anti-Disestablishment Association.*

61. R. V. Heuston, *Lives of the Lord Chancellors, 1885–1940* (London, 1964), p. 316.

62. McCaffrey, 'Liberal Unionism', pp. 54–69: Savage, 'Scottish Politics', pp. 131–5.

63. A. B. Cooke and J. Vincent, *The Governing Passion* (Hassocks, 1974).

64. Mackie, *MacLaren,* I, pp. 83–4; *Life of Henry Calderwood, LL.D., F.R.S.E.,* by his son and Rev. D. Woodside (London, 1910), p. 344.

65. *St. Rollox Division, Glasgow. Address of J. Caldwell, M.P., to the Electors* (Glasgow, 1892), p. 7.

66. *Paisley and Renfrewshire Gazette,* 1 Jun. 1886, *North British Daily Mail,* 10 Apr. 1886; Memorandum by J. J. Reid, 26 Mar. 1886, Rosebery MSS., MS. 10085, ff. 121–2. For Banffshire, J. Allan to R. W. Duff, 25 May 1886, Fetteresso MSS., GD 105/635/18; for Stirling, R. Taylor to H. Campbell-Bannerman, 28 Apr. 1886, Campbell-Bannerman MSS., Add. MS. 41232, ff. 235–8.

67. R. Yellowlees to H. Campbell-Bannerman, 22 Apr. 1886, Campbell-Bannerman MSS., Add. MS. 41232, ff. 212–7; *Address by J. Caldwell,* p. 3.

68. West Perthshire Liberal Association Minute Book, 3 May, 24,30 Jun. 1886, DG/YG/Li.

69. R. Yellowlees to D. Ireland, 17 May 1886 (copy), Campbell-Bannerman MSS., Add. MS. 41232, ff. 251–2; Campbell-Bannerman to J. Campbell, 16 Oct. 1889, Ibid., 41246, ff. 26–7.

70. E.g. J. W. Johnston, Rev. J. G. Crawford, G. Greig to R. P. Bruce, 16,22,25 Jun. 1886, Elgin MSS., 41/10 for Fife West; J. Webster, J. O. MacQueen to J. B. Bryce, 14,29 Jun. 1886, Bryce MSS., MS. Bryce UB 29,28 for Aberdeen South.

71. H. Ivory to Rosebery, 1,5 Apr. 1886, Rosebery MSS., MS. 10037, ff. 143–4, 145–6.

72. R. Yellowlees to H. Campbell-Bannerman, 22 Apr. 1886, Campbell-Bannerman MSS., Add. MS. 41232, ff. 212–7; J. Ross to R. P. Bruce, 2,10 Apr. 1886, Elgin MSS., 41/10.

73. J. Allan to R. W. Duff, 25 May 1886, Fetteresso MSS., GD 105/635/18; E. R. Russell to W. E. Gladstone, 2 May 1886, W. E. Gladstone MSS., Add. MS. 44497, ff. 91–4.

74. J. B. Smith to H. Campbell Bannerman, 20 Apr., 15 May 1886, Campbell-Bannerman MSS., Add. MS. 41232, ff. 211–2, 248–9; J. Ross to R. P. Bruce, 7 May 1886, Elgin MSS., 41/10.

75. P. W. Campbell to W. E. Gladstone, 10 Jun. 1886, W. E. Gladstone MSS., Add. MS. 44116, ff. 103–4.

76. H. Ivory to Rosebery, 23 Jun. 1886, Rosebery MSS., MS. 10037, ff. 155–8; T. R. Buchanan to R. P. Bruce, n.d. (June 1886), Elgin MSS., 41/10.

77. Asquith to Elgin, 10 Jul. 1886, Elgin MSS., 22/20.

78. R. Yellowlees to D. Ireland, 17 May 1886, Campbell-Bannerman MSS., Add. MS. 41232, ff. 251–2.

79. A. R. D. Elliot to A. C. Sellar, — Oct. 1886, Elliot MSS., Acc. 4246/15.

80. R. Yellowlees to H. Campbell-Bannerman, 10 Jun., 20 Nov. 1886, Campbell-Bannerman MSS., Add. MS. 41232, ff. 259–62.

81. R. Cathcart to Elgin, 20 Apr., 31 Oct. 1886, Elgin MSS., 41/7.

82. Same to same, 27 May, 4 Jun. 1887, Ibid., 41/84.

83. R. W. Campbell to W. E. Gladstone, 26 Dec. 1888, W. E. Gladstone MSS., Add. MS. 44116, ff. 163–4; West Perthshire, Liberal Association Minute Book, 1 Jun. 1887, DG/YG/Li. Cf. the similar position in Buteshire, SLA Minute Book, 30 Sep. 1887.

84. H. Ivory to Rosebery, 31 May 1891, also 19 Feb. 1888, Rosebery MSS., MS. 10038, ff. 15–16, 7–8.

85. J. Grahame to H. Ivory, 17 Sep. 1895; Ivory to Rosebery, 22 Dec. 1895, Rosebery MSS., MS. 10038, ff. 66–73, 74–7.

86. J. Patten to Rosebery, 28 Dec. 1886, Ibid., MS. 10042, ff. 210–3; SLA Minute Book. 29 Oct. 1886.

87. Marjoribanks to Elgin, 6 Nov. 1886, Elgin MSS., 41/24.

88. Marjoribanks to W. E. Gladstone, 11 Dec. 1886, W. E. Gladstone MSS., Add. MS. 44332, ff. 166–8; also Rosebery's letter in SLA Minute Book, 17 Feb. 1886.

89. J. Patten to Rosebery, 28 Dec. 1886, Rosebery MSS., MS. 10042, ff. 210–3; Prof. T. Lindsay to Elgin, 4 Dec. 1886, Elgin MSS., 41/8.

90. E. Marjoribanks to Elgin, 16 Dec. 1886, Ibid., 41/24.

91. Elgin to Rosebery, 22 Jul. 1888, Rosebery MSS., MS. 10087, ff. 271–6.

92. Prof. T. Lindsay to Elgin, 4 Dec. 1886, Elgin MSS., 41/8.

93. Elgin to G. Beith (draft), Beith to Elgin, 18, 17 Dec. 1886, Ibid., 41/8; MS. notes by Elgin, n.d. (Dec. 1886), Ibid., 41/7.

94. SLA Minute Book, 11 Jan. 1888.

95. Elgin to W. E. Gladstone, 17 Nov. 1887, W. E. Gladstone MSS., Add. MS. 44502, ff. 115–7.

96. SLA Minute Book, 24 Jan., 30 Nov. 1887; SLA Balance Sheet, 1887, Elgin MSS., 41/31; J. Patten to Rosebery, 12 May 1887, Rosebery MSS., 10042, ff. 214–7.

97. J. Cowan to Gladstone, 24 Jul. 1886, W. E. Gladstone MSS., Add. MS. 44137, ff. 441–2.

98. West Perthshire Liberal Association Minute Book, 3 May 1886, 17 Mar. 1888, DG/YG/Li; SLA Minute Book, 26 Jun. 1889.

99. J. Patten to Rosebery, 12 May 1887, Rosebery MSS., MS. 10042, ff. 214–7: C. MacRae to K. MacKenzie, 14 Sep. 1889, MacKenzie MSS. (Stornoway); J. Ross to H. Campbell-Bannerman, 24 Apr. 1886, Campbell-Bannerman MSS., Add. MS. 41232, ff. 218–9 (Dunfermline).

100. R. Mitchell to H. Campbell-Bannerman, 15 May 1889, Campbell-Bannerman MSS., Add. MS. 41233, ff. 11–18.

101. SLA Minute Book, 14 May 1891.

102. R. Mitchell to H. Campbell-Bannerman, 15 May 1889, Campbell-Bannerman MSS., Add. MS. 41233, ff. 11–18; SLA Minute Book, 30 May 1889.

103. SLA Minute Book, 21 Feb., 4 Mar. 1887.

104. Campbell-Bannerman to R. P. Bruce, 14 Jun. 1886, Elgin MSS., 41/10.

105. SLA Minute Book, 30 Nov. 1887.

106. SLA Balance Sheets 1888–9, Elgin MSS., 41/31.

107. SLA Minute Book, 1 May, 27 Jun., 2,8 Oct. 1890, 27 Mar., 6 May 1891.

108. SLA *Annual Reports,* 1888, 1889; SLA Minute Book, 12 Jul. 1887, 24 Jan. 1888.

109. Mrs. C. M. Beith to Elgin, 23, 26 Feb. 1889, 14 Oct. 1890, Elgin MSS 41/8; Lord and Lady Aberdeen, *'We Twa',* pp. 271–5.

110. G. Bell to Elgin, 11 Jan. 1892, Elgin MSS., 41/8.

111. SLA Minute Book, 16 May, 6 Sep. 1887, 12 Sep. 1888, 26 Jun., 20 Aug. 1889.

112. Ibid., 26 Jun. 1889.

113. H. T. Anstruther to K. MacKenzie, 9, 18 Nov. 1889; MacKenzie to Wolmer, 1 Sep. 1889; Chamberlain to MacKenzie, 9 Sep. 1889, MacKenzie MSS.

114. SLA Minute Book, 30 Sep., also 17 Aug., 6 Sep. 1887.

115. Ibid., 10 Sep. 1890; cf. SLA *Annual Report,* 1890.

116. Campbell-Bannerman to J. Campbell, — Mar. 1890, Campbell-Bannerman MSS., Add. MS. 41246, ff. 28–30.

117. SLA Minute Book, 16 Nov. 1887.

118. A. Morley to Gladstone, 15 Oct. 1887, Gladstone MSS., Add. MS. 44253, ff. 145–6; cf. SLA Minute Book, 16 Nov. 1887.

119. *Calderwood,* pp. 344–50.

120. J. G. Kellas, The Liberal Party in Scotland, 1885–1895 (Ph.D., London University, 1962), Ch. 6; H. J. Hanham, *Scottish Nationalism* (London, 1969), pp. 91–3.

121. SLA Minute Book, 22 Nov. 1889.

122. Campbell-Bannerman to D. Crawford, 16 Nov. 1889, Campbell-Bannerman MSS., Add. MS. 41233, ff. 46–50.

123. J. W. Crombie, J. B. Butchart to Bryce, 3 Nov. 1891, 22 Jun. 1892, Bryce MSS., MS. Bryce UB 29,28.

124. E.g., SLA Minute Book, 7 Feb. 1888.

125. Marjoribanks to Elgin, 9 Sep. 1887, Elgin MSS., 41/84.

126. SLA Minute Book, 13 Oct., 16 Nov. 1887, 7 Feb. 1888.

127. Marjoribanks to Elgin, 14 May 1888, Elgin MSS., 41/24.

128. SLA Minute Book, 7 Feb. 1890.

129. M. Barker, *Gladstone and Radicalism* (Hassocks, 1975), pp. 122-3.

130. SLA Minute Book, 7 Nov. 1889, 7 Feb. 1890, 27 Feb. 1891, 2 Jun. 1892.

131. Marjoribanks to Elgin, 16 Dec. 1886, Elgin MSS., 41/24, cf. same to same, 9 Sep. 1887, Ibid., 41/84.

132. Rosebery to Elgin, 18 Nov. 1889, Ibid., 41/24.

133. J. Bryce to W. E. Gladstone, 29 Nov. 1886, Bryce MSS., MS. Bryce 11, ff. 155-7.

134. Marjoribanks to Gladstone, and reply, 3, 5 Sep. 1892, W. E. Gladstone MSS., Add. MS. 44332, ff. 226-31, 234-5.

135. A. Morley to Gladstone, 13 Jul. 1892, Ibid., Add. MS. 44254, ff. 216-7.

136. Campbell to Gladstone, 20 Jul. 1892, Ibid., Add. MS. 44116, ff. 212-3.

137. Same to same, 3 Oct. 1890, Ibid., Add. MS. 44116, ff. 180-1.

138. See p. 201.

139. J. P. B. Robertson to C. Dalrymple, 11 Sep. 1890, Newhailes MSS., Acc. 7228/235.

140. NUCAS, Eastern District Organisation Sub-Committee Minute Book, 15 Jan. 1891.

141. Laymen's League *Annual Report* (1893), in Hope MSS., GD 364/598.

142. *Disestablishment Banner,* 34 (Oct. 1892).

143. F. Schnadhorst to Gladstone, 21 Sep. 1891, W. E. Gladstone MSS., Add. MS. 44295, ff. 249-52.

144. Liberation Society Minute Book, 8 Jun., 10 Sep., 27 Oct. 1886, A/LIB/7.

145. Haldane to Rainy, 18 Apr. 1888 (Copy), Haldane MSS., MS. 5903, ff. 95-6.

146. Marjoribanks to Gladstone, and reply, 3, 5 Sep. 1892, W. E. Gladstone MSS., Add. MS. 44332, ff. 226-31, 234-5.

147. H. Ivory to Rosebery, 23 Jul. 1895, Rosebery MSS., MS. 10038, ff. 58-61.

148. H. C. G. Mathew, *The Liberal Imperialists* (London, 1973), pp. 98-9, notes the Scottish interest in Liberal Imperialism.

149. Lady Carmichael, *Lord Carmichael of Skirling* (London, n.d., c. 1929), pp. 87-98.

150. R. C. Munro Ferguson to Rosebery, 27 Jul. 1895, to J. Morley, 24 Nov. 1895 (copy), H. Ivory to Rosebery, 23 Jul. 1895, Rosebery MSS., MSS. 10019, ff. 1-2, 36-7, 10038, ff. 58-61.

151. H. Ivorty to Rosebery, 19 Sep. 1895, Ibid., MS. 10038, ff. 72-3.

152. Gibson-Carmichael to H. Campbell-Bannerman, 26 Oct. 1900, Campbell-Bannerman MSS., Add. MS. 41235, ff. 279-80.

153. Munro Ferguson to Rosebery, 19 Oct. 1896, Rosebery MSS., MS. 10019, ff. 52-5.

154. Same to same, 27 Jul. 1895, Ibid., MS. 10019, ff. 1-2.

155. *Disestablishment Banner,* 59 (Dec. 1900); cf. Lady Pentland, *The Rt. Hon. John Sinclair, Lord Pentland, GCSI. A Memoir* (London, 1928), pp. 53-4 for Sinclair's diary entry, 30 Sep. 1898, of a discussion on this with Rosebery.

156. Campbell-Bannerman to H. Gladstone, 12 Oct. 1900 (copy), Campbell-Bannerman MSS., Add. MS. 41216, ff. 22-3.

157. Same to same, 22 Oct. 1900 (copy), Ibid., Add. MS. 41216, ff. 27-8.

158. Master of Elibank to H. Campbell-Bannerman, 31 Oct. 1900, Campbell-Bannerman to H. Gladstone, 12 Oct. 1900 (copy), R. C. Munro Ferguson to Campbell-Bannerman (24 Oct. 1900), Campbell-Bannerman MSS., Add. MSS. 41235, ff. 286-9, 41216, ff. 22-3, 41222, ff. 330-3; *Disestablishment Banner,* 59 (Dec. 1900).

159. Munro Ferguson to Rosebery, 19 Oct. 1896, Rosebery MSS., MS. 10019, ff. 52-3.

160. Munro Ferguson to Campbell-Bannerman, 19 Nov. 1898, 14 Nov. 1900, Campbell-Bannerman MSS., Add. MS. 41222, ff. 278-83, 336.

161. R. C. Munro Ferguson to H. Campbell-Bannerman, 3 Jul. 1897 (copy), Rosebery MSS., MS. 10019, ff. 71–3; Munro Ferguson to Lady Munro Ferguson, 3 May 1897, Novar MSS., 16.

162. Munro Ferguson to Rosebery, 6 Feb. 1898, Rosebery MSS., MS. 10019, ff. 89–92.

163. Munro Ferguson to Campbell-Bannerman, 23 Jan. 1899, 14 Nov. 1900, Campbell-Bannerman MSS., Add. MS. 41222, ff. 291–4, 336.

164. Campbell-Bannerman to H. Gladstone, 21 Jan. 1900 (copy), Campbell-Bannerman MSS., Add. MS. 41215, ff. 216–7.

165. R. C. Munro Ferguson to H. Campbell-Bannerman, 19 Nov. 1899, Campbell-Bannerman to H. Gladstone, 9 Dec. 1899 (copy); Munro Ferguson to Campbell-Bannerman, 10 Dec. 1899, Campbell-Bannerman MSS., Add. MSS. 41222, ff. 311–2; 41215, ff. 165–6; 41222, ff. 313–6.

166. Munro Ferguson tó Campbell-Bannerman, 31 Jan. 1899, Ibid., Add. MS. 41222, ff. 295–6, Munro Ferguson to Lady Munro Ferguson, 7 Feb. 1899, Novar MSS., 18.

167. Munro Ferguson to Campbell-Bannerman, 9 June. 1900, Campbell-Bannerman MSS., Add. MS. 41222, ff. 318–22.

168. Tweedmouth to Campbell-Bannerman, 29 Nov. 1899, Ibid., Add. MS. 41231, ff. 63–4.

169. H. Campbell-Bannerman to H. Gladstone, 9 Dec. 1899 (copy); Tweedmouth to Campbell-Bannerman, 7 Nov. 1900, Campbell-Bannerman MSS., Add. MSS. 41215, ff. 165–6; 41231, ff. 67–70.

170. Munro Ferguson to Campbell-Bannerman (31 Jan. 1899), Ibid., Add. MS. 41222, ff. 295–6.

171. Same to same (12 Sep. 1900); T. Glen-Coats to Campbell-Bannerman, 16 Sep. 1900; Tweedmouth to Campbell-Bannerman, 7 Nov. 1900, Campbell-Bannerman MSS., Add. MSS. 41222, ff. 326–7; 41235, ff. 236–7,; 41231, ff. 67–70.

172. Munro Ferguson to Campbell-Bannerman, 24 Oct. 1900, Ibid., Add. MS. 41222, ff. 330–3.

173. R. B. Haldane to Rosebery, 9 Dec. 1899, Rosebery MSS., MS. 10029, ff. 95–6.

174. E.g. R. Q. Gray, *The Labour Aristocracy in Victorian Edinburgh* (London, 1976), pp. 165–76, 182–3.

175. K. D. Buckley, *Trades Unionism in Aberdeen, 1877–1900* (Edinburgh, 1957), esp. pp. 94–151, 161–74.

176. D. Howell, *British Workers and the Independent Labour Party, 1886–1906* (Manchester, 1983), pp. 143–9; F. Reid, *Keir Hardie* (London, 1978), pp. 117–8; K. O. Morgan, *Keir Hardie* (London, 1975), pp. 24–31.

177. Letters to J. Bryce from: J. B. Butchart, 22 Jun. 1892; 'JD', 18 Jun. 1892; J. W. Crombie, 19 Jun. 1892; W. M. Ramsay, 18 May 1893; Bryce MSS., MS. Bryce UB 28, 29; Buckley, *Trades Unionism in Aberdeen*, pp. 133–51, 172–4.

178. E. Marjoribanks to W. E. Gladstone, 12 Jul. 1895, W. E. Gladstone MSS., Add. MS. 44332, ff. 330–3.

179. H. Gladstone to H. Campbell-Bannerman, 19 Nov. 1899, Campbell-Bannerman to Gladstone, 2 Dec. 1899, Campbell-Bannerman MSS., Add. MS. 41215, ff. 144–50, 156–7.

180. Rosebery to J. Ogilvy, 11 Nov. 1891, Ogilvy MSS.

181. SLA Minute Book, 7 Feb., 20 Nov. 1890; 27 Feb. 1891; 17 Feb., 2 Jun. 1892; 14, 24 Jan., 9 May, 1 Jul. 1895.

182. J. B. Glasier, *William Morris and the Early Days of the Socialist Movement* (London, 1921), pp. 98–9.

183. Howell, *Workers and ILP*, pp. 160–2, 332–40 for brief discussions.

184. J. N. Warrington to J. K. Hardie, 2 Jul. 1893, Johnson MSS., 1893/45.

185. Mann to Hardie, 24 Nov., 5 Dec. 1895, Ibid., 1895/147–8. Buckley, *Trades Unionism in Aberdeen,* pp. 175–8, notes this process of decay after 1895.

186. J. R. MacDonald to J. Penny, 17 Aug. 1899; J. Rose to T. Mann, 28 May 1898, Ibid., 1899/82; 1898/47.

187. M. Bruce to T. Mann, 1 Apr. 1897; J. Macdonald to Mann, 18 Jun. 1898; H. Flowers to Mann, 30 May 1898, Johnson MSS., 1897/13; 1898/61,48A.

188. M. Guthrie to T. Mann, 15 Feb., cf. 22 Feb., 1897, Ibid., 1897/4,5.

189. Hardie to Burns, 24, 22 Mar. 1894, Burns MSS., Add. MS. 46287, ff. 197, 195–6.

190. J. Cronin to Hardie, 21 Nov. 1893, Johnson MSS., 1893/141.

191. For Dundee: R. B. Cunninghame Graham to Hardie, 7 Jan. 1892, Ibid., 1892/1. W. Walker, *Juteopolis* (Edin. 1979), pp. 249–69, stresses the general loyalty to the Liberals of the Trades Council. For Greenock: Cunninghame Graham to J. Burns, 15 Jan. 1892, Burns MSS., Add. MS. 46284, ff. 202–3. Morgan, *Hardie,* pp. 35–6, Reid, *Hardie,* pp. 120–1, discuss union aloofness from the SLP.

192. Howell, *Workers and ILP,* pp. 32–9, demonstrates this lucidly.

193. Buccleuch to Sir C. Dalrymple, 19 Aug. 1895; R. Dundas to Dalrymple, 10 Aug. 1892, Newhailes MSS., Acc. 7228/236, ff. 160–1; 127–9.

194. Cunninghame Graham to J. Burns, 15 Dec. 1890, Burns MSS., Add. MS. 46284, ff. 71–2.

195. SLA Minute Book, 11 Jan., 14, 17 Feb., 9 Jun. 1892.

196. Davitt to Hardie, 25 Mar. 1894, Johnson MSS., 1894/53.

197. Cunninghame Graham to Hardie, 8 Jan. 1892; cf. J. S. Robertson to Hardie, 23 Feb., 8 Mar. 1892, Johnson MSS., 1892/2,9,10.

198. Connolly to Hardie, 28 May, 8, 19 Jun., 3 Jul., n.d., 1894, Ibid., 1894/106,118,127,140,226.

199. SLA Minute Book, 1 Jul. 1895, Gray, *Labour Aristocracy,* p. 180, for Irish-socialist differences in Edinburgh.

200. Davitt to Hardie, 25 Mar. 1894, Johnson MSS., 1894/53.

201. Reid, *Hardie,* pp. 18–20.

202. J. B. Burleigh to Hardie, 30 Jan. 1892; J. Adams to Hardie, 27 Jan. 1894; W. Lowe to Hardie, 13 Feb. 1894; J. H. Maxwell to Hardie, 7 Mar. 1894; W. Henderson to Hardie, 22 May 1894, Johnson MSS., 1892/7, 1894/13, 24, 40, 100.

203. J. MacDonald to J. Penny, 10 Aug. 1899, Ibid., 1899/74.

204. Fletcher to T. Mann, 22, 21 Apr. 1896, Ibid., 1896/42,41.

205. SLA Minute Book, 11 May, 4 Apr. 1894.

206. Cunninghame Graham to Hardie, 9 May 1892, Johnson MSS., 1892/13.

207. Aberdeen South was unopposed in 1886, and Dundee was a two-member constituency.

7

From Conservatism to Unionism: 1882–1900

While, as in England, the split in the Liberal party over Irish Home Rule produced a profound effect on politics in Scotland, Scottish Unionism did not make so rapid an advance in terms of seats won. As Table 7.1 shows, the decisive majority of Scottish M.P.s (unlike English M.P.s) remained Home Rule Liberals after the 1886 election. The 1895 and 1900 elections, arguably, constituted the real breakthrough for Scottish Unionists. In the former their representation rose to 31, and in 1900, for the first time since the 1832 Reform Act, the Liberals were not the majority party in Scotland. In the 1895 contest, the proportionate increase in Scottish Unionist M.P.s was greater than in England, and while more seats were gained in 1900 in Scotland, the number of Unionist M.P.s in England actually fell very slightly. Two leading causes for this Unionist success in the later 1890s may be suggested. Firstly, it was only then that organisational efficiency reached the levels which had been attained in England many years earlier, and secondly, there was a quite appreciable shift in Unionist policies away from the concerns of the preceding quarter century.

Table 7.1. Members Returned, 1885–1900

| | ENGLAND | | | | | SCOTLAND | | | | |
	C	LU	U Total		Other	C	LU	U Total	Lib*	Other
1885	213	—	213	242	1	8	—	8	62	0
1886	278	55	333	122	1	10	17	27	43	0
1892	231	30	261	191	4	9	11	20	50	0
1895	292	51	343	112	1	17	14	31	39	0
1900	287	45	332	122	2	19	17	36	34	0

*This column includes Crofters' Party M.P.s.

I

The drive to improve organisation began in 1882 when, fifteen years after its English namesake, the National Union of Conservative Associations of Scotland (NUCAS) was founded to remedy glaring defects in party machinery.[1] Many constituency associations were all but defunct: in Dunbartonshire, later to be held up as the paragon of efficiency, no meetings were held in the five years before December 1883, when the secretary had not been paid for three years and local agents had not been kept going.[2] Of the burghs, only two were deemed to have efficient organisation in 1883, and sixteen had no funds to fight an election.[3]

Improving organisation became linked with the need to democratise the party, or so a group of younger Tories, led by Reginald MacLeod, Harry Hope and Moir Stormonth-Darling, argued. One critic commented that local bodies were composed of only 'a few men, ardent conservatives, or gentlemen of leisurely position in life', so that 'the Conservatives have 'lost touch' of (sic) the people'.[4] Evidently the trend to broadening the social base of the constituency parties, so prevalent in the early 1870s, had atrophied. With rural deference substantially reduced after the tenant-farmer revolt of the 1860s, Unionists could be very unpopular for still relying on factors and estate lawyers to conduct canvassing. As Harry Hope mused, the dominance of the great house was resented by voters: 'They are very jealous of dictation from above and will not work to order of local magnates'.[5] Moreover, the impending arrival of a wider rural electorate could easily sweep away the Tory county seats, and made the old style of informal, personal organisation irrelevant.[6]

The NUCAS aimed to encourage different elements to become active — particularly hoping to attract the younger generation of new voters — by developing a democratic representative framework in the constituencies.[7] It was clearly felt that a new body, separate from the Scottish National Constitutional Association (SNCA), should be formed to stimulate local voluntary grassroots organisation, as the SNCA was both dominated by the upper classes and lacked any representative system. Hence in the new NUCAS, an ardent party moderniser stressed, 'Local magnates never to act as a body working from a centre. Each to be elected in his own locality'.[8] An additional drawback of relying on the great territorial magnates was that many would give finance only to seats embracing their estates, declining to subscribe to a central party fund.[9] This distortion of resources impeded party development in many seats.

A major innovation by the NUCAS occurred in techniques of propaganda, which altered circumstances were deemed to call for: 'The old order is changing of counties being fought by local men of position who chiefly depend on their personal character and local influence, and while I am old-fashioned enough to think such candidates much the best, it is impossible to deny there is more and more need every day of appealing to the populace by much speaking'.[10] Accordingly, mass meetings addressed by national Tory politicians became a regular feature of the 1880s. Northcote, Salisbury, Churchill, Cairns and Ashmead Bartlett all came north under NUCAS auspices. Salisbury's visit to Glasgow in 1884 was the occasion of a massive display of support, and the city Tories were pleased with the benefits derived from Northcote's trip in 1882: 'These demonstrations have had a most distinct effect in largely strengthening the Association, not only in the number of its membership, but in its influence throughout the city'. Some 2,000 new members were added to the Glasgow Association after both Northcote's and Salisbury's meetings.[11] But there were doubts as to the permanency of these recruits,[12] and so the Scottish National Union produced leaflets to argue its case, since, as one enthusiast argued, 'there is too much disposition among all of you to trust to personal considerations and to undervalue the importance of influencing *opinion*'.[13] The pro-Liberal bias of the press, so frequently lamented by Tories, made leaflets an attractive device to reach voters, and MacLeod urged the NUCAS to publish a leaflet every month on Scottish political issues.[14] By 1885, 26 leaflets had appeared, and 850,000 copies had been distributed.

The launching of the National Union, despite some gains, had only partial success before 1886. By 1885, 140 local associations had joined. Stimulus did occur at the grassroots, as in the Galloway area, where an ex-M.P. reported about 'the little local Conservative Associations, which have been springing up, and which are, I think, the most hopeful symptoms for our side in Scotland'.[15] But in some places, the depth of the support looked shaky: at the Kinross A.G.M. in April 1886, two members attended. In Dundee in 1885 the President of the Association circulated likely supporters in a very defensive tone: 'I desire to draw your attention to the existence of a Conservative Association in Dundee', he began.[16] The NUCAS had set itself the target of running Tory candidates in all the seventy Scottish seats in the 1885 election, but fifteen were not contested. (In four of these there was a desire not to split the anti-disestablishment vote where two Liberals were fighting on this issue).[17] Not all local associations were in practice democratised, as Harry Hope, a tireless advocate of change in that direction, discovered in West Lothian, where he had been chosen as a prospective candidate. His reforming ideas ran up against the opposition of the Earl of Hopetoun, who particularly disapproved of picnics for party workers being held in the grounds of landowners. Hopetoun warned that 'a group of warm Conservatives' were against Hope, and the Earl himself was not disposed to do much electioneering on the candidate's behalf.[18] Hope eventually stood down as candidate, to be replaced by Hopetoun's brother.

The Scottish National Union recognised the limitations of its achievement when it surveyed the 1885 and 1886 elections and sombrely concluded that 'a very great deal still remains to be done with a view to perfecting the system of organisation in the country'.[19] An official of the Union was despatched to England to study how efficient associations conducted their affairs, and the NU devoted much of its time to organisational improvement.[20] Yet little real change seems to have been effected until about 1890. At the end of 1887, MacLeod was still unhappy: 'As I mentioned to you at Castle Douglas I am alarmed at the inadequate idea our more active men in Glasgow have of the degree of organisation necessary for electoral success'.[21] Thus Dunbartonshire was not yet in its halcyon days. For two years before May 1887, no organiser could be got; finances were weak as subscriptions fell steadily between 1886 and 1889; and participation was low, with only 22 delegates out of an eligible 107 attending the 1888 A.G.M.[22] However, early in 1890 the Glasgow Conservative Association reported that after several years of endeavour, 'now, generally speaking, there is in each division a living organisation which, when the time for action comes, will be found ready'. The difficulties encountered and openly referred to in previous years had been overcome, and there was instead 'a marked absence of the ever-recurring points of difficulty which characterised previous years'.[23]

The marked improvement in organisation which began in 1889-90 had several sources. The Liberals had done very well in by-elections between 1886 and 1890, holding on to five seats and winning three Unionist seats. In 1889 a run of particularly bad results highlighted the inadequacies of the Tory machine. In urban Govan, a Unionist loss, 'the fact is', complained MacLeod, 'Sir William Pearce had discountenanced all party work, relying exclusively on his personal position'.[24] A comfortable win in East Perthshire by a weak Liberal revealed the slowness of change in rural seats. MacLeod attacked the reliance there on 'the vicious and destructive system of making the big Factor political secretary' and argued: 'In the future we must and will get rid of the lawyer-factor system under which no political organisation can flourish'.[25] Prompt and decisive action followed, this time being imposed by the national leadership in London. MacLeod had repeatedly drawn Salisbury's attention to Scottish organisational defects in 1889–90. The rising power in national organisation, A. Akers-Douglas, was not only one of the 'Kentish Gang', he also owned an estate in Dumfriesshire, a county with exceptionally poor organisation. As a result, a Scottish agent was appointed who reported to Middleton, the administrator of the English National Union, who paid his salary. The Scottish National Union was apparently not consulted about this, but only 'received intimation' of the appointment of the agent, who was Col. A. B. Haig, ironically a Lowland laird.[26] Haig 'advised' the NUCAS and generally helped to find candidates and distribute funds; and he steered its activities into dynamic channels. In the last department he seems to have succeeded: 'I have heard nothing against Haig either from Fergusson or others, though he is sure to annoy people by stirring things up', Akers-Douglas learned, doubtless with satisfaction. 'This however is what is necessary, especially in a place like South Ayrshire'.[27]

Through Haig, Middleton began to raise the Scottish National Union to the level of efficiency displayed by its English counterpart.[28] Two independent offices were set up in Edinburgh and Glasgow, allowing initiatives to be taken by those who had a more intimate knowledge of local peculiarities. As will be seen, Glasgow and the west seized this opportunity. Under Haig's watchful eye, the two areas of the National Union exercised tighter supervision over constituencies, so that the Eastern District had a sub-committee to monitor local organisational developments. By 1891 the NUCAS had 310 affiliated bodies, with every constituency at last represented. Moreover, the 'system of popular and representative organisation' advocated by the Council of the National Union was being widely adopted, as in the city of Perth, where the Tories embarked with great gusto on a variety of mass organisations designed to reach more voters.[29] An additional sign of genuine growth in support was the rise in subscription levels. The National Union boasted that at £2425 its income from subscribers in 1891 was double the £1198 received the previous year and over ten times the £190 raised in 1884.[30] Constituency parties also tended to do better financially. The unrelenting decline in the income of the Dunbartonshire Association was reversed, so that in 1891 the subscriptions at £497 were 65% above the 1889 figure. Even more significantly, 40% of the 1891 income came from new subscribers.[31] The financial resources of the Scottish Conservatives were boosted by the creation in 1890 of a Political Committee of the

Scottish Conservative Club. For the first time since its inception, the Club acted directly to promote party work, and did so entirely by distributing cash. Extra money was badly needed, as in 1889 MacLeod had calculated that £5000 was needed to fight every seat seriously.[32] Haig was a member of the Club's Political Committee, ensuring that its regular contributions — usually of between £10 and £50 — were allocated to build up organisation and find candidates in constituencies most in need of assistance.[33]

The major development at constituency level in this period was the widespread institution of the Organising Secretary — a full-time paid agent who succeeded in breaking the stranglehold of the laird's factor or the local lawyer over the development of popular and effective party machinery. There were around thirty organising secretaries at work by 1892, and their success was regarded as considerable. The Glasgow constituencies were eloquent in their annual reports of the 1890s in praising the achievements wrought by their paid officials. So pleased were the Dunbartonshire Tories that they raised the salary of their secretary by £20 to £140 in 1891, and in the later 1890s Haig sent the Dunbartonshire man round the backwaters to expound the benefits of having professional experts running the constituency machinery.[34] The main advantages contributed by an organising secretary were intimate local knowledge, full-time devotion to the work, and a high level of competence. Thus, after the 1895 election, Dunbartonshire Tories were given a detailed breakdown of the strengths and weaknesses of the campaign in every district, as well as general points to be applied at the next contest, including lists of suitable halls, of cyclists, and even of formidable hecklers.[35] Probably the most tangible result of using an organising secretary was the expansion of registration work. This had always been done of course, but the general efficiency of the system in respect of the ordinary occupier voter, compiled as it was by the municipal valuator of property, meant that only minor adjustments were made. In the early 1880s the Glasgow Tories, in an electorate numbering 50,000, were adding only a few hundred per year at best, and the net gain over Liberals ranged from 18 in 1882 to 102 in 1885. However, Consevative registrations in Glasgow rose sharply from 469 in 1887 to 3,315 in 1894, and net gains were proportionately higher, up from 177 in 1887 to 2119 in 1894. Activity was greatest in marginal Liberal seats like College (majority in 1892 — 1,046) where 1,135 Conservatives were enrolled in 1894 (a net Unionist gain of 955), while in all of the Glasgow seats only 1,196 Liberal registrations were made.[36] In 1895 College was won by the Unionists, turning a Liberal majority of 1,046 in 1892 into a Unionist majority of 1,145, a figure very close to the 2,418 net registration gains chalked up by the Unionists between 1892 and 1895. Most of these registration gains were lodger voters, and it is testimony to the efficiency of Conservative organisation that they had so comprehensively mastered this complex franchise qualification, while the Liberals were unsuccessful.[37] The National Union constantly stressed the central importance of registration work, and the Conservative Club's Political Committee frequently earmarked grants for this purpose.

Organising secretaries were also active in facilitating another growthpoint of

Scottish Unionism in the 1890s, viz. the expanding of its social base, particularly recruiting working-class support. Sporadic efforts in this direction had been made before 1890. In 1887, having stressed to constituencies the appeal of using working men to address working-class audiences, the Scottish National Union appointed such a man, William MacAllister, but by 1890 the finance for his salary had expired. At that point, as a clear sign of tighter London control, Haig stepped in and undertook to pay MacAllister's salary, at the same time sharing with the Scottish Tories decisions as to his deployment.[38] MacAllister's efforts were augmented by a series of schemes to attract voters to the party by offering greater social, as distinct from political, occasions. A Mr. Martin of Niddrie expounded the rationale in 1897: 'The people would not come out for mere political meetings, but should be attracted by social meetings, with singing and dancing, with a short political address thrown in. His experience was the ordinary man was pretty lukewarm as to Home Rule and Disestablishment, and that he might be secured to Unionism by attention'.[39] A variety of lures were offered in the 1890s — smokers in winters, lantern lectures, exhibitions of the use of the phonograph and cinematograph. Dunbartonshire had a cycling unit: 'the duty of this Corps will be to disseminate amongst the large body of cyclists in the County the principles of Conservatism'.[40] Glasgow's Balfour Political Choir linked music and politics, while the Bridgeton Conservative Association's Flute Band catered for the tastes of that locality. But the most significant development lay in the formation of working men's Conservative Clubs. These had of course been commonplace in industrial England from the 1860s and 1870s, but revealingly only spread in Scotland in the 1890s. Within a year of gaining greater local self-government in 1890, the Western District Tories had established 64 clubs, and by the later years of the decade the West Renfrewshire party was approaching its target of having club premises in every village in the constituency.[41] The setting up of such clubs was a cause which regularly received financial backing from the Political Committee of the Scottish Conservative Club.

Thus the 1890s signalled the attainment of the targets set at the start of the previous decade by Conservative reformers. Firstly, the party machinery was efficient enough by 1894 for Middleton to coax Salisbury to visit Scotland (something he was normally reluctant to do, as in 1890 he refused to speak in Glasgow: 'it is a long way off, and an awful climate'[42]) on the grounds that he should help the Scottish National Union, 'as they are doing good work up there'.[43] Difficulties of course did remain, with some constituencies still ill-organised, but determined efforts were made in the decade to tackle these recalcitrant areas.[44] A second area of improvement was that the social blight cast by the landed classes on the party's growth was less pervasive, as the lairds seem to have participated less in Unionist matters. Haig, for instance, recorded that Lord Home was quite unusual among Scottish peers, since he 'has uniformly done his utmost, both by his personal actions and by his purse, to support the interests of the party in Scotland'. Haig commented in similar vein on a landowner who was being proposed for an honour. The nominee had done some work 'in the ordinary way' for the party — 'more so perhaps than most Perthshire lairds, which is not saying much'.[45] Many landowners still remained on party committees, but increasingly, apparently, as figureheads, with their real power in decline. Perth Tories demonstrated this point when they proceeded to open a Conservative Club in the town despite the disapproval of Lord Stormont, the son of Lord Mansfield, probably the weightiest Tory peer in the county.[46]

II

But organisation of itself was not the sole explanation of the inroads made by Unionists in the 1895 and 1900 elections: policies too were a factor. These two elections marked an important transition, for whereas Conservatism in the 1880s had appeared reactionary, and largely indifferent to the urban-industrial social order, by the mid-1890s a positive Unionism had emerged. This Unionism represented a convergence of new policy stances which were adopted by both Liberal Unionists and Conservatives — although not necessarily for the same reasons — and which blurred the differences in outlook between the two, even if organisational and personal antagonisms made a total fusion impossible at the time.

During the 1885 election contest the Tories did not convey the impression of being a party pursuing policies designed to win support from either the urban middle or working class. The social characteristics of its candidates were hopelessly inappropriate, suggesting the slenderness of local support. Several men with a business background did stand — John Scott, the shipbuilder, stood for Greenock, another shipbuilder, Pearce, won at Govan, W. R. Bousfield, a coal and ironmaster, ran at Mid-Lanark, and two members of the Baird industrial dynasty stood in the Glasgow area. Yet in Glasgow, three of the seven seats were fought by lairds with no obvious local connections, and Partick was contested by a son of the Duke of Richmond. Moreover, the party's policies seemed defensive and negative. As already seen, the Conservatives hoped to play to the full the card of the church in danger, but had to admit that this tactic was unsuccessful. Over-concentration on the threat of disestablishment left the Tories virtually bereft of room for other policies. There is a similar profile to be derived from a study of the pamphlets published on Scottish political questions by the Scottish National Union in 1884–85 and also from a printed series of speeches delivered in 1884–5 by a Conservative candidate for a Glasgow seat, James Somervell.[47] When not defending the Established Church, they tended to castigate the Liberal government for policy failures such as in Ireland, on imperial questions and in economic and fiscal matters. These were neither constructive nor vote-winning topics since, as we have seen, the handling of Ireland or the Empire was losing very few votes from the Liberals before 1886. Somervell's major incursion into alternative ideas was to advocate the restoration of protection for industry from unfair foreign competition, but as the 1906 election was to show, this was not a popular cry in Scotland, where most of industry was flourishing mightily under free trade.[48]

In contrast to England, Tory Democracy, that is, the attempt to engage the working class on the side of the Conservatives by advocating social reforms, seems curiously feeble in Scotland in the 1880s. The Scottish National Union made some token gestures, aiming two out of the 31 leaflets just referred to at the urban working class, but their impact was neutralised by the reported refusal of their intended audience to read them because they were printed by a non-union shop.[49] A bid to bring forward a working man for one of the Glasgow seats in 1885 foundered, Lothian was informed, because 'the feeling there is hostile to it and there is so much jealousy afloat that it cannot be worked'.[50] The main advocate of Tory Democracy, Lord Randolph Churchill, complained that on his tours of Scotland he met a universally hostile response from party notables. In Glasgow, Tory leaders were 'extremely disagreeable', in Edinburgh, 'unpleasant', and 'when I was in Perth in 1887 or 1888 all the county magnates refused to attend the meeting'.[51] A penetrating analysis of the Scottish Conservative party concl;uded that Toryism had made no mass converts among either town labourers ('a select reality') or rural labourers ('Toryism has there been universally regarded as the creed of lairds and law agents').[52]

While the Liberal Unionists after the Home Rule split repaired to some degree this defect in the Tories' electoral appeal by giving a more progressive tone to Unionism, the Conservatives themselves moved only slowly. Thus in 1887, the very year in which William MacAllister was appointed to woo the working class, a delegation of Scottish Tories persuaded the government to prevent the Early Closing Bill applying to large industrial towns, so outraging temperance opinion in Scotland.[53] Indeed the party's resistance to espousing substantial social reforms, as illustrated by that episode, along with the failure to operate a truly democratic party machine, seems to have led many of the proponents of a more dynamic Conservatism in the early 1880s to move out by the end of the decade. One simply withdrew: MacLeod became a State official in 1889. Two found new theatres: R. W. Cochran-Patrick, an admirer of the co-operative movement who had been approached by Ayrshire miners for help in exposing evasions of the Truck Act because of his reputation as a sympathiser of the working classes, became a junior minister at the Scottish Office in 1886.[54] Patrick, however, was not an M.P. after 1885 and he seems to have preferred to try to advance his modern Conservatism within Whitehall by direct implementation of policy, rather than striving to convert the party at large. The most dramatic evidence of dissatisfaction with the stagnation of Scottish Conservatism in the late 1880s came from Harry Hope. Frustrated at every turn, Hope late in 1887 despaired of the Tories ever moving forward. This timidity he deplored, as 'From my former experience in the constituencies I feel sure that there is no great feeling of *Radicalism,* but there is a very strong feeling for continued, well-considered Liberal progress which I admire'. Accordingly he joined the Liberal Unionists, and there established contact with other young Tories who were likewise being drawn into that party.[55]

However, the 1890s saw a transformation in policy akin to that in organisation which had served to make Unionism more responsive to moderate middle and working-class demands. In general the new policy stress was on acceptance of social reforms. The extent of the change can be gauged from several pointers. By 1892, Churchill's admirers assured him that the Edinburgh gang which had spurned him before had been replaced by men alert to the need for vigorous policy. In the West of Scotland, too, the old anti-Churchill clique was in decline: 'Conservative opinion has advanced there of late, under the persuasion of the polls, and they are not so antiquated and sluggish as they were'.[56] In 1893 Churchill received the ultimate accolade of endorsement by official Scottish Conservatism. The National Union anxiously implored Churchill to address their meeting convened to launch a new organisational development designed to encourage grassroots participation.[57] Another pointer to a desire to change the party's image was an apparent distancing of Conservatism from Orangeism, presumably as part of the process of expanding middle-class support. In 1890, an Ayrshire Tory protested to the National Union at what he saw as the party's failure to capitalise on the large Orange vote in many seats, but the Eastern wing of the party decided to take no action. (The response of the Western sectiuon is not known.)[58] Six months earlier, the Council of the National Union refused to accept the affiliation application of the 'Protestant Confederacy and Patriotic Union', run by Alexander Godfrey, a Glasgow Green orator. The reasons for rejecting Godfrey's body were that it was not a Conservative Association, although this had not been applied against the Orange Order some years before.[59]

The adoption of new policies in the 1890s was mainly due to the altered political realities of the period. For one thing, reliance on the older issues was less a guarantee of success than hitherto. The cry of resistance to disestablishment had become both less potent and also more divisive. The Church Interests Committee began around 1890 to disentangle itself from unquestioning support for Conservatives in every seat. Instead, in a shrewd tactical move, the Committee would encourage local branches to support Gladstonians, if they so wished, provided satisfactory assurances on the Church of Scotland were received. This was the course adopted in Kincardineshire, West Lothian, Aberdeenshire East, Kirkcaldy, Aberdeen North, Montrose and Elgin Burghs.[60] The harassment he was subjected to in the 1892 election in Mid Lothian at the hands of the Church party vexed Gladstone. But it was not so widely recognised that the Church Defence lobby had focussed on only a very few selected seats, and elsewhere, as in the foregoing list, did little. Chamberlain (not without an axe to grind) observed to Balfour that 'the friends of the Kirk are not of much importance. Except in Mid Lothian and Berwick they have made no show at all. Look at Border Burghs, West Perth, Roxburghshire etc. etc'.[61] Furthermore, as discussed elsewhere, the cause of disestablishment was not one best calculated to unify all sections of Unionism: Arthur Elliot was told by no fewer than three supporters that many Liberal Unionists had gone back to Gladstonianism in Roxburghshire in 1892 out of support for disestablishment, so losing him the seat.[62] In any event, by 1895 Scottish disestablishment was not a realistic threat, for it had been pushed aside by the Welsh Church question, and the new Liberal leader Rosebery was at best agnostic on the issue.[63] The Scottish disestablishment organ was on the defensive during the 1895 election, denying that its cause had been downgraded, nevertheless admitting that 'a great deal remains to be done in influencing the indifferent and informing the uninstructed in every district of Scotland'. There was a growing feeling that the union of the two non-established Presbyterian churches was more likely to resolve the Scottish Church difficulty than political assault, and the momentum towards union was rapid by 1895, to the dismay of the disestablishers.[64]

Irish Home Rule — the basis of the Unionist alliance — itself looked less of an issue by 1895, for it was clear that the Lords' veto would negate any moves by the Commons to enact legislation. This left the Liberal Unionists in particular with a sharp dilemma. After all, if in practice Irish Home Rule was unlikely to be put through, it became difficult to see why they should persist in remaining aloof from Home Rule Liberals. For the Conservatives, too, the outlook was bleak if they were to be bereft of both Home Rule and disestablishment, but the Liberal Unionists felt the crisis more acutely. For of the seven Unionist losses in 1892, six had been of their number. Many Liberal Unionists were, as discussed below, still distrustful of the Tories, and certainly over-identification with the reactionary party was seen by one defeated M.P. as the cause of his rejection in 1892, for this closeness had driven away his supporters among the Angus fishermen and farmworkers.[65] Thus the search for a distinctive position became vital for the survival of the Liberal Unionists, and social reform was taken up. Shortly before the 1892 election, the East of Scotland Liberal Unionist Association adopted the suggestion of a member that they should emulate Jesse Collings' work in England and set up a Rural Labourers' League in counties like Dumfries, where their majority, 854 in 1886, shrank to 274 in 1892. In 1893, plans were made to send an organiser to work among the fishermen in St Andrews constituency, where the majority had fallen to an exiguous 112.[66] Nor was the urban working class neglected. The new candidate in the Hawick Burghs was stated in 1893 to be 'paying special attention to the working man in Galashiels'. At the end of 1894, the Eastern Association decided to back Chamberlain's programme of old age pensions, the miners' eight-hour day, early shop closing hours and so on.[67]

The reappraisal by the Liberal Unionists of their policies was perhaps not totally unexpected, given the radical elements among their number. But this trend was not restricted to them, as in a sharp change in attitude, the Conservatives also espoused these social reform demands in the 1895 election.[68] In Edinburgh East in the spring of 1895 a Tory drive to build up support included a series of lectures on Chamberlain's social programme.[69] A Liberal journal in Falkirk, where the Liberal Unionists won the burgh seat and the Tories the county in 1895, both fighting on virtually interchangeable progressive policies, noted with concern the novelty of the policies being propounded and the new shared ground occupied by the anti-Home Rule parties: 'It cannot be overlooked that Unionism evidently is more attractive to the Scottish people than Toryism ever was, and that many constituencies that had little favour for the one have given their support to the other ... It is believed that through the amalgamation of the [Liberal] Unionists with the Tories, more progressive ideas have been infused into the party and that the old Tory spirit has given place to one which evinces more regard for the general welfare of the people'.[70]

The Unionists argument was skilfully built up. Firstly, it was pointed out that the Liberal administration of 1892–95 had utterly failed to carry through any substantial social reforms, despite the high expectations aroused, in the fields of housing, pensions, temperance and industrial compensation.[71] The Unionists, by contrast, would certainly introduce reforms. The reasons for this assertion were various. The proven record of the Salisbury government of 1886–92, especially in Scottish matters, was stressed as one of impressive, constructive advance. Here the quiet but diligent work of Lord Lothian and Cochran-Patrick was a great asset in allaying fears either of rash innovations or of total resistance to change. The two men had striven to establish certain features about their regime. They wished to portray their handling of affairs as non-partisan, being actuated only by the determination to do the best possible for Scottish interests. Lothian protested at Salisbury's vetoing the appointment of Rosebery to a Commission: 'I wish Lord Salisbury could have overlooked party politics — he knows nothing about Scotland or Scottish feeling — that is clear'.[72] The spoils of office were firmly held in check. Lothian was ready to appoint the Liberal ex-Lord Advocate, J. B. Balfour, to a judgeship, partly because he was the best legal mind available (in itself an original criterion) but also because it would demonstrate the Conservative preference for efficient justice above narrow party gain.[73] The allocation of honours was also tightly reined in. 'There is also the feeling that we as a party have rather overlooked the merits of our Scottish friends ... ', complained Lothian's successor, 'Our party is not so lavish in Scotland of honours as our opponents'.[74] A good amount of useful, if unexciting, legislation was put on the statute book by Lothian and Patrick, including a Local Government Act which set up County Councils and the first Universities Act for thirty years, as well as minor measures securing better educational provision, a simplification of the judicial process, and better fishery regulations.

In 1895 the Unionists could thus contrast the records of the past two administrations. The Tory victor in Stirlingshire emphasised in his address that the 'first duty' of Parliament was to promote the 'social advancement' of the people, which was more pressing than tampering with constitutional arrangements, or pursuing faddist hobby-horses.[75] Unionist vindication for calling for social reform demands in 1895 was based on the concept of Tory Democracy, so firmly rejected half a dozen years before. The Scottish National Union's handbook for the 1900 elections stated boldly: 'It will be found that the greater part of modern legislation specially affecting the social well-being and daily life of the wage earning class is due to the Conservatives, and has in many instances been carried in spite of determined opposition from so-called Liberals'.[76] This argument was graphically illustrated by a strident Unionist Ayrshire paper which listed many Tory-inspired reforms and came to a climax by praising the 1886–92 government's performance: 'while it increased the duty on sparkling wines and luxuries, it reduced apprentices' and hawkers' licences and Stamp Duty on Health Insurance policies'.[77] Linked to this appeal went the argument that the Tories by their management of the economy had done more than the 1892–95 Liberal governments to raise living standards. The Liberal *Falkirk Herald* regarded this factor as a prime motive for the Unionist gains in its area.[78]

Thus, although the old rallying calls of disestablishment and opposition to Irish Home Rule were still to be heard in the 1895 campaign, much attention was given by Unionist candidates in the Lowland urban areas to demanding social reforms. Successful ones like Arrol (South Ayrshire), MacKillop (Stirling County), Orr Ewing (Ayr Burghs) and Wilson (Falkirk) all advocated the miners' eight-hour day (Cross in Camlachie wished it to apply to railwaymen). Chamberlain's Old Age Pension scheme was universally endorsed; housing reforms, specifically giving to working men the right to purchase rented property, were favoured by Denny (Kilmarnock), Begg (St Rollox), Ferguson (Govan), Wilson and MacKillop. The failure of the Liberals in office to deal with employers' liability was highlighted by Unionists, and the Stirlingshire Liberal M.P.'s alleged backsliding on this issue was believed to have contributed heavily to his downfall.[79] Even temperance, which traditionally the Tories had been cool towards, received sympathetic support from men like Denny and Orr Ewing. Individuals added their own touches to this catalogue. Wilson had worked out a scheme to compensate miners for accidents, 'whereby the full compensation would be given to miners out of the royalties of the mine owners'.[80] It was hence not unreasonable for Denny to point to his opponent's stress on disestablishment, Home Rule and the Lords and conclude: 'He appealed to them whether, having read his address, he was not a more advanced Liberal than Mr. Williamson'.[81] Most Liberal observers agreed that the working-class vote had moved against their party, largely because of Unionist social reform rhetoric.[82] These issues were raised again in the 1900 election, which was not, as we have seen, simply a Khaki contest. The NUCAS handbook for this election gave eighteen pages to social reform, only three to the war, and fifteen and eleven pages respectively to the old warhorses of Ireland and the State Church. Moreover, social reform was placed before these two old topics, coming immediately after the war and foreign policy.

The other geographical breakthrough came in the Highlands. Here, of the eight seats, only one (Wick) was Unionist in 1892, but by 1895 four were, and in addition Moray and Nairn, in some respects having the same characteristics as the Highland seats, was won. In 1900 two more were won (Sutherland, and Orkney and Shetland), although Inverness County was lost, making six (including Moray and Nairn) Unionist. By 1895, much of the acerbity which had existed in landlord-crofter relations in the previous decade had apparently diminished. The crofters' movement had rather lost direction, as the Liberal M.P. and very large landowner Munro Ferguson reported in 1895, predicting a reversion to Tory rule in places like Inverness-shire.[83] Ferguson's observations were made at the start of a by-election in that county occasioned by the resignation of the Crofters' party M.P., Dr. MacGregor, in protest at the failure of the Rosebery government to help landless cottars acquire plots. The Unionists seized on this to prove the powerlessness of Crofter M.P.s to effect real improvements and also the total indifference of Liberals to the land problem in the North. Crofters were urged to acknowledge the inadequacy of the proposed measure, and were assured that once the Unionists took office, they would get a bill bestowing on Highlanders the same rights of peasant proprietorship on favourable terms which had been granted to the Irish peasantry by Ashbourne's Act. Although the Unionist gain in the by-election was partly due to a deep split in the Crofters' party over the choice of candidate, the seat was retained at the general election shortly after against a very formidable Crofters' challenger, who had the inestimable benefit of being closely related to two of the most powerful Free Church ministers in the North.[84]

The Unionists won Moray and Nairn and Inverness Burghs (which included three towns in these two shires) by promising *inter alia* to extend the crofting legislation to these counties, where there were many smallholders, and also by calling for curbs on the rights of landlords to restrict access to mountains and the like.[85] In Argyll, another acquisition in 1895, the Unionists called for an end to evictions and the implementation of large-scale state aid on the model of the Irish congested districts schemes to alleviate the economic backwardness of the Highlands.[86] Admittedly other factors contributed to the Unionist recovery. R. B. Finlay ascribed his triumph in Inverness Burghs to Free Church hostility to disestablishment, while in Argyll and Moray and Nairn, good organisation and vigorous electioneering were felt to have given the edge.[87] But the added ingredient was the new Unionist position on Highland grievances, and in particular the acceptance of the need for sweeping changes in the proprietorial system. Thus in Inverness-shire it was a member of one of the greatest landowning families in the county, J. E. B. Baillie, who stood in 1895, calling for 'wide and radical measures' to take over land for use by crofters. But in no-one was this shift more remarkable than the Duke of Argyll, who had left the Liberals at the outset of the 1880s in protest at proposed Irish land legislation which he feared would destroy the institution of landownership in Britain. In the aftermath of the 1895 election, Argyll urged that the basis of a permanent commitment to Unionism should be developed, and that one way of securing this was to consider the introduction of Land Purchase in the Highlands. 'If we could get a body of men to form a class of capitalists or actual freeholders the gains could be great', he mused, citing his own county, where there were thousands of acres which the many small estates would willingly sell: 'a measure which could provide facilities for the purchase of farms and the purchase of estates at low prices to be broken up might create a very desirable Conservative middle class of Proprietors'.[88]

Besides developing a strong strand of social reform as part of their platform, the Unionists also strove to link that with the other key concepts of imperial unity and a strong foreign policy. This was seen as binding the voters more subtly and materially to Unionism than Home Rule on its own. In addition, a sympathetic stance was taken towards the rights of trade unions, whose general importance was stressed by the rising Unionist politicians of the 1890s, men who themselves embodied as significant aspect of social change in their party. All Unionist candidates in the 1895 election agreed that a strong Empire was necessary for prosperity, and imperial unity had two angles to it. One was of course the retention of Ireland, but now the emphasis was moving focus. In 1891 Lewis McIver,

Liberal Unionist M.P. for Edinburgh West (1895–1909), drew a parallel between the importance of maintaining law and order and public security in Ireland and the condition of the working class in Britain. For the later, it was vital to have protection against violence and robbery, and this had to be provided for them by the state, whereas the rich could always afford to pay for such security. So it was with Ireland, economically so vital to the Scottish working class, especially shipbuilders.[89] Secondly, the expansion of Britain overseas was equally crucial for keeping full employment, for as the Director of the Falkirk Iron Company explained, speaking on the Unionist candidate's platform at Grahamston, the government should 'add colony to colony and thereby open up and develop new markets for their industry'.[90]

The role to be performed in all this economic and social advance by trade unions was stressed as being of fundamental significance. 'You have the right to combine, you have the duty to combine', McIver told them, simultaneously rendering unto God and Caesar by citing as his authorities Matthew v, 5–7 and 34 and 35 Vict c. 22.[91] The new Stirlingshire M.P., MacKillop, confirmed that, despite a tendency to be over-tyrannical in certain cases, overall the contribution made by the unions was great and wholesome, particularly for instilling a sense of moral discipline.[92] McIver tied the two ideas of imperial unity and trade unionism most neatly together into progressive Unionism when addressing working men. He sought: 'To remind you that although work and wages are the most obvious concerns of the workingman, work depends upon trade and wages upon capital, and that the successful maintenance of prosperous relations among those depends on peace and union — peace abroad, which in the last resort means our naval supremacy; peace at home, which means law and order in the streets, conciliation and compromise in the workshops and the factories. (Cheers) Unionism in matters Imperial and Trade Unionism in matters industrial. Within a united Empire safeguarded from external attack and industrial disruption, which gives you the markets for the produce of your labour, combine as working men, not in spasms of anger for the purpose of war with capital, but continuously, and with deliberation, in order to use your strength peacefully to secure your just share of the profits of your labour'.[93]

What made these exponents of the new Unionist doctrines so disturbing for the Liberals was that they were mostly businessmen, far removed from the anti-capitalist Tories of the earlier period like Lord Elcho. For by 1895 the Unionist party M.P.s had changed markedly, as Table 7.2 shows. The promotion of the interests of organised labour was often close to these new men's hearts. Wilson offered to contribute to meeting Smillie's expenses at the 1894 Mid Lanark by-election, but the miners' leader declined, fearing lest it would be exposed as Tory gold by Liberals.[94] Liberal and Unionist accepted that MacKillop won in Stirlingshire in 1895 with the aid of many of the votes cast by miners for their union leader, Chisholm Robertson, in the 1892 contest.[95] In West Fife the idiosyncratic mine owner and laird, R. G. E. Wemyss, stood in 1889 and 1895 as a Unionist on a very advanced Radical platform. He stood down in 1892 only because he wished to give the Fife Miners' Secretary a free run as a Labour candidate, again offering to help foot the bill.[96] In the light of the divided counsels and outmoded policies prevalent in the Liberal party, the Unionists seemed to have established at last a solid position as the majority party in Scotland, as the 1900 election results indicated.

Table 7.2. Background of Conservative and Liberal Unionist M.P.s, 1874–95

1. CONSERVATIVE

	1874			1886			1895		
	Cont.*	New	Total	Cont.	New	Total	Cont.	New	Total
Background									
Land	4	12	16	2	4	6	4	5	9
Business	1	1	2	2	1	3	2	5	7
Professional	0	0	0	1	0	1	1	0	1
	5	13	18	5	5	10	7	10	17

2. LIBERAL UNIONIST

	1886			1895		
	Cont.	New	Total	Cont.	New	Total
Background						
Land	3	2	5	2	1	3
Business	5	3	8	6	3	9
Professional	4	0	4	1	1	2
	12	5	17	9	5	14

*Cont: Continuing
Source: M. Stenton, *Who's Who of Members of Parliament, 1832–1979,* 4 vols. (London, 1976–81).

III

In England, relations between Conservatives and Liberal Unionists speedily settled into a pattern of fairly harmonious co-operation, with squabbles the exception, so that after 1895 the two parties had drawn extremely close together.[97] These two trends, of collaboration and of near-integration, were much less manifest in Scotland, and English Unionist leaders constantly bemoaned the difficulties in reaching a happy liaison. The Liberal Unionist Chief Whip complained to Salisbury about the general problem: 'Scotland gives us more trouble than all the rest of the United Kingdom put together. The LU and C will not work together as they do in England and each section properly mismanages its own affairs'. He concluded that few seats would be won, 'because the spirit is not *yet* right on either side'.[98] This was not just English condescension, for a Scottish

Liberal Unionist peer noted that 'In Scotland it does not do for a Lib Ust to go on a Conserv Platform — In England nobody minds'.[99]

Conflict centred on several clearly defined areas. The first was the question of which party had the right to nominate candidates for seats. This had not been a problem in 1886. In no seat did the Unionists fight each other then, and almost everywhere the allocation of seats was conducted in a spirit of 'mutual forbearance and mutual help'.[100] In East Perthshire, a local Conservative branch resolved to support the Liberal Unionist since 'on the strong ground of patriotism it is the duty of all parties to support at this juncture a Liberal Unionist'.[101] In Wigtownshire, the Liberal Unionist Lord Stair publicly endorsed the sitting Tory, who won handsomely.[102] This amity had been reached by careful negotiations between the leaders of both parties, but while most of the leaders were keen to continue this system of joint action, local activists on both sides were less enthusiastic.[103] For each, the 1886 pact involved reluctant sacrifices of principle: 'We have had some difficulty in finding a suitable candidate for South Ayrshire. I found it was very distasteful to many Conservatives to ask them to support a Liberal who, like North Dalrymple, had stood against Alexander [the Tory M.P.]', reported Sir James Fergusson.[104] It was to overcome precisely this discontent that Lothian induced Salisbury to compose a letter advising Scottish Tories of the need to accept Liberal Unionist candidates without challenge, but even then many Tories announced they did so 'while retaining their own political convictions'.[105] Even greater scruples were harboured among Liberal Unionists.

These differences of principle shaped much of the organisational friction which tended to preoccupy party managers. Apart from Irish Home Rule, there were few common points of reference for the Unionist alliance in the late 1880s, and it was frequently very difficult to arrive at a compromise. There was a fear that a deep policy rupture might drive some at least of the Liberal Unionists back into the Gladstonian fold, an event which some Tory experts felt might follow a bitter attack on their Unionist allies in a Conservative journal in the summer of 1887.[106] By contrast ultra-radical Liberal Unionists could drive off Tory voters. Fraser-Mackintosh in Inverness-shire was said to have this effect, as did the candidate in the 1889 Moray and Nairn by-election.[107] Disestablishment proved the trickiest obstacle, since prominent supporters of the Church of Scotland, like Balfour of Burleigh, distrusted Liberal Unionist leaders like MacLaren, Calderwood and Cross, the erstwhile arch-enemies of the state church.[108] While, as in Stirlingshire, the issue had been put to one side in the 1886 General Election, problems soon arose in subsequent by-elections. In Leith in August 1886, the local Tories defied Salisbury's recommendation to support the official Liberal Unionist, William Jacks, because of his anti-state church views, and instead backed a rival Liberal Unionist, MacGregor, whose opinions on the Church question were more congenial. As a result the Liberal romped home easily.[109] Similar tensions sprang up in West Edinburgh, where Tories were uneasy at helping a disestablisher, feeling that 'we as a party ought not to take any prominent part in support of a Unionist candidate who pledges himself to disestablishment'.[110] Some Liberal Unionists were willing to demote the Church question for the sake of Imperial unity. By 1895 Calderwood, a leading disestablisher of the 1880s, insisted in Inverness that the election was being fought over Home Rule and the land question, but not disestablishment.[111] Other Liberal Unionists were not happy at this low-level approach, and bitterly criticised the Tories for raising the Church in Danger cry, indicating that this could turn them back to Gladstonianism.[112] The attempt to juggle with these centrifugal forces could be just as complex, therefore, on the Unionist as on the Liberal side. MacLeod caught the intricacies neatly when surveying the scene in West Edinburgh: 'A combination of the entire Unionist vote in all its sections would just give us the seat but this is extremely hard to obtain. There is a group of say 200 radical disestablishment radicals who want to forward Mr. Raleigh, who was the advanced candidate in the S Division in 1885. I dread in this case an angry defection from the extreme right'.[113]

In at least two other areas there were sharp collisions in the 1880s, only removed in the 1890s as the new direction of Unionism came about. While the Tories, as has been seen, were not at this point pro-temperance, many radical Unionists were — indeed Cameron Corbett rejoined the Liberals in 1909 over the Licensing question. The loss of Ayr Burghs in 1888 was partly ascribed to the insistance by the Liberal Unionists on running a strong temperance advocate, so alienating Tories.[114] There was also, in the pre-1895 era, a clear divergence on the Highland land question. In Ross-shire the determination of the Tories to put up Fletcher of Rosehaugh, a great proprietor, was vehemently resisted by Liberal Unionists, led by Mackenzie of Gairloch, who argued that 'Only a candidate of advanced Liberal views will be able to divert any considerable part of the Crofter vote away from Dr. MacDonald to the Unionist cause'.[115] Chamberlain deprecated the Tory government's handling of the Crofter difficulty as insensitive and likely to lose the seats of sitting Liberal Unionists and also to 'ruin our chances in the North of Scotland'.[116]

One of the major organisational grievances was that the disparity in strength between the two parties rankled with Tories. One fear was that where a Liberal Unionist sat, it would soon prove well-nigh impossible to maintain Conservative organisation in the seat in good working order.[117] Equally relevant, Liberal Unionist party machinery was frequently held to be, as MacLeod described the case of Inverness-shire (a seat held by a Liberal Unionist), 'a mythical body'.[118] Indeed in 1889 the National Union Council resolved to draw to the attention of its Liberal Unionist counterpart the unsatisfactory state of the latter party's constituency organisation in several areas of the country.[119] This seems to have been a genuine, not a partisan, complaint. The Liberal Unionist Chief Whip was told by a warm supporter in 1890 that the party in Scotland badly needed 'one man at the head who knows about electioneering'.[120] Harry Hope, a Tory turned Liberal Unionist, complained that after nearly four years' membership he had still received no intimation of any party meeting being held in either Fife or East Lothian.[121] It was believed that the success of Liberal Unionist M.P.s in 1886 was mainly a personal vote and, once that was removed, local Liberal Unionist organisation would then be exposed as flimsy in the extreme. This argument was strongly put forward to help explain the loss of Ayr Burghs in 1888.[122] In addition, although the Liberal Unionists had contributed the preponderance of M.P.s, in almost every case it seemed reasonable for the Tories to claim it was mostly their votes which won the seat. But, conversely, Liberal Unionists could argue that their votes were decisive in making the difference between the 1885 and 1886 results. Conservatives were made more uneasy about having surrendered so much to their allies as the long-term allegiance of certain anti-Home Rule Liberals was called into question. The steady trickle of prominent Liberal Unionists back to their original party gave body to these doubts.[123]

There were instances of wholehearted and fruitful co-operation in the 1886–92 period, notably in Kinross-shire, where both sides pooled their resources to improve organisation and to choose a candidate, and the Dunbartonshire Tories sent their congratulations to Hartington in recognition of his work for the common cause.[124] But in rather more places separate activity and collision were the order of the day. Unionist leaders in England received intimation when at last the two wings met together in public — in Ayr Burghs only in November 1888, and in Fife East not until November 1891.[125] But it was perhaps the disputes over the right to choose candidates that caused the most serious damage to the Unionist alliance. These arguments happened at virtually every by-election after 1886, with the Liberal Unionists feeling especially under pressure from the Tories. At Ayr in 1888 the Tories voted for the Liberal Unionist only after a *diktat* to that effect emanating from Salisbury himself, but as the local Conservative press explained, 'that there was a friction and loss of power from this cause it would be idle to deny. There was manifest lack of that unity of aim and concentration of effort which were to be witnessed on the other side'.[126] Govan was another scene of struggle when a previously Tory seat was contested by a Liberal Unionist in 1888, creating bad feelings and leading to defeat. Again, at Partick in 1890 the new Liberal Unionist complained of Tory manoeuvres to stop him standing, while Tories turned the charge back at the Liberal Unionists.[127] Later that year there was distress among the Liberal Unionists in Dumfriesshire, Kincardineshire and especially at Glasgow College, 'where a candidate seems to have been chosen by the Conservatives without any communication being made to the late [Liberal Unionist] candidate or his friends'.[128] On the other hand, Liberal Unionist incursions also took place. Dunbartonshire Conservatives were infuriated in 1890 when in this solidly Tory fastness the Liberal Unionists nominated a candidate upon the retiral of the incumbent M.P. and then insisted that the Tories come to a speedy decision as to what they would do. The Conservatives turned in despair to Alexander Wylie, who had earlier declined the nomination; but now, under great pressure from his party, he agreed to run and was duly put forward as the Conservatives' choice.[129] To resolve these recurrent squabbles a committee composed of leading men from both parties was formed, but its decisions were not always regarded as binding. In Moray and Nairn in 1889 the committee came down in favour of a Conservative standing, but he withdrew because the Liberal Unionists found him unacceptable. In his place the Liberal Unionists put up an ultra-radical who promptly forfeited Conservative support, and a winnable seat was not taken.[130] In the face of these squabbles the leaders of both sides could only groan. 'The Scotch politicians are a hopeless lot' was one of the more polite comments made.[131]

Under the circumstances the setback endured in the 1892 election was not perhaps surprising, but it did not induce greater cordiality, still less promote a desire to merge. Resistance to a merger was particularly noticeable among Liberal Unionists in the West of Scotland. The Eastern Liberal Unionist Association was perhaps more inclined to seek an accommodation with the Conservatives. After the 1892 election the Liberal Unionists agreed to concentrate only on those seats where they entertained reasonable prospects of success. In most of the other seats negotiations with the Conservatives were carried on, in order to establish collaboration in organising constituencies such as Angus, Dumfriesshire and Edinburgh Central. Elsewhere the talks centred on finding mutually acceptable candidates, as in Sutherland, Aberdeen South, and Moray and Nairn. The logical conclusion of this process came only in 1899, when the Liberal Unionists decided to devote their registration work to a mere thirteen seats which were either marginal or had no Conservative organisation.[132] There were still flickerings of the old disputes, however, as in Hawick, where the local Liberal Unionists declined to co-operate with the Tories, and in Edinburgh East.[133] In the latter case relations deteriorated very sharply as late as 1898 because the Conservatives believed the Liberal Unionists were not in practice co-operating on the joint organising committee, but were using it to poach votes from them. When the Liberal Unionists confirmed these suspicions by subsequently embarking independently on a recruitment drive, a total divorce followed.[134]

The West of Scotland Liberal Unionist Association, always the stronger body of the two, adopted a more robustly independent response. A thorough reorganisation was carried out after the losses in 1892, largely under the direction of James Parker Smith, one of the original organisers of the party in the area. This course was chosen rather than, as in the east, seeking some liaison with the Tories. The aims in the west were firstly to get businessmen more involved in party affairs, and to this end regular meetings to discuss policy were held, and a clear command structure of organisation was imposed with an effective committee system. Modernisation was the keynote of the reform of the party machinery, extending even to the installation of a telephone in the central Glasgow office.[135] A corollary of all these shake-ups was an expansion, not a contraction, of constituency asssociations. In 1894–5, sixty-four new branches were opened and membership increased by a substantial amount, while constituency agents were encouraged to be constructive in their outlook. This aggressive approach by the Liberal Unionists brought them rapidly and regularly into conflict with the Conservatives, who protested vociferously at the former's irruptions into such Tory fiefs as South Ayrshire, Argyll and Wigtownshire.[136] Whereas, in the east, moves at constituency level to merge the two Unionist bodies into one were not viewed with disfavour, the West of Scotland LUA Executive frowned upon marriages in Mid Lanark, St Rollox and Camlachie and reiterated the need to keep a separate identity.[137] The upshot of these feuds in the west was that at the end of 1895, after the general election, still no closer unity was achieved, and instead both sides accepted the right of the other to organise everywhere, agreeing that no joint constituency organisation should be created without consultation within the Liberal Unionist party at all levels. A committee of both parties was to adjudicate on problems presented by these regulations.[138] Even so, friction still broke out. In 1899 Liberal Unionists complained of their exclusion by the Tories from doing organisational work in North-West Lanarkshire and Wigtownshire.[139] Nevertheless, after 1895 these incidents were isolated outbreaks, but the greater instances of harmony frequently reflected less an agreed reconciliation than a reluctant recognition by Liberal Unionists of demographic reality. From 1899 a repeated theme in the party discussions was that as the original Liberal Unionists died out (they had been largely a middle-aged group in 1886), replacements were not stepping forward. This was first reported in the smaller villages of Ayrshire and Renfrewshire: 'we are finding it very difficult to get new claims made up for the losses among the old men'.[140] In the 1900 election, assistance in finding Liberal Unionist candidates had to be obtained from the party's London headquarters. Yet even then the Western Association clung to the importance of presenting a distinctive standpoint: 'So long as there are 80 Irish votes for sale and the price is the dismemberment of the British Empire, the 68 Liberal Unionist M.P.s at present elected to Westminster must be supported and maintained by suitable organisation throughout the country'.[141] The sense of separate identity was reciprocated, as instanced by the reaction of a prominent Scottish Tory deploring the decision in 1896 to admit Liberal Unionists to membership of the Carlton Club: 'I thought there was at least one place where one was free from the restraint of having these people about you'.[142]

In short, there were barely suppressed tensions still persisting at the start of the twentieth century between Conservatives and Liberal Unionists in Scotland. Liberal Unionism was in decline because its members were dying out and because the Conservatives had steadily moved in the 1890s from a reactionary position based on landlordism and defence of the state church to a commitment to progressive reform. But this equilibrium was still newly established and hence fairly fragile, so that any developments which might disturb it would be likely to have graver consequences for Unionism in Scotland than in England, where the strength of Unionism was of longer duration.

NOTES

1. D. W. Urwin, 'The Development of Conservative Party Organisation in Scotland until 1912', *SHR,* 44 (1965), pp. 89–111, is a general survey.

2. Dunbartonshire Conservative Association Minute Books, 21 Dec. 1883, GD 260/6/7. Kinross-shire was in a parlous state too: Kinross-shire Constitutional Association Minute Book, 20 Feb. 1882.

3. National Union of Conservative Associations of Scotland [NUCAS] Council, Minute Book, 12 Feb., 25 May 1883.

4. W. E. Hodgson, 'Why Conservatism Fails in Scotland', *National Review,* 2 (1883–4), pp. 238–9, 237.

5. H. J. Hope to H. W. Hope, 23 Jun. 1884, Hope MSS., GD 364/647; cf. J. Rankin, D.D., *Causes of Conservative Failure in Perthshire. A letter to Col. Moray the younger of Blair Drummond* (Edinburgh, 1886), *passim*.

6. 'A Scottish Conservative', 'Scottish Conservatism', *National Review,* 29 (1889), p. 11.

7. NUCAS, *2nd Annual Report* (1883) unpag; Memoranda (2) by H. Hope, both 21 June 1884, Hope MSS., GD 364/17.

8. Second Memorandum by H. Hope, 21 June 1884, Hope MSS., GD 364/17.

9. E.g., Dukes of Montrose, Richmond to Lord Kintore, 31 Oct., 15 Nov. 1885, Kintore MSS., 191.

10. M. T. to P. Stormonth-Darling, 18 Feb. 1884, Stormonth-Darling MSS., 73.

11. Glasgow Conservative Association, *14th, 16th Annual Reports,* 1882, 1884. For similar effects in the south-west: G. G. Walker to H. E. Maxwell, 2 Aug. 1884, Maxwell of Monreith MSS., Acc. 7043/HEM 2.

12. See R. MacLeod to Lord R. Churchill, 8 Nov. 1886, Churchill MSS., RCHL/1/XVI/1984 for the opinion that mass meetings were a substitute for real activity. Glasgow Conservative Association, *15th Annual Report* (1883) admits a falling off in members after the impetus of the previous year.

13. M. T. to P. Stormonth-Darling, 6 Feb. 1884, Stormonth-Darling MSS., 64.

14. NUCAS *Annual Report* 1884 in NUCAS Council Minute Books, R. MacLeod to Lord Cairns, 22 Jul. 1884, Cairns MSS., PRO 30/51/20 for his views on the Liberal press bias. Urwin, 'Conservative Organisation', pp. 102–3, seems mistakenly to put the start of the production of Scottish literature as rather later.

15. G. G. Walker to H. E. Maxwell, 2 Aug. 1884, Maxwell of Monreith MSS., Acc. 7043/HEM 2.

16. Kinross-shire Constitutional Association Minute Book, 30 Apr. 1886; Circular by W. Boase, 28 Feb. 1885 (for Dundee) in Dundee Public Library, Lamb Coll. 17/3.

17. A. Akers-Douglas to R. MacLeod, F. Pitman, 24 Oct., 29 Dec. 1885, Chilston MSS., U 564/C Lp 1/96, 216.

18. Hopetoun to H. Hope, 21, 31 May 1884, Hope MSS., GD 364/688.

19. NUCAS, *Annual Report* 1886.

20. A. Ross to Lothian, 21 Jan. 1886, Lothian MSS., GD 40/16/7, ff. 8–9; NUCAS Council Minute Book, 20 Jan. 1886; R. MacLeod to Lord R. Churchill, 8 Nov. 1886, Churchill MSS., RCHL/1/XVI/1984.

21. MacLeod to A. Akers-Douglas, 3 Nov. 1887, Chilton MSS., U. 564/C 361/1.

22. Dunbartonshire Conservative Association Minute Books, 18 May 1887; 9 Nov. 1889; 24 Nov. 1888; GD 260/17.

23. Glasgow Conservative Association, *20th, 21st Annual* Reports 1888, 1889.

24. MacLeod to Salisbury, 22 Jan. 1889, Hatfield House MSS., 3 M/E.

25. Same to same, 14, 22 Feb. 1889, Ibid., 3 M/E.

26. R. E. Middleton to Sir C. Dalrymple, 14 Jan. 1890 (copy) and two undated memoranda by Middleton are in NUCAS Council Minute Books.

27. H. E. Maxwell to A. Akers-Douglas, 14 Oct. 1890, Chilston MSS., U 564/C 370/3. For more 'stirring up' by Haig — in Dumfriesshire: A. Akers-Douglas to Haig, Rev. J. Paton, 21, 28 Oct. 1895, Ibid., U 564/C Lp4/382, 398. Urwin, 'Scottish Conservatism', p. 102, gives a different estimate of Haig's achievement.

28. P. T. Marsh, *The Discipline of Popular Government* (London, 1978), pp. 183–212, for Middleton's work.

29. NUCAS *Annual Report* 1891; S. Chapman to Lord R. Churchill, 18 Sep. 1892, Churchill MSS., RCHL/1/XXVIII/3999. For similar trends in East Lothian, see A. Ross

to J. Congleton, 16 Mar. 1889, Hope MSS., GD 364/588.

30. NUCAS, *Annual Report* 1891.

31. Dunbartonshire Conservative Association Minute Book, 28 Nov., 16 Sep. 1891, GD 260/6/7.

32. MacLeod to Salisbury, 23 Aug. 1889, Hatfield House MSS., 3M/E.

33. Scottish Conservative Club Political Committee Minute Book, *passim,* GD 309/44.

34. Dunbartonshire Conservative Association Minute Book, 28 Nov. 1891, 6 Jan. 1897, GD 260/6/7; Scottish Conservative Club Political Committee Minute Book, 22 Jul. 1897, GD 309/44. Marsh, *Discipline of Popular Government,* pp. 193–5, discusses the professionalisation of party agents at this time.

35. Dunbartonshire Conservative Association Minute Book, 8 Oct. 1895, GD 260/6/7.

36. Based on Glasgow Conservative Association *19th–26th Annual Reports* 1887–1894.

37. Marsh, *Discipline of Popular Government,* pp. 195–6, explores the importance of registration work.

38. NUCAS Council Minute Book, 15 Sep. 1886, 19 Feb., 16 Nov. 1887, 21 May, 17 Dec. 1890.

39. NUCAS Eastern Divisional Council Minute Book, 24 Feb. 1897.

40. Dunbartonshire Conservative Association Minute Book, 30 Nov. 1898, GD 260/6/7.

41. NUCAS *Annual Report* 1891; West Renfrewshire Conservative Association Minute Book, 3 Feb. 1898. Marsh, *Discipline of Popular Government,* p. 205, for England.

42. Salisbury to Hartington, 9 Nov. 1890, Devonshire MSS., 340.2257.

43. R. E. Middleton to Salisbury, 28 Apr. 1894, Hatfield House MSS., 3M/E.

44. NUCAS Eastern Division Council Minute Book, 29 Jan. 1896, for work in West Lothian, Peebles and Selkirk and West Fife. Urwin, 'Conservative Organisation', pp. 106–9, gives a more critical appraisal.

45. Haig to S. McDonnell, 31, 4 Dec., 1 Jul. 1897, Hatfield House MSS., 3M/E.

46. S. Chapman to Lord R. Churchill, 18 Sep. 1892, Churchill MSS., RHCL/1/XXVIII/3999.

47. There is a collection of these NUCAS pamphlets in the National Library of Scotland; *Political Speeches by Mr James Somervell of Sorn to the Glasgow Electors, February and March 1884* (Glasgow, 1884).

48. *Political Speeches by Somervell,* pp. 53 ff.

49. NUCAS Council Minute Book, 14 Apr. 1884.

50. R. MacLeod to Lothian, 20 Jun. 1886, Lothian MSS., GD 40/16/7, ff. 16–17.

51. Churchill to Sir C. Dalrymple, 21 Aug. 1892, Newhailes MSS., Acc. 7228/232; cf. A. J. Balfour to Salisbury, 19 Dec. 1883, Hatfield House MSS., 3M/E: 'From the little I hear, Randolph was not a great success last night [in Edinmburgh]'.

52. 'A Tory Democrat', *Scotland at the General Election of 1885* (Edinburgh, 1885), pp. 8, 9.

53. A. Akers-Douglas to Salisbury, 4 Aug. (1887), Hatfield House MSS., 3M/E.

54. Hunter MSS., 6/63 for his views on co-operatives; A. Barr to R. W. Cochran-Patrick, 6 Feb. 1888, Ibid., 1/10 for the miners.

55. H. Hope to Tweeddale, 20, 17 Feb. 1887, to J. Reid, 4, 5 Nov. 1887, to Camperdown, 20 Nov. 1887 (all copies); J. Reid to Hope, 6 Nov. 1887, Hope MSS., GD 364/692.

56. J. Chisholm to Churchill, 16 Aug. 1892; for similar changes in Edinburgh, S. Chapman, G. Jamieson to Churchill, 5 Feb. 1892, 26 Mar. 1891, Churchill MSS., RCHL/1/XXVIII/3981; XXVII/3832, 3692.

57. S. Chapman to Churchill, 15 Feb. 1893, Ibid., RCHL/1/XXIX/4074.

58. NUCAS Council Minute Book, 21 May 1890; Eastern Division Organising Sub-

Committee Minute Book, 17 Jun. 1890.

59. NUCAS Council Minute Book, 16 Oct. 1889.

60. J. P. B. Robertson to Sir C. Dalrymple, 11 Sep. 1890, Newhailes MSS., Acc. 7228/235; NUCAS Eastern Division Organising Sub-Committee, 2 Dec. 1890, 15 Jan. 1891.

61. Chamberlain to Balfour, 19 Jul. 1892, J. Chamberlain MSS., JC 5/5/55.

62. J. Melrose, J. Brunton, P. Lugton to A. R. D. Elliot, 28 Apr., 14 Jul., 21 Jul. 1892, Elliot MSS., MS. 19489, ff. 9–10, 33–4, 70–1. Marsh, *Discipline of Popular Government,* pp. 166–7, mistakenly argues that opposition to disestablishment was the basis to Liberal Unionism in Scotland.

63. Cf. Rosebery to R. B. Haldane, 22 Jan. 1892, Haldane MSS., MS. 5903, ff. 194–5.

64. *Disestablishment Banner,* 43, 45 (Jan., Nov. 1895).

65. J. W. Barclay to A. R. D. Elliot, 25 Jul. 1892, Elliot MSS., MS. 19489, ff. 66–7.

66. ESLUA Minute Book, 22 Feb., 6 Apr., 2 Aug., 10 Oct., 5 Dec. 1892, 13 Feb., 18 Oct., 1893.

67. Ibid., 18 Oct. 1893, 21 Dec. 1894.

68. Marsh, *Discipline of Popular Government,* pp. 245–6, notes that although Salisbury did not endorse Chamberlain's programme in its entirety, a good number of Conservative candidates did so.

69. NUCAS Eastern Division Council Minute Book, 17 Apr. 1895.

70. *Falkirk Herald,* 27 Jul. 1895.

71. E.g. *Dalkeith Advertiser,* 25 Jul. 1895, *Dumfries and Galloway Courier,* 10 Jul. 1895.

72. Lothian to R. W. Cochran-Patrick, 25 May 1888, Hunter MSS., 1/1.

73. Lothian to Salisbury, 31 Oct., 5 Nov. 1890, Hatfield House MSS., 3M/E.

74. Balfour of Burleigh to S. McDonnell, 6 May, 13 Mar. 1896, Ibid; cf. Lothian to Cochran-Patrick, 15 Jan. 1890, Hunter MSS., 1/3 for the Scottish ministers' unhappiness at Salisbury's habit of appointing Lords-Lieutenant on party lines.

75. *Stirling Observer,* 10 Jul. 1895; cf. *Ayr Observer,* 9 Jul. 1895; speech by F. F. Begg in St Rollox, *Glasgow Herald,* 9 Jul. 1895.

76. *Handbook of Facts for Electors. A Handbook for Unionist Committee Men* (Edinburgh, 1900), p. 23.

77. *Ayr Observer,* 12 Jul. 1895.

78. *Falkirk Herald,* 17, 24 Jul. 1895; also *Airdrie Advertiser,* 6 Jul. 1895.

79. *Falkirk Mail, Falkirk Herald,* 20 Jul. 1895.

80. *Airdrie Advertiser,* 13 Jul. 1895.

81. *Kilmarnock Herald,* 26 Jul. 1895.

82. E.g. H. Ivory to Rosebery, 19 Sep. 1895, Rosebery MSS., MS. 10038, ff. 72–3; *Falkirk Herald,* 24, 27 Jul. 1895; *Ayrshire Post,* 26 Jul. 1895; *Stirling Observer,* 24 Jul. 1895.

83. R. C. Munro Ferguson to Lady Munro Ferguson, 2 Jun. 1895, Novar MSS., 13. J. Hunter, 'The Politics of Highland Land Reform, 1873–95', *SHR,* 53 (1974), pp. 62–7, traces the reasons for Crofter disunity.

84. *Inverness Courier,* 21, 28, 31 May, 7, 11, 18 Jun., 30 Jul. 1895.

85. *Ibid.,* 9 Jul. 1895 (speech by R. B. Finlay).

86. *Dunoon Observer, Argyll Herald,* 13 Jul. 1895 (both).

87. Finlay to Salisbury, 27 Jul. 1895, Hatfield House MSS., 3M/E; *Dunoon Observer,* 27 Jul. 1895, *Elgin Courant and Courier,* 26 Jul. 1895.

88. *Inverness Courier,* 11 Jun. 1895, for Baillie; Argyll to Salisbury, 27 Jun. 1895, Hatfield House MSS., 3M/E.

89. L. McIver, *Trades Unionism. An Address to the Electors* (Beaufort, 1891), pp. 3–4. This speech was given to working-class voters of Edinburgh South.

90. *Falkirk Herald,* 17 Jul. 1895.

91. McIver, *Trades Unionism,* pp. 5–6.

92. J. McKillop, *Thoughts for the People* (Stirling, 1898), p. 183.

93. McIver, *Trades Unionism,* p. 10.

94. R. Smillie, *My Life for Labour* (London, 1924), pp. 103–5.

95. *Stirling Observer,* 24 Jul. 1895, *Falkirk Mail,* 20 Jul. 1895. H. Pelling, *Social Geography of British Elections, 1885–1910* (London, 1967), p. 395, suggests however that the votes of Glasgow commuters in the west of the county were decisive.

96. A. S. Cunningham, *Randolph Gordon Erskine Wemyss: an Appreciation* (Leven, n.d.), pp. 130–4.

97. Marsh, *Discipline of Popular Government,* gives a general account of this process.

98. Lord Wolmer to Salisbury, 10 Feb. 1889, Hatfield House MSS., 3M/E.

99. Lord Camperdown to H. Hope, 24 Nov. 1887, Hope MSS., GD 364/692.

100. Lothian to R. McLeod, n.d. (draft), Lothian MSS., GD 40/16/7, ff. 4–5.

101. Alyth and Meigle Constitutional Association Minute Book, 17 Jun. 1886; for a similar instance in North East Lanarkshire, R. MacLeod to Lothian, 23 Jun. 1886, Lothian MSS., GD 40/16/7, ff. 21–2.

102. Sir H. E. Maxwell, *Evening Memories* (London, 1931), pp. 177–8. The same happened at West Renfrewshire (J. King to J. P. Smith, 3 May 1886, Smith of Jordanhill MSS., TD 1/346) and Greenock (R. MacLeod to R. E. Middleton, 28 Jun. 1886, Hatfield House MSS., 3M/E).

103. WSLUA, *1st Annual Report* (1886), R. MacLeod to Lothian, 15 Jul. 1886, Lothian MSS., GD 40/16/7, ff. 25–7.

104. Sir J. Fergusson to W. C. Cuninghame, 21 Jun. 1886, Cuninghame MSS., GD 149/413/3.

105. Lothian to Salisbury, 12 Jun. 1886, Hatfield House MSS., 3M/E; Alyth and Meigle Constitutional Association Minute Book, 17 Jun. 1886.

106. J. F. C. Hozier, Lord Hopetoun to Salisbury, 3, 8 Sep. 1887, Hatfield House MSS., 3M/E.

107. D. Cameron, R. MacLeod to Salisbury, 28 Nov . (1890), 3 Oct. 1889, Ibid, 3M/E.

108. Lady F. Balfour, *A Memoir of Lord Balfour of Burleigh* (London, n.d.), p. 116.

109. D. Hunter, A. Smith, A. R. Rennie and T. Wood to Lothian, 23 Jul., 14, 18 (twice), Aug. 1886, Lothian MSS., GD 40/16/7, ff. 35, 58, 60, 61.

110. A. Akers-Douglas to R. MacLeod, 5 Nov. 1887, Chilston MSS., U 564/C Lp 2/33–4.

111. *Inverness Courier,* 11 Jun. 1895; *Life of Henry Calderwood, D.D.,* by his son and Rev. D. Woodside (London, 1910), pp. 323–5, 340–50.

112. J. Ross to Sir K. MacKenzie, 10 Sep. 1889, MacKenzie MSS; Rev. D. Hunter to J. P. Smith, 22 Jan. 1890, Smith of Jordanhill MSS., TD 1/354; J. Melvin to A. R. D. Elliot, 28 Apr. 1892, Elliot MSS., MS. 19489, ff. 9–10.

113. MacLeod to A. Akers-Douglas, 3 Nov. 1887, Chilston MSS., U 564/C361/1.

114. *Ayr Advertiser,* 21 Jun. 1888. In 1893 in a division on the Welsh Local Veto Bill, the Scottish Liberal Unionists supported it, voting against the Conservatives: A. Akers-Douglas to H. Tennent, 17 Mar. 1893, Chilston MSS., U 564/CLp3/258.

115. Sir K. MacKenzie to — Jackson, 22 Nov. 1889 (copy), MacKenzie MSS; cf. H. T. Anstruther to R. MacLeod, 9 Nov. 1889, Ibid.

116. J. Chamberlain to Wolmer, 17 Mar. 1892, Selborne MSS., MS. Selborne 8, ff. 25–6.

117. A. Akers-Douglas to Capt. Boyle, 15 Feb. 1888, Chilston MSS., U 564/CLp2/76; NUCAS Eastern Division Organising Sub-Committee Minute Book, 14 Oct. 1891.

118. MacLeod to Salisbury, 8 Dec. 1890, Hatfield House MSS., 3M/E.

119. NUCAS Council Minute Book, 15 May 1889.

120. C. Cooper to Wolmer, 7 Oct. 1890, Selborne MSS., MS. Selborne 13, ff. 51–2.

121. Hope to A. Gifford, 2 Mar. 1891, also 4 Feb. 1890, Hope MSS.. GD 364/588.

122. *Ayr Advertiser,* 21 Jun. 1888.

123. Cf. A. Akers-Douglas to Capt. Boyle, 15 Feb. 1888, Chilston MSS., U 564/CLp2/76.

124. Kinross-shire Constitutional Association Minute Book, 30 Apr., 15 Oct. 1889; Dunbartonshire Conservative Association Minute Book, 2 Oct. 1889, GD 260/6/7.

125. Sir J. Fergusson to Salisbury, 3 Nov. 1888, Hatfield House MSS., 3M/E; J. Gilmour to J. B. Kinnear, 27 Nov. 1891, Gilmour MSS., GD 383/75/61–4.

126. *Ayr Advertiser,* 21 Jun. 1888.

127. J. P. Smith to R. MacLeod, 19 Jan. 1890, Smith of Jordanhill MSS., TD 1/354; R. E. Middleton to Salisbury, 21 Jan. 1890, Hatfield House MSS., 3M/E.

128. C. Cooper to Selborne, 7 Oct. 1890, Selborne MSS., MS. Selborne 13, ff. 51–2.

129. Dunbartonshire Conservative Association Minute Book, 18 Jan., 7 Feb., 2 Apr., 12 Sep., 5 Nov. 1890, GD 260/6/7; for another rivalry over the Edinburgh and St Andrews Universities seat, see J. P. B. Robertson to A. Akers-Douglas, 23 Oct. 1890, Chilston MSS., U 564/C456/12.

130. R. MacLeod, S. McDonnell, R. E. Middleton to Salisbury, 11 Sep., 3 Oct. 1889; 11, 5, 7 Sep. 1889, Hatfield House 3M/E.

131. W. H. Smith to A. Akers-Douglas, n.d. (c. Jan. 1890), Chilston MSS., U 564/C25/119.

132. ESLUA Minute Book, 10 Jul. 1893, 20 Jul., 4 Oct. 1894, 12 May 1899.

133. NUCAS, Eastern Division Council Minute Book, 28 Jul., 22 Dec. 1897, 29 Jun., 30 Nov. 1898, 26 Apr. 1899, 24 Apr. 1901, 27 May 1903.

134. Ibid., 26 Jan., 23 Feb., 25 May, 27 Jul. 1898.

135. WSLUA Minute Book, 25 Nov., 30 Dec. 1892, 8 Jan., 11, 28 Feb., 10 Mar. 1893.

136. Ibid., 30 Nov., 26 Dec. 1894, 25 Oct. 1895.

137. Ibid., 13 Apr. 1894, 24 Jan. 1896, 22 Jan. 1897.

138. Ibid., 8 Nov. 1895.

139. Ibid., 24 Feb., 7 Jul. 1899.

140. Ibid., 21 Apr., 8 Sep. 1899.

141. Ibid., 9 Nov. 1900.

142. J. P. B. Robertson to Sir C. Dalrymple, 23 Feb. 1896, Newhailes MSS., Acc. 7228/236, ff. 191–4.

8

Edwardian Politics

I

In the 1906 general election, Scotland swung sharply back to Liberalism and remained virtually unchanged in the two 1910 elections, whereas in England there was a clear movement back to Unionism. In 1906 the Unionists fell from having 36 to 10 M.P.s, only marginally better than 1885. In January 1910, whereas the number of Unionist M.P.s in England doubled from the 1906 total of 122 to 234, in Scotland a further seat was lost. This pattern is the more striking as two key components — education and licensing reform — of the process which contributed to the distintegration of the Unionist majority after 1902 did not apply in Scotland. The Education Bill did not cover Scotland, and as already seen, the issues raised by it, which so mightily fanned the resurgence of the Nonconformist conscience in England, had not stirred Scottish Dissenters in the earlier phase of the 1870 and 1872 Bills. Also, the Free and U.P. churches were too preoccupied with the implementation of their recent union to devote much attention to the education agitation. Indeed, as the union already looked like being contested in the courts by the anti-union Free Church party, the leaders of the new merged church would not wish to antagonise a government on whose support they might have to rely for legislative assistance to clear up any confusion. Therefore, it was widely agreed that the education controversy was not very relevant in Scotland.[1] The Licensing Bill similarly did not apply to Scotland, and here again the church union question tended to divert many temperance advocates from the issue.

It was the tariff reform campaign launched by Chamberlain in 1903 which was, almost on its own, the crucial destroyer of the recently cemented Unionist strength in Scotland.[2] There were several reasons for this. Firstly, Unionism was very badly split, with some prominent figures from the landed wing exceptionally hostile. The Scottish Secretary, Lord Balfour of Burleigh, left the Cabinet on this issue, and other lairds who supported his stance included Sir Michael Shaw-Stewart, M.P. for Renfrew West, C. B. Renshaw, M.P. for Renfrew East, and Sir John Stirling-Maxwell, M.P. for Glasgow College. But unlike England, there was far less of a positive response from the industrial and business sections of Unionism. One of the most assiduous critics of tariff reform in Parliament was Col. J. M. Denny, the only Scottish shipbuilder M.P.[3] As Denny stressed, he reflected the apprehensions of the leading sector in the West of Scotland economy about the impact of Protectionism on its profitability. The steel industry, so closely related to shipbuilding, showed little zeal for Chamberlain's scheme, and J. G. A. Baird, one of the great Baird dynasty and a longstanding M.P. for Glasgow Central, resolutely opposed the abandonment of free trade. The organ of the West of

218

Scotland business community, the *Glasgow Herald*, had been firmly committed to Unionism since 1886. It strenuously and repeatedly championed free trade, deriding the tariff reform proposals as misguided and dangerous to the economic wellbeing of the country, and to reinforce the point it published a damning series of articles in 1903 exposing the folly of protectionism.[4] Likewise, during the 1906 election in Dundee, where the jute manufacturers could discern no benefits in protection, the Unionist head of the industry's biggest firm urged support for candidates who would uphold free trade, irrespective of party.[5]

Tariff reformers were not entirely friendless north of the Tweed. The movement enjoyed the backing of some members of landed Unionism, including Sir Herbert Maxwell, M.P. for Wigtownshire, the Hon. Thomas Cochrane, M.P. for Ayrshire North, Lord Minto, and his brother, Hugh Elliot. But remarkably few industrialists pledged themselves to tariff reform, and a sympathetic observer, Hugh Elliot, lamented that at Chamberlain's Glasgow meeting in 1903 only second-rate individuals were present to support him.[6] The second annual meeting of the West of Scotland Tariff Reform League was dominated by the flint glass manufacturers, hardly a central pillar of economic life in the area.[7] The two main organisers of the Chamberlainites in the Glasgow area were not front-rank members of the business community. One was Montague Baird, a brewery director who hailed from Birmingham, and the other was James Parker-Smith, Liberal Unionist M.P. for Partick, a somewhat impoverished landowner and an erstwhile private secretary to Chamberlain. Bonar Law was perhaps the only M.P. with a business background who committed himself enthusiastically to the principles of tariff reform, while, as a counterweight, the rising manager of Scottish Unionism, George Younger, was always sceptical. The two Scottish Unionist M.P.s who crossed the floor on this issue, John Wilson and Alexander Cross, were, significantly, both businessmen. Because these divides were so deep, the struggle for power within both Unionist parties was exceptionally bitter in Scotland. As early as August 1903 Stirling-Maxwell complained to Balfour of Burleigh that there were firm rumours of protectionist candidates being run against Unionist Free Fooders.[8] And indeed by 1905 Chamberlain was urging Parker Smith to act to oust his Unionist opponents: 'Are we going to do nothing in the case of Alexander Cross and others of his kidney?'[9] In the case of Moray and Nairn, Chamberlain advocated that 'the Tariff Reform Association ought publicly to withdraw its support' if the candidate followed the line laid down by party headquarters.[10]

The Free Fooders struck back vigorously. In the 1906 and January 1910 elections Shaw-Stewart ruthlessly deployed his influence as the local laird against tariff reformers in both Greenock and West Renfrewshire. In the latter seat in 1906 he threatened that 'I must hold myself to take any course during the Election that circumstances may render necessary', and as he was the retiring M.P., this was no light matter.[11] On the eve of the first 1910 contest he resigned as vice-president of the constituency Conservative Association in protest at the new candidate's protectionist principles, thereby creating confusion among the voters.[12] In the Greenock constituency Shaw-Stewart resigned as honorary officebearer after a dispute arising from his publicly airing his free trade opinions in the midst of the first 1910 election campaign.[13] It is not certain that the laird of Ardgowan's influence was decisive in causing these normally Unionist seats to be lost, though some claimed it was, and certainly it was a worry for local party managers. Elsewhere, Arthur Elliot, the former M.P. for Roxburghshire, refused to endorse the candidature there of the Unionist Lord Henry Scott in 1906 on the grounds of their divergent positions on tariff reform.[14]

These disagreements went beyond the level of individuals seeking to exercise influence, for there was also an organisational struggle. C. B. Renshaw became the link between the Free Food League nationally and its Scottish adherents. He began his activities by mobilising all Unionist M.P.s sympathetic to free trade in a bid to prevent Chamberlain being invited to visit Glasgow under the auspices of the West of Scotland Liberal Unionists.[15] Despite these frenetic exertions by Free Fooders, in the long run the efforts of the tariff reformers proved more successful. The eastern and western branches of the Tariff Reform League were united in 1908 and recruitment steadily expanded. From only 14 branches in Scotland in 1905, rising to 55 on the eve of the merger, by 1910 there were 182 branches. These were very active, and not just paper entities, as they held a total of 1450 meetings in 1909–10. More importantly, the tariff reformers captured the grassroots. The West Aberdeenshire Women's Tariff Reform League had 1284 members in 1908, when the constituency Women's Unionist Association had 1448 members, suggesting the extent of the protectionist triumph.[16] It was asserted that every Unionist candidate fighting the January 1910 election endorsed Chamberlain's ideas, and protection was also the principal policy of the Scottish Conservative Party.[17] This process was often quite speedy, as the deliberations of the West of Scotland Liberal Unionist Association reveal. In 1903, it upheld Balfour's middle of the road stance, declining to give total agreement to tariff reform, but by March 1906 the executive voted by 20 votes to 5 to accept the resignation of the Duke of Devonshire from the presidency of the Association.[18]

But while the protectionists were enthused by the results of their incessant endeavours, the general result of the tariff reform crisis on the morale of the Unionists was often negative. Many rank and file party workers became lethargic and apathetic after witnessing the confusing and bitter exchanges between the party leaders. In Paisley, disaffection was extreme and extended to the defection of many Unionists to the Liberal camp, including a Vice-President of the Association.[19] The Scottish Conservative agent had detected these discontents as already prevalent in August 1905 and had used them to counsel Balfour against going to the country in the autumn of that year.[20] The 1906 election was characterised by a widespread lack of commitment among Unionist party workers. A meeting at the Scottish Conservative Club at the start of the campaign to drum up workers for the contest in the Edinburgh seats produced a 'very discouraging' response; and only those already active volunteered.[21] Likewise in Kirkcaldy, the Conservative Association Annual Report stated: 'The Committee thinks it right to say that although some of the Committee worked hard — and to them all thanks are cordially given — a great many did not give the assistance which was expected of them'.[22] This indolence persisted after the polls, and the Dunfermline Conservatives reported in October 1906 that they faced imminent collapse as no-one could be induced to become an office-bearer.[23]

II

The reaction of the Conservatives to the electoral rebuff of 1906 was to undertake a rigorous scrutiny of organisational and propaganda techniques which resulted in marked improvements in both fields.[24] At the centre, the changes were simple, swift and brutal. Col. A. B. Haig, the Party Agent for some fifteen years, was replaced in 1906 by Guy Speir, an advocate with a landed background. However, dissatisfaction was soon voiced at what was seen as his overconfidence and his assumption of powers not previously exercised by Haig. 'His ways are mysterious', complained Balfour's secretary after Speir had sent the party leader on a 'fruitless' mission to Aberdeen during the January 1910 campaign.[25] However, the problem was as much structural as personal, for it had been pointed out in 1906 that if the Agent were resident in Scotland, with an office there, he would be able to keep close links with local parties and dispense advice.[26] In the general review of Unionist organisation in the whole of Britain carried out in 1911 the force of these arguments was accepted. A Scottish Whip was set up with the object of uniting more closely the constituency and parliamentary wings of the party and with the duty of exercising general oversight of party machinery in Scotland.[27]

Constituency parties were subjected to a systematic dissection to pinpoint weaknesses after 1906. A good example is West Aberdeenshire, where a detailed post mortem was conducted among activists to examine why this seat, which had seen spectacular advances by the Unionists in the 1890s, had remained Liberal in 1906 with a majority of 3,158, against 1,139 in 1900. The key themes which emerged from the constituency study were substantially borne out by a special report on all the eastern Scottish seats commissioned by the NUCAS. For the latter, 'the chief weakness which is displayed in every constituency is the apathy of the committee men, most of whom are such in name only. This may be attributed to two causes; first, ignorance of the duties they should perform, and second, slackness on the part of ward, parish or district secretaries'.[28] The parish, or ward, committees, so vital for efficient running of a constituency party, were indeed hopelessly defective. In Berwickshire, no minute books were kept and no regular meetings were held, while in West Renfrewshire there was minimal contact between the parish level and the constituency central body.[29] Too much reliance was placed upon the constituency organiser, and he received inadequate support, especially in those seats where he was not a full-time worker but a local solicitor with limited energy and time.[30]

Besides ramshackle organisation, too many constituency parties had an inadequate social mix. This was partly because the eclipse of the lairds, so pronounced a feature of the 1890s, seems to have been reversed. From West Aberdeenshire, a proponent of reform expressed the difficulty trenchantly:

'Proprietors and factors take a far less prominent part in management'.[31] From the other end of the country, a defeated candidate in Berwickshire in January 1910 contrasted Scotland unfavourably with Lancashire, where he had been M.P. for St Helens between 1885 and 1906. 'In many Scottish Committees', he informed Balfour, 'there is a 'County-family' feeling of exclusiveness still somehow maintained, quite unsuited to these democratic days. The idea is in some fashion conveyed, not intentionally, that the landed proprietors and 'county families' are a class apart and above the middle classes of the county towns, the tenant-farmers, the farm servants and the working classes generally'.[32] The need to make local parties more representative and therefore attractive to new men was recognised as paramount. 'Then we must get the proper kind of members', argued a West Aberdeen Tory. 'What we want is young fellows (married men of course, and householders) who are mixed daily amongst the millworkers. Now this class are mainly all Liberals — our committees are composed of older men who vote all right, but don't exert themselves'.[33] Attempts were made to redress this imbalance, as at Cairnie in West Aberdeenshire, where a token two farm servants were added to the Conservative committee, but it was reported that this did not silence the anti-landlord propaganda used by Liberals to denigrate Unionism.[34]

The re-energising of constituency organisation was generally impressive in its speed and thoroughness. Full-time professional organisers were briskly installed everywhere, the existing part-timers being dispensed with, as in West Aberdeen, where after sixteen years of running the local association the agent was informed in 1907 that he was too old and should step down forthwith.[35] By 1913 there was scarcely a constituency in the east of Scotland without its professional organiser. Parish and ward committees were revived and extended into new areas, as shown by the formation of a Cowcaddens ward by Glasgow College in 1911, and the launching of a Burntisland section in 1909 by Kirkcaldy.[36] The wards were given more scope yet kept in closer touch with constituency officials.[37] By 1909 one Glasgow seat had been divided by the party association into 150 sections of 100 voters, with each member of the executive responsible for three sections.[38] The work of constituencies was carefully monitored by NUCAS, which encouraged improvements with the assistance of the Scottish Conservative Club, which would withhold financial grants until proof of progress was given.[39]

Marked advances were achieved in the effort to bring in new supporters. Membership rose quite appreciably in, for instance, all the Glasgow seats, with four of the seven actually doubling in size between 1901 and 1911. But equally significant was the reaching out to tap the relatively new areas of women, working men and youth. Traditionally the Primrose League had served as the vehicle for involving women in party work, but after 1906 it was increasingly seen as ineffective, probably because of the rapid turnover in adherents and also perhaps because it seemed more interested in social than political activities.[40] There was instead, as in Kincardineshire, a desire to exert direct control over the women's efforts in the belief that they would render 'more real work and assistance than the Primrose League ever gave at an Election'.[41] The new movement seems to have begun in 1906, when the East of Scotland Women's Liberal Unionist Association dropped the word 'Liberal', and thereupon enjoyed a steady accession of Conservative women members. Within two years some twenty-two constituency branches had affiliated, with the largest, West Aberdeenshire, claiming 1900 members in 1909.[42] In the west, the process was slightly slower, for while some, notably West Renfrew and Mid Lanark, had formed women's wings around 1906–8, most of the Glasgow seats only moved after 1910.[43] Unlike the Primrose League, much of the work centred on political education: over the years Kinross women heard a series of lectures on the leading issues of the day and, as was stated of the first meeting, 'By their close attention those present testified to their interest in the lecture and the earnestness of their desire to learn the rudiments of political warfare'.[44] The other portion of their work was in dealing with registration and distributing literature (which they had totally taken over in West Renfrew by 1911), but they were not much used in canvassing or street meetings.[45]

There was a widespread feeling that Unionism was failing to capture the imagination of the young, and this was aired in the press.[46] Unionist Clubs, offering billiards and card games, which had been the mainstay of support in the 1890s, were in decline as a result of economic and social change. West Renfrew Tories noted in 1910: 'The Political Clubs (10 in number) are still being carried on, but generally speaking your Committee regret that these institutions do not prove the useful political factor they did before the advent of tramways and easy locomotion between the village and towns, and the greater facilities for enjoyment and recreation now provided for the young men of the villages'. An indication of the problem was the case of Barrhead, whose club membership had dropped from 308 in 1903 to 142 six years later.[47] The remedy, as seen by West Renfrew, was easier to prescribe than to fulfil: Tories should 'induce more of the young men to become interested and enthusiastic in the general work of the party'.[48] In Glasgow, the solution was to create branches of the Junior Imperial Unionist League, which flourished best, apparently, in working-class areas like Bridgeton and Camlachie, where League members were active in holding open-air meetings on the eve of war.[49] While the Junior Imperialists do not seem to have been as active as their Liberal counterparts, the Young Scots, their existence does testify to the resilience of the party and indicate the extent to which it was endeavouring to recover lost ground in the years before the war.

Winning working-class men to Unionism was a prime objective in the post-1906 scheme. Two approaches were to be developed. On the one hand, propaganda was carefully angled towards working men and, on the other, organisations with a specific working-class appeal were initiated. There was a clear opinion that the proletariat would prove responsive to tariff reform and general anti-socialism if the message was projected in the correct manner. Firstly, speakers to working-class audiences were to be, wherever possible, of the same class. The Conservative Club put up £100 p.a. from 1909 to help pay for trade union lecturers, and NUCAS used this cash to employ W. P. Templeton, a woodturner from Falkirk, who spoke throughout Scotland. Templeton was widely regarded as successful in his work, and his efforts were supplemented by others. Willie Dyson, an English National Union working man speaker, gave an effective address in 1908 on tariff reform and socialism to shipyard workers in Yoker. In Kincardineshire a year earlier, several working men spoke from the platform at a series of Unionist meetings, and produced the view that 'the speakers were capable men and had a very good reception from the audiences addressed'.[50]

The other weapon used in the propaganda campaign was the inculcation of Unionist principles through the press. The power of Liberal journals — notably the *People's Journal* and the *Daily Record* in the rural east and urban west respectively — was regularly blamed for Unionist difficulties.[51] Initially the counterblast was sporadic and uncoordinated. The Conservative Club gave £100 to assist a NUCAS scheme to place anti-socialist articles in the *Glasgow Weekly Herald*, which would then be distributed to 'publicans, innkeepers, blacksmiths, hairdressers and certain selected radicals'.[52] In 1913, however, a major breakthrough was achieved with the appearance of *The People's Politics*, which was designed to be read by working men and was wholly devoted to advocating the Unionist cause. At first, only 10,000 copies were to be disposed of by local parties, but within six months in the west of Scotland alone 55,000 copies were required to satisfy demand.[53]

Some constituencies seem to have enrolled working men as ordinary members: for instance, Glasgow Blackfriars and Hutchesontown claimed in 1910 that they formed 'a large preponderance' of the association. But more success was claimed for the device of creating separate organisations specifically fashioned to enlist working-class Unionists. In Glasgow, in the aftermath of the January 1910 elections, when it was reported that 'working men were in many cases somewhat disenchanted through the lack of sufficient encouragement', and young men were felt to have been 'not perhaps fully utilised', the Democratic Unionist Association was created to meet these needs. Its aims were 'to advocate Unionist principles by democratic propaganda, especially with regard to social reform and the development and defence of the industrial interests of the British Empire', and to demonstrate that Unionism was the friend of the working class because it promulgated these goals without fomenting class hatred. Its work involved establishing political libraries, training speakers and holding meetings around Glasgow. Within one year it claimed to have enrolled 500 members.[54] The Workers' League was a body intended to cover all of Scotland and was founded under NUCAS auspices — also in 1910. The League was to train speakers and form lodges for its members in constituencies. It is not apparent whether the undertones of Orangeism are intentional in the word 'lodge'.[55] By 1911 a West of Scotland Unionist asserted that the Workers' League was achieving much, but little more was heard of it thereafter.[56] Certainly by 1913 there was a new body in existence, secretly financed by the Scottish Unionists. This was the Scottish Labour Federation, which had 3,000 adherents at the outset, and was expected to have 5,000 shortly thereafter. The Federation engaged in extensive agitation at factory gates and street corners to repudiate socialism by denouncing it as anti-religious and by calling for a trade union movement devoted to industrial peace and social reform along the lines put forward by Unionist leaders. It is not easy to gauge how effective its good works were, as the only full report of its operations was written by the organisers, but the Federation did receive a further grant of £100 from the Conservative Club in 1914 in recognition of its important work.[57]

These wide-ranging and imaginative schemes left the Unionists in a dilemma after the general elections of 1910. By then, party organisation in most seats had been developed to new heights of efficiency, and so the failure to record many gains from the Liberals had therefore to be assigned to other factors, and two solutions were suggested.[58] One answer was to step up propaganda work, not just that produced for consumption by working men, but also in order to reach a broader audience. Kincardineshire Conservatives perhaps carried this furthest. They resolved not to contest the seat in December 1910, but instead to concentrate on a three-year programme of educational work, which was to be funded by a special annual grant of £150. In that period, regular meetings were held to expound Unionism, and a newspaper (*The Mearns Leader*) was launched to spread the Tory evangel.[59] In the West of Scotland in 1913, 50,000 leaflets were distributed to electors, and 165 meetings were held in a similar propaganda blitz.[60] The Unionists were therefore determined not to despair in their commitment to victory, and little sense of defeatism was being shown despite the 1910 electoral disappointments.

Another upshot of the 1910 elections was a sweeping reform of the central organisation of Conservatism, part of a process also carried out in England. As we saw, the creation of a Scottish Whip was part of this shake-up. Merger with the Liberal Unionists was deemed more necessary than ever, and by 1911 the initiative was with the Conservatives, as the Liberal Unionists were much weaker in organisation. Financially, their base was very narrow. In the West of Scotland Association after 1906, there were only three large subscribers, and the death in 1912 of the head of the Coats family removed by far the biggest contributor.[61] The decline in support as the older generation died off continued to wreak damage in previously thriving areas like Dunbartonshire, and in 1911 an internal memorandum confessed that outside Glasgow and environs 'there are not really any effective Liberal Unionist organisations in existence'. Even within Glasgow there were symptoms of decline. Glasgow College, in 1886 the most vigorous of all, 'had fallen asleep' by 1910.[62] Efforts to resuscitate constituency activity were usually abortive, as when a meeting to start up again in Ayrshire South flopped, although 'probably the Golf Championship at Prestwick had something to do with it'.[63] In many seats, indeed, this problem had been acknowledged by the merging of the two Unionist parties. This trend, began in 1902 or so, had accelerated after 1906, and by 1911 at least a dozen had done so, and although Liberal Unionists in particular insisted that these were only temporary mergers, it was very rare for these to be reversed.

These difficulties on the Liberal Unionist side served to intensify the constant friction over candidates and seats. The Tories constantly complained about the dilatoriness of their fellow Unionists in producing nominees for those seats which lay within the Liberal Unionist patrimony. In Edinburgh East the inability of Liberal Unionists to find a man by the end of 1904 led the Conservatives to warn that they would run someone if no prompt action took place. In 1908, this was repeated in North-East Lanarkshire, where the Liberal Unionists reported in alarm: 'No candidate in sight. The Conservatives are so pushing all along the line, that we must do something or be cut off'. In the following year the Tories put up H. J. MacKinder for Glasgow Tradeston, a traditional Liberal Unionist seat, in protest at Liberal Unionist indecision. By January 1912, almost all the seats in the West of Scotland, except Glasgow St Rollox, had Conservative candidates, and even in that sole seat the Tories were pressing for a joint initiative.[64]

Yet the Scottish Liberal Unionists did not enter into amalgamation with unbridled enthusiasm. The main worry was fully explained in a memorandum compiled in 1903, just before the tariff reform row erupted, by the Western Association. The 'wavering' of Liberal Unionist votes, it argued, was disturbing, especially as the Liberals had downgraded Irish Home Rule, so that there might well be a drift back. The best means of forestalling this was to retain the separate identity of Liberal Unionism. A plan to have Chamberlain speak in Glasgow under the banner of both Unionist parties was therefore rejected, as it would only 'give colour to a profound and widespread impression that the Liberal Unionists of the west are no longer a distinct party, but part and parcel of the Conservative party'.[65] After the 1906 election, a proposal to join with the Tories was not seen as feasible, and even in 1911 there was still resistance to the idea. Steel-Maitland and Younger were told that the western Liberal Unionists wished to remain independent, in order to 'emphasise the point that Liberal Unionists were constructive politicians and Conservatives were defensive politicians by born nature'.[66] Two extra factors had now entered the equation, however. Some important Liberal Unionists, led by Parker-Smith, after the experience of fighting seats with two Unionist parties, had become convinced of the greater efficiency which would flow from having one united Unionist organisation in each constituency.[67] Secondly, fears that the gathering power of the Tories would soon result in the swamping of Liberal Unionists led to the conclusion that better terms might be secured for a merger if the Liberal Unionists co-operated. But unease about the extinction of a Liberal Unionist identity remained. The Eastern Association, always more favourable to liaison with the Conservatives than in the West, pronounced itself opposed to a merger, until the formation of a united Unionist party in England and Wales left little option but to accept a *fait accompli*, albeit reluctantly.[68] The Western Association acceded to going in with the Tories in October 1912, after taking care to ensure that one third of all committee posts would be earmarked for former members of its party in the early years of the new body. Its final report still took a defiant line, insisting that 'Liberal Unionism, embodying the root principles of the old Liberal party, retains its hold in the west of Scotland.[69]

The Scottish Unionist Association, formed in 1912, therefore incorporated both parties and hoped to reap considerable benefits. There was indeed much activity, notably in propaganda work like the *People's Politics*. By February 1914 candidates had been selected for all but one of the West of Scotland constituencies. But the Unionist machine may not have been quite as efficient as it appeared. The merger had not eliminated the Liberal Unionist identity. In 1922 a Unionist M.P. remarked: 'I never was a Tory, but from 1907 when I entered politics as a Liberal Unionist I have held to that view, only accepting Toryism as modified by it'.[70] Even if no strong animosity existed, the exercise of carrying through the merger must have diverted time and energy from direct political work. The level of improvement among local parties is difficult to estimate. There are clear examples of a new vigour, as in West Aberdeenshire, where in 1914 the prospective candidate was holding four meetings a week, and in Kincardineshire, where by 1913 the apathy induced by the 1910 elections had been shrugged off. The registers were by then well maintained, and regular political meetings were being held.[71]

It is possible, however, to point to less satisfactory aspects, one of which was finance. Many constituency associations still depended on a few very large subscribers, as for instance West Renfrew, where the death of Lord Blythswood resulted in a loss of one quarter of the party's annual income.[72] In 1909 in East Lothian only thirty landowners contributed, and their total came to £100. This seems to have been typical of the east of Scotland, for in 1913 Lord Dalkeith complained about the 'inadequate' level of financial commitment shown in most seats.[73] Younger confirmed this when he drew attention to the reliance of Scottish Conservatives on 'a good deal' of cash support from national funds in London.[74] Morale was not always high. The East Fife candidate despaired in 1914 of his party workers — 'timid and impossible people ... *chicken-hearted*' — while a party report shortly before noted with unease the 'lack of cordiality which was apparent to the candidate in many instances' among supporters.[75] Despite the claims made in 1910 that they were at maximum efficiency, several constituency parties were found to be gravely defective after 1910. In 1912, three of the five Edinburgh and Leith seats were deemed unsatisfactory, and in that same year West Fife 'for various reasons' was in a deplorable state. Early in 1914, Mid Lothian (a Conservative seat after 1912) was still lethargic; in the Liberal marginal seat of Roxburghshire there had still not been a canvass of supporters as a prelude of instituting a new Unionist Association; and Peebles and Selkirk, another highly marginal Liberal seat, was inadequately developed.[76]

III

Next to the Unionists themselves, the greatest political casualty of the tariff reform movement was Liberal Imperialism. After the 1900 election rout and Rosebery's Chesterfield speech in December 1901, which heralded the frontal challenge to official Liberalism, the Liberal League mounted a full-scale attack on the established party in Scotland.[77] As in the prelude to the 1900 election, the focus of Liberal Imperialist effort was in the areas of organisation, policy and candidates. At the very start of 1901 Haldane began these moves in Glasgow, where he found a good local organiser who was given the duty of forming branches. Grey delivered a major speech in the city in December 1901, and exactly one year after his first foray, Haldane reported his pleasure in progress made in the west to Rosebery.[78] In Edinburgh, where Haldane detected that 'pro-Boerism is stronger in reality than in Glasgow', developments were less rapid. By late 1902, however, after Rosebery had been induced to make a speech to advance the cause, a branch was set up in the capital, complete with offices and a zealous secretary.[79] With rival organisations in the two major cities, the Liberal League was obviously challenging the power of the Scottish Liberal Association (SLA). At times the strategy of the former was one of boycott: 'In Scotland they have held aloof from the general party meetings and functions, and confined their attendance and support exclusively to Grey's and Asquith's meetings and those of their own set', Gladstone learned.[80] At other times the opposite approach was preferred: 'I'm not sure', wrote the immediate past Chairman of the SLA, 'but I think that there's a chance of capturing the organisation, or at any rate in making it split in such a way that there'll be nothing worth having left'.[81] There were indeed many who suspected that Haldane, Munro Ferguson and Dr C. M. Douglas, the League's chief Scottish organiser, were conspiring to undermine the vitality of Liberal associations so as to engineer a secession from the SLA.[82] The SLA retaliated by trying to prevent Liberal Imperiaists from operating under official party auspices, but these efforts diverted attention from the need to reorganise the party generally after the 1900 electoral setback.[83]

The incessant activities of the League infuriated the party leadership. At different times Campbell-Bannerman referred to their Scottish efforts as 'untiring', 'intolerable', and felt they caused 'much devilment' from being 'actively hostile'.[84] Herbert Gladstone was despondent in autumn 1902: 'The League seems to occupy the field in Scotland so far as organisation goes'.[85] But it is not clear if the threat was as grave as he feared. Inside the League, all was not sanguine. The paid organiser told Rosebery only a few months later, 'I am seriously concerned at Scotch affairs. Positively we are making no progress and opportunities are being lost'.[86] Despite the support it received from wealthy men like Sir Charles Tennant and Sir Thomas Glen-Coats, finances were not good. Rosebery complained that 'Scotland does not give us a shilling — indeed it extracts what it can from our meagre funds', but his scheme to get nine Scots to put up £1,000 each was dismissed by Haldane as hopelessly facile; Haldane thought it more realistic to raise that sum among thirty men.[87]

The size of support for Liberal Imperialism is not easy to ascertain. The Edinburgh Liberal League had 340 members at the outset, a not inconsiderable following, but incapable of comparison with official Liberal support in the city.[88] As important as numbers, at least in the eyes of the Liberal Imperial leaders, was the quality of backing gained. In Glasgow, Haldane noted, prominent businessmen who had long withdrawn from active Liberal work had re-entered. These included Joseph Maclay, and ex-Lord Provost Sir James Bell, both very large shipowners, and Robert Lorimer, head of a huge locomotive building concern. Equally striking, for the first time since 1886, Glasgow University professors, including Jones, Phillimore, Gray and Barker, committed themselves to the Liberal side.[89] The success of the League in recruiting those who had remained indifferent to orthodox Liberalism was in part due to its policy stance. The stress in Liberal Imperialism on efficiency doubtless evoked interest among businessmen, but that section of Rosebery's Chesterfield speech which reappraised the priority to be given to Irish Home Rule also elicited a positive response. Haldane had stated from the beginning that his plan of campaign in launching the League in Glasgow would be to stress that Rosebery and his followers 'explicity exclude the Home Rule policy of 86 and 93 as having been made impossible by the action of the Irish'. The impact of this approach was confirmed by Lorimer: 'I had been alienated from my old party not only by the Irish Home Rule proposals but also by the methods of the Irish. Your Chesterfield speech, to my great delight, revived the hope of co-operation with my old friends . . . '[90]

Even if Liberal Imperialism did not establish a vigorous grassroots organisation, its challenge to orthodox Liberalism could also be sustained by getting League candidates adopted for seats. When this happened, as could easily be managed in those seats where party machinery was thin, mainstream Liberals were placed in the dilemma of either voting for a man whose policies were unpalatable, or of abstaining and so ensuring a Unionist win. The North-East Lanarkshire by-election of 1901 showed this problem starkly. Harmsworth, a strong Liberal Imperialist, secured the nomination, but lost the seat, to Bannerman's delight. It was moreover widely believed that many Bannermanites voted for Smillie, the Labour candidate, or else did not poll.[91] As a result of this episode, Liberal headquarters tried to vet applications from prospective candidates more stringently. By 1903, this seemed to be working. 'We are completely checked in Scotland', complained Munro Ferguson, 'by want of candidates, where the supply of them is the only safeguard against humiliation, the CBites having a free hand in dealing with constituencies, while we have not'.[92] Although one or two Liberal Imperialist candidates were smuggled in, only nine of the Scottish Liberal M.P.s returned in 1906 were identified as such. Nevertheless the potential for trouble was extensive, as the Orkney and Shetland by-election of 1902 showed. Here the official Liberal candidate, MacKinnon Wood, was opposed by J. C. Wason, the sitting Liberal Unionist M.P., who now styled himself an 'Independent Liberal' and was enthusiastically helped by C. M. Douglas, the Liberal League organiser in Scotland. To the general consternation of the Liberal leaders, Wason retained the seat.[93]

That such internal strife did not continue was probably due less to the organisational blocking of Liberal Imperialism by the SLA than to the launching of the tariff reform crusade. At once the Liberals drew together at all levels. The SLA convened a meeting in Glasgow in defence of free trade in the summer of 1903, in which all wings of the party were invited to participate, with a direct approach made to the League. A joint organising committee was formed, and the successful collaboration was followed late in 1904 by the wings of the party combining to co-ordinate work at the general election.[94] Evidence of this new unity abounded. The Bannermanite leaders invited Rosebery to agree to permit

R

one of his sons to stand for Mid Lothian, so evocative a seat for all Liberals, and when Rosebery consented, all sections backed Lord Dalmeny warmly.[95] After a lapse in correspondence of some five years' duration, Munro Ferguson patched up his quarrel with Campbell-Bannerman over the former's Liberal Imperialist sympathies while acting as Scottish Whip. During the 1906 election campaign Ferguson assured his leader that he looked forward to being returned for Leith as the supporter of a free trade government.[96] Campbell-Bannerman enthused at the spectacle of Liberal Leaguers speaking at meetings alongside their former Liberal antagonists, and the most astonishing sight of all was the presence of C. M. Douglas sharing a platform with orthodox Liberals at a Scottish Free Trade League meeting in January 1904.[97] Although in 1905 Munro Ferguson and others wished to keep the Liberal League alive in Scotland as a means of exerting power over a future Liberal government, little activity ensued. Instead, the League wound itself up very quickly after the 1906 election in Scotland, closing its Edinburgh office in May of that year. This was well in advance of the demise of the English League, and suggests the Liberal party in Scotland was more united than in England in 1906.[98]

<h2 style="text-align:center">IV</h2>

The acute setbacks suffered by Unionism and the eclipse of Liberal Imperialism promoted the Liberal recovery after 1903 and their sweeping victory in the 1906 contest. How far this was a temporary respite, largely due to exogenous factors, rather than to any significant re-shaping of the Liberal party, has been a matter of scholarly debate.[99] In October 1902, Lord Tweedmouth, the incoming President of the Scottish Liberal Association, 'expressed surprise' at various defects in the party's organisation. A report was presented to the SLA at that meeting of the responses to a questionnaire circulated among constituency associations. Of the 31 in the west of Scotland, one fifth (6) had no central constituency organisation; only one half (16) had an Executive Committee 'thoroughly representative of the constituency'; and in only 13 seats was it felt that the constituency was 'adequately covered' by local committees. In the 35 east of Scotland associations the position was less critical, (although one fifth (7) gave no reply, probably indicating the absence of any organisation), with almost all respondents satisfied with the representativeness and efficiency of constituency parties.[100] Between 1902 and the 1906 election there was a good deal of reconstruction and overhauling of party machinery under Tweedmouth's direction. The Master of Elibank built up Mid Lothian to a peak of efficiency which he maintained for nearly a decade, as well as performing similar feats in Peebles and Selkirk.[101] His work was only one instance of a widespread resolve to revitalise the party, not just to sit back and rely on a tidal wave of disaffected Unionist Free Traders to deliver a Liberal majority. Seats which the last of the lairds had controlled through a personal network of support were the objects of particular attention. In East Perthshire, the new candidate found that 'everything under Kinloch had gone to sleep', for, as the Scottish Whip added, 'he does not I think realise how greatly organisation has improved since he began'.[102] Also, in Aberdeenshire East, the new candidate found in 1902 that the condition of the local party 'bordered on paralysis', and he set about reviving it, to win handsomely in 1906.[103] After a tour of the eastern area in the late summer of 1905, the SLA Secretary reported that organisation in the vast majority of seats was in a very healthy state and drew attention to the new energy being manifested on all sides.[104]

The great victory of 1906 did not lead to complacency, and improvements in party machinery were constantly sought thereafter. Bannerman's death in 1908 afforded the opportunity to set up a Stirling Burghs Liberal Association which would be 'representative of all the Burghs, [and] which would enable it to give expression to its views and to take concerted action with regard to a candidate in a more businesslike way than had been the case in the past'.[105] Edinburgh West was urged to put its organisation on a proper footing in 1906, and in Roxburghshire no effort was spared to keep the party in full fighting trim to resist Unionist designs on the seat.[106] In the January 1910 contest, the *Glasgow Herald*, no friend to the party, praised the quality of Liberal organisation in places as far apart as Sutherland, Wigtownshire, Hawick and Montrose.[107] The attempts to improve standards continued after 1910, as seats with defective organisation were badgered by the SLA to appoint organisers to tackle their problems properly. Such seats included West Perthshire, St Andrews and West Fife.[108] While these instances disclose a far from perfect organisation — probably the Unionists were better equipped in most seats — what is significant is that the Liberal party was acting with determination to try to eliminate defects, as at Leith, where after the loss of the seat at a by-election in February 1914 it was stated that local machinery was in the process of being overhauled and 'brought up to date'.[109] A good example of this pattern after 1910 is Glasgow Bridgeton, where the new M.P., MacCallum Scott, found that there was very little organisation. Much depended on the association's secretary, whom he dissuaded from resigning, and encouraged to keep 'pegging away' at developing party activity.[110] By 1913 Scott saw results — 'I have at last got the Liberal Association doing some work' — and the following year he praised the secretary for further improvements.[111] In Aberdeen, the Liberal Association languished between 1908 and 1911. The strongly Liberal ward of Rosemount in 1909 observed that 'in the present circumstances, all attempts at organising would, we believe, be futile'. However, by 1913 the party had stirred itself, and planned an aggressive publicity campaign to recruit support and to persuade voters of the justice of the Liberal government's legislative programme.[112]

More precisely quantifiable assessments of Liberal organisational strength are available to some degree. Thus membership was not everywhere in decline in the pre-war decade. Dundee increased its membership from 1,100 in 1907 to 1,279 in 1908 (about 15%); Glasgow Central rose from 662 in 1904–5 to 1,020 the next year. A small town like Galashiels could produce 120 party workers in 1905.[113] But these examples are all taken from the high point of Liberalism. In 1911 MacCallum Scott found the utmost difficulty in persuading Bridgeton Liberals to turn out to distribute leaflets, indicating a lethargic support.[114] While no membership figures are available for the last few pre-war years, when Liberal fortunes were ebbing, subscription levels can in part be helpful. As late as 1913 the Glasgow Liberal Council recorded a record number of subscribers and also the highest amount raised thereby. Subscriptions to the national organisation confirm the trend. In 1907 the East of Scotland section of the SLA had 1,273 renewed subscribers and 166 new ones, a total of 1,439; in 1911 the figures are 1,348 continuing, 176 new, making a total of 1,524. In the West, whereas in 1907 there were 844 subscribers (695 continuing, 149 new), in 1911 there were 962 (826 continuing, 126 new).[115] Against these evidences of a steady level of financial strength must be placed some cases of weakness. The Bridgeton Liberal Association could not meet the £10 annual registration costs in 1912; while in 1911 St Andrews Liberals could not guarantee to find £30 to pay for an organiser.[116] On the whole, however, the picture until the outbreak of war is of the routine work of local parties being carried on without any appreciable diminution. The general temper and spirit of the party may be gauged from Bridgeton where in 1914, despite its problems, MacCallum was encouraging consideration of new devices to reach voters. A supporter suggested that workers should be addressed at factory gates, which was eagerly leapt on: 'I believe there is something in it. I would reach quite a different class from the loafers who hang about a Cross Meeting, and there would be no Junior Imperialist horseplay. It might also spike the guns of the Labour Party'.[117]

The important groups of women and young men, both essential for the future health of the Liberal party, were also in a rude state of health on the eve of war. The Scottish Women's Liberal Federation (SWLF) was invaluable in the 1910 elections, canvassing and dealing with registration work, as well as providing a panel of 40 speakers, all of whom were regularly employed during the year. There were no signs of a deceleration in support in the women's work: in 1904 the SWLF had 11,000 members in 70 branches, but by 1914 this had increased to 25,000 in 174 branches, with most of the upsurge occurring after 1908, when 103 branches contained 14,291 members.[118] A measure of the levels of activity in these branches, in order to test whether a live organism existed behind these statistics, may be drawn from branch reports inserted in the *Scottish Women's Liberal Magazine.* In 1909, 75 branches are reported as holding 132 meetings, and in 1913, 87 branches met on 148 occasions. Equally relevant is the geographical distribution and level of activity, to indicate whether Liberalism was being driven out of the urban centres into the periphery. In 1909 the north-east and Highlands area had 18 branches, holding 28 meetings between them, but by 1913 this had dropped to 6 branches and 11 meetings. In the urban-industrial west Lowlands (Glasgow and the counties of Ayr, Lanark and Renfrew), whereas in 1909, 55 meetings were held by 25 branches, by 1913, 39 branches held 64 meetings. Similarly, Edinburgh and the Lothians, which in 1909 had been less active than the rural north, with only 4 branches and 10 meetings, had overtaken the latter by 1913 with 10 branches and 20 meetings.

The Liberal party organisation for younger men was an even more remarkable and growing success. The Young Scots were formed immediately after the 1900 election defeat, as the result of a letter in the *Edinburgh Evening News* which called for a movement to reach young Liberal men. At a meeting in Edinburgh on 26 October 1900, it was resolved to form a society 'for the purpose of educating young men in the fundamental principles of Liberalism and of encouraging and stimulating them in the study of social science and economics'.[119] The society grew steadily, and, like the women's body, did not falter in the immediate pre-war period. In 1909 there were 29 branches, by 1912, 49. Membership is only listed for 1910, when 2,500 were enrolled, a figure said to be double the 1909 level.[120] This compares with the ILP's 143 branches and between 2,500 and 3,000 members in Scotland in 1910. Most of the Young Scots branches in 1912 were to be found in industrial centres. Glasgow and the four western counties of Ayr, Dunbarton, Lanark and Renfrew had one half (23), while the Highlands and north-east had only one seventh (7).

The role of the Young Scots was twofold: one was to spread ideas and formulate policies (which is discussed later), the other was to help in organisational effort, in which they proved invaluable. Between 1903 and 1906 they were central to the free trade campaign on Scotland, organising meetings and distributing literature. Haldane observed in 1904 of the Young Scots: 'They are the only body that is actively at work in Scotland and we need every battalion to fight an enemy that has already got ahead of us'. Harcourt also praised the Young Scots in that year for their work, and Bannerman commended them for their 'invaluable work' during the 1906 election.[121] In 1911–12 they were still very involved in this work, when a vigorous propaganda campaign saw five leaflets issued in the year and 83 speakers on their list. Their activity at elections remained the most noteworthy aspect of their work, and in 1910 they concentrated on Unionist-held seats and Liberal marginals. Their influence at by-elections was great. At Ayr North in 1911 they sent in 'numerous' workers, and at Mid Lothian in 1912 the Liberal agent was delighted to see young men in large numbers working everywhere throughout the constituency.[122] The most emphatic testimonials to the impact of the Young Scots came from Unionists. The future Unionist organiser in the Borders recalled their role in the pre-war years: 'For many years this Society was the spearhead of the Liberal attack in Scotland. In almost every town there was a branch and a vigorous activity was carried on ... It was subtle propaganda but in its way extremely effective'.[123] In North Ayrshire the Unionist chairman remarked after the 1911 by-election that his party would need to get its organisation into good working order, 'especially by bringing in more of the younger generation than they had been bringing in recently to oppose the Young Scots and others on the Radical side who had made their fight so strenuous'.[124] A further contribution to the general health of the party by the Young Scots was in the provision of a rising generation of M.P.s and candidates. J. W. Gulland and J. M. Hogge, both Chief Whips of the party, had been early office bearers in the society.

No slackening in the efficiency and vigilance of the central Scottish Liberal body, the SLA, is obvious in the period. The Secretary, W. W. Webster, had held his position since the 1890s and was experienced and competent. The assistant secretaries were highly esteemed for their detailed knowledge of constituency matters and were invaluable at co-ordinating general election operations.[125] Until the start of the war the SLA kept up its main role of inducing constituencies to put their machinery onto a businesslike footing, and in 1910 did much to sponsor a major step forward by establishing a Scottish Liberal Agents Association. This was designed to professionalise the agents, who had to pass an examination before being admitted.[126] Propaganda work was likewise maintained. In 1911 it organised lecture tours in the Borders on free trade and Scottish Home Rule; in 1912, Irish Home Rule was the subject of a speaking campaign; and in 1914 a Land Campaign Committee expedition was planned — along with another Scottish Home Rule tour — in the east of Scotland.[127]

V

As important for the long-term future of the Liberal party as the vitality of its organisation were two related questions. First of all, there is the issue whether the party had managed to adjust its policies from a commitment to traditional Liberal demands to those of social reform, in order to win back voters (especially working-class ones) on a permanent basis, as distinct from the temporary recruits produced by tariff reform. Linked to this is the question of how favourably these changes in policy direction were received by the party rank and file and also by Scottish M.P.s.

The two old-fashioned issues, which had predominated in late nineteenth-century Scottish Liberalism were of course disestablishment and temperance. The union in 1900 of the Free and United Presbyterian Churches, prime advocates of disestablishment, removed much of the pressure of the Church of Scotland. Many Free Church anti-disestablishers, like Andrew Jameson, Lord Ardwall, remained quite happily in the new United Free Church, because they felt that disestablishment was now irrelevant.[128] In addition, the Boer War had turned attention away from the question of state-church relations, as the Disestablishment Council for Scotland admitted.[129] Principal Robert Rainy, the foremost clerical champion of disestablishment and head of the UFC, revealed the declining importance of the issue when he exchanged opinions in September 1900 with his son, who had just been selected as Liberal candidate for Kilmarnock: 'P.S. — would it not be well to take the line of *asserting* that religious equality *must* come to the fore again ere long?' His son replied by reporting on the state of public opinion in the constituencies: 'Land Values, Temperance and Religious Equality come in opposite order to the importance I attach to them. I confess the moral questions interest me most'.[130]

In 1904, however, Rainy senior was forced to admit that the demand for religious equality had made little progress in the present circumstances since the nadir of 1900.[131] One reason was the free trade controversy, but equally important was the legal case involving the UFC. The minority of the Free Church, which had declined to merge in 1900 and instead maintained a separate identity, successfully sustained in the law courts their claim to ownership of all the property of the pre-1900 Free Church. The only means by which the majority (now in the UFC) could hope to achieve redress was by persuading the Government to reverse the courts' decision by legislation. The consequences of the Free Church case for the political cause of disestablishment were totally negative. Firstly, there was the paradox of the UFC which justified the case for disestablishment by denying the right of the civil magistrate to interfere in church matters, being obliged and willing to call in the selfsame civil magistrate to its aid. This strengthened the opinion of many that disestablishment was politically and morally no longer tenable.[132] Liberal politicians on the other hand drew clear conclusions from the episode, most of which counselled caution about getting at all involved. Partly this was because, as Campbell-Bannerman put it, the whole question was too beset with old enmities to be easily solved, and partly because some felt that if the Unionist government were left to itself, it would alienate both Church sides in its efforts to deal with the difficulty, and so doubly benefit the Liberals.[133] The need for cautious handling of the topic penetrated even the General Council of the SLA, normally a fervent supporter of religious equality. At its annual policy-making meeting in October 1904 the Chairman intimated that it had been decided to withdraw the customary resolution 'in view of the present difficulties and excitements, especially in the Highlands'.[134]

As indicated by that speech, the peculiarity of the Highlands was an additional factor operating to remove disestablishment from the immediate agenda of Liberal policies. The 'Wee Frees' were strong in the Highlands: 144 of their 190 congregations were north of the Highland line, and they constituted some 10% of the religious adherents in the Highlands. The Wee Frees were solidly anti-disestablishment, as were the Free Presbyterians, the Episcopalians and the Church of Scotland. The last body had been growing markedly since the 1890s, so that a careful survey in 1902 described the state church as 'distinctly the strongest body in the Highlands'. In all, these opponents of disestablishment constituted 57% of the Highland church population.[135] The eight Highland seats were very important for the Liberals: in the debacle of 1900, almost all were marginal on one side or the other.[136] It was therefore necessary to avoid the contentious topic of disestablishment if these seats were to be won for Liberalism. In the Ayr Burghs by-election of 1904, the silence of the Liberal candidate on the Church question was explained by the large Wee Free vote in Oban, Campbeltown and Inveraray, and this tactic may well have contributed to the Liberal capture of the seat by 44 votes.[137] Instead of the Church, the free trade question was played to the full in the Highlands: in the 1906 election in North Uist, a Wee Free stronghold which had gone Unionist in 1900, the Unionist *Glasgow Herald* detected 'a strong feeling among the crofters against Protection'.[138]

With the return of the Liberals to office, the SLA reverted to its traditional stance, unanimously urging the severance of state links with the Church of Scotland within the lifetime of the government.[139] Little heed was paid to this, and by 1909 disestablishment was seen on all sides as having been cast aside, as the foremost propagandist of the cause, the Rev. B. Martin, confessed: 'The multiplicity of important new public questions, home and foreign, have had the effect of throwing somewhat into the shade older questions — such as Disestablishment — long debated and matured for treatment'.[140] One cause of the loss of support, in addition to the points made by Martin, was that the full logic of the Free Church case had begun to work itself out. Many in both the Church of Scotland and the UFC concluded that reunion was the only possible outcome of these events, and the Church Union Society began to attract widespread support. In 1907 the Church of Scotland raised the question of reunion, and in 1909 the UFC General Assembly agreed in principle to enter into negotiations for a full merger on the establishment basis. Principal Rainy's son recognised this new context in a letter to *The Times* of 6 October 1909: 'I frankly confess that as a practical question and for the reasons given above [i.e. the church union movement], it is for the time being dormant'.[141]

The steady push to full church union had a devastating impact on the Disestablishment Council for Scotland. Its annual income fell from £797 in 1899–1900 to £468 in 1908–9 and to £193 in 1910–11, and after 1909 its journal, the *Disestablishment Banner*, ceased to appear monthly, instead coming out annually.[142] At the 1912 UFC General Assembly only thirteen voted against the detailed proposals for union, and the cause of religious liberty had effectively passed from the Scottish political scene. In that year the SLA by only one vote decided to keep it as an issue for immediate legislation rather than assigning it to be dealt with by a Scottish Home Rule Parliament.[143] Neither the Women Liberals nor the Young Scots, with 40 and 83 speakers respectively in 1911–12, offered a single lecture on the topic, and the *Liberal Women's Magazine*, which between 1907 and 1914 carried 189 articles on Liberal policy, did not have any on the Church question. John Buchan — admittedly not an impartial observer — summed up in 1913: 'The high flying doctrine of spiritual (which includes temporal) independence has faded today out of the intellectual air ... The old tenets of the Liberation Society have few adherents today north of the Tweed'.[144]

Temperance was never dropped quite so dramatically from the party's policy slate. The SLA continued to proclaim its necessity in annual resolutions right up to the start of the war. Among the topics offered by the eighty-three Young Scots speakers, it came fourth, with eight willing to lecture on it, and it came second, after female suffrage, on the Women's list of forty, with ten ready to talk on it. The *Women's Magazine* also printed several articles on the topic. Its retention, unlike disestablishment, was probably not a great vote loser, at least not in the sense of driving working men seeking a realistic solution to social problems into the Labour Party, for the ILP element in particular was taunchly teetotal, notably Tom Johnston and Willie Graham. The latter was once mortified when a waiter in a restaurant brought him not the glass of water he had ordered, but a glass of Watney's. Even after the war the ILP in Scotland retained a strong prohibitionist policy, as at the 1923 Scottish conference, where delegates voted by a two to one margin for prohibition in preference to the alternative of public ownership of the drink trade.[145]

As we saw, the challenge to free trade provoked a strong response in Scotland between 1903 and 1906, and this might suggest that there would be little sympathy for the transition to social reform measures which so preoccupied the Liberal administration after 1908. The SLA, however, duly pronounced in favour of the individual items in the legislative programme. In 1911 an amendment calling for a Royal Commission to enquire into how injury to legitimate interests could be averted before the National Insurance bill was carried found no seconder.[146] However, it could be argued that the SLA by its nature was not likely to be overly critical of a Liberal government's legislation, and that grass-roots opinion might be divergent. As a sign of this, the SLA's vote on the Osborne decision revealed a less than wholehearted commitment to promoting the rights of labour, which the progressive movement required. The SLA was split equally on a vote between one resolution calling for resistance to any bid by unions to amend the judgement through legislation and another urging the conceding to the unions of 'all reasonable grounds of complaint', provided that the rights of individual members were not interfered with. Finally, a heavy majority opted for 'upholding the law as defined in the Osborne Judgement, so as to defend the political liberties of trade unionists', but the call for resistance to a campaign against the Judgement was dropped.[147]

There is a detectable shift in the issues discussed by both the Young Scots and the Women Liberals. In the former's 1911–12 handbook, there is a section containing articles dealing with issues of concern to Liberals. After chapters on Home Rule and foreign policy, but before temperance, education and other older themes, come three essays on social questions: MacCallum Scott called for a minimum wage; J. D. White for rating reform; and the Rev. J. Glasse for Scottish poor law reform.[148] In its section arguing for Scottish Home Rule, much emphasis was put on the need for national regeneration demonstrated by the 1911 census, the very language used by Lloyd George and social radicals.[149] In 1914 the Young Scots held a meeting in Glasgow on housing policy to argue for building houses by municipal authorities, not just pulling down existing slums.[150] Against this, it should be noted that few of the 83 speakers on the society's 1911–12 speakers' list offered social reform themes: 8 in all on unemployment, social reform, labour questions, poor law reform and housing. For temperance alone there were also 8 speakers. The Women Liberals did better: out of their 40 speakers, 15 were willing to talk on social policy. The drift in content of the articles in the Liberal Women's journal is also instructive. In 1909 there were 17 items on free trade and temperance, 7 on social policy and 2 on female suffrage. By 1912 there were 7 on free trade and temperance, 15 on social policy and 12 on women's suffrage.

It is hard to say very much about opinion at the level of constituency members, as the records of only one association survive. The Aberdeen Liberals did take a view of the 1909 Budget which clearly showed an awareness of the social radical dimension, declaring that Lloyd George's proposals 'will secure for this and future years the money needed for the navy and social organisation, will vindicate Free Trade, will relieve local burdens and will promote land reform'.[151] When in 1912 members were asked which Cabinet minister should be invited to address the SLA annual conference (being held in Aberdeen, it was the host association's right), it is interesting that they opted first for Lloyd George, and then for Churchill, the two main proponents of the New Liberalism.[152] Although the Aberdeen President did resign over the Insurance bills, he did so not on the grounds of opposition to the principle of state interference but because as a doctor he resented the manner in which the proposals affected his profession.[153]

Elsewhere the evidence is less detailed. It has already been noted that subscriptions to the Glasgow Liberal Council were buoyant in 1913, and this must be placed in the context of the Glasgow Liberals' unequivocal stance on social reform. The 1909 Budget was hailed by them as a 'fair and equitable' solution to the dilemma of financing social reform and also defending the Empire; the Insurance bills were seen as ensuring a long stay in office. The Coal Mines Minimum Wages Act of 1912 was also, and more controversially, welcomed, the mover of the resolution rebuking 'the stalwarts of the not wholly extinct Manchester School' for denying that Parliament could fix wages. In the following year the Glasgow Council extended and reaffirmed its position by advocating the extension of Trade Boards to a whole range of industries, particularly sweated occupations.[154] It seems likely, then, that most of the rank and file Liberals were not reluctant followers of the new social radical policies enacted by the Liberal movement, implying that the adjustment to twentieth-century politics had been acehived before 1914 without breaking up the party. The very limited swing to Unionism in Scotland (1.8%) as compared to England (4.9%) in the January 1910 election reinforces the view that the Budget and its social reform implications were popular in Scotland.

A further signpost to constituency feeling may be found in the opinions of the M.P.s chosen by local parties. Dr Farquharson, who stood down in 1906, may be taken as a fair representative of the old laissez-faire school. 'The Trades Dispute Bill', he wrote in 1912, 'is an admitted blunder, and if we can shake ourselves clear of the superstitious fear and dread of the working man, the sooner it comes out of the statute book the better . . . ' Minimum wage laws were bad, and would be used as a stepping stone to further demands by trades unions, who found it hard 'to adhere to an honest agreement'. His views have a breathtaking honesty, as over the early closing of restaurants: 'The defenders of this kind of grandmotherly legislation retort by saying that the public houses are closed early and that it does not do to make one law for the rich and one for the poor. I hold an entirely different opinion. The social fabric is built up on this principle, and if those who are below us cannot keep within the bounds of moderation, we can and should get the reward for our sense of decency and self-restraint'.[155]

Herbert Gladstone reported with some relief to Campbell-Bannerman, after scrutinising the new intake of 1906, that most were men of the centre, with only two whiggish types coming in, one (E. P. Tennant) sitting for a Scottish seat.[156] Gladstone's definition of the centre must have been fairly catholic if he included James Annand, M.P. for East Aberdeenshire. Annand had published several works attacking state interference, the new liberalism and the sacrifice of middle-class interests, which were drawn together in his *Forgotten Liberalism* (1899). His Liberalism was unashamedly of the older school: 'If I were to lay down a policy for the Liberal party which would last half a century, I would look beyond the far-reaching constitutional reforms which are to be accomplished to the vast material possibilities that remain undeveloped in connection with the land, to the enlarged freedom of thought and worship still to be won in the establishment of complete religious equality and the purification of the schools from the taint of sects and to what yet may be done to foster the world's hatred and horror of war and abate the scourge of drunkenness'. His main remedy for the poor was to make litigation more readily available to them.[157] The strength of attachment to his views is shown by his biography being commissioned at the request of a group of Scottish admirers.[158] But Annand, like Farquharson, sat for a heavily rural seat, where the pressure to respond to the needs of labour was not much felt, and it is to urban areas that attention should be turned.

Although the 1906 intake of M.P.s did not have a large quota of New Liberals from Scotland, from 1908 these new social radical M.P.s entered Parliament in ever-increasing numbers. The most prominent instance is of course Churchill's return for Dundee in that year in lieu of a worthy but colourless local. But simultaneously there was an even greater symbolic change, when Bannerman's successor at Stirling was Arthur Ponsonby. Ponsonby's manifesto included the ritual obeisance to free trade, the House of Lords etc., but, he announced, 'it is upon these vital questions of Social Reform that I am chiefly interested ... Further, so long as there are hungry children to be fed, and aged poor to be saved from destitution, as long as men are overworked and underpaid, as long as there are men willing to work who are unemployed, as long as families are crowded together in small insanitary hovels and large tracts of land are left to waste, as long as the wealth of the country is so unevenly distributed that while a few thousands of men are able to amass great riches, some millions of our fellow countrymen are left in want, there is a vast field for us'.[159] Within a month of his election a friend suggested he should be following Hardie, not Asquith, and later in the same year another wrote: 'how I wish that there was a stronger Socialist party and that you could join it and lead it'.[160]

Ponsonby was an Englishman, and another by-election in 1908 confirmed a new pattern. While after 1886 Scottish seats had been used as safe bolt-holes for distinguished Liberals (Morley, Trevelyan, Childers, Birrell), the new candidates from England tended to be less well-known — Churchill apart — but politically more left-wing. Morley's elevation to the peerage created a vacancy at Montrose, which was filled by R. V. Harcourt (a nephew of Lewis Harcourt), who was described in 1913 as making up a 'radical gang' along with Ponsonby, and three more Englishmen — Barran (elected in 1909), W. G. C. Gladstone (1911) and Molteno (1906).[161] The general elections of 1910 and the subsequent by-elections prior to 1914 positively opened the floodgates to social radicals. W. M. R. Pringle won North-West Lanark in January 1910 with an election address praising Government for its legislative aid to the working classes and supporting the Minority Report on the Poor Law.[162] MacCallum Scott won Bridgeton in December 1910 and soon decided that 'I ought to get up some issue which specially affects the workers of Scotland'. So, between 1911 and 1914 he was preoccupied with propounding his case for the social radical remedy of the Minimum Standard in wages, health, housing, education and the poor law.[163] The interest in establishing a minimum wage was shared with the Scottish Miners, who persistently called for its introduction between 1911 and 1914.[164] J. D. White and D. Holmes, both elected in 1911, were part of this process, as was J. W. Pratt, who won West Lothian in 1913.[165] The Scottish ILP's house journal, *Forward*, commented on Pratt: 'our chief objection to him is that he has chosen to associate himself with the Liberal party, which as John William Pratt himself knows, is controlled and directed by capitalists and their tools. In one respect Mr Pratt is a dangerous man. His platform ability, his knowledge of the socialist case, and his strong humanitarian (if not socialist) sympathies could be used with damaging effect against Labour candidates on behalf of the Liberal aspirants for Parliament'.[166]

Moreover, some who when first elected did not display any noticeable interest in the progressive movement of ideas showed distinct signs of going in that direction as time passed. J. W. Gulland published a book in 1906, the year he became an M.P., on the social mission of the UF Church. In the era of the Minority Report on the Poor Law, Gulland still felt confident that a return to Thomas Chalmers' church-based scheme would tackle poverty most effectively, and he identified the main causes of poverty as drink and gambling, the traditional laissez-faire analysis.[167] By 1911 Gulland was endorsing the Insurance bills — 'a monumental measure of social advancement' — as demonstrating as baseless the allegation that Liberals had concentrated on constitutional reform at the expense of social reform.[168] Even Munro Ferguson was going left as his mentor Rosebery moved right. In 1909 Ferguson agreed with R. T. Reid that unemployment and housing were the major issues facing the country, and by 1912 he had concluded that the coal mines should be nationalised and that a minimum wage in the industry was sorely needed.[169]

VI

One pointer to the extent to which Scottish Liberals had willingly embraced Radical social policies was the development of policies specifically relevant to Scottish conditions. The House Letting Act was intended to alleviate the rigours of the widespread missive system under which tenants were committed to a minimal six-monthly rental period, and were subject to heavy penalties if they broke the lease by moving without giving four months' notice. As such it was praised by the organ of the Edinburgh Trades Council for ending 'an abominable system', and in the 1910 election the SLA published a leaflet outlining the bill's contents, because it was reckoned to be a good vote-winner.[170] The more significant political aspect of the measure was that it also removed the franchise disqualification which had hitherto followed from the practice of this category of tenants not paying rates directly, and this point was also stressed by Liberal candidates such as Sir Robert Laidlaw in West Renfrewshire.[171] Thus Scottish Liberals were proudly and consciously extending the right to vote to a section of the working class, contrary to the widespread belief then and now that such an act would be inimical to them and beneficial to Labour. This hardly betokens a want of confidence in the response of the working class to the Liberal social reform programme.

In two other fields Scottish Liberals also displayed an assurance that they were providing the momentum in policy initiation and that they were driving the appeal of Labour into retreat, while simultaneously erecting a bridge between old and new Liberalism which would permit both to coexist peacefully in one party. The advocacy of Scottish Home Rule, until then something of a fringe theme, was taken up with mounting clamour after 1902.[172] The new impetus stemmed from the Young Scots, who altered their constitution in 1909, adding to a general commitment to 'Progressive Politics' and 'Liberal principles' a specific aim, *viz.* 'to further the National Interests of Scotland and to secure for Sctland the right of self-government'. During the 1910 elections, they announced that they would make Scottish Home Rule a test question, and their conference that year had its scope restricted solely to the topic. In 1911 the Young Scots reached new heights, opposing the candidacy of Gladstone at Kilmarnock and the projected candidacy of Masterman at Tradeston because they were Englishmen. Their Propaganda Committee became more and more devoted to publishing Scottish Home Rule leaflets, culminating in 1912 in *60 Points for Home Rule.*[173] The cause was supported by more senior Liberal forces. In May 1912 a deputation of Liberal M.P.s met Asquith and the Scottish ministers to plead the necessity of a speedy granting of a separate Scottish legislature.[174] At the instigation of the M.P.s the SLA joined a committee of various Liberal organisations to carry out propaganda work throughout Scotland, while a ginger group of M.P.s maintained pressure in Parliament between 1912 and 1914 to ensure that the issue did not slip from prominence.[175]

The agitation was raised to such a level that in May 1914 the Scottish Unionist Whip suggested that all party candidates should be given guidelines on how to handle the questioning on the topic which, he predicted, would be omnipresent at the next election.[176] Yet, on the other hand, many Liberals, even keen supporters, doubted its electoral impact. As a candid member of the M.P.s' deputation which met Asquith said: 'I admit, and I think that most of my colleagues will admit, that there is no such enthusiastic body of opinion behind the Home Rule movement as might seem to justify the urgency of our cause'.[177] On the previous day J. M. Hogge went further when addressing the Young Scots' conference: 'The only people in Scotland in favour of Scottish Home Rule were the branches of the society. They were living in a fool's paradise if they thought that the average Liberal member cared anything for securing Scottish Home Rule within this parliament'.[178] Popular feeling is difficult to assess, but certainly James Bryce was informed by his brother, the M.P. for Inverness-shire, that his constituents did not press the matter at all, and Scottish Home Rule was rarely mentioned as a factor affecting the outcome of any of the numerous by-elections in the 1910–14 era.[179].

Although championing the cause of Scottish Home Rule seems to have been an issue of greater interest to professional politicians than to voters, its advantages to the Liberal party were various. Firstly, as noted before, it helped to make Irish

Home Rule more palatable if it could be presented as merely the first instalment in a process of devolution which would shortly be extended to Scotland.[180] This was the line taken by J. M. Robertson and Dr Chapple, M.P., in the Young Scots literature.[181] This may help to explain the insouciance with which Scottish Liberals regarded the Irish Home Rule difficulty after 1910. Plans were mooted in 1912 to hold open-air meetings in the constituencies on the Irish bill, but: 'there had however been very little response, as there seems to be a general apathy all over, the prevalent feeling apparently being that the opposition to Home Rule having now largely subsided, there was not much necessity for carrying on a strong propaganda in its favour'.[182] A second element was that Scottish Home Rule helped to unite sections within the party. Munro Ferguson, who between 1906 and 1911 had been critical of the land reform schemes of the Liberal government, joined with advanced radicals like Hogge and Pringle in planning discussions on how to work up opinion on Scottish self-government both at Westminster and in the country at large.[183]

Thirdly, while most of the interest in devolution was couched in traditional Liberal language of the recognition of the right to national identity, it was possible to link the demand with social reform. The inefficiency of Parliament in dealing with Scottish business was stressed, as before, but this was given a new twist by adducing the evidence of the 1911 census, which was read as proving the case for a policy of national regeneration. 'So the diseases of our social and economic system grow, and spread a blight over our country. The great solitudes of the north, once the home of a grand and heroic race, the overcrowded city slums, the emigrant ships are terrible witness to the neglect and mismanagement of Scottish business', argued the Young Scots in their National Manifesto.[184] The final motive for fighting on Scottish Home Rule was to appropriate for Liberalism a policy which many Labour party people also backed. MacDonald and Hardie had of course long been devolutionists, and in 1918 the Scottish Labour Party put the issue at the head of their programme. A good number of those who left the Liberals for Labour after the war had the attainment of self-government as one motive — for instance the Rev. James Barr. Before 1914, however, the Scottish Home Rule Council was very firmly wedded to the Liberal party, the chairman of the former, Robert Murray, being an active member of the SLA Executive. An ardent nationalist like R. E. Muirhead — a man with strong socialist affinities — was on the very eve of war still prominent in the Young Scots, where he argued that Labour candidates should only be supported when the Liberal would not endorse Scottish Home Rule.[185]

Liberal support for Scottish self-government partially represented the putting down of markers for the future, so pre-empting Labour. The more immediate source of Liberal strength was the land question. Recent work on British politics has indicated how Lloyd George's attempt to mobilise a Land Campaign between 1909 and 1914 should be seen as a contribution to continuing the social and economic social regeneration scheme of the New Liberalism, and this argument had considerable relevance to Scotland.[186] The older radical views on the land problem — essentially demands to end monopoly landownership and stimulate instead small holdings and peasant proprietorship — had particularly strong support in Scotland. In each of the political episodes discussed in this book, landownership and alleged abuses thereof have bulked large. So it was consistent with this historic standpoint that the major focus of interest in Scottish legislation after 1906 was the vicarious fortunes of the Scottish Small Holdings Bill.[187] For John Sinclair, the Liberal Scottish Secretary, 'one need stood first: what Scotland wanted most was land for the Scots'.[188] The Bill strove to extend the principles of the Crofters' Acts to the Lowland smallholder in order to arrest rural depopulation. It was violently opposed by landowners, including Rosebery and other Liberals like Elibank. The Scottish Land and Property Federation was created in November 1906 by proprietors to proect themselves against state encroachments on their rights. The Federation's officials were all leading Unionists, like Buccleuch, Atholl, Mackintosh of Mackintosh and Sir Robert Anstruther, and this along with a sustained campaign by *The Scotsman*, which published seventy-seven articles hostile to the bill, merely stiffened the resolve of Scottish Liberals to pass the measure.[189] The SLA expended a great deal of effort in organising meetings, lobbying ministers, publishing leaflets and passing resolutions, all calling for the passage of the bill.[190] The use by the Lords of their veto was condemned during the 1910 elections as much for having killed the land bill as for rejecting the Budget.[191] The intense amount of support for the Small Holdings Bill and the accruing political benefits to the Liberal party were perhaps best recognised in a report drawn up by a deputation from the National Executive of the Labour Party which came up from London in 1911 to attend a conference it had itself convened to discuss the future of the Labour Party in Scotland: 'We were also asked to pay more attention to rural questions because the Land Question in Scotland dominates everything else. Scotland has stood by the Liberal Government so solidly because it hates the House of Lords and the landlords, and as soon as the Veto Bill has been passed and a Scottish Land Bill placed upon the Statute Book, the political field in Scotland will be open to any main possession'.[192]

But these hopes were not at once realised, for by the time that the Small Holdings Bill was going through its final parliamentary stages, the Liberal party had taken up the land question in a new, more radical form, stemming from the 1909 Budget. The stress had now switched from Cobdenite economics (free trade in land) to Hobsonian economics (the right of the state to appropriate the unproductive surplus arising from the activities of the community). These far-reaching concepts were warmly embraced from the outset. The Glasgow Liberal Council had praised the Budget for proposing to tax land in order to fund social reform, thereby relieving the burdens on industry, and as noted, the Aberdeen Liberals took a similar approach.[193] For some leading Unionists, their party's signal failure in Scotland was largely due to the land clauses of the Budget which had kindled radical enthusiasm.[194] As will be seen below, the land question in its radical guise continued to be deployed by Liberals at subsequent by-elections, with a deal of success.

The attractions of the radical land campaign were manifold. Firstly, by keeping land to the fore, it concentrated all shades of Liberalism on an issue which fostered unity. Indeed, the new programme, with its emphasis on a constructive approach to rural regeneration, even enticed back to full-hearted support several Liberal landowners who had been noticeably cool towards the earlier Small Holdings act. The Master of Elibank was one who had been unhappy about the bill, regarding the smallholders as probably lost to the Liberal party thanks to the legislation, 'inasmuch as they are secured in the fruit of their industry'.[195] But, surprisingly, he had no serious qualms about Lloyd George's ideas on land. Munro Ferguson, who, with his very large estates, had bitterly opposed Sinclair's Land Bill, threw himself vigorously into the new land movement. Ferguson was an expert on afforestation, one of the leading planks in the rural regeneration programme.[196] His links with the young radicals, nursed by the home government lobby, were reinforced here, and he discussed with MacCallum Scott a project to involve leading men in Scotland in the intricacies of land taxation and forestry.[197]

Also, concentration on the idea of land value taxation enabled the challenge of the socialist analysis of capitalism to be sidestepped. The unearned increment enjoyed by landlords was used to explain many of the causes of urban as well as rural social distress in a convincing manner. A Liberal party worker recorded the attitudes she encountered while canvassing in Clydeside in the January 1910 election: 'Every phase of the present evils in large towns — as slums, insanitary homes, impossibly high rents, restricted enterprise and trade depression — was explained to masses of hearers, mainly victims of the evils enumerated'.[198] The SLA took up this theme at its 1912 General Council meeting, and it passed a resolution claiming that land value taxation would provide for better housing and improved agriculture.[199] MacCallum Scott was very excited at the prospect of taking the land question into an urban setting, as he felt it would have major vote-catching appeal in Bridgeton.[200] The Glasgow Liberal Council was told in 1912 that land value taxation could have averted the recent bitter miners' strike, and could finance social reforms of a more sweeping and fundamental nature than hitherto.[201] The effect on the housing crisis (on which the ILP was making much headway) of site value taxation was particularly emphasised by Liberal enthusiasts, since it would reduce the cost of feuing land for building purposes, so increasing the supply of urban housing.[202] For businessmen and industrialists, site value taxation was presented as having a positive aspect. In January 1914 the SLA decided to form a Land Campaign Committee to spread the argument that land taxation would lead to a transfer of much of the burden of taxation away from industry and enterprise, so stimulating expansion.[203] This argument struck a chord among those who felt that the rating system was iniquitous, antiquated and detrimental to the efficient running of local government.[204]

The land value taxation movement had been inspired by Henry George, who had deeply influenced early Scottish socialists, and although the Scottish Liberals had virtually adopted the single tax agitation in the 1890s, there were still many socialists who were keen advocates of the principle. One such was Councillor Alston, who just before the war became the ILP-nominated candidate for Camlachie, the Glasgow seat most expected to be won by Labour.[205] Initially the 1909 Budget compelled the Labour party in Scotland to fall in behind the

Liberals. George Barnes, M.P. for Blackfriars, firmly supported Lloyd George; the ILPer George Carson, the former Secretary of the Scottish Workers Representation Committee, and Secretary of the Glasgow Trades Council, was also joint secretary of a Budget Democracy Committee, which 'recognise(d) the value and importance of the Land and Valuation Clauses of the Present Budget'.[206] In the January 1910 election campaign, the press noted a profound change in Liberal–Labour relations wrought by the Budget: 'the street corner socialist no longer seeks to shout down his Radical protagonist on the other side of the street'.[207]

Increasingly, as the social radical elements in the Land Campaign became more apparent, the Labour party began to feel that it was losing much ground to the Liberals, and two of the most prominent ILPers in Scotland voiced these fears. From the centre-right of the party, Joseph Duncan expressed alarm in 1911 that the land agitation 'was completely overshadowing Labour's campaign for a minimum wage'. By 1912, Duncan was deeply disturbed: 'There is no doubt that we shall be 'dished' again and left to pursue a course of lame criticism that the ordinary man takes to be mere carping'. He predicted that the Liberal land campaign would do well all over Scotland: 'It will be popular and effective electioneering and not all our criticisms will stay the triumph of the Liberal candidates'. The adoption of a policy of land nationalisation, he continued, would probably not have any impact on a well-established Liberal bandwagon, except to buttress it: 'We may make up our minds then that from the party point of view it is unlikely the Land Campaign will bring us any immediate advantages, but rather the reverse ... It seems to me that we are likely to pay the price of our neglect of the land question in having to face a revived Liberalism in Scotland'.[208] From the Marxist wing of the ILP, Neil MacLean, later M.P. for Govan, agreed with Duncan. Labour's Right to Work and Minimum Wage agitations were not stirring the imagination of the voters, and so a new policy was needed. Land seemed to MacLean the obvious choice, but he cautioned that nationalisation should not be advocated, since it was too complex a case to put across effectively. Instead, he rather weakly suggested, landowners would be required to furnish documentary proof of ownership. Another, anonymous, article in the same issue of *Forward* as MacLean's piece reiterated the need to engage seriously with the land question, but argued that any policy should be clear and concrete, for 'We cannot meet them [Liberals] with vague cries for nationalisation ... Let something be done before it is too late to do anything but shout curses at the tail of the Liberal Land Society ... Otherwise, the Liberals will dish us for a generation'.[209] This is hardly the rallying call of a Labour movement confident of its triumph over a decaying political party. No wonder one Glasgow Liberal exulted in 1912: 'In the taxation of land values they had the key to the whole position'.[210]

VII

Given the rapidity and comprehensiveness with which Labour displaced the Liberals as the major electoral force on the left after the First World War, there is a natural inclination to discern evidence of this breakthrough in the period before 1914. There is testimony from all political angles to substantiate this viewpoint. Under the heading *'E Pur Si Muove'*, the editor of *Forward* in 1910 argued that Labour was advancing on its unstoppable onward march. 'Yes, friends, the tide of Democracy is rising. We are winning. We are going to see great changes in Scotland, and we shall all contribute to their making.'[211] While this might be dismissed as a normal piece of morale-boosting, the Liberal Scottish Whip, Elibank, assured the King's Secretary in late 1906 that socialism was a major threat to Scottish Liberals. A secret memorandum compiled for Elibank at the start of 1908 by the Scottish Liberal secretaries alarmingly reiterated the view that 'the Socialist and Labour movements are steadily gaining adherents in Scotland'. The report warned of the long-term threat presented by the new party to the Liberals in Scotland, particularly stressing the increasing association of the trade unions with the ILP, and the impact of extensive socialist propaganda.[212] Bonar Law was similarly assured by a Glasgow correspondent late in 1907 that discussions with a former trade union leader and a Conservative shipyard joiner suggested that Liberalism was being extinguished among working men, and that ceaseless socialist agitation was proving effective.[213] Four general areas need to be examined to evaluate how far these assertions were accurate. These are: firstly, the strength of the ILP, the medium for socialist ideas within the Labour party; secondly, the organisational challenge of the Labour party; thirdly, the nature of trade union and socialist relations; lastly, the electoral pattern and the impact of Labour on the Liberal party.

The vigour of the ILP, stressed by these quotations, is at first striking. The number of branches in Scotland expanded remarkably, rising from 98 in 1906 to 130 in 1913, a faster rate of growth than in the UK as a whole. Yet to many seasoned members of the ILP there were few grounds for optimism. Thus in 1909 a leading Glasgow ILPer felt able to say no more than that the party was not yet dead in Scotland.[214] A more sustained scrutiny of the real position of the ILP came from Joseph Duncan, who was Scottish organiser of the party between 1906 and 1908, the very years when discontent with the Liberal government's lack of radical drive was strongest, and the time when socialists like Pete Curran and Victor Grayson were winning spectacular by-elections in England on a platform of heady socialist rhetoric. Duncan, however, found very little encouragement in his systematic tour of Scotland, even in places where electoral hopes were high. Organisation was poor, even in Dundee, where Labour had won a seat in 1906. Ten months after the election, he found 'The branch is all at sixes and sevens and I had a wallop at them on Wednesday. Perhaps they will organise themselves into better order'.[215] The preaching of the socialist message met with a stony reaction in potentially profitable areas of solid working-class communities. 'I am in for a fortnight's bad work in Lanarkshire. They look to be about the worst places I have tackled in Scotland. They are a cross between bad Irish and bad Scots ... ' A return visit a year later reinforced these impressions. At Hamilton, 'I never saw such a collection of weeds in all my life. The Lanarkshire miner is the most disagreeable animal I ever met with. He is dirty, drunken and conceited. It is no use talking to him. The only thing that will do is Prussic Acid'.[216] The quality and liveliness of ILP members was not always high, as in Stirling: 'This will be new ground. There are socialists but they are all very timid. That is the worst sort of place to tackle'. These premonitory fears were confirmed after meeting the Stirling people: 'The finest collection of cranks I ever struck' was his verdict.[217] By the middle of the 1908 Duncan was glad to assume the position of organiser for the fisherman's trade union, evidently judging this daunting task as preferable to struggling to improve the Scottish ILP.

The number of branches is a misleading index of the vitality of the ILP. Many were based on slender support. The case of Stewarton, an important centre for the North Ayrshire constituency, highlighted this, as the Scottish Secretary of the ILP told the national Secretary, explaining its sudden demise: 'It never was a thriving branch, being dependent mainly on Comrade MacKenzie, who is a small employer. The members for the most part consisted of some of his workmen. Some of them may have left the district or Mac may have got grown tired of paying fees out of his own pocket'.[218] Outlying areas were either highly vulnerable to the loss of a few stalwarts, or suffered from intertia induced by isolation, the latter shown by the frequent requests for 'big' speakers to be sent out to rally interest.[219] Coupar Angus illustrates the former problem. Begun in 1909 with six members and great keenness, within a year five had left the area to look for work, and although two new recruits had come in, the one original member reported that political work was confined to no more than 'a quiet word here and there as the opportunity occurs'.[220] Indeed there was a rapid turnover of branches. Of the 98 branches listed in the 1907 Annual Report, 17 — nearly one-fifth — did not exist three years later. Branches rose and fell with alarming speed. In March 1910 a flurry of work in West Fife resulted in five branches being formed, yet within two months it was reported from one of these towns that 'the ILP is defunct here'.[221] Beith lapsed in 1910, re-formed in 1913, and was dead again in 1914.[222] Between 1910 and 1914 the ILP was losing more branches in Scotland than it was gaining, falling from 143 in 1910 to 130 in 1914. Though several of these were in marginal areas, like Duns and Nairn, others were in important industrial centres which should have survived if the ILP could claim to be advancing, such as Port Glasgow, Gorbals, Airdrie and Bellshill.[223] These lapses were only very infrequently caused by secessions due to dissatisfaction at the weak political stand adopted by the ILP and Labour Party after 1910. In 1911, when 9 out of the 42 lapsed branches throughout the United Kingdom indicated that they were doing so on political grounds, none of the four defunct Scottish branches were among them. Of 69 lapsed Scottish branches between 1910 and 1914, only Forfar and Inverness seem to have quit the ILP to join the more Marxist socialist BSP.

The number of members was also a source of concern. In 1908 Scotland had 14.8% of the total branches but only 10.6% of members, and at 2,720 in 1913–14, the actual number was proportionally lower than, say Wales, which had 1,580 members.[224] Membership movements were irregular. Dundee fell from around 150 in 1908 to 80 or 90 in 1912 and only began to increase again in 1914. Montrose

Burghs, one of the seats regarded by the ILP as a winnable seat (James Maxton became candidate in 1914), was likewise small and fluctuating in supporters. Arbroath fell from 50 in early 1910 to only 30 in August 1912, and Montrose itself showed a similar dip from 15 to 6.[225] By far the largest concentration of ILP support was in Glasgow, with between 1,200 and 1,300 members in 1913, about half of the Scottish figure.[226] It is revealing to contrast this with statistics for the other two parties. The Dundee Liberals had 1,279 members in 1908, yet that city's population was one fifth that of Glasgow. The total Unionist membership in Glasgow in 1911 was 7,375, and in Bridgeton, which after the war was probably the strongest ILP area in the city, the ILP could claim about 20 members in 1909, while the Unionists in 1911 had 868.[227]

Despite the small active membership, the ILP was felt on all sides to be winning an extensive sympathetic hearing through its forceful propaganda. The public meeting was regarded as the speciality of the ILP, much envied by other parties. Regular summer outdoor meetings were held in parks and at speakers' corners, and in winter theatres were hired on Sundays for lectures and debates. Rural areas and seaside resorts were visited by teams of party workers to boost recruitment. Yet the efficiency of these ventures was questioned by many.[228] Duncan noted sourly that while 3,000 turned up at a Glasgow theatre on a Sunday night to hear a lecture on Socialism, all the city's socialist bodies together contained no more than 1,200, and could get no recruits.[229] In 1910 the Clackmannan and Stirling Federation concluded that its summer propaganda meetings were not a success, as despite 52 meetings, not a single new member had been gained.[230] The Angus Federation came to a similar conclusion in 1912 when it reported that its Carnoustie meetings 'seemed only to draw the same people every week and [were] therefore unsatisfactory'.[231] The shrewd Willie Graham argued from his experiences with the Selkirk ILP between 1907 and 1909 that 'the increased interest did not mean in those days a wider acceptance of socialist doctrine', but was merely the reaction to a novelty.[232] The difficulties many branches had in retaining support after the initial launch — usually accompanied by a mass meeting and a prominent national speaker — would suggest that there is some point in Graham's argument.

On the whole, then, the decade before 1914 cannot be seen as one of unchecked gain by the ILP, and this was reflected in problems of organisation. With a small and stagnating membership, thinly spread over too many branches, this was inevitable. When Duncan visited Leith, only one out of the 60 members turned out to support him at a public meeting.[233] On the eve of the January 1910 election, a leading member of the Scottish ILP Executive complained that apathy and bickering were responsible for the 'lack of life' in many Glasgow branches and warned: 'The party must draw itself together. It is ineffective at present'.[234] Looking back from the vantage point of 1921 to the 1900–14 era, a leading activist in what was the centre of Scottish socialism reflected that 'The record of the Glasgow ILP Executive is a struggle with adversity. The party did not seem to make headway'.[235] Elsewhere, the news was no better. When he went to Edinburgh in 1909, Willie Graham found that 'the ILP had not a very strong hold in Edinburgh and district, and the work of establishing the party was of the hard pioneering order'.[236]

Lack of finance seriously limited the work of the ILP. There was not enough money to defray Duncan's expenses on his organising tours in 1906–8. He had therefore to meet his costs from collections taken at meetings. For the same reasons of economy, these meetings had to be outdoors, and so were subject to the vagaries of the Scottish weather, and two consecutive days of rain precipitated a cash flow crisis of major dimension: 'It knocks a bad hole in the finances'. It was a losing battle, as Duncan complained: 'We are far in debt for cash — a debt I have got to bear in wages due. We must work every meeting we can in the summertime so as to get our full reward in collections'.[237] Two years later, the National Administrative Council was informed of the 'bad financial position' in Scotland, where it was evidently more acute than in other areas.[238] Between 1903 and 1911 the Glasgow Federation's income remained at around £230, a figure which was held to be inadequate for proper organisational and propaganda work.[239]

The most critical impact of the cash problem was on electoral work. Repeatedly the desire to put up an ILP candidate was defeated by financial realities, as at Leith in 1913, or in Montrose Burghs, which decided after the January 1910 election that it could not afford to fight again in the near future.[240] It was possible to maintain the nomination of a candidate in the only Glasgow seat contested by the ILP in this period largely because of the personal guarantee given by James Allan, the socialist son of a millionaire shipowner.[241] This problem would go far to explain the remarkably small number of ILP-sponsored candidates in Scotland: 1 in 1906, 2 in January 1910, 1 in December 1910, and 2 in by-elections (Montrose, 1908 and Kilmarnock, 1911). In general, however, even apart from the financial difficulty, the electoral preparedness of the ILP was not impressive. As Hardie observed of the Montrose by-election, 'Burgess as candidate is awful and Duncan [his agent] as good as helpless'.[242] In the two seats fought in January 1910, party officials noted that no proper electioneering machinery existed, and despite the defects exposed during the by-election in 1908, Montrose had done nothing in the intervening eighteen months to improve things.[243] In Camlachie, the ILP's brightest Glasgow hope, disarray also prevailed, as the former candidate, J. O'Connor Kessack, put it in 1913: 'He knew from personal experience that the organisation in Scotland was not worth the name of organisation at all. He had had the misfortune to contest a constituency twice, and on both occasions no organisation existed until the fight actually began'. He added that although a new candidate had been put up for Camlachie, there was still no organisation to speak of.[244]

VIII

The weaknesses of the ILP might not have been of such moment if the Labour Party itself could compensate by being efficient and dynamic. The omens were propitious. The Scottish labour movement had, after all, formed the Scottish Workers' Parliamentary Election Committee before the Labour Representation Committee (LRC) itself was created.[245] Moreover, by the inclusion of the Co-operative section, the Scottish Workers' Representation Committee (SWRC) could be judged as more broadly representative of the whole working class movement than the LRC, which in its initial years expressed admiration and envy at the achievement of the Scottish party in securing the involvement of the Co-operators.[246] The SWRC was established at the instigation of the Scottish Trades Union Congress (STUC), whose Parliamentary Committee had grown frustrated at the disproportionately meagre legal concessions extracted from M.P.s when compared with the time and effort applied, and moreover these small gains were 'conceded as favours rather than recognised as rights'. The Parliamentary Committee then deliberated, and 'after careful consideration they came to the conclusion that the best means by which those questions would receive full attention was to have direct working class representatives in the House of Commons'. After discussions with the ILP, the Social Democratic Federation (SDF) and the Co-operative societies in the autumn of 1899, the launching conference was held on 6 January 1900, with 226 delegates present, 145 drawn from trades unions and trade councils; 28 from Co-operative organisations; 34 from the ILP; and 19 from the SDF. At the meeting there was total unanimity as to the organisational structure and policy programme of the new body. The underlying reasons for this development are complex. Partly it was because in Scotland the unions were relatively weaker than in England, and so were more interested in securing a political presence to reinforce their lack of industrial influence. In addition, Hardie reported that on the crucial committee of the STUC sympathisers of the ILP had become the majority voice. It was felt, indeed, by some that the conference had been 'nobbled', in that socialist-minded delegates in favour of independent representation predominated. The secretary of the STUC Parliamentary Committee complained that Hardie had been allowed to dictate proceedings and his performance had been rapturously received by his supporters.[247] The secretary of the SWRC concluded his account of its origins with the prediction: 'It is not too much to say that the political history of the future will be very different indeed from the past, and that the action of the Scottish Workers' Representation Committee will have contributed very largely to this event'.[248]

Despite this auspicious inauguration the SWRC was a failure, as was widely accepted by 1906. As one union leader told Ramsay MacDonald, 'I do not wish to cast any reflections upon the Scottish Workers' Representation Committee further than to say it certainly does not accomplish the good results that its founders anticipated'. More bluntly, it was 'that useless body'.[249] The loss of support is seen in the dramatic fall in the number of delegates attending the annual conference, which dropped from 190 in 1901 to only 108 in 1906.[250] As we shall see below, Labour did worse in Scotland in the 1906 election than in England, and a large share of the blame was laid at the door of the SWRC. In 1909 it suffered the abject humiliation of having to accept incorporation into the Labour Party on the latter's terms, as the SWRC could not face the threat of having the English party entering directly into electoral work in Scotland.[251]

The problems confronting the SWRC were twofold: firstly there were internal failings and secondly the difficulties of trying to run two entirely separate Scottish and English political parties, several of whose constituent parts operated in both countries. The incompetence of the SWRC is abundantly evident. On the one hand it failed to publicise its presence, as shown by the numerous letters, seeking advice, which were sent to MacDonald at the LRC from local Labour parties set up in Scotland by spontaneous local effort.[252] Yet when the SWRC did make its presence known, the benefits were not apparent, as one local party found: 'We had Mr Carson [the SWRC Secretary] here last night but did not get much satisfaction from him, his Committee seems to be useless, only blocking the way of Labour Representation'.[253] The SWRC was not well led. Carson, the Secretary from 1902, may then have been displaying the traits evident when Emmanuel Shinwell joined the Glasgow Trades Council in 1910. Carson, the Secretary of that body too, was in the habit of barracking speakers from the floor and commenting critically on debates. Certainly by the First World War, Carson was seen to have a drink problem.[254] However, in defence of Carson, it may be noted that in this last he was not a solitary sinner among the SWRC. A trade union branch protested to the Executive of the Committee that reports circulating of the 1904 conference were 'an indictment of the business methods of the Conference, and that many of the delegates present were in a condition to prevent them performing their part of the business'.[255]

The extent of the failure of the SWRC is best measured against the objectives it set itself in 1900 in its first address to the electors, when it undertook to work to foster the formation and growth of local representation committees and also to raise funds for the payment of M.P.s.[256] In reality, it did little to stimulate the creation of local LRCs, rather, as with West Fife, instructing the local men first to form their committee and then come to the SWRC. Only around 1906 does central encouragement become normal, as in the SWRC's efforts to found a party in Kilmarnock.[257] Otherwise, as noted above, local initiatives occurred quite without the knowledge — or interest — of the SWRC. Even when local parties were in being, the SWRC was of little use. It declined to involve itself in placing registration agents in winnable seats.[258] Its conduct of propaganda was low-keyed. In reply to a suggestion that it hold meetings in seats where Labour candidates might stand, it deemed such action not to be part of its policy. Leaflets were published, but in derisory numbers, such as one on Chinese Labour, which was given a print order of 5,000. For the nine candidates in the 1906 election, a total of a mere 1,500 posters and 14,000 button badges were produced by the SWRC.[259]

Perhaps the most telling sign of poor organisation was the SWRC's utter inability to compile a list of candidates for constituencies to consult. So in 1903 Govan was told that 'we had no candidates on our list at present', and in 1905 Partick was referred to the LRC in London. In the 1906 election, the SWRC had not been able to find candidates for three seats, despite the warm interest shown locally in a contest.[260] As late as 1907, Carson wrote to MacDonald asking if he had any men who might be put on the Scottish list.[261]

At the centre of the SWRC's problems was the poor financial state it found itself in, especially as compared with the LRC.[262] In 1905 the SWRC could not afford to send any delegates to the STUC conference in Hawick; in 1906 finances were reported to be 'a matter of grave concern'; and in 1907 things were so critical that 'it was agreed to make a joint representation to the STUC and the Glasgow Trades [Council] regarding the papering and whitewashing of office'.[263] The income from affiliation fees never rose above £100, and donations were usually under £50. A measure of the ineptitude of the SWRC was that it never managed to enrol anything like all of the eligible societies. Carson was talking of approaching non-affiliated unions in early 1905, yet two years later he seemed no further forward: 'We intend to push all the Scottish Societies still outside, and there are many such, to join this year — we hope to be successful'.[264]

The linked problems of finance and trade union affiliation were responsible for the deteriorating relationship between the SWRC and the LRC. At first there were mutual declarations of harmonious co-operation. Thus when the LRC was formed, MacDonald informed the Scottish party that the former 'considered all North of the Tweed sacred to us, and would refer any Scotch unions to us'.[265] Friction soon emerged in respect of the payment of union affiliation fees, which went to whichever party held jurisdiction over a union's headquarters. This gave rise to grave anomalies. Some unions, especially those in shipbuilding, collected fees from a large number of Scottish workers, but were powerless to influence the SWRC, as they were affiliated to the LRC. In the case of the Boilermakers, it was feared the unrest among the Scots at their exclusion from the Scottish party would lead to a total disaffiliation from the LRC.[266] By contrast other unions, either based administratively in Scotland, or even with a purely Scottish membership, desired to join the LRC, which they saw as a far more effective body.[267] Attempts to allocate union affiliation fees between the Scottish and English parties on a more equitable and rational basis were fraught with difficulties. In 1903 an agreement was reached to set up a common Parliamentary Fund, but the method of collecting fees was not fully settled, and while the LRC accused the SWRC of not passing on dues collected in Scotland, the Scots believed that the basis on which the scheme worked left them with inadequate funds to function properly in Scotland. This dispute rumbled on with mounting acerbity on both sides, and it occupied a great deal of the SWRC's time, which could well have been devoted to other tasks.

At the LRC MacDonald exploited this dispute and the trade union unease at the waste it involved in order to vindicate greater intervention by his party in Scottish affairs. He called for 'some rearrangement so that the movement for Labour consolidation may go ahead in Scotland as it has done in the South'.[268] In the North-East Lanark by-election of 1904, MacDonald threw the resources of the LRC behind the SWRC candidate, John Robertson. Although this was, as he admitted to the candidate, 'more or less irregular', MacDonald's real motives emerged in his instructions to an LRC underling: 'Do your best to hustle Christie [a printer] so that we may show the Scottish fellows that we can handle things'.

The assistant secretary of the LRC was to see the chairman, Shackleton, and: 'Explain to Shackleton, 1) the deadness of the Scottish Committee, 2) the imminent necessity of our taking over the whole country ... '[269] The poor performance of Scottish Labour candidates in 1906 confirmed MacDonald in his strategy of working on trade unions in Scotland to withdraw support from the SWRC and transfer to his party. In February 1906 he told the secretary of the Scottish Engine Keepers in strict confidence that while the union was at present ineligible to join the English party, 'I am strongly of opinion that the arrangement will have to be revised, as Scotland is not being well handled'. Accordingly, the Engine Keepers should apply to affiliate to MacDonald's party, so as to enable the latter to 'open the general question upon that'.[270]

Between 1906 and 1908 the squabble over the distribution of affiliation fees simmered on.[271] MacDonald maintained contact with disgruntled union leaders in Scotland. A special sub-committee of the Labour Party Executive drafted an addition to the Annual Report to be presented to the 1908 conference as follows: 'During the past year we had frequent requests from some [Scottish] unions to allow them to become associated with us, and our experience has shown us that there are serious difficulties in limiting our field of action in the way prescribed by this agreement'. The conclusion was that there should be uniformity, and this could only be obtained by having both countries administered by one party.[272] The SWRC resisted this demand for a merger, but the long-awaited collision came in 1908 at the Dundee by-election. This was a double-member constituency; one member, Alexander Wilkie, was Labour, and the vacancy arose from the elevation of the other, Liberal, M.P. to the peerage so as to let Churchill return to the House. The Labour Party's policy in such two-member seats (where Labour and Liberal each held one) was that 'both seats in double-barrelled constituencies should not be fought at present'.[273] However, the Scottish party did not accept this ruling and instead endorsed the local party's decision to run a Labour candidate against Churchill. This decision caused consternation among the Labour party in England, for whereas Dundee was the only two-member seat in Scotland, 11 of the 27 Labour M.P.s south of the border owed their election to understandings with Liberals in this type of seat. If, as was feared, the Liberals should regard developments in Dundee as justifying retaliatory moves in England, the effects could be dire for Labour. The National Executive Committee (NEC) in London took prompt action. While a separate Scottish party existed, there were 'no safeguards against the springing of candidates upon the movement at by-elections'. Accordingly, MacDonald sent a telegram to the Scottish section announcing that 'his committee had met and decided to affiliate Scottish societies and place their own candidates in the constituencies there'.[274] Two unions — the Scottish Ironmoulders and the Blacksmiths — thereupon transferred their allegiance from the SWRC to the Labour Party. Faced with the threat of a disaffiliation stampede, the Scottish party voted to dissolve itself at its annual conference in February 1909, leaving the Labour Party as the sole party in Britain. The Scottish Ironmoulders' secretary observed in confidence to MacDonald: 'You will see that our action has brought matters our way'.[275]

After the merger, the improvements were not always apparent, although few would go as far as George Barnes, who claimed in 1914 that 'since that absorption there was not the slightest doubt in his mind that the Scottish movement had not been in the same strong position [sic] as before'.[276] Part of the cause was the inordinate delay before the NEC decided, first, how liaison with and control over Scotland should be established and then, how best to implement the scheme. It was not until some thirty months after taking in the SWRC that the NEC gave consideration to running Scottish affairs. A report to the NEC in August 1911 accepted the partial validity of Scottish complaints about remote and insensitive treatment from London, and also noted the presence of different political questions in Scotland which London-produced propaganda did not cover. The report recommended that a Scottish Committee should be set up to advise and act with the NEC on Scottish matters, in a move designed to meet the resentment felt about the loss of local influence ever since the demise of the SWRC.[277] Eight months later the NEC discussed these proposals, and broadly endorsed them. However, it was not until 1914 that the Scottish Advisory Council (SAC) was established, thanks in part to a complicated set of negotiations over the powers and composition of the Council.[278] It was an appropriate end to this episode that the inaugural conference of the SAC had to be postponed from 5 August 1914, because Britain's involvement in World War One inconveniently began on that day.[279]

The upshot of this lack of direction before 1914 from a Scottish centre meant that local parties, not in a very robust state at the end of the reign of the SWRC, were given only fitful attention by the party's organisers. As a result, organisation in Scotland lagged substantially behind the levels attained at this time in England. In 1911 the NEC was informed that although the members in Scotland were in excellent heart, 'The political organisation in Scotland is not what it might be. It appears that between elections it is allowed to rust and is brought into activity only after elections are decided upon. The steady and persistent work of local Labour Parties is not so marked in Scotland as in England'.[280] In confirmation of this point, the National Agent had just two months previously strongly advised the NEC against sanctioning a candidature in Glasgow Tradeston because no recent organisational or even propaganda work had been undertaken in the seat, and in 1912 St Rollox was also to be left unfought 'in view of the absence of satisfactory organisation in this constituency'.[281] Shortly before the outbreak of war, there were indications of some advances, but these were patchy. Several local parties had begun to do serious registration work, which had been singled out by the West Fife agent as the key to victory there in December 1910, and which he urged others to develop if they hoped to win.[282] A step forward in co-ordinating effort came with the creation in 1913 of the Glasgow City Labour Party, but its initial impact was qualified, in the estimate of the SAC Secretary, by being 'vast, inexact and duplicated' in both activities and membership.[283] In 1914 a delegate to the party conference remarked that 'everybody knew that Scotland was in need of better organisation', and at the same time the SAC Secretary informed London that in five of the seats in which it was intended to field candidates 'immediate action seems required to prevent errors'.[284]

One of the most persistent and vexing weaknesses of pre-war Labour in Scotland lay in the lack of organisation in mining seats. On the one hand, as the political agent of the miners' union noted, 'the miners were fighting county seats and in these constituencies the only political organisation that existed was the Miners'.[285] Yet the miners would not organise properly, only moving on the very eve of an election. Keir Hardie was clear on this in 1906: 'If he were asked to explain why all the miners' candidates in Scotland were defeated, he would say that it lay at the door of the Miners' Federation. Elections could not be won with ten minutes' preparation. They refused to spend money beforehand in organising the constituencies which they were to fight ... That had to be remedied'.[286] Apart from West Fife, little was done, and in almost every year between 1906 and 1914 the litany was repeated. These criticisms were most loudly voiced after by-elections, as in 1912, following the Mid Lothian contest, when the NEC reiterated its worries about 'the unsatisfactory state of Labour organisation in most of the [Scottish] mining constituencies'.[287]

The poor condition of the Labour Party in mining seats leads on to another topic. It might be contended that despite these manifest organisational defects, a broad working-class unity had been forged, linking socialist and trade unionist in a common struggle whose momentum was strong enough to burst through institutional weaknesses. Examination of the electoral results will give clear pointers to the validity of this claim, but the extent of unity of purpose and outlook between the two wings of the Labour movement can also be assessed in other ways. Right up to the eve of war, in reality, there was a gulf between trade unionist and socialist in Scotland. Barnes, the M.P. for Glasgow Blackfriars, had no time for Glasgow socialists: 'I have noticed things in Scotland going from bad to worse this last year or so. There is that raw declamatory sort of thing which is getting more general, and which the newspaper, which has just been started here, encourages [i.e. *The Forward*]. There is the absence of organisation, and there is the boose [sic], and the three together are preparing Scotchmen for a fall'.[288] Barnes was the secretary of the engineers' union and also an ILPer, but clearly the former factor predominated in his outlook. Again, the delay in securing agreement on a constitution for the SAC was in good measure due to trade union suspicions that the socialist societies were manipulating the basis of representation to the detriment of the unions. At the 1913 Labour Party conference, the proposed structure was referred back after leading Scottish trade unionists opposed it. Smillie warned that 'in his opinion it was absolutely unfair to the Trade Union movement in Scotland'. Another miner, and a Labour candidate in three elections, complained that 'about 20 small organisations with less than 1,000 members would have double or three times the representation of the Scottish Miners Federation with 80,000 men. He submitted they could not unite the organisation upon the representation proposed'.[289]

The socialist wing did not always display unalloyed admiration for the trade unionists. Wilkie, the Shipwrights' secretary and Dundee M.P., was denounced roundly by local ILPers. When he was selected, the local ILP was said to be in a state of 'incipient revolt' because Wilkie's political ideas were so retrograde. The decision to fight the second Dundee seat in 1908 was partly instigated by the local ILP, one of whose members rhetorically demanded of Hardie: 'Was the Labour Party formed for the express purpose of gaining seats for a few egotistical Trade Union secretaries or was its purpose to become a large and national party?'[290] An article by P. J. Dollan in *The Forward* in 1911 bemoaned the dead hand which was laid upon many ILP branches if trade union officials became involved. Also in that year Dollan pointed out that whereas the industrial unrest in England and Wales had promoted working-class political consciousness, it was difficult to say the same of Scotland, where the concepts of boycotting and sympathy strike were unknown. The Glasgow dockers, he said, won their strike only because of the resolution shown in England, Wales and Ireland; the railwaymen's action failed in Scotland because of blacklegs, but in England the strike was solid, and the seamen's strike in Scotland was similarly lacking the unity demonstrated in England.[291]

IX

The permanence of the Liberal recovery between 1906 and 1914 and the challenge of Labour can be tested through examination of electoral trends in the period. It is instructive to compare the results with England and Wales in order to get a sense of the relative performance of the Scottish parties. In the 1906 election Labour fought 9 seats in Scotland (out of 70) and won 2: in England and Wales, 45 constituencies were fought (from a total of 490) and 27 were won. Thus the Scottish performance was proportionally less successful. Between 1906 and 1910 Labour in England made two spectacular gains, at Colne Valley and Jarrow, but these were not emulated in Scotland. Five months before these two English results, Labour came a poor third in Aberdeen South, taking 19.5% of the poll (compared to 33.1% in Jarrow and 35.2% at Colne Valley). The Aberdeen Labour Party had entered the contest with high hopes, as neither of the other two candidates was felt to be very strong. However, Fred Bramley was not any stronger as Labour's choice: he was too flippant for the earnest Aberdonians, and some disaffection amongst activists resulted from Bramley's forming a liaison with the wife of the ILPer with whom he was staying during the campaign.[292] The other two by-elections fought by Labour in Scotland came in May 1908, some ten months after Jarrow and Colne Valley. At Dundee, in circumstances of a local Labour Party divided on the question of fighting the second seat, a poll of 24.9% was reasonable, but only ensured third place. At Montrose, 29.4% gave Labour second place, and this was one of the best results for Labour (apart obviously from seats won) in the entire pre-1914 era. Nevertheless, the Liberal, who won 46.7% of the vote, was well ahead, and certainly expressed no apprehension about winning comfortably.[293]

In January 1910, Labour fought 11 Scottish seats, 2 more than in 1906, and won 2, whereas in England and Wales, 67 were fought and 38 won. Here, the march of Labour south of the border is much more marked. In the second election of that year, Labour fought a mere 5 seats in Scotland, winning 3, but in England and Wales, 51 seats were contested and 38 held. Again, the shrinkage in seats fought is clearer in Scotland, but the capture of another seat (West Fife) was a distinct bonus. The overall interpretation of these results seems fairly straightforward. If the 1910 elections saw, as Blewett contends, the containment of Labour by the Liberals, this was very much the case in Scotland.[294] Two of the seven seats not won in 1906 were not fought again before 1918 (Falkirk and Paisley). Four were fought again, in January, but not in December, 1910, and in all of them Labour's vote fell sharply, as Table 8.1 shows. Of the three seats fought at by-elections between 1906 and January 1910, only Montrose was tackled again, but there was a swing of around 4% to the Liberals from Labour, and the seat was not fought in the later 1910 contest. Three seats were contested in January 1910 which had not been fought in 1906, but only in West Fife did the party poll reasonably well, coming second with 36.7% of the vote. The December 1910 results showed no advances, apart from the three seats won. In Mid Lanark Robert Smillie polled 17 fewer votes and kept his share of the poll at around 25%, coming well behind the other two. At Camlachie, where Labour had won about 30% in the two previous elections, there was steep decline to 18.1% of the vote.

There were fourteen by-elections between December 1910 and the declaration of war in 1914. Ten of these were in seats with either a Labour tradition or a strong working-class presence, and this facilitates examination of the argument as to whether the Liberals were under mounting pressure from Labour or were still withstanding the challenge. In five of these ten, no Labour candidate was promoted, including two seats, Govan and North Ayrshire, which had been fought in January 1910. Govan was one of Labour's gains in the 1918 election, yet in 1911 it was not worth contesting. Of the five which were contested, the Labour share of the poll varied between 16% and 20%, apart from Leith, where it reached 24.5%. Two yardsticks can be applied to assess the pattern of these results. Firstly, where comparison with previous contests in these seats is possible, Labour was not doing well. Lanark North-East is the most graphic instance, with almost the same number of votes being got in 1911 (2879) as in 1901 (2900) but the share of the poll dropping from 21.7% in 1901 to 16.3% a decade later. Only in Leith could Labour be said to be improving its position. A second form of measurement is comparison with England, and here Scotland was polling less well for Labour. Consistently the percentage share of the vote won by the party in Scotland was lower, as Table 8.2 reveals. However, in one respect the impact of Labour was being felt more acutely by the Liberals in this phase: in three of the Scottish by-elections where they intervened, the Liberals lost the seat to the Unionists by a margin less than the Labour vote. Labour in England had been inflicting this kind of indirect damage on the Liberals in elections since 1906, but apart from Camlachie, this was not at all the case in Scotland until Mid Lothian in September 1912.

Various reasons may be adduced for the relatively weaker electoral showing by Labour in Scotland between 1906 and 1914. Firstly, as we saw, there were acute organisational weaknesses, which plagued the party far longer than in England.

Table. 8.1. The Labour Vote in Scotland, 1901–14

	1906	1910 Jan	1910 Dec	By-Election	
Aberdeen,South				(1907)	1740 (19.5%)
Ayrshire, North	2684 (20.8%)	1801 (12.9%)			
Dundee	6833*	10365*	8957*	(1908)	4014 (24.9%)
Falkirk	1763 (17.5%)				
Fife, West		4736 (36.7%)	6128* (53.0%)		
Glasgow, Blackfriars	3284* (39.5%)	4496* (61.7%)	4162* (59.5%)		
Glasgow, Camlachie	2568 (30.0%)	2443 (28.9%)	1539 (18.1%)		
Kilmarnock				(1911)	2671 (19.3%)
Lanarkshire, Govan	4212 (29.0%)	3545 (23.3%)			
Lanarkshire, Mid		3864 (25.7%)	3847 (24.7%)		
Lanarkshire, N-E	4658 (29.2%)	2160 (11.8%)		(1901)	2900 (21.7%)
				(1904)	3984 (27.9%)
				(1911)	2879 (16.3%)
Lanarkshire, N-W	3291 (23.9%)	1718 (9.7%)			
Lanarkshire, South				(1913)	1674 (16.8%)
Leith		2724 (18.9%)		(1914)	3346 (24.5%)
Mid Lothian				(1912)	2413 (16.7%)
Montrose		1888 (26.6%)		(1908)	1937 (29.4%)
Paisley	2482 (23.1%)				
Aberdeen, North (SDF)	1935 (25.1%)	1344 (16.9%)			

*Labour victory.

Secondly, a large number of Labour M.P.s elected in England owed their presence at Westminster to the understanding reached with Liberals in two-member

Table. 8.2. *Labour's share of poll in Scottish and English by-elections, 1911–14*

		By-election	Previous contests	
26 Sep. 1911	Kilmarnock	19.3%		
3 Nov. 1911	Keighley (1)	28.9%	(1906)	26.6%
13 Nov. 1911	Oldham	24.6%		
20 Jun. 1912	Holmfirth	28.2%	(1910 Jan)	14.9%
13 Jul. 1912	Hanley	11.8%		
26 Jul. 1912	Crewe	17.7%	(1910 Jan)	9.5%
10 Sep. 1912	Mid Lothian	16.7%		
18 Mar. 1913	Houghton-le-Spring	26.2%		
11 Nov. 1913	Keighley (2)	29.8%	see above	
12 Dec. 1913	Lanarkshire, South	16.8%		
26 Feb. 1914	Leith	24.5%	(1910 Jan)	18.9%
20 May 1914	Derbyshire, N-E	22.5%		
30 Jun. 1914	Durham, N-W	28.2%		

constituencies. In 1906, 11 of the 27 who won did so in this manner, but in Scotland, with only one such constituency, the path for Labour was harder. Moreover, in England the MacDonald–Gladstone arrangement of 1903 smoothed the way for Labour to fight a number of seats without a Liberal also in the field, and vice versa. In 1906 this helped Labour to win a good spread of seats otherwise probably unattainable. In Scotland, no such agreement existed, and the pact specifically excluded Scotland, where both parties' organisations were separate independent units. In 1903 the SLA did appoint a committee to consider the matter, and this accepted the need to retain the unity of the Progressive vote. While in most seats this would be best represented by the Liberals, in certain seats, where there was a substantial working-class vote which could be relied upon to vote for a Labour candidate, 'justice and wisdom' dictated pulling together behind that man.[295] At the instigation of Lord Tweedmouth, a Conciliation Committee was formed by the SLA, which he stressed would intervene in disputes between the two parties only when asked to do so. Six months before the 1906 election, Tweedmouth informed an enquirer that this committee had never met, not even to deal with Camlachie, the most intractable conflict.[296]

Thus everywhere in Scotland Labour faced Liberal, so detracting from the former's prospects. The absence of a pact was not so much because Liberalism was stronger in Scotland: the 1900 results had, after all, been the party's worst since 1832. It was in part because the SWRC, as we have seen, was, for reasons mainly of its own making, far less of a threat than the LRC. But perhaps as important a factor was the timing of consideration of the need for an arrangement in Scotland. The SLA only began to discuss this matter after Chamberlain's tariff reform campaign had radically altered the electoral opportunities for Liberals. The Gladstone-MacDonald concordat was reached in March 1903, about two months before Chamberlain's new departure. The Scottish Liberals only considered the matter in June, and did not appoint the Conciliation Committee until January 1904. The basis on which the committee indicated it would seek to accomplish settlement was in terms not applied in England: '[it] should endeavour to secure support on behalf of a candidate professing to stand on Free Trade lines, even although the candidate had not in the past been a supporter of the Liberal Party'.[297]

A third factor which prevented Labour making a breakthrough was the discernible trend (already referred to) from 1908 for social radicals to be nominated by Liberals as candidates. *The Forward* attributed the diminution by one third in Labour's vote at Camlachie in the December 1910 contest (when Labour fell by 904, and the Liberals rose by 660) to the introduction of J. M. Hogge, a Liberal whose policies it described as so advanced that he captured erstwhile Labour voters. In 1908, in the same seat, there had been much agitation among the ILP when the eminent Radical, Leo Chiozza Money, was chosen by the Liberals in a bid to unite the Progressive forces in the seat. The Scottish secretary of the ILP predicted that they would lose against Money, but might win if the alternative Liberal candidate were chosen.[298] Money was not chosen, the other man stood, and in January 1910 the Labour Party kept its vote at the 1906 level.

The advance of Labour was further held in check by the continuing divisions among the working class. The Irish nationalist vote, which had so grievously disappointed the socialist movement in the 1890s by its fickleness, remained a source of dismay in the pre-war decade.[299] Indeed, the trend in some seats seemed to be to move away from voting Labour. In North-East Lanark in 1906 it was reported by an impartial source that despite instructions from the official Irish Nationalist movement that its supporters should cast their franchise for the Liberal, many Irish trade unionists nevertheless 'feel bound to support the Labour candidate, and as a matter of fact are doing so and carrying with them no inconsiderable number of Irishmen'.[300] Labour polled its highest ever in this seat, adding some 25% to its vote in the 1904 by-election. This proved the peak in the seat, and in January 1910 *The Forward* pointed to the instructions issued to Irish Home Rulers to vote Liberal as the reason for Labour's low votes in several seats, including North-East Lanark.[301]

The Irish vote became ever more estranged from Labour as the Third Home Rule Bill proceeded on its tortuous legislative circuit. Thus the wholehearted support given in the 1911 by-election in North-East Lanark by Irish Nationalists to the Liberals drove *The Forward* to call for any informal alliances between Labour and the Irish to be broken. It argued that the Irish party in Scotland was controlled by 'publicans, slum property-owners, pawnbrokers, model lodging house-keepers and provision merchants ... That is why I say that the Irish Party, as a party, must be fought by Socialists and Labourists'.[302] At the Mid Lothian by-election in 1912, the Scottish organiser of the Irish party assured the Liberal candidate that, after an exhaustive canvass, 'with 12 exceptions you are getting the entire Nationalist vote. I have been all over the constituency and never in its history were so many Nationalist meetings held or the people so unanimous'.[303] The Irish Nationalists were also active in the South Lanark contest on behalf of the Liberals, and were believed to have secured the delivery of the Irish vote to

Liberals in Kilmarnock, St Rollox and Govan.[304] West Lothian, with its solid mining vote, seemed a good prospect for Labour when a contest occurred in late 1913. On investigation it emerged that the local miners' union were not affiliated to the Labour Party and, added a local ILPer, 'are likely to remain so until the Irish Home Rule question is settled, their membership being largely made up from both the Irish factions'.[305]

Even amongst those sections of the working class who were identified with Labour, the degree to which they had become socialist or even were irretrievably lost to the Liberals is questionable. It is instructive that all three Labour M.P.s were solid trade unionists, with quite close affinities to the Liberal Party. The views of George Barnes, who won Glasgow Blackfriars, on Glasgow socialists have already been cited. In 1902 he had been invited to stand for Labour in Dundee, but declined, allegedly stating that 'he was prepared to accept but only on condition that he was adopted by the Liberals. If there was to be a Liberal on the field, he would not stand'.[306] During the First World War, Barnes joined the Coalition government and had the distinction in the 1918 election of standing as a 'coupon' Labour candidate. Alexander Wilkie, the victor in Dundee, was secretary of the Shipwrights' union. As noted earlier, he was anathema to local socialists, and the leading Radical journal in the area observed that 'Mr Wilkie is a politician with whose opinions no Liberal can seriously quarrel'.[307] Wilkie retained links with the Liberal Party at least until 1908, when it was complained that he was vice-chairman of the Heaton Ward Liberal Club in Newcastle-upon-Tyne.[308] Willie Adamson, who took West Fife from the Liberals in a straight fight in December 1910, was assistant secretary of the county miners' union. The local Liberal newspaper praised him during that campaign as a fine upholder of Liberal principles, and the Fife miners' political agent (himself a Labour M.P. after the war) reprimanded the Unionist candidate for misrepresentation during the earlier 1910 election: 'no man knew better than he [i.e. the Unionist] the composition of the Labour Party, he knew it was not a socialist party'.[309]

There was a marked disposition in general to prefer the vote-attracting qualities of a trade unionist to those of a socialist from the ILP. At the Govan by-election of 1911 (which was the first seat in Clydeside to be won by the ILP in their post-war sweep, being taken by Neil MacLean in 1918) the ILP's Scottish secretary argued that a trade unionist might carry the seat, but, as the national organiser of the ILP remarked after a visit to the seat, 'absolutely nothing can be done in Govan by the ILP'.[310] In Leith in 1914 the message was still the same: ILP party officials had admitted six months before that they were in no position to promote a successful candidature. *The Forward* agreed that only 'a good Trade Unionist or kindred leader' could hope to unite the Labour voters.[311] So overwhelming was the presence of trade unionism that only 7 out of the 34 separate contests entered by Labour between 1906 and 1914 were fought by ILP nominees.

The preponderance of trade unionists among the Labour Party candidates was regarded by many Liberals as affording some reason for feeling that no irreparable gap had opened up between their party and organised labour in Scotland. Only a very few trade union candidates were socialists — Robert Smillie was the most prominent example. There was not a great deal of evidence that Labour voters were attracted by socialist ideals. Thus at Kilmarnock in 1911, where the ILP had nominated the candidate, the *Glasgow Herald* reported that his vigorous advocacy of undiluted socialism was turning many voters away from Labour. The *Herald* viewed this result with dismay, as a small Labour vote would jeopardise the hopes it entertained that the Unionist might win if the progressive vote were evenly split.[312] *The Forward* complained that in this election only one third of trade union members voted Labour.[313]

When Labour did win seats before 1914, as seen, the candidates were not socialistic in outlook. Nor did they rely on socialists or socialism to draw voters to Labour. Wilkie was warmly endorsed by local trade union leaders and based his victorious strategy on superior organisation centring on the officials and activists of his own union.[314] The local Liberal press described how when Wilkie won the nomination, his 'energetic body guard of canvassers and agents at once set on foot a thorough scheme for the organising of the Labour vote'.[315] In West Fife, as noted earlier, Labour's close and almost unique attention to the electoral register contributed mightily to victory. In Glasgow Blackfriars, where Barnes relied heavily on his Engineering union members for electoral work, there was an added factor behind his capture of the seat in 1906. As the defeated Unionist, Bonar Law, explained it, the key to the result lay with the 1,500 to 2,000 Irish voters in the constituency, which embraced the Gorbals and the Bridgegate, two of the densest Irish settlements in the city. These had largely gone Unionist in 1900, in order to deliver a reprimand to the Liberal candidate, A. D. Provand, who was deemed to be insufficiently committed to Irish Home Rule. In 1906, the Liberals persisted with Provand, whose opinions had altered little, and now the Irish switched to Barnes, who was firmly in favour of Home Rule, and the delivery of this Irish block vote, together with the natural Labour vote, was enough to tip the seat in Barnes' direction.[316]

Liberals found it quite easy to live with these Labour M.P.s: in Dundee, Wilkie and Churchill fought together after 1908; at Blackfriars, the Liberals declined to run against Barnes after he first won the seat, so that the Unionists faced what they termed 'an unholy alliance'; and in Fife West, the local Liberals counselled against opposing Adamson as he had given no offence.[317] In many seats, indeed, the relations between trade unions nominally affiliated to the Labour Party and the Liberals were often remarkably warm. At Camlachie, where a sort of pact had existed in 1900, the Liberals sought a 'mutual arrangement' to be applied to the next contest, whereby a 'progressive' candidate would run, but the insistence of the local ILP that their nominee, Joseph Burgess, be the candidate proved unacceptable to the Liberals, as Burgess was 'an irreconcilable socialist'. The Liberals were willing to accept John Hodges, the Camlachie-born leader of the steelmen's union, and emphatically not a socialist, as an alternative candidate, while Burgess would be given a free run in Gorton, a seat where he had local connections. Although this deal fell through, the willingness of the Camlachie unions to explore this solution with the Liberals profoundly worried the ILP. Two of its top national officials felt compelled to reprimand Camlachie LRC for infringing the autonomy of the party, adding tartly: 'It should hardly have been necessary to inform your committee of this fact'.[318]

The Mid Lothian by-election of 1912 was another revealing episode suggesting that Liberals could still feel that their links with the unions were not totally ruptured, even although in this instance they were electorally at loggerheads. Labour put up as candidate the county minders' leader, Robert Brown. Three or four years before he had been repudiated by Edinburgh socialists as unworthy to be a party candidate, and during the by-election he made it plain that he saw himself as a Labourist, not a socialist. Brown recalled with pride having worked to secure Gladstone's return in 1892 and also having appeared on the Liberal platform in 1906. He confessed that he had been disenchanted with the Liberal party for some years, but the main grounds he cited for this disillusion were not political ideology, but the Liberals' reluctance to promote working-class candidates. Brown had been on the executive of the Mid Lothian Liberal Association until 1908, when the national vote by the miners to disaffiliate obliged him to resign. Elibank, the M.P. who retired in 1912, stated that he would not have stood in the way in January 1910 had Brown wished to run.[319] When he announced his decision to retire, Elibank telegrammed local Liberals upon hearing rumours that Brown might come forward. He undertook to induce Alexander Shaw, the prospective Liberal, to withdraw and strove 'earnestly to advise my old Liberal supporters to concentrate on [Brown]'. He added that although Brown had been mainly associated with the mining union, 'he is a thoroughly experienced politician of wide sympathies, sound common sense and strong progressive views. He is a fine type of Scot, deservedly held in high popular esteem and respect, and possessing the confidence of all sections of the community'.[320] There were still, despite Brown's departure four years earlier, six miners' representatives sitting on the council of the county Liberal Association in 1912, and Elibank pressed the need for 'consolidation', as no Liberal could win without the miners.[321]

The gap between the vote predicted by the Labour Party in elections — which was usually derived from the known trade union membership in the seat — and the actual number of votes case for the party could also be read by Liberals as an encouraging sign that the working class was not solidly hostile to them. Thus at Mid Lothian, with over 5,000 miners and an unspecified number in the Farm Servants' Union, it was confidently anticipated by Labour that they would poll far in excess of 3,000 and come a good second, whereas they polled 2,413 and trailed badly in third place.[322] Again in Leith, 5,000 were expected to go to the ballot box for Labour, when only 3,346 did so, and *The Forward* bewailed the desertion of Labour by the miners in Lanarkshire South.[323] Perhaps these factors go toward explaining the insouciance of Liberals in regard to Labour's challenge. In Leith in 1909, the right-wing Liberal, Munro Ferguson, was faced with the selection by an enthusiastic Labour Party of William Walker, an influential trade unionist and ILPer who was also a powerful orator. Ferguson observed languidly: 'I see the Labour candidate is adopted for Leith. We'll have to look in there occasionally this autumn'.[324]

The last years before the First World War (1911–14) have been the subject of debate as to the proper interpretation of the movement of votes between Labour and Liberal. Some contend that the Liberals were continuing to withstand the Labour threat, as in the two 1910 elections, while the other argument is that by 1914 Labour was in a far stronger position and would have undermined the Liberals at the ensuing General Election. A third approach is to say that there was a drift away from the ILP and the Labour Party by the working class, in protest at the parliamentary paralysis of Labour, towards the more intransigent socialism of the British Socialist Party (BSP). The last point may be dealt with first. The BSP was active in Scotland, particularly on Clydeside, where John MacLean held sway, and in Aberdeen, where Thomas Kennedy led the party. However, membership remained very small, and as already noted, there were only isolated instances of ILPers joining the BSP in disgust at their party's flabbiness. In 1914, the BSP announced plans to contest six seats at the next election, where before it had stood only in North Aberdeen in 1906 and January 1910. (Its vote fell, incidentally, by one third in the second election.) The party seemed unlikely to do very well in any of these six, most of which were solidly Liberal — notably Kirkcaldy, Falkirk, and Orkney and Shetland. In Montrose, the ILP was already in the field, and apart from Aberdeen North the only place they might expect to acquit themselves well was Greenock. But none of these was at all winnable.

The weak performance of Labour in Scotland between 1911 and 1914 was a problem the party was well aware of. Even *The Forward*, normally the most bullish of papers, found it difficult to raise two cheers when looking at by-election results. Results like South Lanark were seen as 'disappointing', while Leith, easily the party's best performance in the sequence of results, was given a guarded response, being analysed as 'encouraging if not highly exhilarating'.[325] At Labour's 1914 conference an Edinburgh delegate perhaps expressed the prevailing opinion: 'Unfortunately Scotland was so imbued with Liberal principles that it was a harder fight there than in any other part of the country'.[326] Yet it may be wondered whether the Liberals might not have experienced some doubts of their own. The impact on the Liberals of Labour in causing the loss of three seats was a worrying trend. Moreover, there had been confidence in 1912 that the Mid Lothian miners were still basically well-disposed towards Liberalism, and that the presence of a Labour candidate in the 1912 by-election was in large part due to the inept handling of Elibank's retiral. Yet in 1914 Mid Lothian was one of the handful of seats which Labour was determined upon contesting at the next election. Again, in neighbouring West Lothian, the miners in 1914 at last moved to affiliate to Labour and set in motion a project to have a Labour candidate selected before the dissolution of Parliament.[327] Lastly, the result at Leith was a possible portent. Here, where the local Labour Party had doubled its membership and had won places on municipal and parochial bodies, a candidate fighting, as *The Forward* described it, on a clear and firm socialist platform, had won the highest share of the poll for Labour in all of the by-elections of that Parliament in Scotland. As no other contests occurred thereafter before war began, no firm conclusion may be drawn.

On the other hand it certainly cannot be maintained that Labour in Scotland was as strongly poised as in England to damage the Liberals at the forthcoming general election. MacKibbin and others have pointed to the preparations made by Labour to stand in perhaps 150 seats which were Liberal-held, signifying that the era of pacts and progressive alliances was over and that the Liberals might expect to lose many seats.[328] In Scotland, Labour's plans to fight seats did not enjoy uninterrupted momentum. In 1912 the party talked of standing in seventeen seats, including six where the Scottish Miners' Federation would have a free hand. By 1914, the Miners had dropped from six to two (West Fife and North-East Lanark) because the financial burden was too great. Of the remainder, six were categorised in 1914 as 'uncertain'.[329] In sum, at the outbreak of war Labour in Scotland would field a maximum of seventeen and a likely minimum of seven or eight candidates (including three M.P.s). If some figure in between were to be treated as the probable figure — say twelve or thirteen — this would be only just above the eleven candidates of January 1910. By contrast, in England and Wales, where sixty-seven candidates ran in January 1910, there were apparently to be twice as many. Scotland still lagged well behind the rest of Britain. Equally interesting are the feelers put out in 1914 by the Glasgow ILP to the Liberals to reach some sort of accommodation about candidates. MacCallum Scott was approached by prominent ILPers asking him whether the Liberals would accede to an ILP proposal not to run any Labour men in the city apart from Barnes, the sitting M.P., and in Camlachie, in return for the Liberals not fighting these two seats. Scott, evidently seeing this as a confession of weakness on the part of Labour, said that Liberals would only contemplate withdrawing in Camlachie if the Labour Party in addition pulled its candidates out in Leith, Mid Lothian and South Lanark. No further response by Labour is noted, perhaps because of the imminence of war.[330]

NOTES

1. C. Dilke to J. Ogilvy, 7 June 1902, Ogilvy MSS.

2. A. Sykes, *Tariff Reform in British Politics, 1903–13* (London, 1979), is a full survey of the movement.

3. Denny to A. J. Balfour, 20 Feb., 21 Nov. 1905, 12 Nov. 1908, Balfour MSS., Add. MSS. 49857, ff. 165–8, 49858, ff. 43–4, 49860, ff. 17–23.

4. *Fiscal Facts and Policy* (Glasgow, 1904), is a collection of these pieces.

5. W. Walker, *Juteopolis* (Ediburgh, 1979), pp. 281–2, cf. 77–8.

6. H. F. H. Elliot to Minto, 15 Oct. 1903, Minto MSS., MS. 12374, ff. 71–2.

7. *Glasgow Herald*, 3 Mar. 1906.

8. J. Stirling-Maxwell to Balfour of Burleigh, 15 Aug. 1903, Balfour of Burleigh MSS., 197.

9. Chamberlain to J. Parker-Smith, 13, 17 Mar. 1905, Smith of Jordanhill MSS., TD 1/116.

10. Same to same, 11 Aug. 1905, Ibid., TD 1/127.

11. W. Renfrew Conservative Association Minute Book, 24, 9 Nov. 1905.

12. Ibid., 30 Nov., 10 Dec. 1909.

13. C. B. Renshaw to J. P. Smith, 20 Dec. 1909, Smith of Jordanhill MSS., TD 1/377;

Balfour of Burleigh to Lansdowne, 1 Oct. 1909 (copy), Balfour of Burleigh MSS., 33.

14. Elliot to Scott, 6 Jan. 1906 (rough copy), Elliot MSS., MS. 19494, ff. 229–31.

15. Renshaw to Balfour of Burleigh, 22, 26 Sept. 1903, Balfour of Burleigh MSS., 190.

16. Cluny Castle MSS., 67, 132, for the annual reports of the two bodies.

17. *Glasgow Herald*, 5 Apr. 1909, 31 May 1910.

18. WSLUA Minute Book, 30 Oct., 3 Dec. 1903, 7 Mar. 1906.

19. Ibid., 28 Jun. 1905.

20. A. B. Haig to J. Sandars, 6 Aug. 1905, Balfour MSS., Add. MS. 49857, ff. 269–70.

21. Scottish Conservative Club, Political Committee Minute Book, 26 Jan. 1906, GD 309/44.

22. Kirkcaldy Burghs Unionist Association Minute Book, *Annual Report*, 1905–6, MS. 36617.

23. NUCAS, Eastern Division Committee Minute Book, 31 Oct. 1906.

24. D. Urwin, 'The Development of Conservative Party Organisation in Scotland until 1912', *SHR*, 44 (1965), pp. 102–11, discusses this process.

25. J. Sandars to A. J. Balfour, 1 Jan. 1908, Sandars to J. Short (1 Jan. 1910), Balfour MSS., Add. MSS. 49765, ff. 90–5; 49766, ff. 62–8.

26. Scottish Conservative Club, Political Committee Minute Book, 7 Mar. 1906, GD 309/44.

27. Unionist Organisation Committee Report (1911), pp. 30–2, Steel-Maitland MSS., GD 193/80/4.

28. NUCAS, Eastern Division Committee Minute Book, 'Special Report on the Eastern Division, April 1906'; cf. J. A. S. Cameron to G. Cruden, 20 Jan. 1906 (copy), Cluny Castle MSS., 68.

29. NUCAS, 'Special Report … '; W. Renfrew Conservative Association Minute Book, *Annual Report* 1908; J. Henderson to G. Cruden, 20 Jan. 1906 (copy), Cluny Castle MSS., 68.

30. NUCAS, 'Special Report', particularly West Lothian, and Peebles and Selkirk; Sir A. Grant to G. Cruden, 12 Nov. 1907 (copy), Cluny Castle MSS., 68.

31. J. A. Henderson to G. Cruden, 20 Jan. 1906, G. A. Anderson to Cruden, 22 Jan. 1906 (both copies), Cluny Castle MSS., 68.

32. H. Seton-Karr to Balfour, 5 Feb. 1910, Balfour MSS., Add MS. 49860, ff. 213–7. J. Ramsden, *The Age of Balfour and Baldwin, 1902–40* (London, 1978), pp. 48–9, for Kincardineshire.

33. J. A. S. Cameron to G. Cruden, 20 Jan. 1906 (copy), Cluny Castle MSS., 68; cf. NUCAS, 'Special Report', for the same.

34. J. Pirie to G. Cruden, 22 Jan. 1906 (copy), Cluny Castle MSS., 68.

35. Sir A. Grant to G. Cruden, 12 Nov. 1907 (copy), Ibid., 68.

36. Glasgow Conservative Association *Annual Report* 1911; Kirkcaldy Burghs Unionist Association Minute Book, 30 Sept. 1909, MS. 36617; cf. W. Renfrew Conservative Association Minute Book, 4 Mar. 1910, 27 Jun. 1911.

37. W. Renfrew Conservative Association Minute Book, *Annual Report* 1908; Kincardine Unionist Association Minute Book, 18 Dec. 1907.

38. Glasgow Conservative Association *Annual Report* 1909 (College).

39. E.g. Scottish Conservative Club, Political Committee Minute Book, 24 Mar. 1909, for West Lothian, GD 309/44.

40. *21st, 29th Annual Report of the Scottish Primrose League* (1906, 1914).

41. Kincardineshire Unionist Association Minute Book, 18 Dec. 1909.

42. Women's Unionist Association for Eastern and Northern Scotland, *Annual Reports*,

1907, 1908, Cluny Castle MSS., 132.

43. W. Renfrew Conservative Association Minute Book, 28 Jun. 1906; *Glasgow Herald,* 5 Oct. 1909; Glasgow Conservative Association *Annual Reports* 1910–12.

44. Kinross Women's Unionist Association Minute Book, 11 Apr., 29 Apr. 1908, 25 Jan. 1909, 20 Apr., 1 Dec. 1911, 11 Dec. 1912.

45. W. Renfrew Conservative Association Minute Book, 21 Jun. 1908, 27 Jun. 1911; SUA Eastern Division Council Minute Book, 10 Jun. 1913.

46. *Glasgow Herald,* 31 Jan. 1911.

47. W. Renfrew Conservative Association Minute Book, *Annual Report* 1910, 11 Jul. 1910; cf. *Annual Reports* 1905, 1907, 4 Mar. 1910. Cf. Ramsden, *Balfour and Baldwin,* pp. 49–50.

48. W. Renfrew Conservative Association *Annual Report* 1910.

49. Glasgow Conservative Association *Annual Reports* 1910–12, 1914.

50. R. Spencer to Mrs Cuninghame, 24 Mar. 1908, W. Renfrew Conservative Association Letter Books; Kincardineshire Unionist Association Minute Book, 18 Dec. 1907.

51. E.g. Report of the Sub-Committee of West Aberdeenshire Conservative Association on Reorganisation, 6 Jul. 1906, Cluny Castle MSS., 68; J. P. Smith to E. Starkie, 22 Jan. 1910 (not sent), Smith of Jordanhill MSS., TD 1/130.

52. Scottish Conservative Club Political Committee Minute Book, 27 May 1908, GD 309/44; cf. R. Spence to J. Cuthbertson, 18 May 1908, W. Renfrew Conservative Association Letter Book.

53. SUA Western Division Council Minute Book, 2 Apr., 1 Oct. 1913, Eastern Division Council Minute Book, 13 Jan. 1914; Scottish Conservative Club Political Committee Minute Book, 23 Apr., 22 Oct. 1913, GD 304/45.

54. *Glasgow Herald,* 6 May, 9 Jun. 1910, 3 Feb. 1911; WSLUA Minute Book, 15 Apr. 1910.

55. NUCAS, Eastern Division Council Minute Book, 25 May 1910; ESLUA Minute Book, 25 May 1910.

56. K. A. Oliver to A. B. Law, 17 Nov. 1911, Bonar Law MSS., BL 24/3/49.

57. G. Younger to A. B. Law, 9 Oct. 1913; Report of Scottish Labour Federation, n.d., Ibid., BL 30/3/12,42/N/11; Scottish Conservative Club Political Committee Minute Book, 25 Mar. 1914, GD 309/45.

58. E.g. *Glasgow Herald,* 5, 9, 12, 25 Oct., 6, 10 Nov., 18, 21, 24 Dec. 1909, 1 Jan. 1910; W. Renfrew Conservative Association Minute Book, 3 Feb. 1910; NUCAS *Annual Reports* 1909–10.

59. Kincardineshire Unionist Association Minute Book, 4 Nov. 1910, 25 Feb. 1912, 25 Jan. 1913, 16 Feb. 1914.

60. SUA Western Division Council Minute Book, 2 Apr. 1913.

61. WSLUA Minute Book, 17 May 1912.

62. Ibid., 18 Dec. 1908, 17 Feb. 1911, 21 Oct. 1910.

63. Ibid., 7 Aug. 1908.

64. NUCAS, Eastern Division Council Minute Book, 30 Nov., 14 Dec. 1904; WSLUA Minute Book, 7 Jan. 1908, 23 Apr. 1909; 5 Jan., 2 Feb. 1912.

65. WSLUA Minute Book, 18 Feb., 20 Mar, — May 1903.

66. Ibid., 22 Mar. 1907, *21st Annual Report* (1906), 19 May 1911, cf. Memo dated 8 Feb. 1911.

67. J. P. Smith to his mother, 16 Jun. 1907, Smith of Jordanhill MSS., TD 1/230; WSLUA Minute Book, 25 Feb. 1910.

68. ESLUA Minute Book, 18 Jan. 1911, 13 Jun. 1912.

69. WSLUA Minute Book, 30 Oct. 1912, *27th Annual Report.*

70. P. Ford to A. Chamberlain, 19 Oct. 1922, A. Chamberlain MSS., AC 31/2/102.

71. A. F. Irvine and R. R. MacDonald, Circular Letter, 23 Feb. 1914, Cluny Castle MSS., 68; Kincardineshire Unionist Association Minute Book, 25 Jan. 1913.

72. R. Stevenson to G. W. Tod, 26 Nov. 1908, to J. Lilburn, 11 Jan. 1909, W. Renfrew Conservative Association Letter Book.

73. NUCAS, Eastern Division Council Minute Book, 24 Nov. 1909; SUA, Eastern Division Council Minute Book, 18 Oct. 1913.

74. *Glasgow Herald*, 25 Nov. 1911.

75. E. Sprot to A. B. Law, 2 Apr. (1914), Bonar Law MSS., BL 32/2/7; SUA Eastern Division Council Minute Book, 18 Oct. 1913.

76. NUCAS, Eastern Division Council Minute Book, 28 Feb., 27 Nov. 1912; SUA Eastern Division Council Minute Book, 22 Apr., 24 Jun. 1914.

77. H. C. G. Matthew, *The Liberal Imperialists* (London 1973), pp. 98–9, notes the interest shown in Scotland by Liberal Imperialists.

78. Haldane to Rosebery, 3 Jan. 1901, 9 Jan. 1902 (copies), Haldane MSS., MS 5905, ff. 52–5, 158–61; cf. J. Sinclair to H. Gladstone, 12 Dec. 1901, H. Gladstone MSS., Add. MS 45995, ff. 27–30.

79. Haldane to Rosebery, 3 Jan. 1901 (copy), Haldane MSS., MS. 5905, ff. 52–5; letters to Rosebery from R. Munro Ferguson, 22 Jun. 1902, T. D. Gibson- Carmichael, 4 Jun., 15 Jul. 1902, W. Haldane, 8 Sept. 1902, Rosebery MSS., MSS. 10019, ff. 146–7; 10168, ff. 144–7, 192–7, 209–10.

80. J. Sinclair to Gladstone, 'Christmas Day', 1901, 7 Oct. 1902, H. Gladstone MSS., Add. MS. 45995, ff. 34–9, 51–60; for Rosebery's similar attitude, see R. Munro Ferguson to Rosebery, 22 Jun. 1902, Rosebery MSS., MS. 10019, ff. 146–9.

81. Sir T. D. Gibson-Carmichael to Rosebery, 28 Feb. 1902, and cf. R. Munro Ferguson to Rosebery, 15 Oct. 1902, Rosebery MSS., MSS. 10168, ff. 85–6, 10019, ff. 158–9.

82. H. Ivory to Rosebery, 25 Sept. 1902, Ibid., MS. 10168, ff. 231–4; Sir H. Campbell-Bannerman to W. Robertson, 5 Oct. 1901 (copy), Campbell-Bannerman MSS., Add. MS. 41226, ff. 17–18.

83. R. Munro Ferguson to Rosebery, 18 Sept. 1902, Rosebery MSS., MS. 10019, ff. 158–9.

84. Campbell-Bannerman to H. Gladstone, 28 Sep. 1902, to J. Sinclair, 9 Oct. 1902, to W. Robertson, 23 Oct. 1902, Campbell-Bannerman MSS., Add. MSS. 41216, ff. 231–3, 41230, ff. 58–9, 41226, ff. 32–5. Cf. Bannerman to Sir W. V. Harcourt, 11 Oct. 1902, Harcourt MSS., MS. Harcourt Dep. 77, ff. 179–81.

85. Gladstone to Campbell-Bannerman, 1 Oct. 1902, Campbell-Bannerman MSS., Add. MS. 41216, ff. 234–5.

86. W. Allard to Rosebery, 2 Jan. 1903, Rosebery MSS., MS. 10169, ff. 1–2.

87. Rosebery to R. B. Haldane, and reply, 5, — Sep. 1902, Haldane MSS., MS. 5905, ff. 228–9, 242.

88. W. Haldane to Rosebery, 8 Sep. 1902, Rosebery MSS., MS. 10168, ff. 209–10.

89. J. P. Maclay, R. Lorimer to Rosebery, 1 Mar. 1902, 27 Nov. 1905, Ibid., MSS. 10168, ff. 109–10, 10170, ff. 158–9; R. B. Haldane to Rosebery, 9 Jan. 1902, Haldane MSS., MS. 5905, ff. 158–61.

90. Haldane to Rosebery, 3 Jan. 1901, Haldane MSS., MS. 5905, ff. 52–5; R. Lorimer to Rosebery, 27 Nov. 1905, Rosebery MSS., MS. 10170, ff. 158–9.

91. Campbell-Bannerman to D. Crawford, 1 Oct. 1901 (copy), H. Gladstone to

Campbell-Bannerman, 24 Sep. 1901; 'Sir Henry Campbell-Bannerman's Leadership. Notes from Scotland by W. W. [ebster]' (typed, n.d., c. 1922), Campbell-Bannerman MSS., Add. MSS. 51217, ff. 151–2, 41216, ff. 130–3, 41252, ff. 234 *et seq.*

92. Munro Ferguson, W. Allard to Rosebery, 22, 2 Jan. 1903, Rosebery MSS., MSS. 10019, ff. 167–8, 10169, ff. 1–2.

93. Munro Ferguson to Rosebery, 18 Sep. 1902, Ibid., MS. 10019, ff. 154–7; J. Sinclair to H. Gladstone, 7 Oct. 1902, H. Gladstone MSS., Add. MS. 45995, ff. 51–60.

94. SLA Minute Book, 25 Jun., 3 Aug. 1903, 27 Jan., 19 May, 28 Jul. 1904.

95. Elibank to Rosebery, 17 Jan. 1903, Elibank MSS., MS. 8801, ff. 23–6; Tweedmouth to H. Gladstone, 1 Jun. 1903, H. Gladstone MSS., Add. MS. 46022, ff. 51–4.

96. Ferguson to Campbell-Bannerman, 11 Dec. 1905, Campbell-Bannerman MSS., Add. MS. 41222, f. 338.

97. Campbell-Bannerman to W. Robertson, 24 Oct. 1905 (copy), Campbell-Bannerman MSS., Add. MS. 41226, f. 74; Campbell-Bannerman to H. Gladstone, 30 Nov. 1905, H. Gladstone MSS., Add. MS. 45988, ff. 209–10; *Ayr Advertiser*, 28 Jan. 1904.

98. R. Munro Ferguson to Lady Ferguson, 24 Jul. 1905, Novar MSS., 26; SLA Minute Book, 1 Mar. 1906; cf. G. Cunningham to W. Allard, 2 Feb. 1906, Rosebery MSS., MS. 10171, f. 16.

99. E.g. P. F. Clarke, *Lancashire and the New Liberalism* (London, 1970); N. Blewett, *The Peers, the Parties and the People* (London 1972), H. V. Eny, *Liberals, Radicals and Social Politics, 1892–1914* (London, 1972), H. Pelling, 'Labour and the Downfall to Liberalism', in *Popular Politics and Society in Late Victorian and Edwardian Britian* (London, 1969).

100. SLA Minute Book, 29 Oct. 1902.

101. Elibank to Rosebery, 17 Jan. 1903, Elibank MSS., MS. 8801, ff. 23–6; J. Golder to A. Shaw, 18 Sep. 1912, Craigmyle MSS; SLA Minute Book, 29 Jan. 1903.

102. T. R. Buchanan to H. Campbell-Bannerman, n.d. (1903), Campbell-Bannerman MSS., Add. MS. 41237, ff. 81–2; J. Sinclair to H. Gladstone, 7 Jan. 1903, H. Gladstone MSS., Add. MS. 45995, ff. 61–5.

103. J. McCallum, *James Annand, M.P.: A Tribute* (Edinburgh, 1908), pp. 142–4.

104. SLA Minute Book, 4 May, 14 Sep. 1905.

105. Ibid., 19 Nov. 1908.

106. Ibid., 28 Jun. 1906; 9 May, 11 Jun. 1907.

107. *Glasgow Herald*, 8, 26 Oct., 7, 20 Dec. 1909.

108. SLA Minute Book, 5 May, 17 Nov. 1910, 8 Jun., 9 Nov., 7 Dec. 1911, 6 Feb. 1913.

109. Ibid., 9 Apr. 1914.

110. A. M. Scott Diary, 19 Oct. 1911; A. MacCallum Scott to R. Cumming, 3 Dec. 1912 (copy), MacCallum Scott MSS., MS. 1465/2, 185.

111. Scott Diary, 14 Apr. 1913, Scott to R. Cumming, 5 Oct. 1914, Ibid., MS. 1465/4, 197.

112. Aberdeen Liberal Association Minute Book, 22 Feb. 1909, Report by Committee (end 1913), MS. 2472.

113. Dundee Liberal Association *Annual Reports*, 1907, 1908; *Glasgow Herald*, 18 Apr. 1906; T. Shaw to A. Shaw, 31 Jan. 1905, Craigmyle MSS.

114. Scott Diary, 5 Mar., 19 Apr. 1911, 14 Apr. 1913; Scott to P. Young, 26 Nov. 1912, MacCallum Scott MSS., MS. 1465/2,4, 484.

115. SLA Minute Book, 7 Feb. 1907, 24 Mar. 1911.

116. A. MacCallum Scott to R. Cumming, 30 Sep. 1912, 6 Oct. 1913, MacCallum Scott MSS., MS. 1465/182, 189; SLA Minute Book, 8 Jun. 1911.

117. Scott Diary, 19 Jan. 1914, MacCallum Scott MSS., MS. 1465/5.

118. *Liberal Year Books*, 1905, 1909, 1915.

119. *Young Scots Handbook* (1911–12), p. 5.

120. *Glasgow Herald*, 11 Apr. 1910, 6 May 1912.

121. Haldane to Rosebery, 28 Sep. 1904 (copy), Haldane MSS., MS. 5906, ff. 134–5; W. V. Harcourt, H. Campbell-Bannerman to J. Gulland, 24 Mar. 1904, 10 Mar. 1906, Gulland MSS., Acc. 6868.

122. *Ardrossan and Saltcoats Herald*, 22 Dec. 1911; J. Golder to A. Shaw, 19 Sep. 1912, Craigmyle MSS.

123. T. N. Graham, *Willie Graham* (London, n.d.), p. 39.

124. *Ayr Advertiser*, 28 Dec. 1911.

125. E.g. W. Lang Todd to Tweedmouth, 15 Mar. 1905, Campbell-Bannerman MSS., Add. MS. 41231, ff. 90–1.

126. *Liberal Year Book*, 1914, p. 15.

127. SLA Minute Book, 18 Jul., 17 Oct. 1912, 21 Jan., 30 Apr., 16 Jun. 1914.

128. J. Buchan, *Andrew Jameson, Lord Ardwall* (Edinburgh, 1913), pp. 113–6.

129. *Disestablishment Banner*, 58 (Jul. 1900).

130. R. Rainy to A. R. Rainy, and reply, 20, 18(?) Sept. 1900: Mrs A Rainy, *Life of Adam Rolland Rainy, M.P.* (Glasgow, 1915), pp. 169–71.

131. *Disestablishment Banner*, 70 (Jul. 1904).

132. E.g. Buchan, *Lord Ardwall*, pp. 115–6.

133. R. B. Haldane, R. Rainy to H. Campbell-Bannerman, 3 Nov., 2 Aug. 1904, Campbell-Bannerman MSS., Add. MSS. 41218, ff. 155–8; 41237, ff. 287–8; J. A. Bryce to J. Bryce, 22 Aug. 1904, Bryce MSS., MS. Bryce Adds. 10, unfol.

134. SLA Minute Book, 22 Oct. 1904.

135. 'A Member of the Royal Scottish Geographical Association', *The Geography of Religion in the Highlands* (Edinburgh, 1905), p. 23 and App.

136. The Liberals retained Ross-shire by a majority of 1903 votes; Caithness by 28; and won Inverness-shire from the Unionists by 301. They lost Sutherland by 472, Orkney and Shetland by 40 and Wick by 213; while Inverness Burghs were retained by the Unionists on a margin of 360.

137. *Ayr Advertiser*, 14 Jan. 1904.

138. *Glasgow Herald*, 2 Jan. 1906.

139. SLA Minute Book, 5 Oct. 1906.

140. *Disestablishment Banner*, 84 (Jun. 1909).

141. Mrs Rainy, *A. R. Rainy*, pp. 292–6.

142. *Disestablishment Banner*, 58, 84, 86 (Jul. 1900, Jun. 1909, Jul. 1911).

143. SLA Minute Book, 29, 30 Nov. 1912.

144. Buchan, *Lord Ardwall*, pp. 115–6; cf. R. Farquharson, *The House of Commons from Within and other Memories* (London, 1912), p. 39, for a comment on the 'deadness' of disestablishment at the time of writing.

145. *Glasgow Herald*, 7 Jan. 1923, cf. *Foward*, 20 Oct. 1923.

146. SLA Minute Book, 21 Jul. 1911.

147. Ibid., 22 Oct. 1910.

148. *Young Scots Handbook* (1911–12), pp. 78–86.

149. Ibid., p. 40.

150. *Glasgow Herald*, 9 Feb. 1914.

151. Aberdeen Liberal Association Minute Book, 16 Sep. 1909, MS. 2472.

152. Ibid., 8 Oct. 1912.

153. Ibid., 9 Jan. 1913.

154. *Glasgow Herald*, 8 Jul. 1909, 6 Apr. 1912, 12 Apr. 1913.

155. Farquharson, *The House of Commons from Within*, pp. 185, 197.

156. Gladstone to Campbell-Bannerman, 21 Jan. 1906, Campbell-Bannerman MSS., Add. MS. 41217, ff. 294–5.

157. G. B. Hodgson, *From Smithy to Senate, the Life Story of James Annand, Journalist and Politician* (London, 1908), pp. 125–31, 157–60, 223.

158. McCallum, *James Annand, M.P.*, p. 15.

159. Ponsonby's Election Address, 1 May 1908, Ponsonby MSS., MS. Eng. hist. c. 657, f.1.

160. 'John', '?' to A. Ponsonby, 9 Jun., 20 Dec. (1908), Ibid., MS. Eng. hist. c. 657, ff. 82–3, 177–8.

161. Scott Diary, 10 Aug. 1913, MacCallum Scott MSS., MS. 1465/4.

162. His Election Address is in Pringle MSS., Hist. Coll. 226/I/39.

163. Scott Diaries, 16 May, 13 Aug. 1911, 15 Apr., 21 Oct. 1913, 10 Jul. 1914, MacCallum Scott MSS., MS. 1465/2,4,5; cf. *Young Scots Handbook* (1911–12), pp. 78–80.

164. R. P. Arnot, *A History of the Scottish Miners* (London, 1955), pp. 120–2.

165. Scott Diary, 10 Aug. 1913, MacCallum Scott MSS., MS. 1465/4.

166. *Forward*, 25 Oct. 1913.

167. J. W. Gulland, *Christ's Kingdom in Scotland, or the Social Mission of the United Free Church of Scotland* (Edinburgh, 1906), Part 2.

168. *Ardrossan and Saltcoats Herald*, 29 Dec. 1911.

169. R. C. Munro Ferguson to Lady Ferguson, 21 Oct. 1909, 15, 22 Mar. 1912, Novar MSS., 34, 41.

170. *The Balance*, 2 (Oct. 1909); SLA Minute Book, 17 Nov. 1910.

171. *Glasgow Herald*, 27 Dec. 1911; Laidlaw's election Address, 4 Jan. 1910, is in Gilmour MSS., GD 383/9/10.

172. H. J. Hanham, *Scottish Nationalism* (London, 1969), pp. 94–103.

173. *Young Scots Handbook* (1911–12), pp. 6–16, 38–42; *Glasgow Herald*, 26 Apr. 1909, 5 Sep. 1910, 1 May, 7 Jul., 7 Sep. 1911; Mrs Rainy, *A. R. Rainy*, pp. 347–50.

174. 'Deputation of Scottish Liberal Members of Parliament to the Rt. Hon. H. H. Asquith, K.C., M.P.', Asquith MSS., MS. Asquith 89, ff. 3 *et seq.*

175. SLA Minute Book, 12 Sep., 17 Oct. 1912, cf. 16 Jun. 1914: Scott Diary, 26 Jul. 1912, 22 Jul. 1913, 1 Jul. 1914, MacCallum Scott MSS., MS. 1465/3,4,5.

176. G. Younger to A. B. Law, 19 May 1914, Law MSS., BL 32/3/36.

177. 'Deputation ... ', speech by J. A. M. MacDonald, Asquith MSS., MS. Asquith 89, ff. 7–9.

178. *Glasgow Herald*, 6 May 1912.

179. J. A. Bryce to Lord Bryce, 19 Oct. 1913, Bryce MSS., MS. Bryce Adds. 10.

180. P. Jalland, 'United Kingdom Devolution: Political Panacea or Tactical Diversion?' *EHR* 94 (1979), esp. pp. 762–4, for this.

181. *Young Scots Handbook* (1911–12), pp. 49–56; Young Scots Society, *60 Points for Scottish Home Rule* (Glasgow, 1912), points 2, 3.

182. SLA Minute Book, 16 May 1912.

183. Scott Diary, 26 Jul. 1912, 22 Jul. 1913, MacCallum Scott MSS., MS. 1465/3,4.

184. *Young Scots Handbook* (1911–12), pp. 36–42; cf. *Scotland's Fight for Freedom: The Two Vetoes* (Young Scots Society Leaflets, N.S., No. 3) (Glasgow, n.d. (c. 1910)).

185. *Glasgow Herald*, 18 May 1914.

186. B. B. Gilbert, 'David Lloyd George's Reform of British Land Holding and the Budget of 1914', *HJ* 21 (1978), pp. 117–42; H. V. Emy, 'The Land Campaign: Lloyd George as Social Reformer, 1909-14', in A. J. P. Taylor (ed.), *Lloyd George — Twelve Essays* (London, 1970), pp. 35–70.

187. J. Brown, 'Scottish and English Land Legislation, 1905–11', *SHR* 47 (1968), pp. 72–85.

188. Lady Pentland, *The Right Hon. John Sinclair, Lord Pentland, G.C.S.I.: A Memoir* (London, 1928), p. 84.

189. *Scottish Land and Property Federation, Its Objects and What It Has Achieved* (Edinburgh, 1919), pp. 2–4; Lady Pentland, *Sinclair*, pp. 89–91.

190. SLA Minute Books, 28 Aug., 5 Oct. 1906, 2 May, 29 Jun. 1907, 25 Mar., 30 Jun., 8 Sep. 1908, 3 Jun., 14 Sep., 4 Oct., 25 Nov. 1909, 6, 7 Oct. 1911, 15 Feb. 1912.

191. *Glasgow Herald*, 12 Dec. 1910, for Argyllshire.

192. 'Report on Scottish Conference', 5 Aug. 1911, Labour Party MSS., NEC Minute Book.

193. *Glasgow Herald*, 8 Jul. 1909; Aberdeen Liberal Association Minute Book, 16 Sep. 1909, MS. 2472.

194. J. P. Smith to Mrs Smith, 19 Jan. 1910, Smith of Jordanhill MSS., TD. 1/231; H. F. H. Elliot to Lord Minto, 23 Jan. 1910, Minto MSS., MS. 12374, ff. 112–5.

195. Elibank to Rosebery, 16 Jan. 1908, Elibank MSS., MS. 8801, ff. 167–71.

196. R. Munro Ferguson to Lady Ferguson, 13, 15, 16, 17, 20, 21 Aug. 1907, Novar MSS., 28; R. C. M. Ferguson, *Afforestation* (London, 1909).

197. Scott Diary, 26, 28 Jul. 1912, MacCallum Scott MSS., MS. 1465/3.

198. Mrs Macrae, 'The Election in the West of Scotland', *Scottish Liberal Women's Magazine*, Apr. 1910, p. 76.

199. SLA Minute Book, 29, 30 Nov. 1912.

200. Scott Diary, 21 Oct. 1913, 7 Jan. 1914, MacCallum Scott, MSS., MS. 1465/4,5.

201. *Glasgow Herald*, 6 Apr. 1912.

202. A. D. Kinloch to R. B. Outhwaite, 2 Feb. 1914; A. D. Kinloch, 'Land Enquiry (Scotland). Summary of Preliminary Report' (typescript, n.d. — c. 1912), Kinloch MSS., 1/18.

203. SLA Minute Book, 21 Jan. 1914; cf. *Glasgow Herald*, 8 Jul. 1907, for similar points made by the Glasgow Liberal Council.

204. A. D. Kinloch to R. B. Outhwaite, 2 Feb. 1914, Kinloch MSS., 1/18.

205. *Bazaar to Promote the Taxation of Land Values* (Glasgow, 1902), pp. 17–27, outlines the SLA's relations with the 'single taxers'; for Alston: J. L. Kinloch to J. Fels, and to Councillor J. W. Pratt, 4 Mar., 11 Dec. 1909, Kinloch MSS., 1/19.

206. G. Barnes to J. L. Kinloch, 20 Feb. 1909, G. Carson and J. Busby to Kinloch, Aug. 1909, Ibid., 1/19.

207. *Glasgow Herald*, 20 Sep. 1909.

208. *Forward*, 19 Aug. 1911, 3 Aug. 1912.

209. *Ibid.*, 3 Aug. 1912, cf. 20 Dec. 1913.

210. *Glasgow Herald*, 6 Apr. 1912.

211. *Forward*, 31 Dec. 1910.

212. Elibank to Knollys, 7 Nov. 1906 (draft); 'Confidential: Memorandum on the Socialist and Labour Movements in Scotland' (endorsed Feb. 1908); Elibank MSS., MS. 8801, ff. 99–102, 145–51.

213. F. C. Gardiner to A. B. Law, 21 Nov. 1907, Bonar Law MSS., 18/3/47.

214. W. M. Haddow to J. B. Glasier, 12 Mar. 1909, Glasier MSS., I. 1,1909/63.

215. J. Duncan to Mabel, 9 Nov. 1906, 16 Jun. 1907, Duncan MSS., Acc. 5490/1, ff. 109–11, 182–4.

216. Same to same, 5 Aug. 1907, 22 Jun. 1908, Ibid., Acc. 5490/1, ff. 198–9, 5490/2, ff. 74–5.

217. Same to same, 12, 29 Nov. 1906, Ibid., Acc. 5490/1, ff. 112–4, 115–6.

218. W. Stewart to F. Johnson, 30 Jul. 1907, Johnson MSS., 1907/194.

219. E.g. P. Laidlaw to J. K. Hardie, 18 Dec. 1908, Johnson MSS., 1908/523.

220. A. Wilson to F. Johnson (23 Sep. 1910), Ibid., 1910/461.

221. *Forward*, 12 Mar., 14 May 1910.

222. ILP Archives, 53 and 57, 'Lapsed Branches',

223. Ibid.

224. ILP, *17th and 22nd Annual Reports* (1909, 1914).

225. Angus District ILP Minute Book, 26 Apr. 1909, 19 Mar. 1910, 22 Apr., 26 Aug., 26 Oct. 1911, 18 May, 24 Aug. 1912, 1 Feb., 20 Dec. 1913.

226. *Forward*, 5 Apr. 1913.

227. J. Paton, *Proletarian Pilgrimage* (London, 1935), p. 166; Glasgow Conservative Association *Annual Report* 1911.

228. Cf. D. Howell, *British Workers and the Independent Labour Party, 1888–1906* (Manchester, 1983), pp. 338–9.

229. J. Duncan to Mabel, 12 Nov. 1907, Duncan MSS., Acc. 5490/2, ff. 24–6.

230. *Forward*, 22 Oct. 1910.

231. Angus ILP Minute Book, 27 Jan. 1912.

232. Graham, *Willie Graham*, pp. 40–1.

233. J. Duncan to Mabel, 28 Sep. 1906, Duncan MSS., Acc. 5490/1, ff. 94–7.

234. *Forward*, 1 Jan. 1910, cf. 30 Dec. 1911, for complaints of lack of enthusiasm.

235. W. M. Haddow, *Socialism in Scotland: Its Rise and Progress* (Glasgow, n.d.), p. 49.

236. Graham, *Willie Graham*, p. 51.

237. J. Duncan to Mabel, 17 May 1907, 26 Mar. 1908, Duncan MSS., Acc. 5490/1, ff. 165–8; 5490/2, ff. 59–60.

238. ILP NAC Minute Book, 22–3 Nov. 1910, Coll. Misc. 464/1/6.

239. Haddow, *Socialism in Scotland*, pp. 49–51.

240. F. Johnson to W. Grant, 8 Aug. 1913 (copy), Johnson MSS., 1913/170; *Forward*, 2 Apr. 1910.

241. ILP NAC Minute Book, 25 Mar. 1913, Coll. Misc. 464/1/7; cf. Haddow, *Socialism in Scotland*, pp. 50–1 for Allan's 'helpful' role as Chairman of the Glasgow ILP, 1910–13.

242. J. K. Hardie to J. B. Glasier, 11 May 1908, Glasier MSS., I. 1,1908/39.

243. G. Dallas to ?, 16 Oct. 1909, F. Jowett to J. Burgess, 27 Nov. 1909, Johnson MSS., 1909/447,547(ii).

244. Labour Party, *Report of 13th Annual Conference* (1913), p. 79.

245. In 1902 the Committee was re-titled the Scottish Workers' Representation Committee (SWRC). The latter's acronym has been used in the text, even for the 1900–2 period.

246. G. Carson to J. r. MacDonald, 1 Mar. 1904, Labour Party MSS., LRC/13/438; LRC *Annual Report* 1900–01, p. 2.

247. J. K. Hardie and J. B. Glasier to NAC of the ILP, 8 Oct. 1898 (draft), Johnson MSS., 1898/96: M. H. Irwin to J. R. MacDonald, 4 May 1899, MacDonald MSS., PRO 30/69/5/9.

248. 'Statement of Steps leading up to the Calling of the First Conference'. SWRC Minute Book, Mf. MSS. 141.

249. J. Cassels, A. Gardiner to J. R. MacDonald, 12, 15 Mar. 1906, Labour Party MSS., LP/GC/2/31; LRC/MISC.2/2/2. The writers were secretaries of, respectively, the Scottish Engine Keepers and Scottish Painters unions.

250. SWRC, *1st, 6th Annual Reports*. The 1901 figure is adjusted to allow for the subsequent withdrawal of the SDF and of many Co-operative societies, who were therefore ineligible to affiliate in 1906. There were 247 delegates at the 1901 conference.

251. F. Bealey & H. Pelling, *Labour and Politics, 1900–1906* (London, 1958), pp. 293–7.

252. S. MacArthur to J. R. MacDonald, and reply, 18, 21 Nov. 1904; J. S. Robertson to MacDonald, 17 Apr. 1905, Labour Party MSS., LRC/17/353–4; LRC/22/35. MacArthur wrote on behalf of Patrick LRC, Robertson of Clydebank LRC.

253. J. Kelly to MacDonald, 23 Apr. 1903, Ibid., LRC/8/340. Kelly was secretary of St Rollox LRC.

254. E. Shinwell, *Conflict Without Malice* (London, 1955), pp. 41–3; B. Shaw to J. S. Middleton, 11 Oct. 1914, Labour Party MSS., LP/SAC/14/32.

255. SWRC Minute Book, 9 Apr. 1904, Mf. MSS. 141.

256. *Address and Manifesto* of the SWRC. n.d. (1900), Labour Party MSS., LRC/1/373/2.

257. SWRC Minute Book, 9 Jun. 1900, 12 May 1906, Mf. MSS. 141.

258. SWRC Minute Book, 20 Aug. 1904, Ibid.

259. SWRC Minute Book, 30 Sep. 1905, 25 Jun. 1904, 9 Dec. 1905, Ibid.

260. SWRC Minute Book, 12 Dec. 1903, 10 Dec. 1904, Ibid., cf. Labour Party MSS., NEC Minute Book, 2 Dec. 1904; SWRC, *6th Annual Report* (1906).

261. Carson to MacDonald, 10 Apr. 1907, Labour Party MSS., LRC/MISC 2/1/60.

262. R. Charlton to J. R. MacDonald, 23 Apr. 1903, Labour Party MSS., LRC/8/105; SWRC, *6th Annual Report* (1906).

263. SWRC Minute Book, 15 Apr. 1905; SWRC *6th Annual Report* (1906), p. 10; SWRC Minute Book, 6 Jul. 1907, Mf. MSS. 141.

264. Carson to MacDonald, 6 Jan. 1904 (i.e. 1905), 23 Jan. 1907, Labour Party MSS., LRC/19/406; LP/GC/11/358.

265. SWRC Minute Book, 28 Apr. 1900, Mf. MSS. 141.

266. D. C. Cumming to MacDonald, 25 Mar. 1904, Labour Party MSS., LRC/13/49.

267. J. R. MacDonald to J. Thomson, and reply, 28, 29 Nov. 1907; J. M. Jack to MacDonald, 14 Jun. 1904; Ibid., LRC/MISC/2.2.15,16; LRC/15/140. Thomson was Secretary of the Blacksmiths' Union, Jack of the Scottish Ironmoulders.

268. MacDonald to J. Thomson, 28 Nov. 1907, Ibid., LRC/MISC 2/2/15.

269. MacDonald to J. Robertson, 12 Aug. 1904, to J. S. Middleton, 4 Aug., 20 Jul. 1904, Ibid., LRC/16/346,294,285.

270. MacDonald to J. Cassels, and reply, 23 Feb., 12 Mar. 1906, Ibid., LP/GC/1/34, 2/31.

271. SWRC Minute Book, 15 Dec. 1906, 7 Mar. 1908, Mf. MSS. 141.

272. Labour Party MSS., NEC Minute Book, 18 Jan. 1908.

273. Ibid., NEC Minute Book, 28 Apr. 1908.

274. SWRC Minute Book, 6 Jun. 1908, Mf. MSS. 141; Labour Party MSS., NEC Minute Book, 28 Oct., 25 Nov. 1908.

275. J. M. Jack to J. R. MacDonald, 2 Feb. 1909, Labour Party MSS., LRC/MISC 2/1/100/1.

276. Labour Party, *Report of 14th Annual Conference* (1914), p. 100.

277. Labour Party MSS., NEC Minute Book, 'Report on Scottish Conference, 5 August 1911'.

278. Ibid., NEC Minute Book, 'Special Scottish Report' (1912): 4, 8 Nov. 1912, 27 Jan. 1913; Labour Party, *Reports of 13th, 14th Annual Conferences* (1913, 1914), pp. 77–9, 26–7 respectively.

279. Labour Party MSS., NEC Minute Book, 5 Aug. 1914, 16 Sep. 1915.

280. Ibid., NEC Minute Book, 'Report on Scottish Conference, 5 August 1911'.

281. Ibid., NEC Minute Book, 27 Jun. 1911, 14 Feb. 1912.

282. *Forward*, 5 Oct. 1912.

283. B. Shaw to J. S. Middleton, 6 Jul. 1914, Labour Party MSS., LP/SAC/14/8, cf. R. I. McKibbin, *The Evolution of the Labour Party, 1910–24* (London, 1974), pp. 29–31.

284. Labour Party, *Report of 14th Annual Conference* (1914), p. 100; B. Shaw to J. S. Middleton, 2 May 1914, Labour Party MSS., LP/SAC/14/7.

285. Labour Party, *Report of 13th Annual Conference* (1913), p. 82.

286. *Ayr Advertiser*, 1 Feb. 1906.

287. Labour Party, *Report of 13th Annual Conference* (1913), p. 4.

288. Barnes to J. R. MacDonald, 15 Oct. 1907, Labour Party MSS., LP/GC/20/108.

289. Labour Party, *Report of 13th Annual Conference* (1913), pp. 77–9.

290. J. Carnegy, D. Turnbull to J. K. Hardie, 12 Mar. 1905, 17 May 1908, Johnson MSS., 1905/23, 1908/180.

291. *Forward*, 17 Jun., 23 Sep. 1911. The first article appears under Dollan's pseudonym, 'Myner Collier'. Walker, *Juteopolis*, pp. 312–3, notes the absence of industrial strife in Dundee's jute industry between 1912 and 1914.

292. J. F. Duncan to J. K. Hardie, 7 Jan. 1907, Johnson MSS., 1907/5.

293. R. V. Harcourt to L. Harcourt, 10 May, 'Monday' (1908), Harcourt MSS., MS. Harcourt Dep. 681, ff. 240–1, 270–1.

294. N. Blewett, *The Peers, the Parties and the People*, Ch. 12.

295. *Scotsman*, 20 Nov. 1903.

296. SLA Minute Book, 13 Feb. 1903, 7, 27 Jan., 30 Mar. 1904, 29 Jun. 1905.

297. Ibid., 30 Mar. 1904.

298. *Forward*, 17 Dec. 1910; W. Stewart to J. K. Hardie, 30 Nov. 1908, Johnson MSS., 1908/493.

299. I. Wood, 'Irish Nationalism and Radical Politics in Scotland, 1880–1906', *Bull. Scot. Lab. Hist. Soc.* 9 (1975), pp. 21–38, is helpful.

300. *Motherwell Times*, 12 Jan. 1906.

301. *Forward*, 29 Jan. 1910.

302. *Forward*, 4, 25 Mar. 1911.

303. J. O'D. Derrick to A. Shaw, 9 Sep. 1912, Craigmyle MSS.

304. *Forward*, 29 Nov. 1913; *Glasgow Herald*, 28 Sep., 23 Dec. 1911, 27 Feb. 1912.

305. J. S. Taylor to F. Johnson, 27 Oct. 1913, Johnson MSS., 1913/225. For Dundee, see Walker, *Juteopolis*, pp. 138–9, 145–7, 282, 378–81.

306. Letters to J. K. Hardie from J. Reid, T. Wilson, W. F. Black, 26 Mar., n.d., 10 August 1902, Johnson MSS., 1902/27,87,88.

307. *People's Journal*, 1 Apr. 1905. Despite the date, there is no reason to think that this is not a serious article.

308. Labour Party MSS., NEC Minute Book, 29 Jan., 18 Mar. 1908.

309. *West Fife Echo*, 2 Feb. 1910.

310. F. Johnson to J. B. Glasier, 5 Dec. 1911, Glasier MSS., I. 1,1911/40; J. S. Taylor to Johnson, 7 Dec. 1911, Johnson MSS., 1911/336.

311. F. Johnson to W. Grant, 8 Aug. 1913 (copy), Johnson MSS 1913/170; *Forward*, 14 Feb. 1914.

312. *Glasgow Herald*, 28 Sep. 1911.

313. *Forward*, 2, 30 Sep. 1911.

314. Walker, *Juteopolis*, pp. 200, 280, 287–8.

315. *People's Journal*, 4 Mar. 1905.

316. Law to J. Chamberlain, 19 Jan. 1906, J. Chamberlain MSS., JC 21/2/16; A. MacKay to Law, 22 Jan. 1906, Bonar Law MSS., BL 21/1; *Glasgow Observer*, 13 Jan. 1906.

317. Glasgow Conservative Association *Annual Report* 1910; SLA Minute Book, 26 Jan. 1911.

318. SWRC Minute Book, 20 Jun. 1903, Mf. MSS. 141; J. Burgess to J. K. Hardie, 19 Jun. 1903, Hardie to A. E. Fletcher, 23 Jun. 1903 (copy); Burgess to Hardie, 27 Sep. 1903; F. Johnson to J. Fraser, 25 Apr. 1904 (copy), Johnson MSS., 1903/137A,142,187,1904/14a; T. F. Wilson to W. Barry, 16 Mar. 1904, J. Fraser to Wilson, 21 Apr. 1904, R. Shanks to Lord Tweedmouth, 8 Feb. 1905, J. K. Hardie — Shanks correspondence, 4 Apr. — 14 May 1905 (a bundle of press-cuttings), Pringle MSS., Hist. Coll. 226/I/3,5,9,10–17; F. Johnson and J. B. Glasier to J. Fraser, 25 Apr. 1904 (copy), Johnson MSS., 1904/14A.

319. *Dalkeith Observer*, 15, 22, 29 Aug. 1912; Midlothian Liberal Association Minute Book, 15 Apr. 1908; Elibank to A. Shaw, 14 Aug. 1912, Craigmyle MSS.

320. *Dalkeith Observer*, 15 Aug. 1912.

321. *Ibid.*, 15 Aug. 1912; Elibank to A. Shaw, 14 Aug. 1912, Craigmyle MSS.

322. *Forward*, 17 Aug. 1912.

323. *Ibid.*, 14 Feb. 1914, 20 Dec. 1913.

324. R. C. Munro Ferguson to Lady Ferguson, 12 Aug. 1909, Novar MSS., 33.

325. *Forward*, 20 Dec. 1913, 28 Feb. 1914.

326. Labour Party, *Report of 14th Annual Conference* (1914), p. 100.

327. W. Lothian Miners' Association Minute Book, 22 Nov. 1913, 22 May 1914, Acc. 4312/1.

328. MacKibbin, *Evolution of the Labour Party*, pp. 72–87.

329. Labour Party MSS., NEC Minute Book, 'Special Scottish Report' (Aug/Sep. 1912), 10 Oct. 1912, 7 May 1914; *Glasgow Herald*, 7 Jan., 7 Apr., 11 Jun. 1914.

330. Scott Diary, 25 Apr. 1914, MacCallum Scott MSS., MS. 1465/5.

9

The Arrival of Labour: 1914–24

I

The breakthrough achieved by the Labour Party in Scotland after the First World War was sudden and emphatic. 'So far as anyone could see before 1918', wrote an erstwhile ILP organiser from the vantage point of the mid-1930s, 'viewing the situation realistically, the slow, if steady, progress of the Labour Party would continue making inroads into the strength of the other parties, but the real challenge seemed still many years ahead'.[1] What was striking about the advance made by Labour in Scotland was what appeared to be both its quantitative and qualitative dimensions. In the 1918 election only seven Scottish seats were won by the party, whereas fifty-two were won in England and Wales. In 1922, 113 seats were gained in the latter, while Scotland returned the disproportionately large tally of twenty-nine, as well as one Communist who was endorsed by the local Labour party. In the 1923 and 1924 elections, Scotland's share of Labour M.P.s remained high.

Table 9.1.   Labour M.P.s, 1918–24

	1918	1922	1923	1924
England and Wales	52	113	157	125
Scotland	7	30*	34	26
TOTAL	59	143	191	151

* Including 1 Communist, who was endorsed by the local Labour party.

But in 1922 Scotland had not just swung to Labour; it had apparently embraced militant socialism more warmly than the rest of the country. The 1918 M.P.s had been highly moderate men. The two who had held their seats before 1914 —Wilkie (Dundee) and Adamson (West Fife) — had both been firm supporters of the war. Of the five new men, F. H. Rose (Aberdeen North), James Brown (Ayrshire South) and Duncan Graham (Hamilton) had also been 'war patriots'. Two ILPers were returned: Willie Graham (Edinburgh Central) was, as is discussed later, in no sense an extreme socialist, while Neil MacLean (Govan), though more left-wing, was described by Unionist officials in Glasgow as not 'so objectionable as some'.[2] The 1922 intake was quite different, for of the thirty-two ILPers in this Parliament, nearly half were from Scotland. Within Scotland, the ILP's main base

277

was the Glasgow area, where ten of the city's fifteen seats were won by Labour, as well as nearby constituencies like Dumbarton and West and East Renfrewshire. With a couple of exceptions, these M.P.s were all ILP members. The 'Clydesiders' soon won a reputation for their vehement socialism and for their frequent flouting of parliamentary convention in order to draw attention to their political demands. The most notorious such episode came in June 1923 when Maxton and Wheatley led a group of Clydesiders in attacking the Conservatives as murderers for seeking to cut Government expenditure on Scottish social welfare.[3]

The success of the ILP in the Clyde area seemed linked with the wartime unrest in the same locality, when the Government had encountered vigorous resistance to their labour policy.[4] The emergence in 1915 of the Clyde Workers' Committee with its leadership of Marxists had been a serious threat, and the general strike of January 1919 in Glasgow reinforced the image of Clydeside as politically and industrially militant. It seems clear that the wartime events on the Clyde did move many of the rising generation of ILPers to a more left-wing brand of socialism than the ethical socialism so typical of the movement before 1914. By the later stages of the war the Labour Party leaders were worried at the tendency for the movement in Scotland, plainly led by men like Maxton, Johnston and Kirkwood, to advocate policies whose radical demands were felt to be unacceptable.[5] By 1918 old ILP hands like Glasier found themselves out of touch with the new ILP elements: 'I suppose we have got to approve the nomination of Neil for Paisley and Martin for Dunbartonshire', he complained, 'though for myself I don't know either of these comrades from Adam'.[6] Hence the results of 1922 suggested a continuous thread of extreme socialism at work. So grave was the position revealed by that election that *The Times* took the unusual step of sending a special correspondent to study the swing to Labour on Clydeside. The journalist reported the results were not accidental, but the fruits of long years of propaganda and unremitting effort by the socialists.[7]

Thus the great triumph for the Scottish ILP in returning so many of its members to Parliament in 1922 would suggest a large and thriving movement, especially in Glasgow. Yet when the ILP held its 1920 Annual Conference in Glasgow, the chairman of the city's party sounded a cautionary note, seeking to disabuse delegates of the widespread assumption that they were meeting in a centre of socialism second to no other town in Britain. In fact, Dollan stressed, there was a very low level of labour representation on elected municipal authorities, so that the delegates should 'realise that all the talk of Glasgow being the Petrograd of Britain was a great deal of moonshine and they in Glasgow had very little to give in the way of encouragement because they were looking to the conference to give them encouragement ... '[8] These deeply pessimistic remarks by Dollan came at a point when the ILP's strength in Glasgow was at a higher point that at any time in the past or the near future. Its membership climbed to 2,992 in 1920–21, but collapsed to 1,370 in the next year, and although an undefined increase was reported in subsequent years, it was not until the later 1920s that the 1920 level was regained.[9] By contrast, in 1922 the Glasgow Unionists had some 20,000 members. Even the ILP's recovery in active support in

1922–3, as it confessed, came only after the election results. Indeed on the eve of the general election, the ILP still seemed in the doldrums. Nearly half the branches had stopped sending delegates to the Glasgow Federation meetings during the setback of 1921, and in September 1922 (two months before polling), after considering what to do about lapsed branches, 'it was agreed that no attempt be made to re-form the branches at present'.[10] Even propaganda work, so frequently seen as the real basis of the ILP's support in Glasgow, was not prospering in the run-up to the 1922 election. In 1921–22 less vigorous efforts were recorded, meetings were felt to be eliciting a declining response, and sales of literature were dwindling. It is interesting to note that unemployment and the economic recession were held responsible for this apathetic reaction — a contrary interpretation to that often advanced to explain the ILP electoral gains in 1922.[11]

The general position of the ILP in the rest of Scotland was little better. Scotland contained around a quarter of all the ILP branches, but this figure is misleading. Firstly, the average membership of each branch in Scotland, at 20, was well below that of 50 in England, so that in 1923 one authoritative calculation estimated that Scotland's 171 branches had 3,500 members, about an eighth only of the United Kingdom total of 27,000. This is borne out by affiliation fees, based on membership. In 1923 Scotland paid £322 from its branches. Yorkshire, with under half that number — 73 — paid £354, while Lancashire's 100 branches contributed £431. Secondly, with such a low average membership, many Scottish branches were probably not functioning at all well, and the national ILP report for 1923 complained that reports from Scotland were so inadequate that the Division's data could not be properly analysed.[12] A survey in 1927 for the NAC revealed that many areas (in addition to mining communities, where the protracted strike of 1926 had depleted the ILP) were not strong. These included North Lanarkshire, Edinburgh and the Lothians, and Renfrewshire, as well as most rural and agricultural districts.[13]

The ILP was not a body with a uniform outlook, and because some of its most colourful Scottish exponents were undoubtedly left-wing, this was not universally true of the entire movement in Scotland. Opinion in the Scottish party encompassed a broad spectrum. There were, to be sure, self-styled Marxists like Neil MacLean and John Paton, and also non-Marxist left socialists such as Maxton, Wheatley and Kirkwood. But there were also ILP socialists of a more moderate hue, among whom were a centrist group including Keir Hardie's brother George, the M.P. for Springburn, who in the 1923 election viewed the first priority in his campaign to be taxation of land values, the old pre-war Liberal cry. Thus Hardie stood in contrast to Wheatley, who in the same paper on the same day looked to nationalising the basic utilities and state control of foreign trade.[14] Others, like Willie Graham, were not far removed from radicalism. Graham, his brother relates, dismissed the Clydeside rebels as 'merely advertisement men'. Instead he 'held firmly to the view that there was little in the way of fundamental difference between the Radical and the Constitutional socialist ... He had nothing but contempt for the extremist, to whichever party he might belong'.[15]

Another strain in the ILP somewhat removed from the Clydesiders' version was typified by the Rev. James Barr, the M.P. for Motherwell from 1924. A pre-war Radical, Barr listed in 1948 nine individuals who influenced his political development. The first three were Liberals (Gladstone, Bright and Campbell-Bannerman). Three British socialists — Hardie, Henderson and Snowden — followed, being praised for their advocacy of temperance, their religious beliefs and their opposition to class-war rhetoric. The last three were a mixed bunch —Archbishop Davidson, Van der Verde, the Belgian socialist, and T. P. O'Connor, the Irish Nationalist.[16] Barr's political style was not that of a doctrinaire socialist. A local Liberal remarked: 'Man, I was at a meeting of Mr Barr's in Wishaw, and he hardly touched on politics. He would be fine company on holiday'.[17] The climax of his 1924 election address reads like a pastiche of Ramsay MacDonald: 'I am for the rebuilding of the home, the saving of child life. I stand for advancing progress and many-sided social reform. My watchword is ever 'Forward Yet!' Let us concur with heart and hand in ever bettering, ever uplifting the masses of the people, in rebuilding the old wastes and repairing the waste cities, the desolations of many generations until 'the child's sob in the silence' shall give place to the peal of merry laughter, and happy tended boys and girls shall play in the streets of our new Jerusalem'.[18] Several other pre-war Liberals joined the ILP in the post-war years. These included J. Dundas White, who sat as Liberal M.P. for Tradeston until his defeat in 1918, John Kinloch, secretary to Josiah Wedgwood the eminent Radical, Arthur Ponsonby, M.P. for Stirling until 1918, and A. M. Scott, a Lloyd George Liberal whip after 1918. None of these men seems to have been converted to socialism to any dramatic extent. White, for instance, was an obsessive land-taxer whom both Phillip Snowden and Bruce Glasier felt was essentially self-seeking in joining the ILP.[19] Scott's grounds for joining the ILP in 1924 were, in essence, that Labour was the natural continuation of pre-war radicalism. As he was leaving the Liberal party, he drafted a letter to Asquith calling on him to urge Liberals to support Labour if no Liberal stood in a seat, as Labour was against protection. As he told MacDonald, he had become alarmed at the recent drift of the Liberal party, and hoped other concerned Liberals, following his example, 'will take the step of enrolling themselves in the Labour party as the only Party which is capable of becoming an effective instrument of reform'.[20] It is noticeable that it was reform, not socialism, that he looked to Labour to achieve.

The shrewd Scottish organiser of the ILP made this point in debunking the myth about the 1922 M.P.s: 'The candidates were an exceedingly diverse selection, they had nothing whatever of the homogeneity of outlook and action expressed by such picturesque titles as 'the Clydesiders' or 'the Scottish Rebels'. The men from Clydeside, as from all the other districts, were men of the Right, the Centre and the Left, as their temperaments, experiences and habits of thought dictated'. While some, he noted, laid great stress on socialism, for others 'socialism was a remote ideal of little practical import; they were in fact a representative section of the general body of Labour candidates'.[21]

Two of the leading 'Clydesiders' did not sit for seats in the Clyde area. Tom

Johnston sat for West Stirlingshire, and Emmanuel Shinwell for West Lothian. These were both mining seats, having no connection with the special factors held to have made the Glasgow situation unique, and neither seat was particularly noted for socialism before 1922. Johnston's moderation in the campaign is noted below, and Shinwell was reportedly issuing 'unequivocal repudiations' of Bolshevism to placate his voters.[22] Nor were all the Labour victors in Glasgow left-wingers. The *Glasgow Herald,* no slouch at spotting extremists, pronounced the St Rollox M.P. James Stewart 'a moderate type of Labourist'. Probably the two most right-inclined of Glasgow Labour M.P.'s sat for seats which might well have been expected to choose strongly left-wing socialists. Tradeston, which contained an area well worked by John MacLean, and included among its residents Neil MacLean, Shinwell, George Buchanan and J. P. Hay (M.P. for Cathcart), had Thomas Henderson as M.P. Henderson was a Cooperator, and the seat was organised by the local Cooperative movement, with little direct participation by the ILP. Partick was a centre for shipbuilding workers and had been very militant during the various rent strikes both during the war and in 1922. The Labour candidate who succeeded in 1923, Andrew Young, was another moderate in the eyes of the *Glasgow Herald.* Invited in 1923 by that paper to explain why he should be voted for, Young stressed 'that taxation of land values is especially ours', condemning the Liberals for not pursuing the question after 1909.[23]

The return of ten Labour M.P.s for Glasgow in 1922 tended to exaggerate the true extent of popular support for the party. As Table 9.2 demonstrates, Labour won just over 50% of the vote in the twelve seats it fought, entitling it in strict proportionality to a mere six gains. In 1924, when Labour held eight seats, the

Table 9.2.   Seats won and share of votes, Glasgow, 1922–4

	1922	% of		1923	% of		1924	% of	
	Cands.	Poll	M.P.s	Cands.	Poll	M.P.s	Cands.	Poll	M.P.s
Labour	12	52.0	11	12	54.4	9	12	50.7	8
Liberal	12	19.3	0	7	13.4	0	2	6.8	0
Unionist	8	28.7	1	9	32.2	3	10	42.5	4

Only the twelve seats contested by Labour in 1922 are used in Table 9.2, for reasons of consistency in comparison. The figures for all the Glasgow seats are:

	1922	% of		1923	% of		1924	% of	
	Cands.	Poll	M.P.s	Cands.	Poll	M.P.s	Cands.	Poll	M.P.s
Labour	12	43.5	11	14	49.9	10	15	48.6	8
Liberal	16	25.7	1	10	15.2	0	2	5.5	0
Unionist	10	30.8	3	12	34.8	5	13	45.9	7

party's share of the percentage vote had barely moved. Thus the party benefited in 1922 (and 1923) from the existence of a three-party system, but by 1924, when a two-party framework had been reimposed, its representation was reduced to a more realistic level.

Furthermore, not all of those who earned reputations as fiery left-wingers necessarily fought election campaigns on such a full-blooded platform. In 1922 James Maxton's address barely used the word socialism, instead preferring to stress his involvement in local community affairs, such as education.[24] When the victorious Tom Johnston declared his adherence to the Clydeside group in Parliament, a Stirling paper complained that throughout the West Stirling contest he had 'resented the idea of his name being associated with the 'red menace'', but now he had dropped the guise of moderate opinion adopted to lure non-socialist voters.[25] Before 1922, Wheatley pre-eminently owed his influence in Glasgow, as John Paton remarked, to his 'consistent moderation of statement and devotion to the intensely practical', while 'the heated discussions on high policy and the demand for maximum programmes seemed to have left him cold'.[26]

While the gains made by Labour in Glasgow and its environs, where there was a shared industrial base of shipbuilding and engineering, may be held to be in part attributable to the experiences of wartime crisis, Labour's post-war election victories in Scotland were to be found over many parts of the rest of the Lowlands. As with Glasgow, the evidence that an irresistible tide of socialist consciousness was at play is not entirely confirmed. Thus between 1918 and 1924 eleven seats were held in which the mining vote was sizeable, and here, although strenuous efforts were made to win these districts for Marxist socialism — notably by John MacLean — even ILP socialism did not make a great deal of headway. Jennie Lee, herself sprung from a Scottish mining community, recounted that when she entered Parliament, she and the other ILP M.P.s met with great hostility from the Scottish miner M.P.s.[27] Thus in Lanarkshire, in 1918, Robert Smillie had to withdraw as candidate in Hamilton because of his anti-war views, while the failure to win Bothwell in that contest was ascribed in part to heavy voting against Labour by miners who took umbrage at Smillie's proposal to cooperate with 'a certain political element'.[28] The victor of 1922 in Rutherglen, William Wright, also eschewed visionary socialism. His address was principally on the housing question and pensions for the blind, irrespective of age. He would build baths at all the collieries so as to avoid the men bringing dirt home with them.[29] In Fife, Willie Adamson comfortably rebuffed a challenge by socialist miners to wrest the West Fife seat from him in 1923.[30]

A revealing insight into the miners' political position was given by the Dunfermline contest in 1918. Arthur Ponsonby, the Left-Liberal M.P. for Stirling and Dunfermline Burghs from 1908, had strenuously opposed the war, collaborating with Snowden, MacDonald and Morel in the Union of Democratic Control. Ponsonby was disowned by the local Liberals and chose to fight Dunfermline in 1918, which had been divorced from Stirling, having instead added to it several Fife mining towns like Cowdenbeath. Ponsonby ran as an independent, but had the backing of the local ILPers who worked enthusiastically for him. The attitude of the miners was quite hostile to Ponsonby. During the war, the Stirling miners had withdrawn from that town's Trades Council when the local ILP had tried to get the Council to champion Ponsonby's stand against the war.[31] When the Dunfermline Labour Party decided not to contest the seat, so enhancing Ponsonby's prospects of victory, 'the Miners had after the meeting formed a Committee to promote the candidature of Mr W. Watson'.[32] Watson got 5,076 votes, Ponsonby got 3,491, and the Coalition Liberal won by 1,810 votes. Watson's support was said to have come overwhelmingly from the mining townships: 'The miners must practically have voted solid for him, even although many of them do not approve of his candidature. They are very highly organised and put loyalty to their union before all other considerations'.[33] Ponsonby joined the ILP immediately after the polling was over, saying he had not wished to join before in case he would induce Labour voters to support him merely because he was a Labour candidate.[34] MacDonald, deeply shocked by the whole business, commiserated with Ponsonby: 'This is really a terrible revelation of the mind and spirit of sections of the Labour Party, and makes me very unhappy lest the fine ideas of liberty and catholicism we associate with the party are all humbug'.[35] In 1922 Watson won the seat.

Another fifteen seats went to Labour at some point between 1918 and 1924. Again, the spectrum of political views held by the M.P.s was wide, ranging from Newbold, the Communist at Motherwell, to Frank Rose in Aberdeen North, who was the subject of a complaint by the miners to the Scottish Council of the party in 1920 on the grounds that he opposed nationalisation of the mines.[36] In addition, the share of the poll gained by successful Labour candidates outside the Clydeside belt was not significantly different to the performances attained in the Glasgow region. Thus there was a widespread movement towards Labour throughout the urban and industrial areas of Scotland, of which Clydeside was but a part.

It seems likely that Labour's growing support came not only from the spread of socialism among the Scottish working class. John Paton recorded that smallholders in Arran in 1922, though strong individualists, would go to Labour because 'Toryism was a stench in their nostrils'. He felt these sentiments were widespread in helping Labour that year, as 'vast numbers of working class Liberals, their old allegiance destroyed, were without a political anchorage: it was inevitable that they should turn to the Labour Party as the instrument by which they could express their old opposition to the Tories. Their new attachment to Labour did not rest on any particular support of its programme so much as their hatred of Toryism'.[37] Others echoed this. At the 1921 Kirkcaldy by-election, the Labour victor agreed that 'a large number of Independent Liberals had voted for him, not on grounds of principle, but on ordinary political grounds. He was prepared to admit that a very large number of sincere Radicals in the constituency voted for Labour outright'.[38] It is also somewhat surprising to find a firebrand like Kirkwood in 1924 appealing to Dumbarton Liberals not to cast their vote on behalf of the hereditary enemy, Conservatism, but to turn to Labour.[39]

As the triumph of Labour does not seem to have been due to a marked and universal socialist mood, alternative explanations must be sought. One view would put the accent on the bundle of issues adventitiously at work in the 1922 election. Harvie and MacLean have recently argued that there were two elements.[40] Firstly, the very high levels of unemployment, deteriorating industrial relations, typified by the engineers' strike of 1922, and the bleak economic outlook, all disabused working people of their trust in the Coalition government. Secondly, there was the refusal of the Liberals and Tories to promise to oppose any legislation designed to cancel a recent House of Lords decision which had ruled that the rent increases imposed on Scottish tenants were illegal. Labour, who had been instrumental in having the rents test case taken through the courts, pledged it would ensure that the repayment to tenants of excess rents would not be blocked by statute. This interpretation was prevalent at the time, especially among Liberal and Unionist politicians. Thus, on unemployment, the Liberal M.P. swept aside by the Maxton landslide in Bridgeton had few doubts about its central importance: 'I simply could not stand up to the tragic figure of the man and woman who had been out of work for a year and had only 15/- a week dole ... I had no remedy, no solace, no answer for them. I was conscious in my heart that in their place I would revolt like them'.[41] The rents issue caused agitation in Unionist circles. Bonar Law and his entourage received a flow of warnings from senior Scottish managers about the dire electoral effects likely to follow from the Lords' verdict. 'The position of the Government Candidates in Glasgow and in Scotland generally is becoming very critical as a result of the Rent Act decision', reported Sir Michael Bruce.[42] In the Conservative postmortem on the rout in Glasgow, grassroots opinion concurred with the brass-hats. Maryhill Tories considered the rents case and unemployment the two prime causes of defeat.[43]

To both defeated camps this analysis had the immense attraction that it was possible to conclude that the vote for Labour was emphatically not a vote for socialism, so that these voters could be won over or back. 'The great Labour poll', reflected MacCallum Scott, 'did not indicate the conversion of the electors to socialism. The Labour programme was practically the old Radical programme. On an advanced programme we could recover the lost ground'.[44] But the statistics of the subsequent elections do not sustain fully this overall argument. Thus in the 1924 contest, when the Tories won seven of the fifteen Glasgow seats, Labour in fact was still polling as well in terms of votes cast. In 1922, 166, 637 Glaswegians voted for Labour, and in the same twelve seats in 1924 Labour polled 167,993 with an almost identical turnout on a comparable electorate. Yet in that later election the rent question was no longer alive, and if unemployment was not dead, it was a less prominent issue than in 1922. Moreover, the jobless total began to increase about two months before polling, and should have rebounded on Labour as the outgoing administration responsible for this failure. Furthermore, the rent issue was particularly sharp in the Glasgow area, and one or two other urban seats. But in many other constituencies it does not seem to have been a major topic, yet Labour still polled well in 1922. The successful M.P. for Rutherglen did not refer to it, nor did the victor at Coatbridge, while E. D. Morel won at Dundee on a programme which stressed foreign policy issues before domestic ones. Of the twenty points in his manifesto, the first seven relate to external affairs. The rent issue is not mentioned at all by Morel, although he found space to call for the abolition of road taxation.[45] Thus the remarkable feature is the stability of Labour's vote, despite the shifting weight given to different issues in different places.

II

The elections of the immediate post-war period may be regarded as marking a watershed in the electoral sociology of Scotland, as indeed they do for England.[46] From the standpoint of the Labour Party in Scotland, the important development was the growth of a strong and wide sense of working-class solidarity or consciousness, but not necessarily the formation of an equally powerful socialist consciousness. The pointers towards this trend to working-class identity might include a reduction in the various gradations and divisions within that class, so that its coherence became greater.[47]

One clear indicator of the drawing together of the working class can be seen in the rapid unionisation which accompanied the First World War. Membership of trade unions throughout Britain doubled between 1914 and 1920 from 4,145,000 to 8,348,000. It is difficult to disaggregate these figures in order to establish the position in Scotland, but it seems very likely that there was little deviation from the overall pattern of growth. Furthermore, the new recruits were largely drawn from the less skilled portions of the workforce. It was this section of the working class who had been most likely to be excluded from holding the franchise before 1918, and accordingly their mass accession to the electorate under the Fourth Reform Act had a considerable impact on the political balance in constituencies, especially urban seats.[48] In Scotland there was more male disfranchisement before 1918 than in England and Wales. In 1911, 69.9% of adult males in English county seats had the vote, in Scotland only 62.5% had, and in burghs the respective figures were 59.8% and 57.3%. By 1921, the overall figures were very high and very close. England enjoyed 94.9% male enfranchisement, Scotland 94.1%, implying a greater change in the latter. Moreover, the influx of new male voters was larger in Glasgow and Dundee (which in 1911 had 52.4% and 48.1% male enfranchisement respectively) than in Edinburgh (69.1%), and it may be significant that Labour was relatively unsuccessful in Edinburgh after 1918, but very strong in the first two.[49] The new class of male voters may well have felt a natural loyalty to their unions, under whose aegis their standard of living rose in wartime, as discussed below. As one paper not sympathetic to organised labour reported in 1918 of developments in Roxburgh and Selkirkshire, recent advances in wages and hours of work had been obtained by trade unions, 'so that the workers have in this way become accustomed to combined effort in protecting what they believe to be their own interests'. The paper predicted that Labour's vote would benefit from this process.[50] Although the Borders are far removed from the industrial central belt, it may not be too fanciful to see this as a general condition.

That there was some correlation between high unionisation and Labour voting strength is suggested by the evidence of the geography of union membership gathered by the STUC for its 1925 conference. Those areas where the proportion of employed males in trade unions exceeded the overall average of 36.9% were all Labour strongholds (with the exception of Edinburgh, which had 37.9%), and those with a lower degree of unionisation were Labour's weaker spots. So while Dundee had 49.5% unionisation and Labour representatives, the surrounding Perth and Angus area, with 19.1% in unions, returned no Labour M.P.s; and while Aberdeen city had a Labour M.P. and 45.6% organised in unions, the north-east, without any Labour successes, had a mere 13.3% in unions.[51] The sense of solidarity was probably enhanced by the fact that around 80% of all Scottish male trade union members belonged to only 36 out of a total of 227 unions.[52] During the war, too, the initial tensions between organised labour and the socialist wing diminished and a measure of joint action was developed, doubtless encouraging the identification of the Labour Party with trade unionism in the eyes of many new recruits to the latter. Thus in November 1914 a plan to put the Scottish office of the Labour Party in with that of the ILP was counselled against for fear of 'a good deal of confusion arising that might militate against the success of your work among the Trades Unions'.[53] By 1917 the joint campaign over the food crisis launched by the Labour Party and the unions together resulted, as Ben Shaw (the party's Scottish secretary) reported, in there being 'a better spirit shown and more tolerance than had been the case hitherto since the war began'.[54]

By the early 1920s wage differentials, one of the crucial causes of the pre-1914 stratification within the working class, had been substantially eroded, both relatively and absolutely. As Table 9.3 shows, the ratio of weekly wages between skilled and unskilled men had shifted in favour of the latter, and in cash terms also the gains made by the unskilled were very striking. With greater equality of income, the implications for status and standards of living are obviously profound. At the same time as lifestyles were becoming more widely shared, experiences previously restricted to the poorer sections of the working class became prevalent also among the artisans. This was especially the case with the wartime and post-war housing crisis on Clydeside. Recent analyses of this problem have noted that rent strikes and housing protests were strongly pursued in areas such as Partick, a locality of skilled workers. Moreover, housing problems were felt acutely by women, and their active involvement, it has been argued, sharpened their political education, paying ample dividends for Labour in 1922.[55]

Although the influences produced by domestic factors during the war fostered working-class solidarity, for many this of course was not the case, as they would be engaged in active service. Scotland, indeed, contributed a disproportionately large share of Britain's military forces.[56] Thus at Aberdeen South in 1917, it was recorded that the male labour force was either enlisted or transferred to Invergordon for naval work.[57] Among those on military service a solidarity was nurtured which was to be carried home and kept alive in a civilian context. The Glasgow rail strike of 1919 shows revealing signs of this. The strike committee produced a bulletin which carried reports from branches, many of which are couched not in terms of political demands, but of the cameraderie of the trenches.

Table 9.3.   *Wage differentials, 1914–20*

	1914	1920	Place
Fitters and Turners, and their Labourers	100:60	100:80	Glasgow
Bricklayers and their Labourers	100:62	100:84	Glasgow
Shipwrights and their Labourers	100:55	100:76	Glasgow
Rivetters and their Holders-Up	n.a.	100:88	Glasgow
Railway Drivers and Porters	100:52	100:67	U.K.

Source: *British Labour Statistics, Historical Abstract, 1886–1968* (London, 1971).
All of the above figures are based on time wage rates, and do not necessarily reflect actual earnings.

Muirkirk was 'ready to take a Coalition front bench. No shirkers at this dug-out', while Motherwell brushed aside the Premier's intervention: 'Lloyd George's poison gas attack repelled'.[58] The existence of several ex-servicemen's associations served to perpetuate these feelings, and a number of Scottish Unionists felt uneasy at the political leanings of bodies like the Discharged Soldiers' and Sailors' Federation, whose leaders, Younger warned, 'seem to be making it their business to go about everywhere and foment agitation . . . and who are at present a source of real danger'.[59] The significance of the soldier vote was probably not fully felt until 1922, when turnout — around 60% in 1918 — rose sharply in many seats to 75%. After the 1918 contest, Law had enquiries made about his own seat, Glasgow Central, where turnout had been 52.9%. The serviceman vote was only 27.7% (2,060 out of 7,446), but other voters polled 58.4% (20,313 out of 34,887). By 1922 turnout rose to 69%, and it seems likely that many of these additional voters came from those on the Absent Roll in 1918. Many of these, Law's agent confirmed, had been unable to vote then because of administrative hurdles, which would not apply in subsequent contests.[60]

A further force for unity was the lesser prominence of the Irish question, which before 1914 frequently placed the Irish Nationalist voters in the Liberal camp, and Orangemen in the Unionist. The feeling had been that these sectarian factors militated against the Labour party before 1914 in West Lothian.[61] In 1922, however, Shinwell became Labour M.P. for the constituency. Many Irish Nationalists had gone for Labour in 1918, on the grounds that while a vote for the coalition was a vote for Carson, 'it had been abundantly clear to Irish Nationalists for some time past that they would serve Home Rule best by voting Labour at the next election'.[62] Even though the Nationalist leadership urged backing the Liberal in seats like St Rollox and Springburn, the local branches resolved to support the Labour candidates, whose municipal records were praised for being sympathetic to Irish and Roman Catholic grievances.[63] With the signing of the Irish Treaty, the way was open for the Irish Catholic community to accept its class identity. As its Glasgow organ expressed it, 'the Catholics of this country are chiefly workers. They belong mostly to the toiling masses and therefore they are *prima facie* sympathetic towards the Labour movement and towards a sane and sound Labour policy'.[64] By 1924 the ILP learned that the Catholic Socialist Society was wound up, its activists being absorbed into the broader socialist movement, 'and furthermore ... the average Catholic in Glasgow is sympathetic to our party'.[65]

It is also possible that Labour began to attract the votes of working-class Orangemen. The Orange Order loosened its close ties with the Unionist party in 1922, when in protest at the Irish Treaty it set up a separate party. Although thereafter it generally recommended its supporters to vote Unionist, the lack of official ties was felt by many Conservatives to lead to seepage of working men's votes to Labour. This was argued by Maryhill Tories in explaining the loss of the seat in 1922, and in Paisley in 1924 up to a third of the previous Tory vote went Labour in a constituency with a firm Orange presence.[66] In 1923, *Forward* claimed that in Scotland 'there are literally thousands of Orangemen who are members of the Labour Party', and many were also in the ILP. *Forward* argued that by contrast with Ireland, where the order was the tool of the ruling classes, in Scotland it was not pledged to uphold capitalism, only the Protestant faith.[67] This desire of the ILP paper to acknowledge Orangeism as a respectable aspect of the working-class movement would have been unthinkable at an earlier date.

This unification of various working-class organisations is well illustrated by the close links established between the Labour Party and the cooperative movement. Before 1914 the cooperators had generally kept their distance from the party, but events in war altered this. The cooperatives felt discriminated against in the allocation of food to retailers and by the imposition of a tax on their profits. In October 1917 the STUC, the Scottish Labour Party, the Cooperative Union and the Scottish Cooperative Wholesale Society formed the Scottish Cooperative and Labour Council at the prompting of the cooperators who felt driven to the same conclusion as the unions that they must organise politically to defend their rights.[68] The Labour Party saw this development as suggesting 'an entente cordiale with a sort of militaristic combination in the background ... '[69]

The importance of the cooperators lay not so much in the financial help they could give as in the access Labour gained to the rich range of educational and social institutions sponsored by the cooperative movement. Most party leaders in Scotland visited the Men's and Women's Cooperative Guilds with the active encouragement of the societies involved. By 1922 the cooperative journal remarked: 'We maintain that visits from leading Labour men have been not only the means of imparting to members of the [Men's] Guild a realisation of the importance of politics to the movement but of enabling members to grasp in its proper perspective the significance of Cooperative and Labour representation in public bodies'.[70] Labour's victory in Dunfermline in 1922, in the view of the local press, was partly due to the candidate's wooing of female cooperators: 'If he can organise the women's vote by working his way into the Cooperative Women's Guilds and inducing them to ally themselves with the Labour Party, he does not hesitate to do so'. In 1924, the town's Cooperative Choir was also alleged to have been a vital ingredient in Labour's electoral victory.[71] In a clear bid to draw support, much Labour propaganda laid stress on the idea of a Cooperative Commonwealth as the goal towards which the party was striving.[72] It was claimed in 1922 that 24 out of the 29 Scottish Labour M.P.s were also cooperators, and one society — Kinning Park — contained six M.P.s.[73]

It is also possible to detect a cohesive working-class identity in literary evidence, whose reliability may be the greater for having been drawn from neutral or hostile sources. The *Glasgow Herald* observed in 1922: ' ... the Motherwell and Wishaw women have felt the pinch and amid the failure of policies and the confusion of creeds it is perhaps not surprising that a purely class appeal should be succeeding'. In Rutherglen it detected Labour advancing because 'a large section of the electorate, undetermined in its views, is open to the affective influences of sentiment'.[74] North Lanark was felt to have been lost in 1924 because while the party's vote had remained solid in the industrial centres, it had been eroded in the 'clachans and roadside houses' where presumably working-class solidarity might be less.[75] An interesting incident — almost pre-modern in some ways — occurred at Greenock, where Labour supporters in the intensely working-class Third Ward held a carnival procession at the height of the 1922 election, with many dressed in 'fantastic costumes'.[76] Another instance of the intensity and localism of this community sense was observed by John Paton. He claimed that the M.P. for the Gorbals (the poorest area in Glasgow), George Buchanan, although a skilled engineer whose brothers were in professional or highly trained occupations, felt compelled to adopt the rougher speech and behaviour of his constituents. Buchanan did this, according to Paton, because 'he's merged himself in the community he represented'.[77]

The methods of organising election campaigns reflected these attitudes. It has recently been argued that one of the reasons for the decline of the Liberals after 1918 was that their message was irrelevant to the new electorate who were less moved by rational political discourse than by instinctive class feelings.[78] This can be taken further: the very techniques of traditional political debate seemed ill-adjusted to new conditions. A Liberal M.P. noted that mass meetings, ideal for communicating with the pre-1914 voters were unsuited to the expanded electorate comprising 'the more floating and vagrant element among the men and a large body of women, few of whom are interested in old-style politics'.[79] Labour had developed techniques to reach the voters in, so to speak, their natural habitat rather than the artificial context of large meetings. Rosslyn Mitchell's style excited press comment in the Glasgow Central contest of 1922. He eschewed the large public set-pieces, instead convening five or six 'gatherings' a day, where he explained party policy in an informal manner. No one chaired these happenings, instead Mitchell 'just enters the meeting-place, and after some casual conversation, he begins his address'.[80] A major area of contact pioneered by Labour was workplaces. In 1918, Graham was the first candidate in any Edinburgh contest to hold meetings in factories and workshops.[81] Asquith's campaign manager in the Paisley by-election was worried by this device: 'I do not think that sufficient watch has been kept over the activities of Labour in the workshops. I have had the greatest difficulty in getting any details of what they are doing or of the literature they are selling'.[82] At Partick in 1924, women voters were reached by holding back-green meetings in daytime.[83]

The broad involvement of many sections of the working class in electioneering was repeatedly stressed by contemporaries, and perhaps most fully brought out in a description of the Edinburgh Central campaign in 1922, where a careful observance of demarcation lines was adhered to. While the NUR men, being largely unskilled, were allocated general duties, the members of the Railway Clerks' Union addressed envelopes in, no doubt, impeccable copperplate, and volunteers from the Shop Assistants' Union formed canvassing teams, where their salemanship skills would be ideal. The cooperative women, mainly working class, worked an open horse lorry on polling day, but a motor car loaned for the day by a sympathetic doctor was driven by the more middle-class ILP ladies.[84]

The presence of a working-class consciousness is quite distinct from any commitment to full socialism. One of the most straightforward methods to attempt to assess whether the latter existed in Scotland in the 1922–24 period is to look at seats where the voters had on offer alternative left-wing candidates. These are shown in Table 9.4. In Greenock in 1924, the Labour candidate, Geddes, was in fact a Communist, and the ILP ran Stephen Kelly against him. Kelly was a Roman Catholic, and Greenock had a large Catholic population. Kelly was also the solicitor responsible for handling the 1922 rent restriction case, so decisive in that year's election results. Nevertheless, Geddes kept a clear majority of the working-class vote. In nearby Paisley, the ILP ran a nominee in 1923 against Biggar, the official Labour candidate, complaining that Biggar was too right-wing, and that as a rent-collector he was not the most suitable man to represent the working class. The ILP purposely selected a Dumbarton councillor closely involved in the rents agitation, but he was still comfortably seen off by Biggar. One interpretation of the contrasting results in these two seats is that the left-winger did better in Greenock and the right-winger in Paisley because they both had the endorsement of the local Labour Party, while the ILP did not.

This view of working-class electoral loyalty to the party label rather than policy content can be tested at Kelvingrove. In 1923 Ferguson, the Communist, seems to have taken two-thirds of the vote given in 1922 to the Liberal, when no Labour candidate stood. In a by-election in May 1924, Ferguson stood as the Labour Party candidate, and made only a modest advance. In October 1924 he was replaced by an ILP centre-socialist, on the grounds that Ferguson's extremism was frightening potential voters away. Yet Labour's poll was not markedly better. The element of blind fidelity to Labour comes out quite strongly in this seat. The Glasgow Catholic newspaper had in 1923 urged that 'where Communists are nominated no Catholic should go anywhere for any Communist candidate'. Six months later, with Ferguson, still a Communist, fighting under Labour colours, the paper's view was that 'in such a situation, and where the candidate stands not as a Communist but as a Labour candidate, the Irish vote will probably (and warrantably) be polled in support of the Labour nominee'.[85] Motherwell shows similar characteristics. Here the hardline Communist, Newbold, did well in 1922 and 1923 on an uncompromising platform. This did not necessarily mean that the voters there were swept along in a tide of Marxist-Leninist zeal, as the secretary of the local Labour organisation explained: 'In the first place one can give an

Table 9.4.   *Election Results in Four Constituencies, 1922–24*

Votes   % of Poll

GLASGOW, Kelvingrove

	Comm	La	Li	U	(T/O)	Comm	La	Li	U
1922	—	—	11,094	13,442	(64.5)	—	—	45	55
1923	10,021	—	4,662	11,025	(68.2)	39	—	18	43
1924 (By)	—	11,167	1,372	15,488	(70.5)	—	40	5	55
1924 (Gen)	—	12,844	—	18,034	(77.5)	—	42	—	58

GREENOCK

	Comm	La	Li	U	(T/O)	Comm	La	Li	U
1922	9,776	—	10,520	8,404	(84.8)	34	—	37	29
1923	10,335	—	16,337	—	(78.4)	39	—	61	—
1924	7,590	5,874	12,752	—	(77.8)	29	22	49	—

PAISLEY

	ILab	La	Li	U	(T/O)	ILab	La	Li	U
1922	—	14,689	15,005	—	(78.0)	—	49	51	—
1923	3,685	7,977	9,723	7,758	(77.1)	13	27	33	27
1924	—	17,057	14,829	—	(84.1)	—	54	46	—

MOTHERWELL

	Comm	La	ILi	NLi	U	(T/O)	Comm	La	Li	NLi	U
1922	8,262	—	5,359	3,966	7,214	(81.5)	33	—	22	16	29
1923	8,712	—	4,799	—	9,793	(77.4)	37	—	21	—	42
1924	—	12,816	—	—	11,776	(82.3)	—	52	—	—	48

Note.   Comm: Communist; La: Labour; Li: Liberal; U: Unionist; ILab: Independent
Labour; ILi: Independent Liberal (Asquithian); NLi: National Liberal (Lloyd
George-ite); T/O: Turn-out.

unhesitating 'No' to the question has Motherwell gone Communist'. He
contended that Newbold won because a united front of Socialist and Labour
bodies was forged after the Trades and Labour Council could not find a Labour
candidate. 'Under the circumstances', the secretary concluded, as if it were the
most natural thing, 'the Council did the only thing possible in deciding to support
the Communist candidate'.[86]

However, 1924 in Motherwell gives a further hint as to working-class voting behaviour. Then Barr, whose politics were quite different to Newbold's, collected 4,000 more votes. These were, so the Catholic press claimed, the votes of Roman Catholics who had declined to vote in 1923 for a Communist. It is likely that Kelly's poll in Greenock in 1924 was also in good part a religiously-derived support, as Kelly was a Roman Catholic facing a Communist.[87] Here is a sign that working-class unity was not totally solid when religion and extreme politics were involved, but these were infrequent clashes. The Glasgow Catholic newspaper, while passionately committed to Labour, was in no sense socialist. It denounced Wheatley for the 'SHEER LUNACY' of suggesting capitalism would end shortly, and worried lest extreme Labour men would drive away many who were attached 'to the basis of our civilisation, which is founded upon private property, as opposed to Communism and Socialism'.[88] This lack of socialist commitment was echoed by other Labour Party activists commenting on working-class political opinion. In Dundee, the chairman of the local party informed the M.P. of the position in Lochee, the most working-class quarter of the city: 'Yon is our weakest spot socially [i.e. in terms of party activity], but it is a mighty fine place when votes are being counted'. Later that year he argued: 'our position is we are certain of a growing support among the intelligent voters. There is a big section none too intelligent'.[89] The leader of Motherwell's Labour Party agreed: most of those who supported Newbold in 1922 were not politically conscious, 'for only in a dim and hazy fashion do they understand the meaning of the words 'Socialism' and 'Communism''.[90] There was political apathy also in South Mid Lothian and Peebles. Here, in a seat held by Labour with 7,882 votes in 1923, a bid at the height of the election to get the *Daily Herald* read by a suggested target of 490 subscribers failed, and only 220 could be found willing to take the party's own paper.[91]

The passivity of Labour voters is also conveyed in the accounts of canvassing techniques frequently deployed at election time. From Gorbals in 1922, it appeared that a new canvassing procedure was adopted: 'As a rule arguing with voters was discouraged, and our folk chose to guide rather than to bludgeon. The candidate's name was reiterated, the Labour programme explained, and if time permitted, the Capital Levy made simple'.[92] Similarly in Partick, canvassing teams operated as if on a time and motion study. Fifteen pairs of canvassers were detailed to cover an entire tenement block, spending five minutes at each house, where they were not to argue or debate, only to arrange to convey voters to the polling station.[93]

Paton, the ILP Scottish organiser, harboured few illusions about the import of the elections. Of the vast crowd which gathered at Glasgow Central Station to see the city's Labour victors of 1922 off to Westminster, he commented: 'The great majority of them had little real understanding of the purposes of these men they were cheering. Socialism probably conveyed as little meaning to them as did the higher mathematics — that mattered less than nothing. What they did understand was that they'd witnessed a portent: a working class party of formidable power had emerged; whether or not they'd voted for it, they could identify themselves with it in its moment of victory'.[94]

III

One consequence of this presence of a solid working-class vote, but with little positive ideological content, was that organisational control of the official party machinery would bestow mastery over the selection and return of Labour candidates. The ILP perceived this basic fact early in the post-war era, and acted upon it. In January 1919, just one month after the general election, the Glasgow ILP Federation instructed all its branches to plan for the next one by acting promptly to secure candidates and to raise funds.[95] Eight months later the National Administrative Council of the ILP sanctioned the Scottish Council's request to run as many candidates as they wished, subject to financial viability.[96] Paton, a central figure in the implementation of this venture, recalled the rationale. He and other party officials urged branches to proceed apace with nominating candidates, even if they had no cash and feeble organisation, because 'we knew that if our members were to wait on funds being gathered, we'd be forestalled in the great majority of constituencies by candidates having the great financial resources of Trades Unions behind them. It was true that most of these would also be members of the ILP but we preferred that they should not only be members but nominees for whom the Party took financial responsibility and could look to for allegiance'.[97] As is already clear, the ILP were widely successful in achieving this objective. Yet the recent work of MacKibbin has demonstrated that the new constitution of the Labour Party brought into being at the end of the war was drafted carefully in order to prevent precisely such dominance being exercised by the socialist ILP element over the Trade Union wing.[98] In reality, none of these hurdles created at constituency level operated in Scotland according to plan: if the unions were to hold the socialists in check, it would have to take place at other points in the party's organisation.

Firstly, finance was to be a factor inhibiting the ILP: unions would subsidise only their own nominees, and few constituency parties would be able to function without grants from sponsoring unions. Cash, however, proved in the event to be no barrier in Scotland. When Paton fought North Ayrshire in 1922, there was 5/10 (34p) in the Election Fund, but small weekly collections in Labour areas meant that the total bill of £190 was paid off less than a fortnight after polling.[99] In 1923, the average election bill in Glasgow was £243 for Labour, £577 Conservative, £626 Liberal.[100] The costs of elections could be kept low for two reasons. In the first place there were sizeable pools of volunteer workers ready to contribute to the campaign. Squads of mass canvassing teams were easily assembled, and worked assiduously. Partick had 300 canvassers out every night in the 1924 contest, while in 1922, forty teams of ten apiece delivered the vote in Camlachie on polling day, and Gorbals boasted of fielding 250 canvassers.[101] Then, the normal running costs of an election were minimised by Labour's new campaigning style, already described. Few large meetings meant no expensive hall hires, and little literature was printed as the spoken word was preferred, and also because propaganda was continuous, not restricted to the campaign period. Labour's Dunfermline victory in 1922 came partly in this way: 'He does not depend upon a spurt at election time. His spade work is unceasing'.[102]

Another device intended to curtail the influence of the ILP within the Labour Party was the innovation in the new constitution of individual membership. The individual members' section was normally allocated a disproportionately large number of delegates to sit on management committees compared to that given to affiliated bodies. At Greenock, for example, there were ten such delegates, representing ninety five individuals, out of the management committee total of around seventy.[103] Because of this favourable weighting, it was anticipated that trade unionists would take out individual membership (as well as affiliating through their union), and thereby swamp the ILP activists who were believed to be small in numbers, but powerful because of union indifference. The chairman of the Scottish party — a trade unionist — certainly took this view when outlining the advantages of the new constitution to Dundee trade unionists: 'The bulk of the Labour Party was made up of solid Trade Unionists who had made the party what it was ... In his opinion the tail had wagged the dog far too long in Dundee ... He hoped that the Trades Union group present would turn out to LRC [sic] meetings. If a certain wing captured the Labour Party they would have themselves to blame'.[104] The ILP seems to have formed the same opinion, for the Scottish Advisory Council of the Labour Party tried to reassure the former that individual members should not be regarded with suspicion but seen as potential recruits to the ILP.[105]

The individual members' sections proved very disappointing. The Scottish Council repeatedly deplored the failure to develop this side of party organisation. In December 1919 it issued a circular to all trade union secretaries urging assistance to boost the 'more or less forlorn attempts' being made. In its report for 1922–23 it reiterated the call for trade unions to do more to develop individual membership.[106] Its concern is borne out by the evidence from constituencies, where the numbers were derisory. Maryhill in 1918–19 had 12 individual members, so that Greenock's 95 in 1924 seems quite huge.[107] The backwardness of the individual membership sections in Scotland can be measured by analysing the affiliation fees paid by constituency parties to the national Labour Party. In order to secure accreditation, all constituency parties were required to submit a fee of £1.10/- based on a minimum figure of 180 individual members. If there were more members than 180, appropriately higher dues were paid. In England in 1921, 65 constituencies paid more than the minimum fee, and by 1924 this had risen to 104, while for Wales the increase was from 3 to 6. For Scotland, too, the figures rose, but only because they could move in no other direction: from 0 in 1921, they reached 2 in 1924. Thus while by 1924 England and Wales each had about one-fifth of all parties in this category, in Scotland the proportion was about one-thirty-fifth.[108]

Indifference, as has been seen, was a factor, but at times outright hostility also greeted efforts to develop the individual section. It was not until 1924 that individual section delegates attended meetings of the Paisley Labour Party, whereupon the trade union representatives voted to give no financial support beyond the cost of the initial meeting to launch the section.[109] At about the same time, the Penicuik Labour Party branch sent affiliation fees of £1.10/- for individual members to the South Mid Lothian constituency party, to the utter incredulity of the treasurer in this mining seat: 'He expressed surprise at the amount, but was assured that the membership of the party would warrant that amount'. It was later confirmed that Penicuik (population: 5,000) had 75 individual members.[110] The most obvious area where individual membership sections were needed was in recruiting women, who after their considerable involvement in the rents campaign should have been ripe for organising. In 1918 a women's organiser was appointed to the Scottish office of the party, but the reports record slow progress. In November 1921, the women's organiser reported that 'The work in Scotland is showing more hopeful signs but it is very slow'. In June 1922 improvements were being made, but considerable resistance by the ILP and trade unionists to the whole idea was still being encountered. There was a steady expansion, so that, by early 1924, 44 women's branches had been formed, as well as 13 joint branches. Membership in the former was perhaps between 2,500 and 3,000, still a fairly low figure compared to that reached by the Unionists.[111]

Feeble resistance to the activities of the ILP within the Labour Party was compounded by the apparent apathy of trade unions, which meant that they failed even to deploy fully their potential power either by affiliating all their branches to constituency parties, or by involving themselves in the work of these parties. In 1919 the Scottish Council of the Labour Party wrote to nationally affiliated trade unions requesting them to encourage branches to join constituency parties. There was so poor a response to the initial plea that a follow-up appeal was made. Only one union responded clearly and positively, and no more than five or six expressed even vague interest.[112] Even the most politically active centres like Glasgow suffered from these problems. The city party found it difficult in 1919 to stimulate trade union branch participation in constituencies, and after several efforts it resolved the following year to circularise all union branches to explain the nature of the political role of the movement: 'It was felt by the Executive Committee that a very considerable number of delegates did not realise the importance of giving effect to the constitution, and that in fact many of the delegates did not understand the constitution'.[113] This does not seem to have been very successful. Exactly a year later, the resignations of two Glasgow constituency party secretaries were reported. Both gave the same reason, viz. 'Affiliated Organisations and Trade Unionists in these Divisions could no [sic] be got to attend the meetings of the parties and take an interest in the work'.[114] In June 1922 the resuscitation of these two parties was accompanied by a general discussion of 'methods of stimulating greater interest among Trade Union branches affiliated'.[115] These problems obtained elsewhere. In 1923, at a meeting to revive the near-defunct Paisley Labour Party, a Communist Party delegate blamed the crisis on 'the lack of interest being shown by the industrial delegates to the Local Party'. The union representatives present voiced opposition to a scheme to appoint a political organiser for Paisley and Renfrewshire, and they were accused by the ILP of also refusing to combine political work with the discharge of their industrial duties.[116]

In Dundee a ballot of the affiliated membership of the Labour Party was held in 1918 to decide whether a second Labour candidate should be run in this two-member constituency: 906 voted in favour, 371 against, and as the total eligible to vote was around 23,000, this represented a turn-out of just under 6%.[117]

A general consequence of these factors was that constituency Labour Parties were often feebly supported and prone to lapse. In 1921 the SAC issued a grave warning about these parties: 'Indeed many of them are clinically in a state of suspended animation until an approaching local election gives them a jolt'.[118] In June 1922, three Glasgow constituencies — Central, Partick and Hillhead — were stated to have no Labour Party organisation.[119] Where there was no Labour Party in a constituency, it was the ILP which normally assumed the role of keeping the Labour interest alive. Thus in Partick in 1922, the Labour Party was 'presently moribund and the ILP is practically acting in its place meantime'.[120]

Hence this range of fatal flaws in the structure designed to prop up union influence at constituency level actually served to facilitate control being placed firmly in the hands of socialist elements. Indeed, sometimes the increase in individual membership was due to manipulation by a socialist body seeking to increase indirectly its delegate total on management committees. In Motherwell in 1924, when the selection of the parliamentary candidate was about to be settled, the women's section, previously containing about fifty members, was suddenly inundated by a single application filed for membership on behalf of over a hundred women. This was openly acknowledged by the local Communists to be a manoeuvre to secure the women's delegates' votes for their nominee.[121] In Dundee, it was reported in 1923 that Communists had taken over the women's section and were moving in on the men's section, with the result 'that it is now almost possible for them to capture the various offices in the group and by a majority vote rule the actions of the party'.[122] A counter-offensive was launched by moderates within the Dundee party which succeeded in averting a Communist takeover.[123]

Another form of delegate manipulation arose from the casual manner in which trade unions fulfilled their affiliation commitments to the Labour Party. In 1923 it was discovered that the miners' union had vastly over-affiliated to the Shettleston Labour Party, thereby acquiring a decisive influence on the management committee. However, the Party's ruling body in Glasgow felt that no irregularity had occurred, 'due to the fact that representation in accordance with the rules cannot be strictly given effect to until returns of all members of Unions have been made to the Central Labour Party [i.e. in London] for the purpose of allocating them to their respective Parliamentary Divisions'.[124] Thus local union secretaries could do as they pleased in the interim. The M.P. for Shettleston, John Wheatley, was of course an ex-miner. Again, it was possible to affiliate dubious or paper bodies to local Labour Parties which could act as a covert way of getting more representatives on to management committees. In Greenock, the Unemployed Workers' Association was permitted to affiliate, and its delegate was Geddes, the Communist candidate. Another kindred body affiliated at Greenock was the Labour Housing Association, and these ploys were not stopped by the weak local constituency officials. Instead it was the Scottish Council which would insist on the disaffiliation of these bogus societies. In Greenock, the Council forced the disbandment of the local party because of these irregular affiliations, and reconstituted it when assurances were received that the Council's rulings on valid affiliations would be complied with.[125]

Perhaps the most outrageous instance of this exploitation of the eligibility difficulty was to be found at Kelvingrove. Here in 1923–4 a bitter struggle for control of the constituency party management committee was waged between the ILP and the Communist Party, the goal being to secure the nomination of the candidate for the seat. The NEC in London was so concerned about developments that it appointed an investigative committee comprising the party chairman, a leading trade unionist and the chairman of the Scottish Party. They reported back in some horror on the loophole afforded by the system of affiliating the cooperative movement in Glasgow. The basis of representation at constituency level was related to the number of members of cooperative retail societies in the constituency. In Kelvingrove, with around 4,000 cooperators, this meant twenty delegates were entitled to attend the local party, a number of considerable influence as there were only around eighty members in all on the party management committee. Nomination of this score of cooperative delegates was vested in the membership of the local Cooperative Party, which prior to the May 1924 by-election numbered in the region of a hundred. Membership of the Cooperative Party merely required membership of a cooperative retail society, residence in the constituency and intimation of the desire to join the Cooperative Party. In the period just before the selection of the candidate, nearly a hundred new members joined the Cooperative Party. This influx was admitted by both the ILP and the Communist Party to be a planned move to swing the Cooperative delegation in their respective favours. The NEC committee concluded that 'the basis of affiliation and the method of representation of the cooperative movement on the divisional Labour parties in Glasgow cannot be regarded as satisfactory and lends itself to exploitation'.[126] A somewhat similar process occurred with the ILP, who purposely chose in Glasgow to establish separate branches in each municipal ward, rather than at parliamentary constituency level. As there were usually three or four wards in each constituency, the ILP could affiliate several branches and so have more delegates on the constituency committee. This consideration would of course also apply to the various branches established throughout Scotland, of which, as we have seen, there was a disproportionately large number.

In these ways, the nomination of candidates could be engineered by the ILP, but other factors reinforced this trend. Even in Glasgow, widely regarded as the centre of political awareness, there was a feeling that trade unions were not fully *au fait* with the Labour Party's constitution. Confirmation of this came in 1923 when the Railwaymen's union intimated that it intended putting forward a candidate for the forthcoming municipal elections. The Trades and Labour Council had to write to the NUR to point out that it was up to constituency Labour Parties, not the Trades Council, to put forward a candidate's name, and that only a body affiliated to the appropriate constituency could induce the local party to do this.[127] It is surprising to find such a large union so ignorant of rudimentary procedures. In addition to ignorance, there was the ever-present lack of interest on the part of organised labour. The choice of a Communist candidate for Motherwell in 1922 came about as a *pis aller* for the Trades Council, as the secretary explained: 'Every effort was made to put an official Labour candidate in the field. On no less than three occasions circulars were sent out to the branches affiliated to the Trades Council inviting them to send in nominations. Only one nomination was received, and this was found not to be in order'.[128] There were nearly twenty different unions on the Trades Council. With the impact of the recession beginning to take effect from 1921, the trade unions were preoccupied with resisting onslaughts on their industrial strength, and it may be that they preferred to concentrate on protecting their primary *raison d'être* than to get embroiled in political infighting.

On occasions when a union did have a nominee, his selection as a parliamentary candidate could be frustrated by sectional rivalries. Even where a seat had a single dominant industry, there was no guarantee of the relevant union having its way. In Kirkcaldy, the linoleum workers' leader lost the nomination to the socialists' champion, and in Motherwell in 1924 the ILP's James Barr captured the nomination from the steel workers' leader. In each case, it appears that there was a hostile alliance of smaller unions, while the larger union would not have delegates in ratio to its membership. By contrast, in mining seats, where each pit, having its own section of the union, would be entitled to send delegates, the control enjoyed by the Miners' Federation was total. In South Mid Lothian and Peebles, the Labour Party was founded at a meeting chaired by a miner and attended mainly by miners. It was decided to contest the seat after a talk by the miners' political organiser, the resolution to look for a candidate being moved by a miners' delegate. There was only one nominee, put forward by the miners, and when financial difficulties pressed, it was to the area Miners' Federation that the constituency party turned. Some three years after forming the party, the miners realised that other unions in the seat, such as the Farm Servants, the Carpet Workers and the Power Workers, should be invited to affiliate, but control of the executive remained firmly entrenched with the miners.[129] In South Ayrshire, a safe miners' seat, the constituency Labour Party had an Executive Committee of nineteen, eleven of whom were miners' delegates.[130] In mining seats, there were few successful bids by socialists to control the nomination process.

The ultimate tactics which were resorted to in trying to dominate the selection process involved bending or breaking the rules. It was alleged that at the 1924 Greenock nomination meeting four delegates ignored their explicit mandate and voted for the Communist.[131] In Paisley in 1923, the Chairman announced that the various nominations had been thinned down by an undefined process to one name to be presented to the formal nomination meeting. This one individual was Harry Pollitt, the Communists' choice.[132] At a meeting to select a candidate for the Cowcaddens ward in Glasgow in the municipal elections of 1923, only one valid submission — from the Horse and Motormen's Union — had arrived by the closing date. At that meeting, however, the St Rollox ILP delegates succeeded in having the deadline extended by one month to allow them to put forward a name.

Not unnaturally, 'to this, the Horse and Motormen's Association took exception' and withdrew their man, leaving the ILP in sole command.[133]

Thus these complex tissues of factors permitted the ILP, as the most dynamic, determined and politically oriented grouping within the Labour Party, to wield power and influence out of proportion to its actual size or to the support its ideas had among the working class. In a few cases, however, the ILP's drive to dominate met with a challenge from other political groups, and it is from these clashes that much of the detail of the *modus operandi* can be gathered. The most serious contender was the Communist Party, which had a considerble following in Scotland. This was in part derived from the leaders of the Clyde Shop Stewards' movement like Willie Gallacher, Arthur MacManus and Tom Bell, who increasingly found inspiration in Leninism after the Bolshevik seizure of power in Russia. In addition, John MacLean's Marxist evangelical work converted a number of the Scottish working class to Communist doctrines, even if his own relations with the British party were somewhat fraught.

The rift between the ILP and the Communists was in part over ideology, and in part over control of the Labour Party organisation in certain constituencies. As to the former, a gradual but eventually quite emphatic gulf opened up. Between 1917 and 1920, the ILP in Scotland appeared quite well-disposed to the embryonic Communist movement. The party's NAC was uneasy at the readiness of the branches in the Motherwell constituency to nominate the Communist Newbold as candidate for the seat in 1918 and 1919. The Scottish Council was urged to exercise some oversight of the choice of candidates in an effort to prevent such incidents recurring.[134] However, at its regional conference held in January 1920, the Scottish ILP resolved to leave the Second International, as a prelude to joining the Third (or Communist) International. Significantly, the ILP declined to leave the Labour Party.[135] By 1921, this ardour began to cool. At the Scottish conference in January of that year, the ILP seemed to distance itself from the Soviet position on public ownership by stressing the basis should not be control by the workers directly involved, but control in the interests of all citizens and society as a whole.[136] A month later, a request by John MacLean for support in calling a general strike in protest at the deterioration in wage and employment levels was not responded to by the Glasgow ILP. In June, 'no action' was decided by the same body to be the appropriate answer to an appeal by the Communists for financial and political backing in the face of attacks by the government on the new party.[137] In August 1921, there was a public debate in Glasgow on the ILP and the Communist versions of socialism, with representatives of both parties speaking.[138] In December, the Glasgow ILP voted by 27 votes to 4 to cooperate with the Trades Council rather than the Communist Party in a protest against restrictions on the right to hold public meetings.[139]

In August 1922 James Maxton and Patrick Dollan published a statement of the goals of the ILP in Glasgow, in which the Communist approach was rejected: 'The party does not advocate the use of force as a means to Socialism ... It is evolutionary rather than cataclysmic. It keeps an open mind and is not bound by iron dogmas'.[140] This is a less sweeping view than that adopted by the ILP in a draft manifesto of 1917 to be circulated round Clydeside workshops, when it announced that the war had shown 'the futility of patchwork reforms within the capitalist-profiteering system'.[141] The Communists naturally retaliated, shrewdly probing the ILP's vanity in 1922 by heckling Dollan as to whether a socialist could be a magistrate.[142] By 1924 the breach seemed irreparable when during the Kelvingrove by-election in May, the Communists vigorously denounced the 'middle-class ideology of the Independent Labour Party'. The ILP countered by, among other things, running a couple of articles in *Forward* by Herbert Morrison outlining the reasons why there could be no question of permitting the Communist Party to affiliate to the Labour Party.[143]

In addition to these policy differences, the challenge which the Communist Party offered to the ILP's position within the Labour Party was a vital component in the divergence. The Communists were a disciplined body, ready to exploit the loopholes and anomalies in the constitution of the Labour Party, and so were obviously a threat to the ILP. The individual sections of the Labour Party, so often a weak point, were in several places in the grip of Communists. At Motherwell in 1924, Willie Gallacher's nomination came from that section, while at Greenock, all ten such delegates voted for the Communist Geddes in a close contest to win the candidature.[144] Again, organisations were often affiliated which proved to be little more than Communist fronts. The Unemployed Committee at Greenock was controlled by Geddes, and the Housing Association at Motherwell was similarly Communist-controlled. The Boilermakers' union, in Scotland virtually in the pocket of the Communist Party, afforded a further avenue to promote the party's interests. Aitken Ferguson was sponsored at Kelvingrove by the union, and at Paisley the union, having affiliated to the city Labour Party in the summer of 1923, had nominated Harry Pollitt for the seat by early September.[145] By such devices the Communists were able to consolidate their position in a number of seats, so challenging the primacy of the ILP. By November 1923, the Greenock newspaper remarked that: 'A rather peculiar situation exists locally regarding the Labour Party. Many Labourists claim that there is now no Labour Party in Greenock, but that the organisation is in the hands of the Communists'.[146] To compound the frustration felt by the ILP, there were allegations that the Communists were attempting to infiltrate the Scottish ILP. In June 1923 Dollan explained to the NAC that action had been taken to deal with this difficulty.[147]

Resistance to the Communist presence in the Labour Party did come, as we saw, from the Catholic elements within Labour. But as this lobby lacked any institutional form, it could do little constructive blocking within the Labour Party machinery, so that its only real power lay in threatening to withhold electoral support. As also noted earlier, trade union loyalty to the chosen candidate, together with trade union inactivity in Labour Party matters, meant that the unions could seldom offer serious opposition. In most places, it fell to the ILP to tackle the Communists, which they did in a variety of ways, and with a reasonable degree of success. The first and most obvious level of action was within the constituency affected. In Greenock, an ILP official explained early in 1923 that they were determined to be ready to run their own candidate in the next election.[148] In Dundee in 1922 Gallacher furiously denounced the local ILP for repudiating him in the election and evidently preferring to seek common cause instead with Edwin Scrymgeour, the Prohibition candidate.[149] Another possible course to pursue at the constituency level was to try to break up the party machinery. Greenock saw this carried out. When in 1923 the Communist Geddes secured the nomination over the ILP's choice, John Paton, by what were claimed to be dubious practices, the ILP led the secession of several affiliated bodies in protest.[150] This helped to get the Scottish Advisory Council to pronounce the local party to be operating unconstitutionally, so that it was disbanded and only allowed to re-form once it had been purged of its Communist power bases.[151]

Attention was drawn on a wider scale to the activities of the Communists through the medium of the ILP's Scottish journal *Forward.* In its columns frequent exposures of Communist malpractices were reported. The issue of 27 October 1923 described the 'Amazing Situation' in Greenock, and issued a dramatic warning, in order to alert ILPers elsewhere: 'The Labour Party in Scotland is faced in two or three important centres with a definite revolt ... ' whose object was to place Communists as Labour candidates.[152]

As a final resort, appeals to the Labour party's higher echelons — the SAC or the NEC — could be made. This was a shrewd move, for both these bodies, and particularly the all-powerful NEC, were always anxious to prevent Communist incursions. So at Paisley in 1923, Ben Shaw, the SAC secretary, attended the nomination meeting, and his ruling that Harry Pollitt's candidature would not be ratified by the Labour Party led to the Communist not being endorsed.[153] It is instructive to note that the NEC inquiry into the means whereby the Communist Ferguson won the nomination at Kelvingrove was launched at the instigation of the ILP.[154] The case of Greenock is a similar one. Against this background of tension, it is not perhaps surprising that violence broke out on occasions between Communists and ILPers. The ILP's insistence on running Stephen Kelly at Greenock in 1924 against Geddes provoked the worst episodes. At one meeting Kelly was struck on the back by a missile and confined to hospital for several days. Shortly afterwards, a significant statement was made to the Labour Party's Scottish Council by two of the more left-wing ILPers: 'Mr Kirkwood also made a statement urging an extreme fighting policy as the only way to combat the Communists, in which he was supported by Mr Maxton'.[155] By then, however, the ILP were in the ascendant: at Kelvingrove, Motherwell and Paisley they had forced the Communists to cede control of the nomination of candidates. Only in Greenock did the Communists still pose a major challenge to the ILP's influence.

Paisley had not only a Communist threat to the ILP, which indeed was dealt with fairly smoothly. The ILP felt it was also strongly challenged there by the Cooperative Party. The general role of the cooperative movement in contributing to the consolidation of working-class support for the Labour Party in this period has already been discussed, and the Cooperative Party, which began in Scotland in 1917, had been allocated certain constituencies to contest. One was Glasgow Tradeston, where the headquarters of the Scottish cooperative movement were sited, and where many of the electors were cooperative employees; so that the party's claim to that seat appeared virtually impregnable. Another constituency was Paisley, where at the by-election of 1920 and the general election of 1922 the Cooperative Party candidate was given a free run by Labour. In 1923, however, the ILP felt compelled to promote a rival candidature, on the grounds explained earlier, viz. that J. M. Biggar, the Cooperative nominee, was unacceptable because of his alleged activities as a rent factor in evicting tenants.[156] The ILP did indicate that if the Co-operative Party had chosen a different, more politically congenial, candidate, their own action would not have occurred.[157] The Cooperative Party took heed of this hint, and replaced Biggar with Hugh Guthrie, expressing the hope that the new man would find favour with the ILP. Guthrie was a long-standing ILP stalwart in the West of Scotland, who had recently served on the NAC of the ILP. Now, however, the ILP were still not satisfied, and led a successful campaign to have Guthrie dropped, replacing him with their own nominee as the sole Labour candidate (and victor). This was Rosslyn Mitchell, not a man detectably further to the left than Guthrie: indeed Mitchell was a pre-war Liberal who only joined the ILP in 1918.

The reasons given by the ILP for this persistence in 1924 were quite different, obviously, from those advanced in 1923. Now it was contended, firstly, that the Cooperative Party had no active membership in Paisley, so that those in the Labour Party, who were going to do the electioneering, should have a say in the choice of the candidate they were to work for.[158] Secondly, and perhaps more centrally to understanding the deeper motives behind this conflict, the ILP argued that the Cooperative Party should not remain outside the Labour Party, but should affiliate directly and merge its identity with the main party.[159] The Cooperative Party had begun in 1922 to show signs of seeking to assert its independence from the Labour Party by establishing a greater political role. In that year, a women's political organiser was appointed, Political Study Circles were formed, and propaganda was built up in an effort to increase the Cooperative Party's influence.[160] In 1923, at the prompting of its chief Scottish agent, the Party began to consider increasing the number of seats to be fought in future. Among the constituencies surveyed were Greenock, Perth, Kilmarnock, Angus, three Glasgow seats and one in Edinburgh.[161] Although almost none of this materialised, this expansionist tendency may well have seemed alarming to the ILP. Certainly the refusal to reach any compromise in a series of protracted negotiations between the various political groupings in Paisley seems to have come mainly from elements identified with the ILP.[162] The Labour Party NEC became alarmed lest the Paisley dispute should lead to a breakdown of the harmonious relations established on a national basis with the Cooperative Party. First of all, Shaw of the Scottish Council tried to induce the ILP to withdraw Mitchell's candidature, and when that failed, a high-powered delegation from the NEC went north to try to get Guthrie approved by the Paisley Labour Party. This too failed in the face of Mitchell's threat to run, whatever was decided, so long as Guthrie was the Cooperative Party's candidate, and not that of the Labour Party.[163]

With the withdrawal of Guthrie, and the defeat at Partick of one of their two sitting M.P.s, the 1924 election effectively demolished the hopes of the

Cooperative Party to fashion a separate presence in Scotland. In several other seats — Kilmarnock, Clackmannan and Edinburgh North — similar decisions by the local Labour Parties to put forward their own candidates meant that 'as a consequence our [Co-operative] candidates did not receive the necessary support'.[164] Accordingly, as the Scottish party chairman explained in February 1925, 'politically they were not making the progress they would like', a view echoed in a report made three months earlier to the London headquarters of the Cooperative Party.[165] The only option, it was argued in Scotland by a leading member of the party, was to join the Labour Party, since 'we could not put forward a candidate without the permission of the Labour Party', and negotiations to arrive at some arrangement were set afoot in January 1925.[166] But the grassroots support was withering very quickly. When Guthrie retired from Paisley, the Cooperative Party was warned that unless vigorous propaganda work was undertaken, support would quickly ebb. One year later the Paisley party did indeed appear to be defunct. No Cooperative candidates stood at the municipal elections, and the party committee appeared to be composed of active Labour Party members, so that there was no substance of independence left.[167]

Paisley represents in microcosm the power of the ILP within the Labour Party. In this burgh both the Communist and the Cooperative parties had been skilfully outmanoeuvred. One local trade union delegate was in no doubt as to this process: 'Comrade MacPhee stated that he thought that there was quite a lot of underhand methods being used in this election and that there was only one party in it and that was the ILP. He appealed to council to take control of their own affairs from this [sic] on'.[168]

NOTES

1. J. Paton, *Left Turn!* (London, 1936), pp. 141–2.

2. Memo. to A. B. Law, 30 Dec. 1918, Bonar Law MSS., BL 95/2 for West of Scotland. J. Paton, *Proletarian Pilgrimage* (London, 1935), pp. 311–3, for Rose.

3. K. Middlemas, *The Clydesiders* (London, 1965), pp. 128–32, discusses these and similar scenes.

4. J. Hinton, *The First Shop Stewards Movement* (London, 1973), is excellent on this, as is I. MacLean, *The Legend of Red Clydeside* (Edinburgh, 1983), pp. 5–110.

5. E.g. the report by E. P. Wake on the SAC Conference (? 1916), B. Shaw to J. S. Middleton, 3 Apr. 1917, Labour Party MSS., LP/SAC/14/212,295; SAC, *Annual Report 1915–16*.

6. Glasier to F. Johnson, 24 May 1918, Glasier MSS. I, 1.1918/50.

7. *The Times,* 28 Dec. 1922.

8. P. J. Dollan in *I.L.P. Annual Conference Report 1920,* pp. 18–19.

9. Glasgow ILP Federation *Annual Reports,* various dates. In August 1922 Gorbals ILP reduced its affiliation fee to the Trades Council because of the fall in its members: Glasgow Trades and Labour Council Minute Book, 2 Aug. 1922.

10. Glasgow ILP Federation Organising Committee Minute Book, 12 Sep. 1922.

11. Glasgow ILP Federation. *Annual Reports,* 1921–2, 1922–3.

12. ILP *Annual Report* 1923, esp. pp. 63,17.

13. Special Report to the Organisation Committee, n.d., ILP NAC MSS., 65.

14. *Glasgow Herald,* 3 Dec. 1923.

15. T. N. Graham, *Willie Graham* (London, n.d.), pp. 134,93–5.

16. J. Barr, *Lang Syne* (London, 1949), pp. 313–48.

17. *Glasgow Herald,* 25 Oct. 1924.

18. *Parliamentary Election 1924. Motherwell Division;* cf. *Glasgow Herald,* 27 Oct. 1924 for a reference to his 'wife and weans' socialism.

19. Snowden to J. B. Glasier, 13 Dec. 1919, Glasier MSS. I, 1.1919/104.

20. Scott Diary, 18 Oct. 1924; Scott to J. R. MacDonald, 5 Dec. 1924; cf. Scott to W. Graham, 14 Nov. 1924; MacCallum Scott MSS., MS. 1465/15,378,259.

21. Paton, *Left Turn!,* pp. 110–1.

22. *Glasgow Herald,* 10 Nov. 1922; cf. E. Shinwell, *Conflict Without Malice* (London, 1955), pp. 88–90.

23. *Glasgow Herald,* 10, 3–5 Dec. 1922.

24. There is a copy of his address in MacCallum Scott MSS., MS. 1465/96. Cf. *Glas. Herald,* 7 Nov. 1922.

25. *Stirling Journal and Advertiser,* 23 Nov. 1922.

26. Paton, *Left Turn!,* p. 149.

27. J. Lee, *Tomorrow is a New Day* (London, 1939), pp. 124–5.

28. *Hamilton Advertiser,* 23 Nov. 1918, 4 Jan. 1919. It is possible the latter reference is to Irish Nationalism rather than to socialism.

29. *Rutherglen Reformer,* 3, 10 Nov. 1922.

30. *Dunfermline Press,* 1 Dec. 1923.

31. For this episode, J. L. Morgan to Ponsonby, 3 Nov. 1915, Ponsonby MSS., MS. Eng. hist c.663, ff. 147–8.

32. Labour Party MSS., SAC Minute Book, 2 Dec. 1918; *Dunfermline Press,* 30 Nov. 1918.

33. R. Hay to Miss Longbourne, 7 Feb. 1919, J. Davidson, D. Milne to A. Ponsonby, 29 Dec. 1918, 6 Jan. 1919, Ponsonby MSS., MS. Eng. hist c.667, ff. 161–2, 119, 147–50.

34. *Dunfermline Press,* 21 Dec. 1918.

35. J. R. MacDonald to A. Ponsonby, n.d. (1918), Ponsonby MSS., MS. Eng. hist c.667, f. 103.

36. Labour Party MSS., SAC Minute Book, 9 Feb. 1920.

37. Paton, *Left Turn!,* pp. 124–8, 142–4.

38. *Fife Free Press,* 26 Mar. 1921.

39. *Glasgow Herald,* 27 Oct. 1924.

40. C. Harvie, *No Gods and Precious Few Heroes* (London, 1981), pp. 31–2; MacLean, *Legend of Red Clydeside,* pp. 164–73.

41. Scott Diary, 16 Nov. 1922; cf. Scott to W. H. Miller, 23 Nov. 1922 (copy), MacCallum Scott MSS., MS. 1465/13,403.

42. Bruce to Law, 10 Nov. 1922; cf. G. Younger, J. Gilmour to Law, Sir R. Horne to J. C. C. Davidson, 9, 8 Nov., 8 Dec. 1922, Bonar Law MSS., BL 113/11/7,6,5,14.

43. Maryhill Conservative Association Minute Book, 20 Nov. 1922; cf. SUA Western Division Council Minute Book, 6 Dec. 1922.

44. Scott Diary, 23 Nov. 1922, MacCallum Scott MSS., MS. 1465/13.

45. *Forward,* 9 Dec. 1922 for the first two. (It is noticeable that several of the Glasgow winners do not see the rent question as decisive); for Dundee, *Morel and the Labour Programme* (Dundee, 1922); Morel MSS., F 2/1/13.

46. Cf. P. F. Clarke, 'The Electoral Sociology of Modern Britain', *History* 57 (1972), pp. 31–55.

47. B. A. Waites, 'The Effects of the First World War on Class and Status in Britain, 1910-20', *Jnl. of Contemporary History* 11 (1976), pp. 27–48, is helpful.

48. N. Blewett, 'The Franchise in the United Kingdom, 1885-1918', *Past and Present* 32 (1965), pp. 27–56; H. C. G. Mathew *et al,* 'The Franchise Factor and the Rise of the Labour Party', *EHR* 91 (1976), pp. 723–52.

49. Mathew *et al,* 'Franchise Factor', pp. 727–33.

50. *Glasgow Herald,* 27 Nov. 1918.

51. STUC *28th Annual Report* 1925, p. 34.

52. *Ibid.*

53. J. S. Middleton to B. Shaw, 2 Nov. 1914 (copy), Labour Party MSS., LP/SAC/14/44.

54. B. Shaw to J. S. Middleton, 30 Apr. 1917, Ibid., LP/SAC/14/298. Cf. Labour Party SAC *Annual Report* 1916–17 (draft) for further instances, Ibid., LP/SAC/14/347.

55. S. Damer, 'State, Class and Housing, 1885-1919', in J. Melling (ed.), *Housing, Social Policy and the State* (London, 1980), pp. 98, 103–4; J. Melling, 'Clydeside Housing and the Evolution of State Rent Control, 1900-39', *Ibid.,* pp. 143, 148–51, 153–4; Melling, *Rent Strike* (Edinburgh, 1983), pp. 109–10.

56. Harvie, *No Gods . . . ,* pp. 10–11.

57. J. Duncan to W. Stewart, 28 Feb. 1917 (copy), Johnson MSS., 1917/44.

58. *Glasgow and District Railwaymen's Strike Bulletin* 5 (2 Oct. 1919).

59. G. Younger to A. B. Law, 24 Sep. 1918, Bonar Law MSS., BL 95/2.

60. R. Stewart to J. C. C. Davidson, 19, 27 Dec. 1918, 'Analysis of Vote, Central Division of Glasgow', n.d. Ibid., BL 21/6/64 (93,98,95).

61. See p. 261.

62. *Glasgow Observer,* 7 Dec., 30 Nov. 1918; cf. *Hamilton Advertiser,* 30 Nov., 7 Dec. 1918.

63. *Glasgow Observer,* 14 Dec. 1918; cf. 'Election Results in the West of Scotland', 30 Dec. 1918, Bonar Law MSS., BL 95/2.

64. *Glasgow Observer,* 17 Nov. 1923.

65. A. Currie to F. Brockway, 17 Jan. 1924, Johnson MSS., 1924/17. MacLean, *Legend of Red Clydeside,* pp. 183–201, explores very fully the role of Irish Catholics in the Glasgow Labour Party.

66. Maryhill Conservative Association Minute Book, 20 Nov. 1922.

67. *Forward,* 3 Feb. 1923.

68. See the printed circular of 8 Oct. 1917 in Labour Party MSS., SAC Minute Books; cf. Ibid., 17 Mar., 11 Aug. 1917, 9 Feb. 1918. P. J. Dollan, *Jubilee History of the Kinning Park Cooperative Society Limited* (Glasgow, 1923), pp. 95–9, 112–3, for a local case-study.

69. B. Shaw to J. S. Middleton, 12 May 1917, cf. 19, 29 May 1917; Labour Party MSS., LP/SAC/14/305,308,319.

70. *Scottish Cooperator,* 25 Nov. 1922.

71. *Dunfermline Press,* 18 Nov. 1922; *Forward,* 15 Nov. 1924.

72. E.g. *Labour News for Kirkcaldy District of Burghs,* 20 Jan., 24 Mar. 1923.

73. *Scottish Cooperator,* 25 Nov. 1922; Dollan, *Kinning Park,* p. 183.

74. *Glasgow Herald,* 7, 11 Nov. 1922.

75. *Forward,* 8 Nov. 1924.

76. *Greenock Telegraph,* 16 Nov. 1922.

77. Paton, *Left Turn!,* pp. 226–7.

78. Mathew *et al,* 'Franchise Factor', pp. 747–50.

79. Scott Diary, 12 March 1921, MacCallum Scott MSS., MS. 1465/12.

80. *Glasgow Herald,* 9 Nov. 1922.

81. Graham, *Willie Graham,* pp. 71–2.

82. W. M. R. Pringle to Mrs Pringle, 8 Feb. 1920, Pringle MSS., Hist. Coll. 226/III/12.

83. *Scottish Cooperator,* 25 Oct. 1924.

84. Cf. *Forward,* 9 Dec. 1922.

85. *Glasgow Observer,* 1 Dec. 1923, 17 May 1924.

86. *Motherwell Times,* 24 Nov. 1922.

87. *Glasgow Observer,* 1, 15 Dec. 1923, 18, 25 Oct. 1924; *Greenock Telegraph,* 24 Oct. 1924. Newbold's own MS. autobiography stresses the support he received from Irish Nationalists in 1922, but records that after that election, Irish unity disintegrated. Newbold MSS., Folder marked 'Autobiographical Details of Newbold's Life'.

88. *Glasgow Observer,* 11 Oct. 1924, 15 Dec. 1923.

89. J. Ogilvie to E. D. Morel, both n.d. (early 1923), (c. Dec. 1923), Morel MSS., F 2/1/8.

90. *Motherwell Times,* 24 Nov. 1922.

91. South Mid Lothian and Peebles Labour Party Minute Book, 27 Oct. 1923, Acc. 4312/23.

92. *Forward,* 9 Dec. 1922.

93. *Scottish Cooperator,* 25 Oct. 1924.

94. Paton, *Left Turn!,* p. 144.

95. Glas. ILP Federation, Election Committee Minute Book, 19 Jan. 1919.

96. ILP NAC Minute Book, 22–24 Sep. 1919.

97. Paton, *Left Turn!,* pp. 106–7.

98. R. I. MacKibbin, *The Evolution of the Labour Party, 1910–24* (London, 1974), pp. 131–61.

99. Paton, *Left Turn!,* pp. 115–8, 139–40.

100. Glasgow ILP Federation *Annual Report* 1923–4; cf. *Forward,* 22 Dec. 1923.

101. *Scottish Cooperator,* 25 Oct. 1924; *Forward,* 2, 9 Dec. 1922.

102. *Dunfermline Press,* 18 Nov. 1922.

103. *Forward,* 25 Oct. 1924.

104. *Dundee Advertiser,* 28, 29 Aug. 1918.

105. Labour Party SAC, *6th, 9th Annual Reports* (1919–20, 1922–23).

106. *Address by Scottish Council Executive to All Trades Union Secretaries* (8 Dec. 1919), Labour Party MSS., SAC Minute Books; SAC, *9th Annual Report* (1922–23).

107. Maryhill Labour Party Minute Book, list of affiliated bodies at end, MS. 891024.

108. Based on the lists contained in the *Annual Reports* of the Labour Party. The two Scottish seats in 1924 were Dundee and Kirkcaldy.

109. Paisley Trades and Labour Council Minute Book, 2 Apr. 1924.

110. South Mid Lothian and Peebles Labour Party Minute Book, 29 Mar., 12 Apr. 1924, Acc. 4312/23.

111. 'Report on Women's Organisation' (Nov. 1921, Jun. 1922), Labour Party MSS., NEC Minute Book; cf. SAC Minute Books, 7 Jan. 1924.

112. SAC *6th Annual Report* (1919–20), cf. B. Shaw to J. S. Middleton, 13 Apr. 1920, Labour Party MSS., SAC Minute Book.

113. Glasgow Trades and Labour Council Minute Book, 11 Nov. 1919, 10 Feb., 5 Oct. 1920; *Annual Report* 1919–20.

114. Glasgow Trades and Labour Council Minute Book, 18 Oct. 1921.

115. Ibid., 14 Jun. 1922.

116. Paisley Trades and Labour Council Minute Book, 27 Jan. 1923.

117. Labour Party MSS., NEC Minute Book, 27 Nov. 1918.

118. SAC *7th Annual Report* (1920–21).

119. 'Report on Organisation of Women in Scotland' (June 1922), Labour Party MSS., NEC Minute Book.

120. Glasgow Trades and Labour Council Minute Book, 9 Feb. 1922.

121. SAC *10th Annual Report* (1923–4); *Motherwell Times,* 16 May 1924; Labour Party MSS., SAC Minute Books, 28 Apr. 1924.

122. *Dundee Advertiser,* 10 Feb. 1923.

123. J. Thomson to E. D. Morel, 17 Dec. 1923, 20 Jan. 1924, Morel MSS., F2/1/10.

124. Glasgow Trades and Labour Council Minute Book, 4 Mar. 1923.

125. Labour Party MSS., SAC Minute Books, 3 Nov. 1923, 4 Feb., 10 Mar., 28 Apr. 1924; SAC *10th Annual Report* (1923–24).

126. Labour Party MSS., NEC Minute Book, 21 Jul. 1924.

127. Glasgow Trades and Labour Council Minute Book, 24 Jan. 1923.

128. *Motherwell Times,* 24 Nov. 1922.

129. South Mid Lothian and Peebles Labour Party Minute Book, 7 Jun. 1919, 24 Jan., 28 Feb., 20 Mar. 1920, 28 Jan., 15 Apr. 1922, 7 Apr. 1923, Acc. 4312/23.

130. A copy of the constitution (1917) is in Labour Party MSS., AFF/09/18.

131. *Foward,* 25 Oct. 1924. This is of course a very hostile source.

132. Paisley Trades and Labour Council Minute Book, 5 Sep., 14 Nov. 1923.

133. Glasgow Trades and Labour Council Minute Book, 14 Aug. 1923.

134. ILP NAC Minute Book, 12 Nov. 1918, 12 Jun., 22–24 Sep. 1919; cf. Newbold MSS., 'Autobiographical Details of Newbold's Political Life', for confirmation.

135. *Glasgow Herald,* 5 Jan. 1920; Paton, *Left Turn!,* pp. 30–5.

136. *Glasgow Herald,* 4 Jan. 1921.

137. Glasgow ILP Federation Minute Book, 18 Feb., 10 Jun. 1921.

138. *Glasgow Herald,* 31 Aug. 1921.

139. Glasgow ILP Federation Minute Book, 23 Dec. 1921.

140. *Forward,* 19 Aug. 1922.

141. Glasgow ILP Federation Minute Book, 30 Nov. 1917.

142. *Forward,* 2 Sep. 1922.

143. *Ibid.,* 31 May, 27 Sep., 4 Oct. 1924.

144. *Motherwell Times,* 17 Oct. 1924, *Forward,* 25 Oct. 1924.

145. Paisley Trades and Labour Council Minute Book, 5 Sep. 1923.

146. *Greenock Telegraph,* 13 Nov. 1923.

147. ILP NAC MSS., 8 Jun. 1923, cf. also 28–30 Aug. 1924.

148. J. I. Duff to J. L. Kinloch, 1 Apr. (1923), Kinloch MSS., 1/30.

149. *Dundee Advertiser,* 2 Nov. 1922, cf. 30 Oct. 1922.

150. *Greenock Telegraph,* 13, 15 Oct., 15 Nov. 1923; *Forward,* 27 Oct. 1923.

151. Labour Party MSS., SAC Minute Book, 3 Nov. 1923, 4 Feb., 10 Mar. 1924; NEC Minute Book, 8 Jan., 17 May 1924.

152. *Forward,* 27 Oct. 1923, 25 Oct. 1924.

153. Paisley Trades and Labour Council Minute Book, 14 Nov. 1923.

154. Labour Party MSS., NEC Minute Book, 21 Jul. 1924.

155. Labour Party MSS., SAC Minute Book, 29 Nov. 1924.

156. *Paisley Gazette,* 23 Jun. 1923; Paisley Trades and Labour Council Minute Book, 6, 13 June 1923; Cooperative Party Minute Book, 13 Feb. 1924.

157. Paisley Trades and Labour Council Minute Book, 16 Nov. 1923.

158. *Paisley Gazette,* 30 Aug. 1924.

159. Paisley Trades and Labour Council Minute Book, 2, 20 Sep. 1924.

160. Cooperative Party Minute Book, 5 Apr., 15 Aug. 1922.

161. Ibid., 7, 31 Mar., 11 Apr., 2 May, 17, 24 Nov. 1923.

162. E.g. *Paisley Gazette,* 3, 17 May 1924; Cooperative Party Minute Book, 26 Sep. 1924; ILP NAC Minute Book, 28–30 Aug. 1924.

163. Labour Party MSS., NEC Minute Book, 2 Sep. 1924; Paisley Trades and Labour Council Minute Book, 22 June 1924.

164. Cooperative Party Minute Book, 16 Oct. 1924.

165. Ibid., 21 Feb. 1925, 17 Dec. 1924.

166. Ibid., 18 Oct. 1924, 12 Jan. 1925.

167. Ibid., 16 Oct., 15 Nov. 1924, 20 Oct. 1925.

168. Paisley Trades and Labour Council Minute Book, 8 Oct. 1924.

10

Realignment on the Right: 1914–24

Just as precipitate as the breakthrough achieved by Labour between 1918 and 1924 was the transformation of the position of the Unionist party in Scotland. In the last pre-war election there were nine Unionists and fifty-eight Liberals, but by 1924 the tables were permanently reversed: now there were thirty-six Unionists and only eight Liberals. For many at the time, and since, the decline of the liberal party was inevitable, as the humiliating rout of the party in the 1918 elections indicated. In all, Liberals standing without benefit of the coupon won only 8 seats. Asquith was bundled out of East Fife after a tenure of over thirty years, and the ex-Secretary of State for Scotland, Mackinnon Wood, lost his deposit at St Rollox, where he had sat since 1906.[1] All of this seemed to confirm the contention that the party had little appeal in the new political context. The party had been badly split during the war, its ideals and policies were outmoded in the post-war world, its organisation had become hopelessly dilapidated. In sum, it represented a past political tradition which had little appeal to young people. Its eclipse was therefore steady, as politics naturally polarised between the other two parties.[2]

There is plenty of evidence from Scotland to commend the various elements of this interpretation. Local parties were in some cases divided over the entry into war and its conduct, as the example of Ponsonby in the Stirling Burghs demonstrates. Because he opposed not the entry into war, but certain aspects of the government's handling of it — notably the abandonment of free trade — W. M. R. Pringle was informed that the North-West Lanarkshire Liberals were unhappy. 'I am afraid that your chances at an election would be very small indeed', he was warned, 'and we could not get men who would work for your return'.[3] In Aberdeen South, the M.P., G. B. Esslemont, refused to support the Military Service Bill in 1916, despite powerful grassroots support for the measure, and within a year he had resigned on the grounds of ill-health.[4] The allocation of the coupon in the 1918 election served to deepen divisions within Scottish Liberalism. Despite the disposition of M.P.s on the eve of war, there were thirty-six Unionist and only twenty-eight Liberal Coalitionist candidates. The effects of this maldistribution, which reflected the strength of Asquithianism among Scottish Liberal M.P.s — Lloyd George's adviser counted out of a total of fifty-four only twenty-two who were loyal to the Government in 1918 — were serious.[5] Coalition-minded Liberals found themselves frequently fighting — and defeating — their former colleagues either in direct confrontation, or by working on behalf of the

Tories. Thus the Aberdeen Liberal Association resolved to support the government candidates, yet in the South constituency this meant helping the Unionist, an Edinburgh advocate, against the sitting Liberal, a local businessman.[6]

These problems were exacerbated by the formal split in the Liberal party in 1920. In the first place, the departure of several prominent figures to join Lloyd George's party was dismaying. They included Sir William Robertson, a former President of the SLA who had been Campbell-Bannerman's close confidant, and also Sir Robert Lockhart, a longstanding mainstream Liberal who in the past had opposed both Liberal Unionism and Liberal Imperialism. The disarray in some constituencies was considerable. In Aberdeen, the Asquithians refused to have any contact with the Coalitionists, while in Edinburgh North the Asquithians ousted the Lloyd George Liberals from office, deselected the prospective candidate and chose instead one of their own kind.[7] Relations were worsened by the SLA's decision to expel any branch which did not renounce the Coalition and all its works. Some seventeen constituency parties either disaffiliated or were treated as though they had. That is to say, nearly one-quarter of the constituency organisations broke away, of whom a disproportionate one-third were in the Highlands or the North-East, two areas where Liberalism had remained electorally strong.[8]

A further deterioration occurred as the Lloyd George wing adopted aggressive tactics in trying to set up rival Liberal Associations. William Sutherland, M.P. for Argyll, carried out most of this work, and he operated in a ruthless manner. Reviewing his work in March 1921, he informed Lloyd George that he had already created a firm organisational base in Scotland. It was his proudest boast that 'We have pretty completely broken up the SLA and I took the best man away (Gibb) and had a hand in securing the resignation from the Association of its leading members and so weakened it practically beyond repair'.[9] Not only did the Lloyd George Liberals form rival organisations, they also worked to destroy the prospects of electoral advance for the Asquithians. At the Paisley by-election of 1920, the initial attitude of the Unionists was not to challenge Asquith, a decision which incensed Lloyd George's managers, who forthwith gave 'definite instructions that at all costs a Coalition candidate — Liberal or Unionist — must be produced'.[10] In Edinburgh North, the Coalition Liberals determinedly threw their weight behind the Unionist candidate, even although as the director of a whisky firm he was held to offend the susceptibilities of some followers of Lloyd George.[11] This support was crucial in defeating Runciman, the Asquithian, and thereby undermining the morale of the Independent Liberals after the fillip received by Asquith's triumph at Paisley three months previously. 'If we can pull this off on top of Paisley', explained Runciman, 'we do more than stagger them in Scotland and will give a general breadth and character to the revival'.[12] The 1922 general election marked the nadir of internal Liberal strife. In sixteen seats Liberal fought Liberal, generally in a bitter atmosphere. Churchill complained that an Asquithian was put up in Dundee simply to make the seat unwinnable by him.[13] The spectacle of Unionists and Coalition Liberals working, if anything apparently more closely together than in 1918, was profoundly discouraging. When Donald

MacLean visited Glasgow and Edinburgh immediately after the general election he found that 'the result of the election had rather depressed many good Liberal workers and their outlook was despondent'. He noted that in Glasgow matters had been very difficult, with the city Liberal Club deeply divided.[14]

These difficulties were confirmed by the decay of party organisation. At the centre, the SLA appeared paralysed by the traumatic events. In 1920 it was agreed that 'very little was being done in the way of organisation and propaganda', while the Secretary pointed out that the party had no great speaking power at present and that there was a dearth of literature.[15] The SLA suffered from acute financial problems. In 1920 subscriptions were about £400 below the best pre-war years, and in 1922 grants had to be halved because 'several very good friends who had rendered valuable financial assistance were unwilling to subscribe any considerable sums as their contributions would depend on how the Federation faced the question of reunion'.[16] With the centre immobile, the rot at the constituency level went on unchecked. In several places the Liberal party appeared defunct. In West Stirling, no Liberal party had been evident since the 1918 election, and by 1923 it was said to be kept alive only in Bridge of Allan, where the Pullar family, prominent in Perth Liberalism before the war, had settled. The Liberals in the Stirling and Falkirk constituency were reported in 1922 to be still in 'the state of hibernation which has existed since the days of the war'.[17] In Aberdeen, the lack of adequate subscriptions to maintain proper organisation led the Secretary to threaten to resign in despair.[18] The existence after 1920 of two distinct Liberal parties simply increased the sense of organisational collapse, especially as the Lloyd George Liberals often seemed a stage army. In Kirkcaldy, a prominent local Liberal complained in 1920 of the party: 'It was not merely in abeyance, it was extinct'. At a by-election the next year, when a Lloyd George Liberal stood, Sutherland was reduced to ranting about his party's poor condition: 'No organisation. Nobody who knows anything about electioneering. The outlying parts quite neglected. You give orders and nothing happens'.[19]

Linked to this decline in Liberal activity was a loss of faith in the relevance of Liberal policies. A sympathetic correspondent commented to Pringle on the eve of his defeat in 1918: 'You remind me of 'the shades of night were falling fast etc.' and on the banner which you bear, inscribed the strange device 'Free Trade''.[20] A self-styled 'Old Radical' expressed this view in 1924 when he warned that it was not enough to fight elections on old warcries: 'The electors must be definitely shown what Liberalism is to do for the nation generally and for various classes particularly. The average elector must have as clearly in his head as an aeroplane sailing across the sky what Liberalism intends to do when next in power. Unless he has that idea, some clearer definiteness of Labour or Conservative will scoop his vote'.[21] This of course was the standard criticism levelled at Asquith in his 1918 and 1920 election campaigns.[22]

The upshot of these various discontents was to leave rank and file Liberals demoralised and rootless. MacCallum Scott observed with concern his constituency Secretary's steady disillusionment with the Liberals. Partly this was because of the faction fighting within the party, and partly because he was, Scott detected, 'restive and out of sympathy with Liberalism' in any form. Six months later he resigned from his office in the Bridgeton Liberals.[23] The general image presented by the Liberals was that of an ageing party. Meeting a local Liberal in Dunoon in 1920, MacCallum Scott reflected: 'He is a prosperous old-fashioned Liberal — a very conservative type in Scotland. The salt of the earth for virtue but quite out of touch with all modern tendencies'. When Scott stood at Partick in 1923, the same observation was made: 'There are a number of good old-fashioned Liberals of a past generation approaching superannuation. But there are no young recruits'.[24] Aberdeen had the identical problem, for here in 1920 there was a general view that younger members should be encouraged to take a more prominent part in the party's affairs, but this does not seem to have been successful, since in the next year it is apparent that there were no young men available to hold open-air meetings. The Liberals' profile seemed confirmed in 1922, when the Chairman of the South Aberdeen seat intimated his wish to stand down, because his 'defective hearing' impaired his effectiveness in the chair.[25]

While there is impressive evidence to sustain the claim that the Liberals were in irreversible decline and were supplanted by the Unionists, who were more politically relevant and better organised, with the Coalition serving as a preliminary phase in the transition, there are, however, indications that this was not a smooth and continuous process from 1918 to 1924. Firstly, there were abundant signs that the relations between Unionists and Coalition Liberals were not always harmonious, nor did they betoken a near-convergence of identity even before then. There were strong feelings on both sides in 1918 that the coupon arrangment was only temporary. At Kilmarnock, local Unionists sought assurances from the sitting Coalition Liberal M.P., Alexander Shaw, that he would not adhere unreservedly to free trade. Munro, the Scottish Secretary, agreed with Shaw that the Tories had no right to impose protectionism as a precondition of support, but he did warn that it might not be possible to return to pre-war verities. Shaw then came back to Munro, stressing his great hopes that the Liberal Party would re-unite after the war.[26] Likewise MacCallum Scott took care to base his 1918 election campaign on the specific point that 'I was clear that the Coalition did not mean the merging of the parties'. He reiterated the point that he would only follow the Government in its pursuance of the peace settlement and so long as it conformed to the policy lines laid down by Lloyd George.[27] This view was also upheld by the rank and file, as at Aberdeen, where the decision to support the Coalition candidates was deemed only to relate to the conclusion of the Versailles settlement. They resolutely refused to 'give further support except to measures which were consistent with Liberal principles'.[28]

The absence of Liberal enthusiasm for Coalition unity may have been in part connected with the distribution of the coupon in a manner unduly favourable to the Unionists. Even the Tories seemed a trifle embarrassed by their share, for a letter from an indignant Unionist candidate demanding to know why he had been denied the Coalition's approval, had the comment endorsed on it by Bonar Law that it was 'on account of our having so many in Scotland'.[29] Lloyd George's Scottish political manager agreed with this, pointing out in 1920 that 'There never was any doubt that, in this respect, Scottish seats were badly handled by the Coalition in 1918'.[30] Nevertheless, there was still great bitterness on the part of the Unionists when they were refused the coupon endorsement, a further sign that there was as yet no wholehearted alliance between the two Coalition parties. In Bridgeton, the recipient of the coupon was the sitting Liberal, MacCallum Scott, and not his Unionist opponent, Hutchison, who had been nursing the seat for some years. When Scott met Hutchison, the latter confessed himself 'greatly disappointed at the situation. He had worked hard and built up a great organisation. If he withdrew it would collapse'. Many of his supporters, he told Scott, would not find it easy to actually work for a Liberal, but the Tories would withdraw their candidature. However, two months after this interview the local Tories changed their mind and pronounced Scott unacceptable. They then appealed to their Central Office for assistance in fighting the seat. Younger finally sorted the dispute out in Scott's favour, and the Bridgeton party publicly asked Conservative electors to vote for Scott, but somewhat weakened this appeal by adding a rider denouncing Tory headquarters for mishandling the whole affair. Scott then approached the Unionists for help in the campaign, received it, and in thanking them for their assistance, significantly acknowledged the difficulty involved in breaking party ties.[31] In Cathcart, where J. W. Pratt, a Liberal with a poor constituency record, was awarded the coupon, the local Tories also erupted in fury. 'I may say it is the bitterest pill I have had to swallow during my whole political life', thundered the disappointed Unionist candidate, while the President of the constituency Association was equally incensed: 'I have swallowed and can swallow many disagreeable things, but cannot swallow Pratt, therefore, as I cannot reconcile myself to support him, I propose going down to Gorbals and help George Barnes against the Bolshevist MacLean'. The Unionist threat to run their candidate as an independent Unionist was squashed only when Bonar Law fired off an angry telegram.[32] While distaste for Pratt's poor record may explain Unionist recalcitrance in Cathcart, dogged opposition was also shown by East Aberdeenshire Tories to the Liberal M.P., Cowan, whose credentials as secretary of the Liberal War Committee should have been unimpeachable.[33]

This intransigence on the part of the Unionists stemmed, it seems, more from awareness of the continuing gap between Liberal and Conservative after the war than from confidence that most Liberal seats were ripe for the seizing because of the collapse of the latter. For the Unionists were aware how vital to their representation in Scotland was the collaboration with the Lloyd George Liberals, and at the time of the break-up of the Coalition in 1922 this Tory dependence upon Liberal goodwill, and not *vice versa*, became apparent. At a meeting in July 1922 of junior Unionist ministers held to review the implications of the dissolution of the Coalition, the opinions given respecting Scotland were unanimously and almost uniquely gloomy. Gilmour, the Scottish Chief Whip, reported: 'Great difficulty in holding many seats without help of Liberal ... ' and predicted a 'catastrophe' unless action were taken to avert collisions over nominations for seats. From the west of Scotland, Mitchell-Thomson detected some ill-feeling amongst Tories about prolonging the Coalition, but he stressed that Unionists 'can't hope to hold our Glasgow seats without Liberal help'. Surveying prospects in the east of Scotland, the Solicitor-General confirmed that 'Scottish Conservatives could run great risk if they went forward as pure Conservatives'.[34]

It is instructive that at the famous Carlton Club meeting of Unionist M.P.s which led to the end of the Coalition, Scottish M.P.s were overwhelmingly against the break-up. Overall, 185 Tories voted to terminate the links with the Lloyd George Liberals, and only eighty-eight opposed this, but the figures for Scotland are quite divergent from the norm. Only six went with the majority, while seventeen sided with the minority, and of the six anti-Coalitionists, two were the prime architects of that policy, Bonar Law and Younger. Austen Chamberlain, the leader of the defeated faction, was reassured by many Scottish Tories that his position was fully supported north of the border, one instancing a private luncheon held for organising secretaries in west of Scotland constituencies where opinion was unanimous for retaining the Coalition.[35] Somewhat intrepidly, Bonar Law's constituency agent proffered the same advice: 'As regards the Coalition Liberals, the feeling that I hear expressed on all hands is that in the Glasgow Divisions, as indeed in Scotland generally, the utmost effort should be made to avoid a cleavage'.[36] Accordingly, as the *Times* correspondent found, the 1922 contest in Scotland, in contrast to England, was noteworthy both for the perpetuation of the electoral agreements already made, and for the instigators: 'There is no question of the pact existing between the Coalition Parties here. It is openly proclaimed. The Unionists took the initiative in announcing they proposed to fulfil in the letter and in the spirit every pledge they had given to the opposite side'.[37] Bonar Law's agent was also emphatic that the desire to respect the existing arrangements flowed from the Unionist camp.[38] In Scotland, the pact was applied in forty-six seats, or nearly two-thirds of all constituencies, but in England in only ninety-five, or under one-fifth.[39]

The reaction of many local Liberal parties to their internal split showed how well grounded was the Unionists' apprehension that Liberalism was still a vibrant force. Even after the formal rift of 1920, several refused to follow the line laid down from the centre by both camps. While, as already seen, friction did occur in some places, elsewhere there was a widespread desire to avoid a complete breach, just as there had been at the time of the Home Rule divide in 1886. Many Independent Liberal associations were quite content to leave the National Liberals within their organisation, as for instance Banffshire, which firmly refused to expel the Lloyd George followers. Elsewhere, the Asquithians professed themselves happy to stay in constituency parties where the Coalitionists prevailed, as at Kirkcaldy and Dunfermline. Argyll confused matters by proclaiming its loyalty to the Asquithian SLA, yet wholeheartedly backed its National Liberal M.P.[40] The re-unification of the Liberal party in Scotland after 1922 was in general speedy and harmonious. At Perth, for instance, both wings came together to select R. M. Mitchell as their candidate, and one of the bitterest National Liberal critics of the Independent Liberals in 1922 publicly declared his approval of the candidate.[41] From the other side, in Partick, where in 1922 the Asquithians had lost the seat to a Lloyd George Liberal, both groups pulled together to back the campaign of another Liberal identified with the Coalition, MacCallum Scott.[42] Indeed in only three seats (Argyll, Inverness, and Ross and Cromarty) were the differences found to be unbridgeable in the 1923 election.[43] The official decision to come together was not taken by the two Liberal parties in Scotland until 1924, but within two months it was announced that all the constituency parties had resolved their conflicts, with the solitary exception of Argyll.[44]

The commitment to the concept of Liberal unity thus demonstrated in 1922–24 was reinforced by another trend. It would be misleading to assume, from the evidence already cited of an enfeeblement of Liberal organisation after 1918, that this decline was an uninterrupted process. There were signs of a recovery under way from 1922. At the central level, the Secretary of the SLA concluded after the 1923 election that party organisation was in a better state than for several years, and in that election he had found that 'there was marked keenness and determination to fight as compared to 1922'.[45] In some respects this turnround in fortunes seems to have preceded the re-union. The 1921 annual meeting of the SLA was declared to be the best-attended ever, and from 1922 an upturn in subscriptions was recorded.[46] The financial position was of course materially improved with the accession of the Lloyd George-ites. This source bore the cost of contesting the Kelvingrove by-election in April 1924, which came to £888. Moreover there were funds now to pay the salaries of two organisers for the east and west of Scotland.[47]

Signs of movement could also be seen in the constituencies. Thus in some places membership showed no signs of slipping. In 1923, there were 1662 members of the Dundee Liberal Association, and the alarming fall of one-eighth in 1924 was explained as due solely to a delay caused by the introduction of a new format of membership card.[48] Although this was not much of an improvement on the 1908 figure of 1279, particularly given the vastly expanded electorate, it was immensely superior to the individual membership of the city Labour party, which probably did not exceed 300. While Paisley's performance may have been distorted by the presence of Asquith as M.P., nevertheless the number of Liberal party members there rose from 1,600 in 1921–22 to 2,000 in 1923–24.[49] Elsewhere, although less quantifiably, there were indications of an organisational revival in 1923–24. The Govan Liberals were said by the *Glasgow Herald* in January 1923 to have 'taken a new lease of life'. Maryhill met in December of that year to re-form, determining on a canvass of the constituency to secure new members. Hillhead early in 1924 claimed to be doing better than ever before.[50] East Renfrewshire was another constituency which revived in 1923, while in 1924 both West Stirling and Perth constituencies appointed organisers to put recovery on a professional footing.[51] Of course there were still areas of lethargy. The SLA in 1924 found that efforts to promote local speakers and meetings had 'not been at all satisfactory', and only a handful of constituencies were taking literature for distribution.[52] Yet at the same time one of the new organisers subsidised by the Lloyd George funds was clear that the state of constituency organisation had 'certainly' improved in the recent past.[53] The pointers are therefore rather confusing, but a good number of them contradict the thesis of the accelerating disintegration of Liberal machinery. In particular, they make the reverses suffered in the 1924 general election more striking, and suggest that other factors were decisive.

This resurgence of Liberal organisation reinforces a related point. The Unionist advance was not everywhere to be ascribed to superior organisation. The SUA acknowledged this point in 1923, complaining: 'It must be admitted that the existence of the Coalition hampered the growth of Unionist organisation which almost vanished during the war, and it was not easy for the Unionists to remain loyal to their allies and at the same time to reconstruct an efficient party machine'.[54] In that year the Western Division stated that in several seats pre-war standards of organisation had not yet been regained; and from the east a prevailing lack of involvement was deplored as the SUA remarked on 'the apathy of the mass of professing Unionists, who although ready to criticise the Party and its organisation, will not rouse themselves to work, or pay for the essential staff'.[55] At the end of 1921, for instance, a survey of the seats in the east found three to be in good organisational shape, eleven adequate, six poor and eight non-existent.[56] In the west, there were still nine seats which had no candidates only three weeks before polling day in 1924 — although this did not prevent three of them being won by the Tories.[57]

Unionist organisation was thin on the ground both in seats where there was a tradition of efficient machinery and in new seats which were won after the war. So, Dunbartonshire, which in the twenty years preceding 1914 had been held up as the paragon of constituency organisation, was singled out in 1922 as 'an example of a constituency where the Association was being kept going by a few private individuals'.[58] West Renfrewshire is equally striking, for it too had a strong party machine before the war, and had been a Unionist seat from 1885 to 1906. Labour won here in 1922, and were not dislodged until 1924. Moves to organise the seat for Unionism only began in late 1923, but efforts to inaugurate branches in the main population centres met with a muted response. Exactly twelve months after starting the organisation drive, the constituency organiser lamented: 'I am experiencing great difficulty in raising support among the so-called supporters of the Unionist cause'. Three months before the seat was won, he reported to the chief Scottish Unionist organiser that 'the Local Associations in the Constituency are still in a state of resuscitation', and even after the victory he confessed to grave misgivings about the condition of organisation in Port Glasgow, the biggest town in the seat.[59]

West Aberdeenshire was gained by the Tories for the first time in 1923, yet with an organisation that was at best rudimentary. Less than three weeks before the polling day a meeting of Tories was held, and it was felt that 'it would be a mistake not to put a candidate in the field'. However, as one of the possible candidates could not reply immediately, the only other available and acceptable man was started, but evidently with no high hopes.[60] The formation of a proper organisation did not commence until January 1924 — after the victory — and even then progress throughout that year was slow. A month before the 1924 election, only twelve of a projected forty-two local parish committees were in good enough shape to distribute leaflets.[61]

A particular and rather surprising weakness of the Unionists was finance. In 1920–21, the Eastern Division recorded a deficit of over £1,000 and feared it might have to curtail its activities.[62] It was only in 1923–24 that subscriptions and donations to Scottish headquarters began to grow in a marked manner, rising from £6,112 in the previous year to £7,364 in 1923–4, and advancing to £8,463 in the next.[63] Constituencies were equally impoverished. West Renfrewshire in 1922–23 had half as many subscribers and half as much subscription income as in 1912–13: 39 individuals gave £228 5/6 against £357 18/6 donated by 80 subscribers a decade earlier.[64] West Aberdeenshire in the first nine months of 1924 had gathered £61 in membership fees.[65]

However, Unionist organisation was improving by 1924 and also had two especially strong areas — women and young people. As to the first, the SUA *Annual Report* for 1923–24 concluded that 'there is a general and marked improvement throughout the whole country, not only in organisation, but also in general activity'.[66] Indeed, the mobilisation of women on behalf of Unionism was perhaps the party's greatest organisational success in this period. In 1920 Lady Baxter proposed to the Eastern Council that small, local village meetings be held for women: 'She was most emphatic that women should be fully informed of the horrors of Bolshevism, and that it was neither wise nor kind to protect them from such knowledge, however unpleasant'. The meeting agreed, although it was gnomically observed that 'moonlight had a considerable bearing on the probable attendance'.[67] After this slightly bizarre start, a women's organiser was soon appointed, and although initially some resistance to her efforts was reported, steady headway was made.[68] By 1924 there were 200 women's branches in the eastern area alone, and the west had a flourishing movement too.[69] The activities of these women's sections generally had two distinct sides. On the one hand, a good deal of educational work was done to instil Unionist ideas and policies. Even in a small town like Kinross, this thirst for information was evident. In March 1924, delegates were sent from the town to attend a study school at Perth, where they were to take notes for the rest of the group to use. A month later they resolved to convene a local study school lasting two days.[70] The other focus of women's work was in canvassing and electioneering. The SUA commended the efforts of women during the 1923 election as a 'fine example of earnestness of effort ... [They] are showing much less diffidence than formerly in standing alongside the men in party warfare'.[71]

The Unionists also developed a thriving youth and children's movement. The Junior Imperial League was revived in the west of Scotland at the end of 1919, after having been allowed to lapse during the war. By 1921 it had a permanent organiser, as well as a motor van available to it, so that it expanded to comprise eight-two branches in 1924–5, covering nearly all the western constituencies. The League was intended to counter the spread of socialistic doctrines among young men, and in Glasgow itself the branches of the League held meetings to consider current political issues and to develop skills in public speaking.[72] For those between eight and sixteen years, the Young Unionists were founded — a movement apparently confined to the Glasgow district at first. It boasted eleven branches by

1925, with 600 members in Bridgeton alone.[73] In these areas of women and youth, the Unionists do appear to have achieved a greater impact than the Liberals managed, but even so, and even acknowledging the patchiness of the Liberal strength, the factors ensuring that Unionism would win and Liberalism lose in Scotland were not so simple as they may have appeared in 1918 or 1922, for their electoral recovery in 1923 suggested that the Liberals were by no means a spent force.

II

The essence of the conflict between Liberal and Unionist after the war was into which one the middle class vote would be channelled. This, rather than organisational defects or antediluvian policies, was what settled the fate of the Liberals, whose relegation was not necessarily pre-ordained. Three outcomes of the post-war uncertainty were possible: the middle class vote might consolidate behind one or the other party, depending on which appeared the more effective opposition to Labour. The third response, however, was that a Centre party might evolve, linking men of moderate and middle opinion in an aliance to resist the extremes of both left and right. By 1924 a variety of developments dictated that the struggle be resolved in favour of the Unionists. But before that sequence of events is examined, the emergence of middle class solidarity must be first explored.

It was quite apparent that the Liberals had lost almost all of their pre-war following among the working class as a result of growing working-class consciousness. The clearest illustration of this was the fate which befell W. M. R. Pringle at Springburn in the 1918 election. Pringle's programme was advanced, for in addition to the customary calls for better housing, temperance reform, land value taxation and Home Rule all round, there were policies which were indistinguishable from demands being made by Labour. Thus, he looked for higher wives' and children's allowances, equal pay for women, a capital levy on all wealth over £2,000, and for public ownership of the railways, mines and canals.[74] Moreover, Pringle had been a stout defender of the Clyde Workers' Committee and had remained a consistent proponent of Irish Nationalism throughout the war. This record and platform were insufficient to stem wholesale defections by working men to Labour, which polled 7,996 against Pringle's 1,669.[75] Similarly, in 1922, although the Liberal at Motherwell was said to have concentrated more on the rents issue than the Communist candidate, focusing upon the question which is sometimes alleged to have won Labour so many seats in that election, this did not prevent the Liberal from coming third.[76]

But parallel with this working-class consciousness there may be detected the emergence of middle-class consciousness, if only in the negative sense of a desire to combine in order to resist the advance of Labour and socialism. In urban-industrial centres, not surprisingly, this developed quite quickly. In 1918 in West Stirling, the Unionists put the defeat of the Labour candidate as their first priority, and shortly afterwards they received hints from the Liberals that they should combine to field one candidate. As the Tory party secretary explained after a joint meeting, 'It was certainly the first occasion on which the Conservatives of

Stirlingshire conferred with the Radicals on the subject of a joint candidature and they conferred with us not on account of the war but because of their fear of the Labour vote which they used to pander for so much'.[77] At Dundee, Professor Seggatt expounded the Liberal rationale in 1922 for continuing to back the Lloyd George ministry: 'Of course they were all disgusted with the Coalition, but they might get something worse'. On the eve of the election he amplified the point: 'The election of Labour members in a city like Dundee was not at present conducive to the general welfare'.[78] The Dundee Unionists at this election, although unhappy at the choice, felt constrained to back the two Coalition Liberals, as the alternative was a Labour gain.[79]

Paisley also displayed these sentiments. At the 1920 by-election, Lloyd George was assured that the Asquithian Liberals were more hostile to Labour than they were to the Coalition.[80] At about the same time, Bonar Law received a report on the middle-class mind in Glasgow which reinforced this impression. The Unionist Scottish Whip had discovered that 'among the businessmen of Glasgow the opinion is strongly held that the treatment of Labour by the Government has shown weakness'. Both there and in Edinburgh there were clarion calls for Lloyd George to make a decisive stand by explicitly repudiating nationalisation and also by acting to withdraw the concessions made to organised labour during the war.[81] A survey of the attitudes of 'Important People' in Wester Ross revealed kindred sentiments. At Aultbea the Free Church minister and the local hotelier made common cause in looking for united action to resist Bolshevism and 'the forces of unrest prevalent today'. For others in the area, this last category included crushing the miners.[82]

As the last example suggests, this solidarity of outlook among the middle class also existed in rural areas, and one of the major successes of the Unionists in ousting the Liberals came with the capture of twenty-two county seats in 1924, against only six in the previous election. Most of these seats were heavily agricultural in their social composition.[83] It is hard to see any specific policy issue which might have swayed the farming vote. In 1923, there were indeed schemes carefully fashioned by the Tories to capture the agricultural interest. Protection was presented as beneficial to the farming industry, and, more directly, a subsidy of £1 per acre ploughed was proposed for Scotland. Yet the party did poorly in these seats. Protection had little economic or political appeal in Scotland. Cereal growing was less important than in England, and, as a farming journal observed, 'There is no affinity of thought between even the most conservative of Scottish farmers and the dominant party in the English agricultural unions [i.e. the NFU]'.[84] The subsidy was blamed by A. C. Murray for his defeat as a Liberal in West Aberdeenshire, but this was one of the subsidy's very few successes.[85] The *Glasgow Herald* found that many farmers regarded it as a blatant bait, and moreover it may have backfired in east-coast and Highland seats, where the fishing communities were said to be angry at preferential treatment being accorded to those on the land.[86] The Liberals indeed held 14 county seats, and the Unionists only 6, in 1923, a reversal of the 1922 position, when these were 9 Liberals and 15 Coalitionists.

The break-up of the great estates and the resultant purchase by tenant-farmers of their own farms may on the face of it be seen as a factor turning farmers away from the attraction of a Liberalism based on anti-landowner sentiment. A leading estate factor calculated that, in the two years after the armistice, four million acres of Scottish land — a fifth of the total — came on to the market as owners found the combination of increased taxes and higher costs squeezing income.[87] As an instance, Lord Aberdeen's annual tax bill rose from £800 in 1870 to £19,000 in 1919, while rentals had not even doubled in that period.[88] As farmers' profits were believed to have risen by 500% between 1914 and 1920, it was clearly possible for many to buy, and the statistics show that owner-occupiership of farms doubled between 1914 and 1925 among holdings of more than 50 acres.[89] But the actual figures are less impressive: in 1925 there were 9,289 farms worked by owner-occupiers, of which 4,986 were 50 acres, but there were 76,161 holdings in Scotland that year, 25,630 of which exceeded 50 acres.[90] Thus, even among the more prosperous farmers ownership was restricted to no more than one-fifth. The reason appears to have been that with limited capital, most of which was committed to plant and machinery, it was obviously preferable to lease.[91]

What seems to have swung the farmers' vote to Unionism was, in the first place, a profound dislike of Labour's agricultural policy. The farmers' press pronounced in 1922: 'They know neither of what they speak nor whereof they affirm. There is nothing in it at all but sheer fatuity'.[92] Next year it singled out Snowden's land nationalisation project for contumely, calling on 'all shades of opinion opposed to socialistic theories of State politics' to combine against it.[93] There was also deep unease at an alternative Labour scheme to create smallholdings in the hope of reversing the trend to consolidation of farms into larger units. This proposal caused considerable alarm to the Inverness-shire branch of the NFU during the 1923 election.[94]

Equally significant in sharpening class lines in rural Scotland was the growth both in numbers and determination of trades unionism among farm workers. The Scottish Farm Servants' Union grew from 6,000 members in 1911 to 23,000 in 1919, and its militancy increased too. From subservience and isolation before 1914, the self-confidence and self-respect of the agricultural workers developed during the war as they participated in several Government-sponsored joint committees set up to deal with countryside problems. As the union's leader, Joseph Duncan, commented, 'from an inarticulate class they progressed rapidly until they had a voice in communal affairs'.[95] Relations between master and man tended to deteriorate in this period, especially as smaller farms fell in number and small-scale rural industry and crafts also declined. The upshot, according to Duncan, was that 'society tended to become stratified horizontally. The gulf between the farm workers and the farmers broadened until both were moving in different circles'.[96] The union resorted to more aggressive tactics in pursuit of its industrial demands. A strike in East Lothian in 1923 for a wage increase excited widespread comment at the time as witness to the new spirit among the men and the low state of industrial relations generally in farming.[97] This industrial activity had two disturbing sides to it, so far as farmers and landowners were concerned.

Firstly, it signified the steady integration of the farm workers into the broader labour movement and the corresponding decline of the traditional appeal to the community of rural interests. This trend had been consciously begun by the union in 1917 when it resisted a Government scheme to foster agricultural unity by tying wage levels to grain prices.[98] Joseph Duncan became a prominent figure in the STUC after 1918, so marking the identification of the union with the rest of organised labour. Secondly, with this went a stronger political link with the Labour Party. The South Mid Lothian Labour Party, which had first been formed almost exclusively by miners, received in 1922–23 a considerable influx of support from farm labourers, who were consequently given representation on the executive.[99] Socialist ideas were believed to be widespread among the rural workers. Scottish Unionists were warned in 1923 that 'the young ploughmen in Forfarshire seemed mostly to be tending towards Socialism', and in Ross-shire the Liberal Party organiser found support for Labour in places like Marybank and Portmahomack. At the latter, 'I appealed to farm servants as a Highlander not to surrender to Bolshevism'.[100] The farmers' paper took particular exception to Labour's plans for minimum wages in agriculture, and attacked both its stress on restricting hours of work and its general tendency to preach class war.[101]

III

Although by 1924 the Unionists and not the Liberals had clearly become the almost exclusive recipients of this unified middle class vote, this only came about after fluctuating fortunes for both parties. Admittedly, in the first phase of post-war politics (down to 1923), the general movement did seem to be increasingly towards the Unionists. In the 1922 general election the Coalition electoral pact was maintained. While in this contest the Lloyd George Liberals improved on their 1918 position by fielding 36 candidates, against 28 in 1918, the longer perspective suggested that they would ultimately be absorbed into the Unionists, on the analogy of the experience of the Liberal Unionists after 1886. In most constituencies, even where they held the seat, Coalition Liberal organisation was regarded as a paper fiction. The Lloyd George Liberal Party organiser in Scotland pointed out in 1922 that the Tories 'complain (quite rightly) that as a rule the Coalition Liberals have no sort of organisation which can act for them'.[102] The Unionist Scottish Whip confirmed this in 1922: 'our organisation is (often the only) organisation'.[103] In some places electoral collaboration led quite rapidly to a merger, with the Unionists preponderant. The Unionists and Coalition Liberals in Burntisland reported in 1922 that they had merged, and called on the other parts of the Kirkcaldy constituency to follow this pattern.[104] In municipal contests this process was well advanced.[105] By 1920 the Glasgow Good Government Committee (representing some sixteen bodies ranging from the Tories and Liberals to the YMCA, the Rotary Club, the National Council of Women and the Middle Class Union) ran anti-Labour candidates; and Dundee and Edinburgh operated similar arrangements.[106]

As late as the summer of 1923, the Unionist leaders were still disposed to continue the 1922 election agreement between the anti-Labour parties. Younger let it be known that in his opinion, 'if the parties in the North have any sense they will make a mutual arrangement with regard to seats at the next General Election'.[107] However, the 1923 elections exposed the precarious basis of Unionist hopes that Liberalism was defunct in Scotland. As noted, the drawing together of the two Liberal parties was accomplished smoothly, for, as one of Lloyd George's aides had remarked during the 1920 Paisley by-election, Coalition Liberals were still, in the main, Liberals: 'Old associations, friendships, business, trade and church connections, are all based upon the habits of mind of Scottish Radicalism'.[108] The emergence of tariff reform as an election issue hastened and reinforced Liberal re-union, and also reminded Unionists that their own supporters could not be wholly counted on. In the business seat of Glasgow Central, Unionist Free Traders were still flourishing, and they tried to stop a protectionist Tory fighting there, for fear the Liberal would draw off enough free trade votes to let Labour slip in.[109] A major worry for the Unionists was the stance taken by the *Glasgow Herald,* the voice of business Unionism. As the *Times* noted, 'that journal has assumed an attitude of strong hostility to the Government's fiscal policy'.[110] The *Herald* ran a series of articles by H. Quigley which predicted that many Scottish industries faced ruin if protection were implemented.[111]

The Conservatives found their support seriously eroded in a number of seats, including Kelvingrove, Hillhead, West Edinburgh, North Mid Lothian, and several rural constituencies.[112] Moreover, there were obviously far fewer seats where a Liberal-Unionist pact could be made. Where this was achieved, as in Kirkcaldy, it entailed the Unionists backing the Liberal who made no concessions to protectionist sentiments.[113] The result of the 1923 elections was that with only 14 Scottish seats, the Unionists had been overtaken by the Liberals with 22, whereas in 1922 the Coalition had led the Liberals by 26 to 14. With the absence of an electoral understanding, and the Unionists apparently moving rightwards on fiscal policy, there was the alarming sign for Tories of talk of a more centrist party being formed to check Labour. Among Tories who mooted this idea, which inevitably gave the Liberals a more significant role, were the Duchess of Atholl and Colonel Lithgow, the shipbuilder.[114]

To win back these sorts of voters, the Unionist party re-tailored its strategy in a more progressive and at the same time a more middle-class direction. Firstly, die-hardism was firmly repudiated by the party, with the objective of demonstrating as groundless the fears of moderate opinion about the extent of ultra-right wing influence within Scottish Unionism. The editor of the *Scotsman,* the pillar of Unionism, stressed to John Gilmour the dangers of being seen as a reactionary party: 'The Die-hards have already made it very hard for us in Scotland. If their influence prevails in the future as it has in the past, Unionism in Scotland will be ruined'.[115] In practice the Party had already accepted this analysis. There was little support for the diehard opposition to the Irish Treaty, a stance which might have been expected to win backing in Scotland, in view of the impact of the first Home

Rule bill on the country. A bid to get the 1922 Annual Conference of the SUA to deplore the surrender to Sinn Fein and its tactics found few supporters, and approval for the negotiations was carried heavily.[116] The three M.P.s who can be clearly identified as diehards received instructive treatment from the party. One, T. S. Adair, stood down at Shettleston in 1922. Captain Sprot, Asquith's vanquisher in 1918, lost East Fife in 1922 and, failing to regain it in 1923, was replaced by A. D. Cochrane, the son of a pre-war progressive Liberal Unionist M.P. Cochrane won the seat in 1924. Sprot, significantly, was picked in 1924 to contest North Lanarkshire, where there was a large working class Orange presence, and he defeated the sitting Catholic Labour M.P., Sullivan. Gideon Murray, the third ultra, resigned the Coalition whip over Ulster early in 1922, to the indignation of his constituency association (St Rollox), which then began proceedings to select another candidate. Murray appealed to Bonar Law for help, but Law declined, urging Murray at the 1922 election to seek a seat in England. Law explained that he felt he would have difficulties enough in defending his own opposition to the Coalition in his Glasgow Central constituency without having a diehard standing nearby.[117] While diehards did still exist, their power was largely confined to backwaters such as Roxburghshire and Selkirkshire.[118]

Another indication of the shift in the Unionist appeal may be seen in the radical revision of the traditional approach to working-class voters. Prior to 1914 this had been mainly aimed at the Orange vote, and in the first three or four years after the peace this policy seemed to be maintained. In 1917 a party organiser in the east pressed upon Steel-Maitland, a very influential figure behind the scenes, the importance to Unionism of the Orangemen.[119] In 1919 the secretary of the West Renfrew party received from the Glasgow Unionist organiser a list of all the Orange lodges in the constituency, presumably to ensure that all members were registered.[120] The Orange Order kept its seat on the Glasgow Conservative Association Executive. But from 1922, distancing manoeuvres can be discerned. In January 1922, the Glasgow Orangemen intimated their decision to leave the Conservative Association because of the Irish Treaty, but the Scottish Unionists, while expressing regret, made no determined effort to woo the Order back to the fold.[121]

Relations between the Unionist party and the Orange movement were quite tense in places by the 1922 election. Gilmour, in whose seat the headquarters of Scottish Orangeism was sited, and who had a lodge named after him, was reported as being closely scrutinised by the lodges, who suspected him of backsliding on the Irish question.[122] In Motherwell, where sectarian feelings were always high, the sitting Unionist M.P. criticised Orangemen for their intransigence, whereupon he was tartly reminded of the electoral importance of that body. The M.P. did not stand again at the 1922 contest, and an extreme Protestant, Hugh Ferguson, who ran as a sort of independent right-winger, received no formal Unionist backing. Ferguson stood again in 1923, when the leading local Unionists — Lord Belhaven and Provost Keith — tried to prevent his being adopted as a Tory. They were unsuccessful, and Ferguson won, largely because Catholic voters declined to vote for the Communist. But in 1924, when no Liberal stood, it is significant that

Ferguson collected only about 40% of that vote, a far lower proportion than in nearby seats where Unionism presented a less sectarian profile, and so could receive respectable Liberal votes.[123] The divorce of the Orange movement from the Conservative Party was formalised by the creation of an Orange and Protestant Party in 1922. While in practice. as in 1924, the new party instructed its members to vote against Labour everywhere, and to vote Unionist in three-way fights, the Unionists themselves were absolved from direct complicity with Orangeism.[124] Although in one or two seats some covert deployment of popular Protestantism was adopted by Unionists — notably at Shettleston and North Lanark in 1924 — this was very much a local initiative, not official Unionist policy.[125]

Even serious efforts by the Tories to recruit a more 'respectable' working-class vote, initiated after the war, met with a similar experience of diminishing interest from around 1922. The *People's Politics,* a propaganda paper circulated among the working class before 1914, was revived in 1919, and the party pronounced its work to be of 'immense value'. At the Scottish Whip's prompting, the Scottish Conservative Club subsidised its production costs.[126] Alarmed at the relative lack of working-class presence in Scottish Toryism compared to England — a fact highlighted by a St Andrews Summer School held in 1920 — the SUA was spurred to action. A Conservative trade unionists' society was launched, a Workers' League was formed with annual grants from the Conservative Club, and a People's League was also established.[127] All of these bodies — essentially anti-socialist — were run down quite drastically in the ensuing years. The *People's Politics* was axed in the summer of 1921.[128] After 1921 the Workers' League seems to have slipped from the priority list of the SUA, only re-emerging in 1924 as a recipient of aid.[129] In January 1923 the People's League had its finance cut off, and in October that year the Conservative trade unionists' organisation was similarly treated.[130] In part this rundown may — almost certainly did — reflect the lack of impact being made by Unionism in the new post-war political context among its former areas of working-class support. This is borne out by the fall in circulation of the *People's Politics,* which had a circulation of only 25,000 in the west (one half of the 55,000 readership there in 1913), while in the east it numbered only 13,000 readers.[131] But there would seem to have been, besides a decision simply to cut losses, a general policy also of trying to woo middle-class Liberal votes.

A further pointer to this re-positioning of Unionism *vis-à-vis* the working and middle classes is the social background of candidates. At the 1922 Scottish Unionist Conference, a resolution from Edinburgh Central, a working-class seat, called for an increase in the number of working-class candidates.[132] However, as the crucial 1924 elections showed, the Conservatives were not seriously prepared to implement such a policy. Four working men stood as Tories: three being picked for the impenetrably safe Labour seats of Gorbals, Govan and Dumbarton burgh. The fourth was selected for the not particularly proletarian constituency of Banffshire, a seat moreover uncontested by the party since 1910. This candidate, W. P. Templeton, was the Unionists' paid working-class speaker, and his nomination for Banff was very much a second choice for him. He had initially been earmarked to fight Kirkcaldy, and his rejection there sheds light on the general motives of the Tories at this time. Templeton was picked by the Kirkcaldy Unionists to fight a seat which had no Tory tradition, but he soon established a superior claim because the two Liberal parties (the Lloyd George-ites evidently retaining a separate identity here) could not find anyone to stand, and because all the anti-Labour parties had agreed to field only one candidate. As a seasoned speaker, Templeton made a favourable impression at Kirkcaldy, 'but at Buckhaven, the place was deserted, everyone being away at a pierrot entertainment'.[133] At the last moment the Liberals contrived to produce a potential candidate, an ex-M.P. for Leeds, and at the selection meeting the Unionists, led by Sir Michael Nairn, the largest employer in the town, opted for the Liberal. The reason for this appears to have been that the Tories felt this man would make a greater impact on the middle-class voter than the somewhat rough-hewn Unionist proletarian.[134] It is pleasing to record that while the Liberal lost at Kirkcaldy, Templeton won at Banff.

As indicated by the Kirkcaldy case, there was now a tendency for the anti-socialist vote to combine behind the Tories, but before that could happen they had to moderate their policy stance after protection had tainted them in 1923, so that Liberals would be prepared to vote Unionist. Both the Eastern and the Western Divisional Councils of the Unionist party produced policy resolutions in 1924 on social reform, which were patently designed to demonstrate the new Tory progressivism.[135] These moves were all the more striking as they came after a five-year period in which such topics were not much raised at Tory conclaves. In May, the Western Division demanded action by a future Tory administration on housing, 'the most vital and pressing problem of the day'.[136] This was a far remove from the view of the diehard Gideon Murray, who regarded the immediate post-war working-class housebuilding projects as far too lavish in the provision of unwanted facilities such as sitting-rooms and separate kitchens.[137] The Eastern Council called for better provision of allowances for the aged, widows and children, 'realising', as they put it, 'that on our production and successful operation of such a scheme depends to an incalculable extent the permanent betterment of social conditions'.[138] The 1924 annual Scottish Conference sought an inquiry into child assault in Scotland. Here were signs of an appeal to socially-concerned Liberals, and somewhat similar Liberal-tinged policies had been demanded in 1923. These included profit-sharing and co-partnership in industry, aid for fisheries, and improved transport and land-tenure provision in the Highlands, but of course these had all been overshadowed at that year's election by protection.[139] To allay Liberal fears on tariff reform being sprung on the unsuspecting party, the Western Council in 1924 made a plea for closer consultation between the leader and the party through its representative organisations before any new policies were launched. The Tories claimed that with this procedure 'it will be impossible for any drastic change of policy to be carried into effect'.[140]

With this background of moderation and middle-class appeal firmly sketched in, the Unionists were able to remove the Liberal threat in the 1924 election, when the number of Scottish Liberal M.P.s fell from 22 to 8, and the Unionists correspondingly rose from 14 to 36. Various factors were at work in effecting this result. On the one hand, the Liberals found themselves financially straitened. In 1922, the Independent Liberals spent £21,913 fighting 48 seats in Scotland, but in 1924, only £12,055 on 35 seats. By contrast in England and Wales in 1922, £95,010 was spent on 294 seats, but in 1924 this had risen to £104,899 on 296 seats.[141] The SLA had received warnings earlier in the year of the need to increase its financial resources, and the Lloyd George merger had undoubtedly helped. But the cost of contesting a third general election in as many years was too great. MacKenzie Wood, one of the party's Scottish organisers, stated only a fortnight before polling that he was unable to plan any electioneering activities because he had no idea how much cash was available. When MacCallum Scott asked about the financing of his putative candidature at Moray and Nairn, Wood could give no specific assurances, and this prompted Scott not to go forward.[142] Another ingredient in the Unionist success was the impact produced by Labour's decision to stand in nine hitherto uncontested seats, where the Liberals were generally the incumbent party. In at least seven of them the Unionists supplanted the Liberals, although securing less than half of the votes cast.[143]

But these were minor elements in the electoral pattern of 1924. A major determinant of the outcome was the reaction to Asquith's decision at the start of 1924 to support the Labour government. This outraged many of those who had voted Liberal, and their discontent led them to revise their estimate of the best means of combating socialism. In his own constituency, Asquith received a letter from five leading local businessmen, both Unionist and Liberal, appealing to him not to keep Labour in office. The letter, mainly inspired by William Galbraith, the multiple grocer and active Liberal, warned that the electors did not want socialistic legislation and that the Baldwin administration should therefore be left in office in order to keep businessmen satisfied.[144] That letter was written in January 1924, and by the time of the election in October its prescience was apparent, as on all sides and in all areas the dissipation of the Liberal vote was confirmed. The main Liberal newspaper in the Glasgow area, the *Daily Record*, which had consistently backed the party hitherto, now threw its support unequivocally behind Unionism. The Liberals had had their chance in 1923, and had failed, so now: 'Liberalism has paid dearly for its mistakes'. As no single strand of the fabric of society would be safe if Labour was returned, readers were pressed to vote for the Tories, who alone offered the prospect of providing firm, stable government. Therefore, wherever possible, Unionists should be voted for, particularly in three-way fights, and the Liberals were only to be supported if no Tory was present.[145]

In rural areas, too, the same mood of middle class unity was found. The leading farmers' organ, which in 1923 had tacitly endorsed the Liberals, now attacked Asquith for his alleged lack of any serious reference to agriculture in his election campaigns. Taking this along with its onslaught on the menace of socialism, the implication in 1924 was obviously approval of the Tories as the means of resisting Labour's threat to 'all that is best and most precious in our Scottish heritage'.[146] In many seats there were reliable reports of staunch Liberals throwing in their lot with the Tories as the only sure guarantee of denying Labour power. In West

Perthshire, the sizeable Lochtayside Liberals were moving as a body across to the Tories, while around Kirriemuir and in other strongholds of Angus Liberalism a surge to Unionism was also noted.[147] Dumfriesshire and Galloway were seats which the Liberals held in 1923, but lost to the Unionists in 1924, largely, it was said, because many Liberals switched to exclude Labour from office.[148] Proof positive that the Liberals had lost the central elements of their middle-class support was furnished by a letter sent to Sir Donald MacLean by an erstwhile supporter. The writer explained that he would not vote Liberal but would instead go for the Tory in Peeblesshire, and added: 'My brother-in-law (a United Free Church minister) tells me that all the UF ministers he meets who voted Liberal last election are going to vote Tory next election to keep the Socialists out'.[149] The flight of the U.F. clergy from the Liberal party was the equivalent of the Barbary apes leaving Gibraltar: an Empire had fallen. After all, it was emphasised by the local press that when the Liberal fightback in Dundee was mounted in 1922, a significant clue to its seriousness was the presence of many United Free Church clergymen on the platform.[150]

The drift of middle-class voters to Unionism was rendered easier by the altered image of Unionism. In Dunbartonshire, for instance, it was reported that the abandonment of tariff reform made it very likely that Liberals would now vote Unionist.[151] As a natural outcome of this, it was possible to resurrect the Unionist-Liberal pacts which had lapsed in 1923, and at this election the Unionists predominated. Robert Horne explained to Balfour that Scotland had been given *carte blanche* in these matters, 'without interference from Central Office'. Gilmour and Horne had decided to issue a statement to the press in response to numerous enquiries from Tories as to how they should vote in seats where their party was not fighting. Their address claimed that the differences between Liberal and Unionist were 'inconsiderable' when contrasted with the 'fundamental disagreement' between both and Labour. Therefore, they continued, 'both are now making common cause in certain constituencies against the common foe, and Unionists should vote Liberal if no Unionist stood so that the views of Great Britain on socialism might be clearly ascertained and the influence of Marx and Russian and German socialism could be eliminated'.[152] There were in all around ten such seats, but far more important, there were thirty-five seats where no Liberal ran, and one deduction to be drawn from the Gilmour-Horne letter was that Liberals should reciprocate in these places.

The absense of Unionist-Liberal conflict in so many seats was due to pacts, albeit of an unofficial nature. Their existence was referred to as a matter of public knowledge in the press, and in some seats they did receive semi-official acknowledgement. The St Rollox Unionists, for instance, reported that they had been required by Scottish headquarters to surrender their right to fight the seat.[153] It was, however, the Liberals who abandoned the claim to a contest in most seats, because, as the Kirkcaldy Unionists put it, the Liberals had little hope of regaining that seat after they had supported MacDonald's government.[154] A good instance of the willingness of Liberals to swallow many of their cherished principles for the greater good of defeating Labour came from West Lothian. Here, as Shinwell noted bitterly, the Liberals voted solidly against him, an ardent advocate of temperance legislation, preferring to exercise their franchises in favour of the Unionist, who was the secretary of the Scottish Brewers' Association.[155] It was appropriate that the most spectacular casualty of the Liberal rout was Asquith himself. The Liberals found themselves after the election confined to five seats located in the Highlands and Islands, and three Lowland seats which benefited from the absence of Unionist candidates. The eclipse of the party which had been so dominant almost uninterruptedly since 1832 was now complete, and Scottish politics took on a new complexion.

NOTES

1. S. R. Ball, 'Asquith's Decline and the General Election of 1918', *SHR*, 61 (1981), pp. 44–61.

2. Important studies of this theme include T. Wilson, *Downfall of the Liberal Party, 1914–35* (London, 1966); M. Cowling, *The Impact of Labour, 1920–24* (London, 1971); C. Cook, *The Age of Alignment* (London, 1975); M. Bentley, *The Liberal Mind, 1914–29* (London, 1977). Of specific Scottish interest, in addition to Ball's article (1), see W. Walker, 'Dundee's Disenchantment with Churchill', *SHR*, 49 (1970), pp. 85–108.

3. J. Rabone to W. M. R. Pringle, 6, 15 Dec. 1915, and Pringle to Rabone, 11, 19 Dec. 1915 (copies), Pringle MSS., Hist. Coll. 226/II/23,25,24,26.

4. Aberdeen Liberal Association Minute Book, 21 Jan. 1916, 26 Feb. 1917, MS. 2472.

5. F. E. Guest to D. Lloyd George, 20 Jul. 1918, Lloyd George MSS., LG F21/2/28.

6. Aberdeen Liberal Association Minute Book, 25 Nov. 1918, MS. 2472; cf. Sir J Fleming, *Looking Backwards for Seventy Years, 1921–1851* (Aberdeen, 1922), p. 76.

7. Aberdeen Liberal Association Minute Book, 8 Dec. 1919, MS. 2472; W. Sutherland to D. Lloyd George, n.d. (Apr. 1920), Lloyd George MSS., LG F22/1/26.

8. SLA Minute Book, 8 Dec. 1922.

9. W. Sutherland to D. Lloyd George, n.d. (Mar. 1921), Lloyd George MSS., LG F22/3/14.

10. F. E. Guest to D. Lloyd George, 15, 16 Jan. 1920, Lloyd George MSS., LG F22/1/3,4. In the event a Unionist candidate stood.

11. W. Sutherland to D. Lloyd George, n.d. (Apr. 1920), Lloyd George MSS., LG F22/1/26.

12. W. Runciman to W. M. R. Pringle, 20 Mar. 1920, Pringle MSS., Hist. Coll. 226/III/15.

13. W. S. Churchill to C. P. Scott, 3 Nov. 1922, M. Gilbert, *Winston Spencer Churchill*, Companion Vol. IV (London 1972), III, pp. 2116–7.

14. 'Copy. *Scottish Liberal Federation*. Visit of Sir Donald MacLean to Edinburgh and Glasgow', Gladstone MSS., Add. MS. 46474, ff. 16–18.

15. SLA Minute Book, 3 Mar. 1920.

16. Ibid., 30 Apr. 1920, 28 Dec. 1922.

17. *Stirling Journal*, 22 Dec. 1923, 16 Nov. 1922.

18. Aberdeen Liberal Association Minute Book, 13 Apr., 25 May, 5 Oct. 1920, MS. 2472.

19. *Fife Free Press*, 25 Sep. 1920; Scott Diary, 3 Mar. 1921, MacCallum Scott MSS., MS. 1465/12.

20. R. V. Houston to W. M. R. Pringle, 5 Oct. 1918, Pringle MSS., Hist. Coll. 226/II/102. As is discussed below, this is a travesty of Pringle's policy position in 1918.

21. *Perth Courier*, 23 Sep. 1924. 'Old Radical' is T. M. Reid.

22. Ball, 'Asquith's Decline', pp. 55–7; R. Kelley, 'Asquith at Paisley: The Content of British Liberalism at the End of its Era', *Jnl. of Brit. Studies*, 4 (1964), pp. 133–59.

23. Scott Diary, 29 Jan. 1921; Scott to R. Cumming, 8 Jun. 1921; cf. Cumming to Mrs W. J. Forsyth, 12 Oct. 1919 (copy), Cumming to Miss Grant 16 Oct. 1919 (copy), MacCallum Scott MSS., MS. 1465/12, 207, 320, 321.

24. Scott Diary, 5 Mar. 1920, 29 Nov. 1923, Ibid., MS. 1465/11,14.

25. Aberdeen Liberal Association Minute Book, 23 Mar. 1920, 11 Apr. 1921, 4 Apr. 1922, MS. 2472.

26 D. More to A. Shaw, 18 Sep. 1918, Shaw to R. Munro, 19 Sep. 1918, Munro to Shaw, 22 Sep. 1918, Craigmyle MSS.

27. Scott Diary, 22 Dec. 1918; Scott to R. B. C. Johnson, 10 Aug. 1918, to G. Younger, 15 Nov. 1918 (copies), MacCallum Scott MSS., MS. 1465/9, 178, 492.

28. Aberdeen Liberal Association Minute Book, 25 Nov. 1918. MS. 2472.

29. Capt. A. M. Shaw to A. B. Law, 5 Dec. 1918, Bonar Law MSS., BL 95/4.

30. W. Sutherland to D. Lloyd George, n.d. (May 1920), Lloyd George MSS., LG F22/1/33.

31. Scott Diary, 3 Sep., 22 Dec. 1918; Scott to A. Donaldson, 11 Dec. 1918, 25 Jan. 1919, to W. Hutchison, 27 Nov. 1918, 25 Jan. 1919, to G. Younger, 15 Nov. 1918 (all copies), MacCallum Scott MSS., MS. 1465/9, 211–2, 332–3, 492. The evidence of the letters to Donaldson contradicts Scott's diary entry for 22 Dec. 1918, claiming that he did not approach the Unionists for help.

32. MacInnes Shaw, Capt. J. C. Black to A. Bonar Law, 6,4 Dec. 1918; E. F. Bird to Miss Watson, 3 Dec. 1918, Bonar Law MSS., BL 95/4.

33. F. E. Guest to J. C. C. Davidson, 6 Dec. 1918; 'Editor, *Buchan Observer*' to A. Bonar Law, 8 Dec. 1918 (telegram); J. Adam to E. F. Reid, 8 Dec. 1918, Bonar Law MSS., BL 95/4.

34. Undated memorandum in A. Chamberlain MSS., AC 33/2/4.

35. M. Kinnear, *The Fall of Lloyd George* (London, 1973), App. I, for the Carlton Club list. J. MacLeod, P. Ford. V. L. Henderson to A. Chamberlain, 17, 19, 19 Oct. 1922, A. Chamberlain MSS., AC 33/2/72, 102, 100.

36. R. Stewart to A. Bonar Law, 23 Nov. 1922, Bonar Law MSS., BL 22/1/73.

37. *The Times*, 1 Nov., 25 Oct. 1922

38. R. Stewart to A. Bonar Law, 23 Nov, 1922, Bonar Law MSS., BL 22/1/73.

39. Kinnear, *Fall of Lloyd George*, App. II.

40. SLA Minute Book, 25 Jul. 1922, 13 Feb. 1923, 6 Jul. 1921.

41. *Perth Courier*, 2 Oct. 1923.

42. Scott Diary, 14, 15 Nov. 1923, MacCallum Scott MSS., MS. 1465/14.

43. SLA Minute Book, 19 Dec. 1923.

44. Ibid., 26 June. 1924.

45. Ibid., 19 Dec. 1923.

46. Ibid., 1 Apr. 1921, 22 Jun. 1922.

47. Undated Memorandum, MacLean MSS., MS. Dep. c467, ff. 83–8; SLA Minute Book, 2 Jun. 1924.

48. *Dundee Advertiser*, 12 Nov. 1924.

49. Paisley Liberal Association *Annual Reports* 1921–2, 1923–4.

50. *Glasgow Herald*, 25 Jan., 17 Dec. 1923, 12 Feb. 1924.

51. *Ibid.*, 14 Apr. 1923; *Stirling Journal*, 16 Oct. 1924; *Perth Courier*, 8 Jan. 1924.

52. SLA Minute Book, 9 Sep., 8 Jul. 1924.

53. Ibid., 7 Oct. 1924.

54. SUA *Annual Report* 1922–23.

55. Ibid.

56. SUA, Eastern Division Council Minute Book, 8, 27 Jul., 30 Nov. 1921.

57. SUA, Western Division Council Minute Book, 8 Oct. 1924.

58. Ibid., 4 Oct. 1922.

59. W. Perry to: R. Blaikiston-Houston, 6 Nov. 1923; R. Kennedy, 10 Nov. 1923, 4 Jan. 1924; W. L. Blench, 26 Dec. 1923, Lt.-Col. P. J. Blair, 20 Jun. 1924; L. Shedden, 26 Sep. 1924; J. W. Martin, 9 Dec. 1924, West Renfrewshire Conservative Association Letter-Books.

60. Kincardine & West Aberdeen Unionist Association Minute Book, 16 Nov. 1923.

61. Ibid., 19 Sep. 1924.

62. SUA Eastern Division Council Minute Book, 27 Apr. 1921.

63. SUA *Annual Reports* 1922/3–1924/5.

64. West Renfrewshire Conservative Association Cash Book and Ledger.

65. Kincardine & West Aberdeen U.A. Minute Book, 19 Sep. 1924.

66. SUA *Annual Report* 1923/4.

67. SUA, Eastern Division Council, 21 Jan. 1920.

68. Ibid., 18 Jul. 1919, 24 Mar. 1920.

69. SUA *Annual Reports* 1922/3, 1923/4.

70. Kinross Women's Unionist Association Minute Book, 11 Mar., 8 Apr. 1924. Cf. SUA *Annual Report* 1924/5.

71. SUA *Annual Reports* 1922/3, 1923/4; Kinross Women's Unionist Association Minute Book, 14 Oct. 1924

72. SUA Western Division Council Minute Book, 5 Nov. 1919, 4 May 1921; SUA *Annual Reports* 1921/2, 1924/5; Glasgow Conservative Association. *Annual Reports* 1923, 1925.

73. SUA *Annual Reports* 1923/4, 1924/5; Glasgow Conservative Association, *Annual Report* 1925.

74. There is a copy of his election address in Pringle MSS., Hist. Coll. 226/II/118.

75. 'The Trouble on the Clyde', an undated draft speech or articles; R. V. Houston, G. P. Collins to Pringle, 30 Dec. 1918, 5 Jan. (1919), Pringle MSS., Hist. Coll. 226/V/6, II/125, III/3.

76. *Glasgow Herald*, 7 Nov. 1922.

77. J. Monteith to Lady Steel-Maitland, 23 Aug., 27 Sep., 6 Oct. 1918, Steel-Maitland MSS., GD 193/24/16.

78. *Dundee Advertiser*, 13 Jun. 1922.

79. *Ibid.*, 27 Oct. 1922; W. S. Churchill to A. Mond, 31 Oct. 1922, M. Gilbert, *Churchill*, Companion to Vol. 4, III, pp. 2018–9.

80. F. E. Guest to D. Lloyd George, 15 Jan. 1920, Lloyd George MSS., LG F 22/1/3. Guest is citing the report of J. W. Pratt.

81. J. Gilmour to A. Bonar Law, 16 Mar. 1920, Bonar Law MSS., BL 96/4.

82. This report (c. 1921), probably by W. M. Cameron, is in Strathcarron MSS., MS. Eng. hist. c. 492, ff. 34–41.

83. M. Kinnear, *The British Voter* (London, 1968), pp. 119–24.

84. *Scottish Farmer*, 8 Nov. 1924, 8 Dec. 1923.

85. A. C. Murray, *Master and Brother: Murrays of Elibank* (London, 1945), pp. 190–1; Murray to Lord Reading, 15 Dec. 1924 (copy), Elibank MSS., MS. 8808, ff. 165–8.

86. *Glasgow Herald,* 5 Dec. 1923; cf. *Scottish Farmer,* 8 Dec. 1923; Duchess of Atholl, *Working Partnership* (London, 1958), pp. 134–5.

87. *Scottish Farmer,* 24 Dec. 1921.

88. *'We Twa'. Reminiscences of Lord and Lady Aberdeen* (London 1925), II, pp. 323–5.

89. *The Agricultural Output of Scotland, 1925.* P.P. 1928–9 (3191) V, pp. 46–51.

90. *A Century of Agricultural Statistics* (London, 1968), Tab. 12.

91. *Scottish Farmer,* 10 Dec. 1921.

92. *Ibid.,* 4 Nov. 1922; cf. 25 Nov. 1922, 8 Nov. 1924.

93. *Ibid.,* 7 Apr. 1923, 3 May 1924.

94. *Highland Times,* 29 Nov. 1923.

95. J. Duncan, 'The Scottish Agricultural Labourer', in D. T. Jones *et al, Rural Scotland during the War* (London, 1926), p. 220.

96. *Ibid.,* pp. 218–9.

97. Lady A. Balfour to Lord Balfour, 12, 18 Apr. 1923, Balfour MSS., (Whittingehame) 230; *Scottish Farmer,* 2 June 1923.

98. Jones, *Rural Scotland,* pp. 141–5.

99. South Mid Lothian and Peebles Labour Party Minute Book, 28 Jan., 15 Apr. 1922, Acc. 4312/23.

100. SUA Eastern Division Council Minute Book, 27 Jun. 1923; W. M. Cameron to J. I. MacPherson, 'Report on Campaign in Easter Ross 4–8 April' (1921), same to same, 30 Aug. 1922, Strathcarron MSS., MS. Eng. hist. c. 492, ff. 18–20. 170–1.

101. *Scottish Farmer,* 4 Nov. 1922, 25 Oct., 8 Nov. 1924.

102. W. Sutherland to D. Lloyd George, n.d. (Apr. 1920), Lloyd George MSS., LG F22/1/26.

103. 'Memo of Conference of Under Secretaries of State, 22 Jul. 1922', A. Chamberlain MSS., AC 33/2/4.

104. Kirkcaldy Unionist Association Minute Book, 7 Dec. 1922, MS. 36617.

105. C. Cook, *The Age of Alignment* (London, 1975), pp. 49–87.

106. 'Municipal Elections in Scotland' (n.d.), Lloyd George MSS., LG F167/3/2.

107. A. Young to J. Gilmour, 4 Jun. 1922, Gilmour MSS., GD 383/18/3. Young is quoting from a letter to him from Younger.

108 'Paisley By-election, 15th Report' (n.d.), Lloyd George MSS., LG F167/2.

109. *Glasgow Herald,* 16 Nov. 1923; *Times,* 20 Nov. 1923.

110. *Times,* 27 Nov. 1923.

111. *Glasgow Herald,* 3 Dec. 1923.

112. *Ibid.,* 27 Oct. 1924.

113. *Fife Free Press,* 1 Dec. 1923.

114. Duchess of Atholl to Lady Waring, 28 Dec. 1922, Waring MSS., GD 398/137; W. Perry to Col. J. Lithgow, 24 Sep. 1924 (copy), West Renfrew Conservative Association Letter Books.

115. A. Young to J. Gilmour, 29 May 1923, Gilmour MSS., GD 383/18/2.

116. SUA Central Council Minute Book, 19 Jan. 1922.

117. G. Murray, Viscount Elibank, *A Man's Life* (London, 1934), pp. 236–7.

118. A. Young to J. Gilmour, 7 Jun. 1923, Gilmour MSS., GD 383/18/4. For an outbreak of die-hardism in neighbouring Berwick and East Lothian, see Lady A. Balfour to Lord Balfour, 26 Nov. 1923, 20 Jan. 1924, Balfour MSS. (Whittingehame), 230.

119. H. R. Elliott to A. Steel-Maitland, 3 Sep. 1917, Steel-Maitland MSS., GD 193/274.

120. R. Stevenson to L. Shedden, 27 Jun. 1919 (copy), West Renfrewshire Conservative Association Letter-Books.

121. SUA Western Division Council Minute Book, 11 Jan. 1922.

122. *Glasgow Herald*, 8 Nov. 1922.

123. *Motherwell Times*, 10 Mar., 24 Nov. 1922, 16 Nov. 1923.

124. *Glasgow Herald*, 22 Feb., 12 Oct. 1922, 22 Oct. 1924.

125. *Forward*, 15 Nov., *Glasgow Herald*, 30 Oct. 1924 — both for Shettleston; *Glasgow Herald*, 27 Oct. 1924 — for North Lanark.

126. Scottish Conservative Club, Political Committee Minute Book, 28 May 1919, 16 Feb. 1921, GD 309/45; SUA Eastern Division Council Minute Book, 20 Dec. 1920.

127. SUA *Annual Report* 1920/1; SUA Eastern Division Council Minute Book, 23 Jun. 1920; SUA Council Minute Book, 6 Oct., 10 Dec. 1920.

128. SUA Eastern Division Council Minute Book, 5 Apr. 1921.

129. SUA Eastern Division Council Minute Book, 13 Feb. 1924.

130 SUA Western Division Council Minute Book, 10 Jan. 1923; P. J. Blair to L. Shedden, 25 Oct. 1923, Shedden MSS., envelope marked 'Thomas Russell'.

131. SUA Western Division Council Minute Book, 4 Feb. 1920; Eastern Division Council Minute Book, 1 Oct. 1919.

132. SUA Central Council Minute Book, 19 Jan. 1922.

133. 'Memorandum re Proposals regarding Representation of the Burghs', 5 Sep. 1924, Kirkcaldy Burghs UA MSS., MS. 36620.

134. Kirkcaldy Burghs UA Minute Book, 30 Sep., 14 Oct. 1924, MS. 36617.

135. J. Ramsden, *The Age of Balfour and Baldwin* (London, 1978), pp. 188–21.

136. SUA Western Division Council Minute Book, May 1924.

137. Murray, *A Man's Life,* pp. 243–4.

138. SUA Eastern Division Council Minute Book, 10 Nov. 1924.

139. SUA Central Council Minute Book, 31 Jan. 1923, 13 Nov. 1924.

140. SUA Western Division Council Minute Book,, 7 May 1924.

141. Based on the information in Asquith MSS., MS. Asquith 14.

142. Scott Diary, 12 Oct. 1924 (entered at 3 May 1924), 10 Oct. 1924, MacCallum Scott MSS., MS. 1465/15.

143. Cook, *The Age of Alignment*, pp. 310–33, 338–40, discusses this.

144. *Glasgow Herald*, 7 Jan. 1924.

145. *Daily Record*, 14, 20, 24, 31 Oct 1924; cf. 10, 14, 20 Dec. 1923 for demands for a Conservative-Liberal coalition rather than a Labour administration.

146. *Scottish Farmer*, 5 Jul., 8 Nov. 1924.

147. *Glasgow Herald*, 27 Oct. 1924.

148. *Ibid.*, 27 Oct. 1924.

149. J. Ward to D. MacLean, 26 Apr. 1924 (copy), H. Gladstone MSS., Add. MS. 46474, ff. 87–8.

150. *Dundee Advertiser*, 24 Mar. 1922.

151. *Glasgow Herald*, 27 Oct. 1924.

152. R. S. Horne to Balfour, 21 Oct. 1824, accompanied by draft circular letter by Horne and Gilmour, — October 1924, Balfour MSS. (Whittingehame), 19.

153. Glasgow Conservative Association *Annual Report* 1925 (St. Rollox).

154. 'Memorandum re Proposals Regarding Representation of the Burghs', 5 Sep. 1924, Kirkcaldy UA MSS., MS. 36620.

155. E. Shinwell, *Conflict without Malice* (London, 1955), 88; *Forward*, 15 Nov. 1924.

Appendices

Appendix A. *A Glossary of Religious and Ecclesiastical Terms as used in the text*

Auld Kirk: The Church of Scotland.

Broad Church: The new theological and liturgical developments which spread through the Church of Scotland from the 1860s and 1870s, seeking to modify traditional Calvinistic doctrines and to make the Presbyterian act of worship less austere. The movement was particularly marked in the better-off parishes of larger towns.

Church Defence: Numerous semi-political organisations formed in the 1880s to champion the establishment principle and to protect the Church of Scotland from the disestablishment and disendowment assaults launched on it by the Free and United Presbyterian Churches.

Church Extension Scheme: An attempt by Chalmers in the 1830s to combat the rise of Voluntaryism by providing more Church of Scotland places of worship, particularly in areas of rapid population growth.

Church Liberal (also *Liberal Churchmen*)*:* Members of the Established Church who supported the Liberal Party. They were by no means necessarily liberal in theological beliefs.

Church of Scotland: The established Presbyterian church that suffered a number of secessions in the eighteenth and early nineteenth centuries, mostly in protest against patronage. The outgoing churches were Voluntary. The biggest single breakaway, however, came in 1843, when the Free Church was set up. There was in the majority of these fissions very little theological controversy. The Church of Scotland was reunited with the United Free Church in 1929.

Disruption: The withdrawal in 1843 from the Church of Scotland of a large section of the Evangelical or Non-Intrusionist wing, who then formed the Free Church.

Dissenters: In Scotland most Protestant Dissenters were Presbyterians. Before 1843, the Presbyterian Dissenters were Voluntaries, thereafter the Free Church were a significant part. As the tables in (B) below show, the main English and Welsh Dissenting churches —Methodists, Baptists, Congregationalists — were of very small size in Scotlnd.

Erastian: One who would subordinate church jurisdiction to the state. A term of abuse used against upholders of the status quo in the Church of Scotland in the 1830s and 1840s.

Established Church: The Church of Scotland.

Evangelicals: In the 1830s, the party opposed to the Moderates within the Church of Scotland. They were led by Chalmers, and were later in the decade also known as the Non-Intrusionists. Many were subsequently to join the Free Church in 1843.

Free Church of Scotland: Formed in 1843 and composed mainly of the Non-Intrusionist element who left the Church of Scotland because of their adherence to the principle of spiritual independence. The Free Church remained initially committed to the concept of state endowment of religion, but rejected the existing Church of Scotland as erastian. Its strongholds were in the Highlands and in the Lowland towns. After abortive union negotiations in the 1860s, the Free Church merged with the U.P. Church in 1900 to form the United Free Church. The Free Church minority who remained outside the new church retained the title of 'Free Church', and were commonly known as the 'Wee Frees'.

The Free Church Case: A prolonged legal dispute in the 1900s between the United Free Church and the continuing Free Church ('Wee Frees') over which was the rightful owner of the property of the old Free Church.

Free Church Constitutionalists: That section of the Free Church which opposed the Union negotiations with the United Presbyterian Church in the 1860s. They did so on the grounds that the latter were Voluntaries, whose principles the founders of the Free Church had explicitly repudiated. Their resistance forced the abandonment of the Union talks.

High Church: The Non-Intrusionist or Evangelical wing of the Church of Scotland in the 1830s. A reference to their political pretensions rather than to their liturgical practices.

Low Church: Those in the Church of Scotland and elsewhere who disagreed with the progressive modernising tendencies of the Broad Church movement.

Moderates: The dominant party in the Church of Scotland from the middle of the eighteenth century until the 1830s, when the Evangelicals emerged as a serious opposition. Moderates accepted lay patronage and sometimes preached distinctly non-evangelical doctrines. In general by the 1830s they were very closely identified with the Tory Party.

National Church: The Church of Scotland.

Non-Intrusionists: Those in the Church of Scotland in the later 1830s and early 1840s who upheld the right of congregations not to have imposed upon them against their will a minister chosen by the patron of the living. Many joined the Free Church in 1843.

Patronage: By an act of 1712 the right to appoint a Church of Scotland minister to a parish church lay with the patron of the living. About one third of the parishes were under Crown patronage, and there were a number of institutional patrons, such as town councils. The majority of patrons, however, were private individuals, normally the largest landowner in the parish. The Veto Act of 1833 tried to modify the lay patronage system, and an act of 1874 abolished it entirely.

Spiritual Independence: The principle that the state church should be supported, financially and otherwise, by the state but should not be subject to any legal control by the state. The doctrine was espoused by the Non-Intrusionists and, later, by the Free Church.

State Church: The Church of Scotland.

Synod: In the United Presbyterian Church, the supreme governing body, akin to the General Assembly in the Established and Free Churches.

Union Negotiations: (1) The discussions between 1863 and 1873 aimed at uniting the Free and United Presbyterian Churches. These failed because of the opposition of the Free Church Constitutionalists. (2) The successful talks which in 1900 led to the merger of the two churches.

United Free Church: The church formed in 1900 by the union of the Free and United Presbyterian Churches. A minority of the former remained outside the new Church, retaining the title 'Free Church', and were popularly known as the 'Wee Frees'. In 1929 the majority of the United Free Church merged with the Church of Scotland.

United Presbyterian Church: Formed in 1847 by a merger of the largest secession churches, the Relief and United Secession Churches, the church was the champion of the Voluntary principle. Its support was mainly found in Lowland urban communities, and was drawn from the middle and lower middle classes. In 1900 the United Presbyterian Church joined the bulk of the Free Church to create the United Free Church.

Use and Wont: The form of religious instruction given in Church of Scotland parochial schools before 1872. It was based on the Bible and the Shorter Catechism.

Veto Act: An act of the General Assembly of the Church of Scotland passed in 1833 and designed to mitigate the grievance felt over lay patronage by permitting a congregation to object to a patron's proposed presentee.

Voluntaries: Those who argued that the state should give no support to any church. The largest number of Voluntaries in Scotland were Presbyterians.

Wee Frees: Those Free Church members who refused to join the United Free Church in 1900. They were predominantly located in the Highlands.

Appendix B. Church Support in Scotland, 1878, 1900, 1924

Some statistics of support for the main churches are given below. No earlier reliable comparative figures are available, but it is unlikely that there were significant changes in the relative sizes of the churches in the preceding period, with the exception of the Roman Catholic Church. Here the steady influx of Irish immigrants meant that its support rose from 190,000 in 1841 to over 310,000 in 1876.

It is striking how few members the non-Presbyterian Dissenting churches had in Scotland, and the contrast with Wales is particularly marked. It is equally revealing how much stronger Anglicanism was in Wales compared with Scotland. In reading the figures below, it should be borne in mind that the population of Wales was less than one half that of Scotland.

		1878	1900	1924
1. Presbyterian				
Church of Scotland	(Roll)	516	662	760
Free Church	(Communicants)	238	60	n.a.
U.P. Church	(Communicants)	175		
U. F. Church	(Communicants)	—	493	535
2. Episcopalian	(Members)	56	116	145
	(Communicants)	25	46	60
[Church of Wales]	(Communicants)	[86]	[141]	[172]
3. Non-Presbyterian Dissent				
Methodist		5	8	10
[Wales]		[26]	[34]	[41]
Baptist		9	17	22
[Wales]		[81]	[107]	[129]
Congregationalist		—	30	36
[Wales]		—	[148]	[164]
4. Roman Catholic		311	413	600

These figures are rounded to the nearest thousand.
Roman Catholic figures are for 1876, 1899 and 1922.

Based on R. Currie *et al, Churches and Churchgoers* (London, 1977).

Bibliography

Plan of Bibliography:

A. Manuscript Sources
    1. Personal Papers
    2. Records of Organisations

B. Printed Sources
    1. Official Papers
    2. Newspapers, Periodicals and Journals
    3. Reports
    4. Addresses, Manifestoes
    5. Biographical Works
    6. Other Primary Works
    7. Secondary Works

C. Unpublished Theses

A. *MANUSCRIPT SOURCES*

1. *PERSONAL PAPERS*

Abercairney MSS., Scottish Record Office.
Abercromby of Forglen MSS., Scottish Record Office.
Lord Aberdeen MSS., British Library.
Adam of Blair Adam MSS., Blair Adam, Kinross-shire.
Ailsa MSS., Scottish Record Office.
Airlie MSS., Scottish Record Office.
Sir James Anderson MSS., Mitchell Library, Glasgow.
Ardgowan MSS., Strathclyde Regional Archives Office, Glasgow.
Asquith MSS., Bodleian Library, Oxford.
Earl Balfour MSS., (1) British Library, (2) Whittingehame, East Lothian.
Lord Balfour of Burleigh MSS., Brucefield, Clackmannanshire.
Ballindalloch (MacPherson Grant) MSS., Ballindalloch, Banffshire.
Berry of Tayfield MSS., Tayfield, Fife.
Blackwood MSS., National Library of Scotland.
Bonar Law MSS., House of Lords Record Office, London.
Brodie of Brodie MSS., Brodie Castle, Morayshire.
Brougham MSS., University College Library, London.
Bryce MSS., Bodleian Library, Oxford.
Buccleuch MSS., Scottish Record Office.
Bught MSS., Scottish Record Office.

John Burns MSS., British Library.
Hill Burton MSS., National Library of Scotland.
Cameron of Lochiel MSS., Achnacarry, Inverness-shire.
Campbell-Bannerman MSS., British Library.
Campbell of Succoth MSS., Strathclyde Region Archives Office, Glasgow.
Chadwick MSS., University College Library, London.
Austen Chamberlain MSS., Birmingham University Library.
Joseph Chamberlain MSS., Birmingham University Library.
Chilston MSS., Kent County Record Office, Maidstone, Kent.
Lord Randolph Churchill MSS., Churchill College Library, Cambridge.
Clerk of Penicuik MSS., Scottish Record Office.
Cluny Castle MSS., Cluny Castle, Sauchen, Aberdeenshire.
Gibson Craig MSS., Edinburgh Public Library.
Lord Craigmyle MSS., London.
Craik MSS., National Library of Scotland.
Crawford and Balcarres MSS., John Rylands Library, Manchester.
Cuninghame of Caprington MSS., Scottish Record Office.
Cunninghame Graham MSS., Scottish Record Office.
Dalhousie MSS., Scottish Record Office.
Earl of Derby MSS., Queen's College, Oxford.
Devonshire MSS., Chatsworth, Derbyshire.
Disraeli MSS., Bodleian Library, Oxford.
Drummond of Hawthornden MSS., Scottish Record Office.
Duff of Braco MSS., Aberdeen University Library.
Joseph Duncan MSS., National Library of Scotland.
Dundas of Ochtertyre MSS., Scottish Record Office.
Earl of Dundee MSS., Birkhill, Fife.
Henry Dunlop MSS., New College Library, Edinburgh.
Earl of Elgin MSS., Broomhall, Fife.
Elibank MSS., National Library of Scotland.
Ellice MSS., National Library of Scotland.
Elliot MSS., National Library of Scotland.
Fettercairn MSS., National Library of Scotland.
Fetteresso MSS., Scottish Record Office.
Forbes of Callendar MSS., Scottish Record Office.
Gilmour of Montrave MSS., Scottish Record Office.
H. Gladstone MSS., British Library.
W. E. Gladstone MSS., British Library.
Earl of Glasgow MSS., Kelburne, Ayrshire.
J. Bruce Glasier MSS., Liverpool University Library.
Messrs. Glen and Henderson MSS., Linlithgow, West Lothian.
Glynne-Gladstone MSS., Flint County Record Office, Hawarden, Clwyd.
Sir James Graham MSS., Bodleian Library, Oxford (microfilm).
Grey MSS., Department of Diplomatic and Palaeography, Durham University.
J. W. Gulland MSS., National Library of Scotland.
Haldane MSS., National Library of Scotland.
Hamilton of Rozelle MSS., Glasgow University Archives.
Harcourt MSS., Bodleian Library, Oxford.
Hatfield House MSS., Hatfield, Herts.

Home of Wedderburn MSS., Scottish Record Office.
Hope of Luffness MSS., Scottish Record Office.
George Howell MSS., Bishopsgate Institute, London.
Hunter of Hunterston MSS., Hunterston, Ayrshire.
Messrs. Innes and MacKay MSS., Scottish Record Office.
Francis Johnson MSS., British Library of Political and Economic Science, London
    (microfilm).
Sir James King MSS., King's Sombourne, Hants.
Kinloch MSS., Mitchell Library, Glasgow.
Kintore MSS., Rickarton, Kincardineshire.
Lauderdale MSS., Thirlestane, Berwickshire.
Leith-Hay MSS., Scottish Record Office.
Lloyd George MSS., House of Lords Record Office, London.
Linlithgow MSS., Hopetoun, West Lothian.
Lord Advocates' MSS., Scottish Record Office.
Lothian MSS., Scottish Record Office.
Sir James Lumsden MSS., Arden, Dunbartonshire.
Lynedoch MSS., National Library of Scotland.
Macaulay-Black MSS., National Library of Scotland.
Ramsay MacDonald MSS., Public Record Office.
MacKenzie of Gairloch MSS., Conan, Ross-shire.
MacLean MSS., Bodleian Library, Oxford.
MacLeod of MacLeod MSS., Dunvegan, Skye, Inverness-shire.
Mansfield MSS., Scone, Perthshire.
Maxwell of Monreith MSS., National Library of Scotland.
Minto MSS., National Library of Scotland.
James Moir MSS., Mitchell Library, Glasgow.
Moncrieff MSS., Tulliebole, Kinross-shire.
Monro of Allan MSS., Scottish Record Office.
Moray MSS., Darnaway, Morayshire.
Morel MSS., British Library of Political and Economic Science, London.
David Murray MSS., Cardross, Dunbartonshire.
Lord (J. A.) Murray MSS., National Library of Scotland.
Murray of Polmaise MSS., Scottish Record Office.
Newbold MSS., John Rylands Library, Manchester.
Newcastle MSS., Nottingham University Library.
Newhailes MSS., National Library of Scotland.
Novar MSS., Evanton, Ross-shire.
J. Ogilvy MSS., Dundee Public Library.
F. S. Oliver MSS., National Library of Scotland.
Oswald of Dunnikier MSS., Hockworthy, Devon.
Peel MSS., British Library.
Ponsonby MSS., Bodleian Library, Oxford.
Portland MSS., Nottingham University Library.
Pringle MSS., House of Lords Record Office, London (microfilm).
J. J. Reid MSS., National Library of Scotland.
Robertson-Aikman MSS., The Ross, Lanarkshire.
Rosebery MSS., National Library of Scotland.
Alexander Russel MSS., National Library of Scotland.

E. R. Russell MSS., Liverpool Record Office.
Lord John Russell MSS., Public Record Office.
Rutherfurd MSS., National Library of Scotland.
Sandars MSS., Bodleian Library, Oxford.
Saunders MSS., Churchill College, Cambridge.
A. MacCallum Scott MSS., Glasgow University Library.
Selborne MSS., Bodleian Library, Oxford.
Shedden MSS., Scottish Conservative Party Offices, Edinburgh.
Sinclair of Ulster MSS., Scottish Record Office (microfilm).
J. B. Smith MSS., Manchester Public Library.
Smith of Jordanhill MSS., Strathclyde Region Archives Office, Glasgow.
Stair MSS., Scottish Record Office.
Stansgate MSS., House of Lords Record Office.
Steel-Maitland MSS., Scottish Record Office.
Stewart of Ardvorlich MSS., Ardvorlich, Perthshire.
Stirling of Keir MSS., Strathclyde Region Archives Office, Glasgow.
Stirling-Maxwell of Pollok MSS., Strathclyde Region Archives Office, Glasgow.
Stormonth-Darling MSS., Lednathen, Angus.
Strathcarron MSS., Bodleian Library, Oxford.
Telfer-Smollett MSS., Balloch, Dunbartonshire.
Tweeddale MSS., National Library of Scotland.
Waring MSS., Scottish Record Office.
Wemyss MSS., Scottish Record Office (microfilm).
Whitelaw MSS., Glasgow University Archives.,

2.   RECORD OF ORGANISATIONS

(i)   *Political*

Conservative Party

(a)   *Central*
National Union of Conservative Associations of Scotland MSS., Scottish Conservative
    Party Offices, Edinburgh.
Scottish Unionist Association MSS., Scottish Conservative Party Offices.

(b)   *Constituency*
West Aberdeen and Kincardineshire Unionist Association MSS., Aberdeen University
    Library.
Alyth and Meigle Constitutional Association MSS., Perth County Library.
Dunbartonshire Conservative Association MSS., D. MacIntosh MSS., Scottish Record
    Office.
Edinburgh Conservative Association MSS., Scottish Conservative Party Offices.
Glasgow Conservative Operatives' Association MSS., Scottish Conservative Party Offices.
Kincardineshire Conservative Association MSS., Aberdeen University Library.

Kinross Women's Unionist Association MSS., Kinross Antiquarian Society, Kinross.

Kinross-shire Constitutional Association MSS., Kinross Antiquarian Society, Kinross.

Kirkcaldy Burghs Unionist Association MSS., St. Andrews University Library.

Maryhill Conservative Association MSS., Scottish Conservative Party Offices.

West Renfrewshire Conservative Association MSS., Messrs. MacRobert, Son and Hutchison, Paisley.

(c) *Ancillary*

Primrose League, Scottish Branch MSS., Scottish Conservative Party Offices.

Scottish Conservative Club, Political Committee MSS., Scottish Record Office.

Co-operative Party

Scottish Parliamentary Representation Committee MSS., Co-operative Party (Scottish Section) Offices, Glasgow.

Independent Labour Party

(a) *Central*

ILP National Administrative Council MSS., British Library of Political and Economic Science, London (microfilm).

(b) *Constituency*

Angus Federation ILP MSS., Arbroath Public Library.

Arbroath ILP MSS., Arbroath Public Library.

Glasgow Federation ILP MSS., Mitchell Library, Glasgow.

Labour Party

(a) *Central*

Labour Party National Executive Committee MSS., Labour Party Head Office, London (microfilm).

Labour Party, Scottish Advisory Council MSS., Labour Party Head Office.

LRC and Labour Party Correspondence MSS., Labour Party Head Office (microfilm).

Scottish Workers' Representation Committee MSS., National Library of Scotland (microfilm).

(b) *Constituency*

Edinburgh Labour Representation Committee MSS., National Library of Scotland.

Glasgow Trades and Labour Council MSS., Mitchell Library, Glasgow.

Maryhill Labour Party MSS., Mitchell Library, Glasgow.

South Mid Lothian and Peebles Labour Party MSS., National Library of Scotland.

Montrose Burghs Labour Representation Committee MSS., Arbroath Public Library.

Paisley Labour Representation Committee MSS., Paisley Public Library.

Paisley Trades and Labour Council MSS., Paisley Public Library.

Liberal Party

(a) *Central*
East and North of Scotland Liberal Association MSS., Edinburgh University Library.
Scottish Liberal Association MSS., Edinburgh University Library.

(b) *Constituency*
Aberdeen Liberal Association MSS., Aberdeen University Library.
Mid Lothian Liberal Association MSS., St. Andrews University Library.
Paisley Liberal Association MSS., Paisley Public Library.
West Perthshire Liberal Association MSS., Dundee City Archives.

(c) *Ancillary*
Scottish Liberal Club MSS., National Library of Scotland.

Liberal Unionist

(a) *Central*
East and North of Scotland Liberal Unionist Association MSS., Scottish Conservative
    Party Offices.
West of Scotland Liberal Unionist Association MSS., Scottish Conservative Party Offices.

(ii) *Other*
Beith Parish Records, Glasgow University Archives.
Mid and East Lothian Miners' Association MSS., National Library of Scotland.
West Lothian Miners' Association MSS., National Library of Scotland.
Scottish Trades Union Congress MSS., National Library of Scotland (microfilm).
Society for the Liberation of Religion from State Control MSS., London County Record
    Office.

B. *PRINTED SOURCES*

1. OFFICIAL PAPERS

1. *Parliamentary Debates*

Hansard, 3rd Series.

2. *Reports from Committees*
Select Committee on Fictitious Votes, P.P. 1837 (215) XII, 1837–8 (590) XIV.
Select Committee on Free Church Sites, P.P. 1847 (237, 311) XIII.
Commission on Landlord's Right of Hypothec, P.P. 1865 (3546) XVII.
Select Committee on Game Laws (Scotland) Bill, P.P. 1867 (426) X.

House of Lords Select Committee on Hypothec in Scotland, P.P. 1868–9 (367) IX.
Select Committee on Parliamentary and Municipal Elections, P.P. 1868–9 (74) VIII.

3. *Other*
The Agricultural Output of Scotland, 1925, P.P. 1928–9 (3191) V.

2. *NEWSPAPERS, PERIODICALS AND JOURNALS*

1. *NEWSPAPERS* (Short Titles)
*Aberdeen Free Press, Aberdeen Herald, Airdrie Advertiser, Ardrossan & Saltcoats Herald,
   Ayr Advertiser, Ayr Observer, Berwickshire News* (Duns), *The Bulletin* (Glasgow),
   Caledonian Mercury (Edinburgh), *The Commonwealth* (Glasgow), *Cumnock
   Chronicle, Daily Record* (Glasgow), *Dalkeith Advertiser, Dunfermline Press, Dundee
   Advertiser, Dundee Chronicle, Dundee Courier, Dundee Warder, Dundee Weekly
   News, Edinburgh News, Falkirk Herald, Fife Free Press* (Kirkcaldy), *Glasgow
   Chronicle, Glasgow Constitutional, Glasgow Herald, Glasgow News, Glasgow
   Observer, Glasgow Sentinel, Greenock Advertiser, Greenock Telegraph, Hamilton
   Advertiser, Highland Times* (Inverness), *Inverness Advertiser, Inverness Courier,
   Kelso Chronicle, Kilmarnock Journal, Kilmarnock Standard, Lanarkshire Catholic
   Herald* (Glasgow), *Midlothian Journal* (Dalkeith), *Motherwell Times, North British
   Daily Mail* (Glasgow), *North Briton* (Edinburgh), *North of Scotland Gazette*
   (Aberdeen), *Northern Liberal* (Perth), *Paisley Advertiser, Paisley & Renfrewshire
   Gazette, Paisley Herald, Perthshire Advertiser* (Perth), *Perthshire Courier* (Perth),
   Perthshire Journal (Perth), *Ross-shire Advertiser* (Dingwall), *Rutherglen Reformer,
   Scotsman* (Edinburgh), *Scottish Guardian* (Glasgow), *Scottish Press* (Edinburgh),
   Stirling Journal, Times (London), *West Fife Echo* (Dunfermline), *Witness* (Edinburgh).

The National Library of Scotland has a nine-volume collection of provincial Scottish
   newspapers covering the general election campaigns of 1892, 1895 and 1900.

2. *PERIODICALS AND JOURNALS*
*The Balance, Disestablishment Banner, The Forward, Glasgow & District Railwaymen's
   Strike Bulletin, Labour News for Kirkcaldy and Fife, League Journal, North British
   Agriculturist, The Protestant, The Reformer, Scottish Cooperator, Scottish Farmer,
   Scottish Liberal Women's Magazine, Scottish Standard, Social Reformer, United
   Presbyterian Magazine, United Secession Magazine.*

3. *REPORTS*

1. *Annual Reports, Rules and Constitutions, etc.*
Ayr Labour Committee (1924).
Dundee Conservative Association (1869, 1883, 1885, n.d.).
Dundee Liberal Association (1878, 1882, 1888, 1907–8).
Dundee Year Book (1891).
Edinburgh Trades and Labour Council (1920–1).
Falkirk Trades Council (1907).

Forfarshire Constitutional Association (1878).
Glasgow Central Liberal Association (1885).
Glasgow (Workingmen's) Conservative Association (1869–1926).
Glasgow Conservative Operatives' Association (1839).
Glasgow Independent Labour Party Federation (1917/8–26/7).
Glasgow Labour Party (1914/5–15/6).
Glasgow Law Amendment Society (1851).
Glasgow Liberal Association (1879–83).
Glasgow Political Union (n.d., c. 1832).
Glasgow Presbytery Church Political Defence Committee (1885).
Glasgow Protestant Missionary Society (1880).
Glasgow United Evangelistic Association (1875, 1878, 1880, 1883, 1887, 1889).
Glasgow United Trades (later Trades and Labour) Council (1881/2–85/6, 1900/1–11/2, 1917/8–25/6).
Glasgow Voluntary Church Society (1835).
Glasgow and West of Scotland Liberal League (n.d., c. 1902–3).
Labour Party, Scottish Advisory Council (1917/8–23/4).
Leith Burghs Labour Party (1906, 1909).
Liberal Anti-Disestablishment Association for Scotland (c. 1886).
A Narrative of Facts Relating to the Work done for Christ in connection with the Orphan and Destitute Children's Emigration Homes in Glasgow [i.e., by W. Quarrier] (1872–90).
Paisley Trades and Labour Council (1916).
Perth Trades and Labour Council (1914/5).
Scottish Central Board for Extending the Principle of Voluntary Churches and of Vindicating the Rights of Dissenters (1837–9).
Scottish Council of the Society for the Liberation of Religion from State Control (1883).
Scottish Liberal Association (n.d., c. 1881, 1888).
Scottish National Constitutional Association (1868–9, 1871–2, 1874–5, 1877–82).
Scottish Orangemen's Historical Directory (1913/4).
Scottish Permissive Bill Association (1865/6–84/5).
Scottish Temperance League (1866/7–83/4).
Scottish Unionist Association (1920/1–24/5).
Scottish Workers' Representation Committee (1901–7).
West of Scotland Liberal Unionist Committee (1886–94).
West of Scotland Loyal Constitutional Union (1834).
West of Scotland Protestant Alliance (1874/5–95/6).
Young Scots Handbook (1911–2).

2. *Annual Conferences and Meetings*
Glasgow Liberal Association.
Independent Labour Party.
Labour Party.
Scottish Trades Union Congress.

3. *Reports of Meetings, Speeches, etc.* (in chronological order)
Report of the Proceedings at the Public Dinner in Edinburgh to the Rt. Hon. Earl Grey on the Occasion of his Visit to Scotland, 15 September 1834 (Edinburgh 1834).

The Durham Festival. Glasgow, Wedneday, October 29, 1834 (Glasgow, 1834).

The Glasgow Election (n.p., n.d.).

J. Cleland, *Description of the Banquet in Honour of the Rt. Hon. Sir Robert Peel, Bt., M.P.* (Glasgow, 1837).

D. MacLaren, *Substance of a Speech delivered at a Public Meeting of Dissenters held in Edinburgh on the 14th July 1841 to devise measures for Protecting the Civil Rights of Dissenters from the Unjust Encroachments of the High Church party and their Abettors in Parliament* (Edinburgh, n.d.).

The National Education Association of Scotland (n.p., n.d.).

State Education at Variance with Civil and Religious Freedom. Report of the Speeches delivered at a public meeting held in Glasgow on Thursday, May 31, 1855 to oppose the Lord Advocate's Education Bill for Scotland (n.p., n.d.).

A. Bannatyne, *Address delivered by Andrew Bannatyne to the Glasgow Legal and Speculative Society* (Glasgow 1856).

Scottish Freehold Movement. Public Meeting in Queen Street Hall, Edinburgh, on Thursday 25 December 1856 (Edinburgh, n.d.).

Report of the Proceedings at the Non-Electors' Festival on the Occasion of presenting a Time Piece to George Armitstead, Esquire, on Wednesday, June 10th 1857 (Dundee, 1857).

Union Soiree (n.p., n.d.).

Scottish Chamber of Agriculture, *Discussion on the Report of Her Majesty's Commissioners on the Law relating to the Landlord's Right of Hypothec in Scotland, in and so far as regards Agricultural Subjects and the Minutes of Evidence on which it is based* (Edinburgh, 1865).

C. Scott, *What Should the Working Man Do With His Vote? A Lecture delivered by request to the Working Classes of Edinburgh by Charles Scott in the Queen's Hall, Edinburgh, on Tuesday, 25 June 1867* (Edinburgh, 1867).

The Union Question. Speeches Delivered at a Meeting of office-bearers of the Free Church on the Present Position of the Union Question (Glasgow, 1868).

H. Renton, *The Principles of the United Presbyterian Church on National Education, particularly in regard to Religious Instruction. A Speech delivered to the U.P. Synod, Edinburgh, May 11, 1869,* (Edinburgh, 1869).

National Education. The Bible in the School: Authorised Report of the Public Meeting held in the City Hall, Glasgow, on Mondy, 25 April 1870 (n.p., n.d.).

Free Church of Scotland Defence Association, *Speeches delivered at a Meeting of Free Church Office-bearers Held in the Evening of 3rd March 1870 in the Large Hall of the Religious Institution Rooms, Glasgow* (Edinburgh, 1870).

Full Report of the Great Free Church Public Meeting of those upholding Free Church Principles, and Unfavourable to Union on the proposed Basis, in the City Hall, Glasgow, on Wednesday evening, 11th January 1871 (Glasgow, 1871).

Scottish Education Bill. The Bible in the School. Report of a Public Meeting held in the City Hall, Glasgow on Thursday, 13th April 1871 (Glasgow, 1871).

W. Kidston, *The Captious and Ensnaring Question* (Edinburgh, 1871).

J. A. Campbell, *The Education Question. An Address to the Glasgow Workingmen's Conservative Association on 30th October 1871, introductory to a Course of Popular Lectures* (Glasgow, 1871).

Report of a General Meeting of the Members of the Scottish Educational Association Held in the Craigie Hall, Edinburgh, on Tuesday, November 14th 1871 (Edinburgh, 1871).

Report of a Meeting of the Scottish Educational Association held in Edinburgh on

Monday, 28 October 1872, to Receive and Dispose of the Report of the Acting Committee (Edinburgh, 1872).

A. Whitelaw, *Report of a Speech on Religious Instruction, Delivered at a Meeting of the Glasgow School Board, 8th December 1873* (Glasgow, 1873).

Vaticanism: a full Report of the Great Public Meeting in relation to the present attitude of the Papacy and its bearings on Civil Allegiance and National Prosperity and Freedom held in the City Hall, Glasgow. 5th October 1873 (Glasgow, 1873).

Report of a Special Meeting of the 'Six Hundred' of the Glasgow Liberal Association for the Consideration of the Land Law (Ireland) Bill held on 22nd April, 1881 (n.p., n.d.).

Political Speeches by Mr James Somervell of Sorn to the Glasgow Electors, February and March 1884 (Glasgow, 1884).

G. Beith, *The Church Question* (Glasgow, 1885).

Scottish Disestablishment Association. *Address by the Rev. Principal Cairns, D.D., United Presbyterian College, Edinburgh, at the Conference Held at Edinburgh on 21 May 1885* (Edinburgh, 1885).

The Church of Scotland. Report of a Meeting of Scottish Laymen of Different Religious Denominations opposed to the Disestablishment and Disendowment of the Church of Scotland, held in St. Andrew's Hall, Glasgow (Glasgow, 1885).

Government of Ireland Bill. Proceedings in the Chamber of Commerce and Manufacturers of the City of Glasgow on 19 April 1886 (Glasgow, 1886).

An Educational Retrospect. Being an Address delivered by the Rt. Hon. Lord Moncrieff, Lord Justice Clerk of Scotland, on the occasion of the opening of the Kent Road Public School, 24th April 1886 (Glasgow, 1886).

J. Guthrie Smith, *Home Rule in Ireland, the Colonies and the United States. An Address delivered in the College Division, Glasgow, 17th December 1886* (London, n.d.).

J. Parker Smith, *The Causes of the Union with Ireland* (London, 1887).

A. B. McGrigor, *The British Parliament, Its History and Function. An Address delivered to the College Division Liberal Unionist Association, 28 January 1887* (Glasgow, 1887).

The Preservation of British and Irish Industries. A Meeting held in Glasgow, 28 October 1887 (Glasgow, 1887).

L. McIver, *Trades Unionism. An Address to the Electors* (Beaufort, 1891).

J. MacKillop, *Thoughts for the People* (Stirling, 1898).

East Renfrewshire. Address by Mr R. Laidlaw, M.P., to his Constituents (n.p., 1907).

4. *ADDRESSES, MANIFESTOES*

1. *Candidates' Election Addresses*
The Scottish Conservative Party offices have an extensive collection of manifestoes issued by all parties at the general elections of 1918, 1922, 1923 and 1924.

2. *Other*
Church Defence and Anti-Patronage Electoral Association: *To the Electors of the City of Edinburgh* (c. 1840).

Glasgow Reform Union: *Address* (6 June 1865).

National Association for the Vindication of Scottish Rights: *Address to the People of Scotland and Statement of Grievances* (1853).

Scottish Board of Dissenters: *Address* (1846).

Scottish Chamber of Agriculture: *The Land Laws as they affect Landowners, Farmers, Workers and Consumers; addressed by the Directors to the Constituencies* (1879).

Scottish Council of the Liberation Society: *The General Election and Disestablishment* (1880).

Scottish Disestablishment Association: *Statement by the Executive Committee* (1874).

Scottish National Reform League: *Address by the Executive Council to the People of Scotland* (1867).

Scottish Permissive Bill Association: *Address to the Electors and Rate-Payers of Scotland* (1861).

United Presbyterian Church Synod: *Parochial Schools (Scotland) Bill. Statement by a Committee on National Education* (1869).

United Presbyterian Church Synod: *Disestablishment and Disendowment of the Established Churches of England and Scotland. Statement by the Committee of the Grounds which Justify and Demand Prosecution of this Object* (1873).

5. *BIOGRAPHICAL WORKS*

1. *Collective*

R. V. Heuston, *The Lives of the Lord Chancellors, 1885–1940* (London, 1964).

G. W. T. Omond, *The Lord Advocates of Scotland. Second Series. 1834–80* (London, 1914).

M. Stenton, *Who's Who of Members of Parliament, 1832–1979,* 4 vols. (London, 1976–81).

2. *Individual* (arranged by alphabetical order of subject)

Lord Stanmore, *Correspondence of Lord Aberdeen, 1838–43* (private, n.d.).

M. E. Chamberlain, *Lord Aberdeen* (London, 1981).

T. McCrie, *Memoirs of Sir Andrew Agnew of Lochnaw, Bt.* (London, 1850).

Sir A. Alison, *Some Account of My Life and Writings,* 2 vols. (Edinburgh, 1883).

J. Nicolson, *Arthur Anderson, a Founder of the P. and O. Company* (Paisley, 1914).

G. B. Hodgson, *From Smithy to Senate: the Life Story of James Annand, Journalist and Politician* (London, 1908).

J. MacCallum, *James Annand, M.P.: a Tribute* (Edinburgh, 1908).

Duke of Argyll, *Autobiography and Reminiscences,* 2 vols. (London, 1906).

Sir R. Purvis, *Sir William Arrol: a Memoir* (Edinburgh, 1913).

T. Martin, *Memoir of William Edmonstoune Aytoun, D.C.L.* (Edinburgh, 1867).

Lady F. Balfour, *A Memoir of Lord Balfour of Burleigh, K.T.* (London, n.d.).

G. N. Barnes, *From Workshop to War Cabinet* (London, n.d.).

J. Barr, *Lang Syne* (London, 1948).

T. Smith, *Memoir of James Begg, D.D.* (Edinburgh, 1888).

A. Nicolson, *Memoirs of Adam Black* (2nd edn., Edinburgh, 1885).

Autobiographical Recollections of Sir John Bowring, with a brief Memoir by L. B. Bowring (London, 1877).

J. H. Gillespie, *James Brown, a 'King o' Men'* (Edinburgh, 1939).

A. Gammie, *From Pit to Palace* (London, 1931) [James Brown].

N. L. Walker, *Robert Buchanan, D.D. An Ecclesiastical Biography* (London, 1871).

J. Burgess, *A Potential Poet? His Autobiography and Verse* (Ilford, n.d.).

J. Burn, *The Beggar Boy* (London, 1882).

C. L. Warr, *Principal Caird* (Edinburgh, 1926).

A. R. MacEwen, *Life and Letters of John Cairns, D.D.. LL.D.* (London, 1895).

Life of Henry Calderwood, LL.D., F.R.S.E., by his sons and Rev. D. Woodside (London, 1910).

Hon. Mrs. Hardcastle, *Life of John, Lord Campbell, Lord High Chancellor of Great Britain,* 2 vols. (London, 1881).

J. A. Spender, *The Life of Sir Henry Campbell-Bannerman, G.C.B.* 2 vols. (London, n.d.).

J. Wilson, *C.B: a Life of Sir Henry Campbell-Bannerman* (London, 1973).

W. Wilson, *Memoirs of Robert Smith Candlish, D.D.* (Edinburgh, 1880).

Lady Carmichael, *Lord Carmichael of Skirling* (London, 1929).

W. Hanna, *Memoirs of the Life and Writing of Thomas Chalmers, D.D., LL.D.,* Vols. III-V (London, 1851-3).

S. Brown, *Thomas Chalmers and the Godly Commonwealth* (London, 1982).

Rev. J. S. M. Anderson, *Memoir of the Chisholm, late M.P. for Inverness-shire* (London, 1842).

M. Gilbert, *Winston S. Churchill* (London, 1977), Vol. IV, *Companion.*

Journal of Henry Cockburn, Being a Continuation of the Memorials of his Time, 1831-54 (Edinburgh, 1874).

Letters chiefly concerned with the affairs of Scotland from Henry Cockburn to Thomas Francis Kennedy, M.P., 1831-54 (London, 1874).

C. Gibson, *The Life of George Combe,* 2 vols. (London, 1878).

J. C. Gibson, *The Diary of Sir Michael Connal, 1835-93* (Glasgow, 1895).

C. A. Cooper, *An Editor's Retrospect* (London, 1896).

C. Cowan, *Reminiscences* (private, 1878).

Sir M. E. Grant Duff, *Notes from A Diary, 1851-72* (London, 1897).

M. MacKay, *Memoir of James Ewing, Esquire, of Strathleven* (Glasgow, 1886).

R. Farquharson, *In and Out of Parliament* (London, 1911).

R. Farquharson, *The House of Commons from Within and Other Memories* (London, 1912).

Sir J. Fleming, *Looking Backwards for Seventy Years, 1921-1851* (Aberdeen, 1922).

G. A. Gibson, *The Life of Sir William Tennant Gairdner, K.C.B.* (Glasgow, 1912).

J. Morley, *Life of William Ewart Gladstone,* 3 vols. (London, 1903).

R. S. L. Gower, *My Reminiscences* (London, 1883).

R. S. L. Gower, *Old Diaries, 1881-1901* (London, 1902).

T. N. Graham, *Willie Graham: The Life of the Rt. Hon. W. Graham* (London, n.d.).

D. K. & C. J. Guthrie, *Autobiography and Memoir of Thomas Guthrie, D.D.* (pop. edn., London, 1877).

R. B. Haldane, *Autobiography* (London, 1929).

A. Thomson, *Life of Principal Harper, D.D.* (Edinburgh, 1881).

J. Hodge, *Workman's Cottage to Windsor Castle* (London, 1931).

George Hope of Fenton Barns. A Sketch of his Life compiled by his Daughter (Edinburgh, 1881).

A. Oliver, *Life of Rev. George Clark Hutton, D.D.* (London, 1910).

J. C. Watt, *John Inglis, Lord Justice General of Scotland* (Edinburgh, 1893).

J. Buchan, *Andrew Jameson, Lord Ardwall* (Edinburgh, 1913).

T. Johnston, *Memories* (London, 1952).

W. Stewart, *J. Keir Hardie: a Biography* (London, 1921).

K. O. Morgan, *Keir Hardie* (London, 1975).

F. Reid, *Keir Hardie: the Making of a Socialist* (London, 1978).

D. Kirkwood, *My Life of Revolt* (London, 1935).

J. Lee, *To-morrow is a New Day* (London, 1939).

T. Pinney, *Letters of Thomas Babington Macaulay,* Vol. III (London, 1976).

G. O. Trevelyan, *Life and Letters of Lord Macaulay* (London, 1876).

G. Wilson, *Alexander MacDonald, Leader of the Miners* (Aberdeen, 1982).

D. Marquand, *Ramsey MacDonald* (London, 1977).

C. MacKay, *Forty Years' Recollections of Life, Literature and Public Affairs from 1830 to 1870,* 2 vols. (London, 1877).

J. B. Mackie, *The Life and Work of Duncan MacLaren,* 2 vols. (Edinburgh, 1888).

J. M. MacLean, *Recollections of Westminster and India* (Manchester, n.d.).

D. MacLeod, *Memoir of Norman MacLeod, D.D.,* 2 vols. (London, 1876).

Lord MacMillan, *A Man of Law's Tale* (London, 1952).

Edward Marjoribanks, Lord Tweedmouth, K.T: Notes and Recollections (private, 1909).

J. Mavor, *My Windows on the Street of the World,* 2 vols. (London, 1923).

Sir H. Maxwell, *Evening Memories* (London, 1931).

P. Bayne, *The Life and Letters of Hugh Miller,* 2 vols. (London, 1871).

J. B. Glasier, *William Morris and the Early Days of the Socialist Movement* (London, 1921).

Sir H. Maxwell, *The Hon. Sir Charles Murray, K.C.B. A Memoir* (Edinburgh, 1898).

A. C. Murray, *Master and Brother: Murrays of Elibank* (London, 1945).

G. Murray, Viscount Elibank, *A Man's Life* (London, 1934).

J. Paton, *Proletarian Pilgrimage* (London, 1935).

J. Paton, *Left Turn!* (London, 1936).

N. Gash, *Sir Robert Peel* (London, 1972).

V. Phillips, *My Days and Ways* (private, n.d.).

W. Reid, *Memoirs and Correspondence of Lyon Playfair* (London, 1889).

The Life Story of William Quarrier. A Romance of Faith (Glasgow, n.d.).

Mrs A. Rainy, *The Life of Adam Rolland Rainy, M.P.*(Glasgow, 1915).

P. C. Simpson, *The Life of Principal Rainy,* 2 vols. (London, 1909).

T. Raleigh, *Annals of the Church of Scotland* (London, 1921).

Marquess of Crewe, *Lord Rosebery,* 2 vols. (London, 1931).

R. Rhodes James, *Rosebery* (London, 1963).

S. Walpole, *The Life of Lord John Russell,* 2 vols. (London, 1889).

E. Shinwell, *Conflict without Malice* (London, 1955).

J. Grant, *Memoirs of Sir George Sinclair, Bt., of Ulster* (London, 1870).

Lady Pentland, *The Rt. Hon. John Sinclair, Lord Pentland, G.C.S.I. A Memoir*(London, 1928).

L. Stephen, *The Life of James Fitzjames Stephen, Bart., K.C.S.I. A Judge of the High Court of Justice* (London, 1895).

Principal Story: A Memoir by his Daughters (Glasgow, 1909).

Rev. G. Smeaton, *Memoir of Alexander Thomson of Banchory* (Edinburgh, 1869).

J. Anstruther Thomson, *Eighty Years' Reminiscences,* 2 vols. (London, 1904).

Mrs. (M. O. W.) Oliphant, *A Memoir of the Life of John Tulloch, D.D., LL.D.* (3rd and cheaper edn., Edinburgh, 1889).

J. C. Smith & W. Wallace, *Robert Wallace: Life and Last Leaves* (London, 1903).

Mrs E. H. Perceval, *The Life of Sir David Wedderburn, Bt.* (London, 1884).

A. S. Cunninghame, *Robert Gordon Erskine Wemyss: an Appreciation* (Leven, n.d.).

C. Grosvenor and Lord Stuart-Wortley, *The First Lady Wharncliffe and her Family,* 2 vols. (London, 1927).

6.   *OTHER PRIMARY WORKS*

The Earl of Aberdeen's Correspondence with the Rev. Dr. Chalmers and the Secretary of the Non-Intrusion Committee from 24 January to 27 May 1840 (Edinburgh, 1840).

Analysis of Election. Names of Electors who voted for Messrs Hastie and Haly at the Late Election, 12 July 1852. By Order of the Non-Electors' Committee (Paisley, 1852).

The Approaching General Election: Being the Past and Present State of the Various Political Parties in Edinburgh and the Probable Result of the Contest (Edinburgh, 1866).

(P. Arkley), *Scotch County Courts* (n.p., n.d.).

Association for Promoting the Religious and Social Improvement of the City, *Report on the Religious Condition of Glasgow* (n.p., n.d.).

G. N. Barnes, *Robert Burns* (London, n.d.).

G. N. Barnes, *Karl Marx* (London, n.d.).

Bazaar to Promote the Taxation of Land Values (Glasgow, 1902).

J. Begg, *The Crisis in the Free Church* (Edinburgh, 1855).

J. Begg, *National Education for Scotland Practically Considered, with Notices of Certain Recent Proposals on the Subject* (Edinburgh, 1850).

J. Begg, *Recent Educational Struggles in Scotland: the altered Policy of the Free Church on the Subject of National Education. With a Correspondence between Dr. Blaikie and Dr. Begg* (Edinburgh, 1872).

G. Beith, *The Crofter Question and Church Establishments in the Highlands, viewed socially and politically* (Glasgow, 1884).

A Book of Remembrance. The Jubilee Souvenir of the Glasgow United Evangelistic Association's Evangelical and Ameliorative Schemes, 1874–1924 (Glasgow, 1924).

British Anti-State Church Association, *Scotland and Its Kirk* (London, 1850).

J. Brown, *What ought the Dissenters of Scotland to do in the Present Crisis?* (Edinburgh, 1840).

Rev. R. Burns, *Free Thoughts addressed to the Electors of the County of Renfrew, with reference to the Church Question* (Paisley, 1841).

R. V. C(ampbell), *Scottish Liberals and Disestablishment: A Proposal for a National Liberal Union* (n.p., 1886).

R. S. Candlish, *A Letter to the Most Noble the Marquess of Lansdowne on the Reform and Extension of the Parish School System of Scotland* (Edinburgh, 1850).

T. Chalmers, *What Ought the Church and the People of Scotland to Do Now?, being a Pamphlet on the Principles of the Church Question* (Glasgow, 1840).

City Election. Correspondence of James MacGregor, Esquire, Secretary to the Board of Trade, with Walter Buchanan, Esquire, relative to the retirement of Mr. Oswald and the Future Representation of Glasgow. From December 1845 till April 1847 (Glasgow, n.d.).

H. Cockburn, *Considerations submitted to the Householders of Edinburgh on the State of their Representation in Parliament* (Edinburgh, 1823).

A Conservative, *Letter to the Lord Advocate on the Scotish [sic] Reform Bill* (Edinburgh, 1832).

D. Forbes Dallas, S.S.C., *Memorandum to Aid in the Conduct of Elections under the Corrupt Practices Acts, 1854 to 1883. Being an Epitome of these Acts compiled by D. Forbes Dallas, S.S.C.* (Edinburgh, 1884).

J. Dawson, *Abridged Statistical Account of Scotland* (Edinburgh, 1862). .

P. J. Dollan, *Jubilee History of the Kinning Park Co-operative Society Limited* (Glasgow, 1923).

A. Dunlop, *Letter to the Freeholders of the County of Dunbarton on Parliamentary Reform* (Edinburgh, 1830).

East and North of Scotland Liberal Unionist Association, *Allotments for Scottish Labourers* (n.p., n.d.).

J. Edmond, *Voluntaryism in the House of its Friends, being a Review of Answers by the United Presbyterian Synod to Reasons of Dissent from Resolutions of May 11, 1855 on the subject of National Education* (Glasgow, n.d.).

An Elector, *Reasons for Declining to Vote in Favour of Mr. Macaulay as M.P. for the City of Edinburgh* (Edinburgh, 1852).

A. R. D. Elliot, *The State and the Church* (2nd edn., London, 1899).

R. C. M. Ferguson, *Afforestation* (London, 1909).

A. E. Fletcher, *The Sermon on the Mount and Practical Politics* (London, 1911).

Friendly Address to the Dissenters of Scotland by Ministers of the Established Church (Edinburgh, 1840).

Friendly Reply to the 'Friendly Address to the Dissenters of Scotland by Ministers of the Established Church', by Dissenting Ministers (Edinburgh, 1841).

Glasgow and West of Scotland Law Amendment Society, *The Demand of the Country for Sheriff Court Reform, Attested by the Resolutions of Public Bodies and the Voice of the Press* (Glasgow, 1853).

J. W. Gulland, *Christ's Kingdom in Scotland, or the Social Mission of the United Presbyterian Church* (Edinburgh, 1906).

W. M. Haddow, *Socialism in Scotland: its Rise and Progress* (Glasgow, n.d.).

G. Hayler, *The Prohibition Movement, 1897* (Newcastle, 1897).

Hints for the Considerate. How should the Members and Adherents of the Free Church conduct themselves toward the Establishment and those adhering to it? (Perth, 1844).

T. J. Honeyman, *Good Templary in Scotland: Its Work and Workers, 1869-94* (Glasgow, 1894).

W. E. Hodgson, 'Why Conservatism Fails in Scotland', *National Review*, 2 (1883–4), pp. 235–43.

G. Hope, 'Hindrances to Agriculture', in Sir A. Grant, *Recess Studies* (Edinburgh, 1870), pp. 376–409.

J. Hope, *A Letter to the Lord Chancellor, on the Claims of the Church of Scotland in regard to its Jurisdiction and on the Proposed Changes in its Policy* (Edinburgh, 1839).

J. P. Hopps, *Education in Scotland and the Approaching Election of a School Board for Glasgow* (Glasgow, 1872).

A. Taylor Innes, 'Why is Scotland Radical?', *British Quarterly Review*, 71 (1880), pp. 107–27.

D. T. Jones, *Rural Scotland During the War* (London, 1926).

J. O'C. Kessack, *The Capitalist Wilderness and the Way Out* (Glasgow, 1907).

Liberal Central Association, *Practical Suggestions for Agents Relative to Registration in Burghs in Scotland* (London, 1874).

Liberation Society, *The Established Church and the People of Scotland* (London, 1879).

List of Tories, Churchmen and Chartists who united at the Late Glasgow Election and Voted for James Campbell and George Mills (n.p., n.d.).

H. A. Long, *Glasgow School Board Elections. Second Edition of 'Wrinkles' showing how the Glasgow Knoxites can capture the poll head at all future elections while the cumulative vote is legal* (Glasgow, n.d.).

D. Lowe, *Souvenirs of Scottish Labour* (Glasgow, 1919).

J. McCosh, *The Wheat and the Chaff Gathered into Bundles* (Perth, 1843).

J. MacFarlane, *Dissenting Neutrality, or the Perthshire Election. Viewed in its Bearings upon the Non-Intrusion Question and the Present and Approaching Duties of Dissenters* (Edinburgh, 1840).

Lord Melgund, M.P., *Remarks on the Government Scheme of National Education as applied to Scotland* (Edinburgh, 1848).

A Member of the Faculty of Procurators of Glasgow, *Sheriff Courts of Scotland. Suggestions addressed to the Lord Advocate* (Edinburgh, n.d.).

A Member of the Royal Scottish Geographical Society, *The Geography of Religion in the Highlands* (Edinburgh, 1905).

H. Miller, *Thoughts on the Educational System, or 'The Battle of Scotland'* (London, 1850).

National Union of Conservative Associations of Scotland, *The Campaign Guide* (Edinburgh, 1892, 1895).

National Union of Conservative Associations of Scotland, *Facts for Electors: a Handbook for Unionist Committee Men* (Edinburgh, 1900, 1905).

A. Ponsonby, *Religion in Politics* (London, n.d.).

The Present Position, Prospects and Duties of the Scotch Farmer viewed in Relation to the Landlord's Right of Hypothec, the Operation of the Game Laws on Grass and Corn Lands and the New Reform Bill (Edinburgh, 1866).

J. Rankin, D.D., *Causes of Conservative Failure in Perthshire. A Letter to Col. Moray, Younger, of Blair Drummond* (Edinburgh, 1886).

E. G. Ravenstein, 'The Laws of Migration', *Journal of the Royal Statistical Society,* 48 (1885), pp. 167–235.

Reasons for Organising a Protestant Confraternity to be Called the 'Knoxites' (n.p., n.d.).

J. Reddie, *A Letter to James A. Anderson, Esquire, Banker* (Glasgow, 1851).

A Reforming Scottish Freeholder, *To the Right Honourable Earl Grey, K.G., on the Inadequacy of the Proposed Number of Representatives Allotted to Scotland* (Edinburgh, 1832).

J. Robertson, *The Macaulay Election, or the Designs of the Ministry* (Edinburgh, 1846).

A Scotch Lawyer, *The Amendment of the Law* (Edinburgh, 1853).

Scotland's Fight for Freedom. The Two Vetoes: Young Scots Society Leaflet, N.S., No. 3 (Glasgow, n.d.).

(F. Scott), *View of the Representation of Scotland in 1831: a Letter to the Scottish Landed Proprietors* (London, 1831).

A Scottish Conservative, 'Scottish Conservatism', *National Review,* 29 (1889), pp. 1–21.

A Scottish Conservative, 'The Scottish Election of 1895', *Scottish Review,* 26 (1895), pp. 359–80.

Scottish Disestablishment Association, *Information for the People* (Edinburgh, 1874).

Scottish Disestablishment Association, *Statistics Relating to the Established Church and School Boards* (Edinburgh, 1875).

The Scottish Land and Property Federation. Its Objects and What It Has Achieved (Edinburgh, 1919).

The Scottish Liberal Members and their Pledges on the Church Question in 1880 (Edinburgh, 1880).

The Scottish Temperance Convention (Edinburgh, 1898).

Scotus, *Reform in the Bankruptcy Law of Scotland* (Edinburgh, 1852).

The Soul of Labour as Voiced by Eight Labour Members of Parliament (London, 1914).

To the Electors of Scotland: the Law of Hypothec (n.d., n.d.).

A Tory Democrat, *Scotland at the General Election of 1885* (Edinburgh, 1885).

Triumph of the Conservative Cause in Inverness-shire (Inverness, 1835).

J. M. Whitehouse, *Essays on Social and Political Questions* (London, 1913).

A. Whitelaw, *National Education* (Glasgow. 1871).

Young Scots Society, *Sixty Points for Scottish Home Rule* (Glasgow, n.d.).

7.   *SECONDARY WORKS*

Arnot, R. P., *A History of the Scottish Miners* (London, 1955).

Bain, W. H., ''Attacking the Citadel': James Moncrieff's Proposals to Reform Scottish Education, 1851-69', *Scottish Educational Review,* 10 (1978), pp. 5-14.

Ball, S. R., 'Asquith's Decline and the General Election of 1918', *SHR,* 61 (1982), pp. 44-61.

Barker, M., *Gladstone and Radicalism* (Hassocks, 1975).

Bealey, F. and Pelling, H., *Labour and Politics, 1900–06* (London, 1958).

Bentley, M., *The Liberal Mind, 1914–29* (London, 1977).

Blake, R., *The Conservative Party from Peel to Churchill* (London, 1972).

Blewett, N., 'The Franchise in the United Kingdom, 1885-1918', *Past and Present,* 32 (1965), pp. 27-56.

Blewett, N., *The Peers, the Parties and the People* (London, 1972).

Brash, J., 'The Conservatives in the Haddington District of Burghs, 1832-52', *Transactions of the East Lothian Antiquarian and Field Naturalists' Society,* 11 (1968), pp. 37-70.

Brash, J., *Scottish Electoral Politics, 1832-1854* (Edinburgh, 1974).

British Labour Statistics. Historical Abstract, 1886-1968 (London, 1971).

Broun-Lindsay, E. C., 'Electioneering in East Lothian, 1836-7', *Transactions of the East Lothian Antiquarian and Field Naturalists' Society,* 8 (1966), pp. 46-60.

Brown, J., 'Scottish and English Land Legislation, 1905-11', *SHR,* 47 (1968), pp. 72-85.

Buckley, K. D., *Trades Unionism in Aberdeen, 1878 to 1900* (Edinburgh, 1957).

Butt, J., 'Working Class Housing in Glasgow, 1900-39', in I. MacDougall (ed.), *Essays in Scottish Labour History* (Edinburgh, n.d.), pp. 143-69.

Cameron, K. J., 'William Weir and the Origins of the 'Manchester League' in Scotland, 1833-9', *SHR,* 58 (1979), pp. 70-91.

Campbell, A. B., *The Lanarkshire Miners* (Edinburgh, 1979).

Campbell, R. H., *Scotland since 1707* (2nd. edn., Edinburgh, 1985).

A Century of Agricultural Statistics (London, 1968).

Checkland, S. & O., *Industry and Ethos* (London, 1983).

Clarke, P. F., *Lancashire and the New Liberalism* (London, 1971).

Clarke, P. F, 'Electoral Sociology of Modern Britain', *History* 57, (1972), pp. 31-55.

Conacher, J. B., *The Peelites and the Party System* (Newton Abbot, 1972).

Cook, C., *The Age of Alignment* (London, 1975).

Cooke, A. B., 'Gladstone's Election for the Leith district of Burghs, July 1886', *SHR,* **49** (1970), pp. 172-94.

Cooke, A. B. and Vincent, J., *The Governing Passion* (Hasocks, 1974).

Cowan, R. M. W., *The Newspaper in Scotland, 1815-60* (Glasgow, 1947).

Cowling, M., *The Impact of Labour, 1920-24* (London, 1971).

Crapster, B. L., 'Scotland and the Conservative Party in 1876', *Journal of Modern History,* 29 (1957), pp. 355–60.

Damer, S., 'State, Class and Housing in Glasgow, 1885–1919', in J. Melling (ed.), *Housing, Social Policy and the State* (London, 1980), pp. 73–112.

Drummond, A. L. & Bulloch, J., *The Scottish Church, 1688–1843: the Age of the Moderates* (Edinburgh, 1973).

Drummond, A. L. & Bulloch, J., *The Church in Victorian Scotland, 1843–74* (Edinburgh, 1975).

Drummond, A. L. & Bulloch, J., *The Church in Late Victorian Scotland, 1874–1900* (Edinburgh, 1978).

Dunbabin, J. P. D., *Rural Discontent in Nineteenth Century Britain* (London, 1974).

Dutton, D. J., 'The Unionist Party and Social Reform, 1906–14', *HJ,* 24 (1981), pp. 871–84.

Dyer, M., ''Mere Detail and Machinery': the Great Reform Act and the Effects of Redistribution on Scottish Representation, 1832–68', *SHR,* 62 (1983), pp. 17–34.

Emy, H. V., 'The Land Campaign: Lloyd George as Social Reformer, 1909–14', in Taylor, A. J. P. (ed.), *Lloyd George: Twelve Essays* (London, 1970), pp. 35–70.

Emy, H. V., *Liberals, Radicals and Social Reform, 1892–1914* (London, 1972).

Englander, D., *Landlord and Tenant in Urban Britain, 1838–1918* (London, 1983).

Ferguson, W., 'The Reform Act (Scotland): intention and effect', *SHR,* 45 (1965), pp. 105–16.

Ferguson, W., *Scotland: 1689 to the Present* (Edinburgh, 1968).

E. J. Feuchtwanger, *Disraeli, Democracy and the Tory Party* (London, 1968).

Fraser, W. H., 'The Glasgow Cotton Spinners, 1837', in J. Butt & J. T. Ward (eds.), *Scottish Themes* (Edinburgh, 1976), pp. 80–97.

Fraser, W. H., 'Trades Councils and the Labour Movement in the Nineteenth Century', in I. MacDougall (ed.), *Essays in Scottish Labour History* (Edinburgh, n.d.), pp. 1–28.

Fraser, W. H., 'Trade Unions, Reform and the Election of 1868 in Scotland', *SHR,* 50 (1971), pp. 138–57.

Gash, N., *Politics in the Age of Peel* (London, 1953).

Gash, N., *Reaction and Reconstruction in British Politics, 1832–52* (London, 1965).

Gilbert, B. B., 'David Lloyd George's Reform of British Land Holding and the Budget of 1914', *Historical Journal,* 21 (1978), pp. 117–42.

Gray, R. Q., *The Labour Aristocracy in Victorian Edinburgh* (London, 1976).

Gregory, R., *The Miners in British Politics, 1906–14* (London, 1968).

Hamer, D. A., *Liberal Politics in the Age of Gladstone and Rosebery* (London, 1972).

Hanham, H. J., *Elections and Party Management* (London, 1959).

Hanham, H. J., 'Mid-Century Scottish Nationalism: Romantic and Radical', in R. Robson (ed.), *Ideas and Institutions of Victorian Britain* (London, 1967), pp. 143–79.

Hanham, H. J., *Scottish Nationalism* (London, 1969).

Harvie, C., *Scotland and Nationalism* (London, 1977).

Harvie, C., *No Gods and Precious Few Heroes* (London, 1981).

Hennock, E. P., *Fit and Proper Persons* (London, 1973).

Hillis, P., 'Presbyterianism and Social Class in Mid-Nineteenth Century Glasgow: a Study of Nine Churches', *Journal of Ecclesiastical History,* 33 (1981), pp. 47–64.

Hinton, J., *The First Shop Stewards' Movement* (London, 1973).

Houston, G., 'Labour Relations in Scottish Agriculture before 1870', *Agricultural History Review,* 6 (1958), pp. 27–41.

Howell, D., *British Workers and the Independent Labour Party, 1886–1906* (Manchester, 1983).

Hunter, J., 'The Politics of Highland Land Reform, 1873–95', *SHR*, 53 (1974), pp. 45–68.

Hunter, J., 'The Gaelic Connection: the Highlands, Ireland and Nationalism, 1873–1922', *SHR*, 54 (1975), pp. 178–204.

Hunter, J., *The Making of the Crofting Community* (Edinburgh, 1976).

Jalland, P., 'United Kingdom Devolution: Political Panacea or Tactical Diversion?', *EHR*, 94 (1979), pp. 757–85.

Kellas, J. G., 'The Liberal Party and the Scottish Church Disestablishment Crisis', *EHR*, 79 (1964), pp. 31–46.

Kellas, J. G., 'The Liberal Party in Scotland, 1876–95', *SHR*, 44 (1965), pp. 1–16.

Kellas, J. G., *Modern Scotland* (2nd edn., London, 1980).

Kinnear, M., *The Downfall of Lloyd George* (London, 1973).

McCaffrey, J. F., 'The Origins of Liberal Unionism in the West of Scotland', *SHR*, 50 (1971), pp. 47–71.

MacDougall, I., *Minutes of Edinburgh Trades Council, 1859–73* (Edinburgh, 1968).

MacHugh, P., *Prostitution and Victorian Social Reform* (London, 1980).

McKibbin, R. I., *The Evolution of the Labour Party, 1910–24* (London, 1974).

MacLaren, A. A., 'Presbyterianism and the Working-class in a Mid-Nineteenth Century City', *SHR*, 46 (1967), pp. 115–39.

MacLaren, A. A., *Religion and Social Class* (London, 1974).

MacLean, I., *The Legend of Red Clydeside* (Edinburgh, 1983).

MacPhail, I. M. M., 'Prelude to the Crofters' War', *Transactions of the Gaelic Society of Inverness*, 49 (1974–6), pp. 159–88.

MacPhail, I. M. M., 'The Highland Elections of 1884–6', *Transactions of the Gaelic Society of Inverness*, 50 (1976–8), pp. 368–402.

Machin, G. I. T., 'The Disruption and British Politics, 1834–43', *SHR*, 51 (1972), pp. 20–51.

Machin, G. I. T., *Politics and the Churches in Great Britain, 1832–1868* (London, 1977).

Marsh, P. T., *The Discipline of Popular Government* (London, 1978).

Mathew, H. C. G., *The Liberal Imperialists* (London, 1973).

Mathew, H. C. G., *et al*, 'The Franchise Factor in the Rise of the Labour Party', *EHR*, 91 (1976), pp. 123–52.

Melling, J., 'Clydeside Housing and the Evolution of State Rent Controls, 1900–39', in Melling, J. (ed.), *Housing, Social Policy and the State* (London, 1980), pp. 138–66.

Melling, J., *Rent Strike* (Edinburgh, 1983).

Middlemass, K., *The Clydesiders* (London, 1965).

Montgomery, F., 'Glasgow and the Struggle for Parliamentary Reform, 1830–2', *SHR*, 61 (1982), pp. 130–45.

Montgomery, F. A., 'Glasgow and the Movement for Corn Law Repeal', *History*, 64 (1979), pp. 363–79.

Moore, D. C., *The Politics of Deference* (London, 1976).

Morgan, K. O., *Consensus and Disunity* (London, 1979).

Pelling, H., *The Origins of the Labour Party, 1880–1900* (London, 1954).

Pelling, H., *Social Geography of British Elections, 1885–1910* (London, 1967).

Pelling, H., *Popular Politics and Society in Late Victorian and Edwardian Britain* (London, 1969).

Price, R., *An Imperial War and the British Working Class* (London, 1972).

Ramsden, J., *The Age of Balfour and Baldwin, 1902–40* (London, 1978).

Rempel, R. A., *Unionists Divided* (London, 1972).

Saunders, L. J., *Scottish Democracy, 1815–40* (Edinburgh, 1950).

Savage, D. C., 'Scottish Politics, 1885–6', *SHR*, 40 (1961), pp. 118–35.

Smith, P., *Disraelian Conservatism and Social Reform* (London, 1967).

Stewart, R., *The Foundation of the Conservative Party, 1832–67* (London, 1978).

Stewart, R. W., *The Politics of Protection* (London, 1971).

Sykes, A., *Tariff Reform in British Politics, 1903–13* (London, 1979).

Urwin, D. W., 'The Development of Conservative Party Organisation in Scotland until 1912', *SHR*, 44 (1965), pp. 89–111.

Vaudry, R. W., 'The Constitutional Party in the Church of Scotland, 1834–43', *SHR*, 62 (1983), pp. 35–46.

Vincent, J., *The Formation of the Liberal Party, 1857–68* (London, 1966).

Waites, B. A., 'The Effects of the First World War on Class and Status in Britian, 1910–20', *Jnl. of Contemporary History*, 11 (1976), pp. 27–48.

Walker, W., 'Dundee's Disenchantment with Churchill', *SHR*, 49 (1970), pp. 85–109.

Walker, W., 'Irish Immigrants in Scotland: their Priests, Politics and Parochial Life', *HJ*, 15 (1972), pp. 649–67.

Walker, W., *Juteopolis* (Edinburgh, 1979).

Walkowitz, J. R., *Prostitution and Victorian Society* (London, 1980).

Waller, P., *Democracy and Sectarianism* (Liverpool, 1981).

Ward, J. T., 'The Factory Reform Movement in Scotland', *SHR*, 41 (1962), pp. 100–23.

Ward, J. T., 'Some Aspects of Working-Class Conservatism in the Nineteenth Century', in J. Butt & J. T. Ward (eds.), *Scottish Themes* (Edinburgh, 1976), pp. 141–58.

Whetham, E. H., 'Prices and Production in Scottish Farming, 1850–70', *Scottish Journal of Political Economy*, 9 (1962), pp. 233–43.

Wilson, A., *The Chartist Movement in Scotland* (Manchester, 1970).

Wilson, T., *The Downfall of the Liberal Party, 1914–35* (London, 1966).

Withrington, D. J., 'The Free Church Educational Scheme, 1843–50', *Records of the Scottish Church History Society*, 15 (1964), pp. 103–15.

Withrington, D. J., 'The Churhes in Scotland, c. 1870–1914: Towards a New Social Conscience', *Records of the Scottish Church History Society*, 19 (1975–7), pp. 155–68.

Withrington, D. J., ' 'Scotland a Half-Educated Nation' in 1834? Reliable Critique or Persuasive Polemic?', in W. M. Humes and H. M. Paterson, *Scottish Culture and Scottish Education, 1800–1980* (Edinburgh, 1983), pp. 55–74.

Wood, I. S., 'Irish Nationalism and Radical Politics in Scotland, 1880–1906', *Journal of the Scottish Labour History Society*, 9 (1975), pp. 21–37.

Wright, L. C., *Scottish Chartism* (London, 1953).

Young, J. D., *The Rousing of the Scottish Working Class* (London, 1979).

C. UNPUBLISHED THESES

G. Brown, The Labour Party and Political Change in Scotland, 1918–29 (Ph.D., Edinburgh University, 1981).

K. L. Cameron, Anti-Corn Law Agitations in Scotland, with particular reference to the Anti-Corn Law League (Ph.D., Edinburgh University, 1971).

J. G. Kellas, The Liberal Party in Scotland, 1885–1895 (Ph.D., London University, 1962).

C. B. Levy, Conservatism and Liberal Unionism in Glasgow, 1874–1912 (Ph.D., Dundee University, 1983).

I. McLeod, Scotland and the Liberal Party, 1880–1900. Church, Ireland and Empire. A Family Affair (M. Litt., Glasgow University, 1978).

F. Montgomery, Glasgow Radicalism, 1830–48 (Ph.D., Glasgow University, 1974).

D. A. Teviotdale, The Glasgow Parliamentary Constituency, 1832–46 (M. Litt., Glasgow University, 1963).

J. C. Williams, Edinburgh Politics, 1832–52 (Ph.D., Edinburgh University, 1972).

Index

Abbreviations used: Cons = Conservative; Eln = Election; ILP = Independent Labour Party;
Lab = Labour; Lib = Liberal; LU = Liberal Unionist; U = Unionist.